1st Edition 2007

D0233568

19/8

Sydney
The Complete **Residents'** Guide

Passionately Publishing...

EXPLORER

Sydney Explorer 1st Edition ISBN 13 - 978-976-8182-90-6 ISBN 10 - 976-8182-90-3

Copyright © Explorer Group Ltd 2007
All rights reserved.

Front Cover Photograph: Pete Maloney
Photography: Pete Maloney, Matt Farquharson, Paul Campbell & Simon Jackson

Printed and bound by Emirates Printing Press, Dubai, United Arab Emirates.

Explorer Publishing & Distribution
PO Box 34275, Zomorrodah Bldg, Za'abeel Rd, Dubai
United Arab Emirates
Phone   (+971 4) 335 3520
Fax   (+971 4) 335 3529
Email   info@explorerpublishing.com
Web   www.explorerpublishing.com

While every effort and care has been made to ensure the accuracy of the information
contained in this publication, the publisher cannot accept responsibility for any errors or
omissions it may contain.
No part of this publication may be reproduced, stored in a retrieval system, or transmitted,
in any form or by any means, electronic, mechanical, photocopying, recording or otherwise,
without the prior permission in writing of the publisher.

Welcome...

Congratulations. You've just made settling into Sydney a cinch by buying this fabulous book. This is your 'where to', 'how to' and 'when to' of life in this spectacular city.

Whether you're looking for car insurance or a weekend in the bush, we've got it covered. The **General Information** chapter gives tips on Sydney's history, geography and culture. You'll also find details of hotels and how to get around. The **Residents** chapter practically unpacks your bags for you. With information on visas, residential areas, schools and money, this section will tell you how to get through all the formalities. Once you've done all the fiddly bits, you can start **Exploring**. This chapter takes you through the city's different neighbourhoods, all the way into the Outback. Here you'll discover Sydney's museums, galleries, parks, beaches and more, along with annual festivals and where to go for weekend breaks. Don't forget to tick off the checklist of 21 must dos on page 147.

If you've still got energy to burn, the **Activities** chapter will sort you out. Learn to surf on Bondi beach, sail on the harbour, or go wine tasting in the Hunter Valley. If you need a bit of pampering and a polish, try out one of the city's luscious spas. Sydney is also a town for those who like a bit of **Shopping**. The city's quirky corner shops, larger malls and glitzy department stores aim to please, as do the popular outdoor markets. We've even added a section on the different areas to shop in, just to make your life that little bit easier.

Then, paint the town red with help from the **Going Out** chapter. Our night owls have reviewed the best restaurants, clubs and pubs to keep you going until dawn. Now that you know where you want to go, look at the **Ferry** map (p. 382) and **CityRail** map (inside back cover) to see how to get there.

And if you think we have missed something (like your favourite basket-weaving club or drag bar), please let us know. Go to www.explorerpublishing.com, fill in the Reader Response form, and share the knowledge with your fellow explorers.

Last and not least, we'd like to say a big fat thanks to all of you for buying this book – without you, all our efforts would be in vain.

The Explorer Team

Explorer online

Life can move pretty fast so make sure you keep up at **www.explorerpublishing.com**. Register for updates on the latest happenings in your city or let us know if there's anything we've missed out using our reader response form. You can also check out city info on other destinations around the world - whether you're planning a holiday or making your next big move, we've got it covered. All our titles, from residents' guides to mini visitors' guides, mini maps to photography books are available to purchase online, so you need never be without us.

Only 6 295 days till my first Volkswagen.

It gets me. I can't quite say why I'm so madly attracted to my Volkswagen. It's like we share an uncommon passion. Sure, it feels so safe and sound on the road, while also looking sleek and styled on the outside. It also feels nice and comfortable on the inside, too!

But it's really more than all that. It's another dimension. A real connection – it's like a soul mate. I guess I can say it's the ONE for me. So why do I always go for a Volkswagen? Because it simply gets me.

"It's that Volkswagen feeling!"
It Gets Me.

I can't quite say why I'm so madly attracted to my Volkswagen. It's like we share an uncommon passion. Sure, it feels so safe and sound on the road, while also looking sleek and styled on the outside. It also feels nice and comfortable on the inside, too!

But it's really more than all that. It's another dimension. A real connection – it's like a soul mate. I guess I can say it's the ONE for me. So why do I always go for a Volkswagen? Because it simply gets me.

For the love of automobiles

Residents' Guides

All you need to know about
living, working and enjoying life
in these exciting destinations

* Covers not final. Titles available Nov/Dec 2007.

Activity Guides

Drive, trek, dive and swim... life will never be boring again

Mini Guides
The perfect pocket-sized
Visitors' Guides

Abu Dhabi
Amsterdam
Bahrain
Barcelona
Dubai mini
Dublin mini
Hong Kong mini
London mini
New York mini
New Zealand mini
Oman mini
Paris mini
Shanghai mini
Singapore mini
Sydney

* Covers not final. Titles available Nov/Dec 2007.

Mini Maps
Wherever you are,
never get lost again

Abu Dhabi mini map
Amsterdam mini map
Bahrain mini map
Barcelona mini map
Doha mini map
Dubai mini map
Dublin mini map
Hong Kong mini map
Kuwait mini map
London mini map
Muscat mini map
New York mini map
New Zealand mini map
Paris mini map
Shanghai mini map
Sharjah mini map
Singapore mini map
Sydney mini map
UAE mini map

* Covers not final. Titles available Nov/Dec 2007.

Photography Books
Beautiful cities caught through the lens

IMAGES of DUBAI · images of ABU DHABI · TELLING TALES · IMAGES OF Geneva

Contents

xi

Contents

moving?

relax.
we carry
the
load.

Door to door moving with Allied Pickfords

Allied Pickfords is one of the largest and most respected providers of moving services in the world, handling over 50,000 international moves every year.

We believe that nothing reduces stress more than trust, and each year thousands of families trust Allied Pickfords to move them. With over 800 offices in more than 40 countries, we're the specialists in international moving and have the ability to relocate you anywhere anytime. Move with Allied to Allied worldwide.

www.alliedpickfords.com

ALLIED
PICKFORDS
The Careful Movers

General
Information

General Information

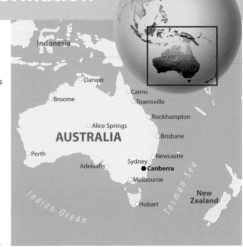

Flat and Wide

Australia is the flattest continent on earth and Sydney does not have towering peaks to boast of. However, some 65km to the west of the city, the Blue Mountains rise from the coastal plains in an aromatic haze of eucalyptus vapour. This is best seen in the early morning, when the Blue Mountains are at their bluest.

See p.224 for tours.

Geography

Sydney is one of the most important ports in the South Pacific. Australia's largest city is also the capital of the state of New South Wales, which covers just over 10% of Australia. Located on the south-eastern coast of the country, Sydney is 33° 55' south of the equator, at longitude 151° 12' east. Sydney lies in the temperate zone. Further inland the climate is drier with hot days and cold nights, while up the coast to the north, the weather is warmer and more humid. The western plains, which cover more than half the state, are generally semi-arid. The wettest parts of the state are along the coast.

The Sydney Statistical Division spreads from the Blue Mountains in the west to the Pacific Ocean in the east; from Lake Macquarie in the north to south of Botany Bay – an area covering over 12,000sqkm. Within that, the Sydney Metropolitan Area is equal in size to London. Bringing the focus in even tighter, the City of Sydney Local Government Area (LGA) covers around 26sqkm, including the central business district (CBD). The LGA was formed in 2004 by the merger of the City of Sydney and the (now defunct) City of South Sydney, despite some resistance by residents.

The A-list cities of the world are each defined by some unique characteristic. For Sydney, it is the harbour. This system of waterways courses through the heart of Sydney from east to west, and divides it into northern and eastern suburbs. The 240km of intricately carved shoreline frames 54sqkm of water.

The CBD at night

Sydney Overview

Anzac War Memorial

Pemulwuy
A Bidjigal man from Botany Bay, Pemulwuy, fiercely resisted the invasion of his land. He led attacks on settlers from 1788 to 1802. In a battle in 1797 at Parramatta, Pemulwuy was shot and hospitalised but managed to escape. He was killed in 1802 and his head was sent to England. The final fate of his head remains a mystery but Pemulwuy's memory lives on, and he is regarded as the first great resistance leader by Aboriginal people.

The compact CBD is on a low ridge, with the rest of urban Sydney spilling out over low hills around the water. To the west of the CBD, on a small, craggy hill, lies the historic Rocks neighbourhood. Further west is Darling Harbour. Beyond the green swathe of The Domain and the Royal Botanic Gardens, Kings Cross occupies the ridge to the east of the CBD, past Woolloomooloo.

Sydney's attraction lies in its mix of city life and a gorgeous natural environment. With a magnificent harbour as focus, sandstone cliffs, pretty bays, long stretches of beach and brilliant natural light, it's easy to see why Sydney is one of the world's great cities.

History

Aboriginal History

The first Aboriginal explorers are thought to have arrived from south-east Asia 120,000 years ago, with human occupation of New South Wales anywhere between 30,000 and 60,000 years ago. The pre-contact Aboriginal population may have been more than 40,000 strong.

The Aboriginal people were hunter-gatherers who managed the land in semi-permanent settlements and lived in separate groups with distinct languages and traditions. These groups mingled for trade, initiations, marriages and political alliances. The traditional owners of the Sydney City region are the Cadigal band. When asked where they came from by the British, the local Aboriginal people answered 'Eora' which means 'here' or 'from this place'. The British used the term to describe the coastal Aboriginal people found around Sydney. Central Sydney is often referred to as 'Eora Country'. Many of Sydney's main thoroughfares, such as George Street and Oxford Street, follow ancient Aboriginal tracks.

European Arrival

In 1770 Captain James Cook charted the east coast of Australia, landing at Botany Bay on April 28. He formally took possession of the eastern part of Australia in August, naming the region New South Wales. Within 20 years, the lives of the local Aboriginal people had been torn apart by disease, dispossession and social upheaval. Today, many Aboriginal people refer to the arrival of the Europeans as 'the invasion'.

On January 26 1788, the 11 ships of the First Fleet dropped anchor in Sydney Cove, marking the beginning of the settlement of Sydney. Under the command of Captain Arthur Phillip, the marines on board (along with 850 convicts) were tasked with building a prison settlement.

The local stream was soon permanently fouled. This forced the local people further out for clean drinking water. Then came the 1789 smallpox epidemic, which killed almost half of the Aboriginal community of Sydney. There were reports of bodies left floating in the harbour. By 1791 there were said to be just three Cadigal people left in the area.

The Rum Rebellion

Until the arrival of Captain Bligh as governor in 1806, Sydney was run by the New South Wales Corps, or Rum Corps, using rum as currency. Governor Bligh forbade the barter of spirits for food or wages and conducted a feud with the corps and John Macarthur. Bligh arrested Macarthur, who promptly persuaded the corps to mutiny. On Anniversary Day in 1808, the (well lubricated) corps marched down Bridge Street to arrest Bligh. Macarthur perched on a gun carriage and the band belted out a stirring tempo. Sydney residents, always keen on a spectacle, cheered on the mutineers. Bonfires burned effigies of Bligh and the governor was arrested. The commanding officer of the mutiny took the title of lieutenant-governor, Macarthur called himself secretary to the colony and they claimed land and convict labour for themselves and their cronies. Bligh was recalled by London and Lachlan Macquarie was dispatched with a regiment to restore order.

3

The Complete **Residents'** Guide

The Europeans survived the smallpox but their settlement teetered on the brink of starvation. It wasn't until the Second Fleet arrived in 1790 that the colony became self-sufficient. After Captain Phillip returned to England, the colony was administered by the New South Wales Corps as their personal fiefdom. It was only when Governor Lachlan Macquarie arrived that order was restored.

A Capital City

Many still mistake Sydney for Australia's capital. But, Canberra has been the federal capital since 1908 and seat of government since 1927. It was chosen as a compromise to appease Sydneysiders and Melbournites who each felt that their city was best. The rivalry still remains though, which you'll notice pretty quickly on arriving.

Self-Sufficiency

Macquarie encouraged exploration and in 1813 the Blue Mountains were conquered, opening up the interior. The British government granted free land, free convict labour and a huge market for any produce. As the colony established itself, Macquarie's civic pride prompted an ambitious programme of public works. Some of the finest buildings of the early convict period were built on his watch.

In 1842, the City of Sydney was established and representative government followed in Australia a year later. By the mid 19th century mineral discoveries, and gold in particular, had shifted the emphasis from pastoral to mining, manufacturing and larger scale agriculture. Sydney was flooded by gold seekers and building activity boomed. Great Victorian piles were constructed from the local Sydney sandstone. In the last half of the century, Sydney exploded from 60,000 to a population of around half a million. By the end of the century, it was one of the largest cities in the western world.

Lachlan Macquarie

Lachlan Macquarie, governor of Sydney from 1810 to 1821, turned a rough and tumble convict station into a city with civic pride. By the time he left, Sydney had an organised police system, decent roads, a bank and a real currency. He had arrived in Sydney at almost 50. His mission was to release the town from the clutches of the Rum Corps. A tall Scot with a proud military background, Macquarie was generally a humane man who believed in the reformation as well as the punishment of convicts. He appointed several educated and successful freed convicts to office, which scandalised the elite of the colony, especially the fiery John Macarthur. They complained bitterly to London, where authorities were concerned by the rising costs of the governor's public works. When London sent a nitpicking official to conduct an enquiry, Macquarie saw the writing on the wall and resigned. But he won't be forgotten easily; there are more than 50 roads, streets and lanes that carry his name.

Federation

On January 1, 1901, federation was achieved and New South Wales became a state of Australia. In Sydney, slums were cleared and the city was smartened up. At this point, Aborigines were believed to be dying out and they were not included in the census of 1901, although cattle were.

As a member of the British Empire, Australia sent 330,000 soldiers (including 300 - 500 Aborigines) to Europe during the first world war. More than 58,000 of them were killed. On April 25, 1915, the ANZACs (Australian and New Zealand Army Corps) landed on the Gallipoli Peninsula in Turkey. During the subsequent eight-month campaign, 27,000 Australian soldiers were killed or wounded. The Gallipoli legend plays a key role in the Australian psyche. This is partly to do with the bravery shown in the face of overwhelming odds, but Gallipoli also marks the start of Australia's psychological independence from Britain.

The second world war saw Australia, as a member of the British Empire and Commonwealth, at war again. This time, troops were sent to Europe, the Middle East,

Sydney Timeline

30,000 to 60,000 years ago	Aboriginal settlement
1770	Captain Cook arrives in Botany Bay
1788	European settlement begins with arrival of the First Fleet
1802	Pemulwuy shot
1807	First wool exported
1808	Rum Rebellion
1809	Governor Lachlan Macquarie arrives in Sydney
1813	Crossing of the Blue Mountains
1838	Myall Creek massacre – 28 Aboriginies shot by white men in northern NSW
1843	First elections
1848	Convict transportation to NSW ceased
1851	Gold rush
1893	Adult male suffrage (with restrictions for indigenous men)
1901	Federation
1902	Adult female suffrage (with restrictions for indigenous women)
1915	ANZAC lands at Gallipoli
1932	Sydney Harbour Bridge opened
1938	First 'Day of Mourning' held by Aboriginal protestors
1942	Singapore falls and 15,000 Australian troops taken prisoner. Darwin bombed and three Japanese midget submarines enter Sydney Harbour
1962	Aborigines given the right to vote in Commonwealth elections
1965	'Freedom Rides'. Students travel through NSW to draw attention to segregation of Aboriginal Australians
1967	Referendum returns overwhelming vote in favour of recognising Aborigines as Australian citizens
1971	Census includes Aborigines for the first time; Aboriginal flag flown for the first time
1972	Aboriginal 'Tent Embassy' erected outside Parliament House in Canberra
1973	The Sydney Opera House opens
1984	*Advance Australia Fair* becomes the national anthem and green and gold Australia's national colours. Homosexuality decriminalised
1987	Royal commission held into Aboriginal deaths in custody
1991	Council for Aboriginal Reconciliation established by an act of parliament with bipartisan support
1992	Sydney Harbour Tunnel opened
1993	Bid succeeds for 2000 Olympics
1994	Royal commission established to investigate corruption in the NSW Police Service
1997	Report into 'stolen generation' tabled in federal parliament
2000	Olympic Games held in Sydney
2001	Australia supports invasion of Afghanistan. Tampa crisis erupts when Australian troops seize control of a Norwegian vessel carrying rescued asylum seekers
2002	Bali bombing
2003	Iraq invasion. Australia part of 'coalition of the willing'
2005	Cronulla beach riots

North Africa and the Pacific. On February 19, 1942, Darwin was nearly destroyed by Japanese bombers. On May 31, 1942, three Japanese midget submarines entered Sydney Harbour. A torpedo destroyed a Royal Australian Navy depot ship, killing 21 people. On June 8, two of the submarines shelled Sydney and Newcastle but did little damage. When America entered the war, it made Australia the Allied base in the Pacific. This was the beginning of Australia's shift in reliance on Britain to the US.

Progress for Some

The period from the late 40s to the early 70s was an era of dramatic growth, which saw Australia's relationship with the US develop, strengthened by Australia's involvement in the Vietnam war. By 1972, when Australia withdrew, economic hardships were taking their toll. The Governor-General's dismissal of the Labor government of Gough Whitlam caused the most serious constitutional crisis in Australia's history. The years that followed saw steady growth as business began to dominate public life in Australia. John Howard's government took the country into the new century on a policy of economic liberalism and social conservatism.

But the era after the second world war was not such good news for the city's Aboriginal population. Until the 1960s, Aborigines fell under the control of the NSW Aborigines Welfare Board. It followed a brutally misguided policy of separating Aboriginal children from their parents in an attempt at integration. These children are known as the 'Stolen Generations'. There are between 15,000 and 20,000 of them in New South Wales, many still searching for their families. The NSW Land Rights Act 1983 finally acknowledged the dispossession of Aboriginal people from their land but the Aboriginal and Torres Strait Islander Commission (ATSIC), which acted for indigenous people on a national level, has recently been abolished by the prime minister.

Olympic Sites

Perhaps the most tangible benefit left to residents by the 2000 Olympics are the sports facilities. You can swim, run and jump around many Olympic sites. Go to the Activities chapter, p.217, to find out how.

Global City

In 1993, Sydney exploded with joy as it was named host for the 2000 Summer Olympics. The city went on to pull off what IOC President Juan Samaranch described as, 'the best games ever'. Images of Sydney at its best were beamed around the world, as the city made the most of its iconic structures and gorgeous natural scenery.

Since those heady days, Prime Minister John Howard has signed the nation up to the 'coalition of the willing' and Sydneysiders, like other Australians, are divided as to the wisdom of this. When terrorists in Indonesia bombed a nightclub in Bali and 88 Australians died, those doubts grew. Later friction between Muslim and Anglo-Australian youths (see p.183) increased these doubts.

But the city remains upbeat and optimistic. Australians have always been curious about themselves in relation to the rest of the world and they pride themselves on performing well in adversity. Sydney can only benefit from facing up to the hard questions about its true identity.

The Rocks

Now one of Sydney's main tourist areas, less than 100 years ago The Rocks was a rat-infested slum. Modern Suez Canal Street was once known as Sewer's Canal and passers-by often dragged into it and robbed. Along Harrington Street, pitched battles would break out between soldiers, sailors and local thugs.

In the summer of 1900, Sydney was struck by an epidemic of bubonic plague and The Rocks, where the first case occurred, was quarantined. Tonnes of garbage were disposed of and over 44,000 rats were caught. Conditions did not really improve though and the area remained almost impossible to police. It was not tidied up until the 70s when it slowly became a popular area of restored historic buildings and souvenir shops.

Economic Overview

Sydney is a major Asia Pacific financial centre with a triple-A sovereign credit rating. The Sydney Futures Exchange is one of Asia Pacific's largest financial futures and options exchanges. The city's economic size is estimated at around US$175 billion (on a par with Singapore), which amounts to 25-30% of Australia's total economic activity. Sydney is the most multicultural city in the Asia Pacific, with a highly skilled and multilingual workforce. More than 30% of residents were born overseas.

Employment

Average Salaries (AUD) – NSW, 2004-05		
Position	Total Salary	Total Package
Chief Executive	222,857	294,330
GM - Division, Region	144,045	177,348
Finance		
Chief Finance Executive	168,023	213,135
Financial Controller	107,471	133,753
Financial Accountant	70,620	83,024
Assistant Accountant	48,396	54,830
Marketing and Sales		
National Sales Manager	99,835	130,727
State Sales Manager	76,170	105,813
Product/Brand Manager	71,233	94,140
Key Account Representative	59,426	82,059
Marketing Assistant	42,697	47,030
Call Centre Operator	37,171	41,475
Information Technology		
IT Manager	90,917	112,794
Project Manager/Leader	90,574	108,269
Network Controller	71,479	80,499
Analyst/Programmer	69,728	78,428
Engineering		
Engineering Manager	93,596	119,772
Professional Engineer	72,309	86,129
Experienced Engineer	60,976	71,054
Manufacturing		
Manufacturing/Production Engineer	81,817	104,031
Logistics Manager	79,996	100,530
General Foreperson	52,599	64,350
Purchasing Officer	44,123	48,989

Source: Australian Institute of Management (AIM) National Salary Survey, October 2005.

In the last quarter of 2006, according to the Australian Bureau of Statistics, Sydney's unemployment rate was 4.6%. The employment rate was 72.3%. According to the UBS Prices and Earnings Report 2006, 14 minutes of work in Sydney buys you a Big Mac hamburger. The global average is 35 minutes, which makes Sydney the world's ninth best city for purchasing power. Sydney is above the average national wage, with a household mean income of $1,360 per week compared to $1,216 per week in the rest of the country. In terms of vacations, Sydney does not do too badly either. The global average number of vacation days and hours worked each year is 20 and 1,844 respectively. Sydney clocks in at 23 days vacation and 1,682 working hours each year.

Sydney Developments

Sydney's population is predicted to grow from the current 4.2 million to 5.3 million by 2031. To deal with the additional pressures this will cause, the government anticipates that New South Wales will need the following:

- 640,000 new homes
- 500,000 more jobs
- 7,500 hectares of extra industrial land
- 6.8 million square metres of additional commercial floor space
- 3.7 million square metres of additional retail space

The government's vision for Sydney in 2031 has Sydney City and North Sydney as the heart of 'global Sydney', while the river cities of Parramatta, Liverpool and Penrith will provide more work, cultural and lifestyle opportunities. The rural land extending to the Nepean-Hawkesbury area and the foothills of the Southern Highlands will be protected, as will Sydney's green areas. Projects in the pipeline include the revamping of the ugly Parramatta Road and the development of a network of major city centres. Some of the projects underway or recently completed include:

- The upgrading of the arterial road network including the Cross City Tunnel, the Lane Cove Tunnel, the orbital motorway network (M4/M7) and the Windsor Road upgrade
- Public transport improvements, including the untangling of rail lines and $1.5 billion for new trains
- Bus reforms – a network of strategic corridors linking key centres such as Parramatta, Bankstown, Liverpool and Penrith
- A $493 million commitment to the first stage of the Northwest Transitway Network
- $100 million for the redesign and development of Parramatta, which will also get a new transport interchange

***Leading Industries** Accountancy and law are all high performers here and Sydney is the number one city in Australia for international corporate headquarters. It also happens to be the contact centre capital of Asia Pacific. In the 70s, Sydney knocked Melbourne off its plinth as the country's financial centre.*

A showcase project for 'global Sydney' is the $4 billion renewal of a 22 hectare port precinct on the western edge of the CBD. Effectively, the project amounts to the regeneration of east Darling Harbour into an upmarket business and residential area. The development is expected to generate $4 billion in new investment in the state and some 30,000 jobs during the construction period of 10 years. The area will house commercial headquarters for 16,000 workers, an 11 hectare headland park and a 1.4km foreshore walk from Woolloomooloo round to the Anzac Bridge. The park is part of a continuing program to keep the headlands free from development. The revamped area has been named Barangaroo, after the feisty wife of Bennelong, one of the First Fleet's Aboriginal contacts. Part of Hickson Road will be renamed The Hungry Mile. Sydney residents made their displeasure known when a sanitised shortlist of names was announced for the area. They wanted – and they got – The Hungry Mile. The name is a memorial to the desperate men that haunted the waterfront, looking for work during the Depression.

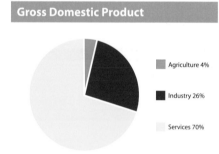

Gross Domestic Product

Agriculture 4%

Industry 26%

Services 70%

Source: Australian Bureau of Statistics

Legacy of the Olympic Games

When Price Waterhouse Coopers analysed the business and economic benefits of the Sydney 2000 Games, the final report was generally positive. Listed benefits included almost $2 billion in post-games sports infrastructure and service contracts, an injection of over $6 billion in infrastructure developments in New South Wales and $1.2 billion worth of convention business for NSW from 1993 to 2007. Inbound tourism spending climbed to over $6 billion during 2001 and the business profile of Sydney, New South Wales and Australia were raised significantly through the equivalent of nearly $6.1 billion worth of international exposure.

Australian business has benefited from involvement in the provision of services for the Salt Lake City Games in 2002, the Athens Olympics in 2004 and the Asian Games in Vietnam in 2003 and Qatar in 2006. The 2000 games provided a showcase for Australian skills, talent and creativity. The benefits in terms of contacts made, international awareness raised, investment committed, partnership and skills acquired, are an enduring legacy that continues to reap rewards for Australia and for Sydney in particular.

Dusk over Sydney's two icons

Accolades

Sydney was again named 'World's Best City' in 2005 by American travel magazine Travel + Leisure. *In 2005 Sydney won the* Condé Nast Traveller *Readers' Choice Awards, earning a world-topping rating of 93.3 out of 100 for friendliness. The city was also voted the UK's favourite overseas city in the* Guardian/Observer Travel Awards *in 2003.*

Tourism

Tourism in New South Wales is worth $23.3 billion; 32.7% of Australia's total tourism income. Tourism generates 185,000 jobs directly, which is 6% of the work force. The Sydney metropolitan area generates around $4.8 billion in tourism export earnings per year. This is more than the total Australian earnings for wool or petroleum. More than two million visitors come to Sydney each year.

By 2020 New South Wales is expected to host up to an estimated 36 million visitors a year, a 22% increase on 2001. On these forecasts visitor growth will outstrip resident population growth. As at December 2005, Sydney City had 121 accomodation spots with 19,370 rooms. This represents a 4.7 % increase in room supply with the re-opening of the Hilton Sydney (577 rooms) accounting for around half of that increase. Sydney has some of Australia's top attractions. The Sydney Opera House and Harbour Bridge are the city's best known icons. Taronga Zoo has some of the best views of the city, beaten only by the bridge and the transparent viewing platforms on the Sydney Tower's Skywalk. A new addition to the entertainment centre at Darling Harbour, Sydney Wildlife World brings some of Australia's unusual flora and fauna to the heart of the city. Sydney Aquarium, also located here, remains a perennial favourite with visitors. The city has a rare spread of tourist treats, from whale-watching in June/July, to shopping, coastal strolls, 37 beaches, numerous art galleries and museums and the world's biggest gay and lesbian mardi gras.

International Relations

Until the second world war, Australia was closely linked to Britain. As the country looked more to the US and immigrants arrived from Europe and Asia, the British connection became weaker. Defence treaties such as ANZUS, made in 1951 with New Zealand and the US, and the South-East Asia Treaty Organisation of 1952, show the change in focus.

Bali

On October 12, 2002, 88 Australians died when terrorists bombed a nightclub in Bali. A joint Australian-Indonesian team was set up to provide a combined response to terrorism. Following the 2004 bombing of the Australian embassy in Jakarta, the Australian Federal Police were invited to work with Indonesian police. On October 1, another bomb in Bali killed 20, including four Australians. Australia provided money and expertise to assist the Balinese after the attack. Efforts are also underway to strengthen the counter-terrorism cooperation between the two countries.

Tiny Tuvalu
There are over 40
consulates represented
in Sydney. The list
includes the
heavyweights such as
the US, Britain, Japan
and France and
extends to smaller
players like Bhutan,
Tuvalu and Tonga.

Today, close engagement with Asia and the stability of the South Pacific are vital. The US is one of Australia's most important economic partners as well as its closest security ally. In 2004, Australia and the US signed The Australia-United States Free Trade Agreement (AUSFTA). The Thailand-Australia Free Trade Agreement was signed in 2004 and The Singapore-Australia Free Trade Agreement (SAFTA) in 2003.

Less than 24 hours after the 2001 terrorist attacks in New York City, NATO invoked article five of the treaty, declaring the attacks to be against all members. Australian Prime Minister John Howard invoked the ANZUS Treaty at the same time. Australia remains a member of the 'coalition of the willing'.

Asian Relations

Establishing Australia's role in Asia and the South Pacific has not been easy. Malaysia proved particularly stand-offish and relations with Indonesia hit an all-time low when Australia led the UN forces supervising East Timor's independence. Though they improved when PM John Howard announced the $1billion Australia-Indonesia Partnership for Reconstruction and Development after the Indian Ocean tsunami. Papua New Guinea, Fiji and the Solomon Islands have all undergone periods of instability recently, causing headaches for Australian diplomats and trade officials.

Government & Politics

Australia is a democratic federal constitutional monarchy. At the time of writing, the NSW state government is left of centre while the federal government is right of centre, which makes for interesting times. Since areas of responsibility are not always clear, the two groups blame each other constantly. The federal parliament consists of the Queen (represented by the governor-general) and two elected houses (the House of Representatives and the Senate). The Australian government is the party, or coalition of parties, forming a majority in the House of Representatives. The prime minister is a member of this house. Since Federation, the two major political parties have been the Australian Labor Party and various conservative parties, known since 1944 as the Liberal Party of Australia (which has often acted in coalition with the Country, or later, National Party). The federal government deals with matters that affect the whole country, like foreign affairs, defence, trade, and social services. Funds are raised through income tax.

State and territory governments make laws in areas not covered by the federal government or the constitution. They raise funds from business and transaction taxes. The leader of a state is called the premier. State responsibilities include police, prisons and education.

Sydney is the capital of New South Wales and the seat of the state's government and parliament. There are over 40 local government areas in the Sydney region. These look after environment protection, rubbish collection, libraries and so on. They raise most of their funds from rates on land and buildings. The leader of the council is usually known as the mayor.

Clover Moore

Clover Moore is a politician who inspires strong passions. As Lord Mayor of Sydney and independent member for Bligh in the New South Wales Legislative Assembly, Moore has campaigned against developers and spoken up for the environment, gay rights and inner city issues. She is an indomitable campaigner who has passionate grass roots support, but critics argue that she should not hold two offices. In February 2004, the councils of Sydney City and South Sydney were merged in what Moore described as a grab by the state government for control of the city. One month later, in a triumphant return, Moore was voted mayor of the new super council of Sydney.

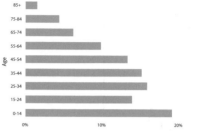

Population

Aboriginal Flag

First flown in 1971, this has a red lower half and a black upper half, with a large yellow circle in the middle. The black represents the Aboriginal people, the yellow represents the sun, and the red the earth and the blood of the Aboriginal people. The flag has no official government standing but is widely known.

Australia's population is ageing thanks to low fertility rates and declining mortality rates. Over the past 20 years, fertility rates have fallen while life expectancy at birth improved by six years for males (to 78 years) and four years for females (to 83 years). Aboriginal life expectancy is around 17 years lower than the national figure. According to the 2001 census, the population of Sydney Statistical Division was 4,128,272. Of these, 2,044,159 were male and 2,101,202 were female. Just 1.1% of the population was indigenous and 31% were born overseas. More than one in four people aged over 15 spoke a language other than English at home.

Population by Principal Language

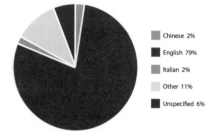

- Chinese 2%
- English 79%
- Italian 2%
- Other 11%
- Unspecified 6%

Time Zones

Adelaide	- 30 minutes
Brisbane	AEST
Canberra	AEST
Hobart	AEST
Melbourne	AEST
Perth	-2
Sydney	AEST
Athens	-8
Auckland	+2
Bangkok	-3
Beijing	-2
Beirut	-8
Colombo	-4.5
Damascus	-8
Denver	-16
Dubai	-6
Dublin	-10
Hong Kong	-2
Johannesburg	-8
Jordan	-8
Karachi	-5
London	-10
Los Angeles	-17
Mexico City	-15
Moscow	-7
Mumbai	-4.5
Munich	-9
New York	-14
Paris	-9
Prague	-9
Rome	-9
Singapore	-2
Tokyo	-1
Toronto	-14
Wellington	+2

National Flag

The Australian flag has three elements on a blue background; the Union Jack, the Commonwealth Star and the Southern Cross. The Union Jack is a reminder of British settlement; the seven points of the Commonwealth Star represent the seven states and territories; the Southern Cross, which can only be seen in southern skies, is a reminder of Australia's geography. The flag was first flown in September 1901 at Exhibition Building in Melbourne, which was the seat of government at the time.

On the New South Wales flag, the badge of state has a silver background with a red cross bearing a gold lion in the centre and an eight pointed gold star on each arm.

Post School Qualifications

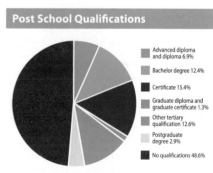

- Advanced diploma and diploma 6.9%
- Bachelor degree 12.4%
- Certificate 15.4%
- Graduate diploma and graduate certificate 1.3%
- Other tertiary qualification 12.6%
- Postgraduate degree 2.9%
- No qualifications 48.6%

Source: Australian Bureau of Statistics

Local Time

There are three time zones in Australia. Australian Eastern Standard Time (AEST) is equal to UCT (formerly GMT) plus 10 hours and followed in New South Wales (except Broken Hill), Victoria, Queensland, Tasmania and Australian Capital Territory. Australian Central Standard Time (ACST) is equal to UCT plus 9.5 hours and followed in South Australia, Northern Territory and Broken Hill (NSW). Australian Western Standard Time (AWST) is equal to UCT plus eight hours. Western Australia follows AWST.

Daylight Saving

Daylight saving time is observed by New South Wales, Victoria, South Australia, Tasmania and the Australian Capital Territory from October to the end of March.

11

Queensland, Western Australia and the Northern Territory do not follow daylight savings. Clocks move forward by one hour.

Social & Business Hours

The working week runs from Monday to Friday. In Sydney, most businesses close over the weekend but many shops remain open on Saturday and with restricted hours on Sunday. Thursday is traditionally 'late night shopping'. Most people work a 36.4 hour week in New South Wales. However, it is not unusual for bright, aspiring corporate types to work long hours and weekends. As a trend across the country, more people are working longer hours without extra pay.

Australians prize their free time. The long weekend is an Australian institution and when any public holiday falls on a Friday or a Monday, the country goes into relaxation mode. State holidays are often set on a Monday. Grocery chains and some of the bigger department stores may open on certain public holidays for a few hours, but pretty much everything closes down on Christmas Day, Good Friday, Easter Monday and New Year's Day. Government departments generally follow hours similar to the business sector but it is a good idea to check before visiting.

Public Holidays

Public Holidays	
Anzac Day	April 25
Australia Day	January 26
Bank Holiday*	First Monday in August
Boxing Day	December 26
Christmas Day	December 25
Easter Monday	March 24, 2008
Easter Saturday	March 22, 2008
Good Friday	March 21, 2008
Labour Day	First Monday in October
New Year's Day	January 01
Queen's Birthday Holiday	Second Monday in June
Not a state-wide public holiday	

National public holidays apply across Australia. There are also public holidays that apply to individual states and territories. Where fixed holidays fall on a Sunday, the public holiday carries over to the following Monday. Local public holidays in NSW also apply within certain council areas and require banks to close. For example, on the afternoon of Tuesday November 6, 2007, a holiday applies to the Muswellbrook Shire Council area for the Musswellbrook Cup Race Carnival. There are 25 of these holidays dotted around NSW through 2007. Unless your contract expressly says you are entitled to these holidays, it comes down to an individual employer's discretion. For a complete listing of public holidays in New South Wales, including local holidays, visit www.industrialrelations.nsw.gov.au/holidays.

Electricity & Water

Other options **Electricity** p.111, **Water** p.111

Sydney's electricity supply is generally very reliable. Electrical current is 220/240 volts AC and three-pin or two-pin plugs are used. These plugs are different to those used in most other countries, so you may need an adaptor. These can be bought locally. If you are using appliances that use 110 volts, you will need a transformer. This is probably best bought in your home country. Laptops often have transformers that automatically switch from 110 to 240 volts but you will still need an adaptor for the three-pin/two-pin plugs.

The Sydney Water (www.sydneywater.com.au) website will tell you everything you ever wanted to know about water in Sydney. A few years ago the city had outbreaks of Cryptosporidium and Giardia organisms in the water system. Sydney Water now publishes a daily report on their website, giving the exact amounts of each of these organisms in the water.

At the time of writing, level three mandatory water restrictions are in force across the whole of Sydney, thanks to the ongoing drought. Sydney Water's website gives precise details on all the restrictions.

Bushfires ◀

Hot dry weather causes anxious moments in the rural areas of NSW, especially when the wind picks up. Australian native plants burn quickly and dramatically, especially eucalyptus trees, which have high oil content and can explode in a bushfire.

Climate

New South Wales lies entirely in the temperate zone so the climate is generally mild, although it can be very hot in the northwest and very cold on the southern tablelands. The western suburbs of Sydney have a reputation for severe storms, and large hail can fall between November and March. Rainfall is spread throughout the year but it is generally wetter from February to June. Summer daytime temperatures can range from 27°C at the coast to 38°C inland. Winter temperatures tend to differ less, although overnight it's colder inland.

Drought ◀

The 1895-1903 drought caused the death of half of Australia's sheep and 40% of its cattle. They say that for every 10 years in Australia there are three wet years and three dry years. At the time of writing, Australia is in the grip of a severe drought. In Sydney, mandatory water restrictions are in place.

Australia has the highest per capita greenhouse gas emission rate of any developed nation. Each person in Sydney creates 27.2 tonnes of carbon dioxide each year. Australia can therefore expect more bushfires, less rainfall and more droughts and floods. The last four years in Sydney have been the warmest on record since 1859. Sydneysiders know about the dangers of the sun but visitors often learn the hard way. According to the Skin Cancer Council of New South Wales, one in 24 males and one in 35 females will develop melanoma (malignant skin cancer) by age 75. You may hear Australians refer to 'slip-slop-slap'. This campaign, which started in the 80s, encouraged people to slip on a shirt, slop on sunscreen and slap on a hat. It is probably the country's most recognisable health message. Indigenous Australians have their own seasonal calendars, which are different to those introduced by the British in 1788.

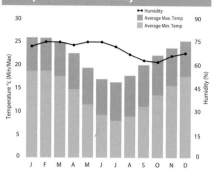

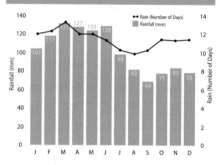

Trees ◀

The topic of trees in Sydney can ruffle all sorts of feathers. Residents are not allowed to cut down vegetation at will, so it is not uncommon for trees that block million dollar views to mysteriously sicken and die for no apparent reason.

Flora & Fauna

If you are out exploring urban Sydney at night, you may see a common ring-tail or brush-tail possum. A surprising number of lizards, turtles and frogs live close to the towns in NSW. Although none of these are venomous, they should not be handled as they are extremely sensitive. Look out for the blue-tongued lizard, a favourite with Sydneysiders. You can sometimes see eastern water dragons near water, although you are more likely to hear them as they slip away. Humpback whale numbers are increasing and they can often be seen off the coast of Sydney. Bottlenose dolphins visit the harbour too.

Birds

Many of Sydney's native bird species have thrived in the urban environment but it's not a good idea to feed them as they can become ill. Look out for pied currawongs, noisy miners, kookaburras (especially at barbecues—they love stealing meat), rainbow lorikeets, galahs, koels, sulphur-crested cockatoos, crimson rosellas,

The Blue Mountains (See p.208)

(See p.208)

WIRES

If you come across injured or orphaned wildlife, phone WIRES (New South Wales Wildlife and Information Rescue Service) on 1800 641 188 or Sydney Wildlife on 9413 4300.

Australian magpies and wattle birds. Watch out for magpies between August and November, when they have chicks in their nests. They become highly protective and will attack anything that poses a threat. These lunatic birds have a tendency to dive-bomb people and cyclists are particularly prone to attack. The birds tend to go for the eyes and one common trick is to paint a fake pair on cycle helmets.

Spiders

Australia's notorious arachnids can be found in urban areas, though they tend to have a tougher press than is really warranted. The Sydney funnel-web can be identified by the silk 'trip-lines' from the entrance to their webs. White-tailed spiders are often found in bathrooms and laundries hunting for other spiders to eat. Their venom is supposed to cause severe ulceration of the skin, but recent research by the Australian Museum suggests that this is rare.

For all spiders, except funnel-webs and mouse spiders, simply apply an ice-pack to relieve pain. If symptoms persist, seek medical attention. For suspected funnel-web or mouse spider bites, a pressure bandage should be applied and the victim kept quiet until medical attention can be given. Funnel-webs often fall into swimming pools and can appear to be drowned, but have been known to survive 24-30 hours under water.

In the case of a redback bite, seek immediate medical attention. Redbacks are common in spring and summer and can be found in garden sheds, under steps or logs and around swimming pools or piles of rubbish. About 600 bites are recorded each year in Australia, though because of their relatively small jaws, most bites are ineffective.

Snakes

You are more likely to see a snake when you are out bushwalking than when you are in a Sydney garden, unless it is very overgrown or borders a golf course. Local inhabitants include the broad-headed snake, the diamond python, the green tree snake and the red-bellied black snake. The brown snake is highly venomous but has not been recorded around the inner city region for more than 50 years.

Blue-Lined Octopus

The blue-lined octopus is common to Sydney. These venomous creatures are very shy and will dart away if they see you. All species are brown and only display brilliant blue markings when they feel threatened. The colour may tempt children to pick them up. There have been several fatalities as a result.

Plants

With colonisation, new plants were introduced, some of which did lasting harm to the environment. Forest red gums are still found in the botanic gardens but their numbers are greatly reduced. The eucalypt is found everywhere, in a number of different forms. There are over 900 species of wattle in Australia. The golden wattle is Australia's national floral emblem and is used as a symbol of remembrance. There are over 1,300 species of myrtle in Australia, including the instantly recognisable paperbarks and teatrees. Another favourite is the scribbly gum. Even if you have never seen this tree before, you will know it by its name. The smooth bark of the tree appears to have been scribbled on by a delinquent child. The marks are made by the larvae of a moth. The Moreton Bay fig and the Port Jackson fig can be found in most public parks and gardens.

Sydney's Bats

Flying foxes can be noisy and smelly when they roost in urban areas. The strong smell comes from an odour the males secrete. The noise is from the 20 different calls which the bats use to communicate. Tragically, their numbers have dropped by 30%

14

Fancy a Bite? ◀

In the last 50 years there have been 61 deaths in Australia as a result of shark attacks. Nine of these were in waters off the coast of NSW. Given the hundreds of thousands of people who swim in Sydney's waters each year, the chances of attack are minute.

in the last 10 years as their natural habitat has disappeared. In Sydney, the best place to see flying foxes is at the Royal Botanic Gardens and in the trees around the Victoria Barracks on Oxford Street in the evenings. There are also colonies at Pymble and Cabramatta.

Environmental Issues

Residents here are passionate about protecting and conserving their natural surroundings, but Sydney is still one of the world's worst generators of waste. The latest New South Wales State of the Environment report (2003) notes that urban air and recreational water quality are generally improving, but levels of smog-forming pollutants and vehicle emissions are too high. Some 267 species of plants and animals within the Sydney region are threatened by the clearing of land for urban development. Sydney uses more water than its reservoirs can provide, and recent droughts have exacerbated this.

Ozone Depletion

Australia has extreme levels of solar UV. In humans, exposure to UVB is associated with eye damage, sunburn, skin cancers and cataracts. The good news is that the use of the most damaging ozone-depleting substances will be largely eliminated in Australia over the next two years. Although the depletion of the ozone layer has reached record levels, it is expected to be fully restored within the next 50-100 years. According to a 2003 report, ozone levels have generally stabilised since the catastrophic falls of the 80s. The level of UVB radiation at the surface though, is estimated to be at higher than normal levels. The bottom line is that even though the ozone hole has stabilised, increased exposure to UVB radiation will continue for some time.

Conservation Bodies

The NSW National Parks and Wildlife Service (NPWS) is the state conservation body. It falls under the Department of Environment and Conservation NSW. The Nature Conservation Council of NSW (NCC) is an umbrella organisation for over 120 conservation and environment groups. It is a non-government, non-profit organisation. Other environmental organisations in the state include:

- Conservation Volunteers Australia (www.conservationvolunteers.com.au)
- Clean Up Australia (www.cleanup.com.au)
- Australian Conservation Foundation (www.acfonline.org.au)
- Volunteer Green Program (www.volunteergreen.org)
- Total Environment Centre (www.tec.org.au)
- NSW Wildlife Information and Rescue Service (www.wires.org.au)
- Local Community Services Association (Local Community Services Association)
- Department of Energy, Utilities and Sustainability (www.deus.nsw.gov.au)
- National Heritage Trust (www.nht.gov.au)

Barrenjoey Lighthouse

Culture

Sydney is a young, vibrant city that throws together innumerable groups and cultures. From corporate climbers to degenerate boozers, sports nuts, surfers and artists, the whole world is here.

The Sydneysider is not afraid of change, quick to challenge pomposity and endowed with a healthy spirit of self-belief. But, this is also a fashion conscious city, and Melbourners may tell you that Sydneysiders are flash and brash; more style than substance.

The city's cultural links to Britain have dissipated with immigration surges from other parts of the world. The original colonists wanted to prove they were worthy of the mother country, but with federation came a budding sense of nationhood. After the second world war, Australia welcomed settlers from Europe. Most of these first arrived and settled in Sydney, and the city's culture was forever altered with large groups of Greeks, Lebanese, Maltese and Italians. A large Jewish community grew up around the Great Synagogue. The late 20th century saw increasing immigration from Asia – a trend that began when Chinese migrants arrived during the 19th century gold rush. Each of these has left a mark on the city, from the Italian speaking shops of Leichhardt, to central Sydney's Chinatown. Today you will find Lebanese communities scattered across Bankstown, Punchbowl and Lakemba. Cabramatta is home to many Vietnamese and the Chinese, Greeks and Italians are found everywhere.

The original inhabitants of Australia, the Aborigines, have their own culture, which developed over tens of thousands of years. They refer to the creation of the world as 'Dreamtime' (when their ancestors rose from the land to become one with nature). Aboriginal people place a profound importance on reliving and recording Dreamtime and ancestral events through traditional song, dance and rituals.

Arabanoo

Arabanoo was one of the first Aboriginal men to enter the western public consciousness. Born around 1758, he was captured under Governor Phillip's orders in December 1788. He was then dressed as a European, taught English and as a friendship grew between the men, Europeans gained their first real information about Aboriginal society and culture.

Mateship

In 1999, a referendum was held on whether or not Australia would become a republic. Australians were also to vote on a new preamble to the constitution. John Howard and poet Les Murray wrote the first draft, including this bit: 'We value excellence as well as fairness, independence as dearly as mateship.' The use of 'mateship' upset just about everybody, including Les Murray. Critics complained it lacked style and insulted women. Some even suspected that the preamble was designed to shoot the debate on the republic out of the water. Both the republic and the preamble were rejected in the referendum. But republican feeling in Sydney was stronger than most parts of the country. Some 68% of voters in the Sydney electoral division wanted a republic, compared to 46% for NSW as a whole.

The Opera House at night

Language

The official language of Sydney is English, but on the streets you may hear anything from Afrikaans to Zulu. Visit Chinatown or even Eastwood and you could easily believe you're in downtown Hong Kong. The most common language spoken at home, other than English, is Arabic, followed by Cantonese, Greek and then Italian. Over one million people in Sydney speak languages other than English at home. There are more than 200 indigenous Australian languages but only 20 of these are actually thriving. The fast erradication of these native languages is mainly due to the fact that only 10% of the next generation are being taught them.

Suckholes

Former prime minister Paul Keating is remembered for his direct parliamentary style, once calling a rival an 'intellectual rust bucket' and, when in opposition, calling the government 'a conga line of suckholes'.

Strine

A true Aussie does not say 'Australian'. A true Aussie says 'Strine'. The Aussie accent is as laid back as the speaker is likely to be. For many years, an English accent was considered the way to go for middle class Australians. Today, the more down to earth version has become fashionable, as a mark of national pride. Australians also have a remarkably infectious habit of lifting the end of their sentences, as if they were asking a question. Be warned, if you live here for any length of time, you will be doing it too. Another peculiarity is the determination to shorten names. For example, relative is shortened to 'rello', musician to 'muso', afternoon to 'arvo', among countless others. The Australian approach to speech is colourful and Sydneysiders love to adapt the spoken word. Australian colloquialisms often raise vivid images, for example: 'flat out like a lizard drinking' (working very hard on a task) or 'standing like a bandicoot on a burnt ridge' (feeling lonely and vulnerable). You may feel like a bit of a 'galah' trying to figure it all out at first but you'll soon catch on.

Basic Strine

Strine	Meaning
A feed	A meal
Arvo	Afternoon
Aussie	Australian
B.Y.O or B.Y.O.G	On invitations or refers to restaurants - means bring your own booze or grog
Beaut/ you beaut	Great/ well done (praise for someone)
Bewdy	Great/ fantastic
Chook	Chicken
Chrissie	Christmas
Come good	Improve
Crook	Sick or something that is cheaply made
Doco	Documentary
Down Under	Australia
Drongo	Idiot
Dummy spit	Tantrum
Dunny	Outside toilet
Galah	Idiot
G'Day	Hello
Gong	Medal
Good onya	Praise for someone but it can also be used ironically
Heaps	A lot, as in 'thanks heaps'
Kindie	Kindergarten
Mexican	Person south of the Queensland border
Mozzie	Mosquitoes
Muster	Round up animal stock
No worries	An expression of reassurance
Oldies/ olds	Parents
Outback	The wild interior of Australia
Pokies	Poker machines
Rapt	Pleased
Road train	Articulated truck with many trailers
Roo	Kangaroo
Salvos	The Salvation Army
Scratchy	Scratch and win lottery ticket
Sheila	A woman
Snag	A sausage
Strewth	Exclamation
Strides	Trousers
Tazzie	Tasmania
Thongs	Flip flops
Too right	Definitely
Tucker	Food
Two-up	A traditional gambling game played by spinning two coins and betting whether they fall as two heads
Wobbly	Tantrum

17

Religion

Freedom of worship has been practised in Sydney since the mid 1800s. Some 30% of Sydney's population are Catholic, 20.2% are Anglican and 11.9% have no religion. The rest follow a number of spiritual paths, from Buddhism to Islam, Baptist, Sikhism and various others. As befitting the city's Christian background, the Christian calendar is followed with major celebrations at Christmas and Easter.

Places of Worship

Baha'i House of Worship (Uniting)	173 Mona Vale Rd	9998 9222	Outer North
Buddhist Centre	52 George St	9699 1555	Redfern
Central Church (Baptist)	619 George St	9211 1833	Central
Christ Church St. Laurence (Anglican)	812b George St	9211 0560	Central
Garrison Church (Anglican)	Cnr Argyle and Lower Fort St	9247 1268	Central
The Great Sydney Synagogue	187a Elizabeth St	9267 2477	Central
Community of St George (Greek Orthodox)	90 Newcastle St	9371 9929	Rose Bay
Lakemba Mosque	65-67 Wangee Rd	9750 6833	Outer West
Pitt Street Church (Uniting)	264 Pitt St	9267 3614	Central
Scott's Church (Presbyterian)	44 Margaret St	9252 7719	Central
St Andrew's Cathedral (Anglican)	Cnr of George and Bathurst St	9265 1661	Central
St Mary's Cathedral (Catholic)	College St	9220 0400	Central
St Patrick's Church (Catholic)	141 Harrington St	9247 3525	Central
St Paul's (Lutheran)	3 Stanley St	9331 1822	Darlinghurst
St Peter-Julian's (Catholic)	641 George St	9211 4100	Central
St Steven's (Uniting)	197 Macquarie St	9221 1688	Central
Surry Hills Mosque	175-177 Commonwealth St	9281 0440	Surry Hills
Sydney Congress Hall (Salvation Army)	140 Elizabeth St	9266 9801	Central
Wayside Chapel (Interdenominational)	29 Hughes St	9358 6577	Kings Cross

Race Relations

Sydney's sunny face of multiculturalism does come with some shadows and Australia's history on race relations is far from perfect. The 1838 Myall Creek Massacre, in which 28 Aboriginal people were killed by a group of white men, and the notorious 'White Australia Policy', which lasted well into the 20th century, stick out as particularly dark episodes. Segregation was enforced on Aborigines until the 1940s, when a policy of integration was introduced. In many cases 'integration' meant taking Aboriginal children from their families, resulting in another dark chapter and the 'Stolen Generations'. On Australia Day 1938, 40,000 Aboriginal people and their supporters marched from Redfern to Sydney Harbour. This was the start of the 'Day of Mourning' protests. But it wasn't until 1967 (after 90% support in a national referendum) that indigenous Australians were permitted to vote. And it was only in 1983 that the NSW Land Rights Act finally acknowledged the dispossession of Aboriginal people. The first National Sorry Day was held on May 26, 1998, to highlight the impact of forcible removal on Australia's indigenous populations.

Tensions still exist, often lying just below the surface. On February 14, 2004, Redfern exploded into violence when a young Aboriginal man, Thomas 'TJ' Hickey, died during a police chase. The riots that engulfed the suburb brought international attention to the problems of Aborigines.

Immigration brought its own problems and Australia has not always been welcoming. In 2001, elite Australian forces boarded a boat (the Tampa) full of asylum seekers. They were dispatched to an internment centre on the island of Nauru. Some were later sent to Papua New Guinea.

As with other countries involved in America's 'war on terror' tensions have developed with the city's Muslim communities. On December 11, 2005, a riot broke out when some 5,000 people gathered to 'reclaim the beach' from groups of Lebanese Muslim youths. The riot was sparked by earlier reports of confrontations. Over the next few nights, violence and vandalism spread through the southern suburbs. Sydney's image as a tolerant, multicultural example to the world took a severe beating.

However, Sydney remains an upbeat and positive city and on a daily basis, visitors and residents from all parts of the world will be made to feel equally welcome.

Clothing

Australia is still trying to outrun its reputation for style crimes. The stereotypical Aussie has a cork hat and stubby shorts that leave little to the imagination. You are unlikely to see this in Sydney, which is the most obviously fashion conscious Australian city.

Generally, dress is dictated by the weather. The winter months – June, July and August - are roughly equivalent to a European autumn, with temperatures dipping into single figures. Summer can see temperatures in the high 30s and with a blistering sun it is necessary to cover up, particularly for young children. An alien landing in Sydney would think that a hat was part of a child's anatomy.

Corporate dress in Sydney is fairly standard, but you will see fewer ties worn during the summer.

The Melbourne Cup causes an outbreak of alarming hats and impossible shoes, despite the fact that the race is run a couple of thousand kilometres away. Sydneysiders also have a thing about fancy dress, so keep a well stocked dressing-up box.

Iconic clothes

You may not see an Aussie with corks around his hat, but there are certain clothes that have achieved iconic status here. Before hitting the beach, men need to decide between boardies and budgie smugglers. Budgie smugglers are Speedos and boardies are the longer shorts worn by surfers. Currently budgie smugglers have the edge in terms of popularity.

Ugg boots have been made in Australia and New Zealand for the past 200 years. These were so-named because they are so ugly. The name is regarded as generic in Australia and consumers were outraged when it was trademarked in the US, Asia and Europe.

Driza-bone waterproof coats were invented by a Scottish sailor over 100 years ago who fashioned them from windjammer sails. These are usually worn with an Akubra hat. Synonymous with the outback, these fur felt hats have been made by Australians for over 100 years.

St Marys Cathedral

Explorer Online

No doubt now that you own an Explorer book you will want to check out the rest of our product range. From maps and vistor guides to restaurant guides and photography books, Explorer has a spectacular collection of products just waitiing for you to buy them. Check out our website for more info.
www.explorer publishing.com

Food & Drink

Other options **Eating Out** p.312

For a long time, Australian and British cuisines were inseparable. Today, few cities can match Sydney for variety. Thanks to its location, Sydney has access to Asian produce to compliment its world famous beef and lamb. An obsession with freshness and quality is reflected in the growing number of certified organic and biodynamic producers. There is no Australian cuisine as such, though as a food ritual, the barbecue is king.

As with many things here, a fusion of different cultures gives 'modern Australian' cuisine – a meeting of the best of the west and east. You will find elements from Europe, Asia and the Pacific. Italian, Chinese, Japanese, Greek, Thai, Malay, French and Vietnamese restaurants can be found in the city and Middle Eastern, Moroccan and Lebanese flavours are increasing in popularity.

The Aussie meat pie

You can also find 'bush tucker' in the city's best restaurants, with wild foods such as bunya nuts, Kakadu plums and warrigal (a spinach-like green). Specialty meats include crocodile and Northern Territory buffalo. Yabbies, a kind of crayfish, are very popular. The local caviar is very tasty, as are barramundi, prawns and Sydney rock oysters.

Before 1970, most of the food served in restaurants reflected the English history of the country. By the early 1980's, relaxed immigration laws saw Vietnamese, Malaysian, Korean, Thai, Chinese and Indian influences.

At the same time, the wine industry was developing. By the end of the 1970s, vineyards all over the southern half of Australia were producing wines that could hold their own against the best in the world. The principal wine-producing areas are in South Australia's Barossa Valley; the Hunter Valley in New South Wales; and Victoria's Yarra Valley. Margaret River in Western Australia produces fine wines too.

Shiraz is the most widely produced grape, followed by chardonnay and cabernet sauvignon. Some of the big producers and their brands are: BRL Hardy, which produces Berri Estates and Hardys; Southcorp which makes Penfolds and Lindemans; and the Orlando Wyndham Group, which produces Jacob's Creek and Wyndham Estate.

Sydney also has a number of celebrity chefs. Guillaume Brahimi presides at Guillaume at Bennelong (see p.325) in the Opera House. Tim Pak Poy can be found at The Wharf Restaurant at the end of Pier 4 in The Rocks. Neil Perry's restaurant, Rockpool, ranked 30th in *Restaurant Magazine*'s world top 50 for 2006. Luke Mangan is executive chef at Glass Brasserie (see p.325) in the Hilton, while Tetsuya Wakuda's Tetsuya's (see p.332) was ranked fifth in *Restaurant Magazine*'s world top 50 for 2006.

Dining by Suburb

Various 'villages' are renowned for their ethnic cuisines. Chinatown offers Chinese, Vietnamese, Thai, Korean and Japanese food. Ashfield is known as Little Shanghai and you can find excellent Chinese and Indian food here. Little Italy in Haberfield serves wonderful Italian food. For Lebanese dishes, visit Punchbowl, Bankstown and Lakemba. Nearby Auburn is home to many Turkish specialities. Spectacular local seafood, including fish and chips, sushi, chilli crab and freshly shucked oysters can be found at the Sydney Fish Market in Pyrmont. The Asian district of Cabramatta is an experience in itself, with its strong Vietnamese influences. Once the centre of the state's drug trade, the tourism slogan refers to it as a 'taste of Asia.' Greek food can be found in Marrickville, and Petersham is good for Portuguese. There is a small Spanish quarter to be found around Liverpool and Kent streets in the CBD. Victoria Street in Darlinghurst is famous for its coffee and Italian cafes. Cookbook author Carol Selva Rajah runs food tours visiting restaurants and shops. Call 9427 5260. Author and TV presenter Maeve O'Meara runs gourmet tours around the city. Visit www.gourmetsafaris.com.au.

The WALKMAN® logo and symbol are registered trademarks of Sony Corporation.

I ⊙ beautiful music

Music now looks as beautiful as it sounds. The new W880i Walkman® phone with up to 900 songs, it's just as beautiful on the inside.

sonyericsson.com/walkman

Sony Ericsson

Visas

Other options **Residence Visa** p.62, **Entry Visa** p.61

Anyone who is not an Australian citizen needs a valid visa to enter the country. They must get this in advance as airlines may refuse permission to board without a visa. An Electronic Travel Authority (ETA) is the same as a visa and allows travel to Australia for a short stay. The ETA is available online from participating travel agencies and airlines, as well as Australian visa offices overseas.

The CBD

Holiday Visas

The tourist visa (subclass 676) is a temporary visa for a stay of three, six or 12 months. This is for people visiting Australia on holiday and not working. It allows you to study for up to three months too. Visas are granted for single and multiple entries. The sponsored family visitor visa (subclass 679) is for people wanting to visit family in Australia. This visa requires formal sponsorship by an Australian citizen or permanent resident and allows people to holiday or visit family. The applicant must have an eligible relative in Australia or an Australian government official willing to sponsor them. The sponsor provides a guarantee that their visitor will leave Australia before the visa expires.

Inquisitive Immigrants
For further details on visas, visit the website of Australia's Department of Immigration and Multicultural Affairs at www.immi.gov.au.

Student Visas

If you want to study in Australia you will need a specific visa, depending on what you are studying. For complete details on each visa, visit ww.immi.gov.au/students/index.htm. Parents or relatives of students can apply to stay in Australia as a guardian of the student.

Professional Training

Sponsored training visas are available for people who want to come to Australia through a professional development programme as a trainee or an apprentice under an employer sponsored agreement. For further information on sponsored training visas, visit www.immi.gov.au/students/sponsored/index.htm.

The professional development visa (Subclass 470) allows sponsored foreign nationals who are professionals, managers or government officials, to attend development training programmes in Australia for up to 18 months.

The trade skills training visa (Subclass 471) is designed to help foreign nationals undertake an apprenticeship in regional Australia. An apprenticeship combines workplace-based training and classroom-based learning.

The occupational trainee visa (Subclass 442) gives you the chance to attend a workplace-based training programme, as long as it will provide additional skills in your current area of work.

Working Visas

Workers have a number of visa options open to them. For details on each category, visit www.immi.gov.au/skilled/index.htm.

The employer-sponsored workers visa is for people with recognised skills seeking to work in the country after being sponsored by an Australian or overseas employer. The professionals and other skilled migrants programme is for people who are not sponsored by an employer but who have skills in occupations required in Australia. Working holiday programmes provide opportunities for people between 18 and 30 to holiday in Australia and support themselves with short term jobs.

There are visas for business-related visits and also for people to establish, manage or develop a new or existing business, or invest in Australia. There are also visas for people to participate in specific professional, cultural or social activities, or to receive medical treatment. Migrants have their own visa classes. For full details, visit www.immi.gov.au/migrants/index.htm.

Migration Agents
There are a host of companies that offer to get you in to Australia. Typically, their services are all things that you could do yourself, but they do remove a bit of the legwork. The website www.work permit.com has a useful points calculator, so you can see how close you are to getting in.

Visa Costs

You must pay a non-refundable charge when you lodge your visa application. For applications lodged outside Australia, ETAs attract a service charge of $20.

For visa applications lodged in Australia, the tourist visa (subclass 676) costs $70. It costs $205 to extend your stay. The sponsored family visitor visa (subclass 679), which is lodged in Australia by the sponsor, costs $70. You can apply online for a tourist visa. Visit www.immi.gov.au/e_visa/visitors.htm.

E-tickets & Electronic Check-in

A number of airlines flying to Sydney airport, including Qantas, offer e-tickets. Check with your airline. Self-service check-in facilities have been introduced for certain domestic flights. Qantas QuickCheck kiosks can be used for domestic flights if you are travelling from Sydney, Melbourne, Brisbane, Canberra and Perth. Check-in at the QuickCheck kiosk and collect your boarding pass. If you are travelling with bags, drop them at a bag drop counter. Qantas Club customers with carry-on baggage can only use QuickCheck kiosks in the lounges. A self-service check-in for international travel will be rolled out in 2007, starting with Sydney Airport.

Meet & Greet

The Sydney Airport Gold Ambassador programme provides help for passengers and visitors to the international and domestic terminals. They will help with any queries you have about check-in, transport, airport facilities or accommodation. The ambassadors are easy to spot as they wear bright gold jackets.

If you want a private meet and greet service, you will need to book ahead with a private company. Taxi companies and limousine services will often be willing to do this. As an example, Getaway Shuttles (www.getawayshuttles.com, mobile 0410 604 935) offers a private meet and greet service with immediate transfer to hotels in the CBD for $120 for up to six passengers. This includes all road tolls.

There are many shuttle bus companies that provide transport between the airport and Sydney suburbs and regional areas. Check the Yellow Pages under Airport Shuttle Services, www.yellowpages.com.au. Check to see if your hotel provides a shuttle service when making your reservation, or call the Sydney Visitor Centre in the International Terminal on 9667 6050.

23

Customs

Australia is extremely strict about quarantine procedures. Food, plant material and animal products from overseas, including some souvenirs, could introduce some of the world's most troublesome pests, so customs officials check thoroughly.

You must declare all food, plant and animal products on arrival (and departure) in Australia. Some may require treatment to make them safe, others may be destroyed. You can dispose of high-risk items in quarantine bins in the airport terminal.

If you're not sure about items you are carrying, ask a quarantine officer or call, for free, on 1800 020 504. Quarantine regulations apply within Australia as well. Do not take fruit, vegetables, flowers, plants, soil or seed with you over state borders. For more information on domestic quarantine, call 1800 084 881. See p.290. Taking medicines subsidised under the Pharmaceutical Benefits Scheme (PBS) overseas that are not for your personal use or for the use of someone travelling with you is illegal and subject to heavy penalties.

It is illegal to export Australian cultural heritage items (some art, stamps, coins, archaeological objects, minerals and similar goods) without a permit. The export of firearms and ammunition also requires a permit.

Online Duty Free
To save time you can do your duty free shopping online. View www.downtown dutyfree.com.au or call 1800 733 000 and get your goodies delivered to the airport. Website www.moodiere port.com compares airport duty free shopping and prices around the world.

Duty Free Allowances

The following items can be brought in to Australia duty free. You can pool your allowance if you are a family travelling together. You get: $900 worth of goods ($450 for people under 18) including gifts (given to you or intended for others), souvenirs, cameras, electronic equipment, leather goods, perfume, jewellery, watches and sporting equipment; 2.25 litres of alcoholic beverages for each passenger aged 18 years or over; 250 cigarettes or 250 grams of cigars or tobacco products for each passenger aged 18 years or over. One opened packet containing 25 cigarettes or less is also allowed. Most personal items such as new clothing, footwear, and articles for personal hygiene (but not fur or perfume concentrates) may also be brought into Australia in accompanied baggage, free from duty. Payment of customs duty and other taxes can only be done at the airport. You may pay in cash, by traveller's cheque in Australian dollars, by personal cheque drawn on an Australian bank, by credit card (American Express, MasterCard, Visa or Bankcard) or by EFTPOS from an Australian bank account.

Leaving Australia

Check-in time is typically two hours before an international flight, but this should be considered a minimum. Sydney is a busy airport and increased security checks can slow things down. Check with individual airlines (see p.41) whether you need to reconfirm your flight. See Air (p.40) for transport to the airport.

Tourist Refund Scheme

The TRS allows tourists to claim a tax refund on goods bought in Australia. You must spend $300 (GST inclusive) or more in one store and get a single tax invoice. Buy goods no more than 30 days before departure and wear or carry them on board the aircraft or ship you are leaving on. Present the goods, tax invoice, passport and boarding pass to a customs officer at a TRS facility. Claims can be made after you have passed through customs and immigration.

Security

Sharp items must go in your checked baggage. Any found at screening will be confiscated. Liquids, aerosols and gels in hand luggage must be carried in containers of 100ml or less. These will need to be taken in a one litre, clear plastic bag and separately screened. Exceptions will be made for some medicines and baby milk or baby food.

In Emergency

For any life-threatening or time-critical emergency, dial 000. This will get you immediate assistance from the police, fire or ambulance services. You can dial 112 as an alternative to 000 if you have a GSM digital mobile phone and are outside your own provider's coverage area.

People who use a TTY (teletypewriter) or computer with modem access to the telephone network can call emergency services via the National Relay Service on 106. This is only for people who rely on text-based communication.

Police

For less urgent matters, telephone the Police Assistance Line on 131 444. Police stations in the city can be found on the corner of George and Argyle streets in The Rocks, on George Street opposite the Town Hall, at the corner of James Street and Day Street in Darling Harbour and at 151 Goulburn Street in Surry Hills.

Medical Treatment

Care in the emergency departments of public hospitals is free to citizens from countries that have reciprocal arrangements with Australia. If you are not from one of these countries, you will be charged $80 for the visit and more for each consultation and test. Countries that have a reciprocal health arrangement include New Zealand, the UK, Ireland, Sweden, Finland, Italy, Malta and the Netherlands. The requirements and entitlements vary, depending on the country you come from and the visa you hold. Visit the Medicare website for more: www.medicareaustralia.gov.au.

Lost Property

Should you lose (or find) property on any public transport service, you can contact the relevant company. For further details visit www.131500.com.au

Quick Fix
The emergency prescription service can be contacted on 9467 7100. To locate a pharmacy near you, visit www.guild.org.au. This is the website for The Pharmacy Guild of Australia. Click on 'pharmacy locator' in the menu box to find the closest pharmacy.

Emergency Numbers

Alcohol and Drug Information Service	9361 8000	Emergency services
American Express	1300 132 639	Lost or stolen cards
Dental Service	9369 7050	Emergency dentist
Domestic Violence and Sexual Assault	1800 200 526	Emergency services
Emergency	000	Emergency services
Kids Helpline	1800 551 800	Emergency services
Lifeline	13 1114	Emergency services
MasterCard	1800 120 113	Lost or stolen cards
Mental Health Central Sydney	1800 636 825	Emergency services
Mental Health South Eastern Sydney	1300 300 180	Emergency services
Mental Health Western Sydney	9840 3047	Emergency services
Mental Health Northern Sydney	1300 302 980	Emergency services
Pharmacy Guild	9467 7100	Pharmacy
Poisons Information Centre	13 1126	Emergency services
Police Assistance Line	13 1444	Police
Rape Crisis Centre	9819 7357	Emergency services
Sexual Abuse Help Line	13 1200	Emergency services
State Emergency Service	13 2500	Extreme weather emergencies
Visa International	1800 450 346	Lost or stolen cards
Youthline	9633 3666	Emergency services

Health Requirements

A yellow fever vaccination certificate is required by travellers over one year of age arriving within six days of having stayed overnight (or longer) in an infected country. No other special immunizations or medications are required for most trips to Australia.

Travel Insurance

Australian medical services are excellent, but they can be expensive for the uninsured. Even those entitled to free healthcare under reciprocal agreements will have restricted access to Australia's public health insurance system. Repatriation, evacuation, ambulance, dental and physio costs are generally not covered. A medical evacuation from Australia to the UK would cost up to $50,000. Extra insurance should be considered essential, at least until you have secured full Medicare cover (for more on this, turn to p.117).

Female Visitors

Sydney is generally safe for women travellers but common sense should prevail. Don't walk alone late at night; do stay alert if you find yourself in a deserted area. Unfortunately Rohypnol and the like have made it to these shores too, so don't leave your drink unattended in bars or clubs. If you travel by train at night, keep in the Nightsafe areas on the platforms and travel near the guard's van on the train itself (this is marked with a blue light). Nightsafe trains operate after 20:00 in the city and 19:00 in the suburbs. These only open the two carriages nearest the guard to passengers. NightRide buses replace trains from midnight. Taxis are generally safe for women on their own, as are buses. Sit near the bus driver if possible.

Embassies & Consulates	
Argentina	9262 2933
Austria	9251 3363
Belgium	9327 8377
Brazil	9267 4414
Canada	9364 3000
Chile	9299 2533
China	8595 8000
Columbia	9955 0311
Czech Republic	9371 8878
Denmark	9247 2224
Egypt	9281 4844
Finland	9327 7904
France	9261 5779
Germany	9328 7733
Greece	9221 2388
Hungary	9328 7859
India	9223 9500
Indonesia	9344 9933
Israel	6273 1309
Italy	9392 7900
Japan	9231 3455
Korea, Republic of	9210 0200
Netherlands	9387 6644
New Zealand	8256 2000
Norway	9200 2159
Pakistan	9299 3066
Papua New Guinea	6273 3322
Philippines	9262 7377
Poland	9363 9816
Portugal	9262 2199
Russia	9326 1866
South Africa	6273 2424
Spain	9261 2433
Sweden	9262 6433
Switzerland	8383 4000
Thailand	9241 2542
Turkey	9328 1155
United Kingdom	9247 7521
USA	9373 9200

Scorched Nippers
The sun can do enormous damage to young skin, so make sure your children wear a hat and maximum protection, waterproof sunscreen. If they are swimming, make sure they wear a rash vest and keep them out of the sun between 11:00 and 15:00.

Travelling with Children

Sydney is very child friendly. Shopping centres sometimes provide dedicated parking bays for parents with strollers and inside you will normally find baby rooms for changing and feeding. Some of the better ones even provide a microwave for warming bottles and a TV to watch while you feed. Many restaurants have children's menus and they will often provide crayons and paper to entertain little ones. You can find some good child-friendly pubs too. Hotels generally offer baby-sitting services and in many resorts, kids' clubs are run during school holidays. Pick up a copy of *Kidfriendly* at the visitor's centres in Sydney. You may also come across a free copy of *Sydney's Child*, often displayed in pharmacies, libraries and childcare centres. This is worth picking up too, or you could visit the website www.sydneyschild.com.au. *Sydney for Under Fives* by Seana Smith has some useful information and tips.

Physically Challenged Visitors

Accessibility
Spinal Cord Injuries Australia has a lot of useful information about accessibility issues throughout the country. Visit their website at www.scia.org.au.

Sydney has a fairly good attitude to accessibility and new and renovated buildings are required by law to include wheelchair access. Most of the city's tourist attractions have good facilities and most car parks provide dedicated parking bays. The website www.accessibility.com.au gives detailed information on accessible venues in Sydney and www.cityofsydney.nsw.gov.au gives contact details for various organisations that may be of help. It also has a map of accessible parking spaces in the CBD. Information about accessible transport can be found at the transport infoline (telephone 13 1500, TTY 1800 637 500, www.sydneytransport.net.au). Accessible Sydney buses display the wheelchair symbol. All monorail trains are accessible. Taxis can be hailed from the street or at taxi ranks. There is no 'lift' fee applicable in New South Wales. To book a wheelchair accessible taxi, call 8332 0200.

Telephone & Internet

Other options **Telephone** p.112, **Internet** p.113

There are 4,000 public payphones in Sydney that accept coins or phone cards. Local calls cost 40 cents for unlimited talk time. Long distance (or STD) calls within Australia are charged at a higher rate determined by the day and time. International calls can be dialed directly using the prefix 0011 then the number, including country code. Calls from a standard fixed telephone service to a mobile are charged a connection fee, with rates depending on the time of day and the mobile carrier. There are also blue payphones that are privately managed by small businesses. These only accept Australian coins.

Where's Wireless?
Wireless hotspots can be found at Sydney Airport, The Rocks, some McDonald's restaurants, Starbucks cafes, some hotels, Qantas Club lounges, Gloria Jeans cafes, Metropolitan cafes and some bookstores.

Area Codes & Useful Numbers

Arabic services	1800 726 001
Beachwatch weather info	1800 036 677
Cantonese services	1800 677 008
Directory enquiries	1223
Greek services	1800 189 129
Indonesian services	1800 429 432
International calls	0011
International enquiries	1225
Italian services	1800 649 013
Korean services	1800 773 421
Mandarin services	1800 678 876
NSW and ACT area code	02
NT, SA and WA area code	08
Operator services	1234
QLD area code	07
Reverse charges	12550
Spanish services	1800 726 002
Talking clock	1194
VIC and TAS area code	03
Vietnamese services	1800 644 500

International calling cards are the most convenient and cheapest way to phone home. Phone cards range in value from $5 to $50. You will find them at newsagents, kiosks or anywhere that displays the Telstra logo. Shop around for the best deal. Within Australia, telephone numbers beginning with 1800 are free, and those beginning with 13 are charged at the local rate.

Internet

Sydney has plenty of places to hook up to the net. Many public libraries offer free internet use, though you may need to be a member. Internet cafes are found all over the city with rates from around $3 per hour. Wireless access is available at the airport. You can access the Sydney Airport website (www.sydneyairport.com.au) and sign up for an account there if your ISP has a roaming agreement with one of the airport's providers. If you are in The Rocks area, you can access free Wi-Fi internet for 30 minutes. You can connect with 802.IIb or Wi-Fi technology and other handheld devices based on wireless LAN technology. For more info, call 9017 6399 or visit www.therocks.com/freewifi.

27

Sydney Tower

The state government plans to introduce free Wi-Fi broadband to the CBDs of key cities in New South Wales within the next three years. Public Networks Australia (PubNet) operates free wireless hotspots at limited locations in Sydney. Visit www.public.net.au.

Mobile Phones

Sydneysiders have taken to mobile phones in a big way. Australia runs GSM, CDMA, W-CDMA and 3G networks. GSM is provided by Telstra, Optus and Vodafone, while CDMA services are provided by Telstra, Orange, AAPT, Optus and Virgin Mobile. Coverage is generally good, especially in urban areas. CDMA services cover more remote areas. See p.112 for more.

A prepaid SIM card is probably the best option for new arrivals as international roaming can get very expensive. The SIM card, used in a GSM mobile phone, will give you a local mobile number and you will pay local rates without a contract. Incoming calls are then free. You can credit extra airtime to your SIM by buying vouchers from news-stands, kiosks and convenience stores. You will need a SIM-unlocked GSM 900/1800 compatible international cell phone. See shopping, p.265, for details of where you can buy these.

Dos & Don'ts

Smoking is becoming a no-no in Sydney. In New South Wales, legislation is up for discussion that will ban smoking in cars with children as passengers. Pubs and hotels have to limit the area in which they allow smoking. Drinking and driving is a very big no-no, as is speeding. Sydney operates driving licences on a points system. Infringements of the law can result in losing points on your driving licence. Once you run out of points, you have no licence. Double points apply on long weekends, making it surprisingly easy to lose your right to drive. You can also lose points for not having a safety belt buckled up.

Crime & Safety

Other options **In Emergency** p.25

Sydney is safer than many big cities. However, common sense should still apply. Keep alert when travelling on public transport after dark. Make use of Nightsafe areas on train platforms and choose a carriage near the guard's van (the one with a blue light). It's a good idea to keep photocopies of valuable documents in a separate place. Don't leave bags visible in a parked car. Avoid dark, deserted areas, especially if your instincts warn you against them. Keep handbags closed and firmly attached to you.

Headline crime rates in greater Sydney have remained stable recently, with only gun crime rising notably. There were 538 robberies with a firearm in the 12 months to June 2006, up from 406 in the previous 12 months. The Roads and Traffic Authority (RTA) has a useful website (www.rta.nsw.gov.au) with lots of information for drivers, including the location of fixed speed cameras. Speed is a major factor in most road fatalities.

Police

The New South Wales Police is Australia's oldest and largest police organisation, with 15,000 officers and more than 500 stations. It is the main law enforcement agency in New South Wales and has far more power than state police forces in other federal countries like the US or Canada. There are three major divisions: field operations, specialist operations and corporate services. All police carry guns. Specialist operations include a mounted unit for crowd control, a rescue unit with an excellent reputation, a marine unit and a highway patrol. The New South Wales police are also the public face of road safety. They are easily recognised by the blue and white chequered band on their cars. The uniform is quite paramilitary in style, with navy blue cargo pants and baseball cap, a light blue shirt and a leather jacket for winter.

Lost/Stolen Property

If you lose your passport, you should report it to the police and your consulate. See the list on p.26 for consulates and embassies in the city. If your airline tickets are lost, get in touch with the airline concerned. For lost or stolen credit cards, contact the relevant firm. See p.112 for contact numbers. Should you lose (or find) property on any public transport service, you can contact the relevant company. For further details visit www.131500.com.au/customerservice/lostandfound. But don't pin your hopes on getting your gear back.

Online Info
There are oodles of websites dedicated to living, shopping, drinking and working in Sydney. Turn to the list on p.50 to begin your online research.

Tourist Information

The Sydney Visitor Centre in The Rocks should be your first stop. It is open from 09:30 through to 17:30, seven days

Tourist Information		
Manly Visitor Centre	Manly	9976 1430
Parramatta Visitor Centre	Outer West	8839 3311
Sydney Harbour National Park	Central	9247 5033
Sydney Visitor Centre	Central	9240 8788

a week (except Christmas and Good Friday). See the table above or visit www.sydneyvisitorcentre.com. There is also a useful information desk with free maps and guides at the airport, though this can get a little swamped when lots of flights are arriving together.

Sydney Tourist Info Abroad

Sydney has three different groups touting its wares across the globe. Tourism Australia has more than 220 people in 21 different countries, with main offices in Sydney and Canberra. It promotes Sydney and the rest of Australia, and some overseas numbers are listed in the table here. It also has quite a detailed website. Have a look at www.tourism.australia.com for more. Tourism New South Wales (www.visitnsw.com.au) deals, as the name suggests, with the whole state. It has a site dedicated specifically to Sydney (www.sydneyaustralia.com), but also promotes areas like the south and north coast, country NSW and Lord Howe Island. Another, www.cityofsydney.nsw.gov.au, comes from the city's council. While it primarily deals with council business, it also has some decent visitor guides and info.

Tourism Offices Overseas		
Canada	Toronto	+1 416 408 0549
Gulf Countries	Dubai	+971 506 446 205
Hong Kong	Hong Kong	+852 2802 7700
New Zealand	Auckland	+64 9915 2826
Singapore	Singapore	+65 6255 4555
United Kingdom	London	+44 207 438 460
United States	Los Angeles	+1 310 695 3200

29

Star Search
The star scheme that rates accommodation in Australia is operated by AAA Tourism. Their site, www.aaa tourism.com.au, gives details of what needs to be achieved to reach a certain star rating.

Places to Stay

Sydney has plenty of accommodation options. There are a range of prices, the quality is generally good and you can find value for your money. Accommodation is spread over the city, but you will find clusters in popular areas like The Rocks, Darling Harbour and the central business district (CBD). The type of accommodation ranges from the ultra-luxurious and modern to the quaint and charming. You will find hotel chains, self-catering apartments, boutique hotels, bed and breakfasts, pub stays and budget and backpacker hostels. Prices vary but there are often special offers and discounts available. These will depend on the time of year and the day of the week. Staying longer usually gets you a better rate and choosing a room without a view will cut costs too. Visit the websites listed to get an idea of what's available.

Hotels

Other options **Weekend Break Hotels** p.214

As of December 2005, Sydney City had 121 establishments with 19,370 rooms, ranging from budget to five-star, chain to boutique, modern to historic. You can usually find a range of prices within the hotel of your choice as well. Your location will depend on what you are looking for in Sydney. If sightseeing is your purpose, The Rocks, Darling Harbour and the CBD will all suit well. If you are after the youth scene, Kings Cross, Bondi and Manly are the places to go. If you have a car, check if the hotel has parking facilities and be prepared to pay a lot for them.

Darling Harbour and Chinatown

Main Hotels

Grace Hotel

77 York St
Central
Map 3-D1

9272 6888 | *www.gracehotel.com.au*
Built in 1930, this elegantly restored, heritage-listed building is a very comfortable base. The staff are friendly and helpful, the business facilities are good and the rooms are spacious and elegant. The management are so convinced of the comfort of the beds, they will even sell one to you if you become addicted to your mattress.

Hilton

488 George St
Central
Map 3-E2

9266 2000 | *www.hiltonsydney.com.au*
After a $200 million makeover, the Hilton has reopened to win a bundle of awards. The new design feels really light and spacious. After a soak prepared by the hotel's Bath Master, you can appreciate the talents of Luke Mangan, one of Sydney's leading chefs, as he does his magic in the restaurant Glass Brasserie, see p.325.

The Hughenden

14 Queen St
Paddington

1800 642 432 | *www.hughendenhotel.com.au*
Another historic Victorian Mansion, this time situated in the heart of Paddington, opposite Centennial Park. This award-winning hotel has 36 authentically restored en-suite rooms. The setting is cosy and intimate, the staff friendly and helpful. Tea is served in the conservatory and a rocking horse and grand piano add a nostalgic touch.

Lord Nelson Brewery Hotel

19 Kent St
The Rocks
Map 2-B2

9251 4044 | *www.lordnelson.com.au*
This historic pub is set in one of Australia's finest sandstone buildings. There are just nine rooms with views of The Rocks. They are on the cosy side and you have to negotiate the stairs with your luggage, but it's worth it for the atmosphere and the location. It is Sydney's oldest pub and six beers are still brewed on site.

The Medusa

267 Darlinghurst Rd
Darlinghurst
Map 4-B3

9331 1000 | *www.medusa.com.au*
This heritage-listed Victorian building houses an outrageously quirky boutique hotel. The startling blend of contemporary and heritage aspects works surprisingly well and has proved to be a magnet for creative types. There are 18 rooms and, quirky or not, each has all the modern comforts you might need.

The Observatory Hotel

89-113 Kent St
The Rocks
Map 2-B3

9256 2222 | *www.observatoryhotel.com*

This multi-award winning hotel drips with colonial opulence. The service here is second to none yet the hotel is unpretentious. They have mastered the art of making you feel at home in five-star surroundings. The hotel's heated pool features a ceiling of fibre optic lights in the outline of the southern hemisphere constellations.

Park Hyatt

7 Hickson Rd
Central
Map 2-D1

9241 1234 | *www.sydney.park.hyatt.com*

This hotel has a great location, literally on the water's edge, under the Harbour Bridge. It feels as if the Opera House is at the end of your bed. Here you will find all the service you could ask for, with a personal butler at your disposal. The rooms are airy, modern and sophisticated, with every high-tech requirement met.

Radisson Plaza

72 Liverpool St
Central
Map 3-D3

9320 4433 | *www.radisson.com*

This hotel is more about location than views. Built in the 19th century and painstakingly restored, the Radisson Plaza has successfully married old world with mod cons to create an air of chic intimacy. There are a choice of rooms, from presidential on down, and despite being in the centre of the city, they are all quiet.

Simpsons of Potts Point

8 Challis Ave
Potts Point
Map 4-C1

9356 2199 | *www.simpsonhotel.com*

This Victorian mansion has been meticulously restored with neat individual touches. The atmosphere is intimate. The location is good and there are lovely night views to be enjoyed. You can walk to the centre of town and there are plenty of good bars and restaurants nearby. The welcome is warm and lots of attention is given to detail.

The Westin

1 Martin Place
Central
Map 3-E1

1800 656 535 | *www.westin.com*

Absorbed into the historic Sydney General Post Office, the Westin combines light and imposing space with historic atmosphere. The rooms are luxurious and great attention has been given to things like extra comfortable beds and perfect shower fixtures. The basement has an exposed section of the city's original water pipes.

Are you always taking the wrong turn?

Whether you're a map person or not, these pocket-sized marvels will help you get to know the city… and its limits.

Explorer Mini Maps
Putting the city in your pocket

Abu Dhabi • Amsterdam • Bahrain • Barcelona • Dubai • Dublin • Geneva • Hong Kong • Kuwait

EXPLORER

Budget Hotels

Sydney does have budget accommodation, but it is harder to find in popular areas like The Rocks and Darling Harbour. The accommodation listed here covers hotel and pub accommodation. Hostel and backpacker establishments are covered separately (see p.38).

100 Cumberland St
The Rocks

The Australian
9247 2229 | www.australianheritagehotel.com
This hotel was built in 1913 but its licence has been in continual use since the early 1800s. The bedrooms are decorated in the period style and the traditional-style bathrooms are shared. Rooms go for $125 per night. Breakfast is included in the rate.

700a George St
Central

The George Hotel
9211 1800 | www.thegeorge.com.au
This hotel is billed as 'hotel services at backpacker prices.' Single rooms start from $57. The location is good and it is five minutes away from Central Station where you can catch the train to the airport. The staff are friendly and the place is well run.

12a Carabella St
Kirribilli

Glenferrie Lodge
9955 1685 | www.glenferrielodge.com
This is a spotlessly clean and comfortable hotel with friendly management and a good location. Single $79 per person. A single economy room, which is smaller, is $65. You can also share four to a room, at $40 per person. Rates include a hot breakfast and shared bathroom facilities.

59 Bayswater Rd
Kings Cross

Hotel 59
9360 5900 | www.hotel59.com.au
A boutique bed and breakfast with a central location. There are only nine rooms, so book ahead. Singles, including a full cooked breakfast, go for $88 per night, with a minimum two night stay. All rooms have a private bathroom and TV, and are air-conditioned. At the time of writing, discount rates were offered for internet booking.

207 Darlinghurst Rd
Darlinghurst

Hotel Altamont
9360 6000 | www.altamont.com.au
The Altamont used to be the hangout of celebs like Mick Jagger. Now it offers accommodation at a budget level. Deluxe rooms start at $119 and include king or queen sized beds. Some rooms open onto a private courtyard and there is a guest lounge and rooftop garden. The location is good too.

22 Allen St
Pyrmont

The Wool Brokers
9552 4773
This heritage-listed hotel was built in 1886 but enjoyed a solid tarting-up in 1991. There are 26 rooms and although there are 19 bathrooms, no-one gets an en-suite. Rates start from $66 for a single and $89 for a double.

Bling Boutiques

Sydney has some very cool boutique hotels. Blue (www.tajhotels.com, 9331 9000), in Woolloomooloo, is a swanky modern hotel in a heritage-listed wharf building. There is a great sense of space and views of either Woolloomooloo Bay Village or the the Sydney Harbour foreshore. Establishment (www.merivale.com, 9240 3100) is so discreet it can be hard to find. Look for a side-alley called Bridge Lane in the CBD. It's where visiting A-listers stay and has a high level of security. The trendy bars provide atmosphere (see p.36), to counter the hush of the hotel. The Kirketon (www.kirketon.com.au, 9332 2011) is cooler than words can muster, and close to vibey Darlinghurst. The service is enthusiastic too. See p.322 for details of the popular Kirketon Dining Room and Bar.

Hotels

Five Star	Phone	Website
Amora Hotel Jamison	9626 2500	www.amorahotels.com.au
Four Points by Sheraton	9290 4000	www.fourpoints.com
Four Seasons	1800 221 335	www.fourseasons.com
Hilton	9266 2000	www.hiltonsydney.com.au
InterContinental	9253 9000	www.sydney.intercontinental.com
Novotel	9934 0000	www.novotel.com
Park Hyatt	9241 1234	www.sydney.park.hyatt.com
Radisson Plaza	9320 4433	www.radisson.com
Shangri-La	9250 6000	www.shangri-la.com
Sheraton on the Park	9286 6000	www.sheraton.com
Sir Stamford at Circular Quay	9252 4600	www.stamford.com.au
Sofitel Wentworth Sydney	9230 0700	www.sofitelsydney.com.au
Stamford Plaza Double Bay	9362 4455	www.stamford.com.au
Stamford Plaza Sydney Airport	9317 2200	www.stamford.com.au
Star City Hotel & Apartments	1800 700 700	www.starcity.com.au
Swissotel Sydney	9238 8888	www.swissotel.com
Sydney Harbour Marriott	1800 222 431	www.marriott.com.au
Sydney Marriott	1800 025 419	www.marriott.com
The Observatory	9256 2222	www.observatoryhotel.com.au
Westin Sydney	8223 1111	www.westin.com

Four and Half Star		
Crowne Plaza Darling Harbour	9261 1188	www.darlingharbour.crowneplaza.com
Grace Hotel	9272 6888	www.gracehotel.com.au
Holiday Inn Sydney Airport	1300 666 747	www.holidayinn.com.au
Novotel Brighton Beach	9556 5111	www.novotelbrightonbeach.com.au
Novotel Rockford	8217 4000	www.rockfordhotels.com.au
Radisson Hotel & Suites	8268 8888	www.radisson.com
Sir Stamford Double Bay	9302 4100	www.stamford.com.au
Stamford Grand North Ryde	9888 1077	www.stamford.com.au
The Blacket	9279 3030	www.theblacket.com
The Sebel Pier One	8298 9999	www.mirvachotels.com.au
The Sydney Boulevard	9389 7222	www.boulevard.com.au
Vibe Hotel	9955 1111	www.vibehotels.com.au
Vibe Hotel Rushcutters	8353 8988	www.vibehotels.com.au

Four Star		
Avilion	8268 1888	www.avillion.com.au
Carlton Crest	9281 6888	www.carltonhotels.com.au
Citigate Sebel Sydney	9213 3820	www.mirvachotels.com.au
Coogee Bay	9665 0000	www.coogeebayhotel.com.au
Harbour Rocks	8220 9999	www.harbourrocks.com.au
Holiday Inn Darling Harbour	9281 0400	www.ichotelsgroup.com
Hotel Stellar	9264 9754	www.hotelstellar.com
Manly Pacific Sydney	9977 7666	www.accorhotels.com.au
Mercure Hotel Sydney	1800 633 948	www.mercuresydney.com.au
Mercure Sydney	9217 6666	www.mercure.com.au
Newport Mirage	9997 7011	www.newportmirage.com.au
Old Sydney Holiday Inn	9252 0524	www.sydney.holiday-inn.com
Quality Hotel Cambridge	9212 1111	www.cambridgesydneyhotel.com.au
Rydges Cronulla	1800 221 038	www.rydges.com
Simpsons of Potts Point	9356 2199	www.simpsonhotel.com
Swiss-Grand Hotel	9365 5666	www.swissgrand.com.au
The Hughenden	1800 642 432	www.hughendenhotel.com.au
The Menzies Sydney Hotel	9299 1000	www.sydneymenzieshotel.com.au
The Sebel Manly Beach	1800 095 602	www.mirvachotels.com

Hotels

Three and Half Star	Phone	Website
Aarons	1800 101 100	www.aaronshotelsandresorts.com.au
Central Park	9283 5000	www.centralpark.com.au
Devere	9358 1211	www.devere.com.au
Hotel Coronation	9266 3100	www.hotelcoronation.com.au
Hotel Ibis World Square	8267 3111	www.accorhotels.com.au
Hotel Unilodge	1800 500 658	www.unilodge.bestwestern.com.au
Mercure Hotel Ultimo	9281 3764	www.mercure.com.au
Metro Hotel Sydney Central	1800 004 321	www.metrohospitalitygroup.com
Pensione Hotel Sydney	1800 885 886	www.pensione.com.au
The Castlereagh Boutique	1800 024 231	www.thecastlereagh.net.au
Travelodge Wynyard	1300 886 886	www.travelodge.com.au
Y Hotel City South	1800 300 882	www.yhotel.com.au
Three Star		
Alfred Park Budget Accommodation	9319 4031	www.alfredpark.com.au
Central Railway Hotel	9319 7800	www.centralrailwayhotel.com
Glenferrie Lodge	9955 1685	www.glenferrielodge.com
Harbour Breeze Lodge	9181 2420	www.harbourbreezelodge.com.au
Maze Backpackers	9211 5115	www.mazebackpackers.com
Russell Hotel	9241 3543	www.therussel.com.au
Sullivans Hotel	9361 0211	www.sullivans.com.au
The Crest Hotel	1800 221 805	www.thecresthotel.com.au
The George Hotel	9211 1800	www.thegeorge.com.au
Two and Half Star		
Highfield Private Hotel	9326 9539	www.highfieldhotel.com
Boutique		
Blue	9331 9000	www.tajhotels.com
Dive	9665 5538	www.divehotel.com.au
Doyles Palace	9337 5444	www.doyles.com.au
Establishment	9240 3100	www.merivale.com
Hotel 59	9360 5900	www.hotel59.com.au
Hotel Altamont	9360 6000	www.altamont.com.au
Kirketon	9332 2011	www.kirketon.com.au
Maisonette	9357 3878	
Manor House	9380 6633	www.manorhouse.com.au
Ravesis On Bondi Beach	9365 4422	www.ravesis.com.au
The Australian	9247 2229	www.australianheritagehotel.com
The Medusa	9331 1000	www.medusa.com.au
The Savoy	9326 1411	www.savoyhotel.com
The Wool Brokers	9552 4773	
Victoria Court	9357 3200	www.victoriacourt.com.au
Vulcan	9211 3283	www.vulcanhotel.com.au
Y Hotel Hyde Park	1800 994 994	www.yhotel.com.au
Pub Stay		
Grand Hotel	9232 3755	www.merivale.com.au
Lord Nelson Brewery Hotel	9251 4044	www.lordnelson.com.au
Royal Sovereign Hotel	9331 3672	www.darlobar.com
The Mercantile Hotel	9247 3570	
The Palisade	9247 2272	www.palisade.com.au
The Wynyard	9299 1330	www.merivale.com.au

Places to Stay

Hotel Apartments

There are many hotel apartments to choose from and you can rent them for short or extended stays. If there is a group of you, an apartment can work out to be cheaper than a hotel. They can be a useful place to base yourself for your first few months in town.

Hotel Apartments

Five Star	Area	Phone	Website
Medina Grand Harbourside	Central	9249 7000	www.medinaapartments.com.au
Medina Grand Sydney	Central	9274 0000	www.medinaapartments.com.au
Meriton Bondi Junction	Bondi	9287 2890	www.meritonapartments.com.au
Meriton Kent Street	Central	9287 2890	www.meritonapartments.com.au
Quay Grand Suites Sydney	Circular Quay	9256 4000	www.mirvachotels.com.au
Quay West Suites	Central	9240 6000	www.mirvachotels.com.au
Saville	Central	9250 9555	www.savillesuites.com.au
Star City Hotel and Apartments	Pyrmont	9777 9000	www.starcity.com.au
Four and Half Star			
Clarion Suites Southern Cross	Central	8281 3000	www.southerncrosssuites.com.au
Grand Mercure	Central	9563 6666	www.grandmercure.com.au
Medina Executive Coogee	Coogee	9578 6000	www.medinaapartments.com.au
Medina Executive Sydney Central	Surry Hills	8396 9800	www.medinaapartments.com.au
Oaks Goldsbrough Apartments	Darling Harbour	9518 5166	www.theoaksgroup.com.au
Oaks Harmony	Chinatown	9211 9303	www.theoaksgroup.com.au
Oaks Hyde Park Plaza	Central	9331 6933	www.theoaksgroup.com.au
Oaks Maestri Towers	Central	9267 9977	www.theoaksgroup.com.au
Oaks Trafalgar	Central	8297 2201	www.theoaksgroup.com.au
Pacific International Suites	Central	9284 2300	www.pacificinthotels.com
Radisson Hotel & Suites	Central	8268 8888	www.radisson.com
Somerset Darling Harbour	Darling Harbour	8280 5000	www.oakford.com
Waldorf Apartment Hotel	Central	8837 8000	www.sydney-south-apartment.com.au
York Apartments	Central	9210 5000	www.theyorkapartments.com.au
Four Star			
Coogee Sands Hotel and Apartments	Coogee	9665 8588	www.coogeesands.com.au
Hotel Stellar	Central	9264 9754	www.hotelstellar.com
Medina Executive Double Bay	Watsons Bay	8353 8988	www.medinaapartments.com.au
Oaks Concierge Apartments	Neutral Bay	8969 6944	www.theoaksgroup.com.au
Quest on Dixon	Central	8281 4700	www.questondixon.com.au
Studio 307 in Hyde Park Plaza Hotel	Central	9599 4776	www.sydney-vacation-rental.com
Waldorf Apartment Hotel	Central	9261 5355	www.waldorf.com.au

Guest Houses

A traditional bed and breakfast is a property where both the owners and their guests live under the same roof. Homestay bed and breakfast accommodation provides up to four guest bedrooms. While there are few in the city itself, there are some to the outer edges. For jaunts further afield, see the Exploring chapter, which begins on p.145.

Hostels

Sydney is something of a backpacker haven, with plenty of places catering to gap year travellers from Europe and young Aussies out to explore their vast backyard. These places tend to be clustered around vibey areas such as Kings Cross, Bondi and Manly. They are the cheapest way to stay, typically offering a bunk bed in a dormitory room. Most will also have large common areas, kitchens and laundry facilities. Official YHA hostels have no age limit but most guests tend to be young independent travellers. In the popular locations, guests may be limited to a stay of up to seven days.

Campsites

Other options **Camping** p.223

There is, unsurprisingly, no camping in the city. But, there are a number of national parks and forest reserves within an hour or so of the CBD. There are also a number of commercial camping sites but these can be overcrowded and if you want the authentic bush experience, you are better off in the parks and reserves. See Camping on p.223.

The 'Coathanger'   *Botanic Gardens*

Places to Stay

B&B Homestay

Four and Half Star	Area	Phone	Website
Arcadia House Bed and Breakfast	Glebe	9552 1941	
Magnolia House Bed and Breakfast	Outer West	9879 7078	www.magnoliahouse.com.au
The Pittwater Bed and Breakfast	Outer North	9918 6932	www.thepittwater.com.au
Glenhope Bed and Breakfast	Outer West	9634 2508	www.glenhope-bnb.com.au
Four Star			
Bed & Breakfast Sydney Harbour	Central	9247 1130	www.bbsydneyharbour.com.au
Marshalls of Paddington	Paddington	9361 6217	www.marshallsbnb.net
Pyrmont Place	Pyrmont	9660 7433	
Clovelly Bed and Breakfast	Clovelly	9665 0009	
Coogee Beachouse	Coogee	9340 7311	www.coogeebeachouse.com.au
Unrated			
Bed & Breakfast Sydney Central	Central	9211 9920	
Paddington Bed and Breakfast	Paddington	9331 5777	www.paddingtonbandb.com.au
Number 71	Bondi	9387 5338	www.number71.com
Greenwich Bed and Breakfast	Outer west	9438 1204	
Linridge Rest	Outer North	9416 1684	www.linridgerest.com.au

Hostels

Name	Area	Phone	Website
Abbey on King Backpackers Hostel	Newtown	9519 2099	www.theabbeyonking.com.au
Big Hostel	Surry Hills	9281 6030	www.bighostel.com
Bondi Beachouse YHA	Bondi	9365 2088	www.yha.com.au
DLux Budget Hotel	Kings Cross	9331 7485	www.dluxbudgethotel.com.au
Dulwich Hill YHA	Inner West	9550 0054	www.yha.com.au
Famous Jolly Swagman Backpackers	Kings Cross	9358 6400	www.jollyswagman.com.au
Glebe Point YHA	Glebe	9692 8418	www.yha.com.au
Manly Backpackers	Manly	9977 3411	www.manlybackpackers.com.au
Manly Guesthouse	Manly	9977 0884	www.ozpitality.com.au
Maze Backpackers/CB Hotel	Central	9211 5115	www.mazebackpackers.com
Pittwater YHA	Outer North	9999 5748	www.yha.com.au
Railway Square YHA	Central	9281 9666	www.yha.com.au
Sinclairs Bondi Budget Accommodation	Bondi	9371 1149	www.sinclairsbondi.com.au
Sydney Beach House YHA Collaroy	Collaroy	9981 1177	www.sydneybeachouse.com.au
Sydney Central YHA	Central	9218 9000	www.yha.com.au
The Globe Backpackers	Kings Cross	9326 9675	www.globebackpackers.com
The Original Backpackers Lodge	Kings Cross	9356 3232	www.originalbackpackers.com.au
Wake Up!	Central	9288 7888	www.wakeup.com.au

Campsites

Name	Area	Phone	Website
Del Rio Riverside Resort	Hawkesberry	4566 4330	www.delrioresort.com.au
Lane Cove National Park	Outer North	9888 9133	www.lanecoverivertouristpark.com.au
Pembroke Tourist and Leisure Park	Outer North	6772 6470	www.pembroke.com.au
Snowline Caravan Park	Snowy Mountains	6456 2099	www.snowline.com.au
Narrabeen Big 4 Holiday Park	Outer North	9913 7845	www.sydneylakeside.com.au

Getting Around

Other options **Exploring** p.146 **Maps** p.369

Hapless Flapper

During construction of the Lane Cove Tunnel, a ten metre deep hole opened up next to the Pacific Highway, causing structural damage to a nearby apartment block. Locals were transfixed by the fate of a cockatiel (nicknamed Tweety) that became trapped inside. It was eventually rescued in a $120,000 operation with a bomb disposal robot.

Public transport in Sydney has not kept up with demand and getting from suburb to city can be frustrating. But the city centre is relatively compact and between the trains, buses, monorail, ferries and your own two feet, navigating the CBD is easy. Taking a car into town is to be avoided. The road tolls are high, parking is prohibitively expensive and the road system, which has numerous one-ways, is tricky. Make sure you take at least one ferry while you are here. It is probably one of the few enviable commutes in the world. Once you move outside the city, a car is essential for independent travel. As a result, the roads can get very congested. The state government's improvement plans include revamping the ugly Parramatta Road, upgrading the arterial road network and public transport and creating fast bus services between key centres such as Parramatta and the CBD. The orbital route around Sydney is part of a plan to divert heavy traffic off congested local roads.

SydneyPass

Aimed at tourists, these three-, five- or seven-day tickets provide unlimited travel on buses, ferries, CityRail trains in the city, Harboursights cruises, Sydney Ferry services, return airport transfers and Explorer Buses (this marvellously monikered firm runs tours across the city and Bondi). Tickets can be bought on Explorer Buses and at Transit Shops (Circular Quay, Wynyard and QVB). Children under four travel free. Prices run from $110 for a three-day adult pass to $410 for a seven-day family pass.

TravelPass

These are best for commuters. A TravelPass gives unlimited travel on trains, buses and ferries within specified zones on a weekly, quarterly or annual basis. Pick up a map from CityRail ticket offices, Sydney Buses Transit Shops or Sydney Ferries ticket offices. The Red TravelPass, which covers the downtown Sydney area, costs $33.00 per week. You may also choose to have a combination of bus and ferry only. This pass does not include the Bondi Explorer or Sydney Explorer buses.

Show Me The Way To Go Home

The State Transit Authority has an excellent information line and website with journey specific information. Call 13 1500 between 06:00 and 22:00 or visit www.131500.com.

DayTripper

This pass allows you to ride the train, bus and ferry all day within the Sydney suburban area for $15.40. You can only use DayTrippers on the Airport Line if you pay an additional access fee. DayTripper passes cannot be used on Explorer Buses or the Manly Jetcat, but they do come with discounts to some of Sydney's most popular attractions. Buy tickets from CityRail stations on the day you travel.

Air

Other options **Meet & Greet** p.23

Sydney is Australia's air transport hub. A curfew on flying after 23:00 makes for a very busy airport during operational hours and delays can be a problem. But, you will be delayed in an airport that benefited from a good spit and polish ahead of the 2000 Olympics. Sydney Kingsford (SYD) was rated the 13th best airport in the world by Skytrax in 2006 and a multi-million dollar revamp is underway that will last until 2010. Direct flights are available across Australia and to Asia Pacific, the Americas and Europe. Australia's size means interstate trips are often made by plane. The journey from Sydney to Perth takes five days to drive but four hours to fly. Budget airlines such as REX (Regional Express), Virgin Blue and Jetstar (a subsidiary of national carrier Qantas) offer low fares flights across the country. See p.41 for contact details.

Airportlink Parking
The airport has short term and long term parking areas open 24 hours a day. Shuttle buses move between the long term parking area and the terminals frequently. For more information call 9667 6010.

Transport Between Terminals

The domestic terminals (T2 and T3) are walking distance apart. The journey between the international (T1) and domestic terminals takes a little longer. The T-Bus shuttle service makes the trip between T1 and T2 in 10 minutes and runs until 20:00 for $5 one way. A taxi ride will take as long but cost $8 - $12. The Airport Link train costs $4.70 and also stops at T3. The trip takes around two minutes. For more information visit www.airportlink.com.au. If you are transferring between a Qantas Domestic Flight (QF400 - QF1599) and a Qantas International Flight (QF001 - QF399) in either direction, you may qualify for the Qantas Seamless Transfer Service. For more information visit www.qantas.com or phone 13 1313.

Transport from the Airport

Airport hotels (such as the Stamford Plaza, Holiday Inn and Mercure Hotel, see table p.35) provide regular free shuttle services for their guests. The Airport Link train (www.airportlink.com.au) connects the airport to the main CityRail network. A single to Central Station costs around $12 for the 13 minute journey. A taxi to Circular Quay will cost around $25. These can be found lined up and supervised just outside arrivals. For buses, see Airport Bus, p.41.

Airport Facilities

Smarte Carte storage is at the northern end of the arrivals level in T1. Costs range from $6 (carry on bag) - $12 (windsurfer) for up to six hours storage and from $8 to $20 for up to 24 hours storage. Call 9667 0926. Baggage trolleys are available free of charge to arriving passengers. Oddly, if you are leaving Sydney they cost $4. The airport has plenty of food outlets, ATMs and money changers. There are baby changing rooms in arrivals and departures, each with a microwave. There is also an area for children to watch TV near Gate 33. There are also free internet kiosks. The medical centre is on level three and is open from 08:00 - 18:00 Monday to Friday, and 08:00 - 15:00 Saturday to Sunday. Telephone 9667 4355.

Security

Any sharp items must go in your checked baggage. Sharp items identified at screening will be confiscated. From March 2007, liquids, aerosols and gels in hand luggage will have to be carried in containers of 100ml or less. These will need to be carried in a one litre clear plastic bag and separately screened. Exceptions will be made for some medicines and baby milk or baby food.

Airlines

Aeroflot	9262 2233	www.aeroflot.com
Aerolineas Argentina	9234 9000	www.aerolineas.com.ar
Aeropelican	13 1313	www.aeropelican.com.au
Air Calin	9244 2211	www.aircalin.nc
Air Canada	9232 5222	www.aircanada.com
Air China	9232 7277	www.china-airlines.com
Air France	1300 390 190	www.airfrance.com
Air India	9299 1983	www.airindia.com
Air Link	6884 2435	www.airlinkairlines.com.au
Air New Zealand	13 2476	www.airnewzealand.com.au
Big Sky Express	1800 008 759	www.bigskyexpress.com.au
British Airways	1300 767 177	www.britishairways.com
Cathay Pacific	13 1747	www.cathaypacific.com
Emirates	1300 303 777	www.emirates.com
Freedom Air	1800 122 000	www.freedomair.com.nz
Garuda Indonesia	1300 365 330	www.garuda-indonesia.com
JAL (Japan Airlines)	9272 1111	www.jal.co.jp
Jetstar	13 1538	www.jetstar.com
Lufthansa Airlines	9367 3800	www.lufthansa.com
Malaysia Airlines	13 2627	www.malaysiaairlines.com.my
Philippine Airlines	9650 2188	www.philippineairlines.com
Qantas	13 1313	www.qantas.com.au
REX (Regional Express)	13 1713	www.regionalexpress.com.au
Royal Brunei Airlines	1300 721 271	www.bruneiair.com
Singapore Airlines	13 1011	www.singaporeair.com
SwissAir	9231 3744	www.swiss.com
Thai Airways	1300 651 960	www.thaiair.com
United Airlines	13 1777	www.ual.com
Virgin Atlantic	1300 727 340	www.virgin-atlantic.com
Virgin Blue	13 6789	www.virginblue.com.au

Airport Bus

The Sydney Buses service between Bondi Junction and Burwood includes the T1 international and T3 domestic terminals. Clearly marked bus stops are located on the arrivals level of each of these terminals. Information about fares, timetables and connections to other parts of Sydney is available at www.sydneybuses.info or 13 1500. The KST Sydney Airporter (www.kst.com.au, 9666 9988) is the largest of

Kings Cross traffic

the many shuttle services that run to and from the airport. A single into the centre of Sydney costs $10 and will stop directly at your hotel or apartment block.

Boat

Ferries are an integral part of the Sydney landscape and regular routes are as memorable as the scenic tours on offer. The trips to Manly, Watsons Bay and Taronga Zoo are particularly impressive. Circular Quay is the hub for all ferry services. During peak periods, the JetCat operates between Circular Quay and Manly. It costs $7.90, compared to $6.20 for a regular single. Ferry services also run up to Parramatta, the trip taking around 50 minutes on the Rivercat. Information about ferry services is available from kiosks at Circular Quay or through the Sydney Transport infoline. Go to www.131500.com.au or call 13 1500. The Sydney Ferries website is www.sydneyferries.nsw.gov.au.

Ferry Tickets

The ZooPass (adult $39, child $21) and AquariumPass (adult $33, children $17, family of four $81) combine a ferry trip with entrance to Taronga Zoo or Sydney Aquarium. These can be bought at the Sydney Ferries office at Circular Quay, as can FerryTen tickets. These cover ten single trips, with no expiry date. There are five different types each covering a different distance. They can save up to 36% on the cost of single tickets.

Water Taxis

This is a fun but expensive way to get about the harbour, so it pays to share the journey. A private trip from Circular Quay to Darling Harbour can cost around $75 for up to four passengers. Alternatively, shuttle rates start around $15 for adults and $10 for children. You can also order a private water limousine service, seating up to 17 passengers - visit www.watertaxis.com.au or call Water Taxis Combined on 9555 8888. Other firms include Yellow Water Taxis (1300 138 840) and Watertaxi (9211 7730).

Need Some Direction?

The *Explorer Mini Maps* pack a whole city into your pocket and once unfolded are excellent navigational tools for exploring. Not only are they handy in size, with detailed information on the sights and sounds of the city, but their fabulously affordable price means they won't make a dent in your holiday fund. Wherever your travels take you, from the Middle East to Europe and beyond, grab a mini map and you'll never have to ask for directions.

Long Distance Coaches

Interstate coaches go from Sydney Coach Terminal (9212 3433) at Central station. It's open from 06:00-22:30 and ticket offices can also be found here. The bigger firms include Greyhound (www.greyhound.com.au, 13 2030); Premier (www.premierms.com.au, 13 3410); and Murrays (www.murrays.com.au, 13 2251). Different firms offer different deals, including hop-on, hop-off tickets across the country.

Bus

State Transit Authority buses, called Sydney Buses, cover most of eastern Sydney. Private bus companies cover the south and the west. Routes are numbered according to their area. So, 100s serve the northern beaches, 200s the north shore, 300s the eastern suburbs, 400s the inner west and south to Rockdale and Miranda and the 500s and 600s the west, including Ryde and Parramatta. When a route has an L, E or X in its number, it means it is an express route or has limited stops. Fares range from $1.70 to $5.50. Main city terminuses are at Circular Quay, Wynyard, Town Hall and Central stations. The two main tourist shuttle buses, the Sydney Explorer (great name) and the Bondi Explorer, provide a guidebook and recorded commentary. Visit www.sydneybuses.info to plan your exact trip or call the Transport Info Line on 13 1500.

Maps

Sydney's CBD is laid out in nice straight lines, and so fairly easy to navigate. The outer suburbs can get a little trickier. Turn to the Maps section at the back of this book to get you started. For a more comprehensive listing, Gregory's Compact Street Directory, *found in most newsagents, is a popular resource.*

Tickets

At a marked bus stop, clearly signal the driver to stop. When you board the bus, insert your ticket into the machine near the driver. You can buy single fares from the driver (excluding "Prepay Only" bus services) but have the correct change ready. TravelTen tickets allow you to buy ten trips at once with no expiry date. DayTripper tickets include unlimited travel on bus, ferry and train services until 04:00. TravelPasses (weekly, quarterly and yearly) allow unlimited travel on different modes of transport in specified zones. BusTripper allows unlimited travel on all regular Sydney buses for one day. Adult, $11.30; child, $5.60. A one day combined Sydney and Bondi Explorer ticket costs $39.00 (Child $19). The ticket includes travel on regular Sydney buses eastwards of Circular Quay. The ticket will also get you discount offers at various popular attractions in the city.

Car

Other options **Transportation** p.136

Central Sydney is not terribly car friendly. The road system is complicated, tolls and parking charges are heavy and public transport will generally get you there quicker. A car only becomes necessary if you're outside the city where public transport is more sporadic.

You are allowed to drive on a current overseas licence for up to three months after arriving in Australia. Then you need a New South Wales driving licence, which normally involves sitting a test. Australians drive on the left hand side of the road. You must have your driving licence with you at all times when driving. If your overseas licence is not in English you need to carry an official translation.

The general speed limit in towns is 60kph but many suburban roads have a 50kph limit. The maximum speed on highways in New South Wales is 100kph and on motorways and freeways it is 110kph. Heavy penalties apply for speeding. The speed limit in school zones is 40kph between 08:00 – 09:30 and 14:30 – 16:00 on school days. Red or orange school zone signs mean that a particular school operates outside these hours.

When covering long distances, be aware of driver fatigue. Police conduct regular random breath checks and if you are driving it is better not to drink at all, though the legal alcohol limit for fully licensed drivers is 0.05g/100ml. Everyone must wear seatbelts and children need child restraints or baby capsules. For further information, contact the Roads and Traffic Authority, NSW on 13 2213.

Car Rental Agencies		
Avis	13 6333	www.avis.com.au
Budget	13 2727	www.budget.com.au
Europcar	1300 131 390	www.europcar.com.au
Hertz	1300 132 607	www.hertz.com.au
Thrifty	1300 367 227	www.thrifty.com.au

Car Hire

Prices are variable but range roughly from $47 per day for a compact manual with air conditioning to $70 per day for a big automatic with air conditioning. This is based on an average for a one day booking using well-known rental firms in December 2006. The rates include GST, vehicle registration fees, basic insurance, unlimited kilometres, recovery fees and allowed extra authorised drivers but did not allow for the age surcharge for drivers under 25. Visit www.carhire.com.au to compare rates.

Toll Roads

Bike Lockers

Secure bicycle lockers have been installed at some CityRail stations. You can rent one for a minimum period of three months for $50 plus a refundable key deposit of $50. Visit www.bicyclensw.org.au or call 9218 5400 for locations.

The following roads carry a toll: M1 Eastern Distributor ($4.50 northbound only), M2 Hills Motorway ($4.40 North Ryde each way, $2.20 Pennant Hills each way), M4 ($2.20 each way), M5 ($3.80 each way), Westlink M7 (30.81 cents per kilometre up to $6.16), Cross City Tunnel ($3.50 each way), the Harbour Bridge and Harbour Tunnel (both $3 southbound only) and Lane Cove Tunnel (due to open April 2007). The Cross City Tunnel, Westlink M7 and the Lane Cove Tunnel tolls cannot be paid in cash. e-tags are available that work on all the roads. Infrequent users without a tag can arrange a temporary pass.

e-tag companies		
Beep Tag	9033 3999	www.crosscity.com.au
Express Tag	9869 4444	www.expresstag.com.au
E-way Tag	1300 555 833	www.tollpay.com.au
Roam e-TAG	13 8655	www.roam.com.au

Cycling

Cycling around the CBD is not for the faint-hearted as traffic can be overwhelming. Most cycling in Sydney is done for recreational purposes and there are a lot of keen cyclists out and about on the weekends. The Roads and Traffic Authority NSW has established a network of bicycle routes around Sydney. Visit www.rta.nsw.gov.au for maps of these and other information for cyclists. *Cycling Around Sydney* by Bruce Ashley, published by Bicycle NSW, gives details on longer rides. Visit the publishers at www.bicyclensw.org.au.

Taxi

Clueless Cabbie

There is no equivalent of the 'knowledge' done by taxi drivers in London, and some cabbies can have a haphazard way of finding your destination. Take a **Sydney Mini Map** with you to help find the way.

Sydney taxis are strictly controlled. Cabbies are licensed and cars are inspected regularly. Taxis are metered, limousines are not. Most cabs take EFTPOS and credit

Taxi Companies		
Legion Cabs	13 1451	www.legioncabs.com
Premier Cabs	13 1017	www.premiercabs.com.au
RSL Cabs	9581 1111	www.rslcabs.com
Silver Service Taxis	13 3100	www.silverservice.com.au
St George Cabs	13 2166	www.stgeorgecabs.com.au
Taxis Combined Services	13 3300	www.taxiscombined.com.au
Wheelchair Accessible Taxis	1800 043 187	www.zero200.com.au

cards but you can save around 10% by paying cash. In the CBD it is generally easier to hail a taxi than call one. Look for a cab with the orange light on and raise your arm. You can call a cab (see table - a charge of $1.50 is payable) or you can find ranks at railway stations, major shopping centres, outside big hotels and at Chalmers Street, Chifley Square and Park Street.

Changeover is at 03:00 and 15:00 and you may find it more difficult to get a cab at these times. Drivers are allowed to refuse fares as they head back to base. Rates in urban areas are set at $1.68 per kilometre, on top of a $2.90 initial charge. Waiting time is set at 72.17 cents per minute. Luggage charges should never exceed 55 cents. Maxi cabs, for six or more passengers, can charge up to 150% of these fares. Passengers in all taxis are liable for any toll fees.

Train

CityRail (www.cityrail.info, 13 1500) trains service the city, suburbs and further afield to the Blue Mountains. CountryLink (www.countrylink.info, 13 2232) provides services throughout NSW and direct trains to Melbourne and Brisbane. Every rail line in Sydney leads directly or indirectly to the City Circle, the underground railway that accesses the CBD and tourist attractions. Trains run every two to three minutes in both directions. There are six stations and a ticket to the city can be used to get on or off at any of these. See p.40 for more on tickets and the CityRail map at the back of the book.

Monorail

The elevated monorail runs through the city, rattling above the streets to Darling Harbour, the Powerhouse Museum and back. To access the Monorail from the city there is a stop on the corner of Pitt and Market Streets. Services run every three to five minutes. Visit www.monorail.com.au or phone 9285 5600. Tickets are available from stations, with a standard fare costing $4.50. Children under five go free.

Light Rail

The Light Rail tram connects Sydney's Central Station to Haymarket, Paddy's Markets, Darling Harbour Star City, Sydney Fish Market and the city's inner western suburbs. Services run every 10 minutes, night and day, every day. Phone 9285 5600 or visit www.monorail.com.au. Tickets are available from customer service officers on the Light Rail itself. Fares start at $3 for a single within one zone. Children under five go free.

Walking

Other options **Hiking** p.232

Sydney is a fun city to walk around as every street brings its own surprises. The CBD is compact enough to be covered in detail in half a day and strolling around is the best way to get your bearings. Pedestrians are catered for with lots of crossings and pedestrian walkways but be aware that buses flash by very close to the kerb. Around Chinatown watch out for the Light Rail, which runs along the street like a tram.

The Light Rail

Mini Marvels

Explorer *Mini Visitors' Guides* are small enough to fit in your pocket but beautiful enough to inspire you to explore. With area information, detailed maps, visitor information, restaurant and bar reviews, the lowdown on shopping and all the sights and sounds of the city these mini marvels are simply a holiday must. Just give the *Sydney Mini* to visiting mates and send them on their way.

Money

The most common methods of payment in Sydney are cash, credit card, debit card and cheque. Foreign currencies are not generally accepted. The Australian Dollar (AUD) is divided into 100 cents. Notes come in denominations of $5, $10, $20, $50 and $100. Coins come in denominations of 5, 10, 20 and 50 cents, and $1 and $2. The Aussie dollar is one of the top ten most traded currencies in the world.

Holey Dollar

In the early days of the colony, a shortage of coins meant that barter (mainly in rum) was the major means of exchange. Governor Macquarie issued the 'holey dollar', a Spanish dollar with a piece cut out of the centre. In 1825 sterling became the official currency. After 1910 the Commonwealth of Australia currency was introduced. Decimal currency and the AUD came into circulation in 1966.

Banks

There are four big banks in Australia, which have branches across Sydney and the rest of the country. These are Westpac, the Commonwealth Bank of Australia, Australia and New Zealand Bank (ANZ), and the National Australia Bank. These have solid representation overseas.

There are a number of other state, regional and city banks and numerous overseas operations. As everywhere, electronic banking is becoming more common, which has reduced the number of branches. Instead, banks tend to offer automated bill payment (BPAY), dial-up services, ATMs, electronic funds transfer, internet banking, smart cards, telephone banking and touch-screen customer service terminals. Some also have currency exchange desks in branches. Banks are generally open from 09:30 to 16:00 Monday to Thursday, and on Friday from 09:30 to 17:00.

ATMs

There are some 460,000 ATMs in Australia. They are often attached to banks, in shopping centres and in some bars and clubs. They normally accept debit cards that operate internationally, such as Cirrus and Maestro. International credit cards such as Mastercard, Visa and American Express are all normally accepted in Australian ATMs for cash withdrawals.

Money Exchanges

Foreign currency can be changed at banks and bureaux de change. Rates differ little, but independent exchanges occasionally have special deals. There are plenty of these in the city and exchange facilities are also available at the airport. Late night exchanges can be found in Central Station, Circular Quay and Kings Cross. Money can be transferred through Western Union. Look in participating newsagencies, Australia Post offices and American Express Foreign Exchanges. No bank account or membership is needed. Call 1800 501 500 (24 hours) or visit www.westernunion.com.au. Traveller's cheques are not generally accepted other than by big stores, tourist shops and hotels.

Exchange Centres

American Express	1300 139 060
Thomas Cook	1800 637 642
Travelex	9264 1267

Credit Cards

Major international credit cards are widely accepted in restaurants and shops or when booking tours and the like. You can also use credit

Exchange Rates

Currency	AUD Buys
American Dollar	0.77
Brazilian Real	1.65
British Pound	0.41
Canadian Dollar	0.87
Chinese Yuan	6.10
Danish Krone	4.50
Euro	0.61
Hong Kong Dollar	6.02
Indian Rupee	34.77
Japanese Yen	90.45
Malaysian Ringgit	2.83
Mexican Peso	8.34
New Zealand Dollar	1.15
Norwegian Kroner	5.06
Singapore Dollar	1.21
South African Rand	5.72
South Korean Won	729.55
Swedish Krona	5.58
Swiss Franc	0.96
Taiwan Dollar	25.75
Thai Baht	28.42
UAE Dirham	2.92

Credit Card Companies

Visa	1800 125 440
American Express	1300 366 105
Diners Club	1300 360 060
MasterCard	1800 120 113
Travelex	1300 137 667
JCB	9247 6399

cards at ATMs to withdraw cash. According to an article in *The Sydney Morning Herald* in November 2006, there are more than 13 million credit cards in Australia. Sydney (89%) and Melbourne (87.6%) are right behind Hong Kong (91.7%) and Seoul (89.4%) in terms of credit card ownership, according to a survey of Asia Pacific by Synovate PAX. Respondents in Sydney billed an average of US$1,650 per month on their credit card.

Tipping

To tip or not is entirely up to you. It is not expected in the same way it might be in America, but it is always appreciated. Tipping is more common in swanky restaurants. If the service is good, tip 10% of the total bill. Taxi drivers are happy if you round up their fare. For porters, work on $2 per bag. You will often see a saucer for tips in cafes. Again, it is not expected, but feel free to add any small change if the service was good. It is not the custom to tip bar staff or doormen, but it will always be appreciated.

Newspapers & Magazines

Australia's media has always taken a robust approach to free speech. On a per capita basis, Australia has one of the highest newspaper and magazine circulations in the world. *The Australian* is Australia's only national daily broadsheet. The opinion pages are particularly strong. The *Australian Financial Review* is the national daily business newspaper, but it also covers politics and arts.

Sydney has two main daily newspapers, *The Sydney Morning Herald* (*The Sun-Herald* on Sundays) and *The Daily Telegraph* (*The Sunday Telegraph* on Sundays). The former is the oldest newspaper in Australia. It has in-depth domestic and international news coverage, solid business and culture reporting. News Corporation's *The Daily Telegraph* is more populist, though not necessarily sensationalist, in its approach. *MX* is given away at CityRail stations. You can buy newspapers and magazines at neighbourhood newsagents, near stations and in shopping centres. Libraries stock magazines and newspapers too. Each suburb has its own local paper, usually provided free to residents.

International newspapers and magazines can be found at newsagents in the city or can be ordered in for a regular delivery.

The Moguls

The two legends of Australian newsprint are Rupert Murdoch and Frank Packer. Murdoch started his empire with his inherited Adelaide journal, *The News*. Rapid expansion across Australian capitals brought *The Daily Mirror*, a Sydney afternoon paper. This brought him onto Packer and Fairfax turf. The Consolidated Press group (publisher of *The Daily Telegraph*) was owned by Sir Frank Packer, and the Fairfax Newspapers group published the *Sydney Morning Herald*. Murdoch then established *The Australian* in Canberra and Sydney. In the early 70s, Murdoch brought *The Daily Telegraph* from Sir Frank Packer and became one of the 'big three' newspaper owners in Australia.

Packer and Murdoch are no strangers to controversy. One of their earlier scandals took place in the 60s. Packer sent some friends and his son Kerry to apply pressure to a small publisher, Francis James, who refused to sell the Anglican Press. James locked himself in his office and called Rupert Murdoch, who sent round some burly friends of his own to throw Kerry and the others out.

The Federal Government has now introduced significant changes to media ownership laws. These will allow two-way mergers between radio, TV and newspaper companies in the same market for the first time in 20 years; a practice that was originally barred to stop the likes of Packer and Murdoch becoming too powerful. These laws will also allow foreign investors to control local media companies, and go into effect in 2007. Moguls and foreign investors started jostling for position as soon as they were announced. It remains to be seen how this power struggle will play out.

48

Media & Communications

Shocked Jock ◀

The book Jonestown *by Chris Masters is an award-winning journalist's expose of Sydney's most powerful radio talkshow host, Alan Jones. He is strident in his opinions, brutish to his callers and has influence with the PM. Masters' book has ruffled more than a few feathers at the top end of town.*

Books

Other options **Websites** p.50

For the most colourful historical guide to Sydney, take a copy of Ruth Park's *Sydney* and start your own private tour at The Rocks. Geoffrey Moorhouse describes the city with true insight, covering the history, culture, social life and political intrigues in *Sydney, The Story of a City*. *The Fatal Shore*, by Robert Hughes, is the granddaddy of Australian popular history books. *Leviathan: The Unauthorised Biography of Sydney*, by John Birmingham, is an entertaining look at the dark side of the city's past. Our own **Sydney Mini Explorer** is a pocket sized guide for tourists and should be a great help to visiting friends and family. The **Sydney Mini Map**, also from Explorer, will help you find your way around the city. Another excellent resource is *Gregory's Compact Street Directory*.

Fiction Books

For popular chicklit set in Sydney, try Maggie Alderson's *Mad About the Boy* or *Pants on Fire*. Di Morrissey is said to be Australia's most popular female author. *Blaze* is one of her blockbusters, set in Sydney. Ruth Park's classic *The Harp in the South* and the follow-up, *Poor Man's Orange*, brilliantly describe Irish slum life in the city. *Puberty Blues* is a story about girls coming of age and is regarded as an Australian classic.

Post & Courier Services

Other options **Post & Courier Services** p.114

Australia Post is the state postal service. Deliveries are made once a day throughout the week, with nothing on the weekend. Allow up to two weeks for letters and postcards to get to Europe or the US, though it doesn't usually take

Courier Companies		
Australia Post	13 1318	www.auspost.com.au
DHL	13 1406	www.dhl.com.au
Federal Express	13 2610	www.fedex.com.au
UPS	13 1877	www.ups.com

this long. Stamps for a letter to either cost $1.85. Post office hours are 09:00 to 17:00, Monday to Friday. The main post office at 1 Martin Place opens until 14:00 on Saturdays. PO boxes can be rented at most post offices and at some newsagents. Stamps are also available in newsagents and supermarkets. Visit www.auspost.com.au or call 13 1318 for more. Most international courier firms are also represented, see table.

Radio

Sydney is pretty well served for radio. Triple J (105.7FM) is perhaps the best known music channel and tries to push new talent. Triple M (104.9FM) plays solid rock. WSFM (101.7FM) plays classics, Mix (106.5FM) is all safe, unobtrusive pop and SBS (97.7FM) follows the lead of its TV partner by producing multicultural shows. On the AM dial, talk is king and 2UE (954) has some of the city's gobbier chatshows. ABC has three channels; NewsRadio (630) provides rolling news, Radio National (576) covers current affairs and 2BL (702) is calmer chat.

Television & Satellite TV

Other options **Television** p.115

Australia has five terrestrial channels. ABC and SBS are government funded. The former is a showcase for Aussie TV talent, but also buys in a lot of BBC programmes from the UK. SBS shows European football, foreign films and has a multicultural programming remit but suffers from poor funding. Both are good for documentaries, news and current affairs. Seven, Nine and Ten are commercial channels, heavy on the ads and US shows. FOXTEL is by far the most dominant pay TV package, and follows the lead of other Murdoch products, with a mix of sports, films and popular American series.

Websites

Business/Industry
www.asx.com.au	Australian Stock Exchange
www.ctc4.com	Commercial Translation Centre
www.dhl.com.au	DHL Worldwide Express
www.immi.gov.au	Department of Immigration
www.nsw.gov.au	New South Wales government
www.scec.com.au	Sydney Convention & Exhibition Centre
www.smartraveler.gov.au	Department of Foreign Affairs and Trade
www.thechamber.com.au	Sydney Chamber of Commerce

Culture
www.amonline.net.au	Australian Museum
www.anmm.gov.au	Australian National Maritime Museum
www.artgallery.nsw.gov.au	Art Gallery of New South Wales
www.bangarra.com.au	Leading Aboriginal dance group
www.hht.net.au	Historic Houses Trust
www.mca.com.au	Museum of Contemporary Art
www.nla.gov.au	State Reference Library with collections of Australian art and manuscripts
www.sculpturebythesea.com	Free, open air sculpture on coastal walk
www.sydneygalleries.com.au	Sydney Galleries
www.sydneyobservatory.com	Sydney Observatory

Directories
www.whereis.com.au	Interactive street atlas
www.yellowpages.com.au	Online phone book

Living and Working
www.ato.gov.au	Australian Taxation Office
www.auspost.com.au	Australia Post
www.bugaustralia.com	Traveling on a budget
www.cbdstorage.com.au	Storage facilities
www.kidfriendly.com.au	Childrens activities
www.nrma.com.au	National Road and Motorist Association

News and Media
www.abc.net.au	Australian Broadcasting Company
www.afr.com	Australian Financial Review
www.dailytelegraph.news.com.au	The Daily Telegraph
www.sbs.com.au	Special Broadcasting Service
www.smh.com.au	The Sydney Morning Herald

Nightlife
www.bestrestaurants.com.au	Restaurants listing
www.cheapdrinks.com.au	Search engine - find bars by type, theme, location, etc
www.darlingharbour.com	What's on in Darling Harbour
www.eatability.com.au	Restaurants listing
www.eatstreetsatnight.com.au	Restaurant listings
www.ksw.com.au	King Street Wharf restaurants and bars
www.manlytourism.com.au	What's on in Manly
www.showbiz.com.au	Preferred seating service for performances
www.sydneycafes.com.au	Cafe and bar information
www.sydneypubguide.net	Pub listings by area
www.therocks.com	What's on in The Rocks
www.ticketek.com.au	Ticket sales
www.ticketmaster.com.au	Ticket sales

Websites

Shopping

www.paddingtonmarkets.com.au	Paddington Markets
www.paddysmarkets.com.au	Paddy's Markets
www.sydney-shopping.com.au	Sydney shopping information

Sydney Information

www.bom.gov.au	Weather forecast
www.cityofsydney.nsw.gov.au	Sydney metropolitan area information
www.cityrail.nsw.gov.au	CityRail
www.discoversydney.com.au	Tourist information
www.sta.nsw.gov.au	Transport infoline
www.sydneyeguide.com	Official e-guide
www.sydneyferries.info	Sydney Ferries information
www.sydney.i4u.com.au	Tourist information
www.sydneyinformation.com	Tourist information
www.visitnsw.com.au	Tourist information

Bondi Beach

Sydney Aquarium

Pyrmont Bridge

Sydney Annual Events 2007/08

Sydney hosts a number of well established events and some quirky one-offs. Those listed below are the most popular with locals and expats alike and cover the period April 2007 – April 2008 (when the second edition of the **Sydney Explorer** will be released).

Royal Easter Show

Sydney Olympic Park
www.eastershow.com.au
April 5 - 18

This is the biggest agricultural show in New South Wales and the largest annual event staged in Australia. Around one million people go each year. The show runs for 14 days over the Easter period.

Australian Fashion Week

Various locations
www.afw.com.au
April 30 - May 4

The leading fashion event of its kind in Australia. Designers enter from all over the world, and particularly from Asia Pacific, to show their latest collections. Many of the shows are invitation only but the whole city is aware of what's happening on the catwalks during fashion week.

Sydney Writers Festival

Walsh Bay
www.swf.org.au
May 28 - June 3

This event has grown exponentially every year. It is held at Walsh Bay, next to the harbour. Featuring local and international authors, there are discussions, panels, readings and book signings. Many of the events are free.

Rugby League State of Origin

Telstra Stadium
www.rleague.com
June 13

This bruising sporting contest between the Queensland Maroons and New South Wales Blues will enter its 28th year in 2007. Club loyalties are set aside for this three-match series as players turn out for the state in which they first played senior rugby. It is considered to be the highlight of rugby league, draws massive TV audiences and is fiercely, brutally competitive. In 2007, the first and third games will be played in Brisbane's Suncorp stadium, with the second game in Sydney. The Blues will be hoping to avenge their 2-1 loss in 2006.

Biennale of Sydney

Various locations
www.biennaleof
sydney.com.au
June - August

A contemporary arts and multimedia festival, the biennale is held on even numbered years. It is renowned for showcasing innovative and challenging local and international art. The festival is held in Sydney's leading museums and galleries including the Art Gallery of New South Wales and the Museum of Contemporary Art. There are outdoor exhibition trails along the harbour foreshore. Most events are free.

Sydney Film Festival

Various locations
www.sydneyfilmfestival.org
June 8 - 24

Held over two weeks in June each year, the festival features the best of world cinema and a plethora of authentic Australian movies.

Sydney Good Food and Wine Show

Sydney Exhibition Centre
www.goodfood
show.com.au
June 15 - 17

Visitors get to sample free food and wine, see live cooking demonstrations from celebrity chefs and win prizes. Take your fill of the latest cooking products, wine tasting, book signings and show bags.

Yulefest

Various locations
www.katoomba-
nsw.com/yulefest.html
June - August

Begun by nostalgic expats, many places in Sydney provide Christmas dinner and all the trimmings in the middle of winter, when the traditionalists believe it should be held. The Blue Mountains are a favourite destination at this time of year.

Annual Events

Telstra Stadium
www.rugby.com.au
July 7

Tri-Nations Rugby

This year, the six match rugby union series between Australia, New Zealand and South Africa sees the Wallabies start with an away game against the Springboks and finish away to the All Blacks. The middle two games of the series are played in Melbourne and Sydney.

Hyde Park to
Bondi Beach
www.sunherald.com
.au/city2surf
August 12

City2Surf

More than 60,000 people compete in the world's largest fun run. The 14km race starts at Hyde Park and finishes at Bondi Beach, just short of the Bondi Pavilion. You can enter as a family or in one of more than 60 categories, covering various age groups and types of team.

Bondi Beach
www.waverley.nsw.gov.
au/info/pavilion/fotw
September 1 - 30

Festival of the Winds

This popular annual event at Sydney's famous Bondi Beach attracts kite enthusiasts from all over the world. Attractions include live entertainment, fairground rides, exhibitions, food stalls and other activities.

Milsons Point
- Opera House
www.sydney
marathon.org
September 23

Sydney Marathon

The Sydney marathon has been going since the 2000 Olympic Games and public support has grown each year. This is the only community road race that allows the public the chance to run across the Sydney Harbour Bridge, offering arguably better views than any urban street marathon in the world.

Telstra Stadium
www.nrl.com.au
September 30

Rugby League Grand Final

This year the match will be held at Telstra Stadium. This is the world's most attended rugby league competition and is considered by many to be the most competitive. It is the climax of the National Rugby League season.

Various locations
www.manly.nsw.gov.au
September 29 - October 2

Manly International Jazz Festival

The festival takes place over the NSW Labour Day long weekend. All sorts of jazz styles are catered for, and many of the events are free. The festival is well established on the international scene and is coming up to its 30th anniversary.

Bondi - Tamarama
www.sculptureby
thesea.com
November

Sculpture By The Sea

This is a free event, staged along Sydney's Bondi to Tamarama coastal walk. You get to stroll along this pretty path and view more than 100 artworks by local and international artists.

The Domain
www.homebake.com.au
December

Homebake Festival

This is a rock/alternative/dance festival featuring only Australian acts, which has been held annually for over 10 years. Audiences get the chance to see emerging talent and smaller bands. The festival is held in The Domain each year in December.

The Domain
www.carolsinthe
domain.com
December 22

Carols in The Domain

This carol concert is held annually in The Domain on the last Saturday before Christmas. More than 100,000 people with candles sing along and various popular performers take to the stage.

Bondi Beach
www.waverley.nsw.gov.au
December 25

Bondi Beach Christmas Party

Travellers get together to celebrate Christmas on the sands rather than in the snow. Entertainment is provided but be aware that alcohol is now a no-no in much of the area, after previous parties got out of hand.

Sydney to Hobart Yacht Race

Sydney Harbour
www.rolexsydney
hobart.com
December 26

Australia's premier yacht racing event attracts competitors from all over the world. The start, in Sydney Harbour, is spectacular and popular viewing. But the race has had a number of tragedies in the past and is not for the faint-hearted.

New Year's Eve

Various locations
www.sydneynew
yearseve.com.au
December 31

Sydney has a world-renowned fireworks display that centres around Sydney Harbour, near the Harbour Bridge (including fireworks shot from the bridge itself). There is a family show at 21:00 and the major fireworks display at midnight. Hundreds of thousands of people gather at vantage points around the harbour, so be prepared to stake your claim hours beforehand.

The Sydney Festival

Various locations
www.sydney
festival.org.au
January

This is a prestigious arts festival held for the month of January each year. The Jazz in The Domain and Symphony in The Domain concerts are held as part of the festival. It includes the Bacardi Latin Festival in Darling Harbour, which contains a week of Latin dancing and music.

Big Day Out

2008 venue TBC
www.bigdayout.com
January

An Australia-wide rock/alternative music festival with a side of dance, plays to more than 60,000 Sydneysiders at a time for one or two days in late January (normally on January 26, the public holiday).

Flickerfest

Bondi Pavilion
www.flickerfest.com.au
January

This international short film festival has now been running for 16 years. Films from Australia and around the world are screened over ten days at the Bondi Pavilion. Since 2003, it has been included as a qualifying festival for the Best Short Film and Best Animation categories of the Oscars.

Twilight at Taronga Series

Taronga Zoo
www.zoo.nsw.gov.au
January - March

Three months of regular twilight performances at Taronga Zoo. Music ranges from tribute acts and show tunes to modern jazz.

Australia Day

Various locations
www.australia
day.gov.au
January 26

A number of events are held in and around the harbour, including a parade of ships and the popular race between Sydney's ferry fleet. There is a fireworks display in Darling Harbour in the evening.

Chinese New Year

Chinatown
www.cityofsydney.
nsw.gov.au
February 7

The new year is widely celebrated by Sydney's Chinese community, with the centre of festivities being Chinatown. The celebrations run for three weeks and include a street parade through the city centre and dragon boat races in Darling Harbour.

Tropfest

The Domain
www.tropfest.com
February 24

The world's largest short film festival. It's a free outdoor event held for the full day, on the last Sunday of February each year, in The Domain.

Gay and Lesbian Mardi Gras

Various locations
www.mardigras.org.au
March 1

This festival, organised by and for the gay community, is one of the world's biggest such events. It lasts for a month and includes sports, cultural and arts events and culminates in the flamboyant Mardi Gras parade in Darlinghurst on the first Saturday of March each year. The festival began as a street protest and has grown into a huge celebration.

Great things can come in small packages…

Perfectly proportioned to fit in your pocket,
this marvellous mini guidebook makes sure
you don't just get the holiday you paid for,
but rather the one that you dreamed of.

Sydney Mini Visitors' Guide
Maximising your holiday, minimising your hand luggage

MOTO**RAZR** *maxx* **V6** Ⓜ

Move faster with 3.5G HSDPA high speed mobile broadband, external touch music keys and a 2 mega-pixel camera with flash. **The new *MOTORAZR maxx* V6. Cutting-edge speed for cutting-edge style.**

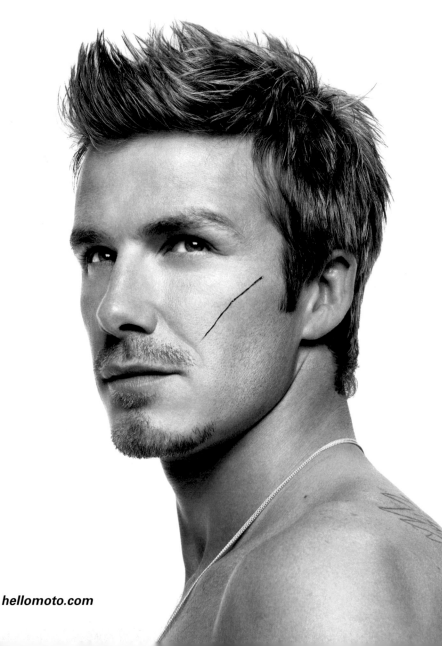

hellomoto.com

Residents

Residents

Pleasure Commute ◀
Thousands of people embark every day on what has to be the most sublime commute in the world: a green and yellow ferry across Sydney Harbour with the ocean breeze flapping your morning paper, and, if it's the season, whales and dolphins swimming alongside.

Overview

Sydney is one of the world's great success stories. What started out as a far-flung, disease-riddled and socially discordant British convict colony has developed, in just two centuries, into a model city.

It has a near-perfect climate; economic robustness; democratic political and legal systems; significant arts and entertainment; third generation communications; scientific innovation; sporting prowess; a thriving international community; high education, health and employment standards; a low crime rate and possibly the most beautiful physical setting of any city in the world.

Living and working standards are among the best on earth and Sydney regularly appears near the top of the Economist Intelligence Unit's survey of the world's most liveable cities.

One big statistic holds Sydney (and Australia) back economically: the country's population is just over 20 million (Sydney is about four million). This, combined with the continuing brain-drain of Australians overseas, has left some gaping holes in the workforce, and openings for talented new residents in key industries, like finance, ICT, biotech and pharmaceutical. Doctors, nurses and hairdressers are also in short supply. However, you're going to have to prove your worth. While the red tape is not overwhelming, the entry rules have been significantly strengthened recently.

Considering Sydney

The pros of living and working in Sydney far outweigh the cons. The joyful climate, abundance of fresh produce, proximity to the ocean, English language, economic wealth and the familiarity of western political, legal, financial and business systems all make it an enviable place to live.

On the downside, there is still a feeling of geographical isolation. Regardless of the city's bravado, it has to fight to get its blip on the world's business and commercial radar screens.

Expats from more affluent nations might balk at the modest salaries: entry-level assistant store managers earn about $34,000, while corporate lawyers with five years' experience get about $136,000. However, as Sydney becomes more desperate for skilled workers it is becoming an employee's market. Glimpse the job market at www.seek.com.au, www.mycareer.com.au, and www.careerone.com.au. See the table on p.7 for average salaries.

The cost of living is generally low (for staples such as food, public transport, taxis, domestic flights, etc), but residents bemoan tax rates and property prices. To work out which tax bracket you are likely to be in see Individual Rates on the Australian Tax Office (ATO) website, www.ato.gov.au or go to p.314.

Property prices rocketed during a recent boom that peaked in 2003. A good two-bedroom apartment in the sought-after eastern suburbs will cost at least $2,000 a month to rent. Mortgage repayments on the same place could be twice as high.

Before you do anything, read the Australian Government's immigration website www.immi.gov.au for details on visa regulations, other entry requirements and how to get the ball rolling.

Before You Arrive

There are 1,001 things to organise before you hop on the plane to Sydney. Start with the essentials, like passports and visas, and then do as many of the rest as you can before you go.

- **Documents** – make sure your passport has at least 12 months to run, get an Australian visa (see p.62), and obtain a photocopy of any sponsorship letters from employers, relatives and/or your spouse.
- **Accounts** – hire a certified accountant or tax agent in your home country with good knowledge of international tax laws. You might have to continue to do tax returns there as well as in Australia.
- **Property** – consider selling property or renting it out.
- **Bank** – inform your bank and keep your account open so you can transfer funds internationally. Sign up for internet banking to keep an eye on your money. Make sure that any regular payments in your home country (credit cards, loans etc) are still catered for.
- **Shipping** – a container of possessions can take three months to reach Sydney from Europe.
- **Change of address** – send your new address to everybody and lodge a mail-forwarding service with your post office to last at least three months.
- **Job search** – the best sites for jobs are www.seek.com.au, www.mycareer.com.au, and www.careerone.com.au. The better-known recruitment agencies include www.hays.com.au, www.juliaross.com.au and www.jobnetwork.com.au (see Finding Work p.73).
- **Home search** – for properties check out www.realestate.com.au and www.domain.com.au (see Housing p.83).
- **Schools** – the NSW Government's School Locator is at www.schools.nsw.edu.au (see Education p.130).

'Roo Spotting

Many new arrivals to Sydney might yearn to see kangaroos hopping down George Street and over the Harbour Bridge but sadly, despite the advertising hype, you will have to drive at least four hours to see your first 'roo. Or, take a trip to Taronga Zoo (p.190) on the north shore.

When You Arrive

You're on the ground in Sydney. The sun in shining, the sky is blue, and the beach is calling. However, there's some boring but essential administration to be done first.

- Apply for a **Tax File Number** (TFN) through the Australian Tax Office (www.ato.gov.au). Do this first. You need a TFN to receive an income in Australia. See p.79.
- Open a **bank account**. All you need is your passport and some additional ID. See p.77.
- Enrol in **Medicare**, the Australian Government's scheme that provides help with basic medical expenses.
- **Driving licence** – permanent residents with a current driving licence from another country can drive for three months after arrival, after which they need a New South Wales licence. This must be in English (so if yours isn't, get an official translation). See p.64.
- **Furnish** your new home and get connected. See Setting Up Home, p.106.
- **School** – by law children must attend school until they are 15 years old so make sure to enrol them early, as places fill up quickly.
- **Community** – there will almost certainly be a social group of your country's expats that you can join. These can be a useful way to learn the basics and help you settle in.
- Register with your **embassy** (p.26), so they know you are here.
- **Centrelink** (www.centrelink.gov.au) can help you find work and provide family assistance payments to residents.

Essential Documents

Certain documents will become particularly worn as you settle in to your new life. You need original photo ID (passport, driving licence) for numerous admin tasks like opening bank accounts, boarding flights, renting cars, checking into hotels, collecting post and even sending parcels overseas.

Make copies of your passport and get them signed by a Justice of the Peace (JP), who'll attest that they are genuine. If you do not know a JP, ask at your local doctor's surgery, chemist (a surprisingly large number of pharmacists are JPs) or police station. They should not charge a fee. It's a good idea to get some copies made of your birth and marriage certificates too, and anything that relates to your children. You can usually get photocopies and passport photos in pharmacies, railway stations, post offices (www.auspost.com.au/InstantPassport) and some convenience stores. It is best to get two sets of four passport photos, just in case you need some spares, and 10 copies of each important document.

Secondary documents include those without a photo that show your address, such as utility bills, bank statements or tenancy agreements.

Your documents should be in English. If you need a translator, the federal government's immigration department (www.immi.gov.au) should be able to tell you where you can find a list. If you already have an immigration agent who speaks your language, ask them.

When You Leave

When leaving Sydney, you will need to inform certain authorities.
- **Moving out** – notify a removal company at least two months before you plan to go, as they can book up well in advance. And don't forget it can take up to three months to ship a container of goods from Sydney to Europe.
- **Winding up a lease** – give the full notice required on your rental agreement so you can claim back your bond. If the landlord refuses to refund the bond and you disagree with the reasons, try negotiating first, and then contact the NSW Office of Fair Trading (www.fairtrading.nsw.gov.au). See the Tenant's Union website (www.tenants.org.au) and p.83 for more information.
- **Disconnecting** – notify utilities at least one month before you are due to leave. They will need a forwarding address to send your final bills to.
- **Finances** – notify your bank, accountant/tax agent and the ATO. If you have one, contact your Australian online share registry (you may not be able to continue to trade shares when you leave).
- **Immigration** – notify your immigration official at least one month before your planned departure. They will advise you if anything needs to be done.
- **Property** – if you own property and want to rent it out, there may be non-resident implications. You will be able to keep a bank account open for mortgage payments. See p. 77.

Mini Marvels

Explorer **Mini Visitors' Guides** are the perfect holiday companion. They are small enough to fit in your pocket but beautiful enough to inspire you to explore. With area information, detailed maps, visitor information, restaurant and bar reviews, the lowdown on shopping and all the sights and sounds of the city these mini marvels are a holiday must.

The CBD

Documents

Be prepared for a lot of form filling and frustration. Despite the easy-going nature of the Australians, their immigration system can be an administrative nightmare.

If you're being sponsored by an Australian company or a multinational with a Sydney branch then they should do most of the hard work for you and larger firms will have human resources staff that are partly responsible for overseeing the smooth transition of your visa.

Entry Visa

Other options **Residence Visas** p.62

Every non-Australian citizen needs a visa to enter Australia. In fact, you need one to board a flight to Australia, as there is no 'visa on arrival' system.

There is a veritable smorgasbord of visas on offer but none is easy to obtain. Most relevant are tourist, work and spousal visas. Your passport must have at least another six months to run but a year is better.

The Media Centre section of the federal government's immigration portal (www.immi.gov.au) has fact sheets that tell you everything you need to know.

The most common tourist visa is an Electronic Travel Authority (or ETA, www.eta.immi.gov.au), which you must apply for from outside Australia. You can apply online in minutes, there is no stamp in your passport and it costs $20.

Family or friends coming to visit you in Australia should get a tourist visa, give your residence address as their abode in Australia (or their hotel address) and tick 'Visiting Family' on the immigration card. For more on visas, see p.22.

Health Insurance

It is all but mandatory for residents to have some sort of private medical insurance. There is a national government healthcare scheme called Medicare (www.medicareaustralia.gov.au) but it only goes so far and does not cover dental and optical care or ambulance transport, and most Australians take out some form of private healthcare as extra cover.

Overseas visitors to Australia are not always eligible for Medicare and often have to pay in full for medical treatment. If you successfully apply, you will be able to claim back any expenses incurred before you were given Medicare cover.

Medicare is not free, however. To help fund it, resident taxpayers pay a Medicare levy (1.5% of taxable income). If you are on a taxable income of more than $50,000 and are single with no dependents and do not also have private medical insurance, then the federal government will charge you an extra 1% on top of your Medicare levy. See www.ato.gov.au for details.

This is the federal government's way of encouraging (some say forcing) you to take out private medical insurance.

There are 38 registered private healthcare funds in Australia. Competition between the big names (MBF, NIB, Medibank and others) is hot and they take up a huge chunk of TV and newspaper advertising.

Packages appear flexible, offering you tailor-made cover and the option of taking out

Health Insurance Companies		
Australian Health Insurance*	1800 221 133	www.austhealth.com
HCF	13 1439	www.hcf.com.au
iSelect	13 1920	www.iselect.com.au
MBF	13 2623	www.mbf.com.au
Medibank Private	13 2331	www.medibank.com.au
NIB	13 1463	www.nib.com.au

* Offers health insurance for temporary residents working in Australia

singles', couples' or family policies, but the fine print reveals restrictions and fees. Waiting periods are common, so you cannot claim until you have been paying into your fund for 12 months or more.

Trawl the websites, talk to staff and check out consumer websites like www.iselect.com.au and www.seia.com.au.

At the time of writing, a standard health cover deal with MBF costs $52 per month. This includes hospital charges such as ambulance, intensive care, operating theatre cover, shared accommodation and most pharmaceuticals. Australian Health Insurance (see table) will offer health insurance for temporary residents.

Residence Visa

Other options **Visas** p.22

DIMA and DIC
The Department of Immigration and Multicultural Affairs (DIMA) and the Department of Immigration and Citizenship (DIC) are one and the same. Visit www.immi.gov.au or call 13 1881.

There is, strictly speaking, no such thing as a residence visa. But, there are scores of different visas which provide some form of residency status: everything from media visas for film producers on long-term projects to retirement visas for over-55s who do not wish to work.

The following are the visas that will allow you to reside in Australia. They give you more rights than a tourist visa: you are able to work, apply for social security, buy property, set up a business, study and stay for longer. It is these visas the authorities keep a close eye on, especially as there is no labour card or ID card requirement in Australia. These visas vary in cost, starting at about $70 and most are renewable. There are two main forms of residency status – temporary and permanent.

Getting Started

To get a visa that will grant you residency you will need to apply either to an Australian diplomatic mission overseas or the Department of Immigration and Multicultural Affairs (DIMA) in Sydney (while you are in Australia). You can also apply for some visas online at www.immi.gov.au.

Each visa application process is different. You may be coming here as the spouse or de facto partner of an Australian citizen, on your own, to retire, or as a sponsored employee. So, you will need to work out which is the most appropriate visa for you. The fact sheets in the Media Centre section of www.immi.gov.au can help.

Visiting Immigration
Most migrants get a case officer at DIMA. He or she will tell you when to apply for permanent residency and what you need to provide. Keep in regular contact and always be on time for meetings. Early mornings are best as case loads will not yet have built up.

Permanent or Temporary?

Visas granting permanent residency are listed in the fact sheets of the DIMA website. Look under the 'Migrating to Australia' labels. This includes those covered by the Skilled Stream, Family Stream and Special Eligibility programmes. Visas giving temporary residency are under the 'Temporary Stay' in Australia and 'Temporary Residence' labels.

Spouse Visas

Spouses of Australian citizens must prove their relationship is genuine and ongoing, which can mean endless declarations from friends and family, a supply of love letters, birthday cards, photos of joint holidays and other romantic keepsakes. All copies of these must be certified by a Justice of the Peace. Immigration can interview you both, asking anything from how you met to the colour of your loved one's eyes and toothbrush.

De Facto Visas

Marriage may be making something of a comeback but the common law or 'de facto' relationship remains very popular in Australia. De facto couples have the same rights as married couples and the same regulations apply. At both the temporary and permanent stages of the application process, the Department of Immigration and Multicultural Affairs (DIMA) must be satisfied that both parties are in a genuine relationship (ongoing for at least 12 months immediately before lodging their application). Dependent family members of the applicant, such as children or lone, aged relatives, may be included in the application.

Sponsored Employees

If you are coming here to work and are sponsored by a company or organisation then you will have to show correspondence with your Australian sponsor including emails, letters of acceptance and work contracts (including start dates). You may well have to show health records or reports of medicals as well. As Australia is tuberculosis-free it is especially sharp on anyone who has TB or TB-like symptoms.

Family Members

Family members of Australian residents may have the right to join their relatives here but they will still need to apply for visas. For example, parents (retired and otherwise) of children who are Australian citizens or permanent residents (with at least two years' residency) can apply for a Parent Category visa. They will almost certainly need to have a medical to prove good health.

Children

If your child is born in Australia they automatically gain Australian citizenship (and hence full residency). If you bring children with you to Australia they will also need to enter on a visa (see www.immi.gov.au). If you bring them out to Australia while you are already living here, the immigration department may need proof that they are really your children.

Health Requirements

All migrants to Australia have to undergo a medical examination that involves chest x-rays and tests conducted by a government-approved doctor. These health checks are at your own expense. DIMA provides a list of registered doctors and medical centres where you can have these tests done.

Student Visas

If you are a long-term overseas student you must provide proof that you can support yourself. This includes evidence that you have enough money to cover living costs (for you and any family members), tuition fees and travel costs. Applicants must also be able to speak English to a good standard, have achieved a certain level of education, and sometimes, convince the immigration department that they are unlikely to breach their visa conditions by working. Students and any family they have in tow must be of good character and have medical insurance. Overseas students must apply for their first student visa from outside Australia.

Labour Card

You do not need a labour card to work in Australia. Your passport, the right visa and confirmation of your employment (like a security pass, company payroll certificate or employee number) should be enough.

ID Card

Australia has no official ID card or residence card. The accepted standard ID is a driving licence with photograph, which in the case of Sydney residents should be issued in New South Wales. It does not hurt to carry your passport as well, especially if you know you will need to give ID.

Working Holiday Visas

The Working Holiday and Work and Holiday Programmes allow people aged 18 to 30 to holiday in Australia and supplement their travel through casual work. The Working Holiday Visa (Subclass 417) costs $185 and a Work and Holiday Visa (Subclass 462 - for tertiary educated visitors) is $175. Both allow you to live and work for up to 12 months and are extremely popular, so expect processing delays.

Driving Licence
Other options **Transportation** p.136

Getting a driving licence is relatively straightforward and should be made a priority. It means you are mobile and you have a second piece of photo ID. However, if you are a new driver and need to start from scratch it can get much more complicated.
Driving tests and licences in Sydney are managed by the New South Wales Government's Roads and Traffic Authority (www.rta.nsw.gov.au). Whether you are a driver or motorcycle rider you will need to make arrangements to get a New South Wales licence. If you intend to stay in NSW and you hold a permanent visa you can use your home country licence for up to three months after arriving, after which you must get a NSW licence. Legally, only one licence can be used for driving. By law you must carry your licence with you when driving: you will be asked to produce it whenever stopped by the police and there may be fines if you do not have it. To get a NSW licence you must be aged 17 years or older. You can apply at any RTA office .

Permanent Licence
If your existing licence is in English, take it with your passport and proof of address (a utility bill or tenancy agreement will do) to an RTA office. Don't worry about photographs, they will take your picture at the office. If it is in a different language you will need to bring along an official translation from the NSW Community Relations Commission (www.crc.nsw.gov.au) or the Commonwealth Department of Immigration (www.immi.gov.au). If you cannot produce your existing licence you must get a letter from your home country's licence issuing authority confirming the details (or possibly from your country's consulate, but this can take months).
At the RTA office you will have to take an eye-test, pass tests on road knowledge and an on-the-road driving test for each class of licence required. You may be exempt from the knowledge and on-the-road tests if you have previously held an Australian driving licence, hold a current New Zealand licence, or you hold a current overseas licence (or one that expired within the last five years) from a country recognised as having comparable standards to Australia. These include; Austria,

Driving Schools		
ABC Driving School	9587 1899	www.abcdrivingschool.com.au
All Professional	9314 6604	www.drivingschool.com.au
A-Vision	9712 5049	www.a-vision.com.au
Bondi Driving School	9369 1090	–
Class A Driving School	9283 8693	–
NRMA Driving School	1300 696 762	www.mynrma.com.au
Peter Finley's Advanced Driving Schools	9873 1773	www.finlays.com.au
Road Runner Driving School	13 1741	www.road-runner.com.au
Royal Driving School	9477 1790	www.royaldrivingschool.com.au
Stay Upright	8824 9980	www.stayupright.com.au
Transport Industries Skills Centre	6297 7187	www.suttonroad.com.au
Trent Driving School	8748 4511	www.ltrent.com.au

Belgium, Canada, Croatia, Denmark, Finland, France, Germany, Greece, Ireland, Isle of Man (licences issued since April 1, 1991), Italy, Japan, Luxembourg, Malta (licences issued since January 2, 2004), Netherlands, Norway, Portugal, Singapore, Spain, Sweden, Switzerland, United Kingdom, USA. For more information, download the guide for international drivers (see www.rta.nsw.gov.au). An unrestricted driving licence costs $41 for one year, $101 for three years or $135 for five.

Temporary Licence
If you have held your existing licence for less than 12 months, you will be issued a NSW provisional P1 licence. If you have held your licence for between one and three years, you get a provisional P2 licence. Before you go to the motor registry, it is worth

getting a letter from your licence issuing authority or consulate confirming your licence details. If the letter is not in English, an official translation, as mentioned above, is also required.

Learner Licence

If you hold a provisional or learner licence from abroad and want to get a NSW car learner licence, you must be 16 or older and provide proof of your NSW address, ID, pass an eyesight test and pass a knowledge test.

Driving Test

New South Wales has a graded licensing scheme. To get a full driving licence, you need to pass three stages: learner, provisional P1 and provisional P2. You need to pass a series of tests, each costing between $34 and $42 for each attempt. You can book your test online at www.rta.nsw.gov.au.

Motorcycle Licence

Procedures for motorcycle riders are similar if you have a licence from one of the countries listed. But if you're starting from scratch you must successfully complete the Motorcycle Rider Training Scheme before getting a licence. There is a full list of training centres on www.rta.nsw.gov.au, or call 13 2213 for your nearest one. There are two levels of training - pre-learner ($69) and pre-provisional ($104). Both levels involve on and off-road training.

Christenings

Christenings and baby naming ceremonies are common in Sydney. On most Saturdays you will see proud parents clutching bundles of joy in parks and outside churches all over the city. There are few more memorable spots than in view of the Sydney Opera House. You'll pay top dollar for such a venue but it's a story your little one can dine out on forever.

Visitors

If you are on a visit or work visa you do not need a NSW driving licence, even if your stay is longer than three months. You are known by the RTA as a 'visitor'. This includes tourists, business people, those visiting friends or relatives and anyone on a working holiday visa, studying or working temporarily in NSW, or on an overseas defence force exchange.

However, visitors must hold a current overseas driver licence. If the licence is not written in English, an International Driving Permit or an English translation from the Community Relations Commission must also be carried with the licence when driving. Your visitor status must remain unchanged and all NSW driving laws apply. You might also need to prove to police that your visitor status is genuine, with your passport, letters from employers or educational institutions, or a written statement from your consulate. The Community Relations Commission is at Stockland House, 175-183 Castlereagh Street. Call on 1300 651 500 or go to www.crc.nsw.gov.au. If you intend to stay in NSW and you hold a permanent visa, you are no longer considered to be a 'visitor' and must get a NSW license.

Birth Certificate & Registration

There are no specific religious laws regarding childbirth and parents do not have to be married. A child born in Australia automatically becomes an Aussie citizen if either parent is a citizen or permanent resident. If not, and the child lives the first 10 years of its life in Australia without leaving, then on its 10th birthday it automatically becomes an Australian citizen.

Once your baby is born, you must register the birth with the NSW Registry of Births, Deaths & Marriages within 60 days. Most hospitals and midwives can provide the forms but it's up to you to get on with it. The registry keeps all records, so you (or your child) can ask for a birth certificate whenever you want. It is best (and easiest) to do this right away, so your newborn has the certificate for life.

To prove you are eligible for the birth certificate, you'll need to show three forms of ID. The bare minimum you will need is a passport as well as a Medicare card and a credit or debit card. If you have an Australian driving licence, bring that as well.

Child Alert

If you believe that an attempt might be made to remove your child from Australia, you can complete a Child Alert Request form (www.passports.gov.au). This warns the Department of Foreign Affairs and Trade, which will then check before issuing a passport or other travel document to the child.

Adoption

Adoption is quite common but can be difficult for those who are not full Australian citizens. A child born abroad will automatically become an Australian citizen if adopted in Australia and at least one of the adoptive parents is a citizen. Children adopted overseas through other processes must have at least one adoptive parent who is an Australian citizen and hold an adoption visa. To help you through what can be an exhausting procedure, check out the adoption support groups on the NSW Government website www.community.nsw.gov.au.

Marriage Certificate & Registration

Same-Sex Marriages
Same-sex marriage is not yet legal but thousands of gay and lesbian couples have held commitment ceremonies. A Certificate of Commitment is a legal document which can be used for property settlement, residency applications and more. Ceremonies can be registered by couples on the new Sydney Partnership Register. See www.cityof sydney.nsw.gov.au.

Marriage has enjoyed something of a renaissance recently, so couples now have to join waiting lists for the most popular venues. Sydney is seen as a great place to get married because of the superb weather and beautiful venues, including the beaches and coves around the harbour. Many get married outdoors at spots like the Botanic Gardens, Observatory Hill, Balmoral Beach or on a yacht on the harbour. Increasingly it is the setting that matters rather than the type of service. Many of these venues are not consecrated ground so religious ceremonies cannot take place. As a result, there has been a rise in the use of celebrants, individuals authorised by the law to conduct marriages who do not necessarily have a religious belief. For a list of wedding services see Shopping on p.265.

If you have a religious ceremony in mind, contact the relevant body. For example; the Catholic Archdiocese of Sydney (www.sydney.catholic.org.au), Australian Federation of Islamic Councils (www.afic.com.au), the NSW Jewish Board of Deputies (www.nswjbd.org) or the Hindu Foundation of Australia (www.hindunet.com.au). Most weddings conducted in Sydney follow the practices of 'western' religions but it is a truly multicultural city so you're likely to stumble over a Hindu or Muslim ceremony, which can be dramatic and full of colour.

The Paperwork

The NSW Registry of Births, Deaths & Marriages records all marriages in New South Wales. Marriage celebrants are responsible for registering the marriage on your behalf within 14 days of the ceremony taking place.

Once this is done, get your marriage certificate by completing the form in the Marriage Certificates section of www.bdm.nsw.gov.au (you will need at least three forms of identification), then print it and mail or fax to the Registry along with your ID: NSW Registry of Births Deaths & Marriages, GPO Box 30, Sydney NSW 2001 (fax: 9699 5120). You can also deliver the form in person to a registry office, courthouse or government Access Centre. A standard marriage certificate costs $38 and is delivered within three working days ($55 if you want it within 24 hours). Prices include GST, postage and handling.

Some women choose to adopt their husband's surname. This is not a legal requirement and does not require a formal change of name at the registry office, though you can if you want to. A standard marriage certificate is usually enough to change personal documents such as your driver's licence and passport. The RTA and Passport Office will not accept the Certificate of Marriage issued by the celebrant on the day of your wedding; you need the formal certificate from the registry. Also, tell the tax office when you do your first tax return after the marriage.

A typical marriage ceremony involves the bride and groom signing declarations that they are over 18 years old, not legally married to others and not directly related to each other. After exchanging vows and rings, the Certificate of Marriage is signed by the bride, groom and two witnesses. This is presented to the husband and wife after the ceremony.

Adventure Weddings

As if pledging yourself to someone for the rest of your life were not scary enough, one Aussie firm has added the element of mortal danger. FreemanX (1300 132 906) can get you hitched as you bungy jump, freefall from a plane or surrounded by sharks. See www.freemanx. com.au for more.

Residence Status After Marriage

Spouses of Australian citizens, whether married or de facto, do not have an automatic right to citizenship. To be eligible, the spouse must be a permanent resident for a certain period of time (this varies, so check with your DIMA case officer). Changes to the requirements for citizenship are due to be made law in mid-2007. Applicants will need four years' residence in Australia immediately prior to an application for citizenship and at least a year as a permanent resident. They can't have been out of Australia for more than 12 months in those four years or more than three months in the year of permanent residency. DIMA has a useful online residence calculator. Go to www.citizenship.gov.au then click Becoming a Citizen, then How Do I Become an Australian Citizen, and finally, Am I Eligible?

The Location

You have plenty of choice about where in Sydney you marry; a church, registry office, courtroom, on a yacht or barefoot on Bondi Beach. If you want a registry office wedding you'll need to book at least a month and a day before the ceremony. Weddings take place in a marriage room, which accommodates up to 12 guests. The registry provides the vows and the ceremony takes 15 to 20 minutes. Bring your full (certified) birth certificates with you. If you were born overseas, a birth certificate or foreign passport is needed.

If you have been previously married, you must provide a death certificate (if you have been widowed) or your final divorce papers. All documents provided to the registry must be originals and in English. Once you have all the paperwork, you can have your initial interview with a marriage officer and he or she will arrange a date and time for the ceremony. If you cannot attend an interview to lodge your Notice of Intended Marriage with the registry, you may be able to post the documents. Call the registry on 1300 655 236 for more.

If you marry somewhere other than a registry office, you must give a marriage celebrant at least one month and one day's notice of an intended date. Civil and religious celebrants are listed on the Attorney General's website; www.ag.gov.au/celebrants. Once you have chosen a marriage celebrant, they will ask you to complete the Notice of Intended Marriage form (they'll give you this).

Death Certificate & Registration

In the Event of a Death

Most deaths occur in a hospital or other care facility and those authorities can take care of the formalities. If the death happens elsewhere, call the person's doctor. A doctor must certify that death has occurred, determine the cause and time, and sign and issue a Medical Certificate Cause of Death. The doctor or an ambulance will then take the body to a mortuary.

Funeral Directors

Next, get in touch with a funeral director. You can find lists of these at the Australian Funeral Directors Association (www.afda.org.au). Don't expect an immediate funeral. First, the doctor must sign and issue a Death Certificate. Only then can the funeral company take charge of the body and prepare for the service.

Claiming Life Insurance

Contact the deceased's insurance policy provider, which will almost certainly need you to present the doctor's Medical Certificate Cause of Death, a Death Certificate from the NSW Registry of Births, Marriages & Deaths, your own proof of identification, and (if applicable) a copy of the coroner's report.

The Funeral

The family has almost absolute choice when it comes to the funeral service. The only exception is if the death resulted in a coroner's investigation (as in some murder cases). Then the authorities might only allow a burial, in case the body has to be exhumed later for further investigation.

In Australia today the number of people choosing to be cremated is increasing and cremations now outnumber burials. Funeral direction used to be solely a family-run business but it is becoming more corporate as further franchises open. It's not exactly 'Funerals R Us' yet but for a more traditional funeral you may want to pick a family-owned business.

Organ Donation

Donating organs often polarises views, with some believing there can be no greater gift and others believing organs are sacred and should be buried or cremated with the body. The choice is yours. You can find out more from Medicare's Australian Organ Donor Register which contains more than 800,000 donor names (www.medicare australia.gov.au).

Investigation and Autopsy

In certain instances (like suspicious deaths) it may not be legally possible for a doctor to issue a certificate. If a doctor cannot determine the cause of death, it is unexpected or happens in an institution, the police and coroner may get involved. A post mortem examination (autopsy) is a detailed examination of the body conducted by a pathologist to establish the cause of death. A funeral director can liaise with coroner's staff for you and be ready when the body is released.

Registering a Death

Funeral directors are legally responsible for registering a death within seven days of the burial or cremation. The NSW Registry of Births Marriages & Deaths then uses the details to produce a death certificate. You can get these by completing an application form in the Death Certificates section of the registry's website (www.bdm.nsw.gov.au – cost $38, but prices are subject to change). Death certificate applications need three forms of identification: a passport, Medicare card and credit or debit card. If you have an Australian driving licence, bring that as well.

It is also possible for a relative of the deceased to complete the death registration process but this is complicated. You will need to provide the deceased's surname, first names, sex, date of death and birth, place of death, address, occupation, marriage details (place, age, full name of spouse), details of children and both parents.

As well as that lengthy list, you will need to supply a Medical Certificate Cause of Death (the one issued by the doctor) stating the cause of death. If the coroner has been involved you must supply the coronial order. If you are not a funeral director and wish to register a death, call 1300 655 236 for a registration form.

Returning the Deceased to Country of Origin

This is known as repatriating the body and in multicultural Sydney is quite popular. It must be organised through a registered funeral director and a death certificate must be issued before the body can be put on a plane or ship.

just arrived? **living here?**
exceptional talent requires unique opportunities

Charterhouse Consulting Team

Martin O'Donnell (+612 9641 2472)
martinod@charterhouse.jobs

Robin Jerome (+612 9641 2424)
robinj@charterhouse.jobs

web www.charterhouse.jobs

SYDNEY ▪ MELBOURNE ▪ SINGAPORE
▪ HONG KONG ▪ DUBAI

CHARTERHOUSE
p a r t n e r s h i p

At Charterhouse Partnership we believe that high achieving organisations and individuals deserve dedication and excellence. Our contract consulting team have been drawn from the most experienced and highly regarded industry specialists and are committed to ensuring mutually beneficial engagements for our candidates and clients.

If your expectations and aspirations know no borders or limits, register with Charterhouse. We are passionate about connecting our industry-leading clients with talent befitting their requirements.

Our reputation has been built on our innovative approach to connecting high-achieving travellers with career opportunities in:

- Accounting
- Financial Services
- Construction Management
- Manufacturing & Supply Chain
- Sales & Marketing
- Technology
- Professional Support

03373

Working in Sydney

Australia is a hard-working nation whose prosperity has been built very much against the odds. The first few generations of convicts and free settlers in the early 19th century overcame immense hardships in a hostile climate smitten by drought and plague. These early Australians became known as 'battlers' and their dogged work ethic is still celebrated.

Today, however, Australia suffers from a brain-drain as talent emigrates overseas from a relatively small population. This presents significant opportunities for expats in certain industries, notably finance, ICT, insurance and business services, pharmaceuticals and biotechnology.

Different industries have built up critical mass in different cities. Sydney is the financial centre of the nation; Australia's New York, if you like. It is home to the Australian Stock Exchange and the Reserve Bank, as well as big multinational banks like Macquarie, Babcock & Brown, Deutsche Bank and ABN AMRO. It is also the focus for the insurance and financial services industries, with AMP and NRMA based here.

Skills Shortage Lists

Doctors and nurses are currently the most sought-after professionals in Sydney, closely followed by hairdressers. Suggestions that this is a government drive to eradicate the mullet should not be taken seriously. Experts in finance, law and biotech and pharmaceutical businesses are also urgently required.

Multinational Workforce

Foreign workers tend to be spread evenly across various industries. Take any large corporation and it is likely to be made up of British, Asian, American and European employees – usually from enough different nations to stage a mini-World Cup during a lunch break.

There are few jobs that are reserved solely for Australian citizens, apart from certain government positions and those requiring in-depth security checks. Usually any job application will contain the words 'applicants must be permanent residents of Australia' and only rarely will they say 'Australian citizens only'.

You will almost certainly need to be a strong if not fluent English speaker. If you are from a non-English speaking country you will have to pass an English proficiency test to get your visa and qualify for employment.

Work & Play

As a rule, the working week is Monday to Friday but store workers and those on shifts will be required to work weekends. Sunday is generally the one guaranteed day off, unless you work in the hospitality industry, when it could be your busiest day of the week.

The lifestyle of New South Wales (NSW) is similar to the lifestyles of North America and Europe, which eases the transition for executives who choose to relocate here. Australia and North America share similar legal systems, education systems and business cultures. These factors are a major attraction for many expats who choose Sydney as a long-term base. As the most multicultural city in Asia Pacific, Sydney has produced a society that is creative, open and friendly.

Workers Wanted

Over the past few years the NSW government has been on recruitment drives in several overseas regions, including Europe and North America, to attract skilled migrants. At the heart of the talent drive is the State/Territory Nominated Independent (STNI) programme, which sponsors skilled migrants to move to Sydney for the first time. The NSW government wants to double the number of skilled migrants coming to the state from 350 a year to at least 700.

There is a strong focus on attracting high value, highly skilled applicants in the fields of finance, information technology, biotechnology, pharmaceuticals and film and television. The labour market is competitive but the competition tends to be between employers rather than employees. This is resulting in some industries (notably the hotel industry) having seriously under-experienced staff in positions of considerable responsibility and being, frankly, out of their depth. It is also, according to some, breeding a culture of superiority among the skilled labour force.

Standard & Cost of Living

Residents moving from more affluent nations might balk at Sydney salaries, which many migrants consider modest. An entry-level assistant store manager can expect about $34,000, while a corporate lawyer with five years' experience about $136,000. However, as Sydney becomes more desperate for skilled workers it is becoming an employee's market. The median graduate wage for 2007 is estimated to reach $45,000. There is little if any difference between salaries offered by Australian companies and multinationals. The only benefits of working for the latter would be the chance to relocate again in the future to a bigger office overseas.

The cost of living in Sydney is generally quite low (for staples such as food, public transport, taxis, domestic flights, etc., see p.79), but tax and property costs are considered high.

Property prices rocketed during a recent boom that peaked in 2003, and this has impacted both buying and renting. For a good two-bedroom apartment in the sought-after eastern suburbs expect to pay at least $2,000 a month. Mortgage repayments on the same apartment can easily be twice that.

Another important financial factor to consider is the tax rate, see p.80. And, if you are working as a freelancer or contractor or have your own business, don't forget the fiendishly complicated 10% GST (Goods and Services Tax). This applies to items such as newspapers and postage stamps and domestic flights (but not international ones). Like VAT in the UK it is almost always included in the marked price and most residents don't even notice it, but it gets complicated if you set up your own business and have (by law) to complete quarterly GST calculations (known as Business Activity Statements). Get the latest GST information from the ATO or an approved Australian accountant.

Aussie CVs
Don't be lulled into a false sense of security by any images of Australia as a laid-back country. With CVs, you should be as formal as if you were applying to be the head of the Bank of England. Australians can be formal and old fashioned so don't shorten words and don't use colloquialisms.

Employment Packages

These are as changeable as the Sydney wind and rely entirely on the company. Feel free to ask for share options, relocation expenses, health benefits, housing costs, cars, start-up allowances, flights home, shipping costs, etc. Yes, it's an employees' market but no, you cannot expect the world. Certainly, the deals will be nowhere as fruitful and attractive as they have been in some Middle East countries. Then again, you can always negotiate. See the table on p.7 for NSW averages.

Backwater Syndrome

The attractions of moving to live and work in Sydney are mixed. Unless you are working in the big banks, you are unlikely to earn a fortune – and you'll be heavily taxed anyway. The cost of living is not high (see above) but certain crucial elements are expensive (housing costs, for example), which makes saving large amounts of money difficult.

For some it may be career development (maybe a chance to work in a regional office rather than a country branch in Asia or New Zealand, for example) but for others it can be a sideways or backward step. Despite Australia being a country of significant innovation it is still considered by many multinational companies as something of a backwater. A recent Innovation Index survey by Fujitsu Consulting in Sydney found that big global companies were willing to spend billions on innovation worldwide but comparatively little in Australia. There are companies like Macquarie Bank and Babcock & Brown who are developing novel financial

71

engineering systems and the rest of the world is taking note, but generally no one is looking at Sydney as a major city; it is in many ways just a regional hub for the Asia-Pacific and new migrants would do well to take the glossy Sydney business hype with a pinch of salt.

Security Hassles

There are very few frustrations when working in Sydney but one you may encounter is the level of security and auditing. In Australia companies and authorities have to be more and more accountable. There has been a determined effort to stamp out corruption and money laundering, although Australia is not clear of this yet. If you work for almost any big company or organisation expect to undergo security checks, have to show electronic passes regularly and generally have your movements monitored in a way you may not be used to.

Researching the Job Market

You can get ahead of the game and research the Sydney job market before you come. As long as you have an internet connection it's not hard. The best three websites are www.seek.com.au, www.mycareer.com.au and www.careerone.com.au. They all have hundreds of vacancies, many of which can be applied for online. Sydney firms will expect international residents to make up a big chunk of their applications.

Working Hours

The working week is 38 hours, usually from Monday to Friday, depending on the field you work in. Sydneysiders tend to start early (between 07:00 and 08:00), especially in the hotter months from November to March, and be out of the door around 16:00 - there's a beach waiting for you at the end of your commute after all.

Public and private sector staff typically get 20 days holiday per year. Employees who have chalked up more than 10 years service are entitled to long service leave which is usually two months paid leave, plus one month for every additional five years. Public holidays are decided by the federal and state governments. Compared to other states, NSW does poorly for non-national public holidays with only two scheduled for 2007 – August 6 and October 1. For more on holidays, see the table on p.12. Overtime varies between the public and private sectors and permanent or temporary contracts.

Business Councils & Groups

American Chamber of Commerce in Australia	9241 1907	www.amcham.com.au
APN Business Information Group	1300 550 470	www.apnbig.com.au
AusIndustry	13 2846	www.ausindustry.gov.au
Australia China Business Council	9247 0349	www.acbc.com.au
Australia Council of Trade Unions	1300 362 223	www.actu.asn.au
Australia India Business Council	9519 4808	www.aibc.org.au
Australia Japan Business Association	9929 9426	www.ajba.com.au
Australia Latin America Business	9252 5251	www.business.gov.au
Australia Singapore Chamber of Commerce and Industry	9215 1090	www.ascci.org.au
Australian British Chamber of Commerce	9247 6271	www.britishchamber.com
Australian Business Limited	13 2696	www.australianbusiness.com.au
Australian Business Research	07 3837 1333	www.abr.com.au
Australian Council Of Business Women	9260 6128	–
Australian Industry Group	9466 5566	www.aigroup.asn.au
Business Capital Financial Group	8831 7400	www.bcfg.com.au
Business Council of Australia	03 8664 2664	www.bca.com.au

Finding Work

The Daily Grind
Sydney works hard but the hours are nothing like in London or Tokyo. The balmy climate and the beach ensure that workers knock off as soon as they can and head home. Most organisations tend to slow down on Friday afternoons, often allowing staff to wear casual clothes and some organise weekly drinks at 17:00. It's highly civilised and something many former expats miss when they return home.

Australia's tough entry laws for migrants mean it is much better to find a job before you apply for a visa. This will make things far easier because your employer will be your official sponsor and will often deal with the immigration department on your behalf. Even if it is up to you to do this, at least you will have a recognised Australian business name to offer in support of your application.

The expat workforce is a pretty even mix of those who were hired from overseas and those who found work once here.

However, even though there is a concerted effort by Sydney businesses and the NSW government to attract migrant workers, do not consider this to be a blanket demand. The needs are in highly specific areas. Not long ago there was a complete lack of interest in arts-based professionals like journalists and a dire need for stonemasons and plumbers. If you tick the right job boxes you should have few difficulties but if not, you could face a rocky road.

When applying for an advertised role, follow the instructions on the advert to the letter. Government job applications can be labouriously detailed but this helps them sort the wheat from the chaff. Some have to be completed online only, with all supporting literature sent as zipped files. You should note down and print out all receipts of applications sent to you from the organisation as proof that you applied on time and through the correct channels.

As with any job application anywhere, the more qualifications and relevant experience you have, the better your chances. And it never hurts to put down at least two reliable referees (email addresses are crucial).

Finding Work Before You Come

The best way to get a view of the job market is through websites like www.seek.com.au, www.mycareer.com.au (the online jobs section of the *Sydney Morning Herald*) and www.careerone.com.au (the News Limited rival). However, there is little point in applying for positions unless you can email or fax all the relevant documents from your home country. Many job ads will ask for applicants who are Australian residents and it is a lot easier to get a job if you are in the country. But don't let that put you off. It is always worth sending in an application and stating that you are currently living overseas and are not an Australian resident but are interested in being sponsored to come to Australia to take the job. While this may make you a little less attractive, companies are after talent and they are used to looking abroad to get it.

Job Hopping
Sydney is an employees' market right now so job-hopping is becoming more common. You might get some grief if you break your contract but unless you do something very serious you're unlikely to face anything worse than some lost pay. Just remember that Sydney is a small town so it is much easier to get a negative reputation as a job-hopper here than in bigger cities.

Finding Work While You're Here

Use the websites above, as well as the daily and weekly newspapers and magazines. If you are after general jobs try the *Sydney Morning Herald*, *The Australian* and the *Daily Telegraph*, especially on Saturdays when they run their big job supplements. On Sunday try the *Sun Herald* and *The Sunday Telegraph*. For finance, business and executive jobs also get hold of a copy of the *Australian Financial Review* on Friday and Saturday.

While you have the papers in your hand (and the weekly business magazine BRW is useful too), read the news stories to find articles about companies and organisations that are expanding and might be hiring staff. Cold calling and talking to human resources (HR) departments to find out about potential jobs is perfectly legitimate and can be successful.

Among the bigger employers are supermarket chains like Woolworths (www.woolworths.com.au) and Coles (www.coles.com.au), the NSW Government (www.jobs.nsw.gov.au) and its many agencies, and firms like PricewaterhouseCoopers (www.pwc.com.au) and Qantas (www.qantas.com.au). All have specific job sections on their websites.

Recruitment Agencies

24/7 Nursing & Medical Services	9314 7744	www.agencynursing.com.au
360HR	9819 6324	www.360hr.com.au
AAA Recruitment	9299 9366	www.aaagroup.com.au
Adecco	9244 3400	www.adecco.com.au
Careers Connections International	8741 0400	www.ccjobs.com.au
Charterhouse Partnership ▶ p.69	9641 2472	www.charterhouse.jobs
EBR Even Better Recruitment	9299 9199	www.ebr.com.au
Hays Specialist Recruitment	8226 9600	www.hays.com.au
Hudson	8233 2222	www.hudson.com
Job Network	13 1715	www.workplace.gov.au
Julia Ross Recruitment	1300 139 922	www.juliaross.com.au
LINK Recruitment	9893 8447	www.linkrecruitment.com.au
Mahlab Recruitment	9241 1199	www.mahlab.com.au
Manpower	9208 8700	www.manpower.com.au
Skilled	1300 366 606	www.skilled.com.au
Slade Group Recruitment	9006 8777	www.sladegroup.com.au
Temp-Team	9299 2600	www.ttas.com.au
Westaff	9251 4888	www.westaff.com.au

Recruitment Agencies
You can and should sign up with recruitment agencies. There are mixed reports from residents who have used them, with comments ranging from 'very helpful' to 'utterly useless'. The general consensus is that the applicant ends up doing most of the work, so do not rely on the agency to even call you back, let alone find you a six-figure dream job. Also, even though they would deny it, some agencies put more than one candidate up for the same job.
Once you are in touch with them, they do an initial interview where they will undoubtedly gush that you are an ideal candidate and they should have a job for you within a week, which is rarely ever the case. Among the biggest in Sydney are Hays (www.hays.com.au) and Julia Ross (www.juliaross.com.au).

Voluntary & Charity Work

There are plenty of opportunities to do voluntary or charity work in Sydney; anything from serving soup to the homeless on Christmas Eve and visiting spinal patients in hospital to planting trees with your family. Around 4.5 million Australians volunteer each year.
You rarely need any qualifications apart from an altruistic view on life and a good heart. For much voluntary and charity work you do not even need a residency visa but you will probably need a home address and usually a contact number. A good place to start looking is Volunteering Australia (1800 008 252, www.volunteeringaustralia.org).
To work with some charities, like some children's charities, you may need to undergo security or police checks but this is rare. And for any work that involves medical procedures some specialist knowledge and qualifications (including recognised certificates) will be needed.
One of the best-known kids' charities in Sydney is the Starlight Foundation (www.starlight.org.au), which helps seriously ill children.

Working as a Freelancer/Contractor

In the ever-flexible Sydney workplace there are plenty of opportunities for freelancers and contract staff. However, there are strict rules too. You will need a visa that allows you to work and be employed (even on a part-time basis) and you may have to set up your own business (through the NSW Government's Office of Fair Trading, www.fairtrading.nsw.gov.au). You may also have to provide proof of insurance and personal indemnity certificates so you are covered in case of an accident at the workplace. This is so you don't sue your temporary employers if an accident occurs. You should also check they have their own certificates in place so they don't sue you if someone trips over your briefcase. Sydney has become litigious of late and there are numerous farcical stories of bizarre accidents that have ended up in court.

Employment Contracts

If you are offered a permanent job then your employer should give you a formal contract within a few days of the offer being made. This document is essential; nothing is binding until both you and the employer have signed it. If you have any doubts, discuss them with your future employer and if you are still unsure, show the contract to an employment lawyer.

Even if you are being hired for short-term contract work you will need a formal contract or at least a written response (an email may be sufficient) from the employer stating that they agree to your terms. Some freelancers offer a 'work and fee proposal' and begin work once the employer has replied in writing, agreeing to the terms.

Leaving your job early can cause problems but the extent of these depends on the employer and the contract. Some contracts state that the employer can claim back benefits paid (although not salary) so read carefully before signing.

You may get a running contract or one with a fixed-term (which could be as long as two or three years). Either way, at the very least it should include the hours of work, the pay scale (salary or total set fee), the names and addresses of the employer and the employee (and/or the employee's company), the date, the ABN (Australian Business Number) of both parties and a brief but accurate description of the work involved. If you have negotiated benefits such as share options, health benefits, housing allowances and/or flights home, these should also be included in the contract.

As this is an employees' market there might be room for rate negotiation but this should happen before you get to the contract stage. If you have doubts about what to charge, you should contact the Fair Pay Commission (www.fairpay.gov.au).

Under Australia's labour laws employers are required to provide a safe and healthy workplace, freedom from discrimination and harassment, standard holidays and time-off, sick leave and the right to union representation. However, things are about to change as the federal Government's amendments to industrial relations laws come into force in 2007. See Labour Law for more.

Regarding salary increases, most (though not all) public sector workers are guaranteed an incremental increase each year. Check with your prospective employer. Private sector staff are at the mercy of their employers but tend to do well through bonus schemes and other performance-linked incentives.

Probation periods are quite common and can run from three months to a year, during which an employee might not have access to all (or any) of the benefits available to a staffer.

Benefits are not the norm here in the way they are in some cities, so expect the vast amount of your remuneration to come in your pay packet. Maternity leave is almost always included in a contract, even if it is short-term. Many men and women are able to take time off without having to resign to care for their newborn or newly adopted child. Parental leave provisions apply to permanent full-time, part-time and eligible casual employees who have had at least 12 months of continuous service with their current employer (see Maternity under the Health section, p.121).

State of the Unions
The power of the unions has diminished under the conservative Howard government. Traditionally, unions have been strong among state government staff, manufacturing and service industries like nursing, teaching and public transport but support is waning as memberships fall. One of Australia's key business figures remains the secretary of the Australia Council of Trade Unions (www.actu.asn.au); currently Greg Combet.

Labour Law

Until now, Australian labour laws have been based on the British and American systems. Workers and employers have rights in the workplace and workers must be given verbal and written warnings before they can be legally dismissed. Unions are legal and active and anyone is free to join (although some companies do not recognise certain unions). A tribunal system is in place to offer both sides the right of appeal and ensure fair play. Both sides have the right to seek legal advice to help fight their case.

The year 2007 will see some major changes to working practices in Australia. The federal government is implementing controversial changes to industrial relations laws. The new law is known as WorkChoices (www.workchoices.gov.au). This has provoked mass protests with tens of thousands taking to the streets. The NSW state government joined every other state and territory in a high court challenge to the proposed changes, claiming they were unconstitutional. The federal government won but NSW continues to oppose WorkChoices. The laws on unfair dismissal, individual employment contracts, the minimum wage, working conditions, workers' access to unions and the powers of the independent Industrial Relations Commission (www.airc.gov.au) will all be affected if the changes go ahead. If you want the Government's view then read www.dfat.gov.au and www.workchoices.gov.au. If you want the unions' standpoint, check out www.rightsatwork.com.au. For a comprehensive view on how these changes will affect you in Sydney, see the NSW Government's website www.industrialrelations.nsw.gov.au.

Employment Lawyers
A full list of
employment lawyers in
Sydney and all their
contact details can be
found on the website
of the Law Society of
New South Wales,
www.laws.law
society.com.au.

Changing Jobs

Changing jobs is quite common because Sydney is currently an employees' market. But it can have significant implications if your contract includes factors other than just your salary. If breaking your contract means losing benefits like housing and flights home then you could be in trouble. The terms of the job you jump to should be as good, if not better, to tempt you away.

Also, as businesses and organisations work so closely in Sydney you might get a reputation as a short-stayer. Some may see this as a sign of ambition but others may consider you unreliable and greedy and that does not go down well in the land of the 'fair go'. Australia still harbours a particular dislike for people who think they are better than everybody else. It's known as the Tall Poppy Syndrome; with the elite as tall poppies, to be cut down and not allowed to tower over the rest of us.

There is no system of 'banning' here whereby an employer can actively and legally prevent you from taking other contracts but they could easily engage their lawyers to restrict or cancel your benefits and make life financially difficult. There may also be visa implications. The immigration department is a little vague on this but you can expect your residence visa to be tied to your employment visa if you have been sponsored to come to Australia to work for a company. If you have come here independently the two are likely to be unconnected.

Company Closure

There has been an explosion of start-up companies in Australia in recent years, on the back of the economic boom. Sydney has not benefited as much as less developed regions (like southeast Queensland, for example) but there has been a healthy growth in the number of ICT, pharmaceutical and biotechnology firms. They carry risk for employees as many only survive as long as their financial backers see merit in feeding them cash. You should always run contracts with such companies through an employment lawyer. If they go broke and file for bankruptcy you should at least get your entitlements paid but if they have no assets you may lose everything and you'll have no legal recompense.

This may also depend on how long you have been with the company and your standing in the organisation.

Of course, they could also find the next cure for cancer and make their staff instant millionaires. If you are on a permanent visa or are a permanent resident, your immigration status will not be affected. If you are on a temporary sponsored work visa there could be trouble and you may need to find another employer to sponsor you so you can stay in the country.

Read the Small Print ◀

As in most countries, banks exist to make money and while your account may seem inexpensive, make sure that you read the small print and avoid going over the limits on your account as charges can rocket dramatically.

Bank Accounts

Getting a bank account and making regular transactions should be one of your first priorities when arriving, so you can establish a credit rating. Without this, it will be more difficult to get a mobile phone contract, loans, mortgage or even cable TV. Sydney is the business and financial capital of the country and you will find offices of every national bank and many from overseas.

Banking in Australia is pretty sophisticated and all Australian banks offer the services you would normally expect, including current, deposit and savings accounts. The day to day account in an Australian bank is generally known as a savings account and while these offer cheque books, electronic transactions are preferred by most people. You will see and hear of EFTPOS (electronic funds transfer point of sale) everywhere. This debit card

ID Documents	
Primary	
Birth certificate	70 points
Citizenship certificate	70 points
Current passport	70 points
Secondary	
Current Australian driver's licence	40 points
Pension concession card	40 points
Student ID card - over 18yrs	40 points
Public utility bill	25 points
Debit card, credit card or passbook	25 points
Current Medicare card	25 points

system allows you to pay for items directly from your account just by swiping and entering your PIN, and is widely accepted. You can also ask for cash back when you pay in most stores or supermarkets with your EFTPOS card.

You will find ATMs throughout Sydney at banks and in pubs, petrol stations and clubs, with most cards compatible across all ATMs. Some machines (usually the freestanding ATMs in pubs) will charge a transaction fee.

Banking hours are generally 09:30–16:00 from Monday to Thursday and 09:30-17:00 on Friday but some banks offer extended hours and are open on Saturday mornings. Travellers' cheques are widely accepted and most banks offer foreign currency exchange. Interest rates and charges vary widely across banks, depending on the type of account and credit. Overdrafts are widely available as long as you have a banking track record, as are loans.

You do not have to be a resident and there is generally no minimum deposit to open a basic cheque account but there is a minimum deposit on more sophisticated accounts. Check bank websites for details as these conditions change continuously. Please note that as a legal requirement you will need 100 'ID points' to open an account. Only one primary document can be used and all documents must be originals. As a guide, a rundown of the points system is above.

Banks

Name	Phone	Web	Online Banking
ANZ	13 1314	www.anz.com.au	yes
Arab Bank	9377 8900	www.arabbank.com.au	yes
Bank of Cyprus	8226 5888	www.bankofcyprus.com.au	yes
BankWest	13 1718	www.bankwest.com.au	yes
Citibank	13 2484	www.citibank.com.au	yes
Commonwealth	13 2221	www.commbank.com.au	yes
HSBC	9006 5888	www.hsbc.com.au	yes
ING Direct	1800 500 240	www.ingdirect.com.au	yes
Macquarie Bank	1800 806 310	www.macquarie.com.au	yes
National Australia Bank	13 2265	www.national.com.au	yes
Reserve Bank of Australia	9551 8111	www.rba.gov.au	yes
St George Bank	13 3330	www.stgeorge.com.au	yes
Suncorp Metway	13 1155	www.suncorpmetway.com.au	yes
Westpac	13 2032	www.westpac.com.au	yes

Financial Planning

Sydney is a relatively expensive city, even on global scales. Housing is costly and with so many exciting things to do, it can be hard to save money. The cost of living, and housing in particular, is significantly lower in other towns and cities in Australia.

But, there are plenty of investment opportunities tied to stocks and shares. Australians love a flutter, and the country is thought to have the highest number of share owners per capita in the world. These schemes range from the very secure to the highly risky and many are also designed to maximise relief from the rather punitive Australian tax system (see Taxation p.79).

It cannot be stressed enough though, that it is critical to obtain the services of a very good financial planner or advisor. The sector is highly regulated in Australia through the Financial Planning Association (www.fpa.asn.au), which has 12,000 members and comprehensive codes of conducts. The FPA's site can direct you to a qualified planner. Your bank will also offer advice or put you in touch with a financial planner, though this person might only advise on the bank's products.

Foreign Investment Review Board

Aussies (and Sydneysiders in particular) are also great property speculators (see Buying Property p.86). But if you are not a resident of Australia you may require Foreign Investment Review Board approval to buy commercial or residential property. This can also apply to shares or businesses assets. It's always best to be cautious and consult with your financial planner or check with the board directly. Visit www.firb.gov.au or call 6263 3795 from 09:00-12:30 and 13:30 to 17:00, Monday to Friday. Infringements are treated very seriously and can result in you being forced to sell your property and a delay in your visa being issued. The FIRB may also request character assessment, in addition to assessing any tax payable as a result of your purchase.

Pensions

If you have a pension in another country you can transfer it to Australia but this is a complicated issue and you should get specialist advice, as tax may be payable.

In general, you are required by Australian law to declare all your income and assets at home and abroad. Pensions are called superannuation here or 'super' for short and are all privately operated. You run them yourselves but your employer is legally bound to pay 9% of your salary into the super fund of your choice. If you do not choose, your employer is required to decide for you.

Financial Advisors

Altitude Financial Services	9976 5299	www.altitude.hillross.com.au
Avenue Capital Management	9955 3577	www.avenue.com.au
CA Financial Services	9955 7288	www.cafinancialservices.com.au
CU Financial Advisory Services	8243 6500	www.cufinancial.com.au
Financial Wealth	9929 0470	www.financialwealth.com.au
FM Financial Solutions	9518 7822	www.fmfinancialsolutions.com.au
Genesis Financial Partners	9925 7222	www.genesisonline.com.au
Omega Financial Solutions	9380 8144	www.omegafs.com.au
Peppertree Financial	8205 7688	www.peppertreefinancial.com.au
TMS Capital	9976 5911	www.tmscapital.com.au

Offshore Savings Accounts

Off-shore banking is an option for residents but the ATO has a worldwide taxation policy so you have to declare any overseas income. Off-shore banking needs are dealt

Buying Abroad

If you want to invest in property outside Australia, you can find suitable agents bunched together in certain communities. For example, stroll through Leichhardt and you'll find 'agenzia immobiliare' catering to the local Italian population. But in general, realtors here only sell properties in Sydney.

Sending Money Home

Be careful when you send your money home. While the Australian dollar is strong at the time of writing, it is anticipated to weaken over the next year or so. A falling AUD will buy you less of your home currency. Regular small amounts are likely to generate bigger transfer and exchange fees than lump sums.

with by specialist companies including www.taxhavenco.com, and your bank can offer investments in a number of tax haven countries. The basic principle is, if you are living here and spending here, it's best to save here, rather than transferring funds to offshore accounts. The Australian authorities keep a watchful eye on large transfers, especially when money goes abroad and such cases have recently been the subject of very public litigation. (See Taxation, see p.79 for more).

Cost of Living

Apples (per kg)	$4.00 to $4.50
Bananas (per kg)	$10.50
Beer (off licence six pack)	$12
Beer (pint)	$4.00 to $8.00
Beer (scooner)	$2 to $5
Bottle of house wine (restaurant)	$18.00 to $20.00
Bottle of wine (off licence)	$10.00
Burger (takeaway)	$6.00
Bus (10 km journey)	$3.70
Can of dog food	$1.60
Can of soft drink	$2.00
Cappuccino	$3.00
Car rental (per day)	$25.00 to $65.00 - dep on size
Carrots (per kg)	$1.50
CD album	$22.00
Chocolate bar	$1.50
Cigarettes (per pack of 20)	$10.00 to $12.00
Cinema ticket	$15.00
DVD (new release)	$33.00
Eggs (12)	$5.00
Film (colour, 36 exp)	$20.00
Fresh beef (per kg)	$12.00 to $28.00
Fresh chicken (per kg)	$6.00
Fresh fish (per kg)	$28.00 - dep on season
Golf (18 holes)	$30.00 to $60.00
House wine (glass)	$6.00 to $8.00
Large takeaway pizza	$6.95
Loaf of bread	$2.50
Local postage stamp	$0.50
Milk (1 litre)	$1.50
Mobile to mobile call (local, per 30 secs)	$0.18 to $0.50
Newspaper (international)	$5.00
Newspaper (local/national)	$1.25 to $2.50
Orange juice (1 litre)	$3.66
Pack of 24 aspirin/paracetamol tablets	$3.00
Petrol (gallon)	$1.15
Postcard	$1.50 - $3.00
Potatoes (per kg)	$3.00
Rice (1 kg)	$1.60
Salon haircut (female)	$80.00 upwards
Salon haircut (male)	$25.00 to $80.00
Strawberries (per punnet)	$4.00 - dep on season
Sugar (2 kg)	$2.80
Taxi (10 km journey)	$15.00 to $18.00
Text message (local)	$0.15
Toothpaste (tube)	$3.00
Water 1.5 litres (restaurant)	$5.00 to $8.00
Water 1.5 litres (supermarket)	$3.00

Financial Advisors

There are many financial planners in Sydney but it is generally best to contact a qualified and accredited professional through visiting www.fpa.asn.au. See table, p.78. The firms listed here have at least one CFP (certified financial planner) on their staff, awarded by the FPA. The CFP is considered the highest standard available to financial planners.

Taxation

The Australian Tax Office, also called the ATO, levies and collects the majority of direct (income tax) and indirect taxes (sales tax - known as GST) in Australia. See www.ato.gov.au.

One of the first things you should do when arriving is apply for a tax file number. Without this you will not be able to receive an income in Australia. You can do this online at the ATO site or call 1300 720 092 to have a paper copy sent to you. Income tax, corporate tax, payroll tax, fringe benefits tax, etc., all apply here (and are comparatively high compared with other western countries). GST is applied at a level of 10% across all goods, and sales taxes on luxury items, including cigarettes, alcohol and petrol, are significantly higher.

The above rates do not include the Medicare levy of 1.5% which is payable if you are entitled to public healthcare. In addition to the above, a minimum of 9% will be deducted from your salary for compulsory superannuation, irrespective of your residency status. If you are leaving Australia for good, you may be able to claim this back through the Departing Australia Superannuation Payment.

If you lease property, taxes will be included in your rent. If you buy, you'll have to pay taxes to the local council

Be Advised
The offices of tax specialists can be found in every suburb. The Australian Financial Planning Authority (www.fpa.asn.au, 1800 626 393) is a good place to start. Get professional advice; the ATO are a mean bunch.

(based on the value of your property and the area in which you live), as well as government stamp duty.

Items like cars can be deducted from your pre-tax income – get a tax advisor to prepare your annual tax return at the end of the fiscal year, which runs from July 1 to June 30, to ensure you make the most of the wide ranging tax breaks available.

Non-residents who leave Australia within the tax year can receive tax refunds.

And if you were thinking about dodging your taxes, be warned - Australia has an extremely

Tax Rates 2006 - 2007	
Income	Rate of Taxation
$0 - $6,000	Nil
$6,001 - $25,000	15c for each $1 over $6,000
$25,001 - $75,000	$2,850 plus 30c for each $1 over $25,000
$75,001 - $150,000	$17,850 plus 40c for each $1 over $75,000
Over $150,000	$47,850 plus 45c for each $1 over $150,000

efficient and diligent tax regime which does not hesitate in pursuing tax evaders.

Legal Issues

Australia is a federation of states, with a legal system modelled on that of England and Wales.

The legal system is made up of commonwealth law and state law, with each having its own courts and jurisdiction. The state of New South Wales, as with all other states and territories, has its own independent legal system. There are three levels of courts: lower courts (local courts), intermediate courts (district or county courts) and High Courts. The complexity and seriousness of the civil or criminal matter determines the court. Decisions made by a court at the lower levels can be appealed at a higher level. The same procedure applies for appeals at the commonwealth level.

Court proceedings are conducted in English but translators can be provided for non-English speakers. The main issues that visitors or expats living in Sydney should be aware of are the seriousness of overstaying their visa, becoming an illegal resident, drug possession and dealing, tax fraud and driving (drink driving in particular) offences. All can carry severe penalties, including heavy fines or even deportation for non-residents or non-citizens.

Drinking & Driving

All states in Australia are stringent in their pursuit of drink drivers or those driving under the influence of drugs. In New South Wales the police have the power to stop drivers for random testing and you will often see this, in particular at weekends and often on Saturday and Sunday mornings, when drivers may feel they've sobered up but still have a blood alcohol level over the 0.05 g/100ml limit. For details of penalties, visit www.rta.nsw.gov.au. A serious first offence can result in a jail term of 18 months to two years. Licence disqualification ranging from 12 months to two years is automatic with heavy fines and subsequent difficulty in obtaining insurance. As the gloriously direct slogan of the Australian Transport Accident Commission once stated, 'if you drink and drive, you're a bloody idiot.'

Divorce

Australian divorce laws are similar to those of the UK and USA. If you are living in Australia, the divorce laws applicable to Australia apply, along with any findings that the court makes with regard to custody of children and maintenance payments. Consult an international divorce lawyer sooner rather than later if this scenario is developing.

Making a Will

Making a will is very easy in Australia. You can refer to a specialist lawyer, do your own using a will kit (try www.legalwills.com.au, www.legalkits.com.au or one of many others) or go through the Office of the Public Trustee (www.pt.nsw.gov.au). If your affairs are complicated, enlist the services of a specialist lawyer as they can also advise you on significant taxation issues so as to avoid death duties, etc.

Adoption

Adoption is relatively common in Australia but the process is rigorous and complicated for non-residents. See the New South Wales Department of Community Services website: www.community.nsw.gov.au/adoption.

Crime

Australia has grown very quickly and experienced dramatic socio-economic change over the last 30 years. This has increased wealth and improved education levels but also increased the disparity between the rich and poor, producing some increasing criminal trends.

A very significant proportion of crime committed in Australia is related to alcohol and other drug use, with indigenous communities experiencing particularly high rates of serious alcohol-related crime. Gun crime is also on the rise.

Petty Crimes

As always, be vigilant and keep an eye on your bag, wallet or purse, but muggings and bag snatchings are infrequent. If you leave such an item on a train or bus, your chances of getting it back are slim but you can contact the relevant lost property office (see p.29) and hope for the best.

Citizen's Arrest

A private citizen can make an arrest where someone has committed (or is trying to commit) a crime including assault, creating public alarm or obstructing a police officer. Annoyance, disturbance or insulting language are not enough for one citizen to arrest another.

Dangerous Areas

Sydney is largely a safe city, with relatively low levels of crime, particularly in the more affluent areas. Kings Cross has been cleaned up in recent years and is a grand spot for a night out but it's strip clubs and open prostitution still attract a mixed bag of revellers. Discarded needles can occasionally be spotted, beggars can be quite vocal and while the main strip is retina-scorchingly bright 24 hours a day, there can be a sense of menace in some of the quieter side streets. The visible police presence is normally enough to stop any serious trouble. Redfern's 'the block' has a troublesome reputation and was the centre of the 2004 Redfern riots (see General Information, p.1). The area is marked by Eveleigh, Vine, Louis and Caroline streets and at the time of writing, proposals were under consideration to ban drinking within these streets in an effort to curb anti-social behaviour. But, as with any city, keep alert, stay away from anywhere that makes you uncomfortable, and all should be well.

Overseas Criminal Records

If you already have a criminal record elsewhere it may well appear here as Australia liaises with other countries on such matters. But if the record is even relatively serious, it is highly unlikely you would be allowed into the country or granted a visa in the first place. If you do get in with a criminal record, it should not stop you from getting a bank account, unless you've dabbled in fraud or tax evasion.

You're Nicked

If you are arrested for any reason, you will be taken to the nearest police station for questioning and possibly charged. Depending on the offence you may be released on bail to appear in court at a later date. Non-residents should contact their consulate or embassy as soon as possible. Residents and citizens will need a lawyer.

A police officer may use as much force as is necessary to arrest you, recognizing that unreasonable force is assault. He or she may handcuff you if you attempt to escape or the officer considers it necessary. A judge or magistrate will decide whether or not the force used was reasonable. Resisting arrest is an offence, but simply lying down and refusing to co-operate is not considered resisting arrest.

Searches

Police can stop, search, and detain you if they have reasonable grounds to believe you are carrying something illegal, or items that may be used illegally such as tools for theft or weapons. They can pat you down, look in your pockets and bags and search your car. Police are only allowed to strip search you in serious and urgent

Law Firms

Freehills	9225 5000	www.freehills.com.au
Gadens Lawyers	9931 4999	www.gadens.com.au
Koffels Solicitors & Barristers	9283 5599	www.koffels.com.au
Law Council of Australia	6246 3788	www.lawcouncil.asn.au
Law Society of NSW (solicitor referral service)	1800 422 713	www.lawsociety.com.au
LawAccess (free govt. helpline)	1300 888 529	www.lawaccess.nsw.gov.au
MacMahon Associates	9217 2400	www.macmahonassociates.com
Mallesons Stephen Jaques	9296 2000	www.mallesons.com
Swaab Attorneys	9233 5544	www.swaab.com.au
Teakle Ormsby Conn	9232 8933	www.teakle.com.au

circumstances and there are strict rules to ensure privacy and supervision. If you refuse to be searched, the police may arrest you and use force to search you. When carrying out a search, the police officer involved is required to provide their name and reasons for the search. A judge or magistrate will decide whether or not the police had reasonable grounds for the search at a later date.

Your Rights

Following your arrest, the police may detain you for up to four hours to conduct investigations, with a possible extension of up to another eight hours. You must then be charged or released. You can give the police your name, address and date of birth, but it is advisable not to answer any other questions unless you have your solicitor present and not to sign any document other than a bail form. When you are arrested, politely insist that you be allowed to contact a lawyer or consulate and that you have the right to have a lawyer present while you are being questioned. The police may take your fingerprints and photographs for the purpose of identification. If you are subsequently acquitted or the charges against you are dropped, you may ask that your fingerprints and photographs be destroyed.

Bail

If you are charged, you will usually be released on bail, with or without conditions. If you are initially refused bail or cannot meet the conditions set, you must be brought before a court to appeal for bail.

You may be refused bail if you have previously failed to appear in court, committed an offence while on bail, parole or probation, or if the offence you have been charged with involves murder, robbery, drug trafficking or domestic violence.

The Bail Sergeant decides whether or not to grant you bail and the police are required to inform you of your right to contact a lawyer, or any other person, in connection with bail. Those denied bail will go to prison until their trial. Prisons are located out of Sydney and a prisoner may find themselves several hours away from the city. While modern in general, they offer few comforts and visiting times are restricted.

Traffic Accidents & Violations

You do not have to answer questions when you are under arrest and in general you have a right to silence. However, if your arrest relates to a motor vehicle, you are required to give your name and address and details of the incident to the police.

Driving Under the Influence

Normally you will be breathalysed and, if you fail, you will be asked to get out of the vehicle and taken to the Booze Buster van and retested. You will then be taken to a police station for blood and urine tests and if the results are still positive, you will face charges and fines. Possession or the sale of drugs in Australia is very serious and can result in a long prison sentence or deportation.

Legal Aid

The Legal Aid Commission of NSW decides who will or will not get free legal representation. Their website has a simple calculator to work out whether you are likely to be eligible. Go to www.legalaid. nsw.gov.au to see if you qualify. The Law Society of NSW (see table) can put you in touch with a private solicitor.

82

Housing

To begin to understand Sydney and the variation in costs and lifestyle in each area, it's best to rent at first. The range of housing available is incredibly varied, as are the suburbs, with some more suited to families and others to singles and couples. Relocation agents can help and chatting to trusted colleagues is also a good way of learning more, but remember; their standards and interests may be quite different to yours.

Renting in Sydney

Renting in Sydney is not always easy, as the most popular areas are often over subscribed. Whether you buy or rent, costs are likely to be high. Most expats tend to settle in the inner city areas or suburbs close to the city, including Surry Hills, Paddington or Newtown - very trendy and upmarket areas, generally more suitable for couples and singles; the eastern suburbs, including Darlinghurst, Double Bay or Rose Bay – from apartments and units to large waterside mansions; the upper north shore including Turramurra, Wahroonga, Pymble or Gordon – wooded and more suburban with large family houses in most areas; lower north shore including Mosman, Cremorne, Crows Nest or Neutral Bay – a mix of apartments, units and town houses with some large houses overlooking the Sydney and Middle harbours; or the Northern Beaches including Manly, Balgowlah, Fairlight, Dee Why, Narrabeen – a mix of houses, townhouses and apartments with a bigger focus on beach life as you head further north. In all these, the key factors are what you're looking for and how much you're willing to spend.

Rents

It is fairly common for expatriate contracts to include an accommodation allowance, but many companies are cutting back on costs and are specifying how long an expatriate can live in an apartment. Some ask for a contribution to the rent or put a cap on what they will pay. If you're lucky, your company will pay for a relocation company to help you settle. If you rent an apartment, also called a unit, the rent will often include water, parking and other 'body corporate' costs, but not other utilities such as electricity and air conditioning. Rents are quoted weekly but are payable monthly. The bad news is that rents are forecast to rise in the coming years as interest rates are on the up and there is increasing pressure on the housing market.

Rental Agreements

Rental agreements vary significantly depending on the landlord, but tend to be for a year with an option of extending. All residential tenancy agreements in New South Wales are covered by the Residential Tenancies Act, with bonds held by the Rental Bond Board, which is operated by the NSW Government's Office of Fair Trading. Disputes are heard by the Consumer, Trader and Tenancy Tribunal. Please visit www.fairtrading.nsw.gov.au for more.

The landlord is always responsible for property maintenance. You may be able to reduce your rent by agreeing to maintain the garden and the pool, if there is one. The landlord can choose how the rent is to be paid, but it is usually done by electronic transfer or cheque to an agent or the landlord in person.

Finding a Home

Most people find a home through an agent (see table, p.84), although rentals are listed in the *Sydney Morning Herald* and the free local papers in

Housing Abbreviations

ac, a/c	air conditioning
br	bedroom
cnr	corner
crpt	carpet
d/h	ducted heating
d/w	dishwasher
dbl gar	double garage
dbr	double bedroom
dep	deposit
det	detached
din rm	dining room
dlug	double lock-up garage
encl	enclosed
ens	ensuite bathroom
ent	entrance, entry
ext	external
f/furn	fully furnished
fib	fibro
gfh	gas-fired heating
gge, grge	garage
ghws	gas hot water service
ingr pl	inground pool
k'ette	kitchenette
ldr	lounge dining room
lug	lock-up garage
mstr	master
ofp	open fire place
oil/htr	oil heater
ono	or nearest offer
pkg, prkg	parking
pol flrs	polished floors

each suburb. After visiting and selecting a property, you will be asked to complete an application form and (more often than not) pay a deposit, which is refundable if you do not secure the property. Another option is the NSW Department of Housing (www.housing.nsw.gov.au), which is still commonly know as the housing commission. But waiting lists are very long and properties are only open to residents.

Shared Accommodation

If you're after shared accommodation, the best place to look is the *Sydney Morning Herald*, as well as the local papers. Also, make use of contacts at work and friends. Needless to say, getting the right place involves luck but don't rush into anything unless you're sure.

Real Estate Agents

Renting through an agent has its advantages; they are licensed and you can be secure in the knowledge that they are aware of their legal obligations. If they are found to be in breach of the law they can lose their licence.

Your search for a house will determine the agent you'll be dealing with. The house will be listed with a realtor and only the landlord pays the agency fees, not you. Very few

Real Estate Agents		
Century21	8295 0600	www.century21.com.au
Elders	–	www.eldersrealestate.com.au
First National Real Estate	9262 2200	www.firstnational.com.au
LJ Hooker	1800 621 212	www.ljhooker.com.au
McGrath	9386 3333	www.mcgrath.com.au
Raine and Horne	9550 0200	www.rh.com.au

realtors will actively search for a property for you and the pressure on rentals means that they can let all their rentals very quickly. Usually, they will advertise the property and then hold a brief open house, sometimes for only 15 minutes, when they will take applications. You or your relocation agent will have to do the work.

Firstly, find an area you like that's within your budget. Then start walking the streets, calling realtors and trawling the newspapers and websites. Don't depend on the agent to call you when they have something suitable, it just doesn't work like that in Sydney.

You can also search on the internet and set up a profile and alerts in www.justlisted.com.au, www.realestate.com.au and www.domain.com.au There are thousands of realtors in Sydney but the market is dominated by large franchises or chains. See table.

The Lease

Leases in Australia are legally binding and you will be required to honour the commitments you've agreed to, including the price, any increases you have agreed to during the term of the lease, the terms of renewal, the deposit, the process in relation to rent disputes, your maintenance responsibilities, other rental costs, the number of persons that are allowed to live in the property and so forth. Leases are generally in English and the notice period will be included in the agreement. Realtors use standard lease agreements. For further details regarding leases and renting see www.fairtrading.nsw.gov.au.

Need Some Direction?

The *Explorer Mini Maps* pack a whole city into your pocket and once unfolded are excellent tools for exploring. Not only are they handy in size, with detailed information on the sights and sounds of the city, but their fabulously affordable price means they won't make a dent in your holiday fund. Wherever your travels take you, from the Middle East to Europe and beyond, grab a mini map and you'll never have to ask for directions.

Before Signing

Make sure you inspect the property very carefully before you move in, noting on the lease or an additional document (a copy of which goes to the landlord), every detail of the condition of the property, walls, paintwork, carpets, electrical equipment etc. This will prevent unscrupulous landlords from claiming for damage that was done before you moved in.

The Complete **Residents'** Guide

Main Accommodation Options

Housing in Sydney can be divided into two categories: standard apartments (units) or town houses and houses. NSW residential tenancies legislation applies to all of these when renting but apartments and town houses are also subject to strata title rules. These affect all the properties in a building or complex and govern the maintenance of the property and how the building is managed.

Prices in Sydney vary substantially depending on the area and the best bet is to search on the websites listed in the Real Estate Agents table on p.84. New or restored properties attract higher rents than older, dilapidated properties. Although facilities will vary, you can expect most rental properties to include window furnishings but few will include a refrigerator, washing machine or dryer.

An extensive range of serviced apartments is available throughout Sydney but these are much more expensive than non-serviced apartments, see p.86. They are however, ideal for the first few weeks while you get to know the city. For further information, visit www.medina.com.au or www.pacificinthotels.com.

Get Approved
If you are not resident in Australia, do not purchase property without securing the approval of the Foreign Investment Review Board (www.firb.gov.au) as the penalties could be costly.

Other Rental Costs

When renting you should bear in mind the cost of the bond and that you may be asked to pay a month's rent in advance. Under strata title rules, water and all local taxes are generally included in the rent for apartments and town houses. These are mentioned in more detail above. Electricity, gas and telephone services will all be paid by you. If you don't have a credit rating, you may have to pay a deposit. Happily, the realtor's commission is paid by the landlord so that's one thing less to worry about.

Buying Property

The housing market in Sydney is currently very strong, even allowing for the recent increases in interest rates. Should interest rates increase further though, it is predicted that there will be a drop in demand and a flattening of prices.

Expats cannot buy property without the approval of the Foreign Investment Review Board (www.firb.gov.au) so renting is the easiest option until you become a resident or citizen.

Property is a good investment but there are several costs on top of the property price. These include lender's fees, inspection costs, stamp duty, insurance, legal fees, moving costs and estate agent fees. Most lenders will also charge a one-off establishment fee on a new home loan.

Be Savvy
The seller can leave the house bare except for electrical fittings, so try and negotiate any white goods, appliances, fixtures and fittings that match the style of the house into the price. It may be expensive to replace them otherwise.

If you don't have a credit rating in Australia it may be difficult to get a mortgage in the first place, and if you do, the lender may charge you a higher interest rate. Most banks also charge monthly or annual account fees.

You will want your house checked over before you buy to ensure it is sound and free of pests (termites in particular). Building inspections range from a few hundred dollars for a small house or flat, to several thousands for a large house. And remember, the NSW government charges stamp duty on the amount borrowed and the purchase price. The legal transfer of ownership will need to be undertaken through a solicitor or estate agent and this can cost in the region of $1,000.

While 100% and 90% mortgages are available, the interest rates are often higher and if your deposit is less than 20%, your lender will probably charge you for mortgage insurance, which will cover them in case you fail to make the payments. Most lenders will also insist that you take out building insurance.

Mortgages

There are many mortgage providers in Australia (see table p.87) but your first port of call should be your bank. See what they say, then shop around. The difficulty for new arrivals can be establishing a credit rating. It is virtually impossible to transfer your rating from your home country, unless your Australian bank has a relationship with your previous bank. Contact your bank at home to check if they have a relationship with any banks in Australia.

Mortgage Providers

ANZ	13 1314	www.anz.com.au
Commonwealth Bank	13 2224	www.commbank.com.au
eChoice	13 1300	www.echoice.com.au
HSBC	9006 5888	www.hsbc.com.au
ING	1800 066 920	www.ingdirect.com.au
Mortgage Australia	1800 180 800	www.mortgageaustralia.com.au
Mortgage Providers	1300 656 600	www.mortgage-providers.com.au
National Australian Bank	13 1312	www.national.com.au
one direct	13 1401	www.onedirect.com.au
Virgin Home Loans	1300 852 123	www.virginhomeloans.com.au
Westpac	13 2032	www.westpac.com.au

The lender will want to know all sorts about you but will be most interested in your earnings. Typically they'll want to know that repayments do not exceed 30% of your (joint) income after tax. They will also check that the house is worth the price you intend to pay. If your mortgage is to be more than 85% of the value of the house, your providers is likely to insist on mortgage insurance too. Terms are normally for 25 years and occasionally 30.

Real Estate Law

Most houses in NSW are sold by auction because sellers think they will get the best possible price, although private treaty sales are becoming more common. When you have found the house you want, you will need the services of a lawyer or conveyancer for the lengthy legal process.

Done Deals
The five day cooling-off period, where you can change your mind after exchanging contracts, does NOT apply to property bought at auction or after it has been 'passed in'.

When you make an offer, you may be asked to pay a deposit as an indication of your commitment. This does not mean that your offer has been accepted, just that you are serious about buying. It does not mean the property is off the market. If another offer is made the agent is required to let you know but the seller has no obligation whatsoever to sell to you, and nor are you obliged to buy. Gazumping is common in Sydney, especially when the market is very hot. If this happens, neither the agent nor the seller is required to compensate you in any way for legal advice, inspection reports, financial applications, etc.

Once your offer is accepted, you will need to exchange contracts. This is where the legalities really begin. At this stage you will be asked for a bigger deposit, which is normally 10% of the agreed sale price. From this stage onwards have your lawyer check all agreements and contracts of sale before you sign. In NSW there is a five day cooling-off period after exchanging contracts where you can change your mind, with a small penalty payable. Settlement, where the property legally becomes yours, normally follows thirty to ninety days after exchanging contacts. If you are buying at an auction, you should be prepared to pay a deposit then and there (still normally 10%) and exchange contracts afterwards. You may hear the term 'passed in'. This means that the seller's reserve was not met and the auctioneer stopped the bidding to take advice and the owner has decided he is not going to sell at that price. The highest bidder has the right to negotiate with the seller and if they can agree a price then the property can be sold.

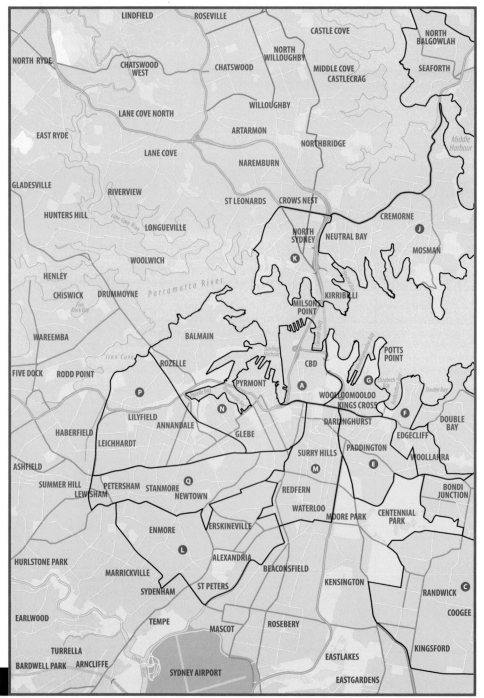

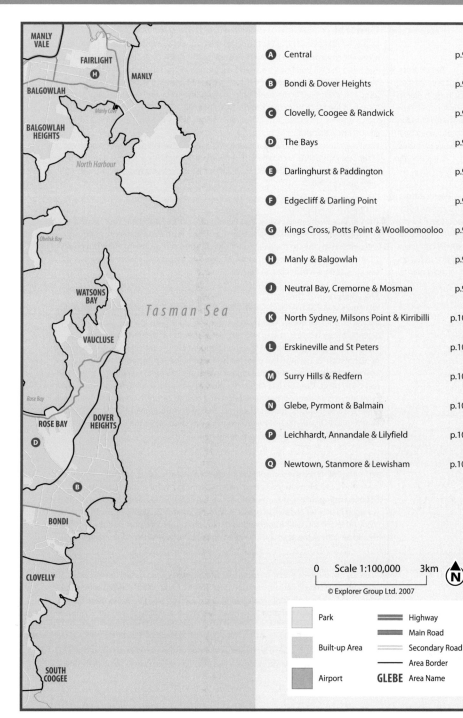

A	Central	p.90
B	Bondi & Dover Heights	p.92
C	Clovelly, Coogee & Randwick	p.93
D	The Bays	p.94
E	Darlinghurst & Paddington	p.95
F	Edgecliff & Darling Point	p.96
G	Kings Cross, Potts Point & Woolloomooloo	p.97
H	Manly & Balgowlah	p.98
J	Neutral Bay, Cremorne & Mosman	p.99
K	North Sydney, Milsons Point & Kirribilli	p.100
L	Erskineville and St Peters	p.101
M	Surry Hills & Redfern	p.102
N	Glebe, Pyrmont & Balmain	p.103
P	Leichhardt, Annandale & Lilyfield	p.104
Q	Newtown, Stanmore & Lewisham	p.105

0   Scale 1:100,000   3km   **N**

© Explorer Group Ltd. 2007

Park	Highway
Built-up Area	Main Road
	Secondary Road
Airport	Area Border
	GLEBE Area Name

Map 2-D4

Central

Sydney's CBD (central business district) is the business and financial centre of Australia. If you like city living, then this has to be one of the nicest inner city areas in which to live. It has the tall buildings, noise and congestion of any CBD but it also has great parks, restaurants, lively bars and the magnificent harbour. It is also pretty safe, and in a trend not often seen in the world's big cities, many empty nesters are now selling their suburban homes to move back to the heart of it all.

Best Points

You are at the heart of the city, with its iconic sites on your doorstep. Nowhere is too far away and you don't have to rely on buses to get about.

Accommodation

Almost exclusively apartments and units with some new high-rise tower blocks. Much of the real estate here is commercial or government property, with corporate high-rises and shopping precincts. The CBD is unlikely to be somewhere you will find housing to suit a young family.

Shopping & Amenities

Worst Points

The CBD can be noisy and congested. Parking costs are very high and some streets can seem spookily deserted on school nights.

The CBD has all the major banks and department stores. Kitting out your home and clothing yourself are also unlikely to be a problem. You'll also find plenty of barbers and salons that cater to the daily commuters. There are few supermarkets but plenty of 24 hour convenience stores. So, while your weekly shop may be more expensive, you can at least do it whenever you fancy.

Entertainment & Leisure

The CBD has the best of the city's museums and attractions and has every imaginable cuisine on offer. Be aware though, that some places are only open during the day, catering to city workers. There are a number of theatres and entertainment venues, including the State Theatre and the Entertainment Centre, see p.366. You're unlikely to go shy of a drink, because there are loads of nightclubs and bars. But, as with many business districts, when the office types have cleared off for the day, some streets can feel oddly quiet. The CBD has some very good facilities for keeping fit and if you like to swim, there is an unusual, partly-underground aquatic centre in Cook and Phillip Park. There are also plenty of commercial gyms and gyms in apartment buildings, plus the Health Club in Martin Place. Fitness First has gyms throughout the CBD (see p.152) and Hyde Park (see p.184) is popular with joggers.

Education

While the CBD is relatively unsuitable for children to live in, some of Australia's best private schools can be found here, or nearby, including Sydney Grammar School, SCEGGS Darlinghurst and James Ruse Agricultural High School. Fort Street Public School is a good choice for children in grades K (for kindergarten or 'kindy') to six. There are also many other schools within commuting distance by public transport, and the journey should be fairly painless as you'll be heading the other way to the commuting hordes.

Transport

The CBD has the best public transport service in Sydney, with buses, the monorail, trams and taxi stands conveniently located. The city circle on the CityRail network does a loop of Hyde Park, the CBD and Circular Quay and you won't be living more than a ten minute walk from a station.

Safety / Annoyances

As in any CBD area, vigilance is advised at all times and in particular at night. The CBD seems to constantly undergo extensive construction, which causes some pedestrian and traffic congestion.

Best Points

Great shopping and food. The glorious beach. An address that will cause envy in all your friends back home.

Worst Points

It's a thriving area so it's all go, all the time and can be crowded down by the beach. Getting from the junction to the beach by bus can be an almighty bun fight.

Bondi & Dover Heights

For many, Bondi epitomises the reasons for moving to Sydney. You can get from the beach to the business district in under half an hour (just) and be home from your day's graft in time to catch the last few rays of sunshine. It is the one area of Sydney that is known all over the world and the spot most likely to cause a tinge of envy when you give the folks back home your new address. The famous beach is eternally popular, while Bondi Junction provides the basics for shopping and transport. Bondi is also close to the CBD and has plenty to keep sports enthusiasts happy. There are lots of gyms, some of the best surf in the world and ocean-side walking and running tracks. Dover Heights is quieter but still pleasant and close enough to the Bondi hubbub.

Accommodation

Bondi Junction, the area's main shopping and business centre, has a mix of semi-detached houses, rows of traditional Victorian terraces, modern and traditional apartments and California-style bungalows. Young families choose this area because of its quiet, leafy streets and off-road parking. Bondi Beach is famous for its distinctive red tiled roofs, though many of these have disappeared as developers put up apartments, duplexes and very smart houses. Dover Heights has some grand art deco houses and roomy, family, detached homes.

Shopping & Amenities

Bondi Junction offers the stunning Westfield Centre, as well as boutique clothing shops, David Jones, Myer, K-Mart, Coles and Woolworths (see Shopping, p.265). Bondi Beach is famous for its stylized surf culture with the trendy and often pricey boutiques of Campbell Parade offering surf wear, beach fashions and souvenirs.

Entertainment & Leisure

There is an amazing choice of recreational activities in the area with Centennial Park (the largest park in Sydney) and Queens Park nearby, the classic surf beach at Bondi (p.182), and the Bondi swimming pool. Here, the winter swimmers of the Icebergs Club (p.244) welcome other hardy souls for seasonal dips. There are also several gyms and fitness centres. Bondi Road offers plenty of eating variety and along Oxford Street, Bronte Road and Spring Street there are many cafes, restaurants and hotels. Bondi's bars tend to attract a cool, laid-back crowd, with a few boozy backpackers thrown in for good measure.

Education

The local state schools are Waverley Public School, Dover Heights High Schools and Bondi Beach Primary. Waverley College, Moriah College, Sydney Grammar, Scots, Cranbrook, Ascham and Kambala are all nearby and Vaucluse High School is commutable.

Southern Bondi

Transport

Bondi Junction is a major public transport hub with buses and trains to the CBD. However, getting a bus beyond the junction, and particularly down to the beach, can be quite a squeeze.

Safety / Annoyances

Bondi is generally a safe area. Nevertheless, it's best to keep your wits about you at Bondi Beach and follow the instructions of lifeguards when swimming. Sunny summer weekends can see hordes of drinkers spilling about the place.

Close to the city and the beach. Great for families, with plenty of natural distractions and a safe atmosphere.

Lots of traffic and major congestion in Randwick when the races are on. Rising house prices.

Clovelly, Coogee & Randwick

The beachside suburbs of Clovelly and Coogee offer an idyllic view of Aussie living. The city is commutable and the beaches are beautiful. Clovelly is not as busy as its neighbour and was once known as Little Coogee. Due to the efforts of a local progress association in 1912, the name was changed to Clovelly after the fishing village in Devon. The area is still quieter than Coogee, which is a popular spot for backpackers and beach lovers. Inland a little, Randwick is famous for its racecourse and the Prince of Wales Hospital, offering a busy commercial centre but quiet residential streets. It is close to both the CBD and beach and is a popular family suburb.

Accommodation

Coogee and Clovelly offer a mix of beachside cottages, quaint semis and beautifully renovated and refurbished 1920s homes. However, these are increasingly being demolished to make way for large, architecturally designed pads with ocean views. There are also some smart new (and some traditionally designed) apartments. Randwick is known for its Victorian and Federation mansions although many have been demolished and replaced by apartments. There are a number of nice semi-detached and terrace style houses and some town house developments.

Shopping & Amenities

You will only find local shopping down by the beach but the Randwick Shopping Centre and Bondi Junction are nearby. Shopping in Randwick is along Alison and Belmore roads, with a good range of food and clothes stores and some specialty Asian food shops.

Entertainment & Leisure

Clovelly's sheltered beach makes it a good choice for families and surfers, with a good ocean pool for swimming. Clovelly is also on the Bondi to Coogee coastal walk and has some great ocean views. There are a number of golf courses nearby including The New South Wales and The Australian. Randwick Racecourse is a popular spot on Melbourne Cup day, with races from late morning and the main event shown on large screens. Randwick offers an international mix of restaurants and local hotels serving good pub grub. Coogee's bars can be a boozy and popular spot for a young crowd.

Education

Clovelly Public School and St. Anthony's School are in Clovelly while the names of Randwick Girls' High and Randwick Boys' High are pretty self explanatory. Others include Randwick High, Randwick Primary, Marcellin, Brigidine College, Emmanuel School, Claremont College and Our Lady of the Sacred Heart, as well as a number of day care and preschool centres. The University of New South Wales is also partly located in Randwick.

Transport

Clovelly, Coogee and Randwick are connected to the CBD by good bus services. Bondi Junction, with its CityRail station and bus terminal, can be reached in 15 minutes.

Safety / Annoyances

These are safe areas, suitable for the most cautious families, though normal safety measures should be followed.

The Bays

Best Points

Stunning views are almost guaranteed. There's easy access to the waters of the harbour. Double Bay has the best boutique shopping in Sydney.

The northern curve of Sydney's eastern suburbs has loads of beautiful bays overlooking the harbour, with a range of residential choices. Watsons Bay still feels like a fishing village, but now has some very expensive property with stunning houses offering fabulous views of the city and out to the ocean. Rushcutters, Double and Rose Bays have some very stylish apartments and elegant bungalows and Double Bay is one of Sydney's most fashionable shopping areas with some great restaurants.

Accommodation

Some of the small fisherman's cottages built from stone and timber amazingly still survive, but these are starting to be dominated by cutting edge mansions and houses, all fighting for the stunning views. Art deco has also left its mark along this shore and bungalows mingle with some big semi-detached and detached homes.

Worst Points

It's expensive and traffic and parking can be problems on busy weekends.

Shopping & Amenities

There is a small village shopping centre in Watsons Bay but Double Bay or Bondi Junction offer a much better selection. Double Bay is something like Sydney's answer to Beverley Hills and the city's boutique fashion capital. Here you'll find all the top international designer brands, with some great antique shops, art galleries and fine food stores.

Entertainment & Leisure

The Watsons Bay Hotel, now owned by Doyles, has a great beer garden with good Aussie and international beers, good food and wine and great water views. Alongside is the world famous Doyles seafood restaurant, dishing up fresh fish and crisp white wines. There's also now another restaurant on the nearby pier.

The walks around the South Head are stunning with amazing harbour and ocean views. Entertainment in Double Bay consists of fashion shopping, socialising and eating. In between, though, you may find some time to visit the gyms in the village or take a run alongside the harbour. The Foreshore walk takes in hidden little coves like Milk Beach.

Education

State schools are available over in Dover Heights, Bondi and Rose Bay with private schools Kambala and Cranbrook nearby. The only school in Double Bay is Double Bay Public School, but nearby are Scots College, Kincoppal, Ascham, SCEGGS Darlinghurst, St Vincent's, Sydney Boys and Girls high schools, Waverley College and Sydney Grammar.

Queens Beach

Transport

There's no CityRail out this way but these bays are only a few kilometres away from the CBD and there are plenty of buses, though these trundle along pretty infrequently outside peak hours. There are, however, a decent selection of services that run along New South Head Road, and Edgecliff and Bondi Junction stations are reachable even in the morning rush. The city can also be reached by ferry from Watsons Bay and Double Bay. It takes a little longer but is a grand way to clear the mind ahead of your daily graft.

Safety / Annoyances

These are safe areas but some construction is ongoing. Traffic and parking are a problem on busy weekends. The absence of rail links within walking distance can lend these suburbs a slightly sleepy feel at other times.

Map 4-B3

Darlinghurst & Paddington

Darlinghurst is a trendy area tucked into a historical setting. Among Sydney's most densely populated suburbs, and linked to Kings Cross by Oxford Street, it is also one of the most cosmopolitan areas, famous for its cafes, smart boutiques, restaurants, bars and non-stop nightlife. Paddington is a little more sedate, but an equally desirable spot, best known for its galleries, leafy streets and beautifully restored terraces.

Best Points

You're close to the heart of it all and you won't be bored. These areas have some of Sydney's best nightlife and its coolest addresses.

Accommodation

You'll find it's mostly apartments and units in Darlinghurst with some new high-rise tower blocks and traditional workers' cottages. Paddington is made up of mostly single and double storey terrace style houses, many from the Victorian and Georgian era and shaded by leafy streets, giving it a distinctive architectural character.

Worst Points

It's loud until well into the wee hours and the houses are quite small.

Shopping & Amenities

Darlinghurst has all the major banks and stores, mainly on Oxford Street, along with some quirkier outlets. Oxford Street is the heart of the city's gay scene and a good shopping strip for those looking for men's clothes. There are also a couple of fetish stores. On South Dowling Street there are a number of young, designer boutiques. There are plenty of gyms in the area, but City Gym on Crown Street is the most famous in Sydney, having been operating for more than 25 years. It is open 24 hours a day. The Paddington end of Oxford Street is one of Sydney's smartest and coolest shopping strips with lots of boutiques selling the latest fashion, books, music, arts, design and food.

Entertainment & Leisure

The Darlinghurst end of Oxford Street is the heart of Sydney's gay and lesbian community and hosts the annual Mardi Gras, which takes place every March. It's a boozy part of town with lots of late bars and clubs and some of the city's best-known gay and lesbian venues (for more, see Going Out, p.361). You will find every type of food imaginable on Oxford Street and Crown Street, including budget restaurants and takeaways offering Chinese, Malay, Indian Thai, Turkish, Vietnamese, Greek, etc., all of which close very late. Paddington has become very well known as a centre for good pubs and plush restaurants with famous hotels including The Lord Dudley, The Four in Hand and The Grand National offering good beer and a fun atmosphere as well as good food. Fox Studios is nearby and has a wide range of restaurants.

Education

Darlinghurst is relatively unsuitable for families but schools in the area include East Sydney High School on William Street, Sydney Grammar School on College Street and SCEGGS Darlinghurst on Forbes Street. Schools available in Paddington include Glenmore Road Public, Paddington Public School and Sydney Grammar Junior School with Sydney Girls & Boys High, Ascham, Kambala, The Convent, St Vincent's, Cranbrook, Scots College and Waverley College all close by.

Transport

The CBD is very close and Oxford Street is a main bus route into town and out to Sydney's eastern beaches.

Safety / Annoyances

As in any inner city area, vigilance is advised, in particular at night and around Oxford Street.

Map 4-F3 ◄

Edgecliff & Darling Point

Edgecliff is a smart area to the east of the CBD, facing onto the harbour. Darling Point's first buildings were not the workers' cottages found in many other inner city areas, but grand mansions for industry, business and political leaders. Sadly, many have been demolished to allow for the construction of (admittedly stunning) new apartments overlooking the harbour. On the harbour foreshore are the Cruising Yacht Club of Australia and the National Trust property Lindesay.

Best Points ◄
Close to the CBD and beaches. Darling Point has some stunning harbour views and huge mansions.

Accommodation

Edgecliff has many refurbished Victorian terraces and cottages, as well as large older-style apartments (some refurbished, some not) and smart modern apartments and townhouses. Darling Point is still dominated by large, smart homes, though these are slowly giving way to big apartment buildings, contemporary duplexes and townhouses.

Worst Points ◄
You'll have to fork out for the lifestyle. The mansions mentioned might give you a clue; it's mighty pricey here.

Shopping & Amenities

The Edgecliff Centre is the local shopping hub with supermarkets, fruit and vegetable and specialty stores. It is close to Double Bay with its smart boutiques, supermarkets, delicatessens, coffee shops and pastry shops. Darling Point has some very small local stores but the Edgecliff Centre and Double Bay are only a short walk away.

Entertainment & Leisure

Edgecliff is very close to the beaches at Bondi, Bronte, Tamarama, Clovelly and Coogee and has the fantastic Centennial Park nearby with horse riding, bike trails, jogging, walking, rollerblading, picnic and barbecue areas, cafes and restaurants. Moore Park Golf Course is nearby, as are Royal Sydney and the Woollahra Golf Clubs. In Double Bay there is the Twin Cinema, and Edgecliff has some good restaurants, including La Bella Casa Pizzeria, Flavour of India and Allegro, but is also very close to the excellent restaurants of Paddington. The famous Bistro Moncur in Woollahra, Catalina in Rose Bay (p.322), Blue Oyster in Double Bay, and Pruniers in Woollahra are all pretty close too. There is only really one restaurant in Darling Point and that is at the Cruising Yacht Club, which has great views of the city skyline.

Education

Schools in the area include Ascham Girls' School at Edgecliff, Double Bay Public School, Scots College and Cranbrook School. St Marks Kindergarten is in Darling Point with Sydney Girls High and Sydney Boys High, Kambala, St Vincents, SCEGGS Darlinghurst, Sydney Grammar and Waverley College only short distances away.

Transport

Edgecliff and Darling Point are only a few kilometres east of the CBD with good services by train from Edgecliff station and direct bus routes into town along the New South Head Road. There is also a regular ferry service from McKell Park in Darling Point to Circular Quay.

Safety / Annoyances

Edgecliff is just up the road from Kings Cross and as in any city area, vigilance is advised, but this is a relatively safe part of town. Darling Point is a comfortable and affluent area. There's some minor ongoing construction work in both.

Map 4-C2

Kings Cross, Potts Point & Woolloomooloo

Best Points

Breathtakingly vibrant and close to the city with great food and drink options. The leafy streets of Potts Point offer a pleasant break from hectic Kings Cross.

These are busy spots just outside the CBD and very popular with younger residents and fabulously convenient for city amenities. Potts Point is leafy and gentrified, Woolloomooloo is quiet but delightfully named and Kings Cross (or 'the cross', as it is affectionately known) is home to an eclectic mix of backpackers, strippers, drunks and prostitutes, so life is never dull. It also has lots of bars, clubs and restaurants.

Accommodation

Mostly units, with some new high-rise blocks and a few older buildings, but also small terraced houses, in particular in Woolloomooloo. There are quiet little enclaves and tree-lined streets with some really good examples of Victorian and art deco architecture. There's an attractive collection of apartments, dating from the 1930s to the present day.

Worst Points

'The cross' is noisy and definitely not for the prudish.

Shopping & Amenities

Kings Cross is an area that sells everything and on the main drag, Oxford Street, there's a Coles supermarket, heaps of convenience stores, pharmacies, newsagents, video stores, takeaways and delicatessens. Macleay Street has the Macleay Street Deli and other trendy food shops. Bondi Junction's Westfield shopping mall (see p.302) is just two stops away on the train.

Woolloomooloo Bay

Entertainment & Leisure

The Bourbon & Beefsteak Bar is the iconic restaurant of The Cross but there are many others in Victoria and Macleay Streets and Challis Avenue. Other classic restaurants in this area include the Bayswater Brassiere. For those who love Italian food, try Mezzaluna (p.330) on Victoria Street. Neil Perry's famous Asian restaurant XO is in Victoria Street and the place to be seen is Hugo's Lounge. See Going Out, p.339 for more.

Education

This area is relatively unsuitable for families to live in, except perhaps temporarily on arrival. However, there are state schools on offer including Plunkett Street, Woolloomooloo and Darlinghurst Primary Schools and Glenmore Road in Paddington, Vaucluse Primary and Double Bay Public School. The nearest state high schools are Sydney Boys and Sydney Girls. Private secondary schools include Sydney Grammar at Rushcutters Bay and private high schools include St Andrew's Cathedral School, Ascham Girls, Scotts College, Bellevue Hill, and Cranbrook Senior.

Transport

The CBD is walkable and Kings Cross has its own CityRail station. Potts Point and Woolloomooloo are well served by buses and a ten mintue stroll from Kings Cross station. There are also plenty of cabs buzzing about ferrying revellers to and from The Cross.

Safety / Annoyances

As in any city area, vigilance is advised, and extra care should be taken around Kings Cross. There is a strong police presence and the glare of lights keeps The Cross startlingly bright 24 hours a day, but beggars can be quite vocal (if not directly threatening), the prostitution is pretty open and you can occasionally spot discarded needles.

Manly & Balgowlah

Best Points

Spectacular location with an amazing harbour and ocean views, plus you've got the beach on your doorstep.

Located on a sand isthmus between the Pacific Ocean and the harbour, Manly offers a laid-back beach culture lifestyle with bush reserves and spectacular views. Nearby Balgowlah and Fairlight are family orientated areas but there are some boutique apartment blocks with spectacular harbour and ocean views that attract a younger crowd. Balgowlah tends to have more houses, with some fabulous new builds and freshly renovated homes.

Worst Points

Getting very expensive and Manly can be congested and noisy.

Accommodation

Manly still has some traditional Federation terraced cottages in the streets behind the beachfront but it appears that the last of the beachfront villas are about to be replaced by a smart apartment block. These tend to dominate the seafront strip on both sides. Balgowlah also offers a range of houses and town houses and families are well provided for.

Shopping & Amenities

The Corso and surrounding streets in Manly's compact centre and around the wharf offer a range of stores selling designer beachwear and souvenirs for the thousands of tourists that visit every day. There are also food stores, delis and supermarkets, with the very smart Warringah Mall a short drive or bus ride away. The Totem Shopping Centre in Balgowlah is undergoing a complete rebuild.

Entertainment & Leisure

Manly has an excellent selection of pubs, hotels, bars and general nightlife with some great restaurants all within walking distance of the Corso, the pedestrian strip that runs between Manly's two beaches. Some of these offer casual dining and others more formal fare, with the Steyne Hotel a particularly popular spot. Balgowlah has a good strip of inexpensive restaurants with the classic French Chez Maurice and the amazing value Balkan restaurant Lukas. The latter offers a five course all you can eat banquet menu for $20 in midweek. Ajmer's is one of the best Indian restaurants in Sydney. For fitness freaks there are few better spots for a run or walk than along the beachfront or up to North Head. Oceanworld has a great shark-feeding programme. The lovely scenery on the Spit Bridge to Manly walk is a fabulous way to discover this area and Middle Harbour.

Education

State schools include Manly Vale Primary, Manly West Primary and Mackellar Girls High with schools in Balgowlah including Balgowlah Boys High.

Transport

Manly is the classic commute from the city with either the ferry or JetCat on offer. There are also buses to the CBD that run across the Harbour Bridge, though these can get very busy and snarled up in traffic in peak hours. This is not a part of town that makes it onto the CityRail network. Getting back from the CBD at night can be a pain, leaving night buses or a pricey cab as your only option.

Balgowlah from The Spit

Safety / Annoyances

Manly and the surrounding areas are very safe, despite the fact that Manly on a Saturday is a pretty lively place. There is a lot of construction going on throughout the area.

Neutral Bay, Cremorne & Mosman

Lying along Military Road on the north side of the harbour, these booming and very popular suburbs offer a range of lifestyles close to the CBD, centred on a collection of very pleasant harbour bays and inlets. Balmoral offers the most amazing views through the Heads to the Pacific and an excellent, safe beach.

Best Points
There's a great village atmosphere and parts of these areas can feel quaintly homely but it's still close to the CBD. If you're close to major bus routes or one of the four ferry terminals, getting over the harbour is easy.

Worst Points
You may feel too isolated. Military Road can get congested and it is all very expensive.

Accommodation

All these suburbs are highly desirable with large Federation mansions, apartment buildings, town houses and the latest in house design, all jostling for that magical harbour view.

Shopping & Amenities

Mosman's main street offers all the latest fashion trends and everything else you would expect in a suburb of this quality. There are markets held every month in Mosman Square. The main food shopping is at Bridgepoint in Mosman or the two Woolworth stores in Neutral Bay.

Entertainment & Leisure

Right along Military Road there are a solid range of restaurants and cafes. Take your pick, from cooking you own steak in The Oaks (see p.356) in Neutral Bay to some of the best pizzas in Sydney at Sopranos at Spit Junction. Sydney's much-loved Taronga Park Zoo (see p.190) is in Mosman, and has an impressive collection of animals, which enjoy some of the best real estate in the area. The giraffes have

a particularly good view. Fitness First has a great gym in Mosman and there are a range of others leisure sites, like Mosman Rowing Club, and heaps of jogging and walking paths along the harbour. Sydney Harbour National Park and Middle and St George's Heads are peaceful spots to appreciate the city's natural gifts. Cremorne also offers one of Sydney's most delightfully restored cinemas, the Hayden Orpheum Picture Palace.

Education

Schools in the area include Mosman, Neutral Bay and Beauty Point Primary Schools, Mosman High and one of Sydney's most expensive schools, SCECGS Redlands in Cremorne, which is favoured by expats.

Transport

Unless you drive your options are limited to either ferry or bus. The former, of course, offers a beautiful journey to work. The latter, while being pretty swift, can be crowded and chug a little slowly through the traffic getting to the bridge. Military Road, which the vast majority of buses cross at some point, can be slow moving. Mosman Bay, Old Cremorne, South Mosman and Cremorne Point ferry terminals all run to wharf four at Circular Quay.

Safety / Annoyances

These are safe areas, but again, proximity to the CBD means some vigilance is required at night. There is a great deal of construction going on, with older houses being replaced by stunning new properties designed to secure that elusive harbour view.

99

Best Points

Amazing location and views, with some very impressive accommodation.

Worst Points

It's very expensive and compact, with parking difficulties during any big events.

North Sydney, Milsons Point & Kirribilli

Famous for spectacular views over Sydney Harbour, Kirribilli and Milsons Point are highly desirable areas and north shore dwellers rightly cherish their spot. So much so, that the area can be viewed as a little bit snobbish, but maybe that's just down to jealousy over the views. North Sydney is effectively a second CBD, with office blocks holding IT, design, publishing, advertising and media firms.

Accommodation

Kirribilli has a range of old and modern apartments, with houses ranging from Federation terraces right through to impressive waterfront properties, although freestanding homes are quite rare. North Sydney has lots of high-rise office blocks and apartment building. There are some very smart apartments in Milsons Point with harbour views. In some parts of North Sydney you will still find fine Victorian architecture and terraced houses. The price of your home, whether renting or buying, will be significantly affected by your distance from the ferry and the water.

Shopping & Amenities

A string of shops run along Kirribilli's Broughton Street, with some spilling out on to Fitzroy and Burton, including a bottle shop, a florist and a small supermarket. All the basics are here and there are more shops near Milsons Point railway station. The nearby offices mean the area is well served for snacks, sandwiches and coffee. In North Sydney there is the Greenwood Plaza which has some fancier shops and fresh food stores.

Entertainment & Leisure

The spectacular art deco North Sydney Olympic Pool includes a gym and is tucked under the Harbour Bridge offering amazing views of Sydney Harbour, the Opera House and Luna Park. There are some lovely little cafes and restaurants offering a choice of international and Australian foods. North Sydney has plenty more restaurants and cafes, although they tend to open to suit the demands of office workers rather than residents. The Civic Centre Park and Charlie Watts Park have modern playgrounds. There are also a few playing fields and tennis courts in the park near the North Sydney Oval. Luna Park recently reopened after many years.

View from the shore

Education

Some of Sydney's leading private schools are to be found here, including Loreto Kirribilli, which has a junior and senior school, St Aloysius College and Monte Sant Angelo College in North Sydney, along with North Sydney Girls' and Boys' High Schools, Wenona Girls and Sydney Church of England Grammar, with The Australian Catholic University and the Northern Sydney Institute of TAFE also nearby.

Transport

The CBD is just over the water. The short ferry hop to Circular Quay from Kirribilli, Luna Park, Lavender Bay or McMahons Point are all very impressive ways to get to work. You can also take the train from Milsons Point and North Sydney stations. While slightly less romantic, this is a quicker way to get across and it still offers decent views.

Safety / Annoyances

The area is pretty safe at most times. There is a lot of construction though and it can be very congested during big events, such as fireworks on the harbour or the start of the Sydney to Hobart yacht race.

Best Points
It's a short trip into town, and there are smart, good value apartments, town houses and renovated old buildings.

Erskineville & St Peters

Erskineville and St Peters were traditionally working class areas, with small houses and big industrial buildings. However, they are currently undergoing redevelopment and benefiting from some steady investment. The old houses are being renovated, and as the big industrial firms have moved out, their old buildings have been left ripe for development. Here you'll find a village-type atmosphere just a stone's throw from the city. This relative proximity to town and the general spit and polish Erskineville and St Peters are getting make them increasingly popular and a prime spot for new cafes, pubs and shops.

Worst Points
It's beginning to get a tad trendy.

Accommodation

This area was originally known for its terraces and semi-detached houses. Some have survived and been renovated but many have been demolished to make way for apartments and town houses, with the old industrial buildings converted into fashionable apartments and lofts.

Shopping & Amenities

There are small shops near the train station and the main shopping strip is along the Princes Highway, but you really need to go to King Street in Newtown for more signs of life. There you'll find some quirky food shops, supermarkets, books and galleries. The St Peters end of King Street has many independent boutiques selling everything from buttons to model toys. In Erskineville you'll also find the Erskineville Hotel and the Imperial Hotel, the latter perhaps better known for its pub, which was made famous in the film *Priscilla, Queen of the Desert* as the popular drag show spot, see p.362 for more.

Entertainment & Leisure

There are great spots for pub food and some pleasant cafes in the immediate area. Nearby King Street has loads of cheap restaurants and some late bars. There is a good mix of ethnic cuisine, with Marrickville and Newtown offering great Greek, Vietnamese, Thai and Lebanese fare. For a spot of sport, there is a pool at Victoria Park. Close to St Peters, Sydney Park is a 44 hectare space that has some excellent sports grounds used mainly for cricket and Aussie rules football, as well as many walking trails, gardens, picnic spots and wetlands. For the more arty types, Erskineville is home to the Tom Bass School of Sculpture and Art, which is the oldest independent sculpture school in Sydney. It hosts exhibitions and workshops as well as classes in life drawing and sculpture.

Education

Schools in the area include Erskineville Public and St Mary's Catholic School, along with Newington College and Trinity College. Sydney University is nearby. St Peters Public School has been around since 1881.

Transport

Erskineville station is on the Bankstown line, just two stops out from Sydney Central. From there you can get to anywhere on the suburban network. St Peters is just one stop further along and about 7 km south of the CBD. Either is about 15 minutes to Circular Quay by CityRail and both are well served by buses.

Safety / Annoyances

While generally fine, there can be quite an eclectic mix of residents and you should pay some extra attention to security.

Map 3-F4 ◀

Surry Hills & Redfern

Surry Hills was once one of the more depressed areas of the inner city, with the quiet streets south of Sydney Central exuding a sullen menace. Redfern is still besmirched by the lingering memories of the riots of 2004 and the reputation of 'the Block', though some lessons have been learnt. This area is a hub for inner city Aboriginal communities and parts of Redfern are allocated to the indigenous population through the Aboriginal Housing Company, an organistion set up in 1973 in an effort to guarantee some urban land rights. The Redfern-Waterloo Authority is charged with revitalising what was for many years quite a deprived area.

Best Points
It's an eclectic community that brings together all of Sydney life and there's lots of exotic eateries.

Worst Points
Congestion can be a problem and while all of Sydney is pretty safe, security is a bit more of an issue here.

Gentrification is coming slowly, as young professionals move in to the area, attracted by its Victorian terraces and proximity to the CBD.

Accommodation

Surry Hills and Redfern offer a mix of trendy restoration and shabby dilapidation, with newly renovated houses next to industrial units and smart apartments alongside restored Victorian terraces. The further south you go along Elizabeth or Chalmers streets, the shabbier the housing tends to become, but some smarter places exist down here too.

Shopping & Amenities

Surry Hills is still the centre of Sydney's garment trade and there are several factory outlets where you can buy plenty of clothes and materials at discounted prices. Supermarkets are limited but there are lots of late opening convenience stores.

Entertainment & Leisure

This area is best-known for the Lebanese and Turkish restaurants on Cleveland and Elizabeth Streets. You will also find everything else, including Indian, Chinese, Thai French, Italian, etc. The watering holes tend to be pubs rather than swanky bars.

Education

There are few schools here. The schools in this area are Crown Street Primary School and Sydney Boys & Girls High.

Transport

From Central Station you can get trains directly to anywhere on the Sydney Suburban Network and on to Newcastle, the Blue Mountains or the Southern Highlands. It also marks the entrance to the six stop City Circle. The walk from Central to Circular Quay can be done in 20 to 30 minutes. Bus services are also reliable and Redfern has its own CityRail station, one stop on from Central.

Safety / Annoyances

Some vigilance is required and beggars and dealers can be fairly visible around Redfern. Neither Surry Hills nor Redfern are particularly car friendly; traffic, parking and congestion are problems.

Glebe, Pyrmont & Balmain

Best Points
The cool address, fashionable restaurants, dappled light of the leafy streets and general pleasantness of the environment.

Worst Points
Property is expensive and the immediate entertainment (beyond eating out) is a little limited.

Glebe is a very trendy suburb filled with magnificent mansions and terrace houses. It's got a very cosmopolitan vibe and Sydney University is right next door. Pyrmont and Ultimo have practically been rebuilt over recent years, with many new apartments in the area. Balmain has been a bit arty since the 60s when it shed its working man's roots and a bohemian air remains, though it is quite quiet and residential.

Accommodation

Glebe has the whole mix including some gorgeous old mansions, classic two storey terraces and Federation cottages. Pyrmont is just a short walk from the CBD across Darling Harbour. This used to be a warehousing area and, while many of these old buildings have been demolished, you'll still find a few here. Pyrmont now offers a mix of town houses and apartments.

Shopping & Amenities

Every Saturday the Glebe markets (p.308) offer all kind of stalls, with the recycling theme flowing down on to Glebe Point Road. Balmain also has its Saturday Market, held in St Andrews Congregational Church in Darling Street, which offers antiques, jewellery and crafts. The Broadway Centre (see p.301) is nearby. Convenience stores have sprung up in Pyrmont to cater for the new units. At 181 Harris Street you will find Simon Johnson's shop (www.simonjohnson.com). This is rated by many as the best food shop in Sydney. It sells speciality items you're unlikely to find elsewhere and runs demonstration classes (for a fee of around $80 to $120) to show the masses how to master their pork hock or knock up exotic desserts.

Entertainment & Leisure

Like many Sydney suburbs you can experience food from around the globe here. The Cat & Fiddle (see p.355) is a well know live music venue and the Friend in Hand Hotel is a quirky spot for a lively schooner. Elkington Park is small but pleasant.

Education

These affluent areas are well served for education with some excellent private schools including Sydney Grammar and St Andrews and state schools like Fort Street. The University of Technology and Sydney University are both nearby. Balmain offers Balmain Primary, Balmain High School, The Montessori School and the Sydney College of the Arts.

Transport

The parts of the inner west that don't make it onto the CityRail network can be a bit of a pain to get in and out of. Buses always appear to take longer than they should, given the proximity to the CBD. But Balmain is reachable by ferry from Circular Quay, bus routes 432/3/4 and 442 pass through and there is a new link to the MLR.

Safety / Annoyances

Some vigilance is required at night in the main restaurant areas and back streets, but generally safe.

Best Points
Great food and a good community feel (particularly if you parli Italiano). Property prices and rents remain reasonable.

Worst Points
Those reasonable prices don't look set to last. Some areas can feel very quiet, and facilities are limited.

Leichhardt, Annandale & Lilyfield

Leichhardt offers a vibrant lifestyle and some strong Italian influences, thanks to the Italian community that has settled in the suburb and nearby in Annandale and Haberfield. Strolling down the street you'll hear old boys chatting in Italian, find Italian food in the shops and delis and restaurants serving homemade Italian fare. You'll also find old restored houses and converted industrial buildings. Lilyfield was formerly an area of boat builders and factories. It is now a residential suburb with weatherboard cottages, freestanding brick houses and terraces that is favoured by young families for its quiet, leafy streets. It's also growing popular with young professionals and students.

The Italian Forum

Accommodation
Leichhardt has some fine Victorian housing, smaller Edwardian semi-detached houses and modern apartments. You will also find some former industrial buildings that have been converted into modern apartments and lofts. Lilyfield has some good family homes.

Shopping & Amenities
The Italian Forum on Norton Street is a must visit. It is designed to resemble an Italian piazza (though with modern architecture) with shops, restaurants, apartments and a good community feel. There are some art and craft shops along Norton Street and a number of good independent bookshops. Many of the convenience stores sell Italian deli goods.

Entertainment & Leisure
If you like Italian food then Norton Street is the place. It's got Sydney's best coffee, cakes, pastries, pasta and pizza. Nightlife tends to focus on this strip and the Italian Forum; this may look a little tacky but has some good spots. To work off some of those extra calories, there's the Dawn Fraser Pool at Elkington Park and Leichhardt Aquatic Centre, near Leichhardt Oval.

Education
The two Leichhardt local Catholic schools are St Columbas and St Fiacres. The state schools are Leichhardt Primary and High schools. In Annandale there is only one primary school and Lilyfield is home to the Orange Grove Public School.

Transport
The nearest CityRail stations are Lewisham, Stanmore and Petersham, all on the Inner West line. There are direct buses into the city and Lilyfield marks the end of the line for the Metro Light Rail.

Safety / Annoyances
This is a relatively safe area but some vigilance is required in the main streets at night.

Newtown, Stanmore & Lewisham

Newtown, Stanmore and Lewisham are trendy suburbs that attract a mix of artists, hippies, students and city types. Newtown in particular is lively with its increased popularity spilling fashionable eateries and kooky shops down to neighbouring Stanmore and Lewisham. The eclectic social mix is reflected (and perhaps caused) by the range of housing. This runs from dinky old cottages to plush new apartments and large detached houses.

Best Points ◀
There's no shortage of nightlife and original shops and you'll be living in one of the city's most vibrant areas.

Accommodation

It's all here. Newtown is highly sought after by the young and upwardly mobile, offering affordable terraces, semi-detached houses and beautifully restored bigger homes, in addition to some very well redeveloped warehouse and industrial buildings. Some smaller cottages still remain.

Worst Points ◀
King Street can be crowded for both pedestrian and automotive traffic. The sheer trendiness of the place might grow to irk you.

Shopping & Amenities

King Street and Enmore Road are the main shopping areas with hundreds of stores, including furnishings, antiques, designer clothes, books, galleries, food, coffee and everything else you can think of. The general trend is towards the arty and bohemian; with Newtown known as the city's capital of second-hand, retro fashion. The shops here are typically small independents, though there are supermarkets for your food shopping.

Entertainment & Leisure

You can merrily eat your way around the world just by strolling down King Street and Enmore Road. You'll find the staples: Thai, Chinese, Indian, Japanese, Mexican, Aussie and some rarer treats like Malay, Balkan and North African. There are some decent bars and it's rare to see King Street quiet. Two of the better known bars, the Bank and Newtown hotels are gay but attract a mixed crowd.

Education

Schools include Newtown Primary, Stanmore Primary and Cardenville Primary. The Newtown School of the Arts attracts a range of would-be performers and Newington is close by.

Transport

There are loads of buses that go straight into the CBD or you can travel by train from Newtown and Stanmore Stations.

Safety / Annoyances

Generally safe, but be careful on the main streets at night for the drinkers and the drunks.

Lewisham street art

Setting up Home

Once you have chosen the part of town you fancy (see Residential Areas on p.88.) and found a home there (see Real Estate Agents, p.84), you can begin the jolly task of moving in. What follows will, we hope, make it all as easy as possible.

Smooth Moves
Use the best movers you can afford, take out good insurance and do not try to bend the rules on importing goods as the penalties are severe.

Moving Services

For local moves, there are plenty of firms (see table) that can be found online (www.sydney-city-directory.com.au is a good start) or in the Yellow Pages. Or, hire a 'man and his van'. If you do (and there is a firm that actually goes under this name; see www.manandhisvan.com.au), it will cost $140 - $160 per hour, for a minimum of three hours, plus half an hour each way to cover travel. This fee will provide you with two furniture movers, the van and some small lifting equipment. Should extra manpower be required, charges are applied pro rata. Otherwise, hire a van and do the legwork yourself. Try www.nqrentals.com.au or any of the car leasing places listed in the table on p.137. It may be easier to store your belongings at first (try www.rentaspace.com.au or www.homeone.com.au) or buy new furniture, see p.286.

Removal Companies			
Allied Pickfords ▶ p.xiv	13 2554	www.alliedpickfords.com.au
Always Moving	0418 248 378	www.alwaysmoving.com.au
Ben Carey Removals	9487 2489	www.bencareyremovals.com
Grace Removals	13 1442	www.grace.com.au

Moving From Overseas

When moving from abroad, bear in mind the strict import laws. You have to tell the Australian Quarantine and Inspection

Relocation Companies	
Crown Relocations	www.crownrelo.com
Home Relocation and Buying Services	www.homerelocation.com.au
Relocation Services Sydney	www.simplysydney.com.au
Wridgways	www.wridgways.com.au

Service (AQIS) of all the items in your shipment and in particular anything that may present a risk. You can check which items are allowed by visiting www.aqis.gov.au. AQIS may inspect your goods, treat items that could contain pests or diseases, or even seize and destroy them, although they may allow you to re-export items of value. Items of concern include: anything made of wood; gardening tools or anything with soil or plant material; carpets, rugs, floor coverings and tapestries; dried flowers; anything made of skin or fur; items containing cotton waste or filling, including sand, straw or water; any food; vacuum cleaners; Christmas decorations, in particular those containing wood or dried plant; any seeds, pods or similar items; feathers and any equipment that has been used with horses or other animals. Any relocation company (see table) should be able to ease some of the strain of organising this.

Furnishing Your Home

Most rental homes are unfurnished and white goods are usually not included. Sometimes a dishwasher is built in. If you're not planning on staying that long in Australia, it might be a good idea to rent furniture. There are a few companies who provide this service. Try www.livingedgerental.com.au, www.phdrentals.com.au or www.rentacentre.com.au. If you're buying furniture, there are several chain stores, including Freedom Furniture, Domain, Harvey Norman, Myer, David Jones and of course IKEA (See shopping p.286 for details). Having items made is expensive and not easy to source.

Second-Hand Items

There is a good second-hand market, with prices significantly cheaper than new. Items are listed in local papers or on notice boards in supermarkets. You can also go

Freebie Furnishings
Local councils have a regular clean up day, in advance of which unwanted items are left on the street for collection. If you have tinker tendencies, you may want to scout out the more affluent areas for discarded gems. According to the SMH, one Sydney man furnished his entire house (in retro style) in this way.

online and search sites such as www.tradingpost.com.au and www.ebay.com.au. Garage sales are listed in local papers and sometimes in the Saturday edition of the *Sydney Morning Herald*.

Tailors

You can get tailors to make up soft furnishings like cushions, throws and even covers for armchairs and settees. There is also the Soft Furnishings Association of Australia. This organisation's website (www.sfiaa.org.au) has a nifty search facility where you can find the closest soft furnishing specialist to you.

Tailors	
Alteration City	9235 2378
Alterations Studio	9232 6988
M K Clothing Alterations	9262 9006
Mei Ling Alterations	9221 5895
Tailor Salon	9232 8951

Household Insurance

Break-ins are on the rise in Sydney, so it is worth getting contents insurance and, if you own your house, building insurance too. You can get either from your bank or direct from an insurance firm, many of which can hook you up online or over the phone. Just contact one of the firms listed. The type and conditions of cover are varied and where you live can have a big impact on cost. Most policies will have an excess and there will be limits to each claim.

Household Insurance		
AAMI	13 2244	www.aami.com.au
ING	1800 815 688	www.ing.com.au
NRMA	13 2132	www.nrma.com.au
QBE	13 3723	www.qbe.com
Suncorp Metway	13 1155	www.suncorpmetway.com.au

Laundry Services

Launderettes are available in some areas, particularly those with lots of backpackers, but are less common than they used to be.
The demise of the launderette can be put down to more people having washing machines. Most apartment buildings also now have communal washing machines and dryers, most of which are coin operated. Costs vary by location but, as a rough idea, you can get a shirt washed and pressed for $3.

Laundry Services		
Bubbles Laundrette	Surry Hills	9698 9286
Castlereagh Dry Cleaners	Outer West	9223 5742
Darlinghurst Laundry	Darlinghurst	9361 0583
Harbourside Dry Cleaners	Pyrmont	9692 8488
Kings Cross Dry Cleaners	Kings Cross	9358 6094
Lawrence Dry Cleaners	Central	9235 1329
T L C Dry Cleaners	Various locations	9223 5678
Wash On The Rocks	Central	9247 6752

Domestic Help

Other options **Domestic Services** p.108

The cost of labour in Sydney precludes most people, except for the very wealthy, from having home help and in particular a live-in maid. More common is having a visiting cleaner and there are a number of franchise operations that have set up recently, including Bebrite and United Home Services, which cover cleaning, gardening and other domestic services.
Advertising in the local paper may also work. It is very difficult, albeit not impossible, to sponsor a maid to come and work for you in Australia, see www.immi.gov.au.

Domestic Help Agencies		
Abbies Housework	1300 308 304	www.abbieshousework.com.au
Absolute Domestics	1300 364 646	www.absolutedomestics.com.au
Bebrite	1300 131 664	www.bebrite.com.au
Easy Life Domestic	6024 0404	www.easylifemacro.com
United Home	1800 204 699	www.uhs.com.au
V.I.P. Home	13 2613	www.viphomeservices.com

107

Smacking
*This is quite a
contentious issue in
Australia. There is a
growing clamour for
smacking to be
banned and while it is
not illegal in NSW, it is
frowned upon in
most communities.*

Babysitting & Childcare

Babysitters and nannies are hard to find. Your best bet may be asking friends or colleagues who they use. Even

Babysitting & Childcare		
Care For Kids	9235 2807	www.careforkids.com.au
Childcare Direct	9526 8810	www.childcaredirect.com.au
Find a Babysitter	1300 789 073	www.findababysitter.com.au
The Australian Child Care Index	07 3289 4614	www.child-care-index.net.au

then, some mums can be reluctant to provide contacts, not wanting to lose their good find. Parents do set up babysitting circles, but even these are sometimes hard to break into. You can advertise locally or ask friends, and these websites: www.bubhub.com.au or www.milestonz.com.au are both useful resources.

Expect to pay between $18 and $25 per hour for a professional nanny. Some may work casually, doing evening babysitting from 18:00 onwards for $18 to $20 per hour. Teenagers would expect to be paid $10 to $15 per hour. Babysitters do not need any qualifications and neither do nannies, but agencies require them to have current and up to date first aid certificates, health clearance from their regular GP and a police clearance or a 'working with children' check from the Department of Community Services in NSW. The child care index (see table) gives listings for carers across Australia.

Domestic Services

Tradesmen can be very hard to find in Sydney. If you buy, it may be worth asking your realtor for the name of a good plumber, carpenter or electrician. If you are renting, your landlord takes care of all the maintenance and you should not commission any work without the landlord's approval. In emergencies, check your lease for who to call. Rates aren't cheap and double time applies on weekends, which can go to triple time over holidays.

The best place to start is either www.etradesman.com.au, the Yellow Pages, or advertisements in your local paper. You should also check the Master Builders Association at www.masterbuilders.com.au or 8586 3555, as they can find services by postcode. They will also provide a list of five recommendations for your area but these are more related to building than maintenance.

There are also some franchise firms. The best known include Hire a Hubby and Jim's Group. For pest control, if the problem is severe you can call you local council but, in general, pest management is the responsibility of the owner of the property. Try www.bestpest.com.au or www.pestcontrolsydney.com.au if that's you.

Domestic Services			
A.P.T Plumbing Services	Outer West	9727 5736	Plumbers & gasfitters
AGL Assist	Various locations	13 1766	Gas & electrics
Energy Electrical Services	Various locations	9962 5145	Electrical services
Hire a Hubby	Various locations	1800 803 339	General maintenance
Jim's Group	Central	13 1546	General maintenance
Scott and Sons	Outer West	9457 9285	Plumbers & gasfitters
SKM Electrical Services	Various locations	1300 772 754	Electrical service
Total Tile Care	Various locations	9905 4360	Tile cleaning

DVD & Video Rental

DVD and Video rental is still fairly common in Sydney with stores in all major retail centres and main streets. The market is dominated by the big players, namely VideoEzy and Blockbuster, which have stores all over Sydney. There are also companies online including, v2direct, BigPond Movies and Quickflix. With these, you choose a payment plan and then start choosing your films. These are sent to you by post or can be download to your PC.

DVD & Video Rental		
Allison Video Sales & Rental	9726 8320	–
BigPond Movies	1800 502 502	www.bigpondmovies.com
Blockbuster	9212 2943	www.blockbuster.com.au
Civic Video	9206 8800	www.civicvideo.com.au
Good Luck Video	9212 1131	–
Hong Kong Video	9281 2519	–
Lucky Thai Sweets & Video	9211 3163	–
Quickflix	–	www.quickflix.com.au
V2direct	–	www.v2direct.com.au
VideoEzy	–	www.videoezy.com.au

Exotic Pets

Exotic pets are not as common in Sydney as you might think and dogs, cats, fish and birds still top the list. It is illegal to keep koalas as pets but wombats make agreeable companions. Snakes, lizards and even spiders are growing in popularity but you'll need a permit from the NPWS to keep one.

Pets

Pets are very popular in Sydney, with a high number of dog and cat owners. Owning a pet is generally straightforward but bringing one into the country is not.

Bringing Pets to Sydney

Regulations change regularly, so check out the Australian Government Department of Agriculture, Fisheries and Forestry website, www.affa.gov.au and click on the Australian Quarantine and Inspection Service (AQIS) bit before you make any plans. Here you can download an information pack with the relevant quarantine requirements, fees and an import permit application. Except for a few countries close to Australia, 30 to 120 days quarantine is generally needed. Also, if you are coming from a country that is not on the approved list the chances are you won't be able to bring your furry friend at all. If you want to take your pet abroad, the regulations related to importing animals into that country will apply and you should check their rules.

Pet Shops

Pet stores are quite common (see Shopping, p293), but most just sell accessories and small pets, leaving the sales of cats, dogs and other animals to speciality breeders and stores. Checking with the RSPCA at www.rspca.org.au is recommended before buying a pet. It gives a few gentle reminders about your responsibilities to a new moggy or mutt.

You do not need a health certificate for your animal but cats and dogs have to be registered, microchipped and wear an ID tag. Please see www.petregistry.nsw.gov.au.

Pet Boarding/Sitting		
A Pet's Friend	9428 4957	Dog walking
A Second Home	8812 5792	Pet boarding
Animal Instincts	9573 1460	Dog walking, petsitting
Don't Fret Pet	1300 307 020	Pet boarding
Home Alone Pet Care	1300 306 756	Dog walking, petsitting
Marendale Boarding Kennels and Cattery	9450 1529	Pet boarding
Pet Carrier International	1300 788 770	Pet boarding
Walkies	0411 148 151	Dog walking
Yappy Dogs	9358 6706	Dog walking

109

Veterinary Clinics

4 Paws	Neutral Bay	9953 1264
Allambie Veterinary Clinic	Outer North	9905 0505
Balmain Village Veterinary Clinic	Balmain	9555 9362
Bankstown Veterinary Hospital	Outer West	9790 1101
Campbelltown North Animal Hospital	Outer West	4628 5055

You should be aware that even if you own your home, many title agreements preclude keeping a dog or other pets. You should check your agreement. If you are renting, check your lease. Some pets are not as well looked after as they should be and there are a number of animal rescue organisations, including www.paws.com.au, www.animaladoption.com.au and www.doggierescue.com.

Dog Walking

You can walk your dog in most locations but many councils insist they are kept on a leash, even in parks and reserves. Dogs are not generally allowed in cafes or restaurants. Local councils can normally provide a list, either online or in print, to let you know where you can and cannot take your pooch. Councils also impose stiff penalties for not cleaning up after your dog, so always carry a bag or some kind of scoop.

Fish & Birds

Most pet stores sell fish and birds (most of which have been bred in Australia) and plenty of equipment to keep them cleaned, housed and entertained. Website www.theprofisionals.com.au has a list of stores and online store www.aquaticlifeaquariums.com.au can also kit you out. For birds, see www.birddealer.com. Also, have a look at Shopping, p.293.

Poop Scoopers

If the thought of fetching fido's effluent from the bottom of the garden proves a little too much, Sydney has a firm that will scoop your pooch's poop for around $15 a week. Dogz Biz covers the north shore and further up the coast and visits homes to tidy up the little parcels that your mutt leaves behind in lieu of rent. Though of course, you have to have a pretty big garden to let it build up for a week. Telephone 0410 699 478 or email info@dogzbiz.biz.

Vets & Kennels

Australia has very professional veterinary care, with a vet's surgery in most areas (see table above). For a local scoop, if you see a well-groomed dog in the area, just ask the owner where they go. There are also specialist centres for a range of animal illnesses, including internal medicine, cancer, ophthalmic, etc., which your vet may refer you to. Vets tend to be expensive and you would be well advised to take out medical insurance for your pet through Petcover (www.petcover.com.au) or Petsecure (www.petsecure.com.au). Petsitting and dog walking services have become widely available and are offered by a range of companies including Walkies at www.walkies.net.au and Don't Fret Pet at www.dontfretpet.com.au. See table, p.109.

Pet Grooming/Training

Canine Excursion	0400 831 232	Pet grooming
Jims	13 1546	Pet grooming
K9 Training	4736 8419	Dog obedience training
Le Belle Pet Salon	9939 4126	Pet grooming
Perky Pets	8902 0908	Dog obedience training
Pet Carrier International	1300 788 770	Pet grooming
Pet Wash 2000	0435 331 010	Pet grooming
V.I.P. Home Services	13 2613	Pet grooming

Grooming & Training

Facilities for dog grooming and training are extensive (see table) with many operations coming to your home and using an enclosed trailer. Services will range from a quick scrub up to a full moggy manicure.

Electricity

Lights Out ◀

The Sydney grid can become overloaded in the summer (as happened in 2004) because of storms and the heavy use of air conditioning. Blackouts can last for several hours, so have an emergency kit ready including torches and candles.

The main electricity supplier is Energy Australia and you can connect online at www.energy.com.au or call 13 1535, but whether they will allow you an account will depend on your credit rating. You now can also obtain electricity from AGL on www.agl.com.au, who also supply gas. Consumers are encouraged to minimise electricity consumption through judicious use of air conditioning in summer and heating in winter. Costs are not extortionate though, and with careful use, you could heat (or cool) a Sydney two bedroom house for around $300 per quarter.

All appliances sold in Australia have the standard Australian two or three pin plug and run on 220/240v 50Hz, but if you wish to operate an overseas appliance an adaptor and/or transformer will be needed. You can get these in a number of stores, including Dick Smith (see www.dse.com.au or Shopping, p279).

The Australian government has committed $2 billion to its climate change efforts, many of which focus on clean energy. As part of this, Blacktown will become the first 'solar city' in New South Wales, getting $15 million for solar projects. But it's all in its early stages and nationwide the scheme is only going to provide enough solar power for 200 homes.

Water

Sydney Water provides water throughout the greater Sydney area. It is effectively a government monopoly, offering generally good service, with very infrequent interruptions and generally high quality. A few years ago, the city had outbreaks of Cryptosporidium and Giardia organisms in the water system. Sydney Water now publishes a daily report on their website, giving the exact amounts of each of these organisms in the water. See www.sydneywater.com.au.

Water Shortages ◀

There is currently a serious water shortage in NSW, with restrictions throughout the state on things like watering your garden. The government is promoting the use of water saving taps and shower heads and you can get a rebate of $650 for installing a rainwater tank. See Sydney Water for more info.

To get connected you need to apply to Sydney Water to have a meter installed. This can only be done by Sydney Water themselves or a qualified plumber. Call them on 13 2092 to make the necessary arrangements. If you live in a house you will have your own meter and will pay your own bill (which can be done online). If you live in an apartment or town house, you will probably have a separate meter, with the payment being the responsibility of the landlord.

Tap water in Sydney is totally safe to drink, and most people drink it, but some prefer to buy bottled mineral water or get water dispensers, which are available from companies such as Neverfail (www.neverfail.com.au). A water cooler and dispenser costs in the region of $150 a year and replacement 15 litre bottle are about $12.

Sewerage

Sewerage systems in urban areas are all connected to the mains with a fee added to your bill by Sydney Water to pay for this. In some more outlying areas sewerage may be dealt with through septic tanks and micro sewerage systems, which can only be installed with the local council's approval.

Gas

To connect your gas or electricity you need to contact AGL at www.agl.com.au. You may be able to get connected online or by calling 13 1245. Connection and disconnection requests should be made three business days in advance. You can opt to pay monthly or quarterly. The cost of gas or electricity will vary depending on the range of appliances you have. For a two bedroom house with gas for cooking and hot water and electricity for everything else, expect to pay about $130 a quarter for the gas and about $300 for the electricity.

Rubbish Disposal & Recycling

Local councils manage the rubbish disposal in Sydney, although generally they contract it out to commercial operators. Recycling is actively practised with separate bins provided in most council areas for paper, cardboard, plastic, bottles and cans. Each council is different and each will provide you with the bins that they want you to use and a schedule of pick up times. There can be fines for not recycling but they are rarely enforced. Landfills are run by private firms either solely or with the government. One such firm is Dial a Dump, which has landfills in Alexandria and Eastern Creek; www.dialadump.com.au, 9519 9999.

Telephone

Talk is (not) Cheap
Cheap mobile deals can be misleading. Look out for special rates that soar after a couple of months and 'free' time that expires quickly because of the high per-minute charge.

Landline services are highly competitive with Telstra (www.telstra.com), which remains partly government owned, and Optus (www.optus.com) the leaders in the field with a plethora of packages incorporating landlines, mobiles, cable TV, etc.

Secondary providers will also vie for your business, some running door-knocking campaigns to win you over. Local calls are untimed and generally at a flat rate but long distance and international calls are timed, with all rates depending on the package you buy. The

Telephone Companies		
3	13 3320	www.three.com.au
AAPT	13 8888	www.aapt.com.au
Dualphone Australia	1300 851 371	www.dualphonecentre.com.au
Nortel Networks	8870 5000	www.nortelnetworks.com
Optus	13 1345	www.optus.com.au
PacificTel	9212 1444	www.pacifictel.com.au
Primus	1300 854 485	www.primus.com.au
SlimTel Mobile Phones	1300 788 840	www.slimtel.com.au
Telstra	12 5111	www.telstra.com
Vodafone	1300 650 410	www.vodafone.com.au

quality of connections between Australia and other countries has been excellent for some time. International calling cards can be found in most newsagents for $5, $10 or $20. There are dozens available, and each one is better for different countries. Internet calls can also offer good rates and, if you don't have access in your home, most net cafes have headsets for making these, though you won't have a particularly private chat.

Hello Mum
Using Skype (www.skype.com) or another VOIP (voice over internet protocol) system for long distance or overseas calls can save you a bundle. If you get the right package, these can even make calling cards seem expensive. But remember that quality can be variable and you need to have broadband internet services.

With the growth of mobile phones, the number of phone boxes has reduced. Phone boxes take cash or phone cards, which you can buy in local stores or online. Charges for using hotel phones for outside calls are significantly higher than normal rates and it is recommended you use a phone card with a 1800 number to access the system, thereby only paying the local call rate.

Extra services are available from both Telstra and Optus, including supplementary lines, fax lines, call waiting, call forwarding, voice mail, etc. It is always best to make international calls in the evenings, overnight or at weekends and look out for special deals over holidays.

If someone is harassing you, get caller ID and ask your provider to monitor the line. If it continues, speak with your provider again and if you know who is doing it, you should consider calling the police.

The Australian Communications and Media Authority are

Cheap Overseas Calls		
Cloncom Connect	1800 355 298	www.cloncom.com
Comfi	7861 4107	www.comfi.com
Hot Calling Cards	7861 4107	www.hotcallingcards.com
IDT Euro Call	1800 182 638	www.cloncom.com
Skytel Traveler	1800 175 972	www.cloncom.com
United World Telecom	7861 4107	www.uwtcallback.com
Worldwide Card Telecom	1800 231 736	www.cloncom.com

the people to complain to if you feel a phone company has done you wrong. The 'tool kit' on their website (www.acma.gov.au) gives hints on finding the best phone, internet and TV deals.

Mobile Phones

The main mobile networks in Australia include 3, Vodafone, Telstra, Virgin Mobile and Optus (see table for all). Each offers multiple options for prepaid, pay-as-you-go and monthly contracts. The main providers all have stores in big shopping malls (see p.291) and stores like Crazy John's (13 2299, www.crazyjohns.com.au) and Mobile Select (1300 134 131, www.mobileselect.com.au) offer deals across networks and handset brands. Comparison site www.phonechoice.com.au is a useful starting point. Most contracts include a phone that you pay for over the term of the contract. Alternatively, you can buy a phone and just pay-as-you-go or pre-pay by loading cash on your account. As a non-resident, it is very straightforward to get a local mobile number, but getting an account may depend on establishing a credit rating. Once you have a number it can be transferred from provider to provider, even if you lose your phone.

Mobile Service Providers		
3	13 3320	www.three.com.au
Optus	13 1345	www.optus.com.au
SlimTel	1300 788 840	www.slimtel.com.au
Telstra	12 5111	www.telstra.com
Think Mobile	1300 284 465	www.thinkmobile.com.au
Virgin Mobile	13 3323	www.virginmobile.com.au
Vodafone	1300 650 410	www.vodafone.com.au

Internet

Other options **Internet Cafes** p.350, **Websites** p.50

Sydney has plenty of providers of internet services of varying cost and quality. The basic principle is to stay away from dial-up as it can't really keep up with newer websites. Broadband deals are widely available and can come as regular cable, wireless or ADSL. The latter has become the most common, with regular cable being hard to secure. Wireless is becoming popular and more reliable.

Plans vary considerably, as does service and reliability. Telstra and Optus both provide solid services and their plans and packages are easy to understand. Packages are available from $14.95, thought these change regularly. All plans provide email accounts and can offer webpages. Wireless broadband is increasing in popularity, but is in its relative infancy with Telstra leading the field and other providers such as Unwired also gaining subscribers. There is no internet censorship in Australia.

Internet Service Providers		
AAPT	13 8888	www.aapt.com.au
Dodo	13 2473	www.dodo.com.au
iPrimus	1300 774 687	www.iprimus.com.au
Optus	13 1345	www.optus.com.au
Telstra	12 5111	www.telstra.com
TPG	1300 360 855	www.tpg.com.au
Unwired	1300 761 881	www.unwired.com.au

Internet cafes are widely available in the CBD and Kings Cross and are generally used by backpackers. Costs can be as low as $1.50 an hour. Global Gossip has probably the most comprehensive network, see www.globalgossip.com for locations. Everywhere Internet also has several spots, see www.everywhereinternet.com.au. A useful internet cafe guide can be found at www.gnomon.com.au.

Bill Payment

All phone and internet bills are monthly and you can pay most providers online, by cheque, or at a bank or post office.

If you miss a payment, the larger providers will send you a reminder and a final notice before terminating your service, but some of the smaller providers may be less tolerant. This really depends on your credit rating, which as a newcomer is hard to establish. Virtually all providers offer internet billing and account access so that you can monitor your spending.

113

Post & Courier Services
Other options **Post & Courier Services** p.49

There is only one postal system in Australia; the government owned Australia Post (www.australiapost.com.au). The service is very efficient for international and domestic mail and there are branches and agencies in most shopping streets.

Domestic city-to-city mail is delivered the next day but mail to more remote locations may take longer. Regular airmail to and from the US takes on average four to six working days, with Europe and the UK taking a day less. A range of express services is also available, including Express Mail for next day guaranteed delivery before noon within Australia and Express Courier International and Express Post International for mailing abroad.

The domestic letter rate starts at 50 cents or $4.10 for Express Mail. Sending a letter to the US will cost $1.85. For a package up to 250g, it's $5.55 to use Airmail and between $11 and $16.50 for Express International. Packages can normally be insured at the post office and recorded delivery and registered post are also available.

While packages have to be taken to a post office, letters can be sent from red Australia Post boxes which are located throughout Sydney. Express Mail has to be deposited in special yellow and red Australia Post boxes only available in some locations, see www.australiapost.com.au. Stamps can be bought at post offices, newsagents and convenience stores throughout Sydney.

PO Boxes & Couriers
PO boxes are operated from post offices and in some areas they are in great demand. Private companies also offer this service, Mail Boxes Etc (www.mbe.com) being particularly popular. Some local convenience stores also hire out mailboxes. All the major international courier companies are represented in Sydney, offering a range of services from same day delivery within Australia to next day international. The level of service is determined by the price.

Within the CBD it is common to use bicycle couriers and to more outlying areas motorcycle, car or van couriers (also known as taxi trucks). Most companies offer online bookings and accept credit cards or accounts for payment. A range of online gift delivery services are also available in Australia; www.wishlist.com.au, www.toysandmore.com.au, www.interflora.com.au and www.vintagecellars.com.au.

Radio
Sydney has a pretty good range of music and chat. See the General Information chapter, p.49, for frequencies, but the main stations are 2CH, 2GB, 2KY, 2UE, 2WS,

FM103.2, Nova and TripleM. ABC, the Government owned broadcaster, offers ABC Radio National and triple j, Classic FM and a local Sydney station called 702ABC Sydney. The combination of commercial and ABC operations ensures an eclectic radio offering in Sydney. SBS also broadcasts a range of news and music in 68 languages and there are local community radio stations, many of which also broadcast in languages other than English. For more see General Information p.49.

Television

The main Sydney free local channels are Channel 9, Channel 7, Channel 10, ABC and SBS. These are in English and offer a wide range of Australian and imported entertainment, current affairs, local and international news and sport. For more detail on what individual channels show, go to the Television heading in the General Info chapter on p.49. Digital TV is also available and requires a decoder box.

Formal censorship of television is limited to issues around sex, nudity and inappropriate language. Shows that are near the knuckle tend to carry warnings before they are shown. There are similar restrictions in advertising, with content restricted before 21:00.

What's on Telly?

Australians love to watch sport on TV, with tennis and rugby the most commonly viewed. Among the favourite TV shows in Sydney are *Australian Idol, Survivor, Lost, Ugly Betty, Grey's Anatomy* and *Heroes*, which at the time of going to press, was the most popular.

Satellite & Cable

Australia has excellent cable and satellite TV services, provided through Optus TV and FOXTEL, which is a partnership with Telstra.

FOXTEL (the shouty capitals are part of the firm's name) is the most common subscription television service and has 45 channels on offer. It claims to cover more than 70% of Australian homes, with 1.27m homes connected directly or through services provided to other providers. FOXTEL also offers a digital service, which provides more than 100 channels and FOXTEL iQ, which allows programmes to be recorded. Optus also offers the FOXTEL digital service. Cable TV packages typically cost around $60 to $70 a month, with some of the more basic schemes available for $40. See the table below for contact details.

Digital satellite TV is also available, provided by Austar, but is generally only used in more remote areas, where cable is not available. Satellite TV packages start at about $70 a month. You can also buy satellite dishes that receive the free-to-air channels and a very wide range of international channels.

If you are living in rented accommodation you will need permission from the owner (and sometimes the council) to put up a dish. Check with both before hooking up or you may find your shiny new dish torn down. With some landlords, you'll even need to get the green light to install cable.

Some live international sports are only covered on SKY Channel Australia, which is only available in some bars and clubs. In Sydney these include Cheers Bar at 561 George Street (www.cheersbar.com.au, 9261 8313; this is a well known six nations rugby union venue), City of Sydney RSL (just down the road at 565), City Tattersalls Club at 198 Pitt Street, Jacksons on George (9247 2727, www.jacksonsongeorge.com.au) and O'Donoghue's Irish Pub on the corners of Kent and Erskine Streets (9279 3133), but please check if they are showing the particular match or event on www.skychannel.com.au. Most hotels have cable or satellite television. Satellite Radio does not seem to have taken off in Australia, but you can tune into most channels on the internet.

Satellite & Cable Providers

Austar	13 2342	www.austar.com.au
FOXTEL	13 1999	www.foxtel.com.au
Optus	13 1345	www.optus.com.au

115

Gaps & Bulk Billing

If a medical practitioner does 'bulk billing', it means they take the Medicare rate without charging you any extra. Many GPs, dentists and other practitioners feel that Medicare payments aren't enough and so charge extra, which is paid by you. This is known as a 'gap'.

General Medical Care

You have two options; government care (including public hospitals and Medicare) and private health care. The relationship between the public and private systems is extremely complex and you need to know your stuff. For example, if you are eligible for Medicare and you are involved in an accident or need surgery, don't also declare any private insurance as it could raise your premiums. The general standard of public and private healthcare in Australia is very good.

Government Healthcare

To claim any state healthcare you will need a Medicare card. Go to www.medicare.gov.au and click the Medicare forms button under the 'quicklinks' heading. Medicare is one of three major national subsidy schemes, the other two being the Pharmaceutical Benefits Scheme and the 30% Private Health Insurance Rebate. Medicare and the Pharmaceutical Benefits Scheme cover all Australians and subsidise many treatments and prescription medicines. The Australian and state governments jointly fund public hospitals and basic and emergency healthcare are provided free. The Private Health Insurance Rebate knocks 30% of the cost of any private medical cover you may take out. Anyone that is eligible for Medicare and pays into a registered health fund is eligible. Be aware though, that the government is extremely vigilant in ensuring that only those that qualify take advantage of the state system.

Medicare offers free treatment in public hospitals and free or subsidised treatment by some GPs, specialists, optometrists or dentists. You're eligible if you live in Australia and hold Australian citizenship, have permanent residency or hold New Zealand citizenship. If you are in the process of applying for a permanent visa (excluding a parent visa) other requirements apply. Contact Medicare to see if you are covered; www.medicareaustralia.gov.au or 13 2011.

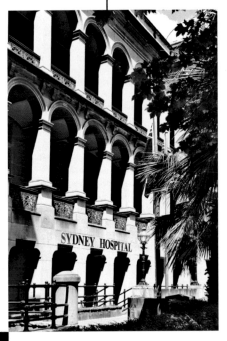

Australia has reciprocal healthcare arrangements with a number of European countries including the UK and Ireland, which provide limited subsidised health services. This typically just includes emergency treatment that you must have before you head back to your home country. It does not apply for students on a student visa and you should not depend on these agreements for medical care.

Visiting the Doctor

If you are eligible for Medicare, GPs or medical centres may 'bulk bill' you. This means they take the amount paid to them by Medicare as their full fee. Others won't and will want immediate payment from you. You then claim back the Medicare payment afterwards and cover the difference yourself. In general, private medical insurance does not cover GP visits but may cover some of the extra cost for medicine not covered by the Pharmaceutical Benefits Scheme.

Private Healthcare

The public system provides excellent emergency and immediate care but many Australians pay for private medical insurance as well. There can be very long waiting lists in the public system and private care can also ensure that you get treated in a particular hospital or by a particular practitioner. And, of course, it normally ensures you get a private room. Private healthcare standards are very high and strictly regulated, as are those in the public sector. Private just gets you more choice, more comfort and (normally) quicker treatment. Public hospitals have A&E departments but in general private hospitals do not. See p.120 for more details of these.

Emergency Services

In an emergency, if an ambulance is required, you should call 000 and the ambulance crew will decide which hospital to take you or the injured party to. If driving yourself, go to the nearest hospital with an accident and emergency department. See p.25 for listings.

Pharmacies

Pharmacies offer excellent advice and are well qualified, but they are restricted and can only supply some medications, including antibiotics, with a prescription from a GP. The emergency prescription service can be contacted on 9235 0333. Or, to find a pharmacy near you, visit www.guild.org.au and click on 'pharmacy locator'.

Health Check-Ups

For day-to-day medical care, you can either use the services of a medical centre or go to a GP. Although, regular GPs are becoming harder to find in Sydney. More common now are medical centres, which have several GPs under one roof and offer other facilities like blood tests and nurses to administer basic treatments. Many of these are owned by major medical corporations and will also carry out well-woman or well-man check-ups.

Health Insurance

If you are not entitled to state healthcare in Australia, it is advisable to take out private medical insurance before you arrive, as medical care is expensive. Medicare will cover the basics and for many that qualify, it is enough. But, if you do need treatment or some form of operation, private cover can speed things along immensely. Employers do not in general offer health insurance as part of an employment package and it is up to you to choose a provider and plan. These range from basic emergency cover to plans that offer full rehab after sports injuries. They can cost as little as $58 a month up to $240 or more for a family plan. Look out for special packages and shop around before deciding which one to go with.

Health Insurance Companies		
Allianz	13 1000	www.allianz.com.au
AMP	13 3888	www.amp.com.au
Australian Unity	13 2939	www.australianunity.com.au
AXA	13 1737	www.axa.com.au
CGU Insurance	13 1532	www.cgu.com.au
Combined Insurance Company of Australia	1300 300 480	www.combined.com.au
CommInsure	13 2423	www.comminsure.com.au

Donor Cards

There is a national information system in Australia that allows organ donors to be identified through their driving licences. All Australian states, but not territories, participate in the arrangement. When you apply for a driving licence you will be asked if you wish to become an organ donor. Alternatively, you can contact the Australian Red Cross at www.redcross.org.au and in Sydney on 9229 4111.

Volunteering

The main emergency services in Sydney all welcome volunteers. The fire brigade (go to ww.nswfb.nsw.gov.au) trains community fire units to protect their homes during a bushfire until the pros turn up. Volunteers in Policing (VIP) provide victim support and help in schools and community events (www.police. nsw.gov.au). Ambulance volunteers (www.ambulance. nsw.gov.au) are invaluable for emergencies in more remote parts of the city and state.

Giving Blood

Giving blood is very common in Sydney and is actively encouraged with ongoing campaigns to secure additional donors. You can give blood in the Sydney CBD Blood Donor Centre at 153 Clarence Street. Further information can be obtained from www.donateblood.com.au or 13 1495.

There is a shortage of all blood groups, partly as a result of the absence of a reliable screening test for Variant Creutzfeldt-Jakob disease (VCJD), the human form of mad cow disease. If you were resident in the UK between 1980 and 1996 for a total time of six months or more, or have received blood transfusions in the UK since January 1, 1980, you will not be eligible to give blood in Australia.

Giving Up Smoking

Smoking is becoming much less accepted in Sydney, and in October 2004 the NSW Government passed the NSW Smoke-free Environment Amendment Act 2004, which will ban smoking in indoor areas of all licensed premises by July 2007. This follows on from the existing smoking ban in all public areas and workplaces. Details on no smoking campaigns in NSW can be found at www.health.nsw.gov.au.

There is also a Quitline on 13 7848 (13 QUIT). This is confidential, and puts you through to telephone advisors that give encouragement and advice on how to quit.

Main Government Hospitals

There are many excellent public hospitals in Sydney and the main ones are listed below. Typically though, where you go is decided by your GP. This will be determined by the specialist they have referred you to. For emergencies, all public hospitals have an A&E facility, but your best bet may be to dial 000.

Canterbury Rd
Outer West

Canterbury Hospital

9787 0000 | *www.cs.nsw.gov.au*

Canterbury Hospital has links to Concord Repatriation General, Royal Prince Alfred Hospitals and the University of Sydney. Around two-thirds of the hospital's population at any one time is from non-English speaking backgrounds. The predominant countries of origin are Lebanon, China, Greece, Vietnam, Italy and Korea. It provides 24 hour emergency services, general medicine, intensive care, surgery, paedi-

Other Government Hospitals		
Auburn Hospital	Outer West	9563 9500
Balmain Hospital	Balmain	9395 2111
Blacktown Hospital	Outer West	9881 8000
Campbelltown Hospital	Outer West	4625 9222
Concord Hospital	Outer West	9767 5000
Health Care Interpretors	Outer West	9757 1800
Hornsby Ku-ring-gai Hospital	Outer North	9477 9123
Liverpool Hospital	Outer West	9828 3927
Mona Vale Hospital	Outer North	9998 0333
North Shore Public Hospital	Outer North	9926 7111
Northern Sydney Health Unit	Outer North	9477 9400
NSW Health	North Sydney	9391 9000
Ryde Hospital	Outer North	9874 0199
South Western Sydney Health Unit	Outer West	9828 3130
St Joseph's Hospital	Outer West	9649 8941
Westmead Hospital	Outer West	9845 5555

atrics, obstetrics and gynaecology, coronary care, day surgery, diagnostic services (including C.T. scanner) and ambulatory care. Community health services and a Tresillian Family Care Unit are also here.

Cnr of Hawkesbury
and Hainsworth Sts
Westmead
Outer West

Children's Hospital at Westmead

9845 0000 | *www.chw.edu.au*

This hospital is dedicated to all aspects of paediatric medicine. It provides community medical care and deals with paediatric emergencies as well as tertiary level paediatric services. The state's liver transplant unit and burns unit, the National Poisons

Information Centre and other state and national services are here. This hospital was once known (and is sometimes still referred to) as the New Children's Hospital.

Darley Rd
Manly

Manly Hospital
9976 9611 | www.nsh.nsw.gov.au
Manly is a teaching hospital for the University of Sydney, so you may find yourself prodded by eager students while you are here. It's also, in quite a quaint sales pitch, 'your hospital by the sea'. It provides community health services to more than 100,000 local residents. Other services include surgery, dental health, care for the elderly, maternity and child care, mental health, drug and alcohol service, cardiac rehabilitation, oncology, a pulmonary clinic, adolescent services and a diagnostic unit.

Barker St
Randwick

Prince of Wales Hospital
9382 2222 | www.sesahs.nsw.gov.au
One of the 13 principal referral hospitals for adults in NSW, the Prince of Wales provides patients with a broad range of medical and surgical services. It's another one linked to the University of NSW for teaching. Services include care for the elderly, intensive care, cardiac services, medical imaging, mental health, rehab and spinal medicine, neurology and oncology. Prince of Wales is on the same street as the Royal Hospital for Women.

Avoca St
Randwick

Royal Hospital for Women
9382 6111 | www.sesiahs.health.nsw.gov.au
The RHW is the only dedicated women's hospital in New South Wales and has an outstanding national and international reputation. It is also a leading research and teaching hospital in the field of women's health. They deliver more than 4,000 babies a year here and care for hundreds of premature babies. The hospital also specialises in treatments for gynaecological and breast cancer. Some 10,000 women rely on RHW for treatment. Other areas of specialisation include menopause and reproductive medicine. It was the first hospital in Australia to open a natural therapies unit.

Missenden Rd
Newtown

Royal Prince Alfred Hospital
9515 6111 | www.cs.nsw.gov.au
The principal teaching hospital of the University of Sydney, the Royal Prince Alfred provides care from Rachel Forster, King George V and Dame Eadith Walker Hospitals as well as its main Newtown campus. It is one of Australia's best-known hospitals, primarily for its work with liver and kidney transplants.

390 Victoria St
Darlinghurst

St Vincent's Hospital
8382 1111 | www.stvincents.com.au
St Vincent's has earned a reputation as a leading teaching and research hospital. It is funded by the Sisters of Charity Health Care Service, which is the biggest not-for-profit health care provider in the country. Its services cover anxiety disorders and addiction health services to do with alcohol and drugs and lots more, ranging from heart surgery and transplant to HIV/AIDS, nuclear medicine, renal transplantation and vascular surgery. The same complex also has the St Vincent's Private Hospital.

Government Health Centres/Clinics		
Bondi Junction Health Centre	Bondi	9387 1644
Chatswood Station Clinic	Outer North	9411 7916
Coogee Medical Centre	Coogee	9665 4519
Darling Street Health Centre	Central	9555 8806
Pennant Hills Health Centre	Outer North	9481 0022
Prince of Wales Clinic	Randwick	9382 8060
RNSH Child & Family Clinic	Outer West	9448 3155

119

High St
Randwick

Sydney Children's Hospital
9382 1111 | *www.sch.edu.au*
Set away from the other Randwick hospitals of RHW and the Prince Albert, Sydney Children's Hospital focuses on all aspects of kids health. It is a teaching centre for paediatric care and the main hub for children's medicine and care in New South Wales. It does the lot, from paediatric emergencies through to longer term care.

8 Macquarie St
Central

Sydney Hospital and Sydney Eye Hospital
9382 7111 | *www.sesahs.nsw.gov.au*
These two hospitals function as the one spot and offer outpatient care and emergency eye care (along with outpatient eye care). They are housed in a rather grand building right opposite Martin Place CityRail station. Other services include care related to drug and alcohol abuse, nutrition, physiotherapy and a hand unit. This is also home to the Sydney Sexual Health Centre.

125 Birrell St
Bondi

War Memorial Hospital
9369 0100 | *www.sesahs.nsw.gov.au*
The War Memorial Hospital is primarily a geriatric rehabilitation centre, so (hopefully) somewhere you're unlikely to see the inside of unless you bring over elderly parents or stay here for a very long time. It has an aged care assessment team and links to St Vincent's and the Prince of Wales. It provides care for those suffering from dementia and has teaching links to the University of NSW. It is run by the Uniting Church in Australia and is a ten minute walk from Bondi Junction.

Other Private Hospitals

Alwyn Rehabilitation	Outer West	9747 5333
Bondi Junction Private	Bondi	9387 6622
Dalcross Private	Outer North	9932 6600
Hirondelle Private	Outer North	9411 1466
Manly Waters Private	Manly	9977 9977
Metropolitan Rehabilitation	Outer West	9569 5622
Prince of Wales Private	Randwick	9650 4000
South Pacific Private	Outer North	9905 3667
St John Of God	Various locations	9747 5611
St Vincent's Private	Darlinghurst	8382 7111
The Hills Private	Outer West	9639 3333

Main Private Hospitals
There are over 100 generally excellent private hospitals throughout Sydney. As is the case for public hospitals, where you end up should really be decided by your doctor. Private hospitals in general do not have A&E facilities. The Prince of Wales and St Vincent's, as listed in Main Government Hospitals, also cater for private patients.

150 Edinburgh Rd
Outer North

Castlecrag Private Hospital
9935 0200 | *www.ramsayhealth.com.au*
The Castlecrag has just 46 beds and speciality areas include orthopaedics, ophthalmology, plastic and reconstructive surgery, urology, ear, nose and throat, oral surgery and palliative care. It is part of Ramsay Health Care, which claims to be the largest private hospital group in Australia.

Rocklands Rd
North Sydney

The Mater Hospital
9900 7300 | *www.matersydney.com.au*
The Mater has a growing reputation for its cancer care and work on joint replacement and sports injuries. It also specialises in maternity and other women's health issues along with cardio vascular care. It is linked to St Vincent's and had its centenary in 2006.

Private Health Centres/Clinics

Bondi Junction Medical Practice	Bondi	9389 9699
CBD Medical Centre	Central	9231 1000
City Clinic	Central	9299 4977
George Street Medical Centre	Central	9231 3211
Holdsworth House	Darlinghurst	9331 7228
Kent Street Medical Centre	Central	9290 3477
St Vincent's Clinic	Randwick	8382 6222
Surry Hill Medical Centre	Surry Hills	9699 3311

120

Westbourne St ◄
St Leonards
Outer North

North Shore Private Hospital

8425 3000 | www.ramsayhealth.com.au

The North Shore is a fairly new hospital and specialises in cardiac surgery and other heart related ailments, along with all the related vascular bits. You can also have plastic and reconstructive surgery here. Other services include physio, nuclear medicine, obstetrics, gynaecology and urology. It's another hospital in the large Ramsay stable.

South St ◄
Kogarah

St George Private Hospital

9598 5555 | www.ramsayhealth.com.au

Based in Kogorah in the suburbs of southern Sydney, the St George is next to the public hospital of the same name. Its services cover general cardiology, ear, nose and throat, neurology, paediatric medicine, infectious diseases, sleep disorders and plastic surgery. It is another Ramsay hospital.

185 Fox Valley ◄
Rd, Wahroonga
Outer North

Sydney Adventist Hospital

9487 9111 | www.sah.org.au

The Sydney Adventist Hospital, while private, is also a not-for-profit hospital. It's still known colloquially as 'the san' (it was formerly called the Sanitarium) and its 350 beds make it the biggest single site private hospital in the state. Around 150,000 out-patients are treated here every year, typically in one of the following areas: radiology, physio, cardiac care, cancer support, diabetes, sports medicine and general surgery.

Dermatologists		
Dr Christopher Kearney	Bondi	9387 6440
Dr Frank Isaacs	Bondi	9389 3377
Dr James Walter	Neutral Bay	9953 9522
Dr Katharine Dunlop	Darlinghurst	8353 3000
Dr Lance Bear	Leichhardt	9550 9357
Dr Rodney Hannaford	Neutral Bay	9960 8344
Dr Stephen Shumack	Central	9221 1477
Dr Susanne Freeman	Randwick	9399 3114
Dr Tanya Gilmour	Manly	9976 0055
Dr Tasman Lipscombe	Central	9247 2887

22-24 Murray St ◄
Bondi

The Sydney Clinic

9389 8888 | www.healthscope.com.au

This private psychiatric care facility is part of the Healthscope organisation, one of the larger private hospital firms in Australia. Patients here are treated for a number of psychiatric conditions, ranging from mood disorders and drug and alcohol addiction to more acute psychiatry conditions.

Maternity

Other options **Baby Items** p.271

Mums-to-be in New South Wales can choose between having their baby in a hospital, birth centre or at home, though some options may be restricted by where you live. For some services there will be a charge while others are covered completely by Medicare. Most pregnant women who do not have private health insurance get a referral from their GP to a public hospital. Then, depending on your health and the hospital you chose to attend, you will be advised by a midwife about your options.

Elective caesarean sections have become more common, mostly for medical reasons, but are not unheard of for cosmetic or convenience reasons. Husbands or partners are encouraged to be there but some hospitals limit the number of people that can attend. You can write your own birth plan and may even be able to bring in soothing music and lightly scented candles.

Government Hospitals

Antenatal clinics in public hospitals are free to Medicare cardholders. They are set up to handle women experiencing both normal and complicated pregnancies. These

121

clinics are very busy and you may find you have to wait despite having an appointment. You may not see the same doctors or nurses each time.

Many major public hospitals also operate midwives clinics that are again free to Medicare cardholders. The midwives in these clinics generally provide care during your entire pregnancy, which many women prefer. If you don't get the same midwife from ante to postnatal care, she is at least likely to be from the same team. Midwifery teams are increasingly being set up in public hospitals, made up of small groups of midwives who work together to provide antenatal, labour, birth, and postnatal care.

Shared Care Programme

Most hospitals now also offer women the option of having their pregnancy care shared between a general practitioner (GP) and a hospital. Hospital midwives and doctors attend the birth and give postnatal care, with the GP providing antenatal care. You can arrange shared care by contacting your local hospital and asking if your GP has a shared care arrangement with them. Women without a Medicare card have to pay for their care. If this is the case, shared care is usually the least expensive option. If you have no Medicare card and payment is a problem then you should discuss this with your hospital; some may be flexible.

Post-Natal Depression

If you are feeling unwell or unable to cope at any time after the birth of your child, go immediately to see your GP or nurse. Beyond Blue is an excellent organisation that will provide guidance and support in cases of post-natal depression. Contact them on 1300 224 636 or by visiting www.beyondblue.org.au. The Bub Hub is also good source of guidance in relation to all pregnancy, birth and parenting issues including PND. They can be contacted on 9977 4480 or www.bubhub.com.au.

Post-Natal Care

Many hospitals have set up early discharge programmes that allow women to go home in the first 48 hours after a normal birth or within 72 hours after a caesarean. A midwife will then visit the home for up to a week. If early discharge is part of a team midwife programme, then a midwife that you have met during the pregnancy will visit you. This programme suits women who are well and feel they will be more comfortable and rested at home. Your midwife or GP can refer you to a paediatrician if required. Breast feeding is allowed in public places generally, but is recommended that you check it out with the manager in a restaurant or similar spot.

Private Hospitals

If you have private health insurance or if you are uninsured but willing to pay, you can choose a private obstetrician to provide your antenatal care and attend your birth in a private hospital. Private obstetricians will also attend births in public hospitals they have visiting rights to. You should check with your health fund provider to see if you are covered for this, but be aware that the costs for private care may not be completely covered (i.e. for a cesarean) and you may have to pay the difference yourself.

Birth Centres

You may be able to deliver at a birth centre, which your GP or a hospital midwife can refer you to. Birth centres are normally in hospitals and staffed by midwives with medical back-up, should complications develop. Some obstetricians and doctors will also help women to give birth in a birth centre. These provide a homelike environment to help you give birth as naturally as possible.

If you choose to give birth at home, you will usually be cared for by an independent midwife. However, if complications occur, you will have to go to hospital. Most midwives will go with you, as long as they have visiting rights to the hospital.

Registering a Birth

All births in NSW must be registered within 60 days. If you give birth in a hospital, the staff there will provide all the relevant information and a registration form (see p.65). There is no fee and the registry keeps a permanent record so you can get a birth certificate at any time. You will have to pay for a birth certificate however. The registry will process the form within 14 days of receiving the application. Call 1300 655 236 or go to www.bdm.nsw.gov.au if you need to know more.

Going Home to Give Birth

You can usually fly up to the end of the 35th week of pregnancy, after which it is inadvisable. The rules vary from airline to airline so plan well in advance and check their rules. Some airlines need a medical certificate with the due date. For multiple births, the airline may not let you fly after the 32nd week. Some also refuse to carry newborns under seven days old. You should also note that some countries place limitations on the entry of non-national pregnant women. For domestic travel, medical clearance is required if you want to travel past the 36th week of a multiple pregnancy.

Hidden Costs

The costs of having a baby vary. If you have Medicare cover and use a public hospital, you do not pay for the doctor, midwife or hospital. If you go private, you will pay for the doctor and hospital, but Medicare and private insurance will meet some of the costs.

If you have a home birth, some GPs will bulk bill (see Health p.116). If not, you may have to pay the difference between their fee and the Medicare rebate. You will have to pay the midwife for a home birth, unless your health fund provides cover. Other home birth costs include attendance of an obstetrician or GP and fees for ultrasounds. If you are transferred to hospital during a home birth, you will have to pay for this cost. There may be an extra cost for antenatal childbirth education classes too.

Maternity / Paternity Leave

If you've been with your employer for more than a year (in one stretch), you are entitled to maternity or paternity leave. This applies to full-time, part-time and some casual staff. Seasonal employees are not normally eligible. The leave tends to be unpaid, but this all depends on your employer.

Mums can take up to 52 weeks maternity leave in one go, starting either during or after pregnancy. Dads get a week, but an extended stint can be taken if dad is the primary caregiver. Adoption leave gives you up to three weeks at the time of placement and more in order to be the child's primary caregiver. All these must be completed before the child's first birthday or the anniversary of adoption.

Maternity Hospitals & Clinics

North Shore Private Hospital	Outer North	8425 3000	Private
North Shore Public Hospital	Outer North	9926 7111	Public
Prince of Wales Private Hospital	Randwick	9650 4000	Private
Royal Hospital for Women	Randwick	9382 6111	Public
Royal Prince Alfred Hospital	Newtown	9515 6111	Public
Sydney Adventist Hospital	Outer North	9487 9111	Private
Sydney South West Private Hospital	Outer West	9821 0333	Private
The Mater Hospital	North Sydney	9900 7300	Public
Westmead Hospital	Outer West	9845 5555	Public
Westmead Private	Outer West	8837 9000	Private

Breast Cancer ◄
The Sydney Cancer Centre at the Royal Prince Alfred Hospital (see p.119) is the leading centre for breast cancer treatment and research in Australia and also has facilities at Concord Hospital. You can contact them on 9515 6677. BreastScreen NSW is a free service for women aged 50 to 69 years. Women outside of this age group will have to pay a fee. You can book a mammogram by calling 13 2050, or through their website; www.bsnsw.org.au.

Gynaecology & Obstetrics

The best way to find a gynaecologist or obstetrician is through your GP or a friend's recommendation. There are nearly 300 in and around Sydney (both male and female) and you can find them yourself through the Royal Australian and New Zealand College of Obstetricians and Gynaecologists. That natty title boils down to the website www.ranzcog.edu.au. A small selection are on the table, along with two of Sydney's better known fertility centres. Contraception can be supplied by your GP under prescription, with all contemporary options available. Some forms (e.g. condoms) can be bought over the counter. The Royal Hospital for Women (see p.119) is also noted for its gynaecological care.

Abortions

Australia has the third highest rate of adolescent abortion in the world. While they are legal in NSW you should consult with an approved clinic or your GP. Options range from a simple surgical procedure under local anaesthetic, to a general anaesthetic or a

Gynaecology & Obstetrics		
Dr Anne MacGibbon	Outer North	9439 0110
Dr Jan Dudley	Randwick	9314 5500
Dr Jennifer Dew	Darlinghurst	8382 6860
Dr Michele Batey	Outer North	9438 3132
Dr Robert Lyneham	Central	9233 7219
Dr Therese McGee	Outer West	9845 8837
Goals For Women	Bondi	1300 886 009
IVFAustralia	Various locations	1800 111 483
Natural Fertility Management	Bondi	9369 2047
Westmead Fertility Centre	Outer West	9845 7484

medical abortion in early pregnancy. Clinics will provide terminations up to 20 weeks but they encourage you to reach a decision within 12 weeks of your last period. Clinics include www.contraceptiveservices.com.au or www.mariestopes.com.au.

Paediatrics

There are many paediatric specialists in Sydney, so it is often best to get a referral from your GP or medical centre. Paediatric care is covered by Medicare but there may be a gap payable. If your baby has been assigned a paediatrician at the hospital where it was born, you can still go to one of your own choosing.

Immunisation

You should check with your GP and clinic regarding immunisation programmes. Australia has an extensive national Australian Standard Vaccination Schedule (ASVS) which is recommended by the National Health and Medical Research Council (NHMRC). The full schedule, which includes jabs at birth, then again at two, four, six and 12 months (which includes the MMR vaccine) can be found at www.mydr.com.au.

Learning Difficulties

If your child has learning difficulties it is important to get expert help and your doctor can provide initial guidance. There is also the non-profit SPELD (Specific Learning Difficulties Association of NSW). It is made up of parents, professionals and adults with learning difficulties. Call 9906 2977 or visit www.speldnsw.org.au. See also p.135.

Paediatrics			
Andrea Ruskin Paediatric	Outer North	9453 9104	Clinic
Australian Paediatric Surveillance Unit	Outer West	9845 3005	Hospital
Central Paediatrics	Newtown	9564 5778	Hospital
Helen Stone Paediatric	Manly	9401 0490	Clinic
Macarthur Paediatric Occupational Therapy	Outer West	9824 8945	Clinic
NSW Health	North Sydney	9391 9000	Hospital
South Western Sydney Public Health Unit	Outer West	9828 3130	Hospital
Sydney Children's Hospital	Randwick	9382 1111	Hospital

Dentists/Orthodontists

Dentistry in Australia is generally excellent, with everything from general check ups to cosmetic surgery available. It is comparable to the UK and US systems and is totally private. There is no recommended scale of fees and prices vary from dentist to dentist. It is actually against trade practices law for dentists to collude in the maintenance of any set fee scale. You may find that your private health insurer offers a deal with free or discounted check ups at selected dentists but this will depend on your plan. You can find a dentist by visiting the site of the

Dentists/Orthodontists		
Australia Square Dental	Central	9247 8679
Chatswood Dental	Outer North	9411 6444
City Dental	Central	9299 6000
City Smile Dental Centre	Central	9264 1592
Dentist At Care	Outer North	9989 8966
Finkelstein Dental Clinic	Central	9232 3900
Marshall Orthodontics	Neutral Bay	9908 2200
Millennium Dental Care	Neutral Bay	9969 5572
Parramatta Dental Care	Outer West	9683 6699
Pyrmont Dental Centre	Pyrmont	9660 3322
Sydney Cosmetic Dentist	Bondi	9369 1236
The Ortho Practice	Central	9221 2181

Australian Dental Association (www.ada.org.au) or going to www.dentist.com.au and clicking on Find a Dentist. Children should have check-ups from when they first grow teeth to ensure that all is well and then every six months after that.

Gap-Free Tests

One optometrist who is popular with expats is Peter Hewett in Mosman. He sells a wide range of eyewear and frames, as well as prescription sunglasses. He doesn't charge a gap on eye tests and accepts the Medicare rate. For an appointment call 9968 4036.

Opticians & Optometrists

Opticians and optometrists are all private in Australia and only eye tests are covered by Medicare. But, most optometrists charge a 'gap', where you pay the difference between what Medicare will pay and what the optometrists will charge.

You will find opticians or optometrists in most main streets and malls in Sydney. Contact lenses are available from optometrists, who also supply solution, as well as in pharmacies and some supermarkets.

The latest laser eye surgery is available too, in clinics like www.theeyeinstitute.com.au or www.lasik.com.au. Costs range from about $2,300 to $3,000 or more per eye. The procedure takes about an hour and a half after which you can go home for a couple of days recovery, although you may have some vision changes for about three weeks before it all settles down. If you suspect your baby is blind or has sight

Opticians & Optometrists		
Dovgan Optometrists	Outer West	9687 0545
Michael Angelos Optometrist	North Sydney	9922 7616
Personal Eyes Optometry	Central	9233 2899
The Eye Practice	Central	9290 1899
The Eyecare Company	Central	9241 2121
You & Eye Optical	Central	9233 6299

problems you should consult your GP or optometrist immediately. For other eyeware, see Shopping on p.280. You must have an eye test to get a driving licence, but that is done at the RTA centre before your test.

Cosmetic Treatment & Surgery

Cosmetic surgery is fairly common in Australia and (as in other parts of the world) becoming more so. There are all sorts of treatments available for both women and men. You can get your breasts augmented or reduced (and this applies to guys as well), tummy tucked, varicose veins erased or nose reshaped. Should your self-esteem take a terrible tumble once you find yourself surrounded by buff young Aussies down the beach, there are plenty of people willing to

Cosmetic Treatment & Surgery		
ADA Cosmetic Medicine	Glebe	9552 1442
Harper Warwick	Manly	9977 1275
L'Image Cosmetic Surgery	Outer West	1300 267 638
Sydney Makeover Clinic	North Sydney	9929 2559
The Clinic	Bondi	9386 1533

125

help you take the short (but deep) cut to a new appearance. Be aware though that cosmetic surgery is less regulated than most medical practices. The industry body is the Australian Society of Plastic Surgeons (www.plasticsurgery.org.au). Clinics that provide some or all of these services include L'image (see www.limage.com.au), The Clinic at www.theclinic.net.au, and Sydney Makeover Clinic (go to www.sydneymakeoverclinic.com.au).

Alternative Therapies

The use of alternative therapies is becoming increasingly popular in Australia, including acupuncturists, complementary medicine, holistic medicine, chiropractors, herbalists and hypnotherapists. The challenge is determining which practitioner to visit and which one will do a good job. You should also discuss alternative therapies with your doctor as GPs in Australia are generally open to these. A useful site that can help you find a suitable practitioner is www.naturaltherapypages.com.au. Also, see the Well-Being section of the Activities chapter on p.256.

Acupressure/Acupuncture

Among the oldest healing methods in the world, acupressure involves the systematic placement of pressure with fingertips on established meridian points on the body. This therapy can be used to relieve pain, soothe the nerves and stimulate the body, as determined necessary by the therapist.

Acupuncture is an ancient Chinese technique that uses needles to access the body's meridian points. It is surprisingly painless and is quickly becoming an alternative to western medicine.

Acupressure/Acupuncture		
Acupuncture Association of Australia	Outer North	8901 0870
Chatswood Medical Acupuncture Centre	Outer West	9411 5011
City Acupuncture	Central	9221 8379
Sydney Bodywork Centre	Central	9299 6688

It aids ailments such as asthma and rheumatism, as well as some more serious diseases. The Acupuncture Association of Australia (www.acupaa.com) has a search facility on its site to help find the nearest practitioner to you.

Aromatherapy

Essential oils derived from plants and flowers can be used in myriad ways to add balance to your health. The oils are commonly massaged into the skin and can be used to reduce bruising and even cure toothache. Some can even be used as insect repellant. They can also be used in prescription medicines, and the scent alone can be beneficial. While no certification is required to practice aromatherapy, you should make sure your practitioner has at least studied plants so they can suggest the best treatments for you. Also, many spas and salons offer aromatherapy facials or massages, which are great for cosmetic and relaxing purposes.

Aromatherapy		
Aromatherapy Clinic Of Sydney	Central	9241 4030
Aromatherapy Park Avenue	Neutral Bay	9953 7617
Aromatica Clinic	Leichhardt	0414 788 583
In Health & Harmony	Neutral Bay	9948 5491

Healing Meditation

Meditation can offer inner peace as well as a disease-free mind and body. With quiet settings and various breathing techniques, movements and mantras, group and individual meditation sessions can be a powerful tool in healing and stress relief. This is becoming evermore popular with Sydney's residents as a means to unwind.

Healing Meditation		
Acharya's Yoga & Meditation	Central	9264 3765
Antara Yoga & Meditation	Redfern	9698 5415
Bodhikusuma-Buddhist & Meditation Centre	Surry Hills	9310 1103
Govindas Yoga & Meditation Centre	Darlinghurst	9380 5155
Kevin Hume Meditation	Darlinghurst	8354 0402
Naturelle	Surry Hills	9310 1909

Homeopathy

Homeopathy strengthens the body's defence system. Natural ingredients are used to address physical and emotional problems. The discipline extracts elements from traditional medicines of various origins but was recently organised into a healthcare system in Europe. Practitioners undergo disciplined training and more and more western doctors are studying and practicing homeopathy.

Homeopathy		
City Health Homeopaths	Central	9267 7889
Johnson Mary	Newtown	9810 8941
Optimum Health Care Clinic	Central	9221 0116
Sydney Homoeopathic Centre	Central	9247 8500

Reflexology/Massage Therapy

Other options **Massage** p.260

Reflexology is a detailed scientific system with Asian origins. It outlines points in the hands and feet that, once manipulated, impact other parts and systems of the body. In addition to stress reduction and improved health, the pressure applied to these points addresses issues in those corresponding parts of the body.

Reflexology/Massage Therapy		
Massage & Float Centre	Bondi	9387 7355
Massage Therapy World Sq	Central	9283 8810
Oriental Spa	Darlinghurst	9380 4268
Sydney Massage Therapies	Outer North	9498 6341
Unwind	Central	0413 558 082

Explorer Online

No doubt now that you own an Explorer book you will want to check out the rest of our product range. From maps and vistor guides to restaurant guides and photography books. Explorer has a spectacular collection of products just waitiing for you to buy them. Check out our website for more info.
www.explorer publishing.com

Physiotherapy

The table here lists a number of physios and sports clinics where you can get clicked, cracked and twisted back into shape, should the Sydney sports scene take its toll. Don't be afraid to ask about the qualifications of whoever is manipulating your muscles and membranes, to check that they are a proper sports physio. A Thai massage will not do as a substitute for proper chiropractic care and could end up doing more damage than good. As with all matters medical, your first port of call should be your GP, who should be able to recommend reliable physiotherapists.

Physiotherapy Clinics		
Bondi Physiotherapy & Sports Injury	Bondi	9130 6914
CBD Sports & Physiotherapy	Central	9223 3122
City Physiotherapy & Sports Injury	Central	9223 1575
Ergoworks Physiotherapy	Central	9251 0822
Spinal & Sports Physiotherapy	Rozelle	9810 2203
North Shore Physiotherapy	Outer North	9437 6043
Physio 4 All	North Sydney	9922 2212
Precision Physiotherapy	Surry Hills	9280 2322
Wynyard Sports & Injury	Central	9262 4147

Back Treatment

Back problems plague many people, whether they are the young and fit sporty types or sedentary people in their later life. As a result, treatment is widely available in Sydney, with specialists from all over the world practising here. Chiropractic and osteopathy treatments concentrate on manipulating the skeleton to improve the functioning of the nervous system or blood supply to the body. Chiropracty is based on the manipulative treatment of misalignments in the joints, especially those of the spinal column, while osteopathy involves the manipulation and massage of the skeleton and musculature. Craniosacral therapy aims to relieve pain and tension by gentle manipulations of the skull to balance the craniosacral rhythm. Pilates is said to be the safest form of neuromuscular reconditioning and back strengthening available. It is also a very popular form of exercise. Check with your gym to see if they offer any classes.

Back Treatment		
Chirosports	Central	9231 2707
City Clinic	Central	9299 4977
Fluid Form Studios	Darlinghurst	8356 9886
Impulse Health Chiropractic	Central	9279 2992
Tokuko Shiatsu Centre	Central	9299 2268

127

Nutritionists & Slimming

If you want to lose weight, you can either speak with your GP, attend one of the many gyms in Sydney that offer weight loss programmes or subscribe to one of the weight loss clubs. See p.128 of Activities for more on these. For weight loss programmes see www.jennycraig.com.au and www.weightwatchers.com.au.

Initially it's best to go to your GP if you have weight to lose or if you have digestive disorders, (e.g. IBS, Crohn's Disease) as he or she will be well positioned to advise you and refer you to a specialist. Personal trainers are also available in most areas and will come to your house or meet you at a beach or park.

Nutritionists & Slimming			
Food & Nutrition Australia	Central	1300 926 212	www.foodnut.com.au
Jenny Craig	Various locations	13 1992	www.jennycraig.com.au
SureSlim Wellness Clinics	Various locations	1300 130 696	www.sureslim.com.au
Weight Watchers	Various locations	–	www.weightwatchers.com.au
Weight-Loss Centre	Central	9233 1555	www.weightlosscentre.net.au

Addiction Counselling & Rehabilitation

Drinking is an integral part of Sydney's culture and, as in any society, this can occasionally lead to problems. The federal and state governments are aware of this, and bars across the city have info on dealing with alcoholism and other such troubles. There are many public and private facilities that treat addictions, but your first port of call should be your GP or local medical centre. Either can refer you to a specialist for counselling or treatment.

Specialist private centres include Psych N Soul (www.addictiontreatment.com.au, 9280 2070) and general information can be found at www.health.nsw.gov.au or www.druginfo.nsw.gov.au. The Alcohol and Drugs Council of Australia provides a range of helpline numbers at www.adca.org.au. A list of centres can also be found at www.adin.com.au, the website of the Australian Drug Information Network.

Australia takes addictions very seriously and contact details for gambling counselling can be found anywhere that has slot machines. The main anonymous meeting groups are all represented here too. For alcohol problems, visit www.aa.org.au or phone 9599 8866. For narcotics issues, see www.naoz.org.au or call 9519 6200. NA also has a recorded

Counsellors/Psychologists		
A A Counsellors	Various locations	1300 300 579
Associated Counsellors & Psychologists	Surry Hills	4160 4169
Australian College of Clinical Psychologists	Central	9221 9292
Making Changes	Central	9231 1785
Solution Focus Psychology & Counselling	Central	9223 6660
Therapeutic Axis	Glebe	9692 9788

info line providing details about meetings. Call 8230 1645 for Sydney specific info or 1300 652 820 for the rest of the country.

For gambling addictions see www.gamblersanonymous.org.au, or call GA on 9564 1574. Smokers hoping to quit should see www.cancercouncil.com.au and www.acosh.org, call 9212 4300, or see p.118. For younger addicts of all types, this is an interesting site; www.reachout.com.au. Reach Out! can also be called on 13 1114.

Counselling & Therapy

Facilities for people suffering from mental health problems are very good and some hospitals have specialised departments, see Hospitals, p.118. If you become depressed or over-stressed for whatever reason, including culture shock and homesickness, speak with your GP, who can advise you, prescribe anti-depressants or refer you to a counsellor. Marriage counselling services are available from Relationships Australia on 1300 364 277 or www.relationships.com.au. Family therapy is available through the Australian and New Zealand Journal of Family Therapy at www.anzjft.com. For child behavioural issues, speak to your doctor, who will be able to refer you to a child psychologist. You can also find a very wide range of counsellors and therapists through www.goodtherapy.com.au.

Psychiatrists

Psychiatrists are slightly different to psychologists because they are trained as medical doctors. After becoming an MD, they do four years of specialist training. They can also write prescriptions. So, they might treat people with drugs as well as talking. Psychologists are PhDs who have trained in using and interpreting psychological tests, but they can't dish out the drugs. The Royal Australian and New Zealand College of Psychiatrists (RANZCP) is the main teaching centre for psychiatrists in Australia.

Psychiatrists		
Bondi Junction Community Health Centre	Bondi	9387 1644
Inner City Mental Health Service	Darlinghurst	9360 3133
Macquarie St Psychiatric Clinic	Central	9241 1977
RANZCP	Balmain	9352 3600
Redfern/Newtown Community Clinic	Redfern	9690 1222

Support Groups

One challenging aspect about living in Australia is it's geographical isolation. Visits back home are usually infrequent and as a result, many groups have recreated home here; Melbourne is said to have the third largest Greek population in the world, after Athens and Thessalonica.

So, while distances to most places are great, culture shock is minimal. The national language is English and the food is similar to other western countries, with almost every other cuisine also represented. Unfortunately, there are very few support groups for expatriates. The informal ones that do exist tend to be run by volunteers and are based in the expatriate communities – mostly in the lower north shore and eastern suburbs. If your move is with an employer, ask the HR team in Sydney if they can put you in touch with people who have recently moved to the city. There are, however, a wide range of more general support groups.

Mothers

There are a number of mother to mother support groups and you can look at www.mumsclub.com.au or www.breastfeeding.asn.au and www.bellybelly.com.au to get you started. In cases of SIDS (sudden infant death syndrome), support is vital. GPs are a good starting point, but you could also try www.thecompassionatefriends.org.au (1800 671 621) or www.sidsandkids.org. Other useful contacts include the Stillbirth and Neonatal Death Support Group, (www.sands.org.au) Sids and Kids Online (www.sidsaustralia.org.au) the Mothers in Support and Sympathy Foundation (www.missfoundation.org). Alternatively you could call the National Centre for Childhood Grief on 1300 654 556.

Bereavement

Some of the groups mentioned above also provide more general support for the recently bereaved. Other respected organisations include Bereavement Care Centre (www.bereavementcare.com.au), Counseling For Loss & Life Changes (www.counselingforloss.com), GriefLink (www.grieflink.asn.au), GriefNet.org (www.griefnet.org), and the National Association for Loss And Grief (www.nalag.org.au).

Support Groups	
Cancer Helpline	13 1120
Centacare Family & Relationship Counselling	9671 2011
Community Bereavement Counselling	1800 013 101
Gay & Lesbian Counselling	1800 184 527
Grief Support	9489 6644
Homicide Victims' Support Group	1800 191 777
Interrelate Counselling and Mediation	6621 4970
Kids Helpline	1800 551 800
Lifeline	13 1114
Men's Phone Line	9979 9909
Nepean Cancer Care Centre	4734 3500
Parents Line	13 2055
Relationship Counselling	9476 8433
Relationships Australia	9418 8800
Salvation Army	9419 8695
Survivors of Suicide	4648 2224

129

Which School?

Check out your selected school's philosophy very carefully. Some private schools place a very strong emphasis on sport for example, and if your child is not sporty, they may not be comfortable. Ask to speak with other parents to ensure the best possible fit for junior.

Education

The Australian school year is the reverse of the northern hemisphere's. It runs from January to December, with four school terms. The longest holiday is midsummer, which runs over Christmas and New Year, with schools and colleges closed for around six weeks. There are also three other two week holidays; in April (around Easter), in winter (typically in July) and also in October.

Every New South Wales public school has a defined local enrolment area, which means that your child is designated to a particular school based on your permanent residential address. Every public school reserves enough places for students in their local area. Call 13 1536 or contact your nearest Department of Education and Training (www.dest.gov.au) office to find the nearest school to you.

Local kids get first dibs, after which, some schools may accept students from outside their enrolment area. This is down to the discretion of the school's enrolment panel, using a range of criteria, including the availability of staff and classroom accommodation. Contact individual schools to find out about their criteria.

School Years

Children must be at school by their sixth birthday. Primary school runs until year six, when children are 11 or 12 years old. They then enter high school, which covers years seven to 12. To get into a selective high school, students must pass the assessment tests held every June. Children can legally leave at age 15, but must complete year ten to gain their School Certificate, or year 12 to get their Higher School Certificate. University entry is based on meeting a set score out of 100 in the HSC. For most medical courses, for example, this is set at 96-99.

To Rooty Hill and Back

Make sure that there are places available in your chosen school before you sign a lease or buy a house, or your children may end up with a lengthy commute.

Enrollment

To enroll your child you will need any reports and evidence of their academic abilities, school records, certificates, and assessments from previous schools. If you can, get a transfer report from their last school. These will all help the school in Sydney assess your child and choose the best class for them.

Most schools, public or private, will allow enrolments mid-term. But, the key issue is whether there is space for your child. In Sydney, as elsewhere, the best schools come with waiting lists. If you have school age children, you should start researching schools as soon as you decide to move to Sydney. If you are using a corporate relocation company they may be able to help and, with private schools, can often secure information (and even places) that might not otherwise be available.

Curriculum

Australia has developed a national curriculum for the whole country. Public and private schools provide subjects in eight key areas; English, Mathematics, Studies of Society and the Environment, Science, Arts, Foreign Languages, Technology and Personal Development, Health and Physical Education. At secondary level, schools have a wider choice, with some private schools offering the international baccalaureate. Around 90% of schools also offer vocational and technical education. All public schools and most private schools follow the Australian national curriculum, but some specialist schools, e.g. Japanese or American schools, follow their own country's curriculum. Many offer after school activities in addition to traditional sports programmes, but these tend to cost extra.

State Schools

Public schools in Australia are those provided by the state and not to be confused with 'public' schools in the UK, which are, in fact, private and fee-paying. Generally,

Careers & Creches
*Childcare creches in
the workplace are rare
in Australia. Many
employers view
families as private
issues and not of their
concern. This
reluctance to subsidise
childcare is helped by
the younger workers
coming into the
market. The trend here
leans strongly toward
career advancement
over marriage and
babies, with many not
settling down until
their late 30s.*

children in public schools start their day at 09:25 and finish at 15:25. Private schools can start and finish earlier. Public (or state) schools are generally free to Australian residents, but holders of temporary visas will be subject to charges. Visit www.schools.nsw.edu.au for information on categories of visas and conditions. Click on Fees and Payment for details of costs, which can be as high as $5,500 per year. All students are likely to be asked to pay for extra items like stationery and sports kit. The quality of public schools varies greatly and you should check with colleagues and friends about the public system in your area.

Private Schools

Private education is increasingly common in Sydney. NSW has 3,106 schools, of which 912 are private. More than 45% of children in Sydney now attend private schools. While Sydneysiders consider private schools expensive, prices are comparable to those in Japan, the UK, the USA, Singapore and Hong Kong, and often cheaper than schools in London, Tokyo and New York. Nevertheless, the better schools on the lower north shore could cost as much as $20,000 annually in years 11 and 12.

Many private schools are affiliated with religious organisations, including the Church of England and the Roman Catholic Church, with those associated with the latter being considerably cheaper. Most private schools have long waiting lists in each year group, but you may be lucky with a school that specialises in expat kids, as spaces are created when families leave. SCECGS Redlands in Cremorne is one such school. Visit www.redlands.nsw.edu.au. You can also search for private schools by location and other criteria on the excellent site www.isd.com.au. Or, see the table on p.133.

Nurseries & Pre-Schools

Children can attend pre-school or kindergarten until age five. These are all privately run, relatively expensive and come with long waiting lists. Prices vary in different areas, from as little as $60 a day to more than $100. Most suburbs will also have a day-care centre for working parents where babies and under-fives can stay from around 07:00 to 18:00. These and pre-schools must be council approved. Your local council can provide a list of what's available in your area. You can also find a centre through www.careforkids.com.au. Visit the NSW Department of Community Services website (www.community.nsw.gov.au) and click on child care for more on standards for child care centres. The nurseries that follow are among those that have good reputation but, of course, there are too many in Sydney for us to list them all. If in doubt, ask other parents.

SDN Children's Services

SDN Children's Services is a well known provider of early childhood education and care. It has centres in Erskineville, Hurstville, Lidcombe, Mosman, Newtown, the northern suburbs, Paddington, Petersham, Pyrmont, Redfern, Surry Hills, Ultimo, Waterloo and Woolloomooloo. It provides early childhood education programmes, long day care for children up to five years old, special education support and additional family support. They can be contacted at www.sdn.org.au or on 9213 2400.

Westfield
101 Grafton St
Bondi

ABC Developmental Learning Centre

9387 5673 | *www.childcare.com.au*

This centre in Bondi Junction takes little 'uns from as young as six weeks, but there are also long waiting lists, so get in touch as soon as possible. The site is well placed for public transport. You can get to the CBD by rail in a few minutes and buses stop here from right across the eastern suburbs.

42 Ethel St
Seaforth
Outer North

Eco Preschool
9948 4289 | *www.ecopreschools.com.au*
Eco Preschool in Seaforth is open from 08:30 to 17:00 and takes children from age two
and upwards. But, it is in a family area and places can be limited. It is NCAC (National
Childcare Accreditation Council) and QIAS (Quality Improvement and Accreditation
System) accredited. Staff tend to have quite a broad knowledge and are up to date on
most modern development theories. Eco has established some admirable beliefs,
including the importance of early learning, making children environmentally aware
and that working with nippers is a privilege.

131 Queens
Pde East
Newport Beach
Outer North

KU Pre-School
9999 4606 | *www.ku.com.au*
KU Pre-School has sites across NSW. This one in Newport Beach is particularly popular. It
is open from 08:30 to 15:30 to children aged between three and five years old. As with
most pre-schools, vacancies are limited and if you want to send your child here, you
should get in touch as soon as possible. KU Pre-Schools follow the emergent curriculum
theory. For more on this, see the entry for Moore Park, which does the same.

319/5 Potter St
Surry Hills

Moore Park Children's Early Learning Centre
9699 6681
Moore Park Children's Early Learning Centre is close to the CBD and a popular spot with
families from south Sydney. It is open from 07:00 to 18:00 and takes babies from six
weeks old. It is NCAC and QIAS accredited. Moore Park follows the emergent
curriculum theory. This is where the interests of children lead learning, rather than a
curriculum decided by a teacher. So, on the simplest level, if the kids get giddy about
the sandpit, the day's learning focuses on building with sand; if they are contemplative
and relaxed, they might do drawing.

WorldTower
87 Liverpool St
Central

WorldTower Child Care
9262 7927 | *www.worldtowerchildcare.com.au*
WorldTower Child Care is something of a working parent's dream. It is near the centre
of town and open 24 hours a day, seven days a week. It is NCAC and QIAS accredited,
and cares for children from six weeks old until school age. The WorldTower Child Care
Centre follows a Reggio Emilia Curriculum. This has a heavy emphasis on learning
through art, the child's environment and a generally collaborative effort between
parents and school. Parent participation is actively encouraged.

Primary & Secondary Schools

Primary Schools
In NSW, children must have turned five before July 31 in the year they start school,
although there are exceptions for gifted and talented children. All children, by law,
have to start school by their sixth birthday. At age 11 or 12, they move up to secondary
or high school. The table that follows gives contact details for some of the bigger
public and private schools mentioned under the Education heading in our Residential
Areas section (see p.88). For other public schools in NSW, go to the website
www.schools.nsw.edu.au. Then, click Finding a Public School to locate the nearest
school to you. For private schools, see www.isd.com.au.

Secondary Schools
Children in NSW can legally leave school at 15. But, to get into further education, they
need to complete year 10 and pass their School Certificate, then go on to finish year 12

and get their HSC (Higher School Certificate). Some private and church schools also offer the International Baccalaureate.

NSW has four types of public school. These are: comprehensive high schools; central schools (for rural kids); specialist high schools (for sports, performing arts, technology and languages after children have passed required tests); and selective high schools. This last group takes kids with the best scores in the Selective High School Test, held in June each year.

Picture Perfect

They say a picture can speak a thousand words. So if you can't sum up a city in a sentence, then grab a copy of one Explorer's stunning *Mini Photography Books*. Each one showcases a unique view of a different city, so the next time you go on holiday you can take home more than just your memories.

Primary & Secondary Schools

Public	Area	Phone	Primary/Secondary
Balmain Public School	Balmain	9818 1177	Primary
Bondi Beach Public School	Bondi	9130 2116	Primary
Darlinghurst Public School	Darlinghurst	9331 4295	Primary
Double Bay Public School	Double Bay	9363 3456	Primary
Erskineville Public School	Erskineville	9557 5206	Primary
Leichhardt Public School	Leichhardt	9560 9440	Secondary
Manly Vale Public School	Manly	9907 9672	Primary
Mosman Public School	Mosman	9969 9325	Primary
Neutral Bay Public School	Neutral Bay	9953 1758	Primary
Newtown Public School	Newtown	9557 4862	Primary
North Sydney Boys' High School	North Sydney	9955 4748	Secondary
Paddington Public School	Paddington	9361 6730	Primary
Randwick Boy's High School	Randwick	9399 3122	Secondary
Randwick Girls's High School	Randwick	8345 8200	Secondary
Ranwick Primary	Randwick	9398 6022	Secondary
Stanmore Public School	Stanmore	9569 1638	Primary
Sydney Boys High School	Surry Hills	9361 6910	Secondary
Sydney Girls High School	Surry Hills	9331 2336	Secondary
Sydney Secondary College	Inner West	9810 0471	Secondary
Private			
Ascham School (for girls)	Edgecliff	8356 7000	Both
Balgowlah Boys High	Balgowlah	9949 4200	Secondary
Cranbrook School (for boys)	Central	9327 6864	Both
Kambala (for girls)	Watsons Bay	9388 6777	Both
Mosman High School	Mosman	9968 1006	Secondary
North Sydney Girls' High School	North Sydney	9922 6666	Secondary
SCEGGS	Various locations	9332 1133	Both
Sydney Grammar School	Darlinghurst	9332 5800	Secondary
The Scots College (for boys)	Central	9391 7600	Both

University & Higher Education

Australia comes 12th globally out of 36 countries ranked by population reaching degree level or higher. Some 28% of the population has managed this, just behind Ireland and ahead of the United Kingdom and Germany. University entry conditions for non-residents are complicated and you should visit the following website to assess your own particular circumstances: www.uac.edu.au/admin/overseas.html. A full list of universities and colleges can be obtained from www.thegoodguides.com.au.

There is also an extensive range of state colleges offering technical and further education, called TAFEs. They offer diploma courses with more of a commercial focus and can be found by visiting www.tafensw.edu.au. There are lots of further education options in the city. A comprehensive list and the courses on offer can be found at www.australian-universities.com and www.uac.edu.au, which also sets out the process for applying. What follows is a brief assessment of the bigger universities.

Universities

Balaclava Road
North Ryde
Outer North

Macquarie University
9850 6410 | www.mq.edu.au

Macquarie University sits in a pleasant stretch of green belt in North Ryde. It is a slightly trendy modern uni, but one that has a strong history of academic achievement and a good research record. Macquarie also houses a research park and the Macquarie Graduate School of Business, which is responsible for producing a big chunk of Australia's MBA's. Macquarie is very popular with overseas students and in particular those from Asian countries. It has 29,000 students, 6,000 of which are international. It offers quite a broad and eclectic mix of departments, including economic and financial studies, Asian languages, culture, media and philosophy and Earth and planetary sciences.

Various locations

University of New South Wales
9385 1000 | www.unsw.edu.au

The University of New South Wales, commonly known as UNSW, is one of the oldest teaching and research universities in Australia, with a good international reputation. This is helped by the relationships (of varying degrees) it has formed with more than 200 other universities around the world. It is known for its research into quantum computing, photovoltaics (renewable energy), HIV, interactive cinema and polymer chemistry. It is close to the city, with its main campus in Kensington, next to Randwick, in the eastern suburbs. While originally viewed as a university strong in science and technology, it has now become recognised for courses in the arts, law, medicine and management.

Various locations

University of Sydney
9351 2222 | www.usyd.edu.au

The University of Sydney is the classic traditional university, redolent of Cambridge, Oxford, Yale, Harvard and other old teaching institutions in grand settings. Established in 1850, Sydney uni has an excellent reputation for teaching and research, and attracts students and staff from across Australia and the rest of the world. Many of the academic staff are recognised as leaders in their fields. The campus is close to the CBD off Parramatta Road and, while made up of a mix of heritage and modern buildings, it is the older sites that give the uni its atmosphere. Its departments cover agriculture, food and natural resources, economics, education and social work, law, the arts and more.

Various locations

The University of Technology
9514 2000 | www.uts.edu.au

The University of Technology Sydney, known locally as UTS, provides courses more closely linked to specific professions in the technical and commercial world, although it has expanded to offer a more eclectic choice over recent years. It has more than 27,000 students spread across three campuses. The main one, known as the City Campus, is close to Central station, with the other two, in St Leonard's and Lindfield, 20 to 30 minutes away by public transport. Faculties include business, sport and tourism, management, architecture and building, midwifery and health, science and international studies.

Various locations

University of Western Sydney
1800 897 669 | www.usw.edu.au

The University of Western Sydney has six campuses around Parramatta, Penrith, Bankstown, Blacktown, Hawkesbury and Campbelltown. UWS links its courses closely to the needs of employers in the west of the city. This part of town is relatively new as a significant residential spot, but has been growing for many years as an industrial and commercial hub, separate to metropolitan Sydney. The Greater Western Sydney area is now the third largest economy in Australia after the Sydney CBD and Melbourne. UWS is the fifth largest university in Australia, with over 32,000 students, 2,800 of which are from overseas. UWS schools include arts, business, and health and science.

Special Needs Education

NSW has good facilities for children with special needs. Your first stop should be www.schools.nsw.edu.au. The NSW Department of Ageing, Disability and Home Care, see www.dadhc.nsw.gov.au, provides advice and guidance and the excellent handbook, *Children's Standards in Action: a resource for service providers working with children and young people with a disability*. This can be downloaded from the department's website. There is also an excellent site (www.raisingchildren.net.au) that aims to help parents with all those questions and queries about bringing up children and providing tips, guidance and options regarding who to turn to when things are not going well.

The choice between a mainstream education and a school dedicated to children with special needs is a mighty conundrum for parents. Your location and the extent of your child's needs will severely affect your options. You may have access to regular classes in mainstream schools, support classes in mainstream schools or a special needs school. Before enrolling your child, you will be asked to contact the student support team at your local council. For all rules on attending state schools go to www.schools.nsw.edu.au/gotoschool/index.php.

The city at night

135

Transportation

Other options **Getting Around** p.40, **Car** p.275

The east coast of NSW is the most populated area in the state and has a comprehensive public transport network, including trains, buses and ferries, linking the cities and suburbs in the greater urban area. Many Sydneysiders commute by car, despite the cost of tolls and parking, which can be high (although some employers will cover these). If you're going to drive, it's best to use the automated tag payment system that covers all tolls on the freeways, bridges and tunnels. For more, see p136. For statewide rail travel visit www.countrylink.info.

Public Transport in Sydney

Sydney's public transport system is pretty comprehensive but relies heavily on buses in the northern and eastern suburbs. CityRail covers most suburbs out west and to the south, and the centre and the CBD is very well served. There are also ferries to and from harbour-side suburbs and the monorail and light rail in the CBD. For bus information, visit www.sydneybuses.info. For ferry information, see www.sydneyferries.info. CityRail trains run to Newcastle in the north, the Blue Mountains in the west, Campbelltown and Goulburn in the south west, and Wollongong in the south. For rail information see www.cityrail.info. There is also an integrated transport information site at www.131500.info. For more, see Getting Around, p.40.

GoGet

GoGet is Australia's first professional car-sharing service. It's an idea so simple and clever, you'll wonder why it's taken so long to catch on. The scheme gives you access to a fleet of cars, taking away the hassle, expense and environmental damage caused by owning. Become a member, then select from a range of plans, depending on your intended usage. Hourly rates begin at $4.40. Visit www.goget.com.au or call 9571 7700.

Driving in Sydney

Driving in Sydney and Australia is on the left, (so right hand drive vehicles), and is like driving in any greater urban area, with traffic congested at times and parking often difficult and expensive. Commuters generally don't car pool and, if not supplied with your job, parking cards can be purchased from a range of companies including www.wilsonparking.com.au and www.secureparking.com.au.

Petrol / Gas Stations

Petrol in Australia is relatively expensive. It's currently around $1.29 a litre although this varies significantly. You can get vouchers from supermarkets and other stores that can reduce the cost by between 5 cents and 20 cents per litre, depending of course on how much you spend. The best way to find the cheapest petrol station in your area is to go to www.motormouth.com.au. In general, petrol stations are self-service. Many have car wash and service facilities, but the most reliable servicing is done at manufacturer's branded centres. Licensed service stations can also do the required RTA testing on vehicles over a certain age.

Outback Driving

Ensure you have plenty of fuel, food and drinking water. Petrol stations are spaced out, and it might take almost a full tank to get from one to another. Take regular breaks to ease the monotony of long empty roads. Never ever leave your car if it breaks down in the middle of nowhere. It gives you shelter from the heat and it is a lot easier to spot than a

136

person walking in the bush. Also, a person uses about four times as much water when walking, and Australia is a big, dry country.

Don't expect your mobile phone to work out in the bush. Efforts have been made to cover populated areas but for vast expanses you won't get a beep. If you're really going to the back of beyond it's a good idea to buy or rent a two-way HF radio or a satellite phone.

Driving Habits ◀
The general standard of driving in and around Sydney is good. But, as in any city, it can occasionally be a little aggressive.

The Basics

- The general speed limit is 60kph in the city and suburbs.
- There are many 40kph and 50kph areas in suburban streets, especially near schools, and the police strictly observe these, with hefty fines imposed for offenders.
- The speed limit outside the metropolitan area is 100kph on normal country roads and 110kph on freeways, but watch out for highly variable speed limits that can be 110kph one second and 80kph the next. There are lots of speed cameras on NSW urban and country roads.
- Holding an overseas licence and claiming not to speak English will not work with NSW Police as they have ready access to translators.
- If you are moving to NSW from another state or overseas, you will need to make arrangements to get a NSW driver's licence. While the rules are different for overseas and interstate residents, in general you can use your existing licence for up to three months, after which you must have a NSW licence in order to drive a vehicle or ride a motorcycle. See www.rta.nsw.gov.au and p.64.
- You may be required to retake a theory or practical driving test, depending on the country in which you held your last licence. Don't try and avoid this as the police will check how long you have been in Australia and the fines are hefty.
- Up to date information about driving in NSW, current and new driving rules, test and licensing requirements can be found at www.rta.nsw.gov.au.

Vehicle Leasing

Leasing in Australia can be complicated so it's best to get specialist advice from your bank or accountant. There are complicated tax rules and lots of types of lease, including novated leases through your employer. These save money, because the lease is deducted from your pre-tax income. For more details on the tax system here, see Taxation p.79. Your credit rating in Australia may also be an issue in relation to the purchase, funding or leasing of any asset, including a car.

Vehicle Leasing Agents

Avis	13 6333	www.avis.com.au
Bayswater Car Rental	9360 3622	www.bayswatercarrental.com.au
Budget	13 2727	www.budget.com.au
City Car Hire	9626 9255	www.citycarhire.com
Discount Car & Truck Rentals	9389 7377	www.discountcar.com.au
Hertz	1300 132 607	www.hertz.com.au
Network Rentals	1800 736 825	www.networkrentals.com.au
Thrifty	1300 367 227	www.thrifty.com.au

The cost of leasing a car is determined by its manufacturer's suggested retail price (MSRP). You would never pay this price if you were buying the car for cash, so there is no reason you should do so for a lease. First, negotiate the lowest possible price on the vehicle and then negotiate the lease terms.

For example, if a car has an MSRP of around $40,000 and the term of the lease is 36 months, at an interest rate of 6.67%, with a residual value of approx $26,000, the monthly lease payment would be approx $480, excluding sales tax, licenses, etc. If you negotiated a price of approximately $34,000, the lease payment would be reduced to around $415.

137

An Aussie Icon
Designed by Ford's
Lewis Brandt, the first
ute was made in 1934.
It has the cabin of a
car and the rear of a
small truck and has
long been a favourite
vehicle for farmers
and tradesmen.

Buying a Vehicle

Locally built cars are limited to Ford, Holden and Mitsubishi, all of which are pretty reliable. These are generally the least costly to buy, with imported cars attracting higher prices. The range of vehicles is immense (although there are still relatively few diesel cars in Australia) with every global manufacturer represented. Australian-built cars still reflect the Australian love of large engines, so the majority sport a v6 or v8, ideal for those long cross-country runs.

Buying and registering a vehicle in NSW is fairly straightforward and dealers normally do all the hard work. The RTA, see www.rta.nsw.gov.au or call 13 2213, is a useful first resource.

The Buying Process

When you buy (or are given) a vehicle that is registered in NSW, you have to transfer the registration into your name within 14 days or pay a late fee. You will need to visit a motor registry with proof of your identity, a completed Application for Transfer form (from www.rta.nsw.gov.au) and proof of acquisition. This can be a receipt or certificate of registration signed by the previous owner, or the previous certificate of registration if the car is coming from another state or overseas. You will need to pay a transfer fee and stamp duty, and you may need to pay extra motor vehicle tax if you have bought your vehicle from someone receiving an RTA concession (such as a pension).

New Car Dealers		
Audi	9931 3400	www.audi.com.au
BMW	9334 4555	www.bmwsydney.com.au
Ford	9331 5000	www.cityford.com.au
Honda	9804 7045	www.hondaeastwood.com.au
MG	9326 9199	www.mgcars.com.au
Mitsubishi	8275 6856	www.mitsubishi-motors.com.au
Nissan	9797 4111	www.nissan.com.au
Renault	9560 1000	www.renault.com.au
Smart	9697 7800	www.smartaustralia.com.au
Toyota	9681 8100	www.westoy.com.au

Importing a Car from Home

Importing and exporting a vehicle is possible but can be difficult. See www.aaa.asn.au, which sets it all out very clearly and concisely. Then, go to www.dotars.gov.au, which lists the detailed requirements for a vehicle to comply with Australian standards. Details on obtaining Green Slips and Blue Slips can be found on the RTA website. To register a vehicle you have imported, you will have to go to a motor registry in person and provide:

Caveat Emptor
Caveat Emptor, or
'buyer beware', applies
when buying a second-
hand car. Make sure
you get it checked out
properly. The Australian
AA (www.aaa.asn.au)
website offers some
useful advice.

- Proof of your identity.
- Proof of your residential address.
- Proof of acquisition (e.g. a receipt or the previous certificate of registration in the same name).
- A valid Compulsory Third Party insurance policy, also known as a Green Slip, with the number plate section blank.
- An inspection report, also known as a Blue Slip, from an Authorised Unregistered Vehicle Inspection Station (AUVIS).
- A completed Application for Registration form.
- Evidence of eligibility for any concessions.
- A Vehicle Import Approval from the Commonwealth Department of Transport and Regional Services.
- A weighbridge ticket.
- If the vehicle is an Individually Constructed Vehicle (ICV) or has been modified to comply with regulation requirements (e.g. converted from left-hand to right-hand drive), a certificate from an RTA recognised Engineering Signatory is needed.

- Payment for registration, including registration fee, motor vehicle tax, stamp duty and the applicable number plate fee.

Dealers

If you want to visit dealers, start at the city end of Parramatta Road and work your way towards Homebush. You will find every manufacturer in Australia represented. Also, you could try an area in Parramatta called Auto Alley which has a big range of dealers. Individual manufacturer websites will also list local dealers. See table.

Private Sales

To buy a car privately, look through the local papers or on one of these websites; www.carsguide.com.au, www.drive.com.au or www.autotrader.com.au, which have largely taken over from the traditional newspaper classified listings. Used cars are generally affordable, with some imports losing value quicker than locally built models. When you

Used Car Dealers			
A1 Car Broker	Various	8215 0516	www.carbroker.com.au
Cars Wanted	Various	1300 722 809	www.carswanted.com.au
Modena Prestige Cars	Darlinghurst	9360 1354	www.modenaprestigecars.com.au
Oz CarSearch.com	Various	8346 6450	www.ozcarsearch.com
Vision Car Wholesale	Manly	9905 2290	www.visioncars.citysearch.com.au

buy a used car, get it checked out by NRAM. Visit www.mynrma.com.au for details. When you sell a vehicle you have to complete a Notice of Disposal form, which is on the back of the Certificate of Registration or obtainable from motor registries. If the buyer is a NSW resident and holds a NSW drivers licence, you can do this online through the RTA web site. It is important that you notify the RTA when you sell a vehicle, so that the police will not fine you for offences you did not commit.

Edit Your Credit
Do not fill out applications at several financial institutions and have all of them checking into your credit history at once. This can make you look desperate and lower your credit score.

Vehicle Finance

Dealers hire purchase and finance rates are often pretty competitive, but it is worth comparing their offer with finance from your bank or other credit providers. Dealer finance might be less hassle but you could end up with an expensive loan and more restrictive terms.

If the banks, building societies and credit unions won't lend to you because you're newly arrived or have a poor credit history, you could consider the 'low doc' loan market. There are a number of non-bank lenders offering such loans. The interest rates on these are generally higher but come down after a

Vehicle Finance		
Aussie Car Loans	1300 769 999	www.aussiecarloans.com.au
Aussiewise Finance Group	1300 723 927	www.aussiewisefg.com.au
Avia Finance & Investment	1300 763 467	www.aviafinance.com.au
Esanda	1300 655 086	www.esanda.com
GE Money	1800 800 230	www.gemoney.com.au
Motor Finance Wizard	1300 227 562	www.1300carloan.com.au
Select Automotive Finance	8356 6700	–
Stratton Finance	1300 132 058	www.strattonfinance.com.au
Wizard	1300 657 355	www.wizard.com.au

139

few years of on-time repayments. Check out Wizard, Aussie Car Loans, Motor Finance Wizard, GE Money and Esanda. For general tips on buying and indications of car prices have a look at the following websites: www.carsguide.news.com.au and www.drive.com.au. The motoring organisation NRMA (www.mynrma.com.au) is well worth joining and the site contains some good reviews and tips. See p.46 for details of local banks.

Vehicle Insurance

You must have basic insurance to register your car, known as Compulsory Third Party (CTP) or Green Slip. This insurance must cover the vehicle owner and driver against liability for personal injury to any other party in the event of a personal injury claim. CTP Green Slip insurance does not cover damage to property or other vehicles.

The best location to secure CTP insurance, which also offers a CTP comparison and shows all the types available is www.greenslips.com.au.

Vehicle Insurance			
AAMI	13 2244	www.aami.com.au
GIO	13 1010	www.gio.com.au
GreenSlips Net	9223 0102	www.greenslips.com.au
NRMA	13 2132	www.nrma.com.au

You are advised to also take out comprehensive insurance, the rates of which are highly variable and depend on you, and the type and value of your car. Insurance is on an annual basis and can be paid monthly with most companies, with excess payable in the event of an accident (this will be determined by you and the insurance company at the outset).

A list of good vehicle insurers is included here, with NRMA being the largest supplier of vehicle insurance in NSW. Try and bring evidence of your good driving and insurance record and any no claim bonus you may have built up overseas. These may not be recognised here, but could influence the premium and policy you're offered.

Spot Check

All vehicles registered in NSW can be selected for an additional inspection by the RTA's Vehicle Identification Inspection Unit (VIIU), just to check that all is above board. You will be told when you register if yours is to be selected.

Registering a Vehicle

When you buy a new vehicle from a dealer in NSW they will register it under the Authorised New Vehicle Inspection Scheme (ANVIS). You will just need to complete the Application for Registration form. The dealer will then give you the Certificate of Registration once everything is completed.

Second hand cars require a bit more legwork, particularly if you buy privately. You will need to transfer registration within 14 days, for which you'll need to present the RTA with a completed Application for Transfer, some ID and proof of acquisition (ie a receipt from a dealer or signed copy of the old registration by the previous owner, see www.rta.nsw.gov.au for more) and a CTP (Compulsory Third Party) insurance policy, also known as a Green Slip, with the number plate section blank.

Your annual renewal (there is no grace period when your current registration ends) can be done online (www.rta.nsw.gov.au/myrta/myrego) or over the phone (13 2213). Check the RTA website (www.rta.nsw.gov.au) for any changes in regulations.

Traffic Fines & Offences

Traffic offences are taken seriously in NSW. You may need to take a test to get a NSW licence, which is a good opportunity to learn the different rules here. There are offences linked to alcohol, drugs, speeding, seatbelts, the condition of your vehicle and obstructing traffic.

Demerit Points

Demerits are penalty points given for a range of driving offences. You start with no points (a clean licence) and collect them if you get caught breaking road laws. For full

Speeding Penalties

Excess Speed	Demerit	Fine
Up to 15km/h	3Pts	$77
16 to 30km/h	3Pts	$231
31 to 45km/h	4Pts	$590
More than 45km/h	6Pts	$1,589

unrestricted licence holders, once you accumulate 12 points your licence is suspended. For provisional P2s it's seven points, and four for provisional P1 licence holders.

Suspentions depend on how many points you get. For full licence holders with between 12 and 15 points the ban is three months. It's four months for between 16 and 19 points, and five months for 20 points or more. For provisional licence holders, the automatic suspension period is three months. If you are driving on busy times like public holidays and long weekends then you'll see signs everywhere warning of Double Demerit Points. That means twice the number of points for the same law infringement. These points almost always come with financial fines too. Driving tests are sometimes required when a licence holder has been disqualified or the licence has been expired for more than five years.

Speeding

If you are caught by a speed camera or police officer, you will get a fine and demerit points (see table). There are also licence suspension periods for exceeding the speed limit by more than 30kph (three months) and by more than 45kph (six months). If the police catch you speeding by more than 45kph, your licence may be immediately suspended and confiscated for six months. If it goes through a court, you could be fined up to $3,300 and given a six-month suspension.

Drink Driving

Blood alcohol laws are complicated because there are three limits: zero, 0.02 and 0.05 grams of alcohol per 100 millilitres of blood. The limit that applies to you depends on your licence and vehicle. Drink driving is taken very seriously and demerit points, suspension, fines, and imprisonment can apply if you're caught. The zero limit applies to all learners and provisional licence holders. The 0.02 limit is for drivers of public vehicles, heavy loads and dangerous goods. The 0.05 applies to everybody else.

Driving Without a Seatbelt

The driver is responsible for making sure that everyone in a car wears a seat belt (where there is one available). Babies under 12 months must be in an approved child restraint.

Breakdowns

Before a breakdown becomes a reality, make sure you are in one of the roadside recovery programmes - NRMA is recommended (www.mynrma.com.au). If you are on a freeway or busy road, make sure that your car is safely positioned and call your recovery service immediately. You should always carry a mobile phone with you and plenty of water to hand if you are going to a remote or off-road area and it's a good idea to advise someone reliable of your route and the time you expect to reach your destination so that they can call for assistance if you don't turn up. See Road Trips, p.211 for advice on longer trips.

Recovery Services/Towing (24 hour)

Active Towing Sydney	9809 5606
Affordable	0401 973 527
ASAP Towing Service	0411 357 035
Austow Towing	0412 956 956
Towcorp	0411 664 665
Towmaster	1300 796 797

141

Traffic Accidents

Other options **Car** p.43

Sydney is a very busy place with heavy traffic, so be vigilant. You are legally required to carry your driving licence with you at all times. The best advice about getting used to driving here is to take your time. Ignore other drivers if they become agitated that you are driving slower than them.

If you are involved in an accident, you are only obliged to call the police if someone is injured. If you feel that the police should be called anyway, then you are free to do so, but if nobody is hurt they may take some time to arrive.

If your car is not fit to be driven, call your insurance company and ask them what you should do. Generally they'll take over and arrange for repairs or advise you if the vehicle is a write off. Don't just take the first tow truck that appears, as they all listen to police frequencies waiting for an accident to happen.

And be warned, if you don't have a valid NSW driving licence (outside of the three-month leeway to apply for one) your insurance will be invalid and you may have to foot the bill.

Repairs

If you have a prang, your insurers should deal with it and tell you where to take your car for assessment and repair. If you are paying for the repair yourself you will need to find a local body shop (see table). Most neighbourhoods have a few to choose from so ask a friend or neighbour for advice.

Repairs		
Casella Motor Repairs	Leichhardt	9560 9155
Cleveland Motor Body Repairs	Darlington	9319 2454
Dino's Motor Repairs	Darlinghurst	9331 2486
Hargrave Motor Repairs	Darlinghurst	9331 3677
Lube Mobile	Various locations	13 3032
Midas	Various locations	13 6432
Ultratune	Various locations	1800 025 715

If your vehicle is new you will probably be covered for one, three or five years of ongoing servicing or repair. If this is not the case, then take you car to the nearest dealer or go to a local garage. Make sure the service book is stamped each time the car is serviced as this can affect the sale value. Popular repair franchises include www.midas.com.au, www.ultratune.com.au and www.lubemobile.com.au. Numbers are listed in the table (for your local Ulatratune garage see their site, the number listed is head office only) and many of these will come to your home or work. The site www.autorepairers.com.au has a directory of garages. When you have your car repaired or serviced you should provide any manuals and warranty information you have.

The cost of a service will depend on the vehicle (for example, how many kilometres it has done). For a small car it can cost from $150 to $250, for a medium car between $200 and $400 and for a large car between $250 and $500. Parts are also expensive and replacing an engine can cost between $2,000 and $10,000, a water pump will set you back $200 to $500 and for a new gearbox, be prepared to shell out between $2,000 and $5,000.

Kings Cross

Dry Cleaners p.74
Divorce Lawyers p.108

Written by residents, these unique guidebooks are packed with insider info, from arriving in a new destination to making it your home and everything in between.

Explorer Residents' Guides
We Know Where You Live

Abu Dhabi · Amsterdam · Bahrain · Barcelona · Dubai · Dublin · Geneva · Hong Kong · Kuwait
London · New York · New Zealand · Oman · Paris · Qatar · Shanghai · Singapore · Sydney

EXPLORER
www.explorerpublishing.com

Raw power, refined.

The new Chevrolet Tahoe refines the raw power of a 355 horsepower Vortec V8 engine and couples it with smooth handling and a quiet ride. Examine Tahoe's luxuriously appointed interior and you'll find refinement in every detail.

CHEVROLET

Tahoe 2007

Exploring

Exploring

Stretching beneath you are pretty beaches and rugged cliffs, the sparkling harbour with its iconic bridge and the graceful sails of the Opera House. This is where it all begins – welcome to Sydney.

This buzzing cosmopolitan city is admired for its natural attractions and envied for its incredible outdoorsy lifestyle. Beneath the splendid surface of its harbour and beaches you'll discover a vibrant cafe culture, historic pubs, fantastic seafood and a wild nightlife. Its short but colourful history is everywhere – in the solid sandstone alleyways of The Rocks, at the Aboriginal rock carvings near Bondi and Manly, and among the eclectic architectural mix of high-rise office blocks and stately Victorian buildings. What really gives Sydney its palpable vibrancy though, is the culturally diverse population. Some Aussie country folk argue that the pace is too fast and the attitude too flashy in the big smoke, but most visitors are won over by the easygoing charm of the locals. These locals have a mix of backgrounds thanks to a massive influx of post second world war immigrants from Europe and, more recently, Asia. As well as adding to the city's cultural flavour they've seriously spiced up the culinary scene. No longer a meat and three veg nation, Sydney is leading the food revolution. Its suburban streets are bulging with exotic eateries and you're never more than a few metres from a Thai, Italian or Chinese restaurant. Homegrown chefs like Bill Granger and Neil Perry are taking the international food scene by storm and the world is swooning over mod Oz creations from Down Under.

In population terms, Sydney is relatively small for a world-class city, but it's growing fast. It stretches nearly 100km from top to bottom and 55km across, making it twice the size of New York. The city is divided into four sections – geographically by north and south, socially by east and west, a relic from the settlement era. The wealthy officers generally lived in the east, while the labourers were stationed out west. Today the well-heeled still cluster among the mansions in the hilly east, while the west and southwest remain the stomping ground of the Aussie 'battlers'. The old-money north, despite its humdrum image, has some of the best beaches and protected national parks. Wherever you wake up, this chapter will guide you to the must-sees of a spectacular city.

Mini Marvels

Explorer *Mini Visitors' Guides* are the perfect holiday companion. They are small enough to fit in your pocket but beautiful enough to inspire you to explore. With detailed maps, visitor information, restaurant, bar and shopping reviews, these mini marvels are a holiday must. Give the **Sydney Mini** to visiting friends and send them off to explore.

The Rocks

Opera House p.174

Map 2-E2

A happy snap in front of the graceful white sails is a nice souvenir but you'll come away with a richer experience by seeing its soaring interiors too. Penny pinchers can go behind the scenes on daily guided tours, but the best way to experience this astonishing building is by seeing a performance.

Sail the Harbour p.193

Sydney is a harbour-centric city, and the views from the water are lovely. You can admire the scenery from a luxury catamaran, or get a bit more involved by learning to sail or hiring kayaks and paddling through middle harbour.

Climb the Bridge p.191

Map 2-C2

It will be among the first questions asked of you by new arrivals and friends back home, 'have you climbed the bridge?' This most iconic of structures is just begging to be conquered. It's not cheap, but the view from the top of the 143-metre iron arch is worth it. Then, you can cross it for free on the footpath.

Taronga Zoo p.190

Other than the native Australian attractions and the exotic overseas imports (even adults go gaga over the giraffes and Asian elephants), locals return for the view across the glittering harbour to the towering city skyline.

Surf Bondi p.191

This famous crescent-shaped strip of sand gave birth to the enduring Aussie cliche of sun-loving, surf-mad larrikins. It's also the symbolic home of the iconic Bondi Surf Bathers Life Saving Club with their natty red hats and skimpy little trunks. So, get into the seaside spirit and learn to ride (or at least paddle) the waves.

Centre Point Tower p.193

Map 3-E1

Go up Centre Point Tower for some of the best views of the city. If you can't afford the Skywalk, or go wobbly at the thought of it, go to the 360 Bar instead (see p.324). A single cocktail in its glam surroundings, 88 storeys up, will buy you the right to savour the panoramic cityscape as the tower slowly revolves.

Paddington Markets p.307

This is where residents snaffle local designer fashion, jewellery and homewares at negotiable prices, laze over a coffee or try a tarot reading. There's no tacky Australiana souvenirs in sight and it's smack bang in the middle of the shopping Mecca of Oxford Street.

Ride the Ferry p.194   *Map 2-D3*

The Manly Ferry is the best value ticket in town. For just $6.20 you get a leisurely half hour ride from Circular Quay to the best-known beach in the northern suburbs. An organised tour will cost plenty more (see p.191) and won't show you anything more beautiful.

Australia Day p.54

Australia Day is celebrated with a passion every January 26, and should always be enjoyed outdoors. Barbecues are fired up and beers are quaffed to celebrate the nation's birthday. Get down to the harbour for most of the action, or the Woggan Ma Gule Morning Ceremony by indigenous Australians at the Royal Botanic Gardens.

Catch a Game p.249

This sports mad city has plenty of big events from basketball to Aussie rules. Try a cricket game at the SCG (p.249, make sure to get your tickets early for the popular New Year's Test) or see the brutal, fascinating spectacle that is the Rugby League State of Origin game at the Telstra Stadium. Or place your bets at the Royal Randwick (p.250) for one of the Australian Jockey Club's thrilling race days, and don't miss the Racing Carnival.

Pub Crawl p.355

The Aussies have worked hard on their reputation as a nation of drinkers. One way for new residents to get to know their city is to explore its watering holes. From rustic, rocker drinking dens to super slick bars, merrily waddle about the pub-packed suburbs of Balmain and The Rocks.

Botanic Gardens p.186   *Map 2-E4*

Picnic in the Royal Botanic Gardens, where local families and canoodling couples unpack hampers every weekend. Directly on the harbour, this grassy expanse is a gorgeous place to wile away a summer's afternoon beneath the famous thick-trunked Moreton Bay Figs.

Fish 'n' Chips p.340

Feast on fish 'n' chips at Watsons Bay. If your funds don't extend to a seafood supper at the longstanding celebrity haunt Doyles (p.340), you can grab some of their delicious tucker at the nearby kiosk and eat in the park. Or, queue at the seafood bistro in the bayfront beergarden at the hotel next door.

The Cross p.97   *Map 4-C2*

Despite its reputation, it's not all debauchery and drugs in Kings Cross. You'll still stumble across some dodgy characters, but the police presence is strong enough to make you feel safe. It's a colourful contrast to the ritzier eastern suburbs and as well as the virbrant bars, there's some great restaurants serving up posh nosh.

Fireworks p.173

Images of the fireworks launching off Sydney Harbour Bridge are beamed around the world every New Year's Eve, and more than one million Sydneysiders spill out onto the streets to see them live. This is the world's second largest NYE celebration (after Rio's massive beach party). Over 80,000 fireworks are set off from the bridge and barges around the harbour.

Take a Dip p.244

The first Sunday in May is the official opening of the winter season, when ice blocks are tossed into the pool, just to make sure it's chilly enough. Members of the Icebergs club take a dip with the media and paying spectators looking on. The loyal (some say loony) locals who do regular morning laps in the dead of winter have become legends.

Eat Pie p.348   *Map 4-B1*

There's nothing more Aussie than a proper meat pie sloshed in thick gravy and mushy peas. Harry's Café de Wheels in Woolloomooloo set up shop in 1945, and soon became a Sydney legend. The famous tucker is as likely to be enjoyed by trendy eastern suburbs kids and celebrities (Pamela Anderson and Frank Sinatra have both stopped by) as merry sailors and hungry cabbies.

Sydney to Hobart p.241

Every Boxing Day since 1945, spectators have taken to the busy harbour in anything that floats to see off the local and international maxi yachts as they sail to Hobart, Tasmania. After a beer soaked start, locals remain glued to the TV to see who tips over and who turns up at the finish. The 1998 race was one of the most tragic – only 44 of the 115 boats made it and six people died along the way.

Walk the Cliffs p.182

Sydney's weather-beaten coastline has some glorious foot trails. Locals never tire of the path from Bondi to Bronte; the ocean views are spectacular and once you've hiked over the hill there are cute cafes where you can refuel. Bondi to Coogee and the Spit Bridge to Manly are just as impressive.

Fish Market p.308   *Map 3-A2*

Sydney is renowned for its fresh seafood and this is where to snap it up straight off the incoming trawlers. On Saturday mornings you'll be crammed in like sardines, but on weekdays you'll only be competing for the fresh catch with local restaurant chefs. The market also has cafes serving up seafood good enough for a trawlerman.

City2Surf p.240

This is one of the few traffic-free days of the year in the city centre, as more than 60,000 locals turn out for a 14km run. It begins in the corporate austerity of the CBD, heading out through the eastern suburbs and on to Bondi Beach, where runners can refuel with a well earned feed.

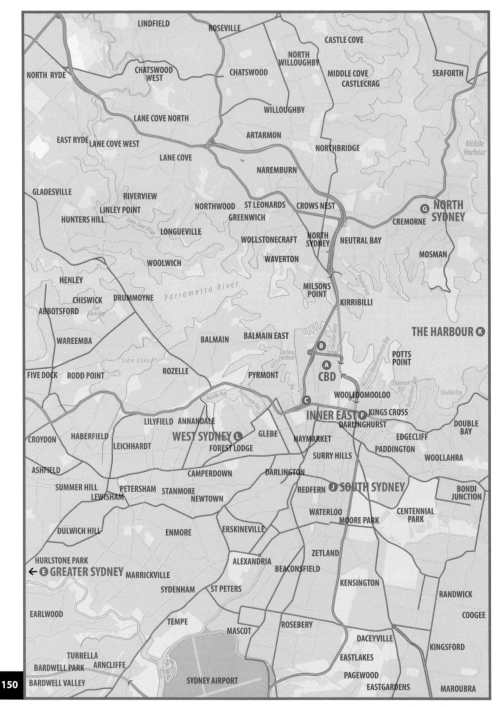

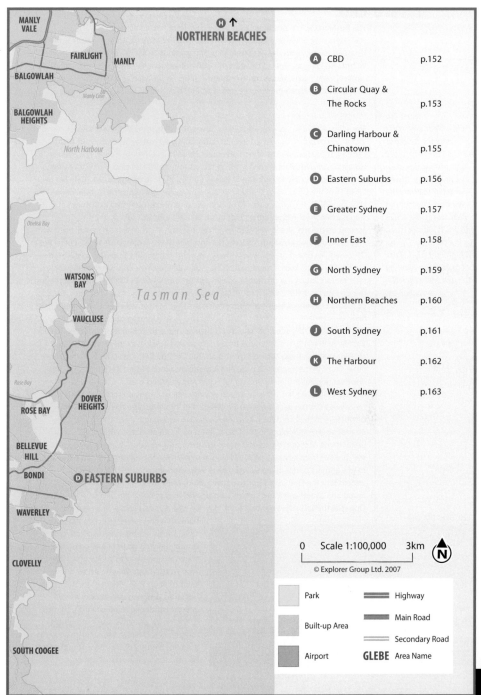

0   Scale 1:100,000   3km   **N**

© Explorer Group Ltd. 2007

Park	Highway
Built-up Area	Main Road
	Secondary Road
Airport	**GLEBE** Area Name

Map 2-D4 ◀

CBD

The bustling Central Business District stretches from Circular Quay to just beyond Town Hall. At its core is Martin Place, the financial heartland of Sydney. It's also a great place to spend money, with the Pitt Street Mall, the gracious Strand Arcade and the Queen Victoria Building all here. In the past the CBD ground to a halt after-hours when office workers went home, but as more residential units go up, such as the World Tower on George Street, there's much more going on in the evenings.

Must Do ◀

On a clear day, don't miss the fabulous views all the way to the Blue Mountains from Centrepoint Tower, (p.300). While the window displays are distracting, the CBD's historic buildings, such as the QVB (p.302), are a highlight. Hyde Park (p.184) is a relaxing place to watch the world go by.

Places of Interest

From Circular Quay, walk up Macquarie Street. It boasts some of Sydney's finest Victorian-era public buildings, erected during the gold rush years of the mid 19th century. These include The Mint, Parliament House, Government House, The Sydney Hospital and Hyde Park Barracks, which has a sunny courtyard cafe. For district views over The Domain, Hyde Park and St Mary's Cathedral, head to Buena Vista Café Bar on Level 14 of the Law Courts building in Queens Square. Don't miss the Art Gallery of NSW (p.165) on the other side of The Domain, or if you're interested in Sydney's colonial history, the Museum of Sydney on Bridge Street (p.176).

Joining Macquarie Street with George Street is Martin Place, a pedestrian mall lined with impressive historic buildings, notably the enormous 1887 renaissance-style General Post Office with its grand clock tower. Halfway up, on the corner of Elizabeth Street, are the Channel Seven studios. Crowds gather here on weekdays to watch the morning show stars performing live in the floor-to-ceiling glass studio (06:00-09:00). In the distance lies the alfresco Lindt Café, which sprinkles real chocolate shavings on cappuccinos. The pedestrian Pitt Street Mall is a shopper's oasis. At the Market Street end is the multi-level Myer department store with fast food outlets beneath. Upmarket rival David Jones is one block away. Between Pitt Street and George Street you'll find the impressive Strand Arcade, built in 1891, which has 3 floors of high-end Aussie designer labels and an excellent cafe, the cosy Strand Espresso. On the Centrepoint side of the mall you'll find more shops in the Imperial Arcade and Skygarden, which has a decent bar at the top. The beautiful State Theatre (see p.173) is just around the corner.

Centrepoint Tower has become a Sydney landmark since it was erected in 1981, and the views from the deck are amazing (see p.300), but to escape the crowds head downstairs to the cafe, which has floor-to-ceiling windows.

Straddling an entire block in the CBD is the stately Queen Victoria Building, Sydney's grand dame of shopping. Its 200 stores get increasingly exclusive as you go up. You can see the QVB from its best angle, all lit-up at night, from the Hilton's Zeta Bar across the road – and the cocktails are superb too. A long shop-lined corridor runs from underneath the QVB direct to Town Hall station, while designer items can mostly be found on Castlereagh Street, which runs parallel to the mall.

Opposite the QVB, the imposing Town Hall was Sydney's first concert hall and still houses an impressive organ dating from 1890. Locals use the steps as a convenient central meeting point before going out and plans are underway to convert the ugly Woolworths opposite into a paved square. West of Town Hall, George Street becomes progressively tackier as you head towards the main cinemas, thanks to the noisy game parlours and garish food chains. Despite the security cameras, it's a notoriously dodgy area at night and bag snatching is not uncommon.

Dusk over the city

Map 2-D2

Circular Quay & The Rocks

Framed by the iconic Harbour Bridge and Opera House, this heritage-rich area is often the first port of call for visitors. In the 19th century, The Rocks was renowned as a place of debauchery; it's claimed you could hear the noise of the gambling houses, opium dens and sly-grog shops a mile offshore. When the bubonic plague hit in 1900, the government bought the area and demolished parts of it in an attempt to control the spread of disease. It was largely abandoned until the 1970s, when a clean-up operation began that created the tourist hotspot it is today. See p.6 for more on its colourful history.

Must Do

Once the city slum, where effluent washed down from one cramped hillside cottage to the next, today this area is home to the Opera House (p.366) and its grand interiors. Take a peek inside and stop for a drink at the luxurious Opera Bar.

Places of Interest

The Harbour Bridge is the widest long-span bridge on earth. When it opened in 1932, the annual average traffic volume in both directions was about 10,900 vehicles per day. By 2005 this figure was 161,000, so a new tunnel was constructed underneath. You can climb the bridge or admire the view from a pylon for a fee. Alternatively, take the footpath for free.

Sydney's other icon, the Opera House (p.174), has only been standing on Bennelong Point since 1973. The forecourt is occasionally used as an amphitheatre for live concerts, and on Sundays market stalls with Australian arts and crafts line the concourse.

Circular Quay is Sydney's main commuter ferry terminal. While it's easy to be distracted by the glittering harbour, keep your eyes to the ground for the Writers Walk plaques, which provide short biographies of famous Australian authors.

Up until 1999, the views across the harbour to the Botanic Gardens (see p.186 and p.201) were unobstructed, but developers then built apartment blocks at East Circular Quay. Dubbed 'The Toaster' by locals, the eyesore does have an upside – swish bars like Aqua Luna have transformed it from a deserted spot after dark to a lively, sophisticated area.

On the western side, past the Museum of Contemporary Art (see p.167), the redeveloped Overseas Passenger Terminal houses some of Sydney's swankiest restaurants and bars. International cruise liners dock here when in town – head up the stairs for gorgeous views.

Writers' Walk

Steel drums in Circular Quay

153

Need Some Direction?
The *Explorer Mini Maps* pack a whole city into your pocket and once unfolded are excellent navigational tools. Not only are they handy in size, with detailed information on the sights and sounds of the city, but their price means they won't make a dent in your holiday fund. Wherever your travels take you, grab a mini map and you'll never have to ask for directions. Pocket the *Sydney Mini Map* to help find your way around your new home.

On Hickson Road you'll pass the Campbells Storehouses, once a depot for incoming produce and now filled with souvenir shops. Past the Park Hyatt (p.32) is Dawes Point, a good spot for harbour photos and further along is the working port of Walsh Bay. Here you'll find the prestigious Sydney Theatre Company (p.366) and the Sydney Dance Company, which holds dance classes that are open to the public. At the end of the pier, the Wharf restaurant (p.336) has killer views and great food.

Exploring the narrow cobblestone alleyways and historic houses of The Rocks is one of the area's highlights; start near the Museum of Contemporary Art at Cadman's Cottage (p.167), the oldest private house in Sydney, now the headquarters of the National Parks and Wildlife Service.

The Sydney Visitor Centre is on Argyle Street (open 09:30-17:30, www.sydneyvisitorcentre.com), near the solid sandstone Argyle Stores, a 19th century complex of boutique souvenir shops. Nearby is the impressive Argyle Cut, a sandstone tunnel connecting Circular Quay with Millers Point, which was hand-chiselled by convicts between 1843 and 1859. Up the Argyle Steps and along Gloucester Walk you'll stumble across petite Foundation Park, home to some incredibly small cottages dating from the 1870s. Near the pedestrian entrance to the Harbour Bridge is Susannah Place Museum, a row of four tiny terrace houses that recreate life in The Rocks in the 1900s.

The Rocks has some excellent historic watering holes, notably The Mercantile on George Street, the Lord Nelson (with its own micro-brewery) on Kent Street, and the Glenmore and The Australian on Cumberland Street. Don't miss the Hero of Waterloo on Lower Fort Street, which used to have secret cellar passageways to the port, allegedly used to ferry unwitting drunks out to waiting ships, where they'd wake up as sailors. Nearby is Garrison Church (p.169), Sydney's oldest, and Observatory Park. To see the southern hemisphere stars through the Sydney Observatory telescope, book a night tour (see p.196). Just south is the National Trust Centre, at the back of which you'll find the SH Ervin Gallery (p.167). The leafy courtyard at The Gumnut Tea Garden, a sandstone cottage built by convicts in the 1830s, is a tranquil sanctuary from the hustle and bustle. George Street is particularly lively on Saturdays when it hosts arts and crafts markets.

Map 3-C2

Darling Harbour & Chinatown

The once dilapidated shipping docks at Darling Harbour have become Sydney's central entertainment precinct. Redeveloped for Australia's bicentenary in 1988, millions of dollars were spent building the much maligned and little used Monorail and the two-storey souvenir hub, Harbourside Shopping Centre. The area had little to offer locals until relatively recently when swish bars and restaurants opened at Cockle Bay and King Street Wharves. Nearby Chinatown is an authentic slice of Asia with bustling markets, fresh yum cha and exotic Asian groceries.

Places of Interest

For visitors, the western side of Darling Harbour, which is dominated by the concrete Sydney Exhibition Centre, is a good place to pick up souvenirs. For more on these, see p.295 in the shopping section.

The National Maritime Museum (p.176) offers an interesting snapshot of Australia's seafaring history. You can see the ships and submarines up close or admire them from a distance at the waterside cafe.

Across the Pyrmont Bridge, The IMAX Theatre (www.imax.com.au) on the Southern Promenade boasts Australia's largest screen (a whopping eight storeys high) and shows 3D as well as 2D films. Nearby are Tumbalong Park (p.186), some green amid the concrete, and the peaceful Chinese Garden, which has a tranquil teahouse among the oriental plants and ponds. Don't miss the aquarium (p.190), which has a stunning Great Barrier Reef Oceanarium including sharks, fairy penguins and seals. Next door is Sydney Wildlife World (p.190), where you'll see both cuddly and deadly Australian natives (safely behind glass) and stunning butterflies.

Must Do
Soak up the sunny summer atmosphere at the swanky bars and restaurants on Cockle Bay Wharf or experience the sounds and smells of Asia in Chinatown. Get a taste of the Great Barrier Reef's beauty at the impressive aquarium (see p.190).

Also worth making time for is the huge Powerhouse Museum (p.176), which has excellent interactive displays covering fashion, arts, science, technology and design.

A ten-minute walk away via Pyrmont Bridge Road is the Sydney Fish Market (p.308), the second largest in the world; more than 14,000 tonnes of seafood is traded here annually. There are guided tours on Monday and Thursday at 06:55 from outside Doyle's Seafood Café – wear closed shoes and if you're not sure what to do with your fresh catch, take a class at the excellent Sydney Seafood School (9004 1111).

Chinatown is a short walk from Darling Harbour but smells and sounds Asian enough to make you feel like you're in a different city. Haymarket was traditionally the centre of Sydney's wholesale district and is still the place to find bargains. From Thursday to Sunday, Paddy's Markets (p.308) sell food, clothes and accessories at over 1,000 stalls. The Entertainment Centre is opposite and above the markets you'll find Market City, a three-level shopping complex full of discount brand outlets; Asian groceries are available on level one, while the third floor has good Chinese food.

The buzzing Dixon Street Mall, framed at each end by red Chinese gates, is particularly lively on Friday nights with outdoor markets (06:00-23:00). Better still is the party atmosphere during Chinese New Year celebrations (January/February, see p.178), when you'll see dragon dancing and live entertainment among the outdoor food stalls. While most of Sydney's kitchens start closing around 21:30, Chinatown always offers a late night bite. Try the BBQ King on Goulburn Street and for the next morning, East Ocean Restaurant on Sussex Street is a Sunday brunch institution (get there before 11:30 to avoid long queues).

Iceberg pool

Eastern Suburbs

The east is home to Australia's quintessential surf culture, complete with bronzed lifesavers. It hasn't always been this way – swimming in the public eye was banned until the early 1900s, when beachgoers were finally granted permission to frolic in the waves in neck-to-knee outfits. The first surf club at Bronte Beach was founded in 1903, and the first person to be rescued at Bondi was Charles Kingsford Smith, who later became Australia's greatest aviator. From the 1930s, the area was home to Jewish and east European immigrants escaping war-torn Europe. You'll still see synagogues and traditional kosher and cake shops scattered about, especially at neighbouring Bellevue Hill. By the early 1970s Bondi was jokingly referred to as 'west Auckland', thanks to a steady influx of New Zealanders.

Must Do

Enjoy Sydney's enviable outdoors lifestyle on the beach at Bondi (p.92), at the hillside cafes overlooking the ocean at Bronte (p.182), or with a drink in your hand at the lively pubs in Coogee (p.93).

Places of Interest

Bondi is one of Sydney's most famous suburbs. Home to humble working class apartments from the 1920s to 1950s, frenzied rebuilding and renovating has seen the area change dramatically since the 1990s (and prices skyrocket accordingly). The well-preserved 1920s Bondi Pavilion gives you a taste of what Bondi used to look like but these days the seaside suburb is a thriving mix of pale British backpackers, topless teenagers sunning themselves, body builders, media types and the odd international celebrity. If you're going swimming be wary of the southern end, which can have a strong riptide (dubbed 'the backpacker express').

The main street, Campbell Parade, has everything from basic takeaways to fine dining, tacky souvenirs and trendy street clothes. The best shopping is on Gould Street, an up-and-coming fashion precinct with trendy shops like Tuchuzy (see p.276) and Jatali. Better for bargains are the massive Bondi markets every Sunday, while the upmarket Westfield Bondi Junction (p.306) is large enough to get lost in for a day.

For drinks with a view, the Bondi Social and North Bondi RSL are hard to beat (get in early to grab an outdoor table) and on the southern end the bistro at Icebergs is a cheaper alternative to the famous see-and-be-seen restaurant above.

For food, fight for a coveted window seat at Trio Café (9365 6044) on Campbell Parade or while away a rainy day at Gertrude and Alice (p.338), which has second-hand books to browse through over coffee. Green's Cafe on Glenayr Avenue is the local's haunt, as it has good home-cooked fare away from the touristy main strip.

From Bondi you can walk to Coogee or Bronte along the well-trodden cliff-edge path for stunning views. Laid-back Coogee has a more relaxed community feel than Bondi and calmer waters (on a rough day there's always the women's-only McIvers Baths or the unisex Wileys Baths). The spirited Coogee Bay Hotel opposite the beach has live music or comedy most evenings, while the Beach Palace Hotel at the northern end has gorgeous water views from the balcony. You can't beat the seafood at A Fish Called Coogee on Coogee Bay Road and Barzura Café is a local favourite.

Clovelly is another safe swimming beach and nearby Gordon's Bay is a great snorkelling spot, teeming with tropical fish. On the headland between Bondi and Bronte is Waverley Cemetery where you'll find the graves of Australian poet Henry Lawson and aviation pioneer Lawrence Hargraves. For great city skyline views, including the Harbour Bridge and Opera House, head to Dudley Page Reserve on Military Road in Dover Heights.

Greater Sydney

Although few tourists venture far from the city, some of Sydney's outer suburbs give an interesting insight into Australia's past and multicultural future. Parramatta has been engulfed by urban sprawl and is now the geographical centre of Sydney. For a taste of classic suburban Sydney, head south to Cronulla. In the south-west lies Cabramatta, once famous as a drug centre and now known for its vibrant Asian food and shops.

Places of Interest

Parramatta became Sydeny's principal farming area when settlers discovered the rich soil there in 1789. Convicts saved settlers from starvation with the first grain harvest in 1789, cultivated in Experiment Farm Cottage. Situated in Harris Park, it is now open to the public. The Parramatta river was an important water source for early settlers and it is again becoming the focal point for the suburb, with lots of developments planned. The RiverCat is the best way to get here as it's faster and far more scenic than the train. Australia's oldest remaining building, Old Government House (1799-1816) still stands in Parramatta Park.

Must Do

Head to Cabramatta for some authentic Vietnamese. You'll feel miles from Sydney here as locals mostly speak and write in their native Asian languages.

Among the busy cafes and shops along lively Church Street is the delightful St John's Cathedral, built in 1803. The helpful Visitor Centre (www.visitsydney.org/parramatta) is on the corner of Church and Market Streets at the Parramatta Heritage Centre.

The RiverCat also stops at Homebush Bay, where the massive $470 million Sydney Olympic Park was built for the 2000 Games. You can get a train here from Central station. Pricey tours of the 85,000-seat Telstra Stadium (see p.112) are held daily unless there's an event and there's also an aquatic centre, tennis centre and Bicentennial Park with walking and cycling tracks.

Cronulla is the last stop on the southern train line and despite the trendy new developments, its relaxed surfing culture hasn't been wiped out. Right on the beach, the Cronulla Kiosk does a decent breakfast, while the Cronulla RSL Memorial Club has cheap drinks and meals with a view. Riots erupted here in 2005 when ethnic groups clashed with Anglo-Australians, and although problems simmer beneath the surface, the gorgeous beach is perfectly safe for visitors and has good surf.

Cabramatta has worked hard to overcome its public relations problems. Once renowned as the drug centre of Sydney (mostly around the railway station, dubbed 'Smack Express'), it is now better known as Sydney's culinary United Nations. A small Asian pocket 32 kms south west of the CBD, nowhere has more Vietnamese food. The arcades leading off the shopping and eating precinct of John Street have everything from tropical fruit to cheap Asian-made clothes. Don't leave without trying a traditional beef pho (Vietnamese noodle soup), sugar cane juice and a bright bean or sticky rice dessert. A good time to visit is during the annual Moon Festival, celebrated around September/October with traditional music, dance, lantern decorations and food stalls (www.fairfieldcity.nsw.gov.au).

Map 4-C2 ◀

Inner East

The inner east is a diverse mix of raunchy red light district (Kings Cross), vibrant gay centre (Darlinghurst) and posh, leafy boulevards (Woollahra). Formerly working class areas like Paddington have become highly desirable suburbs, while the once dilapidated wharves at Woolloomooloo now house fashionably expensive eateries frequented by the social set. The inner east offers stylish shopping and eating options and some of the city's liveliest pubs and clubs.

Place of Interest

Paddington was one of the first parts of Sydney to be settled. Prosperous businessmen set up home here, financing the gracious Victorian-era homes that now line Glenmore Road. Low rents after the second world war made it attractive for artists, but now only the wealthy can afford to live here. Oxford Street is the focal point for funky clothing boutiques. Paddington's shopping reputation grew after the markets were established in the 70s, and they are still great for local designer fashion, jewellery and unique homeware. Dominating the southern side of Oxford Street, the enormous Victoria Barracks was built in the 1840s and still houses soldiers today. Away from Oxford Street is fashionable Five Ways, a Parisian-style quarter popular for its cafe lifestyle. At the junction of Oxford Street and Jersey Road begins Woollahra, which has a distinctly well-to-do air and is the place to hunt for expensive antiques.

Must Do ◀

In summer, make the most of Sydney's balmy evenings by catching a flick at the outdoor cinema in Centennial Park (p.184). For a raucous night, take in the bars of Kings Cross (p.97).

The enormous Centennial Park is a treasured green expanse and hosts Moonlight Cinema (p.364) every summer. Adjoining Moore Park has facilities for tennis, golf, cricket and bowls. Next to the SCG (Sydney Cricket Ground, p.249) is Fox Studios, which houses state-of-the-art TV and film facilities; The Matrix, Star Wars II and III and Mission Impossible were all filmed here. At the Entertainment Quarter you'll find a cinema complex and several bars and restaurants.

Darlinghurst is the centre of Sydney's gay and lesbian scene (p.361) and home to the Mardi Gras (p.178) but it had a more sombre atmosphere in the 1840s when it housed a notorious jail. The lively restaurant quarter on Stanley Street has some good Italian food and is home to one of Sydney's best hairdressers, RAW (p.258). The Palace Cinemas (p.364) on Oxford Street shows mainly art house flicks and across the road are two late-night bookshops, Ariel and Berkelouw (p.273).

Parallel to Oxford Street, William Street is gaining a reputation for designer chic with stores like Collette Dinnigan (p.276). It runs from Hyde Park to the heritage-listed Coca Cola sign in Kings Cross, Australia's most densely populated area. First settled by the upper crust, then bohemian types, it gained its red light reputation when frequented by American servicemen on R&R during the Vietnam War. It has cleaned up in recent years, but its bawdy legacy remains and some of the strip club signs, including Porky's and Showgirls, are heritage listed. The main action is on Darlinghurst Road leading up to the El Alamein Fountain. It still attracts dodgy characters, but the heavy police presence makes it fairly safe. Quieter Kellet Street has some good restaurants and nearby popular bars include Hugo's (p.339). Darlinghurst Road becomes Macleay Street in the decidedly posher Potts Point, which boasts some of Sydney's most stylish restaurants, hotels and art deco apartments. Further down the hill is Woolloomooloo, home to the navy, community housing blocks and fancy new apartments (Russell Crowe owns a penthouse). The Finger Wharves now draw the social set to the ritzy restaurants. Don't miss the famous Harry's Café De Wheels pie shop (see p.348).

Once a sleepy fishing village, Double Bay's manicured, tree-lined streets are now home to Sydney's most exclusive fashion and jewellery boutiques (hence the nickname 'Double Pay'). Thankfully, swimming at picturesque Redleaf Pool by the harbour is free.

North Sydney

Once you cross the Harbour Bridge, the suburbs become leafier and more quiet. While many locals consider the north a little humdrum (this is where the old money lives), it is home to one of Sydney's favourite beaches, Manly, and has some gorgeous waterfront spots, particularly at Kirribilli and Cremorne Point. Crows Nest and Neutral Bay are densely packed with excellent restaurants and the beautiful marina at The Spit offers some fun water activities.

Places of Interest

At the base of the Harbour Bridge is Kirribilli, where Australia's Prime Minister lives. It has a quaint village-like atmosphere that really only comes alive on the fourth Saturday of every month when the markets (p.306) spill over Bradfield Park. To bag the best second-hand designer gear you'll have to be there before 07:30. Just down the road is Luna Park (p.187), Sydney's last remaining theme park.

North Sydney is a bustling business centre on weekdays but a ghost town at weekends. The Greenwood Shopping Centre has some good shops, particularly for fresh food. The small Civic Centre Park near Stanton Library, on Miller Street, hosts outdoor summer noodle markets with live entertainment on Friday nights (November to March until 22:00), and fresh food markets with organic goods on the third Saturday of every month. Crows Nest has endless eating options and Macro (p.282), the biggest organic store and cafe in the area. Some of the best eateries include the noisy Thai Riffic (p.345) on Falcon Street (watch the fireballs in the open kitchen). On Willoughby Road, try Phuong (p.346) for Vietnamese. Tucked away on Holtermann Street (off Willougby Road) is the ultra modern Garfish (p.340), which has top class seafood prepared in an open kitchen.

The dense unit blocks of Neutral Bay and Cremorne are home to many city office workers, and some apartments have stunning water views. Busy Military Road has great restaurants, notably Vera Cruz (Mexican, p.337) and Radio Cairo Café (African, p.315). The Oaks (p.356) on Military Road has a fabulous beer garden and good wood fired pizza. The area's best assets are waterside – the Cremorne Point walk loops past the MacCallum harbourside pool and the lighthouse on Robertson's Point, both offering superb city views. Further up near Mosman is leafy Taronga Zoo (p.190), which also has gorgeous views from its hillside position.

Easily accessible by ferry from Circular Quay, Manly is the jewel of the north with a stunning beach and vibrant cafe culture. A makeover of Manly Wharf has brought trendy restaurants and the swish Manly Wharf Hotel (p.336). You'll find Manly Tourist Information (www.manlytourism.com.au) near McDonalds. The pedestrian shopping strip, the Corso, links the wharf with Manly Beach but the quirkier shops are in the arcades and streets off the main drag. The small Saturday markets on the lower end of Sydney Road have quality goods.

If you're hungry, take away fish n' chips from the Manly Fish Market & Cafe (9976 3777) are sure to satisfy, while the swankier Bluewater Cafe (9976 2051) has a good view. For cheap, healthy burgers, try the vegetarian Green's Cafe (9130 6181) on Sydney Road. The main beach, South Steyne, is lined with shade-giving Norfolk Pines. Follow the footpath south to sheltered Shelley Beach and hike up the headland for stunning ocean views. Even more rewarding is the four-hour Manly Scenic Walkway, which takes you from Manly to the Spit Bridge, past secluded beaches and parkland (the tourist office has maps).

Must Do

The Manly Ferry (p.194) is a cheap and cheerful harbour cruise that gives you the opportunity to explore the lively seaside suburb when you get off. The monthly Kirribilli markets are among the best in Sydney.

Northern Beaches

Extending 30km north of Manly, the northern beaches are among the most stunning stretches of sand in Sydney. This lush bushland area is flanked by beautiful coast on one side and the boating haven of Pittwater on the other; it's only one hour's drive from the city but the strong surf culture and fishing village atmosphere feels a world away from the rat race. It was only in the 1920s, when a tramline from Manly to Narrabeen was completed, that cheap fibro cottages began to pop up among the relatively untouched bushland. You'll still see the odd beachfront shack, but the upper reaches of the private peninsula are increasingly becoming an expensive playground for the rich and famous or wealthy retirees.

Places of Interest

From pretty Freshwater beach, the coast curves around to Dee Why. The lagoon is popular with families and the main strip, The Strand, is jam-packed with eateries, notably Sea La Vie (9984 8644) for breakfast and Moltofino (9981 2061) for incredibly rich Italian hot chocolate. The buzzing, licensed Surf Rock Hotel (www.surfrockhotel.com.au) on Collaroy beach is a good waterfront food option or grab fish 'n' chips from the unpretentious Ocean Master (9970 6188) takeaway on North Narrabeen beach.

Must Do

The northern beaches are among Sydney's best - and they're far less crowded than those in the east. Stop for lunch in the village-atmosphere of Avalon or, like many celebrities, spend the day at the secluded but stylish Palm Beach.

The most beautiful spots lie beyond Mona Vale, where the Barrenjoey Peninsula narrows, offering rolling surf on one side and Pittwater, with its luxury marinas, on the other. The headland above Mona Vale is a fabulous, if windy, picnic spot. Nestled at the base of a cliff, Bilgola Beach is very pretty, while hang gliders head to Warriewood. For some authentic Australian fare, The Copperpan (9999 5740), on Narrabeen Park Parade, does heavenly sausages and homemade strudel. Avalon is the shopping highlight with a range of gourmet dining options and posh clothes shops. It is home to La Banette (9918 2948) on Avalon Parade; a tiny organic store and a sensational bakery with excellent pastries, quiche and sourdough bread. The cosy, U-shaped beach sits between two hills, dotted with stately mansions, and is popular with families. It's one of the few beaches with Norfolk pines offering shade directly on the sand. Even more secluded is Palm Beach, the northern-most point of Sydney; soak up its relaxed vibe, spend the day on the water or catch a ferry to The Basin, a popular camping spot.

The northern beaches will only disappoint if you're into bar hopping – the nightlife is virtually non-existent, although there are some great pubs, notably the Newport Arms (9997 4900). The enormous beer garden overlooking Pittwater makes it one of the most picturesque drinking holes in Sydney and the chic Barrenjoey House (9974 4001) is a nice spot for a sunset drink. The licensed Beachhouse Cafe (9918 7825) in Avalon is opening a cocktail bar in 2007 and has excellent Asian teas and good coffee.

If you really want to escape, for $10 you can get to tiny Scotland Island; ferries go between 08:30 and 19:30 from Church Point wharf and apart from the annual October Fair Day, it's very quiet. Only accessible by water, its isolation has drawn a community of writers and artists. The welcoming hosts at Scotland Island Lodge (9979 3301) offer spacious rooms in a homely atmosphere. There are no shops or restaurants on the island, but Friday nights have a real community feel as locals gather near the quaint old Post Office at Church Point wharf and sink a few beers before heading home in their tinny - a small rowboat with an outboard motor.

Palm Beach

South Sydney

South Sydney is an intriguing mix of seedy and stylish. By the 1940s it languished solely on the seedy side with rough pubs and filthy streets, but as the young and upwardly mobile were priced out of Woollahra and Paddington, they snapped up properties ripe for renovation in Surry Hills. The former industrial area of Waterloo is fast becoming a hip strip. This is yet to happen in Redfern, historically an area plagued with poverty and indigenous social issues.

Places of Interest

Must Do

Sydney's most creative culinary options are away from the waterside tourist traps, and the astounding variety at Surry Hills will satisfy even the fussiest tastebuds.

Surry Hills has well and truly ditched its dingy heritage and embraced a hip restaurant scene, mainly on Crown Street. Here you'll find some of Sydney's most popular restaurants, including Billy Kwong (p.320), and Bill's (p.321); a Sunday brunch institution. Other satisfying options include Longrain (p.322), Tabou (9319 5682), Café Mint (p.338), Red Lantern (p.346) and Bentley Restaurant & Bar on Commonwealth Street (9332 2344). Surry Hills also has a quirky edge – sink into a sagging vintage couch at the homely Lemon Cafe (9380 5242) or play mahjong at the Mahjong Room (9361 3985) on Crown Street while sampling delicious dim sum (only on the first Saturday of every month).

Drinking has long been a popular pastime in Surry Hills but the pubs have got fancy over the years. Among the best is the Crown Street landmark Clock Hotel (9331 5333), which has a breezy balcony and good food upstairs. The Dolphin (9331 4800) and White Horse (8333 9999) nearby are also popular.

The arts scene is thriving here and at the forefront is the Belvoir Street Theatre, an intimate performance space that has a reputation for being radical. The shows often feature big Aussie names like Geoffrey Rush, Hugo Weaving and Cate Blanchett (www.belvoir.com.au). Don't miss the Brett Whiteley Studio (p.166) on Raper Street – following his death in 1992, the artist's coveted contemporary Sydney landscape paintings have achieved record prices.

Surry Hills was once the heart of the fashion and rag trade and there are still some excellent factory warehouses on Fouveaux Street and Kippax Street. For second-hand bargains, the best time to go is on the first Saturday of each month when the markets are held on Crown Street. For antiques, head to the Sydney Antique Centre (9361 3244) on South Dowling Street.

Redfern is the heart of Aboriginal Sydney and has a troubled history. Eveleigh Street, not far from the railway station, has a rough reputation. The government has plans to redevelop the area but riots erupted in 2004 when an Aborigine man died in custody. See p.18 for more on this.

Plans are also underway for a new neighbouring suburb, Green Square. It already has its own railway station and some new residential apartment blocks but the atmosphere is yet to liven up. Waterloo is developing fast, particularly around Danks Street, which boasts some excellent art galleries, cafes like Danks Street Depot (p.347) and food retailers with imported goodies such as Fratelli Fresh (9699 3174).

On the southern fringe of the city, Erskineville is an unofficial gay and lesbian centre. Just 3kms from the CBD and bordering Newtown, it has some old, narrow terrace houses; a relic of its working class past. Its most celebrated pub is The Rose of Australia (9565 1441), an unpretentious spot known for its beer battered chips and relaxed atmosphere.

The Harbour

Flowing between the sandstone cliffs of North and South Head, there are calm bays, national parks and harbour islands to explore on foot or by ferry. Much of the harbour foreshore has been spared from development because of its military significance and is now administered by the Sydney Harbour Trust. Five harbour islands have been joined to the mainland through land reclamation, including Garden Island (the naval base near Kings Cross), Bennelong Point (where the Opera House stands) and Darling Island (now part of Pyrmont).

Must Do

Walking along the serene foreshore is a treat - try the Hermitage Walking Track in the east or Manly Scenic Walkway from the Spit Bridge on the north side.

Places of Interest

The best way to explore the harbour islands is on a National Parks and Wildlife tour (www.nationalparks.nsw.gov.au). They offer regular tours to Fort Denison (p.168), a former penal colony prison visible from Circular Quay, and Goat Island near east Balmain. Water taxis (p.42) will take you to tranquil Clark Island (off Darling Point) and Rodd Island (near Birkenhead Point). Numbers are restricted to both and you'll need to bring your own food and water. Shark Island, off Rose Bay, is serviced hourly (09:45-16:55) by Matilda Cruises (www.matilda.com.au) and has a sandy beach, shelter and good picnic facilities. There's no shop but drinking water is available.

Strewn with celebrity-owned mansions and flanked by luxury marinas, the ritzy eastern suburbs like Rushcutters Bay, Elizabeth Bay and Rose Bay boast some of Sydney's most expensive real estate. Some of its historic architectural highlights, such as the grand Elizabeth Bay House and Vaucluse House (see p.174) are open to the public. Rose Bay is the harbour's largest bay and is popular for sailing, rowing and sail boarding because of its sheltered geographical position. Seaplanes have been taking off from the bay since the 1960s – you'll see them parked near the swanky Catalina waterfront restaurant (p.322). Less busy than the Bondi to Bronte walk is the Hermitage Walking Track, which has

spectacular ocean views. It starts from Bay View Hill Road between the imposing Kambala School and Rose Bay Convent, and takes you via some lovely swimming spots to Nielsen Park, in about one hour. Nielsen Park is a tranquil tree-filled place and has a calm netted bay, but gets busy on weekends. Watson's Bay is a harbour highlight thanks to the fabulous city views across the water and quality seafood at Doyles on the beach (p.340). There's a cheaper Doyle's kiosk nearby, and the lively Watson's Bay Hotel next door also serves their fare. The pub's inviting beer garden is always busy and the adjacent Robertson Park is popular for weekend picnics. On the ocean side are the perilous cliffs of The Gap, sadly a well-known suicide spot. A walking track leads from The Gap to South Head past Camp Cove, a popular family beach, and Lady Bay, a nudist beach.

On the north side, Balmoral is one of the prettiest harbour bays. It's hard to imagine this genteel area was once home to 19th century bohemian artists living in tents. The partially shady bay is divided by Rocky Point, a good picnic spot. Off the sand there's a decent takeaway and bottle shop but the highlight is the mod Oz food at Bathers Pavilion (see p.319). Avoid swimming here after rain as pollution levels rise. Perhaps the best way to admire the tranquil national parkland along the water at Middle Harbour is from a kayak (see p.235). At the 1924-built Spit Bridge, traffic can be slow as the bridge still opens to let tall boats through. From here you can walk to Manly on the Manly Scenic Walkway (see p.188).

West Sydney

Western Sydney is a culturally diverse and entertaining area with some of the best pubs, restaurants and shopping in the city. Shortly after settlement, the wealthy began building grand country estates in the area (many are still standing in Annandale). However, its proximity to the port eventually led to an influx of manual workers, followed by post war immigrants in search of cheap shelter. It still has an eclectic residential mix of up-and-coming professionals, students and new arrivals.

Anzac Bridge

Must Do

See Sydney's alternative side at Newtown and Glebe, with funky fashion and ethnic restaurants. Jam-packed with moody pubs, Balmain is the best place for a traditional Aussie pub crawl. Leichhardt and Haberfield are the best spots to sample authentic Italian.

Places of Interest

Glebe has the highest number of 1860s-70s cottages and terraces in Australia, many with classic lacework verandas. The main street, Glebe Point Road, has a laid-back, village atmosphere, with a strong 'new age' slant and excellent cafes (many cater to the needs of gluten, dairy and wheat-free diets). As well as organic shops, it's packed with alternative healing centres.

Glebe's traditional student culture has been invaded by upwardly mobile thirty-somethings who relish the hip cafe lifestyle and specialty stores like Gleebooks (p.274). Glebe is at its liveliest on Saturdays when the public school hosts markets (p.308). Across the road, Badde Manors cafe is a gem. For a drink, The Nag's Head (9660 1591) just off Glebe Point Road is a cosy, pokies-free pub. Broadway Shopping Centre (p.300) is useful for groceries and also has a cinema.

Nearby Newtown is undergoing gradual gentrification and its former gritty atmosphere has been visibly toned down (although you'll still see some dreadlocked locals with multiple piercings). Busy King Street is great for shopping, from vintage goods to music and clothes – highlights include Newtown Old Wares and Yoshi Jones on King Street and Prettydog on Brown Street. The pub and restaurant scene comes alive at night – try the recently renovated Bank Hotel and Kuletos for cocktails, and Banks Thai (p.344), Thanh Binh (Vietnamese, 9557 1175) or African Feeling (p.315) for a bite to eat. For entertainment, the Dendy Cinema (p.364) often has art-house flicks, while the Enmore Theatre on Enmore Road is an intimate live music venue.

The former working class suburb of Balmain, the birthplace of Australia's Labor Party in 1891, is popular with middle class professionals, particularly local actors and artists. Although largely made up of multi-million dollar houses, the character-filled pubs remain. Among the best are the Exchange Hotel on Beattie Street (9810 1171), the London Hotel on Darling Street (9810 1171) and the recently upgraded Three Weeds in Evans Street, Rozelle (9818 2788). A good time to visit is on Saturdays when the local markets take over the St Andrew's church forecourt.

Leichhardt is the centre of Sydney's Italian community. Norton Street has some of the best Italian grub in town and a good independent cinema, The Palace (p.364). The Italian Forum (a central square overlooked by apartments, shops and cafes) is packed with families on the weekend. The Berkelouw Bookstore (see p.273) has great coffee upstairs, but die-hard caffeine addicts head to the much-loved Bar Italia (9560 9981) at the other end of Norton Street. Further West is the quiet Italian area of Haberfield, a suburb of classic Federation style houses with wide verandas and a few cafes.

Pyrmont is having a slow, expensive overhaul with modern apartment blocks and renovated eateries on Harris Street. The main attraction for visitors here is Star City Casino, a complex of restaurants, theatres, gaming tables and pokies. Check out the tasteless fake palm trees and bright four metre high fish tanks. Nearby Pyrmont Bay Park hosts growers' markets on the fourth Saturday of every month (07:00-11:00).

163

Museums, Heritage & Culture

Sport and surf might be Sydney's first form of entertainment, but culture vultures won't be disappointed here. The city boasts some world-class galleries and museums and scraps with Melbourne to be the arts and cultural centre of Australia. There is an extraordinary range of diverse works, from Aboriginal and Australian art to international touring exhibitions. The performing arts are also highly regarded. The Sydney Opera Company is the third busiest in the world and the Sydney Dance Company and Bangara Dance Company have achieved international acclaim.

Archaeological Sites

Two excavations have been undertaken where the remains of early architecture and engineering have been uncovered. Both offer an interesting peek into colonial life, from household articles of the time to the first waterworks project.

41 Bridge St ◄
Central

First Government House Site

6274 1111 | www.hht.net.au

The remains of First Government House, which was demolished in 1846, were rediscovered in 1983. This was Australia's largest urban archaeological excavation and the ten-year project revealed some long-hidden artefacts such as bricks, bottles, ceramics, tobacco pipes and printing remnants. Australia's first newspaper, *The Sydney Gazette*, was printed here in 1803.

Today, it is home to the Museum of Sydney. First Government Place (the square in front of the museum) is where First Government House actually stood. *The Edge Of The Trees* sculpture by Janet Laurence and Fiona Foley symbolises the first encounter between the indigenous Cadigal people (who watched the strangers struggle ashore from here in 1788) and the First Fleet.

Circular Quay ◄
Central

Tank Stream

8239 2211

The Tank Stream, a stream of fresh water that flowed into Sydney Harbour (roughly between what is now Pitt Street and George Street) is the reason Sydney was founded. Convicts were forced to dig holding tanks in the water stream when the flow turned to a trickle. Years of use led to pollution, and it became virtually an open sewer, forcing authorities to cover it. Although it still flows beneath the city as part of the stormwater system, five markings on the concrete pavement are all that's left to indicate where the watercourse once ran. If you're interested in going underground for a closer look, tours of the water works are run twice a year (usually in April and November).

Art Galleries

Other options **Art & Craft Supplies** p.271, **Art** p.271

Since Sydney hastily erected its first gallery in 1879 (which no longer stands), the city has scrapped with Melbourne to be the country's art capital. The stunning scenery has inspired many of Australia's finest artists, and thanks to renowned institutions like The Sydney College of Fine Arts, it's now nurturing a new generation of budding artists. Make sure you don't miss the Art Gallery of NSW and the Museum of Contemporary Art – both will give you a good insight into what art Down Under is all about.

2 Danks St ◄
Surry Hills

2 Danks Street

www.2danksstreet.com.au

Once a rundown light industrial site, this hip bohemian strip has had an artsy overhaul; ten commercial galleries showcase works here by leading Australian, Aborigine and international artists. Stella Downer Fine Art has interesting contemporary Australian works while the Conny Dietzschold Gallery is known for its quality international and local mix. If hunger pangs strike, try the upmarket Dank Street Depot eatery (p.347), which has simple but satisfying mod Oz food. Open Tuesday to Saturday, 11:00-18:00. Free admission. Wheelchair access.

Art Gallery Rd
The Domain

Art Gallery of NSW

9225 1744 | www.artgallery.nsw.gov.au

This is one of Sydney's most distinctive landmarks and behind the walls of the elegant 1909-built facade lies a rich and controversial history. This gallery houses three floors of Australian, Asian, European and contemporary art, including works by big Aussie names like Arthur Streeton, William Dobell, Sidney Nolan, and Brett Whiteley. Each year it hosts Australia's most prominent and controversial art prize for portrait painting; the Archibald. Don't miss the Asian art section in the glass light box facing Woolloomooloo - a recent $16.4 million extension. There's an excellent collection of works by Aborigines and Torres Strait Islanders on level one in the Yiribana Gallery. The canteen on level one has gorgeous water views (open daily, 10:00-16:30, with evening dining on Wednesdays until 20:30). If you want a free appraisal of any artwork you own, expert staff members are available each Thursday at 10:00 in the Gallery Research Library. Three hours will only scratch the surface of what Australia's second largest gallery has to offer.

General admission is free (charges apply for special exhibitions); open from 10:00-17:00 and until 21:00 on Wednesdays.

275 Pitt St
Central

Arthouse Hotel

9284 1200 | www.arthousehotel.com.au

The Arthouse is slightly different to most other galleries. For starters, it's in a pub, but then again, who said art appreciation has to be stiff and serious? Head to the downstairs Gallery Bar where you can admire the (normally good) artwork with a drink in hand. Art classes are held on Mondays at 18:30 in the Dome Restaurant – it's free but you need to bring your own materials. The pricey but excellent restaurant is packed during business lunch hours.

Open Monday to Tuesday 11:00-00:00; Wednesday to Thursday 11:00-01:00; Friday 11:00-03:00; Saturday 17:00-06:00.

43-51 Cowper Wharf Rd
Woolloomooloo

Artspace

9368 1899 | www.artspace.org.au

Behind the historic facade of the Gunnery Building, and just a few steps from the harbour, lies this slick modern space. Designed to showcase experimental photography and new media, there are 12 stainless steel furnished studios for artists to live in whilst fashioning their work.

Artspace sometimes hosts live performances (some of which are quite controversial), along with book launches and contemporary events like speed dating. Allow at least one hour to see it all. Open Tuesday to Saturday from 11:00-17:00. Free admission. Wheelchair access.

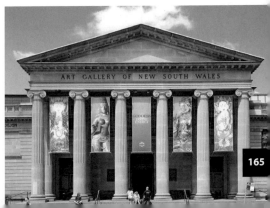

257 Oxford St
Paddington

Australian Centre for Photography
9332 1455 | www.acp.au.com
This is another spot to see experimental, and sometimes controversial, photography and multimedia (see also Artspace). Exhibitions change every six weeks. If you're inspired to learn how to coax art from your own camera, enquire about their vast range of photography workshops, held in state-of-the-art studios. Allow one hour to browse the exhibitions. Open Tuesday to Friday 12:00-19:00, Saturday to Sunday 10:00-18:00. Free admission.

24 Glenmore Rd
Paddington

Australian Galleries
9380 8744 | www.australiangalleries.com.au
The first Australian Galleries opened in Melbourne in 1956, and was one of the few places that showcased emerging post-war Australian artists, including Arthur Boyd and Sidney Nolan, who went on to become international stars. The Sydney branch in Paddington continues in the tradition today, showing contemporary paintings by artists such as Jeffrey Smart and innovative works on paper by new talent.
The works-on-paper gallery is at 24 Glenmore Road, Paddington and is open Monday to Saturday 10:00-18:00 and the painting gallery is at 15 Roylstone Street, Paddington and is open Monday to Saturday 10:00-18:00 and Sunday 12:00-17:00. Free admission on Sundays.

2 Raper St
Surry Hills

Brett Whiteley Studio
9225 1881 | www.brettwhiteley.org
After the gifted and controversial Australian artist died in 1992, his wife turned his studio, once an old T-shirt factory, into a memorial. As well as browsing his awe-inspiring contemporary works you'll get a glimpse into the artist's life with unfinished paintings and objects just as he left them. Poetry readings are held here on Sundays and regular art workshops are open to the public. A couple of hours will pass in a flash here. Open 10:00-16:00, weekends only. Admission is $7 for adults and $5 for concessions.

Harbourside Centre
Darling Harbour

Gavala Aboriginal Art and Cultural Centre
9212 7232 | www.gavala.com.au
This is Sydney's only gallery dedicated to indigenous art, with an extensive collection of modern and traditional styles. The exhibition space has a shop, so you can take home authentic Aboriginal artworks. Choose from iconic boomerangs, masks, statues and ceremonial jewellery. These pieces are a step above the Australiana found in souvenir shops. Keanu Reeves, Prince Harry and The Red Hot Chili Peppers have all stopped by to snap up a hand-painted didgeridoo. Open 10:00-21:00 daily. Wheelchair access.

1 Hickson Rd
The Rocks

Ken Done Gallery
9247 2740 | www.kendone.com
Ken Done's distinctive, bold depictions of the Australian sea and landscape have made him one of the country's most successful commercial artists. His permanent collection, including silkscreen prints as well as canvas and paper works, is on display in the historic Steam Navigation Building at The Rocks. There is a tiny shop in the gallery; for his wearable art, head to the two-level shop further up the road opposite the MCA. Open daily 10:00-17:30.

57-59 Macleay St
Potts Point

Martin Browne Fine Art
9331 7997 | www.martinbrownefineart.com
This bright yellow building caused a stir in the 1970s when a group of local artists moved in and splashed their radical, experimental art all over the walls. Reopened in

2003, as a slick show space for modern Australian art, with its curved walls, a massive open-air skylight and an indoor fish pond, the gallery makes almost as much of a statement as what hangs on the walls. Open Tuesday to Sunday 11:00-18:00.

Museum of Contemporary Art

140 George St
The Rocks

9245 2400 | *www.mca.com.au*
This striking building is a must-do if you're interested in 19th and 20th century art. Sitting right on Circular Quay, this beautiful 1950s Art Deco building has been home to more than 5,000 pieces by Australian and international artists since 1991. Works from the 1960s onwards are on display, including significant contemporary Aboriginal collections. With an outside terrace overlooking the harbour, the MCA Cafe (p.349) is a popular spot for locals to linger over weekend brunch and is open every day; for reservations call 9241 4253. More spectacular still is the view from the Harbour Terrace on level five, which is often booked for functions. Allow two hours for a visit. Open daily 10:00-17:00. Wheelchair access.

Object Gallery

417 Bourke St
Surry Hills

9361 4511 | *www.object.com.au*
Also known as the Australian Centre for Craft and Design, this non-profit organisation showcases funky modern furniture, fashion, glass, ceramics and contemporary jewellery made by the cream of Australia's craft crop. Many of their innovative artists also supply to the gallery shop, called Collect. Open from 11:00-18:00 Tuesday to Sunday. Free admission.

S.H. Ervin

National Trust Centre
Watson Rd
Observatory Hill
The Rocks

9258 0173 | *www.nsw.nationaltrust.org.au*
The hundreds of paintings that don't make it into the coveted Archibald Prize exhibition at the Art Gallery of NSW can be seen here at the Salon des Refusés; an alternative exhibition jokingly dubbed 'The Archibald Rejects'. It took its name from the original Salon des Refusés, which was staged by Napoleon in Paris in 1863, for those artists whose works had been refused by the official Salon – including Cézanne and Manet. Talks are held every Sunday at 15:00 (free with exhibition entry). The 1856 building was once part of a school, but is now the headquarters of the National Trust. They host seven exhibitions celebrating Australian art each year. Open 11:00-17:00 Tuesday to Sunday. Admission $6.

State Library

Macquarie St
Nxt Parliament House
The Royal Botanic Gardens

9273 1414 | *www.sl.nsw.gov.au*
Next door to Parliament House, the Mitchell Wing of the library has exhibitions on Australian historical documents, including the Tasman Map drawn by Dutch explorer Abel Tasman in 1604. The library's 1906-built sandstone Neoclassical facade is linked to the modern extension by a glass walkway. Groups of up to 20 can book a free volunteer-led history and heritage tour of the library (75 minutes, call 9273 1518). Open 09:00-17:00 Monday to Friday, 11:00-17:00 Saturday to Sunday. Free admission. Wheelchair access.

Tim Olsen Gallery

76 Paddington St
Paddington

9360 9854 | *www.timolsengallery.com*
Well-known among the arty crowd, this two-level gallery represents 25 artists; all considered to have either long established reputations or outstanding potential. On display you'll find works by esteemed Australian painter Tim Olsen but the gallery also showcases work in two other premises (Woollahra and Windsor, just a stone's throw from the main gallery). Open Tuesday to Friday 11:00-18:00, Saturday 11:00-17:00.

Forts

Australia has never fought a war on its own shores. As a vast island nation, thousands of miles from its nearest neighbours, Aussies had few occasions to truly fear an invasion, so forts were generally considered unnecessary. However, a few were eventually erected to protect the major harbour entry points.

Congwong Bay
Outer North

Bare Island

9247 5033 | *www.nationalparks.nsw.gov.au*

Built in 1885 to protect Sydney's back door and the colony's water supply in the Botany Wetlands, the fort was decommissioned in the early 1900s and became a home for war veterans for 50 years. Linked by a footbridge to the seaside suburb of La Perouse, it's now part of Botany Bay National Park. The museum in the red-brick clock tower details the story of ill-fated explorer Comte De La Perouse who landed at Botany Bay a mere six days after the First Fleet. Open Wednesday to Sunday 10:00-16:00. Admission: Adult $5.50, child $3.30. You can take a guided tour on Sundays at 13:30 and 14:30. Adult $7.70 child $5.50, families $22.

Sydney Harbour

Fort Denison

9247 5033 | *www.npws.nsw.gov.au*

Dubbed Pinchgut because of the meagre rations available, this is where convicts who committed petty crimes were kept in the early days of settlement. The harbour island was fortified in 1875 for fear of Russian expansion in the pacific. Built from 8,000 tonnes of sandstone quarried from nearby Kurraba Point in Neutral Bay, it was named after Sir William Denison, then Governor of NSW. The fort's canons are still fired daily at 13:00, originally done so sailors could set their ship chronometers. The excellent Blue Rock Café (licensed) is surprisingly  affordable with great harbour views but you can also picnic on the lawn. National Parks offers guided tours to the island, departing from Cadman's Cottage, 110 George Street, The Rocks, Monday to Friday, 11.45-15:00; Saturday to Sunday 11:30-15:00 and 14:30-15:15. (Adults $22, child $18, family $72, incl. return ferry). They also offer catered brunch tours on Saturdays and Sundays from 09:00-11:40 ($47 adult, $43 child).

North Head
Scenic Drive
Manly

North Fort

9247 5033 | *www.northfort.org.au*

This fort was built in 1934, for fear of a naval attack from Japan. The guided tours allow you to explore the maze of tunnels (bring a torch so you can see) or check out the ancient guns at the National Artillery Museum. There's an onsite cafe with stunning water views as well as picnic grounds surrounded by bushland. Tours are held on the fourth Sunday of each month at 10:30 (adult $39, child $29, including lunch).

Temples

Freedom of religion is guaranteed in Australia and you won't struggle to find a place of worship while you're here, see p.349. The most common religion is Christianity, so most of the city's historic churches are Anglican, Roman Catholic or Uniting and many are heritage listed. Being an immigrant society, Judaism, Islam, Buddhism and Hinduism are also represented, mostly out in the suburbs.

173 Mona Vale Rd
Outer North

Baha'i Temple

9998 9221 | www.bahai.org.au

One of only seven Baha'i temples in the world, this 40 metre high landmark has perched on its hilltop home in the northern beaches since 1961. The Baha'i community believes in the oneness of humanity regardless of national, cultural and religious differences – a belief most of multicultural Australia shares. Public services are held every Sunday at 11:00, including performances by the acapella choir and readings from various religious texts (they don't have their own). Volunteer guides are on hand at the visitors centre to show you around the tranquil surrounds. Open Monday to Friday 09:00-17:00, Saturday to Sunday 10:00-14:00.

Cnr Argyle and
Lower Fort St
The Rocks

Garrison Church

9247 1268 | www.thegarrisonchurch.org.au

Officially named Holy Trinity, Sydney's oldest church became known as the Garrison because numerous regiments from the nearby garrison worshipped here after the foundation stone was laid in 1840. Stone was used from the Argyle cut, so the church was quarried from its immediate surroundings. Notable features include the brilliantly coloured east window and the carved red cedar pulpit. It has a small museum featuring historical and military items. Open 09:00-17:00 daily. Free admission.

187a Elizabeth St
Central

The Great Sydney Synagogue

9267 2477 | www.greatsynagogue.org.au

Consecrated in 1878, it was inspired by English synagogues of the time in London and has a beautiful ceiling embellished with hundreds of tiny gold leaf stars. There's also a library that houses some 200 old books including impressive bibles dating back to 1667. The museum houses an interesting collection of Jewish artefacts (textiles, ritual silver and paintings), which you can see as part of the tour. This runs from Tuesday to Thursday at 12:00. Services Friday 17:30, Saturday 08:45.

Berkely Rd
Outer South

Nan Tien Temple

4272 0600 | www.nantien.org.au

Although it's clearly quite new (it was built in 1995), this is still an impressive sight and it's the largest Buddhist temple in the southern hemisphere. The beautiful landscaped garden and the 10,000 or so Buddhas in the main shrine are open to the public. Shoes and hats need to be removed before entering the temple and you should be suitably covered (no skimpy singlets). They also offer weekend meditation retreats from $80, which includes one night's shared accommodation at the onsite three-star lodge. Open Tuesday to Sunday 09:00-17:00. Guided tours $4, Saturday to Sunday at 13:00. Free one-hour meditation and chanting sessions are on Saturdays at 13:00.

Cnr of George
and Bathurst St
Central

St Andrew's Cathedral

9265 1661 | www.cathedral.sydney.anglican.asn.au

Although the foundation stone of the Edmund Blacket-designed cathedral was laid in 1819 (making it Sydney's oldest), the sandstone construction wasn't fully completed

169

until 1874. The twin spires were inspired by England's York Minster and notable features include the windows depicting Jesus' life and images relating to St Andrew. It underwent major restoration work in 1999-2000. Open Monday, Tuesday, Friday and Saturday 10:00-16:00; Wednesday 08:00-20:00; Thursday 10:00-18:30; Sunday 07:30-20:00. Admission is free.

173 King St ◀
Newtown

St James Church
8227 1300 | *www.stjameschurchsydney.org.au*
Originally intended to serve as the colony's first courthouse, this building was converted to a church halfway through its construction. When it was completed in 1824, this colonial Georgian-style, Anglican church became a notable landmark for ships sailing into the harbour. These days it's dwarfed by the surrounding office blocks. Check out the plaques inside, which commemorate Australian explorers and give a small insight into some of the hardships they faced. Guided tours are free, Monday to Friday at 14:30.

Cnr York ◀
& Clarence Sts
Central

St Philip's Church
9247 1071 | *www.stphilips-sydney.org.au*
On one of Sydney's busiest public transport streets and flanked by tall office blocks on both sides, this tiny Victorian Gothic-style church was built by architect Edmund Blacket (who also designed St Andrews Cathedral). Work was disrupted in 1851, when the stonemasons left to try their luck in the gold fields but it was eventually completed in 1856. Open Monday to Friday 09:00-17:00.

Cnr College & ◀
Cathedral Sts
Central

St Mary's Cathedral
9220 0400 | *www.sydney.catholic.org.au*
The original St Mary's catholic church was destroyed by fire in 1865, and rebuilt in 1886. The twin spires you see today were added at a cost of $8 million in 2000 (that's why they're lighter in colour than the rest of the building), to match the original plans drawn up by William Wardell in 1865. Notable features include the large rose window and the terrazzo floor in the crypt, which shows the six days of creation and where exhibitions are sometimes held. This grand building is quite a prominent landmark, sitting just over the road from Hyde Park and marking the entrance to Art Gallery Road and The Domain. It is also the seat of the archbishop of Sydney. The cathedral is open from Monday to Friday, 06:30-18:30 and Saturday 08:00-18:30. There are tours on Sundays at 12:00.

Heritage Sites

Other options **Museums** p.175, **Art** p.271

Sydney has only been around since 1788, but despite its short history it has an impressive range of heritage-listed buildings; from early settlement to more modern architectural wonders. Dotted mainly around the harbour, CBD and eastern suburbs, many of the historic buildings are now surrounded by office blocks or residential units, but most are in top condition and open for public viewing. Some are now museums, while others are used as public spaces. During the year the National Trust (www.nsw.nationaltrust.org.au) hosts a Heritage Festival at various locations around the city.

110 George St
The Rocks

Cadmans Cottage

9247 5033 | www.nationalparks.nsw.gov.au
Now the Sydney Harbour National Park Information Centre, this 1816 house is Sydney's oldest building. The modest cottage was named after John Cadman, a convict who was sent to New South Wales for stealing a horse, only to later become Superintendent of Government Boats. There is a tiny museum dedicated to him in the cottage. The remains of the original sea wall mark where the cottage used to sit, directly on the water, before land was reclaimed. Open Monday to Friday 09:30-16:30; Saturday to Sunday 10:00-16:30.

31 Alfred St
Circular Quay

Customs House

9242 8595 | www.cityofsydney.nsw.gov.au
Thought to be the spot where the local Eora people watched the First Fleet land, Customs House is still the first port of call for people and goods arriving in Sydney. Since some major renovations in 2005, it has become a focal point for tourists and locals with busy eateries (Café Sydney has fabulous food and views) and a public library. It is worth a visit just for the glass covered walkway in the foyer where the continually updated 500:1 scale model gives you an impressive overview of Sydney's CBD. Free admission. Open Monday to Friday 08:00-00:00, Saturday 10:00-00:00, Sunday & public holidays 11:00-17:00.

7 Onslow Ave
Elizabeth Bay

Elizabeth Bay House

9356 3022 | www.hht.net.au
Honoured with the title of 'finest house in the colony' when it was finished in the 1830s, this elegant Greek revival villa was home to Australia's first Colonial Secretary, Alexander Macleay, and his wife Eliza. Once surrounded by an extensive garden of native and exotic plants, it still boasts a sweeping view of the yachts in Elizabeth Bay harbour. Coffee and tea are offered, but it's just a stone's throw from the busy restaurant precinct of Potts Point. Open Tuesday to Sunday 10:00-16:30. Adult $8, child $4, family $17. Wheelchair access.

70 Alice St
Rose Hill

Elizabeth Farm

9635 9488 | www.hht.net.au
This tranquil estate was the birthplace of two iconic symbols; the Aussie homestead with its deep shady verandas, and the country's now declining wool industry. There is a little cafe attached to the museum that sells light snacks. You also have other eating options near the river; just three houses up from the ferry, the Lebanese restaurant Sahra has good food and nice river views (9635 6615). The most scenic way to get here is on a Rivercat from Circular Quay and then it's a 20 minute walk. Visit after 14:00 to avoid school groups. It's open daily from 10:00-17:00. Adult $8, child $4, family $17.

171

Macquarie St
Cnr Bridge St
Central

Government House

9931 5222 | www.hht.net.au

Although no longer home to the government, this elegantly furnished Gothic Revival-style residence is often used for official functions. Designed by prominent English architect Edward Blore, who never set foot in Australia, the sandstone mansion was built in1843. Its most notable feature is the beautiful stencilled ceiling. Open daily from 10:00 to 16:00. Entry is free. Guided tours only. These depart every 30 minutes between 10:30 and 15:00.

10 Macquarie St
Central

The Mint

8239 2288 | www.hht.net.au

Constructed over five years from 1811, when NSW settlers first struck gold, the Mint was built as the southern wing of the Sydney Hospital. It was converted to a mint in 1854 (the first Royal Mint outside of England) with a sandstone coining factory built out the back. It operated until 1926, when the Mint was shifted to the nation's new capital, Canberra. The small museum has closed but the building itself is worth a look. Open Monday to Friday, 09:00-17:00. Free admission.

Macquarie St
Beside Royal Botanic
Gardens
Central

Parliament House

9230 2047 | www.parliament.nsw.gov.au

Sister to the historic Mint, this elegant 1816 sandstone building is one of the world's oldest operating parliament buildings. Originally the northern wing of the Rum Hospital, it housed the NSW legislative council from 1829 and is still used by parliament today. You can watch the politicians battle out their differences (when in session) during question time after the 13:30 tour on Tuesdays. Free admission. Tours run between 09:30 and 16:00. Advance booking is essential.

455 George St
Central

Queen Victoria Building

9264 9209 | www.qvb.com.au

Known as the QVB by locals, this 1898 Romanesque building fills an entire block of the city. It was almost demolished in the 1950s but was remodelled into office blocks before being lovingly refurbished in the 1980s as a shopping complex. The shop windows may be distracting but check out the beautiful period-style tiling on the ground floor, huge stained glass windows, sweeping wooden staircases and the two enormous suspended clocks at either end of the building. Outside the building, on Town Hall Place, is a statue of Queen Victoria clutching her beloved pooch, Islay, which speaks at random in the voice of local radio announcer John Laws. The elegant amenities on level one might be the best public toilets in Sydney. The QVB looks magnificent when lit up at night and the best vantage point is from across the road at the Zeta Bar or Glass brasserie (p.325) in The Hilton. Every December, a multi-storey Christmas tree is erected in the centre of the building; an impressive and much-photographed site. Guided one-hour tours cost $10 and leave from the ground floor at 14:30 daily.

Sydney Opera House

71 Clissold Rd
East Wahroonga

Rose Seidler House

9989 8020 | www.hht.net.au

Built between 1948 and 1950 by Sydney's most prominent architect, Harry Seidler, the cube-shaped, glass-fronted house on legs was ahead of its time with its minimalist ultra modern look. It's still furnished with original kitchen appliances and funky 50s furniture. Open Sunday 10:00-17:00. Adults $8, child/concession, $4, family $17.

Guntawong Rd ◄
Outer West

Rouse Hill Estate

9627 6777 | www.hht.net.au

If you're interested in how life was for early settlers, albeit the wealthier ones, this estate offers a unique insight into country NSW life from the 1800s. The Georgian homestead was occupied by six generations of one family until 1993. It's an hour's drive from the city in the direction of the Blue Mountains, but worth the trip for the peaceful surrounds still untouched by mass tourism. Open 10:00-14:00 Wednesday, Thursday and Sunday by guided tour only, which leaves on the hour. Adult $8, child/concession $4, family $17. Wheelchair access.

49 Market St ◄
Central

State Theatre

9373 6852 | www.statetheatre.com.au

This magnificent 1929 picture palace is lavishly decorated with ornate ceilings, sweeping wooden staircases and wood-panelled floors. You'll need to attend a play or concert to check out the Dress Circle Gallery, which houses artworks by notable Australian artists, such as William Dobell and Charles Wheeler. The impressive crystal chandelier in the Koh-I-Nor auditorium is the second largest chandelier on earth, weighing over four tonnes. Plays and concerts are still held here and there is a Ticketmaster office in the main entrance. The cosy Retro Café next door makes a good pre-show coffee stop. The booking office is open 09:00-17:00 (20:00 on performance nights).

Cnr Macquarie St ◄
and Bridge St
Central

Sydney Conservatorium of Music

9351 1222 | www.music.usyd.edu.au

The conservatory was originally intended to be the servant's quarters and stables of nearby Government House. In 1815, ex-convict Francis Greenaway based the design on a Scottish castle and the large sums spent on construction eventually led to the downfall of both Greenaway and the Governor of the time, Lachlan Macquarie. 'The Con' was completely refurbished in 2000, at a cost of $145 million. From march to November, a one or two dollar donation will get you in to a 50 minute concert by current students on most Wednesdays at 13:10.

The Rocks ◄

Sydney Harbour Bridge and Pylon Lookout

9240 1100 | www.pylonlookout.com.au

Sydney's iconic 'coathanger' was a massive engineering feat for its time and still impresses today. Completed in1932, sixteen people lost their lives building the one mile-long, eight-lane bridge. Although it looks as though the massive pylons support the bridge, they're purely aesthetic; it's the enormous arch that actually holds the road. Every New Year's Eve the Bridge takes centre stage in a spectacular fireworks display (see p.149). If you're not keen to climb the structure itself, at least trudge up the 200 steps to the south east pylon for fabulous harbour views from the lookout (open 10:00-17:00 daily; access from Cumberland Street, The Rocks; adult $9.50, child $3.50 and under sevens free). The pylon also houses a three-level exhibit of the bridge's history. You can walk across the bridge for free.

8 Macquarie St ◄
Central

Sydney Hospital and Sydney Eye Hospital

9382 7111 | www.sesahs.nsw.gov.au

The 'Rum Hospital' is the oldest in Australia and still cares for the sick today. It earned its nickname because it was built by contractors for Governor Macquarie in return for a rum monopoly. One of the original wings is now Parliament House, the other the Mint.

173

Keep an eye out for Il Porcellino, a copy of a boar statue in Florence, out the front on Macquarie Street – it's said that rubbing its snout (or, better still, making a donation to the hospital) will bring good luck. You can cut through the hospital grounds to The Domain and Art Gallery of NSW.

Observatory Hill
The Rocks

Sydney Observatory

9241 3767 | *www.sydneyobservatory.com.au*

This impressive dome-topped 1850s building overlooks Port Jackson (Sydney Harbour's official name) and covers astronomy from two distinct points of view; modern science and Aboriginal sky stories. Night tours, which must be pre-booked, offer the chance to view the sky through a telescope and learn about the Southern Cross. Observatory Hill is a great spot to spend an afternoon. Open daily 10:00-17:00. Free admission to gardens and museum. Night tours; adults $15, child $10, concession $12, family $45.

Bennelong Pt
Circular Quay

Sydney Opera House

9250 7111 | *www.sydneyoperahouse.com*

The Sydney Opera House dates back to 1973, when it was officially opened by Queen Elizabeth II. Danish architect Joern Utzon won a competition with his dramatic design in 1957. Legend has it that his was plucked from the rejects pile by one of the judges. His luck didn't last though. After budget blowouts and political wrangling, Utzon resigned in 1966, and a team of Australian architects finished the job. Critics point out that all the attention went on the majestic exterior, resulting in less-than-perfect acoustics inside. Open 09:00-17:00. The one-hour tours go every half hour. Adult $26, concession $16, online bookings $23. For a glimpse into how productions are staged, a two hour backstage tour goes at 07:00 and costs $140 (no kids), with breakfast.

Cnr George and
Druitt Sts
Central

Town Hall

9265 9189 | *www.sydneytownhall.com.au*

Built as a homage to Victorian England in the 1870s, Town Hall served as Sydney's concert hall until the Opera House opened in 1973, but is now mainly used for public lectures and functions. It was built on the site of an old cemetery and although most of the graves were exhumed before construction began, original graves and headstones were found in 1991 and again in 2003 when restoration work was carried out. Often likened to a wedding cake, the steps in front of the multi-layer building are a popular central meeting point.

Wentworth Rd
Watsons Bay

Vaucluse House

9388 7922 | *www.hht.net.au*

Taking up just ten of its original 206 hectares, Vaucluse House survives as the only 19th century harbourside estate with its original stables and outbuildings. From 1827 until 1853 it was the family home of Australian explorer and statesman William Charles Wentworth and the house still features some original furniture. The cafe overlooking the gardens is a tranquil spot for high tea and they also have a full lunch menu. Open Tuesday to Sunday 10:00-16:30. Grounds open 10:00-17:00 daily. Adult $8, child/concession $4, family $17. Wheelchair access to ground floor only.

Cnr Oxford St &
Greens Rd
Darlinghurst

Victoria Barracks

9339 3000 | *www.awm.gov.au*

Once a jail for military prisoners (and rumoured to be haunted), this vast 1840s sandstone building is still occupied by the army. It is considered a fine example of British military architecture. There are six guided tours including a performance by the military band (weather permitting). Free admission. Open Thursday 10:00-12.30 (museum & barracks), Sunday 10:00-15:00 (museum only).

Museums

Other options **Art** p.271, **Heritage Sites** p.171

Sydney has lots of museums, which showcase the country's colourful social history. These span subjects from Aboriginal art and natural history to colonisation and federation, and culture vultures could spend a week getting around them all.

6 College St ◀
Central

Australian Museum

9320 6000 | *www.amonline.net.au*

This is Australia's oldest museum and a must-see for science buffs. You can explore the natural history of Australia; from dazzling gemstones to the infamous deadly wildlife, including live baby crocodiles. There are several galleries devoted to indigenous Australian artefacts plus free didgeridoo and dance performances on Sundays at 12:00 and 14:00. Dinosaur-obsessed kids can get involved in interactive skeletal displays, while under fives can expend some energy at Kids' Island (admission included in ticket price). Allow at least two hours. Adult $10, child/concession $5, family $17.50-$25. Free for over 55s and under fives. Open daily 09:30-17:00. You can also hire out parts of the museum for functions.

Macquarie St ◀
Central

Hyde Park Barracks Museum

8239 2311 | *www.hht.net.au*

Discover the harsh reality of daily life for Australia's first convicts, housed here until 1848. Afterwards you can soak up some sun in the courtyard cafe, which is often quiet. Visit after 15:00 to avoid school groups on weekdays. Guided tours on request. Allow at least one hour if you plan to read all the details yourself. Adult $10, child/concession $5, family $20. Open 09:30-17:00 daily. Wheelchair access to ground floor.

Cnr Phillip & ◀
Albert Sts
Circular Quay

Justice and Police Museum

9252 1144 | *www.hht.nsw.gov.au*

You would expect some interesting crime stories from a country built by convict labour and this is where to learn all the gruesome details of Sydney's underworld. You can also learn about Aussie bushrangers and there are guns and other artefacts on display. You can't mistake the building, thanks to the somewhat tacky display of cartoon cops and robbers on the roof. Allow about one hour. Open Saturday to Sunday 10:00-17:00. Adults $8, child & concession $4, family $17. Wheelchair access to ground floor only.

University of Sydney ◀
Outer West

Macleay Museum

9036 5253 | *www.usyd.edu.au*

Well respected for its large insect collection (including a flea collected by British naturalist Charles Darwin), it also houses an extensive collection of scientific instruments. If you're interested in creepy crawlies, allow two hours here. Admission is free. Open Monday to Friday 10:00-16:30 and 11:00-16:00 on the first Saturday of every month.

West Esplanade ◀
Manly

Manly Art Gallery & Museum

9976 1420

This small gallery celebrates the beach suburb's sun, surf and sand obsession and offers a visual insight into the history of the area's beach culture. It also houses an eclectic mix of temporary exhibitions, which range from local quilting artists and student projects to indigenous artworks sourced from central Australia. Open Tuesday to Sunday 10:00-17:00. Adult $3.60, child $1.20. Free on Wednesdays.

**Cnr Phillip &
Bridge Sts**
Central

Museum of Sydney

9251 5988 | *www.hht.net.au*

If you're interested in Sydney's short but colourful history, this will be a highlight on your museum itinerary. The objects, pictures and multimedia exhibitions detail early settlement from 1788, including some Aboriginal history. Built on the foundations of the first Government House, thousands of artefacts found here in archaeological digs are on display. There's a good cafe next door with free newspapers. Allow two hours. Open daily 09:30-17:00. Adult $10, child $5, concession $20. Wheelchair access.

2 Murray St
Darling Harbour

National Maritime Museum

9298 3777 | *www.anmm.gov.au*

This museum is easy to spot thanks to its white sail-like roof. It explains Australia's long relationship with the sea; everything from beach culture to Aboriginal fishing methods. Highlights include a sailboat made of beer cans (similar to those raced in the Darwin Beer Can Regatta each year), and a fleet of historic vessels, including the destroyer HMAS Vampire and the submarine Onslow. You'll have to pay a fee to tour the vessels moored outside. Check the website for changing special exhibitions. If you're planning to explore the ships, allow at least two hours here. Open daily 09.30-17:00. The permanent indoor gallery is free. Guided tours from 10:00-14:00. Good wheelchair access to gallery and wharves.

5 Wallaringa Ave
Neutral Bay

Nutcote

9953 4453 | *www.maygibbs.com.au*

May Gibbs is the Aussie version of Beatrix Potter and most will know her much-loved children's bush stories, Snugglepot and Cuddlepie, which were first published in 1918. Gibbs' harbourside house was saved from developers after her death by the efforts of friends and relatives and is now a museum featuring personal memorabilia including notebooks and original editions of her books. The garden tearoom serves light refreshments and has good views across the harbour. Open Wednesday to Sunday from 11:00-15:00, closed December 17 to January 3.

500 Harris St
Darling Harbour

Powerhouse Museum

9217 0111 | *www.powerhousemuseum.com*

Even if you're not a science buff, you'll delight in the thought-provoking exhibits at The Powerhouse. You'll come out feeling like you know a little more about how the world works, from computers and robots to modern transport. Kids will love the fun interactive displays. Even without dawdling, it would take days to see all 380,000 exhibits, which include the world's oldest steam engine and the Strasbourg Clock, a working model of the astronomical clock in Strasbourg's Notre Dame cathedral. Allow at least three hours. Open from 10:00-17:00 daily. Adult $10, child $5, concession $6, family $25. Free for under fives and over 55s. Wheelchair access. You can park for $9 at the Sydney Entertainment Centre if your ticket is validated at the museum entry.

58-64 Gloucester St
The Rocks

Susannah Place Museum

9241 1893 | www.hht.nsw.gov.au

Inside this row of four tiny terrace houses is a time capsule. Here you'll discover what the living conditions were like for some of the local working class of the 1900s. The curators are dressed for the part but the tour through the old kitchens, laundries and dunnies is virtually self-guided. You can purchase replica wares from the recreated 1959 corner store. Open Saturday and Sunday from 10:00-17:00. Adult $8, child $4, family $17.

148 Darlinghurst Rd
Darlinghurst

Sydney Jewish Museum

9360 7999 | www.sydneyjewishmuseum.com.au

There were only sixteen Jewish convicts who arrived on the First Fleet in 1788, but some 30,000 migrants arrived after the second world war. This three-level exhibit traces the displacement of the Jewish people chronologically, from the early days of convict life in Sydney to the Holocaust (which is covered in sometimes distressing detail on the upper two floors) and beyond. There's also a 15-minute introductory film that discusses anti-Semitism through the ages. Allow at least one hour. Adult $10, child $6, concession $7. Open Sunday to Thursday from 10:00-16:00, and Friday from 10:00-14:00.

Festivals

In addition to its obvious natural attractions, Sydney knows how to throw a good party. From small multicultural street fairs in the suburbs to major city-wide celebrations, there is always something to see and experience – much of it for free. Events run from the cultural, musical and artsy, to raucous and boozy summer nights. The biggest yearly bash is the Sydney Gay & Lesbian Mardi Gras; one of the world's most vibrant and colourful festivals and a must-do if you're in Sydney in February. The best way to find out what's happening while you're here is to pick up the *Sydney Morning Herald* on a Friday.

Various locations

Anzac Day

www.dva.gov.au/commem/anzac

Anzac (Australian and New Zealand Army Corps) Day is held on April 25 each year and around 250,000 people turn out to commemorate one of the country's most tragic stories; when 8,000 Australians lost their lives in Gallipoli, Turkey, during the first world war. A dawn service is held at the Cenotaph in Martin Place before war veterans and their descendants march down George Street. This is a passionately patriotic event.

Sydney Showgrounds
Outer West

Big Day Out

www.bigdayout.com

Its title is a dead giveaway; since 1992 this touring festival has been the must-see outdoor music event, featuring local gems and international music giants like the Red Hot Chili Peppers, Nirvana, Nick Cave and Muse. Tickets sell out within hours so get in quick. If you miss out, they hold an online ticket lottery for roughly 10,000 spots, so check the website. It costs $115-$150 plus booking fee.

Royal Botanic
Gardens & Domain

Carols in The Domain

www.carolsinthedomain.com

Local TV hosts and soap stars turn out for this Christmas fest to strut their stuff on stage, belting out carols to a glow-stick wielding crowd. Get there before midday to secure a spot near the front. Alcohol is permitted, but glass bottles are frowned upon. Seats can be hired for $8 plus security deposit for the day but most people bring their own picnic rugs and rations. Admission is free.

177

Chinese New Year

Chinatown

9265 9333 | www.cityofsydney.nsw.gov.au

The Chinese follow the lunar calendar so the date of New Year's Day varies each year, but one thing remains constant, the celebrations and festivities run for three lively weeks. Sydney hosts the largest Chinese celebrations outside of Asia with more than 500,000 people crowding the streets to welcome in the New Year. Most of the live entertainment is centred around Chinatown, but there are also dragon boat races in Darling Harbour, and the annual street parade from Town Hall to Chinatown. Free admission.

Darling Harbour Fiesta

Darling Harbour

This is one of the biggest outdoor parties of the year, as more than 170,000 people don their dancing shoes for four days of flamboyant live Latin entertainment. Young and old come down to rumba and salsa on the harbour foreshore and if you're not blessed with natural Latin rhythm, free lessons are given early in the evening. It's a lively way to spend a summer evening and burn off some of the alcohol you'll inevitably consume.

Darling Harbour Jazz Festival

Darling Harbour

www.darlingharbour.com

Over the Queen's Birthday long weekend (June 10-12) Darling Harbour hosts some of Sydney's biggest festivals. Fans come alive with over 300,000 people tapping their toes to the sweet sounds of bands, gospel groups and well-known jazz performers from Australia and overseas. Last year's line up included legends like James Morrison.

Festival of the Winds

Bondi Beach

8362 3400 | www.waverley.nsw.gov.au/info/pavilion/fotw

Here's your chance to be a kid for a day. If you fancy flying a kite in the festival you can buy one from the stalls in the park or make your own at the workshops in front of the Bondi Pavilion. Even if the kites aren't really of interest, it's still a great day out as there's plenty going on. The crowded pavilion offers multicultural munchies, live entertainment and free dance workshops ranging from belly dancing to Brazilian Capoeira. Free admission.

Flickerfest

Bondi Pavilion

9365 6888 | www.flickerfest.com.au

Fifteen years ago this was just another small festival at a local Sydney high school, but it's now a week long showcase of Australian and international short film and animation. The opening night attracts local film industry heavyweights and some socialites. The film industry snaps up most of the tickets so get in early if you want to join the party. The balcony on the pavilion is a breezy spot for a post-flick drink with unobstructed views over the ocean. Tickets are $15 per screening, $45 on opening night (including screening, drinks and nibbles).

Gay & Lesbian Mardi Gras

Various locations

www.mardigras.org.au

What started as a protest march in 1978 has morphed into one of the world's largest gay pride festivals. The highlight of the month-long celebration is the parade, led by the 'Dykes on Bikes' (a motorcycle parade of mostly bare-breasted lesbians), winding its noisy way down Oxford Street. While the cheeky outfits still attract criticism from conservative sections of the community, it's not all about baring flesh and donning flashy costumes. The dazzling floats often contain political messages and a huge portion of straight Sydney comes to watch or tune into the live coverage on ABC television. Get there a few hours early, as the crowd for the parade can be up to ten people deep. Wear comfy shoes because the party goes on into the wee hours.

Darling Harbour

Greek Festival
www.greekfestivalofsydney.com.au
After the second world war, Australia had a massive influx of immigrants from southern Europe. As well as their fabulous food, the Mediterranean's have brought their lively traditions with them. Each year an estimated 40,000 locals flock to this festival to celebrate all things Greek. You can wander through the many food stalls, sample free live music and watch traditional Greek dancing in all its plate smashing glory. It runs from 10:00-22:00. Free admission.

1 Belgrave St
Manly

Manly International Jazz Festival
www.manly.nsw.gov.au
This is one of the oldest festivals in Sydney. It runs over three days every October long weekend. Around 40,000 people enjoy the free music from five stages and the larger-than-usual Manly markets keep everyone amused between concerts. The event attracts both local and international artists, with a diverse range of jazz. At this time of year it's often warm enough for a swim, and the ocean-front setting is the perfect venue for the music. Free parking is available.

Various locations

Opera, Jazz and Classical in The Domain
Throughout January everyone is invited to plonk themselves on a patch of grass for free open-air performances on three consecutive Saturday nights. It starts off with highlights from Opera Australia's productions, the next night features classical performances by the Sydney Symphony Orchestra and the third and final night serenades Sydneysiders with sweet jazz sounds. Get there early if you want to kick back with some bubbly close to the action.

The Rocks

The Rocks Aroma Coffee Festival
9240 8500
Sydney has some of the best coffee you're likely to taste outside of Italy and caffeine addicts will be hard pressed to hold back from overindulging in the superb $1 coffees on offer at each stall. More than 90,000 people head down to The Rocks to watch Australia's best baristas at work and enjoy the live bands and street entertainment. If it's too frosty to linger in the streets, there are plenty of rustic pubs in the area to retreat into. From 10:00-17:00.

Sydney Showground
Sydney Olympic Park

The Royal Easter Show
9704 1111 | www.eastershow.com.au
Since 1918, over one million fair fans have been flocking to the showground to overindulge in dagwood dogs and homemade lemonade, before mixing it all up with stomach-churning rides. This event plays tribute to everything Australian, but particularly the country's agricultural heritage. Don't miss the impressive fruit displays and, if you've got kids in tow, the cuddly farm animals. Don't bother fighting for a seat to see the Australiana shows. Instead, head to the wood chopping, which is always a massive crowd favourite. Adult $31, child $21.50, concession $25.50 and reduced prices after 17:00. Open 09:00-22:00.

Various locations
St Patricks Day
www.stpatricksday.org.au
There were many Irish among the early settlers in Australia but it's not only those with Irish ancestry that get into the spirit of things – many Aussies leap at the chance to don silly green hats and put away some pints. The Irish pubs around town (like St Patrick's Tavern in the CBD) are packed with revellers from midday, guzzling Guinness and green-dyed beer while crowds cheer on the lunchtime parade from Bathurst Street to The Domain via Hyde Park.

Various locations
Sydney Festival
8248 6500 | *www.sydneyfestival.org.au*
Running over three weeks during the school holidays, this is Sydney's biggest art and culture event. The action-packed programme includes everything from street theatre to art, concerts and kids events. There are plenty of free activities so the strapped-for-cash can still get involved. Many of the high profile events (often starring international names like Cate Blanchett and Ralph Fiennes) sell out early, so you'll need to pre-book. Free festival guides are available from the Opera House, QVB and at cafes around the city. Events are held across Sydney, from the Opera House to Parramatta.

Various locations
Sydney Film Festival
9280 0511 | *www.sydneyfilmfestival.org*
Perfectly timed for Sydney's winter, this is a two-week film fest with over 200 Aussie and international features, documentaries, animation and short films. The hot ticket is for the opening night party ($136 for screening and party or $45 screening only) when a who's who of Australian movie-making goes down the red carpet into Sydney's historic State Theatre. Between flicks, rub shoulders with film industry professionals and soak up the live entertainment or film discussions at World Movies Festival Lounge, 49 Market Street (midday to midnight). For die-hard film buffs, flexipass tickets are available in lots of 10, 20 and 30. Screenings cost $17 and are held at State Theatre, Dendy Opera Quays and George Street Cinemas. See p.364 for more.

10 Hickson Rd
The Rocks
Sydney Writer's Festival
9252 7729 | *www.swf.org.au*
This is Sydney's most prominent literary event, bringing together well-known international social, political and philosophical authors as well as local writing legends. The lively, sometimes heated, seminar discussions are worthwhile (even for non book worms), with wildly varied topics. It's held at various venues around Sydney but mostly centres around the Wharf Theatre precinct at Walsh Bay. Ticket prices change with each event and some are free.

**Royal Botanic
Gardens & The
Domain**
Tropfest
9368 0434 | *www.tropfest.com*
This is Sydney's favourite short film festival and the world's largest. The flicks are shown on a big screen in The Domain – get there early and enjoy the live entertainment from 15:00. If you fancy yourself as a filmmaker, grab a camera and create your own entry. Each short film must include the Tropfest signature item (it was a sneeze for the 2007 festival). This is designed to reduce cheating as well as add entertainment value. If your flick is among the top 16, it could potentially kick-start a new career. It takes place every year on the last Sunday in February. Film screenings from 19:45 at The Domain, Royal Botanic Gardens. Free admission. It costs $40 to enter a film of your own.

Babywear p.98
Bank Loans p.22

Written by residents, these unique guidebooks are packed with insider info, from
arriving in a new destination to making it your home and everything in between.

Explorer Residents' Guides
We Know Where You Live

Abu Dhabi • Amsterdam • Bahrain • Barcelona • Dubai • Dublin • Geneva • Hong Kong • Kuwait

EXPLORER

Beaches

Other options **Parks** p.184, **Swimming** p.244

Other options **Parks** p.184, **Swimming** p.244

Beaches have always been one of Sydney's biggest attractions and deservedly so; with over 30 to choose from, it's a sea and sand lover's paradise.

The volunteer Surf Lifesavers (in bright red and yellow swimming caps) patrol most beaches during summer. Anyone can become a lifesaver – you just need to be over 15 and pass some fitness tests; visit www.slsa.com.au for more information. As well as rescuing swimmers they also keep an eye out for sharks – although few sharks here are aggressive and many beaches have shark nets.

Pollution can be a problem after heavy rain as storm water currents wash up sewage and rubbish, mostly on harbour beaches like Balmoral. Check pollution levels with the Beachwatch Bulletin (1800 036 677) or visit www.epa.nsw.gov.au. If it's the size of the swell you're interested in, log on to www.realsurf.com.

Swimming Stingers

Blue Bottle jellyfish can cause swelling, intense pain and allergic reactions. If you see them washed up on shore, (look for their distinctive blue tails) don't go in the water. If you do get stung, wash the area with hot water and buy a spray-on remedy from a chemists.

Bondi

The most famous of Australia's beaches, no other strip of sand has the same allure. Its mile-long curved expanse of white sand looks even more impressive viewed from the southern hill above the beach. Surfers tend to stick to the southern end where the rocks kick up the waves; the centre is dominated by sunbathers; while families tend to fill up the northern end near the free shallow salt-water pool. Bondi (pronounced bon-dye) is protected by shark nets and there are two sets of flags for swimmers and boogie boarders. The Bondi Pavilion has toilets, showers and changing rooms plus a basic kiosk. If you're looking for more satisfying sustenance, Campbell Parade is packed with cafes, ice-cream and fish 'n' chip shops and fine dining restaurants. The bustling carnival-like atmosphere makes it popular with locals and visitors alike. Don't miss the Bondi-Bronte cliff walk from the southern end of the beach for breathtaking coastal views.

Emergency Rescue

The surf claims several lives each year from strong currents or rips that can drag you out to deep water. If you get into difficulty, don't panic – fighting against a strong current will only tire you out so float with it. Breathe evenly, keep your head above water and raise one arm above your head to signal the lifeguards. Surf lifesavers rescue over 10,000 people each summer and provide first aid to 25,000 beach-goers – just make sure they can see you by swimming in between the flags.

Bronte Beach

Much smaller and less image conscious than Bondi, the family-oriented Bronte has an excellent shady beachside park; perfect for kicking a ball and popular for picnics. The rolling surf can be rough here so steer clear of the rocks at either end. To play it safe, stick to the Bronte Baths, an enclosed free-access pool at the southern end of the beach. Locals converge on the cafe-lined hill to soak up some sun over brunch or bake on the beach where Norfolk pines offer some shade. The mini train ($3) and playground are a big hit with the tiny tots. From here, you can walk north to Bondi or south to Clovelly via the historic Waverley Cemetery, which sits on a headland with incredible ocean views.

Clovelly

This sheltered, keyhole-shaped bay is popular with lap swimmers because of its calm waters. You'll see plenty of snorkellers here too as this spot is well known for the inquisitive blue gropers and tropical fish that lurk beneath the water. Public toilets are on hand but you'll have to bring snacks with you as there are no shops or kiosks directly on the beach.

Coogee

Coogee

Pronounced kuh-jee, this is another safe swimming spot if you don't like big waves or have kids in tow. The area has been greened up by the council and now boasts a playground on the grassy headland overlooking the beach. Big kids are more likely to be attracted by the Coogee Bay Hotel, where the oceanfront balcony is a popular backpacker drinking spot and often hosts excellent live bands. Although its popularity rivals that of Bondi and Manly, its geographical restrictions have helped it retain a cosier community feel and it's yet to succumb to the glitz and glam of its neighbours.

Outer South

Cronulla

This southernmost metropolitan beach and excellent surfing spot has been the focal point of Sydney's recent social unrest. Riots in 2005 erupted here after various ethnic and right wing Australian groups clashed for several days. It has since returned to its generally peaceful state and the incredibly long and popular beach is perfectly safe and great for swimming and surfing. However, it's a long ride from the city if you're travelling by train so if you're not planning to make a day of it, stick to beaches closer to the CBD.

Lightly Toasted

Australia has one of the highest rates of skin cancer in the world and, while it's tempting to bake yourself bronze, hit the shade between 11:00 and 15:00 when the sun is at its strongest. Follow the local slogan of slip (on a T-shirt), slop (on some sunblock), slap (on a hat).

Manly

Manly

Manly vies with Bondi for the title of most popular beach. It was named by Captain Arthur Phillip after the manly physique of the Aborigines he saw there in 1788. The atmosphere is always different, depending on what time of day you arrive. In the early morning and evening, joggers make the most of the long tree-lined walkway above the beach. During the day, it's full of yummy mummies pushing prams and clutching dog leashes. Beach volleyball games are popular at twilight and outside of working hours it's jam-packed with families, teenagers and international tourists.

Locals tend to swim at Queenscliff beach at the very northern end of Manly, while snorkellers stick to the rocky area near Shelley Beach. For lunch, fresh fish 'n' chips is a popular meal (the Manly Fish Market & Café on Wentworth Street is excellent). Parking directly on the beach is expensive.

Outer South

Maroubra

This was the first beach in Australia to host a swimsuit beauty contest back in 1920. While the other eastern beaches have all glammed up in recent years, Maroubra is yet to follow suit. Considered the most Aussie of Sydney's beaches, it's well known for its excellent surf, except after rain. The northern end is dubbed the 'toilet bowl', so it's wise to steer clear after a storm. Grab a meat pie or chicko roll from the nearby take-away stores for a true taste of old Oz.

Coogee Beach

183

Outer North ◀ ## Palm Beach

Bondi may be the home of beach chic but Sydney's secluded northernmost point is a much-coveted address for the rich and famous. Nicole Kidman has been known to holiday here and it's home to sprawling seaside mansions owned by international actors and sports stars like Aussie tennis player Lleyton Hewitt. Flanked on either side by lush green headlands, fans of Aussie soap *Home and Away* might recognise the setting from the show's outdoor scenes. It's a long way from the city centre, especially by bus, but it's worth the hike for the unspoiled beach, excellent fishing and sailing. Parking is relatively cheap and easy to find.

Dellview St, btn ◀ ## Tamarama
Bondi & Bronte Beach
9300 9056

Dubbed 'glamarama', this tiny beach tucked in between busy Bondi and Bronte attracts a similarly uber-cool crowd, but far fewer tourists. Popular with the gay crowd, the bodies here are likely to be the most buffed and bronzed in all of Sydney. The park directly on the beach is a great spot for a traditional Aussie barbecue but it doesn't offer much shade. Despite the peaceful appearance of this cosy cove, be wary of rip tides, particularly near the rocks at either end of the beach. Surfing is prohibited.

Parks & Gardens

Sydney is surrounded by national parks and bushland but the CBD also has plenty of green spaces with a surprising array of bird life, possums and flying foxes. Public parks are generally well maintained, free and tend to have amenities on site. Best of all, you're almost always allowed to lounge or play on the grass. As locals love getting outdoors to make the most of the Mediterranean climate, parks all over town tend to be busy during lunch hours and at the weekend. Bicycles and roller blades are normally allowed and joggers abound, particularly around midday as office workers don gym gear and pound the pavements around The Domain and Botanic Gardens.

Paddington ◀ ## Centennial Park

At the end of the popular shopping strip of Oxford Street, this is Sydney's biggest park and it has a rich history. The Federation Pavilion marks the spot where Australia officially became a nation in 1920. In-line skaters, joggers, cyclists and horse riders make the most of the leafy 220 hectare expanse where pretty lakes teem with ducks and other bird life. There are cafes and a restaurant, plus a kiosk that open at the weekend. If you're here in summer, don't miss the open-air Moonlight Cinema (p.364), which shows mostly art-house films early in the evening, from early December to late February; Ticketek 9266 4800. Bikes and skates can be hired from several places nearby on Clovelly Road, Randwick.

Darling Harbour ◀ ## Chinese Garden
9281 6863 | *www.chinesegarden.com.au*

Created for the bicentenary in 1998, this Chinese-designed garden is a tranquil escape from the bustling crowds at Darling Harbour. The winding pathways take you past ponds blooming with lotus flowers, mini waterfalls and Chinese statues. The teahouse offers a range of oriental refreshments with a few select yum cha choices to snack on, as well as regular cafe fare. Adult $6, child/concession $3, family $15.

Central ◀ ## Hyde Park

On the edge of the city's business district, this grassy expanse was first declared public land by Governor Phillip in 1792 and was used for cricket matches and horse races until it became a park in 1810. These days it's packed with sun-seeking city workers on their lunch hour. The magnificent avenue of Moreton Bay figs is particularly pretty at night

The Complete **Residents'** Guide

when it's illuminated with fairy lights. At the southern end stands a 30m high art deco ANZAC memorial, erected in 1934 to commemorate Australians killed at war – the 120,000 gold stars inside the dome represent each man and woman of NSW who served. You can't miss the grand bronze and granite Archibald Fountain, which was built in 1932 to commemorate the French and Australian world war alliance.

Jubilee and Bicentennial Park

Glebe

One of the few waterside green spots in the inner west, Bicentennial Park offers views of the harbour from a different angle, framed by the new Anzac Bridge. The 6.8 hectare park is popular with joggers and dog walkers and the giant Moreton Bay Fig trees offer good shade. Directly adjacent is Jubilee Park, which has a playground, picnic benches and a sporting oval.

Nielsen Park

Sydney Harbour National Park
The Rocks

9247 5033

Crowded with families at the weekend, this is a peaceful place to picnic during the week and has stunning views across the water to the city skyline, making it a favourite spot for magazine photo shoots. Take a dip in Shark Bay (the name is disconcerting but don't worry, it's netted) or drop into the popular but pricey cafe. It's a prime east-side spot to see the New Year's Eve fireworks from and for a twilight picnic any other night of the year.

Observatory Park

The Rocks

At the foot of the Sydney Observatory, wedding parties often have their photos taken here and for good reason: it's more private than the Botanic Gardens and the elevated position offers sparkling harbour views from Anzac Bridge to the Sydney Harbour Bridge. If it's wet, you can still enjoy the vista from the bandstand that dominates the park, or duck into the Garrison Church opposite.

Royal Botanic Gardens & Domain

The Domain

9231 8111 | www.rbgsyd.nsw.gov.au

This beautiful green expanse with ponds and flourishing flowerbeds is as much loved by locals as tourists. Its initial function was less aesthetic. Settlers used this spot as a giant veggie patch, but it failed to feed the hungry hordes due to poor soil. A great spot for panoramic harbour views is Mrs Macquarie's Chair, a peninsula named after a governor's wife, Elizabeth Macquarie. Legend has it that if a woman sitting here makes a wish it will come true. Keep an eye out for magpies and, if you're here around dusk, the hordes of fruit bats that flock to the gardens. Open daily 07:00 to sunset. There are free 90-minute guided tours each day at 10:30 and a one-hour tour at 13:00; both depart from the Palm Grove Centre. Aboriginal heritage tours depart at 14:00 ($20), from the Moore Room.

Rushcutters Bay Park

New Beach Rd
Darling Point

With pretty views over the multi-million dollar marina, this is a lovely spot to while away a summer afternoon. There's plenty of green space to throw down a picnic rug, a playground, tennis courts for hire (9357 1675), and a kiosk that offers a decent caffeine-fix. Nearby is the Reg Bartley Oval used for cricket, soccer and rugby matches.

Tumbalong Park

Darling Harbour

A little patch of greenery among Darling Harbour's concrete surrounds, this small park often has live entertainment and open air concerts. The free playground and timed acrobatic water features means it's mostly used by families, but it's also a good place for weary shoppers to set down their bags. Occasionally cultural festivals are held here, such as the Thai Songkran Festival in April, which is heaven for Thai food fanatics.

Amusement Centres

Sydney's first and foremost playground is its harbour and beaches, which may be why its amusement parks struggle to stay open. The biggest, Wonderland, closed in 2004, so now there is just one; Luna Park in Milsons Point, just north of the Harbour Bridge.

Olympic Place
Milsons Pt
North Sydney

Luna Park

9922 6644 | *www.lunaparksydney.com.au*

This is Sydney's last remaining theme park and behind the giant laughing face that marks its entrance lies a rocky history. Modelled on New York's Coney Island, it has been shut down numerous times since it first opened in 1935, due to financial problems, friction with local residents and a fire in 1979 that killed seven people. It still retains some of its 1930s flavour and the panoramic views of the harbour and city from the ferris wheel are worth the trip. You can't miss the bright lights at Luna Park if you're crossing the bridge from the city to north Sydney at night. Open Monday and Thursday 11:00-18:00; Friday 11:00-23:00; Saturday 10:00-23:00; Sunday 10:00-18:00; longer hours during NSW school holidays. Free admission. Individual rides $6; unlimited ride day pass $39, child $18-$29 depending on height; unlimited rides for $25 after 17:00 on Fridays.

National Parks & Reserves

Other options **Weekend Breaks** p.202

In Australia, national parks are protected by the National Parks and Wildlife Service. So despite Sydney's ever-expanding size, developers are prohibited from building on these areas, which are popular with locals for bush walking, horse riding or overnight camping trips.

Northern Beaches
Outer North

Bradleys Head

9247 5033

The tripod mast of the original Australian battleship HMAS Sydney marks the end of the headland. Keep an eye out for the cute ring-tailed possums. You'll hear the beach's other noisy inhabitants – rainbow lorikeets – for miles. National Parks offers a two-hour Bush Food tour that departs at 13:30 on the first Sunday of the month, for $13.20 (bookings are essential - 9247 5033), but you can follow the walking track at your own pace anytime.

Forestville
Outer North

Garigal National Park

9451 3479 | *www.nationalparks.nsw.gov.au*

Just 12km out of the CBD, the Davidson picnic area on Middle Harbour is a popular, if busy, fishing spot with public amenities. Camping is prohibited but there is a picnic area and boat ramp. Bring your own firewood if you want to use the barbecues, as there's generally no kindling around. A walk along the Gordon and Middle Harbour creeks is a nice place to stretch your legs and National Parks occasionally offer guided walks. No pets allowed. Parking is $7 per day; bring the right change for the automated machine.

Outer West

Ku-Ring-Gai Chase National Park

9472 8949 | *www.nationalparks.nsw.gov.au*

This national park was once inhabited by two Aborigine tribes, but most of the members were wiped out by smallpox after settlers invaded. As well as Aboriginal rock carvings and cave paintings there are some stunning views from several lookouts; don't miss West Head with its seascape panorama over Barrenjoey Head and lighthouse. The Basin is the park's only campsite and accommodates up to 400 people; often young and sometimes noisy at weekends or during school holidays. It has a public phone, amenities and drink vending machine. If you plan to go horse riding, follow the marked trails as other areas are off limits to horses. Various guided tours are available (adult $3-$10, child $2-$5; 9472 9300). For breathtaking views, you can climb the beautifully restored Barrenjoey Lighthouse. Camping: adults $10, children $5. Entry by car is $11 per day. The landing fee is $3 per day visit if arriving by ferry from Palm Beach.

Lane Cove National Park

Lane Cove
Outer North

9888 9133 | *www.lanecoverivertouristpark.com.au*

A popular camping spot for those who don't want to drive for hours to get out of the city, this peaceful bushland extends from East Ryde to Wahroonga. The river is the highlight and is better for boating than swimming. Drop into the Kukundi Wildlife Shelter to see tawny frogmouths, lizards and flying foxes up close. There are amenities in the park, including a kiosk and picnic spots and you can hire rowboats at the boatshed. You'll need to bring your own wood for the fires. No pets allowed. Park gates open 09:00-18:00. Parking costs $7 per day (you'll need coins for the automated machines). A site with power will cost you $32-$36, or it's $28-$30 for one without.

Sydney Harbour National Park

Sydney Harbour

9247 5033 | *www.nationalparks.nsw.gov.au*

Encompassing sections of park scattered around the harbour; highlights include the 9km Manly Scenic Walkway, a well-marked trail that passes through some excellent swimming spots, or the Harbour Bridge to Spit Walk, which takes you past Bradleys and Middle Heads. The historic harbour islands are also under National Parks protection. Fort Denison (see p.168) is the most popular island and easily accessible but Shark, Clark and Rodd islands are lovely picnic spots.

Zoos & Wildlife Parks

Fairfield City Farm

31 Darling St
Fairfield
Outer West

9823 3222 | *www.cityfarm.com.au*

Though less exotic than other spots listed here, Fairfield is still an interesting place for young minds. The animals here are all of the farmyard variety, with a few koalas thrown in, and the farm runs educational tours and shows. It's a good chance for kids to see where their dinner comes from, with displays of milking, shearing and the like. It's open from 09:00 to 16:30 seven days a week. Shows and tractor rides run from 10:30-15:30. Entry is $16 for adults, $10 for kids, $45 for a family.

Featherdale Wildlife Park

217 Kildare Rd
Doonside
Outer West

9622 1644 | *www.featherdale.com.au*

The chance to get close to some of Australia's native animals is the main appeal of Featherdale, which is more intimate than the Sydney Wildlife Park at Darling Harbour. Here you'll see wallabies, wombats, koalas, dingoes, reptiles and fairy penguins, and many more creatures great and small. It's a 45-minute ride from the city (Doonside station is nearby). Parking is free. Open 09:00-17:00 daily. Adult $19, child $9.50, family $55.

Ocean World

Manly Cove Beach
Manly

8251 7877 | *www.oceanworld.com.au*

More intimate than the Sydney Aquarium, there isn't as much to see but you do get the chance to get involved. If you've ever wanted to touch a python or dive with sharks,

this is the place. You can also watch the sharks and massive stingrays being fed by divers, from the fibreglass viewing tunnel at 11:00 on Monday, Wednesday and Friday. Visit after 15:00 to avoid school groups. Adult $17.95, child $9.50, concession $12.95, family $43.95. You get 15% off the ticket price after 15:30.

Aquarium Pier
Darling Harbour

Sydney Aquarium
8251 7800 | *www.sydneyaquarium.com.au*
Highlights of this amazing underwater world include the penguins, seals and sharks frolicking around the fibreglass tunnels, the glass-bottomed walkway (the closest you'll ever come to walking on water) and the tropical fish in the Great Barrier Reef section. Up to 5,000 people visit here each week and school holidays are exceptionally busy. Donations are welcome to the Sydney Aquarium Conservation Foundation, which supports projects and research into threatened marine creatures like seahorses and turtles. A visit is well worth the steep entry fee. Open daily 09:00-22:00. Adult $26, child $13.50, family $42-$63.

Aquarium Pier
Darling Harbour

Sydney Wildlife World
9333 9288 | *www.sydneywildlifeworld.com.au*
Only open since September 2006, the highlights here include the beautiful butterfly enclosures, cute marsupials and scary spiders and snakes. You can't touch the wallabies or koalas but you can watch them go about their business in the glass enclosure. Be warned that the exhibits require some patience as lots of the 6,000 animals are camouflaged in their glass-encased setting. Don't be alarmed to see snakes or lizards outside their enclosures; roaming rangers have them slinked across their shoulders so you can get up close and personal (10:00-17:00). The 1km track is dotted with interesting animal facts and urban myths. Open daily 09:00-22:00. Adult $27.10, child $13.80, family $64.60.

Bradley's Head Rd
Mosman

Taronga Zoo
9969 2777 | *www.zoo.nsw.gov.au*
Before Taronga Zoo opened in 1916, all the animals, including the elephants, had to be moved from their existing home at Moore Park across the harbour on a flat top barge. Since then it has had several upgrades and expansions and on last count it housed 2,600 animals. The most recent was a multimillion dollar renovation in 2006, which includes a fabulous Asian-style tropical elephant enclosure for the zoo's five elephants. Locals love Taronga as much as tourists for its stunning harbour and city views, as well as the exotic animals. Be sure to show up for the photo opportunities with giraffes (daily 13:45-14:15) or koalas (11:00-15:00). There are many wildlife shows during the day, as well as tours and overnight sleepovers – for the latter you'll need to book ahead. Ask at the ferry terminal for a zoo pass, which will save you a few bucks as it includes the ferry, cable car and entry fee. Open 09:00-17:00 daily. Adult $32, child $17.50, family $84.

13 Namba Rd
Terrey Hills
Outer North

Waratah Park Earth Sanctuary
9986 1788 | *www.waratahpark.com.au*
You can only get in to this wildlife park on a prebooked tour because the animals are left to freely roam the 33 hectare property at all other times. Tours are usually timed with feeds to encourage the koalas, kangaroos and dingos to come out of hiding. If you want to spend more time here, volunteers are always welcome to help with animal care and bush regeneration work. Spotlight evening tours are offered from Thursday to Sunday and they're a good way to see some of the nocturnal animals in action. Adult $16.50, child $11. Free for under 3s.

Tours & Sightseeing

Other options **Activity Tours** p.191, **Weekend Break Hotels** p.214

There are myriad professional tour groups to show you the main sights and a handful who will reveal some of Sydney's hidden treasures. From sailing on the harbour to soaking up the atmosphere of The Rocks or gazing down on the city from giddy heights, there are many unique ways to admire Sydney's beauty. If you're planning to go beyond the city limits, popular day trips include the Blue Mountains, Jenolan Caves, Port Stephens, Hunter Valley and Jervis Bay, see p.202 for more.

Sightseeing & Shopping

Various locations

Shop and Save Tours

9679 2992 | www.shopandsavetours.com

Dotted around the city are bargain warehouses where you'll be able to snaffle designer fragrances, shoes and homeware at reduced prices. Bring cash if you can, as not all the warehouses will take plastic. Pick up from major CBD hotels can be arranged and there's a guide on board who can tailor the trip to the group's shopping wishes. Unfortunately the tours don't run every week and if numbers are too low they'll be cancelled. Half-day tour from 09:00-13:00 or 13:00-17:00; adult $40, child $15, family $100. Full day tour: adult $65, child $25, family $165. Free for children under 5 years old.

Activity Tours

Other options **Walking Tours** p.191

1/980 Victoria Road
West Ryde
Outer North

Adventure Quest Paintball

9808 6333 | www.paintball.com.au

If kitting up in camouflage gear and firing giant globules of paint at your mates is your idea of a good time then the long drive out past Windsor might be worth it. If you've never tried it before, paintball is a war game for grown-ups that can be painful if tender spots are targeted. Two teams shoot exploding balls of vegetable dye at opponents in a bid to catch the other team's flag and while protecting their own. The price includes all the equipment and a cuppa. A private bus can be organized to pick up groups in Sydney. From $65.

128 Ramsgate Ave
Bondi

Bondi Surf School

9365 1800 | www.letsgosurfing.com.au

Surfers are notoriously territorial, so if you're a newcomer learn a few basics before you get on the waves. Nobody will tell you it's easier than it looks but these guys guarantee to have you standing up after three lessons. Time your three lessons as you wish over days, weeks or months. If you already know the basics, improver lessons are also available. Three two-hour lessons cost $165-$185 ($20 less for concessions), depending on the season.

5 Cumberland St
The Rocks

Bridge Climb

8274 7777 | www.bridgeclimb.com

The price is steep but this is a once-in-a-lifetime chance to clamber up the famous 'coathanger' and see Sydney harbour sparkling 134m below. Guided tours up the 39,000 tonne arch run every 10 minutes on most days. They're popular with locals as well as tourists for the awesome views, stretching from the east entrance of the harbour to the hazy outline of the Blue Mountains out west. After gearing up in an

191

unflattering khaki bodysuit be prepared to climb. The chirpy guides will point out some of the sights on the way up (it's a slow one hour steady climb with 1,439 steps so you'll have plenty of time to enjoy the view). You can't take your camera so you'll have to fork out extra for a personal photo (the group photo is free). Monday to Friday $169-$200. Twilight tour $249-$260, exclusive dawn tour $295, first Saturday of every month.

32 Witney St
Prospect
Outer West

Getabout 4WD Adventure Tours
8822 5656 | *www.getabout.net*
Most 4WD day tours don't really go that far into the bush but you do get to traverse more picturesque (and bumpier) roads than on a tour bus. Smaller groups also mean you have more flexibility in the day's itinerary. This firm also offers a guided spotlight tour so you can see some of Australia's bush creatures, such as kangaroos, possums, wombats and owls, which are livelier at night. Day tours are from $225 including lunch and snacks.

Bondi Beach
Bondi

Happy Dolphin Bondi
9365 1050 | *www.happydolphinbondi.com.au*
First-timers can learn to dive in four days from $330 (including equipment) and walk away with a PADI Open Water Diver Certificate. If you just want to see what lurks beneath Sydney's waters, try the four-hour dive from $125 (including equipment) with a professional instructor on hand to show you the ropes. Dives for those with previous experience are also offered. See p.227 for more diving options.

Manly Beach
Opp Pine St, Collaroy
Manly

Manly Surf School
9977 6977 | *www.manlysurfschool.com*
Many of Sydney's competing surfers (ike world champion Layne Beachley) ride the waves around this area but if you're a surfing virgin, you'll be in good hands. The instructors are seasoned surfers with at least 15 years experience and five years of coaching behind them. As well as Manly Beach, lessons are offered further north at Long Reef, Collaroy and Palm Beach. Daily lessons are available throughout the year. Adult $55 one lesson or $330 for 10. Child, $45 one lesson or $300 for 10. Private lessons at $80 per hour are also available.

McCarthy's Lane
Cranebrook
Outer West

Penrith White Water
4730 4333 | *www.penrithwhitewater.com.au*
Built for the 2000 Olympics and the only one of its kind in the southern hemisphere, Penrith's White Water Stadium has serious rapids for keen rafters and kayakers, with both guided and self-guided options. You'll need to be at least moderately fit as just hanging on for 90 minutes is quite a workout. Bring shoes and clothes that will stay on if you fall in the water. Wetsuits can be hired if you don't have your own, but all other equipment is provided. If you need to wear glasses, they sell special straps on site. You'll need to book 10 days ahead and pay a deposit. From $72 per person.

Cockle Bay Wharf
Darling Harbour

Sydney by Sail

9280 1110 | www.sydneybysail.com

Those who don't own a boat in Sydney usually hope to make friends with those who do. It's a spectacular way to spend a sunny summer's day. This professional crew can teach you basic sailing skills over four three-hour lessons from $425, usually run over two full weekend days. If you just want a go at steering or to try your hand at trimming the sails, the popular three-hour trip (10:00-13:00 or 13:00-16:00) is a fabulous way to experience Sydney's bustling harbour (from $130 per person). How hands-on the experience is depends partly on where you're sitting, harbour traffic and how involved you want to get. This is one of the best ways to experience Sydney's stunning harbour and should be top of your list. See Boat Tours p.194 and Sailing p.241.

462 Bunnerong Rd
Matraville
Outer South

Sydney Dive Academy

9311 0708 | www.sydneydive.com.au

Exploring below the surface will open your eyes to a less touristy side of the city. These guys have done thousands of dives around Sydney and they'll take you to some of their favourite spots, such as Bare Island where you'll see rare weedy sea dragons, moray eels and blue gropers. You'll need to pass a medical test but once you've completed the course you'll come away with an international divers certification card. You can hire dive gear for $70 for 24 hours. See Diving p.227 for more.

North Sydney

Sydney Harbour Kayak

9960 4389 | www.sydneyharbourkayaks.com

While the cruises might be faster and more luxurious, kayaking allows you to get up close and personal to harbour life. The friendly guides give you a brief run down on safety and kayaking techniques before you set off. There are several different routes, from the obvious (into the main harbour with views of the bridge and Opera House), to the more remote (taking you into the bays and beaches of Middle Harbour). A generous morning tea is provided during a stop at a secluded beach where you'll feel a million miles from the city. Tours cost $99 including morning tea and depart from Spit Road, The Spit Bridge, Mosman. See also Kayaking p.234.

100 Market St
Central

Sydney Tour Skywalk

9333 9222 | www.skywalk.com.au

Adrenalin junkies might not feel an almighty rush, but seeing Sydney from the outdoor platform is still more exciting than surveying the skyline from behind glass. Only open since 2005, the views from up here are spectacular, and at 260m it's almost double the height of the Harbour Bridge. If you feel queasy, try not to chunder over the safety ledge as you'll be fined $5,000. You're harnessed to safety railings the whole time and the guides let you in on interesting city secrets – like the snipers allegedly stationed on the balcony of the US Embassy since September 2001. Admission includes access to the Observation Deck and OzTrek, a goofy simulated ride through Australia on 180 degree screens. Open from 09:00-00:15. Adult $109, child $85 (must be 10 years or older).

Bicycle Tours

Various locations

Bonza Bike Tours
9331 1127 | www.bonzabiketours.com

Although not an overly bike-friendly city, these tours will have you easily dodging Sydney traffic. You'll cover a larger area including spots other tours miss, like the Walsh Bay wharves, with a welcome pit stop at the charming The Hero of Waterloo pub. Riding through the various parks is enjoyable but the biggest thrill is the 'car park run', a dizzying but exhilarating hurtle down the spiralling five-floor car park under the Opera House. There are regular stops so even the less fit won't find it too tough. Choose between a two-hour Sydney highlights tour ($70, departs 14:00), which takes you around the gardens and harbour, or the Sydney classic tour (three and a half hours, $70, departs 10:30). Tours to the less touristy north side are also available.

Boat Tours

Aquarium Wharf
Darling Harbour

Captain Cook Cruises
9206 1100 | www.captaincook.com.au

Catamarans leave roughly every half hour and tours range from basic sightseeing with live commentary to a la carte dinner cruises. They also have a weekend-long cruise; after dinner and dancing on Friday night the ship docks near the Opera House before drifting up and down the harbour and Parramatta River (you are dropped off to stretch your legs during the day at famous landmarks). The cabins are small but there's plenty of space on the top deck to enjoy the harbour sites. Leaves Friday 18:00, returns Sunday 15:00. From $420 per person twin share, all meals included. Basic sightseeing cruise: adult $24, child $20, concession $12, family $59.

King St Wharf
Darling Harbour

Magistic Cruises
8296 7222 | www.magisticcruises.com.au

These top-class catamarans are the newest on the harbour. The massive windows ensure great views from inside but you can also go on one of the decks to take scenic shots. Basic sightseeing cruises include one free beer. The freshly cooked buffet lunch or dinner cruises have delicious king prawns, oysters and a good selection of hot main meals plus cake, cheese and crackers (alcohol is extra). Table service for drinks is fast and efficient. Thankfully the pre-recorded GPS commentary is much more low-key than traditional live commentary. Mondays and Tuesdays are generally quieter. Boats leave from King Street Wharf and Circular Quay. Adult $25, child $18.50, family $69 for one hour basic sightseeing tour. Lunch cruise: $66. Dinner cruise: $89.

Circular Quay

Manly Ferry
13 1500 | www.sydneyferries.info

This is the locals' cruise of choice. The half-hour trip from Circular Quay to Manly is by far the best value-for-money cruise. There's no commentary, which some might find a blessing, and you can spend a few hours exploring Manly at the other end. In peak summer periods it can be a bit of a squash, but it's designed to be public transport, rather than a cruise with all the bells and whistles. Adult $6.20, child $3.10.

Darling Harbour

Matilda Cruises
9264 7377 | www.matilda.com.au

A day pass allows you to get on and off this cruise as you please at any of the five famous landmarks they visit, such as the fish markets, Taronga Zoo, Watsons Bay and Shark Island. Coffee, cocktail and lunch or dinner cruises are also available at extra cost. If you want to see pretty waterside suburbs that most tours miss, try the Lane Cove River Cruise, which goes from Hunters Hill, under Harbour Bridge to Kirribilli and finishes in Darling Harbour (tickets are available on board). Adult $29, concession $25, child $15, family $75.

Oz Jet Boat

20a Waterview St
Putney
Outer North

9808 3700 | www.ozjetboating.com

These guys started the jet boat craze that's sweeping Sydney harbour. After being kitted out in protective gear (which won't stop you getting wet) get ready to be propelled forward at high speed then tossed about by body-wrenching 270 degree spins, heading east towards Taronga Zoo then West past Goat Island before finishing back at East Circular Quay. Expect to get drenched, give your vocal chords a good workout and get off looking like a drowned (but exhilarated) rat. It's loads of fun. Longer tours (45 minutes: adult $80, child $55, family $240) depart at 13:00 daily. Height restrictions apply for kids. Departs Eastern Pontoon, Circular Quay (between the ferry wharves and Opera House) every hour between 11:00 and sunset. Adult $55, child $40, family $170, for 30 minutes. Pregnant women and those with bad backs, necks or heart conditions cannot ride and children must be over 130cm tall.

Sydney Gondolas

215 Harris St
Pyrmont

9698 8321 | www.sydneygondolas.com.au

A little piece of Venice down under, this is the only tour company offering gondola rides on the harbour. They are cosy but surprisingly spacious (you've got about as much room as in the back of a limo). The coxswain stands behind the partially enclosed cabin so privacy is assured. You can bring your own food (one hour gondola hire, $220 with coxswain and set table) but if you choose a catered cruise, your meal will come straight from one of Cockle Bay's best seafood restaurants, Nick's Seafood (90 minute seafood feast for two; $440).

Sydney Jet Cruiser

32 The Promenade
King St Wharf
Darling Harbour

8296 7333 | www.jetcruiser.com.au

With larger boats than Oz Jet, the spins aren't as dramatic but they do whiz through parts of the harbour at high speed. Part cruise and part joyride, it goes all the way to the heads at the harbour entrance before hitting the gas hard. Expect pre-recorded conversational-style commentary and a party mix medley during the fast action. You won't be given a suit to protect you from getting wet but on calm days you come off fairly dry if you're sitting up front. Adult $44, child $33 (must be 11 years or over and a minimum height of 100cm) for 45 minutes. Pregnant women and those with bad backs, necks or heart conditions cannot ride.

Bus Tours

Other options **Walking Tours** p.199

Various locations ◀

Bondi Beach Explorer

13 1500 | *www.sydneypass.info*

The 30km route will help you cover a large area, but you'll have to pick and choose your stops as it's hard to cover all 19 in a day. The buses run every half hour from Circular Quay to Kings Cross, Double Bay, Rose Bay, Vaucluse, Watsons Bay, The Gap, Bondi Beach, Coogee Beach and back to the city via Centennial Park. Start early as the trip takes two hours even if you don't get off. Commentary is provided. Tickets are available onboard or at STA offices – adult $39, child $19, family $97. Tours from 08:45 to 16:15.

Various locations ◀

City Sightseeing

9567 8400 | *www.city-sightseeing.com*

This is the same outfit that runs double decker bus tours in Europe and you'll have to scramble for seats on the open top deck to film the sights (don't forget a hat and sunnies or you'll fry). This bus offers two routes with a pre-recorded English commentary. The Sydney tour runs from Darling Harbour, through the CBD and Kings Cross, and ends at Circular Quay, while the eastern suburbs tour leaves from Central station and goes to Bondi and Double Bay via Paddington. Tickets are valid for both routes for 24 hours from the time of purchase. You can buy them on board or at The Rocks and Darling Harbour Visitor Centres. Adult $30, child $15, concession $25, family $75.

Various locations ◀

Sydney Explorer

13 1500 | *www.sydneypass.info*

The beauty of this regular route is that you can hop on and off as you please for one price. The air-conditioned buses wind their way through the city's central sights from Circular Quay as far east as Kings Cross, south to Surry Hills, over to Darling Harbour via Chinatown and across the bridge to Luna Park. Commentary is provided and tickets are available onboard or at STA offices. Adult $39, child $19, family $97. Tours leave every 20 minutes from 08:40-17:20.

Various locations ◀

Sydney Night Cat Tours

1300 551 608 | *www.nightcattours.com*

If you want to see Sydney by night but don't fancy wandering around solo, this evening tour covers interesting historical areas and scenic spots for shots of the city lights. It starts with a glass of champers and a lesson on Sydney's colonial past at McMahons Point, stops for snacks en route to the eastern suburbs, and ends at the Opera Bar in Circular Quay for a nightcap. Monday, Wednesday, Friday, Saturday 18:30-22:00. Adult $69, child $55, concession $65.

Culinary Tours

Various locations

Gourmet Safaris

9960 5675 | www.gourmetsafaris.com.au

If you go on just one tour during your stay, make it a Gourmet Safari. It's the only way to discover the city's greatest multicultural gift – the food. Created by respected food author and TV presenter Maeve O'Meara, these tours are run by infectiously enthusiastic foodies who open your tastebuds to the city's best Italian, Portuguese, Vietnamese, Middle Eastern, Turkish and Greek foods, among others. Even locals come away wide-eyed after discovering the amazing traditional handmade cuisine on their doorstep. Expect your bags (and bellies) to be bulging with well-priced goodies. Don't have a big breakfast; you'll need the space for the ample tastings at each stop, as well as lunch. You can choose from full-day bus tours to walking tours of selected suburbs, regional trips and international food tours.

Dolphin & Whale Watching

Ross Smith Ave
Sydney Airport
Outer South

Blue Sky Helicopters

9700 7888 | www.blueskyhelicopters.com

Try your luck at spotting a migrating whale from the sky. Even if you don't see any, the city looks incredible on a clear, sunny day, so if you can afford the hefty price tag it's worth considering. It's $525 for 60 minutes and runs in June, July, September and November only.

Pier 26, Aquarium
Wharf
Darling Harbour

Gray Line Port Stephens

1300 858 687 | www.grayline.com.au

The trip takes you three hours out into the North Sea and chances are you will see some of the 80 or so bottlenose dolphins that call this area home. Buffet lunch is included but bring your swimming gear so you can take a dip (the boat has an attached boom net you can jump in). Tours also stop off at Wildlife Park. From October 1to April 30, Monday, Wednesday and Saturday. Adult $151, child $75.50.

North Ryde
Outer North

Sydney Eco Whale Watching

9878 0300 | www.austspiritsailingco.com.au

Between late May and late July about 6,000 whales migrate north from Antarctica, swimming straight past Sydney, often quite close to the shoreline. These guys know where to find them and are allowed to get within 200 metres of the whales. Be aware that you're more likely to see whales in winter as they cruise closer to the shore on the Eastern Australian Current. You're given a 95% chance of seeing whales but if none are spotted they'll offer you another return trip free of charge. Keep your eyes peeled for dolphins, seals and seabirds too. Boats depart Tuesday to Sunday, 08:00 to 12:00 and 12:30 to16:30.

Helicopter & Plane Tours

Other options **Flying** p.230, **Hot Air Ballooning** p.198

Bankstown Airport
Outer West

Red Baron Flights

9791 0643 | www.redbaron.com.au

If the idea of flying over Sydney Harbour in an open-cockpit Red Baron isn't exciting enough for you, the pilots are more than happy to add some stomach-churning loops and rolls into your scenic flight. Girls with long hair should tie it back or they won't see much. Flights over the harbour start from $395 for 45 minutes.

Seaplane Base
Lyne Park
Rose Bay

Sydney By Seaplane

1300 656 787 | www.sydneybyseaplane.com
If you've ever wanted a VIP experience, this exclusive tour is about as Hollywood as it gets. Based next to Sydney's swanky Catalina Restaurant, see p.322, you can choose between five scenic flights over the harbour and beaches; these include lunch at various posh locations on the northern beaches or in Hawkesbury ($320-$460 per person). Ask about flight training if you fancy piloting a seaplane yourself. Adult $145-620, child $70-$310.

472 Ross Smith Ave
Sydney Airport
Outer South

Sydney Helitours

9317 3402 | www.sydneyhelitours.com.au
You'll need a reasonably strong stomach for the twists and turns on the Thrill Seekers Flight ($199 per person for 20 minutes), and the choppers are doorless so it's not for the fainthearted. Scenic flights over the harbour, beaches and to the Blue Mountains are also available in regular helicopters (20-90 minutes, $189-$675).

Heritage Tours

Moore Room
Royal Botanic
Gardens
The Domain

Aboriginal Heritage Tour

9231 8134 | www.rbgsyd.nsw.gov.au
This one-hour tour shows you around Sydney's magical Royal Botanic Gardens from an Aboriginal perspective. Led by an Aborigine guide, you'll learn about the garden's significance for the Cadigal people, the original indigenous inhabitants of this area, plus you'll get to taste some bush foods and be treated to a live traditional Aboriginal dance performance. Tours cost $20 and depart on Fridays at 14:00.

Congwong Bay
Outer North

Bare Island

9247 5033 | www.nationalparks.nsw.gov.au
Experienced rangers will ferry you across to 'Pinchgut', so called because the convicts imprisoned here were on such meagre rations. The fort only saw a smidgeon of war action but you can still see the (very minor) damage caused by an American cruiser aiming shells at an invading Japanese submarine in 1942. Climb the tower for magnificent 360 degree harbour views and cover your ears at 13:00 for the firing of the canon, a tradition since 1906. There is shade to be found at the cafe, but it's wise to bring hats and sunscreen. Monday to Friday, 11:30 to 15:30. Saturday to Sunday, 11:45-15:00. Adult $22, child $18, family $72. Departs from Cadmans Cottage, Circular Quay.

Hot Air Ballooning

Other options **Flying** p.230

1443 Wine
Country Drive
North Rothbury
Outer North

Balloon Aloft

1800 028 568 | www.balloonaloft.com
The thought of getting up at 04:30 might be off-putting but seeing the sun rise while drifting slowly above the vineyards in the Hunter Valley is worth the sacrifice. Despite

the leisurely pace, the excitement on takeoff is palpable and the humorous pilots point out sights along the way, as well as the odd kangaroo. It's the same temperature at 1,200 feet as on the ground but the gas can heat the top of your head so wear a hat. Unfortunately ballooning is very weather dependent so be prepared to reschedule if conditions aren't right. Although hotel pick-ups can be organised, the Balloon Aloft Bed and Breakfast is a handy option. Run by the Balloon Aloft owners, it's clean and modern and only a short walk to sign in for your flight in the morning. Adult $295, child $180 (including a champagne breakfast).

227b Annangrove Rd
Annangrove
Outer North

Cloud 9 Balloon Flights

1300 555 711 | *www.cloud9balloonflights.com*

Cloud 9's early morning balloon flight goes over the city as dawn breaks. On clear days you'll be able to take in panoramic views across Sydney, the surrounding countryside and the Blue Mountains, before setting down for a champagne breakfast in the historic surroundings of Lachlan's restaurant in Old Government House. A mid-week special costs $260 per person.

Other Tours

Manly

Manly Quarantine Station

1300 886 875 | *www.manlyquarantine.com*

Tour the cemeteries, isolation wards and mortuary by lantern light and be spooked by the bizarre stories in this history-steeped station. For over a century from the 1830s, this is where sick new arrivals were held in a bid to contain smallpox and other deadly diseases. Keep an eye out for the hundreds of wall etchings by former inhabitants. The two hour history tour runs from Wednesday to Friday at 15:00, and on Saturday and Sunday at 10:00 and 15:00. Adult $25, concession $19. Ghost tours run Thursday and Friday at 18:30. Tickets $34 (must be 16 years or over). Family ghost tours run Wednesday to Sunday at 20:00. Adult $25, concession $15.

Kings Cross

Weird Sydney Ghost and History Tours

9943 0167 | *www.destinytours.com.au*

Cruising Sydney's streets for two and a half hours in a massive immaculately-restored Cadillac hearse certainly attracts some attention. As well as giving you snippets of interesting history, learning about Sydney's walking dead is a wacky way to spend a summer evening. It's popular with local groups of guys and gals before a big night out. Ask your driver about his personal ghost encounters (particularly those haunting the hearse). Tours depart from Kings Cross, at the corner of Corner Elizabeth Bay Road and Amos Lane at 19:00 daily, 20:00 during daylight savings. Adult $77, child $38.50.

Walking Tours

Blue Mountains
Faulconbridge Station

Blue Mountains Walkabout

0408 443 822 | *www.bluemountainswalkabout.com*

This tour takes you off the tourist track and aims to teach you about traditional Aboriginal life and Dreamtime stories while you wander through the wilderness. Run by Aboriginal guide Evan Yanna Muru, the 8km trek will take you past ceremonial sites and ancient art and offers bush-tucker tastings. Take water, your own lunch and swimming gear so you can dip in the clear billabong at the waterfall (bear in mind you'll be carrying whatever you bring for the entire day). Moderate fitness is required and be prepared for slippery sections and rock scrambling. The walk begins at 10:00 in the Blue Mountains on Faulconbridge Railway Station platform. Tours are $95 per person.

199

Wharf 6
Circular Quay

Bounce Walking Tours

1300 665 365 | *www.bouncewalkingtours.com*

As well as The Rocks, Bounce do a tour through Kings Cross and the stories of sex, murder, corruption and violence give a good insight into the suburb. It started out as genteel, developed into a bohemian enclave of artists and writers, and then became the sex and drug centre of Sydney. You'll meet in Circular Quay and catch a public bus to Kings Cross (included in the price). They also do a tour tailored specifically to mums with prams. Depart Wharf 6, Circular Quay. Tickets are $25-$40.

23 Playfair St
The Rocks

The Rocks Walking Tours

9247 6678 | *www.rockswalkingtours.com.au*

The Rocks is the main historic area of Sydney (although residents of Parramatta and the indigenous population might disagree). It's worth exploring the hidden alleys and cobbled courtyards on your own, but this tour gives a good insight into what life was like before the tourist shops. It's not an altogether pretty history but it's certainly colourful. Tours depart Monday to Friday at 10:30, 12:30, 14:30 and Saturday to Sunday at 11:30 and 14:00. Adult $20, child $10.50, YHA member $16, family $50.50.

Various locations

Self Guided Walking Tours

www.selfguidedwalkingtours.com

This is the tour for the iPod generation. If you can't bear shuffling along in groups, this is a fun solo stroll. Download the audio tracks from the website for $10, then upload it on to an MP3 player and off you go. As well as historical information and imaginative accounts of past events, you get an authentic Aussie accent. Tours include The Rocks (a wheelchair-friendly version is also available), Harbour Bridge, the Bondi to Bronte Walk and Balmain. Tour maps are very basic but the commentary helps to guide you.

Various locations

Sydney Architecture Walks

8239 2211 | *www.sydneyarchitecture.org*

This is a good way to get to know Sydney's architecture with an expert guiding you on a two-hour stroll around the CBD. As well as details on architectural styles, you'll learn about the history, politics and personal trivia that has made the urban cityscape what it is today. Wear sunglasses as you'll be staring skyward quite often. Wednesday and Saturday, 10:30. Adult $25, concession $20 (includes entry to the Museum of Sydney).

Wine Tours

Other options **Alcohol** p.269, **Wine Tasting** p.248, **The Hunter Valley** p.202

Hunter Valley

Boutique Wine Tours

9499 5444 | *www.visitours.com.au*

This is a great way to see the Hunter Valley and learn about wine. Knowledgeable guides lead you to some fabulous boutique wineries, many of which are family-run and stick to traditional methods, like storing in oak barrels (rather than tossing oak chips into the juice) to produce an authentic flavour. The all-inclusive tour for $99 is the best value and includes lunch. The gourmet option costs $139.

Hunter Valley

Hunter Valley Wine and Dine Carriages

0410 515 358 | *www.huntervalleycarriages.com.au*

This is a fun way to get some fresh air at a slow and steady country pace. The stylish horse-drawn carriages seat up to 10 people and the five wineries visited are smaller than those on the main bus tours. Half-day tours ($50-$75) are also available. Day tours are $85 with a restaurant lunch, $75 with an organised picnic.

Tour Operators

If you don't fancy negotiating Sydney traffic or aimlessly pounding the pavement, there are loads of tour operators who will ferry you around the main sites and beyond the city limits. Prices for tours are non-negotiable and there is little difference dollar-wise between the larger players. The Sydney Visitor Centre (www.sydneyvisitorcentre.com) has hundreds of brochures from credible tour companies, but the tours are best booked direct or through major travel agents. You can expect professional service from all the larger operators, including clean buses and knowledgeable, friendly drivers, but if you want a more personal experience or flexibility to change the suggested itinerary, a boutique operator is the way to go. In case you are disgruntled by a tour experience, you can vent to the Australian Department of Fair Trading and complaint forms can be downloaded from www.fairtrading.nsw.gov.au.

Main Tour Operators

Various locations ◄

AAT Kings
9700 0133 | *www.aatkings.com*

This company has been running coach day trips to the Blue Mountains for decades (from $108 daily, with optional overnight stays at extra cost), the Hunter Valley Wineries and Gardens ($145 daily, with lunch) and Sydney day tours that cover all the main sites. You can opt to include walking, cycling or cruising into package deals with the coach tours.

Various locations ◄

Australian Pacific Touring
1300 655 965 | *www.aussiesights.com.au*

As well as covering the usual Sydney landmarks and offering trips to the Blue Mountains and Port Stephens, they also have southward-bound tours to Jervis Bay (a great place to see dolphins) which go home via the Southern Highlands, an up-and-coming food and wine district. Costs are around $145, Tuesdays, Thursdays and Saturdays.

Pier 26 ◄
Aquarium Wharf
Darling Harbour

Gray Line
1300 858 687 | *www.grayline.com.au*

Well-run, with professional guides that double as drivers, and modern clean coaches, they offer a large range of tours to the Blue Mountains (from $125 daily; $134 including Jenolan Caves on Mondays, Tuesdays, Thursdays and Saturdays). Also available are a huge range of Sydney city sightseeing options, including walking tours of The Rocks combined with scenic harbour cruises.

Other Tour Operators

Aussie Wine Tours	4991 1074	www.aussiewinetours.com.au
Blue Thunder Downunder	9977 7721	www.bluethunderdownunder.com.au
Dolphin Explorer Cruise	4441 5323	www.dolphincruises.com.au
Hang Glide Oz	1793 9200	www.hangglideoz.com.au
Hawkesbury Parachute	4576 6028	www.poweredparachutecentre.com.au
Moonshadow 4WD Tours	4984 4760	www.moonshadow4wd.com.au
Mount 'n' Beach Safaris	9439 3010	www.mountnbeach.com.au
Royal Botanic Garden Tours	9231 8134	www.rbgsyd.nsw.gov.au
Scuba Try Dives	4441 5255	www.deep6divingjervisbay.com
Shopping Spree Tours	9360 6220	www.shoppingspree.com.au
Skydive the Beach	1300 663 634	www.skydivethebeach.com
South Coast Nature Tours	4454 0072	www.southcoastnaturetours.com.au
Surf Camp Australia	1800 888 732	www.surfcamp.com.au
Sydney Seaplanes	1300 732 752	www.seaplanes.com.au

201

Weekend Breaks
Other options **Hotels** p.30

Although there's plenty to keep you occupied in Sydney, you'll get a better sense of the real Australia if you head out into the country. There are many spots near the city; the picturesque Blue Mountains are a welcome relief from Sydney's heat, while the north and south coast have stunning beaches and a laid-back atmosphere. For wine buffs, the Hunter Valley is a must-do while the less touristy Southern Highlands also have an emerging food and wine industry. A short flight away, carefree Byron Bay still rates as a popular escape from the rat race and low-key Coffs Harbour has beautiful beaches and superb national parks. And if you really want to get away from it all, take a trip to serene Lord Howe Island, less than two hours flight from Sydney.

Cellar St ◀

The majority of cellar doors are clustered along Broke Road and Hermitage Road – bike tours are increasingly popular (www.grape mobile.com.au) although some of the narrow, potholed roads may leave you a little saddle sore.

The Hunter Valley
New South Wales' best-known wine region, the Hunter Valley is famous for its citrusy semillion and earthy shiraz and has a growing reputation for its olives. As well as free wine tasting, Sydneysiders come here to sample local produce at sophisticated restaurants and pamper themselves at luxury resorts and spa retreats like The Golden Door (4993 8500, www.goldendoor.com.au).

The majority of Hunter Valley wineries are boutique and many only sell their wine through local restaurants or at cellar doors (most open daily 10:00-17:00). Large wineries like Tyrells (9889 4450, www.tyrells.com.au), McWilliams Mt Pleasant (4998 7505, www.mcwilliams.com.au), Drayton's (4998 7513, www.draytonswines.com.au) and Wyndham Estate (4938 3444, www.wyndhamestate.com) offer guided tours. At family-run cellar doors like Ernest Hill (4991 4418, www.ernesthillwines.com.au), it's often the winemaker filling the glasses. Don't miss Audrey Wilkinson, which was one of the first wineries in the area and has great views over the valley (4998 7411, www.audreywilkinson.com.au).

Two hours' drive from Sydney on the F3 Freeway, Cessnock (population 18,000) is the largest town in the Lower Hunter. It is a mix of miners and winemakers but otherwise unremarkable. For a charming slice of colonial history, take the pleasant forested Wollombi Road to the tiny historic hamlet of Wollombi on the junction between the Hawkesbury and Hunter Rivers. Try the Wollombi Tavern's famous Dr Jurd's Jungle Juice, a secret blend of wine and spirits (4998 3261, www.wollombitavern.com.au). Also worth seeing for its well-preserved old-fashioned shop fronts is Morpeth, 35km north of the wineries. It was an important river port in the 1800s and there are some picturesque riverside lunching options on Swan Street. Don't leave without a fresh loaf from the Sourdough Bakery (www.sourdough.com.au), made by descendants of the famous Australian bakers, Arnotts, in the original Arnotts bakery building.

Pokolbin is the bustling centre of the wine-tasting area and is crammed with cellar doors, fancy resorts, cafes, restaurants and an endless convoy of tours within a 5km radius. The artificial Pokolbin Village (49987670, www.pokolbinvillage.com.au) has a basic cafe, upmarket restaurant and dozens of trinket shops. Just down the road is the popular Harrigan's Pub (4998 4000) and the micro-brewery, Blue Tongue (4955 4411). Delicious local dairy produce is available at the

Hunter Valley Cheese Factory (at McGuigans winery, www.mcguiganwines.com.au, 4998 7744), The Smelly Cheese Shop in Pokolbin Village Resort (4998 6960, www.smellycheeseshop.com.au) or Binnorie Dairy in the Tuscany Wine Estate (4998 6660, www.binnorie.com.au).

There are numerous wine tour companies, some offering exhausting day trips from Sydney, while others operate locally, see p.201. The most unique way to see the landscape is from a hot air balloon, see p.198.

There are food and wine related events in the Hunter every month but highlights include Opera in the Vineyards at Wyndham Estate (October), the Hunter Valley Harvest Festival (March/April), A Day on the Green (November/March) with big name international musicians, Jazz in the Vines at Tyrell's (October) and Lovedale Long Lunch (May). The 25 hectare Hunter Valley Gardens are particularly pretty from July to September during the annual festival of flowers (www.hvg.com.au).

You can pick up a Hunter Valley Wine Country Visitors Guide with a good pullout map from the Visitors Information Centre next to Cessnock Airport (4990 0900 or www.winecountry.com.au).

The Hawkesbury River

Convict Trail ◀

Away from the river are good bushwalking tracks, including the Old Great North Road walk. This was carved out of the rock by convicts, to connect Sydney with the Upper Hunter Valley (www.convicttrail.org). It's accessible to horses, cyclists and walkers but not cars.

One hour's drive north-west of Sydney, the bush-bound Hawkesbury River flows from Brooklyn to the edge of the Blue Mountains. It's one of the earliest colonial settlements in Australia, linking historic towns like Windsor and Richmond and winding past the lush Ku-Ring-Gai Chase and Brisbane Waters National Parks. Somersby Falls is a great picnic spot.

The best way to explore the river is on a cruise. The pick of the bunch is the Hawkesbury Ferries riverboat mail run, which still transports letters as well as sightseers (it departs from Brooklyn Wharf, 9985 7566). The licensed Crab N' Oyster Cruise departing from Kangaroo Point also comes highly recommended (www.crab-n-oystercruises.com.au, $89 including seafood lunch). Houseboats are becoming a popular weekend getaway (www.hawkesburyhouseboats.com.au or www.ripples.com.au) and day trippers often come to try their luck fishing.

Wisemans Ferry is based around ex-convict Solomon Wiseman's home, Cobham Hall, which is now the Wisemans Ferry Inn, although much of the original building remains (4566 4630). A 24 hour car ferry will float you across to Dharug National Park for free – contact the National Parks and Wildlife Service (9542 0649, www.npws.nsw.gov.au) for details on the Aboriginal rock carving guided tours (www.npws.nsw.gov.au). The Wisemans Ferry cemetery on Singleton Road is one of the oldest in the country and some settlers from the First Fleet were laid to rest there.

The Hawkesbury has been supplying Sydney with fresh produce since the late 1700s and is well known for its rock oysters, apples, stone fruit and oranges. A top spot to sample fresh local produce is the fantastic 1825 built colonial style Lochiel Café, Restaurant & Gallery at Kurrajong Heights (www.lochielhouse.com.au), which scored a coveted chefs hat in 2005. The beautiful Mount Tomah Botanic Gardens (www.bluemts.com.au/mounttomah) on the Bells Line of Road has a lovely timber deck restaurant overlooking Wollemi National Park.

The Visitor Information Office opposite the RAAF base on Windsor Street, Clarendon (www.hawkesburytourism.com.au) has a good brochure for self-drive tours that details local farms cultivating everything from berries, figs and walnuts to smoked seafood and goats cheese. Some farms are open to the public year-round, typically from 09:00-17:00, while others are seasonal.

Sleeping options include the National Trust classified, 1887-built Tizzana Winery (www.winery.tizzana.com.au), a gorgeous Tuscan-style bed and breakfast, or try the elegant Victorian-style Loxley on Bellbird Hill (www.loxleyonbellbirdhill.com.au).

Finding Flipper
Port Stephens calls itself 'the dolphin capital of Australia'. Around 150 of the merry mammals live here and are sometimes seen playing from the shore.

Port Stephens

A large natural harbour stretching from the mouth of the Karuah River to the Pacific Ocean, Port Stephens is often also called Nelson Bay, after the area's largest town. There are also 26 unspoilt beaches and bays backed by forested hills. Any of the coastal villages, particularly Shoal Bay, Fingal Bay and Nelson Bay are excellent places to unwind for a weekend. Nearly all of them have a large beachside caravan park.

Nelson Bay (population 8,100) is 223km north of Sydney and has a laidback country town atmosphere. The marina has encouraged a new cafe culture and has live entertainment on Sundays from 12:00-15:00, but the main attraction is the water. Good diving and snorkelling spots include Fly Point for its prolific marine life and Looking Glass, which runs through the middle of Broughton Island. Chinese fishermen established a camp here in the early 1800s and it's still excellent for fishing, particularly marlin. You can also hire boats, kayaks, jet skis and diving equipment (www.portstephens.org.au). Back on land you might be lucky enough to spot a koala around Lemon Tree Passage.

For stunning views, head up to the heritage-listed lighthouse, which has an interesting and free, tiny nautical museum with unique exhibits like an old Morse code machine and a rusty megaphone, which they used to call in boats through the bay until 1984. The Inner Light Tea Rooms (4984 2505) next door has the best ocean views in the district.

To the south are the impressive Stockton Beach sand dunes, the country's largest coastal dune system, stretching 30km to Newcastle with some dunes up to 30m high. Plenty of tour operators make the most of the barren mobile dunes offering everything from camel rides (Oakfield Ranch Camel Rides, 4966 4172) and quad biking (www.quadbikeking.com.au) to sand boarding and four wheel driving (www.moonshadow4wd.com.au). Stockton Beach is also great for surfing.

For bushwalkers, Tomaree National Park (www.nationalparks.nsw.gov.au) stretches nearly 20km between Anna Bay and Shoal Bay along a strip of rocky coastline. Take the walking track near the car park to Tomaree Head for breathtaking views.

The trendiest cafes and dullest food chains are clustered down at the D'Albora Marina in Nelson Bay. AquaBlu (4984 9999) has a generous, good value breakfast and pleasant outdoor seating.

Journey to the Past
For an overview of Newcastle's convict past and major sites, ride the historic replica tram at 10:00 or 13:00 from Newcastle Station. The Newcastle Region Art Gallery is also worth a look (4974 5100).

The Central Coast & Newcastle

A one-hour drive north of Sydney, the Central Coast has spectacular beaches, a lively surf culture and gorgeous national parks. Gosford is the largest town but, other than essential shopping facilities, has little to offer. The bustling seaside town of Terrigal (population 10,000) is the best place to base yourself as it has lots of accommodation options and good places to eat. Everything is centred around the busy 4km beach, lined by tall Norfolk Pines. The Cove cafe at the eastern end of the beach has beautiful ocean views from the veranda and good coffee. Both The Reef restaurant (www.reefrestaurant.com.au) and The Cowrie (www.thecowrie.com.au) have fabulous water views and award-winning cuisine (mains $30-$40). The best takeaway option is The Snapper Spot for beer-battered fish n' chips (4384 3780) or Hungry Wolf's Pizza & Pasta (4385 6555), both on the main street across from the beach. The Crowne Plaza (see table p.35) at the eastern end of the main strip has a huge outdoor beer garden and often has live entertainment.

Don't miss the Neale Joseph Gallery (www.nealejoseph.com) and the gorgeous Art Deco Avoca Theatre (www.avoca-beach-theatre-story.org.au).

Other than the pelican feeding that occurs daily at 15:30, there is little to recommend north of Terrigal until you get to Lake Macquarie, an enormous 24km-long body of water with excellent fishing. South of Terrigal, at Avoca, the scenery becomes hillier and greener and partially dominated by dense national park. For guaranteed wildlife sightings, head to the Australian Reptile Park (www.reptilepark.com.au).

Newcastle is the second largest town in NSW, with a population of 250,000 and growing. It was the largest steel centre in NSW from 1915 until 2000, when much of the steelworks were shut down. The former industrial wharves now house upmarket eateries at Honeysuckle. The city centre and mall generally feels like a ghost town as locals spend their time in the surf, on the beach and in lively suburbs like Cooks Hill. The best places to eat are at bohemian Darby Street, notably Goldberg's Coffee House (4929 3122) with its lovely outdoor garden and Grind Coffee Co. (4929 4710) for well-presented modern Australian food. Darby Street also has some fabulous boutiques like High Tea With Mrs Woo (4926 4883) and Blue Star Elements (4926 1993).

Locals drink at the ultra relaxed The Brewery, which often has good live entertainment and excellent pub grub (www.qwb.com.au). The nearby heritage-listed Customs House has a lovely alfresco cafe and licensed bar. Beaumont Street in Hamilton also has some good Mediterranean eating options.

For district views head to Mount Sugarloaf Lookout where you can see much of the central coast and inland lakes. Don't miss the 5km Bather's Trail Walk from Nobbys Head past Fort Scratchley (only used once, to defend against the Japanese in the second world war) to the large Merewether Baths. On the way you'll pass the Bogey Hole, an excellent swimming spot carved out by convicts. King Edward Park has lovely views out to the ocean where dozens of ships queue to enter the harbour. For more information visit the tourist office at Hunter Street (4974 2999 or www.visitnewcastle.com.au).

Wollongong & Illawarra

Rough and Puff
Golfers will love the picture-perfect 65 hectare golf course at Shellharbour (www.shellharbour links.com.au) and if you're into steam trains and trams, check out the Illawarra Light Rail Museum at Albion Park (4256 4627, www. ilrms.com.au).

Illawarra is an Aboriginal word meaning 'high and pleasant place by the sea', which pretty much rings true. Starting from Sydney's southern end and running all the way to Kiama, the 85km scenic stretch of coast boasts idyllic beaches, tranquil lakes and a string of national parks. The Sea Cliff Bridge, completed in 2005, is the most scenic route south, winding its way along the limestone cliffs with glorious views out to the Pacific Ocean. The best panorama by a long shot is on Bald Hill, a popular hang gliding spot. From here, follow the Grand Pacific Drive along the glittering ocean vista and lush forest to Bulli (the grand old Heritage Hotel is a cool spot for a beer in summer, 4284 5884, www.heritagehotel.com.au) and on to Wollongong.

Dubbed 'the Gong' by locals, Wollongong is the third largest city (population 181,000) and working harbour in NSW. Its working class origins date back to 1844, when 300 convicts laboured on the inner harbour basin, a picturesque spot plagued by pelicans. The hilly north side is greener than the south where the stark steelworks stretch on endlessly at Port Kembla. The pedestrian mall is a few blocks from the beach and has major chain stores and a few cafes, but the pick of the eating options is Levendi (4261 8023), right on the harbour with great gelato and sensational fish burgers. The adjacent park might look appealing for lunch but watch out for the aggressive seagulls. Head up the Cliff Road hill to Verdi's for a caffeine fix (4226 1677) or, for a local pint try Five Islands Brewery (4220 2854, www.fiveislandsbrewery.com). Local maps and information are available at the visitors centre near the mall (1800 240 737 or www.tourismwollongong.com).

Just south of Lake Illawarra, Shellharbour is one of the oldest settlements in this region and developers are now spreading sprawling estates across its vacant acres. Its most enchanting feature is the lively 'eat street' (Addison Street) near the water with buzzing restaurants and an excellent pub, the Ocean Beach Hotel (42961399, www.oceanbeachhotel.com.au).

The delicious Tandoori Junction (4295 3300) has lovely views from the big balcony. The Shellharbour Country Kitchen (4296 3205), a cute 1800s corner store-come-cafe, has good coffee and snacks. Nearby Bushrangers Bay is a popular diving spot.

Around 120 kilometres south of Sydney, Kiama is famous for the blowhole, a natural attraction caused by a south-east wind spurting seawater up to 60 metres in the air through a passageway in the rocks (conditions need to be right for the effect to be dramatic). The blustering southerlies can be fierce in this area, particularly in August and September. Kiama is a sleepy place, popular with baby boomers and busy with families at Christmas. Bombo Beach has some treacherous rips and an ugly railway line directly by the dunes, so locals stick to Surf Beach. Better still, head south to serene Seven Mile Beach, Gerroa. Not far from Gerroa is the enormous Jamberoo Action Park (www.jamberoo.net) with waterslides and rides. Don't miss the Minnamurra Rainforest Loop Walk, an easy 2.6km boardwalk through subtropical surrounds, in Buderoo National Park (www.nationalparks.nsw.gov.au).

Husky Crusts

Don't miss the casual Husky Bakery and Café (4441 5015) in Jervis Bay, which not only has the best pies for just $3.50, but also a sunny wooden deck where you can scoff down delicious hot scones and read the free newspapers.

South Coast

There's a lot to rave about on the south coast – lush forests, rolling green hills, the whitest beaches and abundant aquatic wildlife (including penguins, dolphins and seals). Nowra is the largest town in the area, but nearby Berry (population 1,600) and smaller seaside hamlets like Huskisson are far more charming. Settled soon after Sydney, many are changing rapidly as developers set up sprawling McMansion-type estates. And while traditional takeaways still abound, good espresso coffee and gourmet organic options are thriving in country NSW.

The tourist brochures declare Berry 'a country experience like no other' – a big call but not entirely an exaggeration. A delightful town, its main street is dotted with heritage-listed buildings and gourmet food options – don't miss the Berry Woodfire Sourdough Bakery, a block from the main street (www.sourdough.com.au). For coffee or gourmet sandwiches with local products, you can't beat The Emporium Food Co. with its quaint country-style retro kitchen (4464 1570). Berry can get unbearably crowded on weekends.

Further south through dairy country, sleepy Milton is also a good place to stock up on gourmet goodies and browse the homeware boutiques. Pilgrims Wholefood Takeaway (4455 3421) on the Princes Highway has good, strong organic coffee and the best homemade burgers in town. Next door, The Settling Inn (4455 3449) is a terrific upmarket BYO, famous locally for the twice-cooked duck.

Jervis Bay draws holidaymakers for the many dolphin and whale watching cruises. The nearby town of Huskisson with its clean blue harbour and one of the world's whitest beaches is the spot to base yourself (many dolphin cruises leave from the tiny harbour here).

Kangaroo Valley

Nestled between the South Coast and Southern Highlands, and just 159km south of Sydney, this tiny hamlet is surrounded by dairy farms, dense rainforest and a pretty river. Nature is what draws visitors here. Bird watching is big, as is bushwalking (there are more than 25 walking tracks in the valley) but watch out for snakes in spring and summer. Camping is popular (the Kangaroo Valley Tourist Park is right by the river, near the bridge, 1300 559 977) and the more adventurous will love horse riding up the mountain for fabulous views of the Shoalhaven Gorge (www.kangaroovalleyhorseriding.com), mountain biking (www.kangaroovalleyescapes.com.au) or canoeing down the Kangaroo River (www.kangaroovalleycanoes.com.au).

Driving through the lush scenery is a pleasure in itself. The narrow and winding Kangaroo Valley Road runs along steep sandstone escarpments but it's far more picturesque than the Princes Highway. You'll get good views across to Cambewarra Mountain from a lookout near Nowra.

The village itself (population 350) was classified by the National Trust in 1977, and has a few delightful heritage buildings, such as the sandstone courthouse-come-police station and the Anglican Church of the Good Shepherd, built in 1876 (open by appointment only, 4421 2018). Just east of the town, by the river gorge, is the 1898 built Hampden Bridge, the oldest surviving suspension bridge in NSW, with pretty turreted towers. There are a couple of arts, crafts and homeware shops, traditional takeaways and the decent Valley Bakehouse (4465 1500). For lunch, try the lovely Friendly Inn (4465 1355). Traffic can be slow at the weekends as Sydneysiders converge on the tiny valley town.

Rare Reads

Three kilometres north of Berrima is the enormous Berkelouw Book Barn (www.berkelouw. com.au), with a collection of rare, second hand books and a tranquil cafe.

Southern Highlands

First settled in the 1820s, when farmers discovered the fertile grazing land, this heritage-rich rural area became a desired address for the elite from the 1880s (it now has the highest concentration of pilots in NSW). It still retains its original aristocratic atmosphere with countless English-style estates, young boutique wineries (there are 15 open cellar doors) and award-winning restaurants. For Sydneysiders it's the most accessible slice of rural idyll with a well-to-do air. Don't miss the area's new five-star winery, Centennial Vineyards, with an excellent country-style restaurant attached (4861 8700, www.centennial.net.au). A cheaper lunch option is the 'Vintner's Lunch' with wine tasting at Bou-saada Vineyard near Berrima (4878 5399, www.bousaada.com).

The largest town in the area, Bowral is less grand than the impressive estates that surround it, but it's a good base for wine tasting and just 30 minutes to Fitzroy Falls, a 270m waterfall in the enormous Morton National Park (www.nationalparks.nsw.gov.au). You can admire the cascading falls from several lookouts. Bowral has some interesting antique shops and the Don Bradman Museum (Bowral was his childhood home – 4862 1247, www.bradman.org.au). The Farmers' Market is held every second Saturday, offering local produce like mushrooms, olives, cheese and mayonnaise. Mittagong holds few attractions but from here you can detour a further 66km to the limestone Wombeyan Caves, which are less touristy than Jenolan Caves.

Berrima is by far the highlight of the Southern Highlands as the pretty Georgian colonial town seems to have barely changed since it was settled in 1829. The museum-like streets with delightful sandstone buildings are crammed with restaurants, cafes and antique shops (the old wares at Peppergreen are worth a look). Of particular note is Eschalot (4877 1977, www.eschalot.com.au), which recently won a coveted chef's hat, as did the equally pricey The Journeyman (4877 1911). The old English-style Magpie Café (4877 2008) has good lunch options, or try the lavishly restored (and apparently haunted) White Horse Inn (4877 1204). The 1834 Surveyor General Inn up the road claims to be Australia's oldest continually licensed hotel (4877 1226).

A highlight is the interesting museum in the grand 1838 Courthouse (4877 1505, www.berrimacourthouse.org.au), run by a colourful local character, Colin (ask him about the resident ghost). It's right next door to the 1839-built jail, which is now a low security detention centre for women and you may see uniformed prisoners pottering in the front garden.

Nearby is the lovely Mundrakoona Winery (4872 1311), which also makes Australia's newest award-winning lager, the delightfully named Fish Rock Leather Jacket. The quaint, family-run Howard's Lane winery (www.howardslane.com.au, 4872 1971) where they still prune the vines by hand, is also nearby. If possible, avoid weekends when Berrima is overrun by tourists.

For decent town maps drop into Tourism Southern Highlands in Mittagong. You can also call them on 1300 657 559 or visit the website www.southern-highlands.com.

Blue Mountains & Jenolan Caves

Some 120km west of Sydney, the Blue Mountains really do look a hazy blue from a distance; the colour is caused by the evaporation of oil from millions of eucalyptus trees. An ancient seabed that rose over eons and slowly eroded, the Blue Mountains became a World Heritage Site in 2000. The 1,000m high mountains posed a severe obstacle to early settlers until explorers Wentworth, Blaxland and Lawson managed to forge a path along the steep cliffs and canyons in 1813. Today's Great Western Highway still follows the same route, though the Bells Line of Road is a more scenic drive. The Blue Mountains are a particularly popular winter getaway as it often snows in June, July and August.

Katoomba is the largest town (population 9,000) but the real reason to visit is its proximity to the natural attractions. Nearby are the famous Three Sisters at Echo Point, which overlooks the dense forests of the Jamison Valley. The three pillar-like rocks take their name from an Aboriginal legend about sisters who were turned to stone by a witchdoctor in a bid to stop them marrying men from a forbidden tribe.

Bathurst

Bathurst was founded in 1815 and is the oldest inland town in Australia. It is linked to Sydney by the Great Western Highway. Before this was built, the presence of a navigable route through the mountains was kept secret for fear that convicts may try to escape. As a base for western-bound journeys, lodgings were established and Bathurst has some fine examples of Victorian architecture. Traces of gold were discovered in the 1820s, but this was kept quiet until 1851 by authorities worried that convicts and soldiers would stop working to hunt for treasure.

Originally a coal mining settlement, the mountains suddenly became fashionable when the rail line was completed in 1868, and the well-heeled built grand weekenders with beautiful gardens, particularly around Leura. The incredibly steep Scenic Railway was used to haul coal up the mountain until the 1930s, when it became a tourist attraction. The three-minute descent is still the best pick of the three overpriced rides now offered at the somewhat tacky Scenic World (www.scenicworld.com.au). Once you're in the valley you've got numerous bushwalking options – the Grand Staircase is highly recommended and the easy 3km Grose Valley Cliff Top Walk has spectacular views but won't wear out your legs. You can buy a handy bushwalking map and info guide from Blue Mountains Tourism Authority Information Centres at Glenbrook and Echo Point (1300 653 408 or www.australiabluemountains.com.au). Further down the mountain, Wentworth Falls has a lovely waterfall while the Euroka Clearing near Glenbrook is a great spot to see grazing kangaroos.

Food-wise, the 1816 wood-panelled Paragon Café (4821 3566) in Katoomba has a great atmosphere and delicious handmade chocolates. Just 2km east at Leura is Café Bon Ton (4782 4377) with its rustic home-style cooking and cosy fireplace, and the French-inspired Silks Brasserie (www.silksleura.com) has excellent service and a good value lunch menu. Those with a sweet tooth will love the old-fashioned lolly shop, while the many knick-knack stores will keep antique hunters interested. Outdoors, the colourful formal Everglades Gardens are open year-round (09:00 to sunset, $6). The Leura Gardens Festival opens nine gardens to the public in mid-October.

The spectacular 400 million year old Jenolan Caves, one of the world's oldest and largest underground cave systems, are worth the extra one-hour drive past the ghost town of Hartley. The caves are only accessible by guided tour. The more adventurous should try the discovery tours, which involve climbing and contorting your body through teensy gaps in the rock. Seasoned walkers can retrace the steps of pioneers from Katoomba to the Jenolan Caves on a three-day trek; ask for the Six Foot Track brochure at the Visitor Information Centre ($4.50).

There are numerous excellent bed and breakfast options (see p.39) and stately hotels like The Carrington or luxury Lillianfels. Prices inflate over holidays and festivals, like the folk and blues festival in March and Winter Magic Festival and Yuletide Fest in June. For more information see www.visitbluemountains.com.au.

209

Lord Howe Island

Mountain High

Hikers can attempt to conquer the 875m Mount Gower but you'll need a local guide to help show you the way. There's a golf course and moderately easy walking trails on the north side for the less fit.

Less than two hours flight from Sydney, this crescent shaped island is a great long-weekend getaway. Life on tiny Lord Howe (11km long, 2km wide) is leisurely to the extreme. The 350 residents are limited to the same 25km speed limit as tourists on bikes. At least one resort, Arajilla (see table p.214), hires bikes out to guests ($8.50 per day). Mobile phones don't work here and electricity is limited (there are no streetlights after dark so take a torch).

There are a handful of places to eat, one general store and the local bowling club for drinks. The island boasts kilometres of world-heritage listed rainforest and the southernmost coral reef in the world – divers and snorkellers have plenty to see in the relatively calm waters off the main bay. You can hire an expert guide like Peter Busteed to show you the best spots, from $25 per person, including morning tea and equipment (6563 2298). Don't miss the fish feeding in the shallow waters at Ned's Beach in the late afternoon, when the expectant creatures slap your ankles and nibble your toes with glee.

Camping is not permitted but there are enough accommodation options for all budgets. The comfy Arajilla and Capella Lodges (see table p.214) are at the upmarket end. The best time to visit is September to May, particularly for bird lovers, as seabirds nest on the island.

Credit cards are accepted but there are no ATMs so bring extra cash. It's one of the only destinations in Australia that still weighs you before boarding the flight to Sydney. They also still use paper rather than e-tickets, so don't forget your documents for the return trip. Qantas flies to Lord Howe 5-10 times a week, depending on the season, and luggage is limited to 14kg.

Byron Bay

Whale Spotting

The pretty Cape Byron Lighthouse dominates the headland. It's a popular spot for hang gliding and you might be lucky enough to see migrating whales from June to July and September to November. Call the Byron Bay Headland Trust for information on 6685 6552.

A one-hour flight from Sydney, this sleepy seaside town at Australia's easternmost point was once an oasis for die-hard hippies and surfers. Despite the influx of Sydneysiders, it hasn't lost its alternative culture and laid-back atmosphere. The upscale crowd has encouraged gourmet cafes, day spas and classy boutique accommodation alongside the traditional alternative healing centres. Thankfully the pristine beaches have avoided high-rise resorts.

Byron Bay is popular all year round but particularly over Christmas and during the huge five-day East Coast Blues & Roots Festival at Easter (www.bluesfest.com.au;) so book accommodation well in advance. It's also lively on the first Sunday of each month when Butler Street becomes a massive market.

The 3km Cape Byron Walking Track is highly recommended. You'll get glimpses of the Julian Rocks Island from here, a popular scuba diving location.

Clarks Beach near the cape is good for surfing, as is Watego's, the only entirely north facing beach in NSW. If you can't afford a night at the ultra exclusive Rae's on Watego's (see table, p.214), the attached fine dining restaurant is a treat. A great budget sleeping option is the clean, friendly and central Byron Palms Guesthouse (see table, p.214).

Other good food options are the legendary Beach Café on Clarks Beach for a sumptuous breakfast, Café Wunderbar (6685 5909) for excellent European-style cakes and pastries or the chic Dish Restaurant Raw Bar (www.dishbyronbay.com.au) for cocktails and exquisite meals. The Beach Hotel (66856402, www.beachhotel.com.au) is where the crowds start gathering from midday while the Hotel Great Northern (6685 6454) and the Railway Friendly Bar (6685 7662) are popular with locals.

To see what Byron used to be like, head 20 minutes inland to serene Bangalow, which has retained its low-key community feel. Get Stuff Gourmet on Bryon Street is a classy deli-style cafe with reasonably priced gourmet sandwiches and fresh sweets, while the 1940s Bangalow Hotel does good modern brasserie food in a relaxed setting (6687 1314, www.bangalowhotel.com.au). The enormous Bangalow markets on the fourth Sunday of every month have everything from fresh organic produce and delicious Byron Bay ice cream, to handmade jewellery, wooden handicrafts and clothing. Even more laid-back still is Brunswick Heads – shaded by fragrant frangipani trees. The beer garden at Hotel Brunswick (6685 1236) has live music and simple bar food.

Coffs Harbour

Have a Banana
The state's 'banana belt' since the 1800s, the hills surrounding Coffs are still strewn with banana plantations and you can often pick up cheap fresh fruit at roadside stalls on the outskirts of town.

A one-hour flight north of Sydney, Coffs Harbour (population 60,000) has always been a popular family holiday destination thanks to its pristine beaches and mild climate. The Great Dividing Range meets the sea on this stretch of coast, forming a stunning backdrop to the unspoilt beaches and lively harbour.

The Fisherman's Co-Op (6652 2811) down at the marina has excellent seafood or try Tide & Pilot Oyster Bar & Sea Grill (6651 6046) on Marina Drive.

The steep trail up to the nature reserve on Mutton Island (a path leads up from the marina) affords fabulous views. The island gets its name from the noisy mutton birds that nest here between November and April.

You can arrange to swim with the dolphins or seals at the Pet Porpoise Pool (advance bookings essential, www.petporpoisepool.com). Just north of the city is the kitsch Big Banana (www.bigbanana.com), which has interactive displays, historical information, an ice-skating rink and toboggan run.

The four-level Lake Russell Gallery, 16km north of Coffs has exceptional modern Australian art and craftwork and pleasant tearooms (6656 1092, www.lakerussellgallery.com.au).

Fifteen minutes from Coffs Harbour, the tiny village of Urunga is virtually untouched by tourism. The riverside Anchors Wharf Café on Bellingen Street (6655 5588) serves succulent seafood and steak and does a great breakfast. The Ocean View Hotel is (as the name implies) a good spot for a drink with a view (6655 6221) while the Honey Place on the Pacific Highway is also an interesting stop to learn about bees and pick up fresh honey products (6655 6160, www.honeyplace.com.au).

Further inland is the tiny village of Bellingen (population 2,750), a classic country town with faded weatherboard facades, it is set in a lush valley by the Bellingen River and surrounded by rich pastureland. Well known for its alternative culture, Bellingen is home to many artists and painters and has some fabulous shops. Don't miss The Yellow Shed (6655 1189) in the old Worker's Recreation Hall, and The Old Butter Factory (6655 2150) at the eastern end of the main street. The best bargains are always at the huge Bellingen markets, held on the third Saturday of every month, which have everything from hippy clothes to funky hammocks, woodcraft and jewellery.

Road Trips

Most highways outside of Sydney (except for major freeways) are two-lane roads. Speeding, drink driving and not wearing seat belts are heavily punished, particularly during public holidays. Speed limits are 100-110kph on highways, 50-60kph in town and 40kph in school zones. Watch out for wildlife on the road, especially from dusk to dawn when nocturnal animals like kangaroos are active; they make a big dent. See p.136 for more on driving.

A winding drive 60km west of Coffs is the World Heritage Listed Dorrigo National Park (www.nationalparks.nsw.gov.au), a superb subtropical rainforest with excellent bushwalking. At the park entrance (open 17:00-22:00) is the excellent Dorrigo Rainforest Centre, which has information on walks, souvenirs and a lovely cafe with bush views. From here, the Lyrebird Link Track (400m) connects with the Wonga Walk, an easy 5.8km elevated boardwalk through the forest past several waterfalls and a lovely picnic spot, known as The Glade. Don't miss the Skywalk, a 70m suspended walkway over the upper rainforest. Over 120 species of bird have been counted in the Dorrigo National Park, including the shy lyrebird.

Weekend Break Hotels

191 Mitchell Parade
Mollymook
Outer South

Bannisters Point Lodge
4455 3044 | *www.bannisterspointlodge.com.au*
With stunning views over the Pacific Ocean, this 30 year old motel has been jazzed up to cater for a more upmarket crowd and has been awarded four and a half stars for its efforts. Nearly all the modern, tastefully decorated rooms have wonderful ocean views, as does the pricey Asian-influenced mod Oz restaurant, which just earned itself a coveted chef's hat from *The Sydney Morning Herald*. Surrounded by untouched bushland it's a serene place to spend a weekend. There's a pool with adjacent cocktail and pizza bar, plus a luxury day spa, but some of the rooms are only three and a half stars. Prices range from $350-$700.

Hume Highway
Sutton Forest
Southern Highlands

Eling Forest Winery and Vineyard
4878 9499 | *www.elingforest.com.au*
One of the oldest wineries in the region, this rustic accommodation was built in the 1830s (watch your head through the low doors) and is yet to be star rated. The country-style rooms are clean and well maintained. The blue and white honeymoon suite is the prettiest with a lovely bay window overlooking farmland. The separate two-bedroom 1840s cottage ($70 per person) is quaint but showing its age. The adjacent award-winning restaurant has an excellent menu, extensive wine list (the cellar door is opposite if you want to sneak in some tastings beforehand) and friendly young staff. Breakfast is freshly cooked by the restaurant chef from the a la carte menu. Rooms are $130-$190 per night, including a full breakfast.

Horderns Rd, Bowral
Southern Highlands

Milton Park Country House Hotel
4861 1522 | *www.milton-park.com.au*
Once owned by wealthy retail giants the Hordern family, this enormous five-star estate still offers the finest in country living. It has huge French provincial style rooms, a cosy bar, a billiards room, fine restaurant and large shady verandahs. You may be lucky enough to have the European-style spa, pool, sauna and gym all to yourself as they tend to be under-utilised, but book ahead for the divine skin treatments. The big buffet breakfast is in a beautiful glass-conservatory overlooking the immaculate formal three hectare gardens (well worth an early morning stroll). Grab a free newspaper near reception. Milton Park is outside the eastern boundaries of the tourist map so ask the visitor information centre to help with directions. Prices range from $330-$550 per night midweek (including breakfast) to $425-$650 per night at weekends.

Ekerts Rd, Pokolbin
Hunter Valley

Peppers Guest House
4993 8999 | *www.peppers.com.au*
With its cool, wide verandahs surrounded by tranquil gardens and vineyards, this classic country homestead has a devoted following, so you'll need to book well ahead. As you'd expect in a four and half star guest house, the light, luxurious rooms are tastefully decked out in modern neutrals. Minutes from several cellar doors, there's also a pool, spa and tennis court on site. The bar has a cosy fireplace and the award winning Chez Pok restaurant has excellent French, Asian and Italian-influenced cuisine – book a table on the verandah underneath the grapevines (they have insect repellent to fight off the mozzies). The wine list is extensive and staff can guide you on matching a wine to your meal. Breakfast is a hearty full buffet affair with friendly staff pouring endless coffee. Grab a free newspaper at reception. Rooms are $328 to $328 per night midweek, $792-$992 per weekend (two nights).

56 Tongarra Rd
Albion Park
Ilawarra

Ravensthorpe Guest House & Restaurant

4257 6096 | *www.ravensthorpe.com.au*

Built by the area's first doctor over 100 years ago, this stately English-style home hasn't been star rated yet but it's the kind of place you won't want to leave. The tastefully furnished rooms with high timber-panelled ceilings and modern ensuites overlook the formal garden grounds, vine-covered yard and tennis court. The best deal is the separate cottage (formerly the doctor's surgery), which has a huge spa and its own leafy mini-courtyard for a private alfresco breakfast. It's a dead-set bargain during the week ($149-$179 including a gourmet continental breakfast). Dinner is available in the elegant dining rooms from Wednesday to Sunday. It's close to a tiny airport but with so few flights you'll barely notice.

Crooked River Rd
Gerroa
Outer South

Seven Mile Beach Holiday Park

4234 1340 | *www.kiama.net/holiday/sevenmile*

Spread along the river by Seven Mile Beach, the best windsurfing beach in the region, this popular four-star park offers a range of accommodation from basic camping to spa cabins (from $225) and surf shacks ($110 with shared amenities). The safari tents ($135) are a fun option for not-so-keen campers as they have basic ensuites, wooden floors and proper beds. The front decks overlooking the river are a nice spot for a nightcap. There's a pool and spa on site as well as a decent-sized kiosk, but to satisfy your taste buds you're best walking a couple of hundred metres up the river to Seahaven Café, a cute wooden cottage with deli-style light meals and espresso coffee.

Shellharbour Rd
Cnr Ocean Beach Drv
Shellharbour
Illawarra

Shellharbour Resort

4295 1317 | *www.shellharbourresort.com.au*

Clean and functional with friendly staff, this three and a half star motel is on the main road so it can get a little noisy – but all rooms have ocean glimpses to remind you of where you are. It has all the mod cons – cable TV, fridge, microwave, decent double beds and clean ensuites – and is just a few minutes drive to the Addison Street restaurant strip or Stockland Shopping Centre for supplies. Parking is free. At $109-$120, it's pretty good value.

26 Lea Ave
Wamberal
Central Coast

Terrigal Hinterland

4385 5354 | *www.terrigalhinterland.com.au*

One of only two five-star bed and breakfast options on the Central Coast, this retreat overlooks a lush semi-rural valley but is only minutes from the beach. Each of the two immaculate rooms has large comfy beds with enormous ensuites and the massive spa can't be beaten. Each room has a private entrance and a large shared lounge with snacks, wine glasses and tea and coffee facilities. One of the rooms has full wheelchair access, as does the pool. The friendly owners will do everything to please without being intrusive. Breakfast is fabulous – fresh fruit, as much toast and coffee as you like and heavenly scrambled eggs. Expect to be serenaded by cicadas over summer. Less than five minutes drive from central Terrigal. Rooms are $160-$190 per night.

Travel Agencies		
Best Flights	1300 767 757	www.bestflights.com.au
Flight Centre International	13 3133	www.flightcentre.com.au
Harvey World Travel	13 2757	www.harveyworld.com.au
STA	13 4782	www.statravel.com.au
Travel.com	1300 130 482	www.travel.com.au
Zuji	1300 888 180	www.zuji.com.au

Other Weekend Break Hotels

Sydney has some glorious spots to escape to for weekends away and your accomodation choices range from rustic farmstays to luxury resorts and spas. If you can't find what you're looking for below or in the reviews on previous pages, try the tourist board for each region. Contact details are listed with every area's write up.

Other Weekend Break Hotels

Location	Name	Telephone	Website
Blue Mountains	Carrington Hotel	4782 1111	www.thecarrington.com.au
	Hydro Majestic Grand Mercure Hotel	4788 1002	www.hydromajestic.com.au
	Jenolan Caves House	1300 763 311	–
	Lillianfels Blue Mountains Resort & Spa	4780 1200	www.lilianfels.com.au
	Woolshed Cabins	4787 8199	www.woolshedcabins.com.au
Byron Bay	Byron Palms Guest House	6680 7539	www.byronpalms.com
	Rae's on Watego's	6685 5366	www.raes.com.au
	Victoria At Ewingdales	6685 5388	–
Central Coast	Clan Lakeside Lodge	4384 1566	www.clan.com.au
	Crowne Plaza Newcastle	4907 5055	www.ichotelsgroup.com
	Crowne Plaza Terrigal	4384 9111	www.ichotelsgroup.com
	Kims Beach Hideaway	4332 1566	www.kims.com.au
	Norah Head Lighthouse	13 2975	–
	Star of the Sea Terrigal	4385 7979	www.staroftheseaterrigal.com
	The Bells On Coast	4360 2411	www.thebells.com.au
Coffs Harbour	Boambee Palms Boutique B&B	6658 4545	www.boambeepalms.com.au
	Breakfree Aanuka Beach Resort	6652 7555	www.aanuka.com.au
	Sawtell On the Beach	6655 2002	www.sawtellonthebeach.com.au
	The Sebel Aqualuna Beach Resort	6653 7500	www.mirvachotels.com.au
Hawkesbury Valley	Loxley On Bellbird Hill	4567 7711	www.loxleyonbellbirdhill.com.au
	The Sebel Resort & Spa	4577 4222	www.mirvachotels.com
	Tizzana Winery	4579 1150	www.winery.tizzana.com.au
	Two Rivers Retreat	4575 5372	www.tworiversretreat.com.au
Hunter Valley	Capers Guest House	4998 3211	www.capers.com.au
	Cypress Lakes Resort	4993 1555	www.cypresslakes.com.au
	Harrigan's Irish Pub & Accommodation	4998 4000	www.hvg.com.au
	Splinters Guest House	6574 7118	www.splinters.com.au
	The Carriages Country House	4998 7591	www.thecarriages.com.au
	Wild Edge Retreat	4998 3304	www.wildedgeretreat.com.au
Kangaroo Valley	Clerevale	4465 1621	www.clerevale.123go.com.au
	Tall Trees B&B	4465 1208	www.talltreesbandb.com.au
Lord Howe Island	Arajilla Retreat	1800 063 928	–
	Capella Island Lodge	9918 4355	–
Port Stephens	Marina Resort	4981 4400	www.marinaresort.com.au
	Nelson Bay Bed & Breakfast	4984 3655	–
	Peppers Anchorage	4984 2555	www.peppers.com.au
South Coast	Bellachara Boutique Hotel	4234 1359	www.bellachara.com.au
	Best Western City Sands	4222 3111	www.bestwestern.com.au
	Rydges Wollongong	4220 7800	www.rydges.com
	Sandholme Guest House	4441 8855	www.sandholme.com.au
	Woodbyne Boutique Hotel	4448 6200	www.woodbyne.com.au
Southern Highlands	Berrima Guest House	4877 2277	www.berrimaguesthouse.com
	Links House Boutique Hotel	4861 1977	www.linkshouse.com.au
	Peppers Manor House	4860 3111	www.peppers.com.au
	The White Horse Inn	4877 1204	–

Not big, but very clever…

Perfectly proportioned to fit in your pocket, this marvellous mini guidebook makes sure you don't just get the holiday you paid for but rather the one that you dreamed of.

Hong Kong Mini Visitors' Guide
Maximising your holiday, minimising your hand luggage

Abu Dhabi · Amsterdam · Bahrain · Barcelona · Dubai · Dublin · Geneva · Hong Kong · Kuwait

EXPLORER

Therapeutic Feeding   Essential Medicines   Surgery

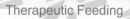

MEDECINS SANS FRONTIERES
أطباء بلا حدود

Providing emergency medical
relief in over 70 countries.

help us help the helpless

Activities

Sports & Activities

Sydney's wealth of activities will keep you engaged and passionate about life. Wherever you go, you'll see people enjoying a city that lends itself perfectly to outdoor pursuits.

With its warm summers and temperate winters, the clear waters and gorgeous beaches of Sydney's beautiful harbour and coastline are a focal point for many residents. Sydneysiders enjoy swimming in the city's amazing open air pools, joining fitness classes at waterside parks or taking to the jogging paths alongside the sparkling harbour.

This giant playground is the setting for everything from sailing, surfing and kayaking to triathlon events, golf and rollerblading. But it's not just about coastal activities. Travel an hour or two in any direction and you'll see how diverse Sydney really is. The nearby mountains, rivers, parks and bushlands offer opportunities for mountain biking, hiking, horse riding and adrenalin sports. The unbeatable campsites and trails open another world of possibilities to intrepid explorers.

Sydney activities don't stop at the outdoor events. You'll find all sorts of indoor sports, clubs and groups, some of the best gyms, most luxurious health spas and alternative pursuits like yoga, pilates and tai chi.

And there are more cerebral activites on offer too. If you're interested in expanding your horizons in your new home, you can take up astronomy, flower arranging or learn

Active Aussies

According to 2006 figures from the Australian Bureau of Statistics, 68% of adults had exercised in the two weeks prior to interview. This included walking (49%), moderate level exercise (36%), and vigorous exercise (15%, more common among men and the younger age groups).

Activity Finder

to paint, cook or dance. Either way, this is a city that can make you wonder what exactly 'spare' time is.

Whatever activity you're interested in, practitioners, instructors and coaches are highly trained and tuition is normally very good. With myriad sports clubs and groups catering to everything from archery to wine tasting, this is one city than can guarantee you'll never be stuck for something to do.

Sports & Leisure Facilities

Take a stroll around Sydney's streets, beaches and parks and you'll quickly get a sense of how much emphasis Sydneysiders place on looking and feeling their best. From the hordes of joggers treading the paths around the harbour to the group training sessions run in many of the city's parks, the place is filled with serious workout fanatics. The sheer number of sport and leisure facilities available reflects that, and there's a dizzying array of gyms, health clubs and sports centres to choose from. Standards are generally high and prices are competitive - just work out where you'll be living or working and choose a gym or health club that's convenient. See p.254 for listings of public and private facilities.

Aqua Aerobics

Aqua aerobics may not look particularly cool, but it's a fantastic way to keep fit without putting a strain on your muscles and joints. Give it a try if you're pregnant or suffer from knee or lower back problems. It's also a great way to lose weight, and you can burn thousands of calories in a single workout. Many of Sydney's health clubs and swimming pools offer aqua aerobics as part of their regular programmes. There aren't many places more spectacular to take part in a class than in the North Sydney Olympic pool. It's at the edge of the harbour, right underneath the bridge.

Aqua Aerobics		
Cook & Phillip Park Aquatic and Fitness Centre	Central	9326 0444
North Sydney Olympic Pool	North Sydney	9955 2309
Victoria Park Pool	Outer West	9298 3090

Observatory Spa (p.259)   *Spa Chakra (p.260)*

Archery

Sydney Olympic Park
Outer West

On Target Archery
9748 8854 | *www.archery.net.au*

Sydney Olympic Park was home to the 2000 Olympics and it's also the base for one of Sydney's leading archery schools. If you're an absolute beginner, you can try an initial hour-and-a-half-long class, before embarking on a three-week course. Each session costs $20. They can also organise team building days and professional coaching, or cater to less formal groups.

Cnr Codrington St &
Darlington Ave
Darlington

Sydney University Archery
9351 4960 | *www.susport.com*

Sydney University Archery club caters for all levels, from beginner right through to expert. It regularly enters competitions through the NSW Archery Association so you can put your new skills to the test and try to establish yourself as part of the archery elite. Training takes place on the campus at St Paul's Oval.

Art Classes

Other options **Art Galleries** p.164, **Art & Craft Supplies** p.271

The University of
New South Wales
Paddington

College of Fine Arts
9385 0684 | *www.cofa.unsw.edu.au*

Sydney's College of Fine Arts runs lots of courses for full-time art students – but they also offer several evening and weekend courses for the general public in areas like landscape painting, life drawing, sculpture, textiles and poster design. Courses run during academic terms. You can view a full list of current courses (and register) on their website.

Various locations

Eastern Suburbs Community College
9387 7400 | *www.escc.nsw.edu.au*

This college offers over 500 courses at centres across the eastern suburbs. Their arts-based courses cover ceramics, crafts, drawing, painting, illustration, fabrics, fashion, glasswork, jewellery, sculpture and more. Visit their website for a complete listing and to register for a course.

117 George St
The Rocks

Julian Ashton Art School
9241 1641 | *www.julianashtonartschool.com.au*

The Julian Ashton is Australia's oldest fine arts school. It's main campus, down in The Rocks, is close enough to the Museum of Contemporary Art for students to stroll off and take in some modern inspiration while learning traditional skills. It offers part and full-time courses in life drawing, oils, watercolours, printmaking, sculpture and modelling. These have a broad appeal and are taken up by students of all ages. For the serious artist, this renowned school offers a range of diplomas and formal qualifications and standards.

Various locations

University of Sydney
9351 2222 | *www.usyd.edu.au*

The University of Sydney runs professional, affordable short courses and their arts programme is led by some of Australia's finest artists. Courses change from one term to the next, but you can choose anything from a part-time, eight-week children's book illustration course to a month-long, full-time introduction to jewellery design. Register online or by phone.

Enjoy the sights of Sydney with Australia's No.1 Lager.

RED EMPEROR AMBER ALE
Bronze Medal, International Section
2006 International Beer Awards

LEATHER JACKET LAGER
Gold Trophy, Best Australian Lager
2006 Australian Beer Awards

Experience all Sydney has to offer with Australia's best lager and it's award winning companion. We at FISH ROCK have created our beers in compliance with the Bavarian Purity Laws, combining Czech Saaz hops, barley, aromatic yeasts and pure mineral artesian waters. The result award winning preservative free, European style beers.

To find your secret fishing spot, **www.fishrockbrewery.com.au**

Astronomy

Observatory Hill
The Rocks

Sydney Observatory

9241 3767 | *www.sydneyobservatory.com.au*

This is Australia's oldest observatory, and it houses a 3D space theatre, a range of telescopes and a planetarium. Nighttime visitors can get excellent views of the moon and other aspects of the southern sky. Admission charges are $15 per adult and you'll need to prebook. If you'd like to learn more about astronomy, they run a variety of part-time courses covering topics such as 'Exploring the Heavens', 'Choosing a Telescope', 'Understanding Relativity' and other astronomical concepts. Visit their website for a full list of current courses.

Belly Dancing

Other options **Dance Classes** p.227

Visit any one of Sydney's many Turkish restaurants and you're likely to witness the art of belly dancing. Often, as soon as your meal finishes, the professional dancers will come out, and may even try to encourage a little audience participation. But if you'd like to learn this ancient Arabian art in a slightly more formal manner, there are a number of courses on offer. Try Amera's Palace Belly Dance Boutique in Newtown (9519 4793), the Arabesque Middle Eastern Dance School in Bondi (9310 1386) or head to Ruby Biscuit in Darlinghurst (9818 5329).

Birdwatching

Other options **Environmental Groups** p.229

Sydney's varied and colourful birdlife can be seen everywhere. Walk the city's streets and you'll be amazed at the cacophony, the preening, the squabbling and the downright cheekiness of its winged inhabitants. Whether you want to see beautiful black cockatoos, brilliantly-coloured parrots, waddling pink and grey galahs or cackling kookaburras, Sydney is an ornithologist's paradise. Perhaps the most impressive winged creatures though are the swarms of squeaking fruit bats you'll see silhouetted against the city skyline as they fly out from the Botanic Gardens at dusk, to roost in the eastern suburbs.

Various locations

Birding Tours

4923 6819 | *www.birdingtours.com.au*

Richard Baxter and Phil Hansbro run all kinds of tours around Sydney and NSW designed especially for bird-lovers. Their North Sydney tour takes you on a search for elusive heath and woodland birds such as the beautiful lyrebird, emu wrens and black cockatoos. A one-day tour (with a minimum of two people) is $250.

Farnell Avenue
Audley Heights
Outer South

Royal National Park Birdwatching

9542 0629 | *www.nationalparks.nsw.gov.au*

Just an hour south of Sydney you'll find the world's second-oldest national park (after the USA's Yellowstone). Packed with incredible diversity, from heath-land walks to beautiful surf beaches and rainforest tracks, it also contains an amazing amount of birdlife. Take a walk with a renowned birdwatcher and see a unique array of birds in their shady rainforest habitats. You might even see the blue kingfisher dive for its lunch, or hear the strange call of the green catbird. Don't forget your binoculars and strong walking shoes. Birdwatching tours run throughout the year and cost around $30 per person.

Bowling

Lawn bowling has regained popularity in Sydney of late – it's even considered trendy these days. Head to one the fashionable eastern suburbs and you'll find a mix of young and old, all making the most of the friendly atmosphere, outdoor setting and licensed bar on sunny weekend afternoons.

Trumper Park
Paddington

Paddington Bowling Club

9363 1150

With its popular outdoor greenside bar, it's hard to know which is the bigger draw here – the bowling or the socialising. The place is often at its busiest on Sunday afternoons. If you live within a 5km radius of the club, you can become a member for just $2 – otherwise you can play without joining. Weekend rates are $10 per person for a three-hour session, and the onsite restaurant can deliver food direct to your table on the green. The club operates from 15:00 to 19:00 on weekdays and from 13:00 to 19:00 on weekends. Bookings are essential.

163-189 Birrell St
Bondi

Waverley Bowling Club

9389 3026

With its three greens, licensed bar and barbecue facilities, this club is one of the largest barefoot bowling clubs in Sydney. On some nights it becomes a live music venue, hosting DJs and bands. Weekend summer sessions run from 12:00 to 16:00 and 16:00 to 20:00. Entry is $10 per session.

Camping

Other options **Outdoor Goods** p.292

You don't need to travel far out of town to get back in touch with mother nature. Sydney's many National Parks are ideal for camping, and many are within an hour's drive of the city. Set up your tent, start up a fire, boil up the billy and get ready for a true wilderness experience amongst the rainforests, meadows, beaches and coastal heaths of Sydney's wild borders.

The best time to camp in this part of Australia is between November and April when the weather is at its warmest. However, winter camping is possible too and what you sacrifice in warmth, you more than make up for in the respite from the flies and mosquitoes.

Many of the designated campsites here are well supplied with toilets, hot showers, barbecue facilities and car parks, though some of the more remote or inaccessible sites are basic. Remember to bring your own gas stove and drinking water, and be aware that because of the danger of bushfires, wood and solid fuel fires are not permitted. There are, however, designated fireplaces in many campgrounds.

223

Blue Mountains National Park

Bruce Rd
Glenbrook
Outer North

4739 6665 | www.nationalparks.nsw.gov.au

Just 24km north of Sydney, the hazy eucalyptus forests of the Blue Mountains are home to a number of excellent camping sites. Euroka, situated at Glenbrook, is famous for its grey kangaroo population, and is well served with amenities. Entry is $5 per night. Perry's Lookdown has some of the best views over the Grose Valley and Mount Banks. The maximum stay here is one night, but camping is free. Ingar campground has the perfect swimming spot at the nearby creek's dam. Again, there's no charge to stay here. Check with the Blue Mountains Heritage Centre for booking information on these and other Blue Mountains sites. Office hours are 09:00 to 16:30. See also p.214 of the Exploring chapter and the camping section of the places to stay table in General Info, p.39.

Ku-Ring-Gai Chase National Park

Bobbin Head Rd
Mount Colah
Outer North

9472 8949 | www.nationalparks.nsw.gov.au

Around 50km north of Sydney, where the Hawkesbury River meets the ocean, this park's campground is at the Basin, near West Head, on Pittwater. It's accessible by ferry or water taxi from Palm Beach wharf, or you can walk about 2km from the West Head road. The excellent facilities cater for up to 400 people and you'll be able to enjoy swimming, bushwalks, mountain biking, birdwatching and much more. Fees are $10 per adult per night and it's possible to reserve your space online (office hours are 10:00 to 16:00).

Royal National Park

Farnell Ave
Audley Heights
Outer South

9542 0683 | www.nationalparks.nsw.gov.au

Driving 30km south of Sydney, you'll be spoilt for choice here. There are three campsites; Bonnie Vale, North Era and Uloola Falls. Bonnie Vale has the most amenities, with drinking water, toilets, showers and picnic tables. Fees are $8 per adult per night and booking is essential. For a more rustic camping experience, try either of the other two. Fees are $3 per adult per night (office hours are 10:30 to 13:30).

Canoeing

Other options **Kayaking** p.234, **Outdoor Goods** p.292

Bushsports

Various locations

9360 0587 | www.bushsports.com.au

Bushsports' exercises include canoeing trips around Sydney Harbour, the Hawkesbury River, the Blue Mountains and Hunter Valley. Groups can range from 10 to 500 people. You'll be briefed on paddling techniques and canoe safety, before teaming up for paddle races and events. They also organise paddling trips along the Colo, Sydney's cleanest flowing river, just an hour north-west of town, and surrounded by national parkland and abundant wildlife. This trip costs $159 per person, with a minimum of eight people required.

Penrith White Water

McCarthy's Lane
Cranebrook
Outer West

4730 4333 | www.penrithwhitewater.com.au

Situated in the foothills of the Blue Mountains, this was the canoe and kayak slalom venue for the 2000 Olympics Games. These days it's open to the public and you'll experience the best in white-knuckle paddling as you navigate the whirlpools and rapids of this man-made course. Each session lasts for 90 minutes and they even have a conveyor belt at the bottom of the course to take you back up to the top. A half-day sampler for beginners costs $66.

Balmoral Beach
Mosman

Sydney Outrigger Canoe Club

04 1615 4246 | www.sydneyoutrigger.com.au

If you're keen to get involved in outrigger canoeing, this club runs regular events and welcomes new members. They offer regular new paddler six-week training programmes at the southern end of Balmoral Beach. During your one to two hour weekly sessions, you'll learn basic paddling skills and safety drills, while paddling on the picturesque harbour. The course costs $120.

Climbing

4-12 Frederick St
St Leonards
Outer North

Climb Fit

9436 4600 | www.climbfit.com.au

Located on Sydney's north shore, this climbing centre and gymnasium has over 200 set routes for all abilities. Beginners will be lead through the basics by trained staff before being set loose on the walls. They also offer free belay instruction. There are no joining fees and casual rates are $15 per session.

7 Unwins Bridge Rd
St Peters

Sydney Indoor Climbing Gym

9519 3325 | www.indoorclimbing.com.au

Sydney Indoor Climbing Gym is the city's largest, and it offers climbing on walls up to 17 metres high. They also have a large bouldering area. Their facilities are suitable for all ages and levels of fitness and expertise, and they can also organise climbing events for birthday parties and adult corporate team building. The centre is open daily from 09:30 until 22:00 (23:00 on Thursdays) and closes at 21:00 on weekends.

Cookery Classes

13 Paul St
Balmain

Cucina Italiana

9555 1904 | www.cucinaitaliana.com.au

This cookery school specialises in traditional Italian cooking. They run courses like the 'Long Italian Lunch', where you'll prepare (and most importantly, get to eat) a full Italian meal. The course costs $120 including lunch and wine. It also has classes for junior chefs, designed to teach your little bambinos how to create simple dishes.

9-11Bungan St
Mona Vale
Outer North

Food Stuff

9999 3033 | www.foodstuff.com.au

Cooking classes are held here most weeknights and on some weekends, and cover subjects such as pasta, cheeses, herbs and spices and themed dishes. Each two-hour class consists of a demonstration and tastings, with recipe handouts so you can recreate three to four dishes at home. Classes start at $70 per person.

Drummoyne
Outer West

Infusions Cooking School

04 1454 7686 | www.infusionscooking.com

This is the place to learn more about middle eastern cooking. Classes are very much hands-on and limited to eight students, for more personal tuition. Choose from classes covering mezze, finger food, main dishes, desserts and Arabic sweets. Course fees start at $80, and costs cover tuition, food, drinks and copies of the recipes.

216 Parramatta Rd
Stanmore
Outer West

Paris International Cooking School

9518 1066

If you want to get back to some cooking basics, French chef Laurent Villoing offers a six-hour course in knife skills, consisting of an intensive introduction to slicing and dicing and even vegetable sculpture. After an introduction to knives, you'll learn the fine art of speed chopping. Once you're doing an approximate impression of a TV chef, you'll prepare (and then hungrily devour) a delicious four-course meal. The course costs $95 per person.

Sydney Seafood School

Cnr Bank St and
Pyrmont Bridge Rd
Pyrmont

9004 1111 | www.sydneyfishmarket.com.au

Seafood makes for a popular meal in Sydney. This school teaches how to prepare and cook the mind-boggling array of species available from the famous fish market. Classes begin with a demonstration, and then in groups of five, you'll recreate the dishes under the watchful eye of the teachers. Courses range from seafood basics to intensive weekend workshops with leading chefs. Their most popular class, the four-hour Seafood BBQ class costs $135 and teaches you everything you need to know to barbecue fish, squid and shellfish to perfection.

Cycling

Other options **Sporting Goods** p.295, **Cycling** p.44

There are plenty of opportunities for cycling in and around Sydney. The city has dedicated cycle lanes, but pedalling around the city's busy central streets can be hazardous and taxis can be pretty casual in their attitude to those on two wheels. For full enjoyment, it's better to take your bike out to some of the excellent cycle tracks along parts of the harbour and in some of Sydney's parks. Don't forget that bikes can easily be taken aboard trains in greater Sydney, opening up possibilities for cycling in places like the Blue Mountains (see p.208 of Exploring and p.224 of this chapter for more). Be aware that you're required to wear a helmet by law here, with on-the-spot fines for cyclists caught with their noggin exposed to the breeze.

Centennial Park Cycles

50 Clovelly Rd
Randwick

9398 5027 | www.cyclehire.com.au

You can take your pick of places in Sydney hiring bikes by the hour, day or weekend, but this is one of the more popular venues. Here you can rent a mountain or hybrid bike and then make use of the pleasant 4km cycle lane around the park, before exploring the off-road tracks beyond it. Prices start at $12 per hour for 60 minutes, with discounted rates for those that fancy holding on to their bikes for longer. The hire shop is open from 08:30 to 17:30 daily.

Manly Cycle Centre

36 Pittwater Rd
Manly

9977 1189 | www.manlycycles.com.au

This shop boasts a grand selection of bicycles for sale, from meaty mountain bikes to speedy racers. It also has a good same-day repair service that might come in handy after testing the limits of your new purchase. You can also hire decent all-terrain bikes to explore the pretty trails around Manly Dam, Red Hill and Oxford Falls. A full day's cycle hire costs $35.

Sydney Cycling Club

Centennial Park
Paddington

www.sydneycyclingclub.org.au

The club lays on regular tours and five training rides a week for its 200 members, leaving from Sydney's Centennial Park. Routes cover 25 to 50km rides out to Watson's Bay at the edge of Sydney's harbour, as well as the main eastern beaches of Bondi, Bronte, Tamarama and Clovelly. The group often finishes with a sociable post-ride coffee or breakfast in the park's cafe.

Dance Classes

Other options **Belly Dancing** p.222, **Music Lessons** p.237

Various locations

Club Salsa

9212 0111 | www.clubsalsa.com.au

Australia's biggest salsa school runs classes around the city, with each lesson structured to take you from the basics to more advanced steps. You can drop in to any of the beginner, intermediate or advanced classes or register for a short-term course. Both singles and couples are welcome.

268 Cleveland St
Surry Hills

Dance Central

9319 2268 | www.dancecentral.com.au

Offering all kinds of classes and workshops, Dance Central covers lots of the more exotic, contemporary styles, including hip hop, funk, dancehall, breakdance, Bollywood and belly dancing, as well as more widely known styles like salsa, samba, tango and swing. They even offer classes in capoeira, Indian classical and Polynesian dance. These are drop-in classes, and entry is $16, or less with a pass for 10 lessons.

Various locations

Fred Astaire Dance Studios

9279 2180 | www.fredastaireaustralia.com.au

This studio specialises in private lessons for singles or couples, with more personalised attention. As the name suggests, the focus here is on the more traditional styles like salsa, tango, foxtrot, cha cha, waltz and rumba. They cater to both beginners and advanced students. The studio even offers special wedding dance lessons, where they choreograph a dance to your favourite song.

Various locations

North Shore Dance Studios

9388 0235| www.dancestudio.com.au

This northern beaches company (with two studio locations) offers both private lessons and group classes in ballroom, latin and salsa dancing. An eight-week beginners course costs $135, while bridal dance training starts from $75 per lesson.

Pier 4
Hickson Rd
Central

Sydney Dance Company Studios

9258 4818 | www.sydneydancecompany.com

This is one of the country's most recognised dance companies and they run more than 60 adult dance classes each week. Classes cover just about every style you can think of; jazz, funk, hip-hop, tap, ballet, contemporary, latin and stretch are all on offer. Whether you're a beginner or more advanced, there's a class to suit. They are run on a casual basis, so you can just drop in whenever you like. The price for each class is $18 per visit, or a multi-pass works out at $15 per lesson.

Diving

Other options **Snorkelling** p.243

While the best diving happens a couple of thousand kilometres up the coast on the world famous Great Barrier Reef, it's still possible to enjoy some excellent dives from Sydney's ocean beaches, and boat dives to shipwrecks off the coast. There are plenty of companies offering training courses, as well as trips for the more experienced. And there's plenty to see in the protected marine areas around Sydney, including giant cuttlefish, huge blue gropers, sea dragons and the occasional shark. For the less adventurous diver, there are some easy dives off the beaches around Manly, Bondi and Watson's Bay. For shipwreck diving, try the Valiant, off northern Sydney's Palm

Beach, an accessible 27 metres down, and home to a variety of anemones, sponges and fish. Dive at the right time of year and you might even catch a glimpse of the humpback whales as they pass (and sometimes enter) Sydney's harbour on their annual migration up the coast.

324 Rocky Point Rd
Bondi

Abyss Scuba Diving
9583 9662 | www.abyss.com.au
Recently voted Australia's best dive operator, Abyss offer regular PADI certificate courses for $445, with discounts for group bookings. They also offer a range of more advanced courses, a refresher, and regular excursions for qualified divers – one of which includes a three-day Great White shark cage diving trip for those brave enough.

10 Belgrave St
Manly

Dive Centre Manly
9977 4355 | www.divesydney.com
This PADI certified training centre offers a comprehensive range of full and part-time courses, and multilingual instructors. Their mid-week, four-day learn-to-dive programme costs $395 and covers theory, pool training, four ocean dives and equipment rental.

West Esplanade
Manly

Oceanworld
8251 7877 | www.sharkdive.oceanworld.com.au
Whether you're a novice or an experienced diver, visit the huge aquarium at Manly for the opportunity to get up close and personal with some of its inhabitants. Choose from a range of 30 minute dives that will bring you face to face with huge grey nurse and wobbegong sharks, moray eels, stingrays, sea turtles and other marine life. Prices range from $180 to $245. Participants must be 14 years or over and bookings are essential.

49 President Ave
Kogarah
Outer South

Snorkel Inn
9588 5042 | www.snorkelinn.com.au
Snorkel Inn run their dive school from southern Sydney, with a choice of flexible learn-to-dive scuba programmes for $365. In addition, they run courses in everything from wreck or night diving to underwater photography and often sell old dive school equipment for reasonable prices.

Dog Training
Other options **Pets** p.293

Adams Rd
Penrith
Outer West

K9 Training
4736 8419 | www.dogobedience.com.au
If your dog jumps, pulls, chews, barks or behaves aggressively, K9 Training offers everything from one-off private lessons to a 14 day in-house training course. Their teaching is dog friendly, humane and positive and they guarantee that if a new problem arises, they'll provide free follow-up lessons for 12 months. One-hour lessons start from $65.

Lot 3, Sixth Rd
Berkshire Park
Outer West

PETS
9834 6613 | www.petstraining.com.au
This dog academy runs a seven-day in-house dog obedience course for $300 (plus boarding), which gives untrained dogs a thorough schooling. Alternatively, private lessons that target specific problems cost $60 each. They even run special agility courses to prepare the Lassies of tomorrow for the world of TV, film and commercial work.

6 Philip Rd
Leppington
Outer West

Sydney Dog Training Centre

9606 2005 | www.sydneydogtraining.com.au

This dog obedience centre offers a series of dog training courses, many of which can be run from your home. They specialise in obedience, behavioural problems, stopping aggression, guard dog training, tricks and agility. Training is done with body signals and voice commands using the clicker technique, and they don't use choke chains. A 21-lesson basic obedience course costs $450.

Environmental Groups

Other options **Voluntary & Charity Work** p.74

18/142 Addison Rd
Marrickville
Outer West

Conservation Volunteers Australia

1800 032 581 | www.conservationvolunteers.com.au

Volunteers with this group work on various practical conservation projects to help improve the environment. Become a member and you could be involved in projects focusing on tree planting, waste reduction and recycling, wetlands or conservation of rainforest revegetation.

Callan Park Nursery
Chapman Rd
Annandale

Rozelle Community Native Nursery

9660 1304

This volunteer group works on nursery projects and reintroducing local plant species to Leichhardt and the surrounding suburbs. They meet at the nursery each Wednesday and Friday from 08:30 to 14:00, as well as the morning of the first Sunday of each month. Send an email with your address details for a postcard containing more information.

Dee Why
Outer North

Youth Lead

9984 8917 | www.ozgreen.org.au

Youth Lead runs three-day seminars designed to give young people the skills, motivation and opportunities to build a sustainable future. This environmental action and leadership programme aims to educate and raise the awareness of people aged between 15 and 25.

Fishing

Other options **Boat Tours** p.194

Sydney offers remarkable variety for keen fishermen, with deep sea, river, estuary, sports and fly fishing all on offer in areas around Sydney harbour, Broken Bay and Pittwater. The fishing is good year-round, with species like john dory, salmon, bonito, kingfish, bass and perch, as well as octopus, crab and many other exotic species all readily available. There's a good choice of charter companies offering excursions for either deep or shallow water fishing. If you'd rather go it alone, there's no shortage of excellent spots to choose from. Be aware that while the water around Sydney harbour is cleaner than it used to be, recent high levels of dioxins have forced a ban on commercial fishing in the harbour. Caution is also advised if you're fishing for personal consumption.

Various locations

Allie Hunter

9891 4246 | www.alliehunter.com.au

Specialists in big game, reef and sports fishing, Allie Hunter has a 34 foot high-speed boat for charter. If it's game fishing you're after, they can take you out in search of marlin, tuna, bonito and sharks (depending on the time of year) for $230 per person

229

(group discounts available). Half-day estuary and reef charters for kingfish, snapper and more cost $115 per person (maximum of 10). All bait and tackle is supplied. Pick-up from Spit Bay, Rose Bay and Watson's Bay.

Various locations ◀ Calmwater Fishing Charters

4385 6879 | *www.calmwaterfishingcharters.com.au*

Catch huge jewfish, flathead, mackerel, salmon and kingfish in the calm bays and estuaries around Sydney's northern beaches. Your boat comes with all gear, bait and licences supplied. A six-hour outing with an expert guide costs $900 (winter season) or $1,200 (summer season). Pick-up from Spit Bay, Rose Bay and Watson's Bay.

Various locations ◀ Justin Duggan's Fly Fishing Tours

9985 1241 | *www.sydneyflyfishing.com.au*

Sydney's only specialist in saltwater fly fishing organises both private tuition and fishing excursions around the Broken Bay, Pittwater, Hawkesbury river and harbour areas. Lessons cost $50 an hour (minimum of two hours), while a full day's saltwater estuary and pelagic tour is $475 per person, with discounts for group bookings. All tackle and equipment is provided.

Flower Arranging

Various locations ◀ Eastern Suburbs Community College

9387 7400 | *www.escc.nsw.edu.au*

This college offers over 500 courses at centres across the eastern suburbs. Their floristry course teaches techniques for creating all styles of both traditional and modern design using seasonal flowers and Australian natives. Visit their website for a complete listing and to register for a place on the course.

7 Seven Hills Rd ◀ Sydney School of Floristry
Baulkham Hills
Outer West   *9686 7287* | *www.sydneyschooloffloristry.net.au*

This school runs courses and workshops in floral art, designed for students wanting to enter a career in this field, and also for people with a hobby-level interest. Courses teach you how to make floral arrangements for the home, fruit and floral arrangements, flower baskets, Christmas wreaths and decorations.

Flying

Other options **Hot Air Ballooning** p.198

Hangar 53 ◀ Airborne Aviation
Camden Aerodrome
Outer West   *4655 7200* | *www.airborne-aviation.com.au*

You can train for the internationally recognised Australian pilot's licence with this flying school, which offers one-on-one training at a pace to suit you. They offer a choice of aircraft, from the standard Cessna to unique planes like the Vintage de Havilland Tiger Moth. For your first trip you'll have a 30 minute trial instruction flight in a Cessna 172. Cost is $140 per person.

685 Comper St ◀ Basair
Bankstown
Outer West   *9791 0111* | *www.basair.com.au*

This western Sydney flying school offers flight training for all licence levels. Budding private pilots can train for the General Flying Progress Test and the Full Private Pilot Licence in their brand new Tecnam aircraft. Training rates are $189 per hour, which also includes fuel, oil and insurance. They also have gift packages, with a three-hour introductory flying lesson for $230 per person. Scenic flights over Sydney Harbour and the Blue Mountains can also be arranged.

Golf

5 Military Rd
Bondi

Bondi Golf Course

9130 3170 | *www.bondigolf.com.au*

With spectacular views of the ocean around Bondi, this is a challenging, nine-hole old-style course designed to help you work on your short game. Recently landscaped and with a new green, it's also a historical landmark complete with Aboriginal stone carvings. You can also do whale-watching here and might be lucky enough to see some making their way to feeding and breeding grounds as you practise your swing. The fee for nine holes is $15, golf lessons are $50 and set hire is $18.50. Both visitors and members are welcome, but booking is essential.

38-42 Balgowlah Rd
Manly

Manly Golf Course

9948 0256 | *www.manlygolf.com.au*

One of Australia's oldest, Manly golf club is a fine example of Georgian-style Mediterranean grandeur. It's a challenging 18 hole, Grade one course, complete with panoramic views and multiple tees, so it's ideal for golfers of all standards. It also offers banqueting services for a range of functions, with space for up to 350 guests. But it's not cheap. This is a members only club, charging a one-off entrance fee of $10,375, with an annual subscription fee of $3,195.

Anzac Pde
Moore Park
Paddington

Moore Park Golf Course

9663 1064 | *www.mooreparkgolf.com.au*

This centrally located Grade 1 club is just 10 minutes from Sydney's CBD. With 18 holes, large greens and rolling fairways, it enjoys great views across the city skyline. It's suitable for all abilities and also contains a driving range, two bars, a bistro and function rooms. Weekend public green fees are $50 for a full round of golf, and there are a number of membership options.

Hang Gliding

Bald Hill
Helensburgh
Outer South

Sydney Hang Gliding Centre

0400 258 258 | *www.hanggliding.com.au*

This is Sydney's most popular centre for hang gliding. Personal instruction in modern gliders will see you taking off from spectacular locations at the edge of Sydney's Royal National Park. Beginners can try a tandem flight, which starts with a 30 minute ground lesson and then half an hour in the air before landing on a nearby beach. This is a great way to try it out before opting for further tuition. The price is $180 on weekdays, and you should wear loose, warm clothing. All other equipment is supplied.

Various locations

Windworks

0408 818 731 | *www.windworks.com.au*

Windworks offers practical training and theory lessons for hang gliding fanatics. Beginners can get in on the action too – the introductory tandem flight lasts for around 30 minutes and costs $150. The northern beaches flights take in views of the area between Manly and Palm Beach, and flights also take off over the Blackheath area of the Blue Mountains.

231

Hiking

Other options **Outdoor Goods** p.292

Walking in the Blue Mountains

This is one city where keen hikers – or bushwalkers, as they're more commonly known, really are spoilt for choice. There are all kinds of opportunities for spectacular walks, both within the confines of Sydney's harbour, and on its outskirts, in places like the Blue Mountains (see p.208) to the west, the Royal National Park (see p.233) to the south, and Ku-Ring-Gai Chase National Park (see p.224) to the north.

A harbour walk is one of the best ways to explore the city, and you can choose from many types of treks along windswept sea cliffs, peaceful forests and overgrown bushland. Large portions of the harbour shore are still quite wild, making you feel like you're a long way from the big smoke. Choice spots include North and South Heads, the National Park around Taronga Zoo and the Manly to Spit Bridge. The Sydney ferries can take you within easy reach of all these spots.

Further afield, there are some truly awesome bushwalks around the cliffs, gorges, waterfalls and valleys of the Blue Mountains, taking from a few minutes to a few days. Try the shorter walking tracks around Katoomba, Blackheath and Wentworth Falls. For the more adventurous, try the three-day hike from Katoomba to the Jenolan Caves along the Six Foot Track.

As with hiking activities in any part of the world, take sensible precautions. Don't forget good walking boots, a map and compass and lots of water. Keep an eye out for some of Sydney's more notorious wildlife – like snakes and spiders – along the way. And telling someone where you're going will make it easier for the area's expert rescue services to locate you if you have any problems. See p.25 for emergency telephone numbers.

166 Katoomba St
Katoomba
Outer West

Australian School of Mountaineering

4782 2014 | www.asmguides.com

Experienced ex-military expedition leaders teach all kinds of traditional bushcraft and survival skills around the Blue Mountains. Their two-day Bushcraft & Trekking course covers subjects like camping, finding food, basic navigation, river crossings, bush hazards and first aid, giving you all the vital information you need to prepare for serious wilderness expeditions and treks. The course costs $275.

Various locations

Auswalk

5356 4971 | www.auswalk.com.au

Auswalk specialise in guided walks around Australia in small groups. They can organise all aspects of your hike, from route planning to accommodation along the way – whether it's a period guesthouse or an alpine ski lodge. Their Sydney walks focus on the areas around the city's bush tracks, bays and beaches, as well as the Hawkesbury River and Blue Mountains. Choose from either guided or self-guided treks (fully planned on your behalf). A guided seven-day tour of the Blue Mountains is $2,050 per person, which includes all planning and accommodation.

Bobbin Head Rd
Mount Colah
Outer North

Ku-Ring-Gai Chase National Park
9472 8949 | www.nationalparks.nsw.gov.au
This is where Discovery Rangers will take you on walks covering everything from Aboriginal culture to exotic wildlife. Hike up to the Barrenjoey lighthouse at Palm Beach, explore the Birrawanna track or take your kids on a bat-watching tour of the eucalyptus forests. Prices range from $5 to $60.

Farnell Ave
Audley Heights
Outer South

Royal National Park
9542 0683 | www.nationalparks.nsw.gov.au
The Discovery Rangers in Sydney's Royal National Park organise a series of guided walks and activities throughout the year. These range from twilight adventure walks to the edge of the rainforest to see gliders, possums, owls and glow-worms, to morning hikes across sections of the park. Prices vary, but generally range between $10 and $20 per person. Bookings are essential.

Darkingung Rd off
Peats Ridge Rd
Calga
Outer North

Walkabout Wildlife Park
4375 1100 | www.walkaboutpark.com.au
This 170 acre sanctuary for some of Australia's native mammals, reptiles, amphibians, birds and insects is just an hour north of Sydney. Their four-hour bush survival course will give you a greater understanding of how to find the things you need to live off the land. Learn about bush tucker, finding water, building shelter, rescue signals and tracking skills. A barbecue lunch is provided and you'll need comfortable clothing and footwear. See their website for further details.

Horse Riding

Centennial Park
Paddington

Centennial Park Equestrian Centre
9332 2809 | www.cp.nsw.gov.au
Located in a leafy city park, this centre offers a number of horse riding options that take you along the 3.6km track. You'll need no experience for a basic one-hour park ride, guided by a professional instructor. They also offer riding lessons in their indoor all-weather arena, and experienced riders have access to 3.5 hectares of fenced grounds within the park. They also run a school holiday pony camp for children aged 5 to 16.

69 Cooks Rd
Peats Ridge
Outer South

Glenworth Valley Horse Riding
4375 1222 | www.glenworth.com.au
Australia's largest horse riding centre has 200 horses stabled on 3,000 acres of land, just an hour's drive south of Sydney. They cater for all levels and you can choose from guided or non-guided riding at a cost of $65 for two hours. Explore the area's unspoilt valley wilderness and the 50km of private trails. Riding helmets and equipment are provided, and you can also organise private lessons, adventure day excursions and even cattle mustering rides.

Otford Farm
Helensburgh
Outer South

Otford Farm Horse Riding
4294 1296 | www.otfordfarm.com.au
Down on the NSW south coast, Otford Farm runs trail rides and riding lessons for all levels. You'll be able to ride through rainforests, by waterfalls and along the cliff tops overlooking the Pacific. A one-hour rainforest trail ride is $40, and they also offer two and three-and-a-half hour rides. Riding lessons are $45 per hour, which includes the horse, a helmet and a guide. The centre is open from 09:00 to 17:00.

233

Ice Skating

Cnr Waterloo and
Herring Rds
North Ryde
Outer North

Macquarie Ice Rink
9888 1100 | *www.macquarieicerink.com.au*
Macquarie ice rink has two-hour sessions throughout the day and evening for $18 per adult, including skate hire. They can also organise parties, private figure skating lessons and kids club sessions for pre-schoolers. Discounted group rates are available.

7 Patty's Place
Jamisontown
Outer West

Penrith Ice Palace
4733 2611 | *www.penrithicepalace.com.au*
Out west, Penrith Ice Palace's 30m by 60m rink holds public sessions, kids' programmes, birthday parties, discos and skating lessons. They also have an ice hockey school and a figure skating club. Weekday sessions are $14, and weekend sessions $16 per adult (skates included).

Jet Skiing

Sydney Harbour is a busy commercial waterway so there are strict rules about the use of jet skis or any other watercraft. It is in fact illegal to ride anywhere around the harbour, including its tributaries. There are restricted zones further out, but even here, you're not allowed to perform any irregular manoeuvres – so no weaving, circling or jumping over swells. If you want to experience the thrill of zipping across the harbour in something fast and furious, try one of the organised powerboat harbour tours instead. See Powerboating on p.239 for more information.

Kayaking
Other options **Canoeing** p.224

Bonnie Vale picnic
grounds
Bundeena
Outer South

Bundeena Kayaks
9544 5294 | *www.seakayak.bundeena.com*
Located 45 minutes south of the CBD, Bundeena rent out kayaks and give guided tours. Bordered by the Royal National Park, you'll be able to explore the pristine Port Hacking waterway and coastline in either open or enclosed kayaks. A full day's hire for a single kayak costs $55. They can also teach you about the area, and about correct kayak handling. The Night Owl two-hour tour of the area's nocturnal wildlife is particularly popular. It departs on Saturday evenings, and costs $77.

Forestville
Outer North

Natural Wanders
9899 1001 | *www.kayaksydney.com*
Natural Wanders arrange personalised harbour kayak tours for small groups. Their popular half-day Bridge Paddle begins at Lavender Bay, then floats under the Harbour Bridge and alongside the Opera House before exploring the bays and beaches of Sydney's north shore. Tours cost $90 per person and leave every Saturday and Sunday at 09:00.

Various locations

Oz Paddle

9949 7400 | *www.ozpaddle.com.au*

Ex-*Celebrity Survivor* contestant and former 'iron man' Guy Leech runs beginners' kayak classes every morning (06:30-07:30 weekdays and 10:00-11:30 on weekends). Individual lessons start from around $70, with discounts for group bookings. They also hire out single and double kayaks for a minimum of one hour. Bookings are advisable on weekdays and essential at weekends. Tours cover Manly Cove, Rose Bay and Balmoral.

Harry's Fish Cafe
The Spit Bridge
Mosman

Sydney Harbour Kayak

9960 4389 | *www.sydneyharbourkayaks.com*

Take a paddle around the secluded coves and bays of Middle Harbour in a hired kayak. Both singles and doubles are available. Prices start from $15 per hour for a one person kayak, or $55 to take the same out for a whole day. As elsewhere, bookings are essential at weekends. They run a Middle Harbour eco-tour, which goes from the Spit Bridge to Garigal Park, with a stop on a secluded beach for tea so you can refuel for the paddle home. You can also take a three-hour introductory course, for $75 per person. This teaches you how to handle your kayak, with advice on the four basic strokes and what to do when you capsize.

Kitesurfing

Other options **Beaches** p.182, **Windsurfing** p.248

Kitesurfing is one of the latest crazes in extreme sports, and it's just taken off in Sydney. Taking its influence from wakeboarding, surfing, snowboarding and kite flying, it's a sport that looks difficult, but is relatively easy to learn. The conditions need to be just right though, and if the wind isn't strong, you'll just spend the day sitting on the beach. It's offered at various aquatic clubs around Sydney, each with unique weather and water conditions, so it's worth checking out a few to find the best school for your skill level. There is no licence system for kitesurfing in Australia, although on some beaches you may be asked for proof that you have public liability insurance. There are some risks attached, but provided you're taught to at least International Kiteboarding Organisation (IKO) Level 1 before going out alone, you shouldn't run into trouble. Landing with a thud on the sand can be quite painful, and the kite can put a strain on your back, arms and shoulders, so it's worth learning how to control the thing before letting it whisk you away. The NSW Kitesurfing Organisation recommends that you seek lessons from an IKO-qualified instructor.

Various locations

East Coast Kite Surf

0410 937 222

This IKO-qualified instructor runs lessons and kitesurfing tours to a number of places around Sydney and surrounding areas. Private individual lessons cost $200 for two hours, while bookings for group classes cost less. Lessons cater to beginners through to advanced kitesurfers, and you can choose from a two-hour class to a full-day tour.

302 Grand Pde
Sans Souci
Outer South

Kitepower

9529 6894 | *www.kitepower.com.au*

Kitepower runs half-day introductory courses from the south Sydney beach of Sans Souci so you can see if it's the sport for you. They recommend you stay on dry land and learn to fly a trainer kite first, and it's possible to hire trainer kites from them, too. The three-hour kiteboarding introductory course costs $210 per person.

Language Schools

Other options **Language** p.17

40 Hunter St
Central

Berlitz Language Centre

9230 0333 | www.berlitz.co.jp

The internationally renowned Berlitz school teaches classes in Spanish, French, Japanese, Mandarin, German, Arabic and more. Classes meet once a week over an eight-week period, and class sizes are limited to eight students. They also offer individual tuition, as well as kids' programmes that use song, games and crafts to keep the little ones engaged.

93 York St
Central

La Lingua Language School

9299 8166 | www.lalingua.com

This excellent school runs conversation-based courses with a minimum of 10 students per class. After each two-hour class, you'll be able to use something you've learned immediately in the outside world. Tutors even teach the expressions and gestures of native speakers. Options cover English, Japanese, Mandarin, Spanish, Italian and French, and most courses last for around eight weeks.

Various locations

University of Sydney

9351 2222 | www.usyd.edu.au

The University of Sydney runs professional, affordable short courses. Their eight to ten week multi-level language classes will teach you skills in Italian, Japanese, Korean, Greek, Russian, Portuguese, Thai and others – in fact, just about every language you can think of. They also have specialised language tours for those wanting to develop their skills while travelling so you could study French in Paris at the Sorbonne, or Arabic in Jordan. Register online or by phone.

Libraries

Other options **Second-Hand Items** p.294, **Books** p.273

31 Alfred St
Circular Quay

Customs House Library

9242 8561 | www.cityofsydney.nsw.gov.au

This impressive library is housed within the historic Customs House building, perched on the edge of Sydney's harbour at Circular Quay. Members can borrow up to 10 books, CDs, DVDs or audio tapes for up to three weeks. The library has the largest collection of local and international newspapers available in a public library. Membership is free for City of Sydney residents.

744 George St
Chinatown

Haymarket Library

9265 9977 | www.cityofsydney.nsw.gov.au

Offering a wide selection of books, CDs, DVDs and magazines, this place also contains an extensive Chinese language book collection. Members can borrow up to 10 items for three weeks. Internet access is available and it's possible to renew books online.

Macquarie St
Central

State Library

9273 1414 | www.sl.nsw.gov.au

The State Library houses over five million items, including monographs, posters, sheet music, audio books, maps, microfilm and computer software. Their book collections focus mainly on Australian history, culture and literature, so if you're looking for resources on Aboriginal studies, Antarctic exploration, genealogy, biography, business, management, health or law, this is the place. To access the collections, you'll need to register for a Reader's Card, which you can do online.

236

456 Kent St
Central

Town Hall Library

9242 8555 | www.cityofsydney.nsw.gov.au

This centrally located library contains paperback books and a collection of magazines and newspapers. Its handy Library Link service lets members request any of the 500,000 items from any of its affiliated libraries. They also have a casual reading lounge and a cafe.

Motor Sports

Brabham Drive
Blacktown
Outer West

Eastern Creek International Raceway

9672 1000 | www.eastern-creek-raceway.com

Just 40 minutes west of Sydney, Eastern Creek International Raceway is the city's only international race circuit. Each year its 4,000-seat grandstand hosts all kinds of events, including rounds of the V8 Supercar Championships and various motorcycle races. It also operates open track days where you can drive your car around the challenging 4km circuit, as well as a range of advanced driver training courses.

Wentworth St
Granville
Outer West

Parramatta City Raceway

9637 0411 | www.parramattacityraceway.com.au

Home to Australia's Sprintcar racing, the 460 metre banked oval at Parramatta City Racetrack is one of the country's fastest. In addition to its regular Sprintcar events, the venue hosts everything from demolition derby and motocross events to monster trucks and stock car racing.

Music Lessons

Other options **Music, DVDs & Videos** p.291, **Dance Classes** p.227

Various locations

All Music

9389 8440 | www.allmusic.com.au

This online resource gives you access to a network of music teachers around Sydney, each with many years of experience. Select from the list of instruments and you'll be able to view the relevant teachers near you. Teachers provide tuition in singing, guitar, piano, violin, cello, drums and more. Lessons cost around $50 per hour and gift certificates are available.

4-22 Showground Rd
Castle Hill
Outer North

Australian College of Entertainment

9680 7577 | www.ace.org.au

This school of performing arts has courses for beginners through to professionals. Private and group lessons are available for the piano, keyboard, harp, guitar, percussion and drums and they teach a combination of practical skills, music theory and performance skills. Their vocal training courses teach modern styles like pop and rock, blues, jazz and country, along with the secrets of posture, breathing, correct diction and lyrical interpretation. Private lessons are also available, and cost $33 for 30 minutes.

Various locations

Eastern Suburbs Community College

9387 7400 | www.escc.nsw.edu.au

This college offers over 500 courses at centres across the eastern suburbs. Their music courses cover a range of disciplines, from Guitar for Beginners and Jazz Vocals to Singing in Harmony and Songwriting Fundamentals. Courses generally last for eight weeks and cost around $140. Visit their website for a complete listing and to register for a course.

St Georges' Church
245 Glenmore Rd
Paddington

Fiveways Music Studio

0438 314 481 | www.fivewaysmusicstudio.com.au

Fiveways Music Studio provides high quality tuition with one-on-one music lessons in a friendly, relaxed environment. They offer vocal instruction, guitar and piano lessons for around $40 per half-hour class.

Paintballing

1/980 Victoria Rd
West Ryde
Outer North

Adventure Quest Paintball Skirmish

9808 6333 | www.paintball.com.au

AQPS runs games from several locations around Sydney. Each game lasts for around 20 minutes and all the equipment and camouflage uniforms are supplied (though you'll need your own footwear). There are a number of packages available, with options for booking either individually or as a group. A 200 paintball package costs $65 per person.

Marsden Park
Outer West

Heartbreak Ridge Paintball

9838 3058 | www.paintball.net.au

Heartbreak Ridge claims to have the best battlefields in Sydney, complete with realistic touches like trenches, cars, barricades and sniper posts. Packages start from $70 per person for a 400 shot game, with extra ammo thrown in for advance and group bookings. Lunch and all equipment are included.

125 Oxford St
Bondi Junction
Bondi

Laser Skirmish

1300 733 585 | www.laserskirmishsydney.com

For a less messy (and less bruising) alternative to paintballing, Laser Skirmish guns use laser sensors rather than paint pellets. Their weekend sessions cater for groups or individuals of 15 or less and their highly realistic battlefield is based out west, near Campbelltown. You'll get a minimum of 270 rounds and prices begin at $40 per person, with weaponry, camouflage outfit and laser packs included.

Parasailing

Sydney's parasailing season runs from November through to April. Rides operate on weekends and on demand during the week. You can choose to go solo, or take a friend on a tandem flight. Either way, it's a fantastic chance to get a bird's eye view of the city. Most of the operators use boats with platforms, from which you're winched out to a distance of up to 450 feet. After your flight, you're safely winched back onboard. For obvious reasons, it's recommended that women don't wear skirts.

11 Wentworth St
Manly

Manly Parasailing

9977 6781 | www.parasail.net

Manly Parasailing is Sydney's main operator, running flights around the harbour from Manly Cove to Watsons Bay, depending on weather conditions. Buy your ticket for a 10 minute flight from Manly Boat & Kayak Hire on the eastern end of Manly wharf. A single parasail is $79, a tandem $129, and group bookings are $55 per person.

37 Nicholson St
Balmain

Live Adrenalin

8755 3100 | www.adrenalin.com.au

Setting off over Sydney harbour, this lot will winch you from a 150m towline, with an optional dip in the water. You can do tandem or solo parasailing. An eight to 10 minute ride costs $130 for the tandem and $80 for the solo. Open November to April. All equipment provided, just wear suitable clothing.

Photography

Australian Centre for Photography

257 Oxford St
Paddington

9332 1455 | www.acp.au.com

ACP's part-time courses, workshops, seminars and lectures cover all manner of basic, intermediate and advanced photography. Whether you're interested in digital design, lighting, black and white, Photoshop or camera use and handling, this place provides a fun, creative environment with excellent tuition. Their Camera Craft 1 Foundation course uses technical and practical tuition to teach you how to get the best from your camera. This 60 hour course is spread over five weeks and costs $390. They also run specialist courses covering architecture, fashion, landscape, portraiture, still life and more.

Focus 10 Photography

Paddington

0407 278 809 | www.focus10.com.au

Focus 10 run travel and digital photography workshops and training courses around Sydney. These cover both theory classes and practical, hands-on training. Their introductory digital photography course teaches you all the skills you need to handle a digital camera and make the most of its various functions. You'll learn all about lighting, composition, creativity and camera handling and after the course you'll be able to take expert pictures of people, landscapes and buildings. The course costs $290 and is run over three weekday evenings and one weekend.

University of Sydney

Various locations

9351 2222 | www.usyd.edu.au

The University of Sydney runs courses that cover both manual SLR and digital photography, giving you practical advice on successful travel and portrait techniques, as well as Photoshop, digital fine art techniques and choosing the right camera. Course costs range from $225 to $445 and you can register online or by phone.

Powerboating

Epic Surf Adventures

Manly Wharf
Manly

8900 1018 | www.epicsurf.com.au

Using the same rigid eight-person inflatable boats operated by police and special forces, these are the only tours that explore the rugged coastline outside Sydney Harbour. Exact routes change according to weather conditions, but you could find yourself riding ocean swells and visiting blowholes, or even catching a glimpse of migrating whales as you speed through National Parks and Aquatic reserves. The 45 minute Ocean Adventure tour is $69 per adult, with lifejackets, waterproof gear and footwear provided.

Oz Jet Boat

20a Waterview St
Putney
Outer West

9808 3700 | www.ozjetboating.com

Operating Sydney's largest and most powerful jet boating fleet, these 23 seat boats take you on an adrenalin-pumping 80kph tour of Sydney's harbour, performing fishtails, sideways slides and power brake stops along the way. Rides depart daily from Circular Quay's eastern pontoon. The 30 minute 'Thrill Ride' tour costs $55 per adult. Weatherproof clothing is provided.

Sydney Jet

Cockle Bay Wharf
Darling Harbour

9938 2000 | www.sydneyjet.com

Sydney Jet operates a choice of two different rides around Sydney harbour in high performance 850 horsepower jet boats. During the ride you'll pass Sydney's harbour

239

icons and picturesque foreshores as your boat performs fishtails and spins. The 40 minute 'Jet Thrill' ride costs $60 per adult and departs daily. Waterproof gear is provided.

Rafting

McCarthy's Lane
Cranebrook
Outer West

Penrith White Water

4730 4333 | *www.penrithwhitewater.com.au*

There are no natural white water areas for rafting in Sydney but this venue was created for the 2000 Olympics. Here you'll navigate the whirlpools and rapids of this man-made course. They have guided rafting for beginners, where your raft will be navigated downstream with the aid of your on-board guide and the eight-person crew, or self-guided rafting, where your team of four navigates the rapids independently. For the latter option they recommend that you are experienced in rafting, and a strong swimmer. Sessions last 90 minutes and the cost is $72 per person.

Rollerblading & Rollerskating

Other options **Beaches** p.182, **Parks & Gardens** p.184

There are some excellent rollerblading and skating venues to be found in Sydney, especially within its many parks. Popular spots include the track around Centennial Park, as well as the Esplanade at Manly beach where you can enjoy spectacular ocean views as you navigate the beachside promenade. Total Skate (36 Oxford Street, near Centennial Park 9380 6356), rents skates for $10 for the first hour or $30 for 24 hours and it's worth asking the friendly staff about a free lesson.

Running

Various locations

City to Surf

1800 555 514 | *www.city2surf.sunherald.com.au*

Australia's largest annual fun run takes to the streets every spring, when thousands of runners turn out to make the 14km journey through the city's eastern suburbs to the finish line at Bondi. Whether you're a serious runner or you're just doing it for enjoyment, this famous run is a highlight of Sydney's calendar and well worth taking part in. It's also a strong fundraising opportunity, with many teams and individuals choosing to support a favourite charity.

Various locations

Sydney Striders

www.sydneystriders.org.au

Sydney Striders welcomes people of all ages. Whether you're a triathlete, orienteer, track runner or marathoner, the club offers around 30 different courses covering some of the most scenic parts of Sydney's north shore, eastern suburbs and inner west. Their Sunday morning runs have a choice of start times and distances – from 10 to 30km. They also organise monthly 10km races and mid-week training, as well as other regular events. Check their website for further details.

Various locations

Sydney Summer Series

9929 0055 | *www.sydneysummerseries.com.au*

This group organises evening running events through the summer in some of Sydney's best harbourside parks and bushlands. The 45 minute events use local features and checkpoints to navigate around a chosen track. Each checkpoint has a different value and the team with the highest score wins a prize. Bring your usual running gear. Compasses can be hired at the event. Visit the website for a route itinerary.

240

Sailing

Other options **Boat Tours** p.194

Sydney's waterways are a haven for boat-lovers and sailing here is popular year-round. It's the perfect way to escape the summer heat, and on a crisp, sparkling winter afternoon, the waters look beautiful. If you're a beginner, there are a number of sailing schools offering basic 'Competent Crew' courses, which will teach you all you need to become a useful member of a cruising yacht. For more experienced sailors, there's a vibrant community fuelled by events like the Boxing Day Sydney to Hobart Yacht Race, when it seems like every boat in Sydney is out on the harbour to see off the competitors.

Aquablue

Level 1, Bridgepoint
3 Brady St
Mosman

9981 4393 | *www.aquabluecharters.com.au*
Aquablue offers an impressive selection of vessels operating out of Sydney Harbour. Their fleet includes multimillion-dollar motor launches, luxury cruisers, yachts and catamarans and tall ships. They're also specialists in providing interactive entertainment options, from an onboard casino with staff to a laser shooting experience.

Ausail

Various locations

9960 5451 | *www.ausail.com.au*
Recognised by Yachting Australia, Ausail's courses are taught aboard luxury Catalina yachts by friendly, patient instructors. An introductory course for absolute beginners costs $440. Other courses cover skipper training, sailing theory, navigation, weather interpretation and more.

EastSail

D'Albora Marinas
New Beach Rd
Rushcutters Bay

9327 1166 | *www.eastsail.com.au*
Australia's largest sailing school, EastSail offers all kinds of Royal Yachting Association courses, from Competent Crew to Day Skipper, Coastal Skipper and Spinnaker courses. Their inshore Competent Crew course comprises four three-hour on-board practical lessons on safety, sheet and halyard use, helming, mooring, docking and anchoring. The courses are run weekly and cost $475 per person, with discounts available for group bookings. If you're interested in chartering a yacht, EastSail also offer charter bareboat sailing yachts (for experienced sailors) or boats with skippers (an additional $55 per hour). Their largest yacht can sleep up to 20. Boats can be taken for a minimum of four hours and a maximum of two days. You can also book from a range of skippered motor cruisers, which take up to 50 people. The magnificent twin-hulled 60 foot MV Yarranabbe is their most luxurious boat – and a good way to cruise around Sydney harbour in real style.

Getaway Sailing School

Drummoyne
Outer West

9181 1911 | *www.getaway-sailing.com*
Getaway is ideal if you're looking for structured, sociable courses with the same instructor and team of students throughout. Their comprehensive tuition covers classroom-based and practical sessions in modern, highly stable 38 foot racer/cruiser yachts. The Competent Crew course operates over two weeknights and two weekends and costs $695.

Matilda Cruises

Darling Harbour

9264 7377 | *www.matilda.com.au*
Head to Sydney harbour and you'll probably see the eye-catching blue and orange sails of the Matilda Cruises catamarans. They offer a variety of sailing packages,

including a seafood and carvery lunch cruise and a late afternoon cocktail cruise. These depart daily from Pier 26, Darling Harbour.

The Spit
Manly

Northside Sailing School

9969 3972 | www.northsidesailing.com.au

Northside offers courses for all ages, with a special focus on students new to sailing. They organise sailing camps for kids and teenagers over school holidays, costing around $375 for a five-day course, as well as adult sailing courses on either dinghies or keelboats. Select from a list of one-day courses and put together a tailored programme to suit. Whether your goal is to race a dinghy at a sailing club or join a crew on a racing yacht, Northside can provide flexible training options. Their one-day Basic Crew course costs £225.

Various locations

Quayside Charters

9341 8226 | www.quaysidecharters.com.au

Specialising in luxury and special event charters, Quayside caters for groups from two to 650 people, with all kinds of vessels available for harbour weddings, whale watching events, New Year celebrations and fishing expeditions. They can also supply fine dining menus, DJs, fireworks and hired entertainers. Special discounts are available for group bookings.

Various locations

Sail Australia

1800 606 111 | www.sailaustralia.com.au

Sail Australia has chartered yachts and cruisers, either bareboat or skippered, for special events, parties and sports fishing. Choose from a number of locations around Sydney, including the beautiful Hawkesbury river. You can also combine pampering treats with your day on the waves, such as a full body massage.

Clontarf
North Sydney

Simply Sailing

9451 2511 | www.simplysailing.com.au

Operating out of picturesque Middle Harbour, Simply Sailing's yachts can be hired for all kinds of functions – from private cruising to corporate racing. You can choose from bareboat and skippered vessels, ranging from 35 to 42 foot. The company can organise everything and they have an overnight anchorage option where after dropping anchor, your skipper is whisked away by powerboat, leaving you to enjoy the peace and tranquillity of an overnight stay on Sydney Harbour.

Scouts & Guides

Various locations

NSW Guides

9698 3322 | www.guidesnsw.org.au

Girl Guide groups are located around Sydney, providing girls aged 5 to 18 with a wide range of regular activities designed to build confidence, develop life skills, make new friends and work within local communities. Patrols within each local unit meet once a week, as well as attending various outdoor adventure activities and camps. Members pay an annual state membership fee, plus occasional camp and activity fees.

Various locations

NSW Scouts

1800 072 688 | www.nsw.scouts.com.au

The Scouts is Australia's biggest, most successful youth organisation. NSW Scout groups meet regularly and organise activities for young people aged 11 to 15 that range from camping and bushwalking to performance arts and community services. There are 590 groups across NSW and more than 16,000 members. You can apply to join one online or over the phone. There's a free trial period of six weeks. Uniforms and some activities cost extra.

Skydiving

Centrepoint

Simply Skydive

9223 8444 | www.sydneyskydivers.com.au

This is the closest skydiving centre to Sydney, with a drop zone just 40km from town. Take a tandem skydive at Penrith Lakes and experience 60 seconds of freefall as you plummet at 220km per hour from 14,000 feet. Once your parachute's opened, you can enjoy the amazing views as you drift back down to earth. Regular mid-week specials cost around $200 for a tandem jump, while weekend prices start from $325.

Bankstown Airport
Outer West

Sydney Skydivers

1800 805 997 | www.sydneyskydivers.com.au

Sydney's main self-contained skydiving centre is also the southern hemisphere's largest. If you're game enough to step from a plane at 14,000 feet on a tandem skydive, you'll enjoy magnificent views of the coast, the city skyline and the Blue Mountains as you hurtle through the clouds. Prices begin at $275 per person for a weekday jump. You can also train for solo jumps here. Courses run every Saturday morning at 07:00, with a mimimum of three people needed for the course to run.

Snorkelling

Other options **Diving** p.227

Whether you're on Sydney's northern beaches or eastern shores, there are some excellent vantage points at places like Manly, Fairlight, Chowder Bay, Balmoral and Clovelly. The fish you're most likely to see are snapper, blue groper, sea dragons and wobbegong, and on a sunny day, the waters are positively teeming. The most popular beaches have aquatic or dive centres, where you can hire out snorkel gear for a minimal charge. Or better still, just spend a few dollars and buy your own mask and fins.

Surfing

Other options **Windsurfing** p.248, **Beaches** p.182, **Kitesurfing** p.235

There can't be many Australian activities more iconic than surfing. It's as Aussie as Vegemite sandwiches, and if you'd like to try this hugely popular sport for yourself, there are a number of surf schools operating from beaches around Sydney's northern and eastern coastlines. They'll generally offer tuition individually or in small groups, teaching you the basics like how to paddle out and get up onto your board before sending you off into the waves to sink or surf. For the many Sydneysiders hooked on this exhilarating sport, it's what summer here's all about. So if you want to feel like a true Aussie, grab your board and head for the waves at Bondi, Manly, Maroubra, Coogee or Bronte.

243

Let's Go Surfing

128 Ramsgate Ave
Bondi

9365 1800

Bondi's only licensed surf school runs a Bondi Surf Experience beginner's course, which teaches you how to safely get up on your board and out on a wave. Classes are limited to six or less and the cost is $59 (low season) or $69 (high season) for the two-hour session. All gear is provided.

Manly Surf School

Manly Beach
Opp Pine St
Manly

9977 6977 | www.manlysurfschool.com

This is Sydney's largest surf school, and it's been voted one of the top five in Australia. They run daily lessons from Manly and a variety of other beaches around Sydney. Safe, stable surfboards and wetsuits are provided and beginners lessons cover how to ride, surf safety and surf awareness. Tuition costs $55 for one lesson, with discounts if you book a course. Private one-on-one tuition costs $80 an hour.

Waves Surf School

Various locations

1800 851 101 | www.wavessurfschool.com.au

Waves Surf School prides itself on offering value for money lessons and surf tours in remote locations, giving you access to some of the best uncrowded waves around. Their one-day surf trip to the Royal National Park south of Sydney costs $75, which includes two surf lessons, over four hours of surf time, all equipment, a buffet lunch, transfers and a 4WD on the beach and sand dunes. They guarantee that you'll be riding a wave by the end of the day.

Swimming

Other options **Leisure Facilities** p.254, **Beaches** p.182

Andrew (Boy) Charlton Swimming Pool

Mrs Macquaries Rd
The Domain

9358 6688 | www.abcpool.org

A beautifully appointed pool, Boy Charlton is sandwiched between the Botanic Gardens and Woolloomooloo Bay, and enjoys great views of both. Named after an Australian Olympic Gold medallist, it's been recently refurbished and its eight lane, 50-metre saltwater heated pool is one of Sydney's best. Complete with cafe and terrace, it also has a toddler pool and offers yoga classes ($15). The pool is open daily during summer. Admission is $5.20 per adult.

Bondi Icebergs Club

Southern end of
Bondi Beach
Bondi

9130 3120 | www.icebergs.com.au

This place is a Sydney institution and swimmers have been doing laps in the famous 'bogey hole' since 1929. Set at the southern edge of Bondi Beach, this open-air venue is actually part rock pool, thanks to the ocean waves that crash over its edge as they roll into the legendary beach. It's also home to the famous Icebergs swimming club, made up of some hardy souls who resolutely swim here all year round. There is a fully equipped gym, sauna and spa onsite with massages, facials and tarot readings also offered. It's open every day except Thursdays, when it's closed for cleaning. The entrance fee is $4.50 per adult.

Cook & Phillip Park Aquatic and Fitness Centre

4 College St
Central

9326 0444

Enormously popular with families on weekends (the leisure pool has a wave machine operating from noon), locals also pop in here for a lunchtime or post-work swim during the week. The Olympic-sized indoor pool also has a hydrotherapy area ($16 with pool use) as well as a gym. It also offers wellbeing services such as massages, acupuncture and yoga lessons. Check out the mural and sculptures by local artists. Adult $6, child $4.40. Open Monday to Friday 06:00-22:00, Sat-Sun 07:00-20:00.

Andrew 'Boy' Charlton pool

McIvers Baths

Beach St
Coogee

This secluded pool is known locally as Coogee Women's Pool because women have been bathing here since 1886. It's the last remaining ladies-only seawater pool in Australia. It boasts spectacular views and is pretty well screened from the surrounding area. Amenities and changing rooms are on site. Open 12:00-17:00. Run by volunteers, you're expected to leave a donation on entry.

North Sydney Olympic Pool

Milsons Point
North Sydney

9955 2309

This 50-metre pool must have one of the best locations in Sydney – set at the edge of the harbour, under the northern end of the famous bridge. It boasts an Olympic sized open-air pool with filtered salt water, as well as a 25-metre indoor pool with sauna, spa, cafe and upmarket restaurant. They also run learn-to-swim classes here. You can choose to pay per visit or become a member. A six-month membership package (for the pool only) costs $330 per adult. Adult $5.10, child $2.50, sauna/spa $6.30; hot showers 50 cents for three minutes. Open Monday to Friday 05:30-21:00; Saturday to Sunday 07:00-19:00. Disabled access.

Sydney Aquatic Centre

Sydney Olympic Park
Homebush Bay
Outer West

9752 3666 | www.sydneyaquaticcentre.com

This is where the world's best swimmers battled it out during the Sydney Olympics in 2000. The purpose-built aquatic centre also has a state-of-the-art gym, large outdoor patio area, cafe, child care facilities and massage services. It gets extremely busy here, and in summer visitor numbers can reach 6,000 a day. Use of the sauna is an extra $12.60. Adult $6.40, child $5.10, family $20 (pool and spa). Open Monday to Friday 05:00-20:45, Saturday to Sunday 06:00-18:45, with shorter hours in winter.

Wylie's Baths

Neptune St
Coogee

9665 2838

This hidden gem is a local treasure and well worth a visit. It's an Edwardian-era bathing pool built into the rocks just south of Coogee beach. Surrounded by a raised boardwalk, and complete with a little cafe, it's also the perfect spot for sunbathing with a gentle breeze that blows through the gaps between the boards. The only slight drawback is the marine creatures that are sometimes washed into the pool. Don't be fazed by the occasional baby octopus or jellyfish that might join you for your morning dip. Entry is $3 per adult. There's also a baby pool a few steps further along the coastal track.

245

Team Building

Various locations

Bushsports
9360 0587 | *www.bushsports.com.au*
Running corporate events for teams of 10 to 500 people, Bushsports' teambuilding exercises include abseiling, canoeing, white water rafting, orienteering, mini Olympics, treasure hunts and more, in Sydney and its surrounding areas. They focus particularly on teamwork, enhancing team spirit and building morale.

Artarmon
Outer North

Corporate Challenge Sydney
1300 859 169 | *www.corporatechallenge.com.au*
This company specialises in team building and corporate fitness activities. You could take part in a buggy rally, sailing expedition, do a speedboat or taxi race, a version of the *Survivor* TV show, treasure trek or similat jaunt. Complete their online enquiry form to find out more about an event you're interested in.

Tennis

Prince Alfred Park
Tennis Courts
Central

Jensen's Tennis Centre
9698 9451 | *www.jensenstennis.com.au*
This tennis club is home to four synthetic grass floodlit courts and hosts all types of matches, competitions and classes for its members. You can visit as a guest, with prices starting from around $14 per hour (with reduced entry if you book online). Alternatively, becoming a member (currently around $48 per month) gives you discounted court hire, tennis lessons, social tennis and weekend competitions. The courts are open daily from 09:00-22:00.

New South Head Rd
Rose Bay

Lyne Park Tennis Centre
9371 7122
This popular public tennis centre is based in Sydney's eastern suburbs and has six floodlit synthetic grass courts. Court hire is $22 if you're playing Monday to Friday before 17:00, and $27 at all other times. The courts are open from 07:30 to 22:30 every day.

Waratah Ave
Rushcutters Bay

Rushcutters Bay Park Tennis Courts
9357 1675
Set just a ball's throw away from the picturesque harbour at Rushcutters Bay, this centre offers four courts for public hire. The cost of each court is $24 per hour after 16:00 on weekdays and at weekends, and $20 at all other times. The venue is open from 07:00-23:00. There is a cafe and childrens' playground nearby.

St James Lane
Glebe

St James Park Tennis Courts
9660 1305
Set just off Glebe Point Road, this public site has two cement courts and a clubhouse (with kitchen and bathroom). Courts are available for hire between 07:00 and 22:00 daily and cost $16 an hour. Free parking. Bookings must be made between 09:00 and 17:00.

Alma St
Paddington

White City Tennis Club
9360 4113 | *www.whitecitytennis.com*
One of Sydney's larger venues, this members-only club has 16 grass courts, six rebound ace courts, six synthetic grass courts and even an 80 year-old lawn court. Membership provides unlimited court use, access to organised social events and

competitive tennis, full use of club facilities and free parking. In addition to the $580 joining fee, the subscription is $1,083 for a full year's membership. The club is open daily from 07:00 to 00:00.

Triathlon

20 Rodborough Rd
Frenchs Forest
Outer North

Triathlon Australia

9972 7999 | www.triathlon.org.au

Australia is world leader in triathlete and Iron Man surf events. It's ideally suited to the Australian outdoor way of life – and especially to Sydney's coastal environment. This unique multi-sport endurance test has been running in Sydney since the 1980s and today competitions take place at various times during the year, run by clubs and sponsors across the city. Triathlon Australia's website has a detailed calendar of upcoming events, as well as a host of information for budding triathletes.

Volleyball

10/318 Sydney Rd
Balgowlah

Sydney Beach Volleyball School

1300 865 539 | www.beachvolleyball.com.au

This place runs regular training classes that teach all the skills and rules you'll need to become a decent player. An initial beginners' class lasts one hour, while their most popular course, the Class'n'Comp is a sociable, six-week course of an hour-and-a-half each week. Here you'll learn the sport's proper techniques, then put them into practice with your teammates in a 45 minute round robin tournament. The course costs $180.

North Ryde
Outer North

Sydney North Volleyball

1300 768 655 | www.snv.org.au

This is the largest volleyball association in Sydney and their north shore-based competitions run regularly between February and December. You can join an existing team or enter your own to compete with others. A membership fee is payable prior to joining.

Wakeboarding

River Rd
Hawkesbury River
Outer North

Black Diamond

4566 4511| www.blackdiamondwakeboarding.com.au

Catering for riders of every ability, Black Diamond is based just an hour north of Sydney on the Hawkesbury River. Here it runs everything from hourly lessons to week-long camps with some of the world's best wakeboarding instructors. Overnight packages include three on-water lessons each day, as well as all meals and accommodation. A one-day package (including three lessons, lunch and a trampoline session) costs $200.

247

Cliftonville Lodge
Resort
Wisemans Ferry
Outer North

Sydney Water Ski and Wakeboard

0418 633 106 | *www.sydneywaterski.com.au*

If you're looking for multiple ways to be pulled through water by boat, you're at the right place. Sydney Water Ski and Wakeboard is on the Hawkesbury River and has all kinds of waterskiing, wakeboarding, tube-riding, knee boarding, free boarding and barefoot skiing options. Beginners use a special boom bar that extends sideways from the boat, allowing for on-the-spot instruction before using a tow-rope. Choose from half and full day courses, with full day trips for $190. All equipment is provided, just bring your swimsuit.

Windsurfing

Other options **Kitesurfing** p.235

The Esplanade
Balmoral Beach
Mosman

Balmoral Sailing Club

9960 5344 | *www.sailboard.net.au*

The geography of this beach means that you're more likely to experience good surfing conditions, as the funnelled wind means faster speeds, and the surrounding heads provide protection from large swells. Balmoral Sailing Club offers windsurfer rental for around $28 to $38 per hour, as well as comprehensive instruction to suit any level. A five-hour introductory weekend course costs $175, which covers lessons, equipment and video analysis so you can see how you've improved (or why you keep falling off).

Palm Beach
North

Sailboarding Safaris

9971 2211

Up on Sydney's northern beaches, Sailboarding Safaris runs windsurfing lessons on Narrabeen Lakes, a haven for watersports surrounded by beautiful parkland and nature reserves. Expect to pay around $150 for a two-hour lesson, or $250 for a five-hour lesson. Buoyancy vests and wetsuits are provided.

Wine Tasting

Other options **Wine Tours** p.200, **Weekend Breaks** p.202

McDonalds Rd
Pokolbin
Outer North

Lindemans Estate

4998 7684 | *www.lindemans.com.au*

This world famous winery has been in the area for 150 years and is open daily for tastings and educational visits. The cellar door itself is set in beautiful grounds, surrounded by vineyards. A range of options for private tastings and functions are available. Open 10:00-17:00.

Cessnock
Outer North

Ultimate Buses Wine Tours

4991 4834 | *www.ultimatebuses.com*

This firm runs regular vineyard tours, as well as transport for private groups of all sizes. Their organised daytrips and social events start from $40 per person for trips to wineries around Cessnock and Pokolbin. Lunch is included.

Dalwood Rd
Dalwood
Outer North

Wyndham Estate

1800 677 366 | *www.wyndhamestate.com*

Established in 1828, this vineyard is the home of Australia's first commercial shiraz plantings. Today it offers tours, tastings and events including Opera In The Vineyard. As Australia's oldest winery, it's a favourite tourist destination and you can bring a picnic to enjoy in the grounds. There's no need to bring your own bottle.

Spectator Sports

If you love sport then Sydney is your dream city. Most spectator sports are played here to the very highest professional level.

Sport is an important social and economical part of the city's culture - many people are fanatical and, like it or not, you will be judged on your level of knowledge and interest. Politicians go to great lengths to convince their electorates they are sport-mad. Anything less is considered un-Australian.

If you've arrived here from the UK, South Africa, New Zealand or any of the other test-playing cricket and rugby nations, you can expect a fairly regular ribbing from your new Australian friends and colleagues. This is largely good natured, but the crowing can get dreary. The new arrival has two choices; either let this slide and claim to only have an interest in one of the few sports that the Aussies haven't mastered (like football), or swat up on your stats and tactical theories and let the badinage begin.

Arguments also rage among Sydneysiders about what is the biggest sport in their city. This is endlessly debatable, but rugby league, union, cricket and AFL are still the big four. Swimming is also a popular spectator sport, and soccer and basketball are gaining momentum. Most sports are male-dominated but swimming and basketball attract women as well as men, and netball is a predominantly female sport. For the main venues, head to Moore Park where you'll find the magnificent Sydney Cricket Ground (SCG) and the Aussie Stadium next door, which hosts rugby league, union and soccer matches. Down the road is Randwick Racecourse where the big horse races take place, and out at Sydney Olympic Park is Stadium Australia, now known as Telstra Stadium because of its telco sponsor. Also on the complex is the aquatic centre, where the big swim meets are held.

If you can't make it to a venue, drop into virtually any pub in town – they are sure to be showing some sporting event, or several on adjacent screens. See p.115 for satellite broadcasters of overseas sports and p.354 for sports bars.

Sports Venues		
Acer Arena	Homebush	8765 4321
Aussie Stadium	Moore Park	9360 6601
Randwick Racecourse	Alison Road	9663 8400
Sydney Cricket Ground	Moore Park	9360 6601
Telstra Stadium	Homebush	8765 2000

Need Some Direction?

The *Explorer Mini Maps* pack a whole city into your pocket and once unfolded are excellent navigational tools for exploring. Not only are they handy in size, with detailed information on the sights and sounds of the city, but their price means they won't make a dent in your holiday fund. Wherever your travels take you, from the Middle East to Europe and beyond, grab a mini map and you'll never have to ask for directions.

Aussie Rules

Australian Rules Football began in Melbourne as a winter exercise for cricketers, which is why it's played on an oval pitch. It's similar to Gaelic Football but there are no direct links.

This is the most family-oriented winter sport. Crowds of at least 35,000 are common for the Sydney Swans at their home stadium, the Sydney Cricket Ground (SCG). It is played from March to August in a series of matches with teams from around the country, leading up the Grand Final, which is always played at the Melbourne Cricket Ground (MCG) in September. The sport expanded from 12 clubs in 1858 to the 16 now battling it out.

The sport is relatively new to Sydney; the Swans started out as a Melbourne team called South Melbourne and migrated north to Sydney in 1981.

Colourful characters include former Swans player Warwick Capper, nicknamed Wazza, who was a larger-than-life sportsman known for his long blond hair and tight shorts, and a penchant for driving a pink Ferrari. For more information on the sport, visit www.afl.com.au.

The Swans

The Swans are the only Sydney AFL team and wear distinctive red and white stripes. Their home base is the Sydney Cricket Ground (SCG) at Moore Park, but they also play some matches at Telstra Stadium. They won the 2005 Grand Final but were just pipped to the post (by one point) for the 2006 title in a thrilling match against Perth's West Coast Eagles. Call 9339 9123 or visit www.sydneyswans.com.au.

Basketball

Basketball has substantial roots in Sydney; the first recorded game was played in 1905. Things began to get serious in 1938 with the formation of the NSW Basketball Association. Ten years later Australia became the 52nd affiliated member of the International Basketball Federation (FIBA).

Australia's men's team is the Boomers and the female team are the Opals; at the Athens Olympics in 2004 the Opals equaled Australia's best-ever result by picking up the silver medal.

Flagship domestic basketball competitions in Australia are the Philips Championship National Basketball League and the Women's National Basketball League. These run from October to March. The men's competition has 12 teams representing all states except Tasmania and the two territories. There are eight teams in the women's league, from each state except Tasmania and the Northern Territory. The National Basketball League has 12 teams, two of which represent Sydney; the Kings and the Razorbacks. For more general information on the sport try www.basketball.net.au, and for Sydney-specific details check out www.sydneybasketball.com.au.

Cricket

Aboriginal Cricket

The first Australian cricket team to tour England, in 1868, was entirely Aboriginal. Their appearance was something of a curiosity, with the UK's Daily Telegraph noting that, 'these Indian fellows are to all intents and purposes, clothed and in their right minds.' They won 14 games, lost 14 and drew 19. One of the players died of TB during the tour and was buried in east London. The first white Australian side did not tour England until 1880.

In Australia cricket is king and it's been popular since the first ball was bowled in a senior match in February 1851. The country pours money and serious energy into training and nurturing talent; no surprise then that the national team are undisputed world champions.

Cricket is a summer sport, played from October to March and domestic competitions are run on a state-by-state basis, as well as local intra-state levels. The world famous Sydney Cricket Ground or SCG (www.cricketnsw.com.au) is home to the New South Wales team (the Blues) and the first recorded match was played there in 1854. The first Test Match – in fact the world's inaugural Test Match - was not until 1877, when an England team toured Australia and were beaten in Melbourne by 45 runs.

The New South Wales team has included cricketing heroes Sir Donald Bradman and the 'voice of cricket', Richie Benaud. Current players include Australian team bowlers Glenn McGrath and Brett Lee.

You'll never have a problem keeping score; cricket is sporting religion here with TV, radio and newspapers following matches ball by ball. For more information on the sport, see www.cricket.com.au.

Horse Racing

If you're a fan of horseracing, make your way to Royal Randwick. This historic racecourse is home to the Australian Jockey Club (9663 8400, www.ajc.org.au). There is racing throughout the year here and at the other course, Warwick Farm, in the city's south-west.

Racing in Australia has always been popular, possibly because it is so closely aligned with betting; Australians are second only to the Japanese in their passion for a flutter. Australia's first organised race meeting was held in Sydney's Hyde Park in October 1810 and lasted three days. The first one at Randwick was a private match between two horses in June 1833. It's an easy course to find and the Australian Jockey Club has

Phar Lap
*Possibly the most
famous horse to race at
Randwick was Phar
Lap; a New Zealand
horse that Australians
claim as their own.
Phar Lap raced
spectacularly from
1928 to 1932.*

details of how to get there by bus and car. Parking can be a nightmare so opt for a bus or taxi; the main entrance for spectators is on Alison Road.

Despite being known as the sport of kings, horse racing in Australia is open to everybody. On big race days you are as likely to be standing next to a shipping tycoon sipping champagne as a labourer with a beer in his hand. Both will be wearing suit and tie as Randwick race days are great opportunities for Sydneysiders to dress up. And don't worry if you can't make it to Victoria for the annual Melbourne Cup (first Tuesday in November) because Randwick stages the next best thing in Sydney, with the main event shown on giant screens and live races throughout the day. For more general information check out www.racingpages.com.au and if you want to follow the form, grab a copy of the pull-out horse-racing sections in the newspapers.

Netball

Thrills, spills and screaming fans; netball is one of the most exhilarating spectator sports in Australia. It's an all-girl affair and there is fierce rivalry between the Australian team and their New Zealand rivals, the Silverferns.

The various city teams around Australia are all named after bird species. If you're a Sydneysider then you follow the Swifts (9646 5666). Join the crowds at Sydney Olympic Park to cheer them on. Games are usually held at the Acer Arena (formerly known as the SuperDome) or the Sports Centre. In August 2004 the world record crowd for netball attendance was set at a Swifts home game at the SuperDome, with 13,439 fans in attendance.

Within the state there is State League and an Interdistrict competition, ensuring plenty of local games too. For more general information check out www.netball.asn.au, and for information in New South Wales, try www.netballnsw.com.

**Rabbitohs
Revival**
The South Sydney
Rabbitohs rugby league
club has made a
remarkable comeback.
Restructuring of the NRL
a few years ago
threatened Australia's
oldest club with closure.
With some high-profile
help from actor Russell
Crowe, a protest by
80,000 fans, and,
eventually, Federal
Court support, the
Rabbitohs survived. The
name comes from the
call of wandering rabbit
sellers once heard in this
part of the city.

Rugby League

Rugby league is a hard, physical game born in the poor northern towns of England but is now more popular in Australia than in its country of origin. It was first played in Sydney in 1907.

There is a continuing tussle between league and its rival, rugby union, for players and support. A number of players have switched between the two codes. While league is viewed as working class, union is considered more the domain of middle class professionals. It's the closest Australia gets to a class war.

Some 16 clubs battle it out through the winter season, leading up to a Grand Final in early October, which is always held at the Telstra Stadium at Sydney Olympic Park and can draw 100,000 spectators.

League is an east coast sport, with New South Wales and Queensland accounting for more than 80% of players nationally, the majority of which are from NSW.

There are eight teams to support (half the national competition): Roosters in the eastern suburbs, Rabbitohs in south Sydney, Manly Sea Eagles, Eels in Parramatta, Panthers in Penrith near the Blue Mountains, Sharks in Cronulla, Wests Tigers in Concord, or Bulldogs in south-west Sydney. For more general information check out the sport's governing body, the National Rugby League (www.nrl.com).

Rivalries

Because there are so many teams in Sydney there is much rivalry. Most of this is in rugby league: the Roosters and the Rabbitohs enjoy feisty local derbies, as do the Eels and the Panthers out west. The Bulldogs are a controversial team you either love or hate. In rugby union there are usually fireworks between the NSW Waratahs and the Queensland Reds, and at a local level try to catch a game between deadly rivals Randwick and Sydney University.

251

State of Origin

Hyped as rugby league's toughest battle, this three-match series has been played since 1980. It pits the two biggest league-playing states, New South Wales ('Blues') and Queensland ('Maroons'), against each other. Players turn out for the state where they first played professionally, so club team-mates are often on opposing sides. The games are ferociously competitive and normally very close. It is rare that one team wins both of the first two games, ensuring the third and final match is the decider, which keeps fans, sponsors and TV executives happy.

Rugby League

Bulldogs	9789 2922	www.bulldogs.com.au
Eels	8843 0300	www.parraeels.com.au
Panthers	4731 5422	www.panthers.com.au
Rabbitohs	8306 9900	www.souths.com.au
Roosters	9386 3210	www.sydneyroosters.com.au
Sea Eagles	9970 3000	www.manlyseaeagles.com.au
Sharks	9527 8270	www.sharks.com.au
Wests	8741 3300	www.weststigers.com.au

Rugby Union

Sydney and rugby union are closely linked; the first game played south of the equator was at Sydney's Hyde Park in 1865.

The Sydney team, which is really a team for the whole of New South Wales, was formed in 1874 and is called the Waratahs (named after a flower found in the state). They're based at Aussie Stadium. The team is the oldest in the southern hemisphere and the seventh largest in the world. The Waratahs play as part of a Super 14 competition involving 13 other teams from Australia, New Zealand and South Africa. A number of Waratahs are also players in the national team, the Wallabies. These include Phil Waugh and Lote Tuqiri.

Union is seen as a family spectator sport with virtually no history of crowd violence, but big attendances are reserved for international matches. Aussie Stadium was a venue for Rugby World Cup in 2003, hosting five games with a total attendance of 170,000. For more general information on the sport, try www.rugby.com.au.

Sailing

With the world's most beautiful harbour on the doorstep, it is no surprise that Sydney has had sailing in its blood for years. A series of competitions are held throughout the year but mainly in the summer months. Some of the more high profile ones, like the Big Boat Challenge, are warm-ups to the sport's iconic contest; the Sydney to Hobart Race. On every Boxing Day since 1945, thousands of spectators have thronged the cliffs of North and South Head to watch the start of the race. The multi-million dollar racing yachts speed across Sydney Harbour, through the heads into the Pacific Ocean, and turn south for Tasmania – 628 nautical miles in total.

It is one of the fastest yacht races, with the record standing at 42 hours, 40 minutes and 10 seconds, set in 2005 by Wild Oats XI. It is also one of the most dangerous as it passes through the treacherous Bass Strait, known for its rapidly forming storms and tumultuous waves. In 1998, five boats were lost and six sailors died, 55 more were rescued from their stricken vessels and more than 60 boats retired from the race.

For more information on sailing in Sydney contact the Cruising Yacht Club of Australia (8292 7800 www.cyca.com.au) and for information on the Sydney to Hobart race see www.rolexsydneyhobart.com.au.

Soccer

Historically soccer has been unpopular, because Aussie rules and rugby dominate the winter season. A switch to a summer season (August-February) means it is now the city's fastest developing sport. It is known as soccer rather than football to avoid confusion with the aforementioned sports (all known colloquially as footie). The national A League includes seven teams (with one from New Zealand). Sydneysiders cheer for Sydney FC (www.sydneyfc.com), who play at Aussie Stadium in Moore Park. The club is comparable to English glamour clubs like Chelsea and Manchester United, attracting celebrity players and fans. Former Man Utd striker Dwight Yorke played for Sydney FC in the opening season of the A League (2005-2006), and former England defender Terry Butcher was manager for the 2006-2007 season. In the same way that Liverpool's die-hard fans have the Kop at Anfield, so Sydney FC's have the Cove at the northern end of Aussie Stadium. The club currently draws crowds of more than 16,500. For more general information, check out the governing body, Football Federation Australia (www.footballaustralia.com.au) or the A League (www.a-league.com.au).

Sydney's Sporting Heroes
Sir Donald Bradman ('The Don') is the city's most famous sports star. From Bowral in the Southern Highlands, he made his mark at the Sydney Cricket Ground and had a career average of 99.94 runs. Current Sydney heroes include cricketers Brett Lee and Glenn McGrath, rugby league stars Anthony Minichiello (Roosters) and Willie Mason (Bulldogs), rugby union players Mat Rogers and Phil Waugh (both Waratahs), and swimmer Ian Thorpe.

Swimming

Australia's swimming teams have dominated the world for several years, with the likes of Ian Thorpe and Leisel Jones becoming international superstars. It is now among the most popular spectator sports, and in Sydney events are held at the Aquatic Centre at Sydney Olympic Park in Homebush Bay. Swim meets are held throughout the year and include national, regional and international competitions. The Sydney 2000 Olympic Games events were all staged in this grand pool too.

You will also get a chance to watch some competitive ocean swims. Although these can draw professional athletes, they are mainly amateur events that any strong swimmer can enter. The big ones are the Cole Classic (Manly Beach), the Bondi-Bronte (Bondi Beach), and the Island Challenge (Coogee Beach), all held in spring and summer. For more details see www.oceanswims.com. For triathlons in and around Sydney, see www.triathlon.venues.org.

Tennis

Australia packs a punch when it comes to tennis, producing big names like Lleyton Hewitt and Pat Rafter in recent years. The big tournament is the Australian Open, held in Melbourne in January. Sydney has a few competitions too, including the Sydney Open at Sydney Olympic Park. Sydney is also the 1880 birthplace of The Association Ground Lawn Tennis Club, which later became the Sydney Lawn Tennis Club (9360 6601), the oldest in Australia. It is based at the SCG in Moore Park. Summer is the season for professional matches (October through to March). The venues vary through the year so the best way to keep up is through the Sydney International Tennis Centre (9763 0777, www.sydneytennis.com.au). See p.246 for details of courts.

253

Sports Centres

Much of Australia's success at competitive international sport can be put down to the access young Aussies get to decent facilities. Visitors from cities in the UK, Europe and even the United States are likely to be amazed by the options here, often provided free (or at least very cheaply) to the public. It goes some way to explaining why a country of 20 million or so regularly beats other, much bigger nations in Olympic medal tables.

Facilities at the city's public sports centres often comprise multipurpose indoor courts for basketball, netball, volleyball or badminton, as well as a swimming pool, tennis courts and a host of community-based events like karate, yoga and youth activities. Designed to be used by anyone and everyone, these centres usually operate on a drop-in basis and fees are generally between $10 and $15 per visit. Sydney's triumphant 2000 Olympic Games required a massive further investment in purpose-built sports venues. Around six million visitors now enjoy the facilities at Homebush each year. You'll find everything from a monster skate park with ramps and tracks to a world class aquatic centre with multiple pools and water playground. Visit www.sydneyolympicpark.com.au for full details of what's on offer and when you can get in.

Cnr Queens Rd &
William St
Five Dock

Five Dock Leisure Centre

9744 2622 | www.fivedock.leisurecentre.com.au

With basketball courts, a gym, free weight room and group fitness classes, this leisure centre also contains an Olympic-standard gymnastic training facility. The staff are well-informed on all aspects of fitness and the InShape For Life programme is designed to help members maintain a healthy weight with regular assessments. Open Monday to Friday from 05:30-22:30 and 08:00-19:00 at weekends.

Cnr Nicholson &
Dowling St
Woolloomooloo

Juanita Nielson Centre

8374 6323 | www.cityofsydney.nsw.gov.au

Located in central Sydney, this recently refurbished complex has a fully equipped fitness centre, which runs fit-ball, spinning and stretch classes, yoga, pilates and karate, as well as a range of youth and adult arts and education programmes. It's open from 10:00 every day except Sundays.

Cumberland St
The Rocks

King George V Recreation Centre

9244 3613 | www.cityofsydney.nsw.gov.au

This sports centre has both indoor and outdoor facilities, including two indoor courts for basketball, badminton, netball and volleyball, outdoor basketball courts, tennis courts and a fully equipped centre for yoga and fitness classes. They run tennis days every Tuesday and provide regular early morning tennis coaching for individuals and groups. The main centre is open seven days a week but the fitness centre is closed on Sundays.

36 Hume St
Outer North

North Sydney Indoor Sports Centre

9437 9909 | www.nsba.com.au

This centre is a community-based association with over 4,000 registered members. With four fully enclosed playing areas and grandstand seating, its facilities are used mainly for basketball, volleyball and badminton. It is home to the Northern Suburbs Basketball Association, a group that has been around for more than 20 years. Hiring a full court costs $50, allowing you to practise for the regular competitions and events held here. The centre is open daily from 09:00.

Gyms

Sydney's obsession with being fit is reflected in the city's booming gym business, and there are plenty of clubs to choose from. From the exclusive top-of-the-range private members clubs to the ubiquitous Fitness First centres, there's something for every budget and taste. With so much choice available, competition for new members is high. You will often be able to take advantage of trial day passes, discounted joining fees and other special offers. Most gyms are modern and well equipped, offering the latest equipment, personal training and classes covering everything from aerobics and circuit training to capoeira, pilates and kick-boxing. But be aware that you'll find most CBD gyms very busy at peak times (like after work) and during the summer, when everybody seems to have joined the quest for the body beautiful.

Australian Institute of Sport
When Australia failed to win a single gold medal in the 1976 Montreal Olympics, the Aussies set up this centre to develop a new generation of elite athletes. Today it offers scholarships to 700 athletes a year. Visit www.ais.org.au.

Gyms			
Balmain Fitness	32 Robert St	Rozelle	9818 3555
Bayswater Fitness	33 Bayswater Rd	Kings Cross	9356 2555
Body Express	Campbell Pde	Bondi	9365 6155
Charing Cross Fitness Centre	213 Bronte Rd	Bondi	9369 2290
City Gym	107 Crown St	Central	9360 6247
Definition Health Club	477 Pitt St	Central	9281 6338
Fernwood Women's Health Club	–	Various locations	03 5445 4500
Fitness First	–	Various locations	1300 557 799
Gold's Gym	23 Pelican St	Surry Hills	9264 4496
Hiscoes Fitness Club	525 Crown St	Surry Hills	9699 9222
Hyde Park Health Club	170 Castlereagh St	Central	9282 8999
KX Fitness	85 Darlinghurst Rd	Kings Cross	9380 6688
LFS Health Club & Spa	30 Pitt St	Central	9251 0144
Living Well Health Club	255 Pitt St	Central	9266 2050
Newtown Gym	294 King St	Newtown	9519 6969
No 1 Martin Place	1 Martin Place	Central	9232 1500
Pyrmont Health Club	19 Harris St	Pyrmont	8514 5888
SHE Health Club	309 George St	Central	9262 6966
Simply Active Fitness Centre	201 Kent St	Central	9247 1317
The Fitness Lounge	600 George St	Central	9264 3665

Well-Being

Alternative health and natural therapies have come of age in Sydney. Studies show that 70% of Australian's are turning to natural healthcare as part of their lifestyle, and this is reflected by the myriad businesses that have sprung up in the last few years. From walk-in massage to clinics offering caviar body wraps, from training in Bikram yoga to courses in psychic development; if you can imagine it, you can probably find it in Sydney.

Yoga, tai chi, pilates, massage, reiki, ayurveda and acupuncture are just some of the most popular activities on offer. In general the standards are very good.

As for the cosmetic side of Sydney's many treatment offerings, you'll find no shortage of beauty clinics, spas and hairdressing salons. This is a city that takes the concept of pampering to a whole new dimension.

Beauty Salons

Other options **Health Spas** p.259, **Perfumes & Cosmetics** p.293

Here, like just about everywhere else in the western world, health and beauty is big business. It's estimated that Australians spent nearly $300 million on anti-ageing cosmetics alone last year. Sydney's residents dedicate plenty of time, energy and money to making themselves as glitzy and good-looking as their city. There are beauty salons in most of Sydney's suburbs, though you'll find the best (and priciest) within the city centre and eastern suburbs. Techniques are advanced and standards high, and whether you're looking for subtle, natural treatments like herbal facials and non-surgical facelifts, or more radical results from Botox, chemical peels and micro-dermabrasion, you'll find it all on offer.

Ayurve

99 York St
Central

9262 3466 | www.ayurve.com.au

This inner city beauty salon, day spa and wellness clinic bases its treatments on the ancient Indian healing system of Ayurveda. It offers treatments for men and women, including waxing, spray tans, therapeutic head, foot and body massage and herbal facials. They can also put together various packages focusing on the inside – with customised nutrition programmes and a variety of Ayurvedic wellness consultations looking at diet, lifestyle, relationships and more. Gift packages are also available.

Fields of Beauty

63 West St
North Sydney

9929 0455 | www.fieldsofbeauty.com.au

This boutique beauty studio offers waxing, manicures, pedicures, bronzing, facials and more, as well as a specialised selection of treatments, from microdermabrasion to laser hair removal. They even have an onsite kinesiologist every Tuesday, who offers natural therapies including chakra work, Chinese and Tibetan medicine and reflexology.

The Paddington Beauty Room

217 Glenmore Rd
Paddington

9356 8700 | www.thepaddingtonbeautyroom.com.au

This place has an excellent and well-deserved reputation. It offers the highest standards in everything from La Prairie and Dermalogica skin treatments for face and body, to laser hair removal, photo-rejuvenation, vascular treatments, eyelash tinting, manicures, pedicures, waxing and bronzing. It's their caviar firming facial that really gives them the edge, and this luxurious, decadent 90-minute treatment uses top quality caviar-based products to lift, firm and illuminate the skin. The salon prides itself on a personal approach and expert care. Staff are friendly, well-trained and highly experienced.

Out-There Alternatives
For a meditation retreat with a difference, head into the Blue Mountains. There you'll find Vipassana, a challenging but highly rewarding retreat from the world. With 10 days of silent meditation, you'll get a chance to quietly reflect on life, the universe and everything. The course is free and the centre relies on donations. Visit www.bhumi.dhamma.org.

Work Visas p.54
Weekend Breaks p.155

Written by residents, the New York Explorer is packed with insider info, from arriving in a new destination to making it your home and everything in between.

New York Explorer Residents' Guide
We Know Where You Live

Abu Dhabi · Amsterdam · Bahrain · Barcelona · Dubai · Dublin · Geneva · Hong Kong · Kuwait

EXPLORER

4 Bridge St
Central

ThaSpa

9247 7077 | www.thaspa.com.au

Whether you're in need of a revitalising facial, quick manicure or a luxurious body wrap, this salon has the full range of beauty treatments for both men and women. Voted Sydney's Best Spa and Beauty Salon, it specialises in anti-ageing, relaxation, detox and well-being treatments tailored to busy professionals, using top skincare brands like Decleor, Thalgo and Priori. Try their ultimate indulgence three-hour 'Tha Escape' package. It includes a facial, eye zone tint, detoxifying body treatment, massage, pedicure, manicure and cranial acupressure massage.

130 Elizabeth St
Central

The Vanity Clinic

9264 1997 | www.thevanityclinic.com.au

Bridging the gap between standard beauty therapy and cosmetic surgery, this city clinic offers non-surgical facelifts, microdermabrasion, oxygen-based skin therapy, biological herbal skin peels, wrinkle correction treatments and lip augmentation, as well as a range of facials and massages for both men and women. Their staff offer a thorough initial consultation using advanced imaging systems to identify the best course of treatment for each individual.

Hairdressers

You won't go short of a good hairdresser in Sydney. There are thousands; from small, personal suburban barbers and boutiques to the trendy, high-end, multi-level salons. While trial and error and word of mouth are usually the best ways to find one you like, these are some of the most highly recommended places for an expert cut and colour.

273-275 Goulburn St
Surry Hills

Brad Ngata Hair Direction

9281 1220 | www.bradngata.com.au

'You're the star' is the simple philosophy behind this private, intimate salon. It's also one of the coolest salon interiors you're ever likely to find. The chill-out lounges, social areas, beautiful furnishings and quirky touches make you feel pretty special. Choose from a range of expert cuts and treatments.

Various locations

Joh Bailey

9363 4111 | www.johbailey.com.au

A hairdresser to the stars, Joh Bailey's impressive client list includes Elle Macpherson, Olivia Newton John and Kylie Minogue. He opened his first hair salon in Double Bay over 20 years ago, which today offers cuts, colours and extensions, plus a range of beauty treatments like facials, waxing and nail care. Branches of his salon have also recently opened within Myer department stores.

30 Burton St
Darlinghurst

Raw Hair

9380 5370 | www.rawhair.com.au

Winner of Hairdresser of the Year 2006, this spacious four-storey salon has two balconies and amazing city views. Each floor provides a different service – level one for example contains an aromatherapy treatment area, with heated, reclining massage chairs, while in level three you'll find the colouring department, complete with complimentary internet access. Services cover haircuts, highlights, tints, straightening, spa treatments and more.

54 Boronia St
Redfern

Ruggeri

9698 5400

This private salon is easy to miss. But step through the frosted glass doors and you'll find yourself in what looks like the dressing room of a 1940s Hollywood starlet,

258

complete with citrus, pink and aqua furnishings and Oriental, black silk embroidered gowns. This luxurious space is home to stylists who specialise in signature cuts and colouring, as well as make-up. The team also work on shoots for editorial and advertising campaigns of key Australian magazines.

Health Spas

Other options **Massage** p.260, **Leisure Facilities** p.254

There's no shortage of spas in Sydney, all promising to bring you back to good health. While specific treatments vary from one place to the next, most spas focus on key services like massage, exfoliation and facials and more unusual treatments. Standards vary, but generally it's worth splashing out for the plusher surroundings of Sydney's best.

Various locations ◀

Aveda Concept Salon & Spa

9222 2177 | *www.aveda.com*

Well known for their skincare and beauty products, Aveda's concept salon is also one of Sydney's top spas. Try one of their signature treatments, like the deluxe Himalayan Rejuvenation treatment, which is two hours of Ayurvedic purification, incorporating an aromatic steam inhalation, exfoliation and friction massage, a special steam canopy and then a continuous stream of warm plant oil over the 'third eye'. It's a strange but deeply soothing sensation. As you relax with complimentary Aveda herbal tea, you will be asked to complete a questionnaire so that you can receive a tailored consultation based on your skin type.

2 Brighton Blvd ◀
Bondi

The Last Resort

9300 6033 | *www.lastresortwellbeing.com.au*

Where possible, this beachside day spa uses organically grown products derived from native plants, fruits, desert salts and marine life. Their health lounge is a good spot to relax before and after your treatment. Here you'll be offered therapeutic teas before your pampering begins. You'll also be given a full lifestyle consultation before treatments, which include therapeutic massages, wraps and facials, as well as natural therapies like colonic hydrotherapy, homeopathy, reiki and clairvoyant readings.

177 Oxford St ◀
Darlinghurst

Millk Studio

8354 0318

This unisex spa is about as hi-tech as they come. Millk is the only Sydney salon to offer the NeoQi Cocoon Spa – a full size space age capsule with built-in infra-red and steam sauna, chromatherapy (light therapy), and both hydro and air bubble massage. Their Square Pulse Light hair removal treatments are some of the best currently on the market. The sheer range of treatments is highly impressive and the spa prides itself on providing a personalised experience.

89-113 Kent St ◀
Central

Observatory Hotel Day Spa

9256 2222 | *www.observatoryhotel.com.au*

Located within one of Sydney's most prestigious hotels, this salon pampers stressed out men and women. Products include Kodo massage (which is inspired by Aboriginal techniques), and Tibetan Bell treatment, which mixes massage and sound therapy. The spa also offers facials, body wraps, mud masks and more. They recommend you arrive early to make full use of their services, and guests who indulge in any one-hour treatment also receive free entry to their luxury pool, spa, steam room and sauna.

259

101 Oxford St
Bondi Junction

Soul Day Spa

9389 5748 | www.souldayspa.com.au

With oriental style decor and a practical, no nonsense approach, this unassuming day spa offers Dermalogica-based treatments including massage, exfoliation and mud wraps. They cater to both men and women, and have a range of mother and daughter, birthday and hen party packages. Their full body Dead Sea salt exfoliation is particularly good for removing dry skin and encouraging circulation. After the ensuing moisturising body treatment, you'll emerge glowing from head to toe.

6 Cowper Wharf Rd
Woolloomooloo

Spa Chakra

9369 0888 | www.spachakra.com

Spa settings don't get much more impressive than this. It's set next to the water, in the five-star boutique Blue Hotel, in the trendy suburb of Woolloomooloo and has views across the harbour and the Botanic Gardens. The spa itself is spacious and elegant, with 12 treatment rooms and a relaxation lounge, as well as hydrotherapy and Vichy showers. If you're staying at the hotel itself, they offer an in-room service.

Massage

Other options **Reflexology/Massage Therapy** p.127

Massage is one of the most ancient forms of medical care. Today, there is a mind-boggling array of techniques to choose from at drop-in centres, private clinics, gyms and health clubs. The treatment is particularly useful for treating poor posture. It's no coincidence that there are so many walk-in centres in Sydney's business district, serving the many office workers who spend hours each day hunched over their computer screens. Be aware that lunchtimes are particularly popular at hot spots in the city's many indoor shopping malls.

1 Booth St
Annandale

Glebe Healing Centre

9566 1222 | www.glebehealing.com.au

Offers all kinds of healing therapies, including aromatherapy, Swedish, shiatsu, remedial and traditional Chinese massage. Whichever type you choose, treatments focus on reducing pain, stimulating blood and lymphatic circulation and aiding deep relaxation. The centre is affiliated with the Australian College of Traditional Medicine.

33 Bligh St
Central

Jobonga Massage & Natural Therapy

9221 0030 | www.jobonga.com.au

In the heart of the city lies Jobonga, a warm and inviting centre decorated in burnt orange tones. You'll be able to choose from aromatherapy, sports, Swedish, lymphatic drainage, pregnancy and reflexology massage. Practitioners are fully accredited and trained, and health club rebates are available.

Neptune St
Coogee

Massage By The Sea at Wylie's Baths

0412 738 483 | www.massagebythesea.com.au

This outdoors, resort-style massage centre runs from Wylie's Baths, an Edwardian-era bathing pool built into the rocks just south of Coogee beach. Stretch out on a massage table on the raised boardwalk above the pool and drift off to the soothing sounds of the ocean as your therapist works some magic.

76 Oxford St
Paddington

The Sydney Ka Huna Centre

9358 3777 | www.kahunacentre.com.au

More and more people are trying Hawaiian-style Ka Huna or Lomi Lomi massage. It's a powerful style of bodywork that will have you virtually floating out of the door afterwards. Walk in and you'll be greeted by soothing music, aromatherapy oils and bright, friendly therapists who work hard to make you feel welcome. This isn't a massage for the prudish, as you'll need to strip right off – though a strategically placed sarong keeps your dignity intact. This unique style incorporates lots of hand, forearm and elbow work by the practitioner and lots of oil, too, so you'll need a shower afterwards. If you're suffering from stress, exhaustion, emotional upset or even just physical aches and pains, this is an uplifting and transformative experience.

163 Commonwealth St
Surry Hills

Zen Living Natural Health Clinic
9280 0363 | *www.zenlivingnaturalhealth.com*
This small healing centre is an oasis of tranquility. Tucked away in the back streets of Surry Hills, it is run by a highly experienced therapist. Massage styles include remedial, sinus, migraine, colonic, chest, lymphatic drainage and more. Try the one-hour hot rock massage, which uses smooth, heated, oiled volcanic stones massaged against your skin, then placed along the spine. It's the perfect massage to give you a warm and fuzzy feeling in the cooler winter months.

Meditation
Other options **Healing Meditation** p.126

For most people, daily life is consumed by endless activity and distraction. But meditation is a powerful way of allowing the mind to go beyond its normal limits. Often described as 'inner wakefulness', the goal is to disconnect from thought, emotion and bodily sensation. Hundreds of recent studies have highlighted a range of remarkable physical effects, from reducing blood pressure to slowing down the ageing process. Feelings of increased calm, peace, clarity, focus and overall happiness have also been reported by millions of people.
Most yoga centres incorporate meditation teachings, and they'll probably offer standalone meditation courses too. Buddhist centres usually offer a mixture of Buddhist teachings and meditation instruction.

Meditation Centres			
Mahasiddha Buddhist Centre	Various locations	9387 7717	www.meditateinsydney.org
Sydney Buddhist Centre	Newtown	9519 0440	www.sydneybuddhistcentre.org.au
The Panditarama Centre	Outer West	9727 2077	www.panditaramasydney.org

Pilates
Other options **Yoga** p.263

Originally devised as a way for dancers to recover after injury, pilates has evolved to become a technique for anyone wanting to improve posture, get long, lean muscles and increase vitality. It's great for lower back pain and joint care and can help conditions involving the respiratory, neural and digestive systems.
Classes teach precise, small movements, focusing on the torso to provide core stability and strength. You'll often use apparatus to help refine these movements, from medicine balls to lengths of stretchy elastic and even full body machines.

167 Bondi Rd
Bondi

Bodhi Maya Pilates Centre
9369 4354 | *www.bodhimayapilates.com.au*
This newly renovated studio offers both apparatus and mat work. The instructors put together personalised programmes, with a choice of one-on-one tuition or groups of no more than four. Every exercise focuses on correct body alignment and core stabilisation.

261

Pilates International

79-83 Myrtle St
Chippendale
Outer West

9699 5509 | *www.pilatesint.com*

Offering private classes by appointment, Pilates International's purpose-built studio is light and bright with big windows and beautiful views. You'll start with an initial consultation – a one-hour session to discover your goals – followed by a choice of either regular appointments or casual visits.

The Pilates Room

25 Ralston Ave
Belrose
Outer North

9975 7766 | *www.pilatesroom.com.au*

With small, intimate mat classes in various locations across Sydney, The Pilates Room offers all levels of training – from basic classes for beginners to Power Pilates, for a really dynamic and challenging workout. Casual classes cost $17. They also offer one-on-one classes, group training, pre-and post-natal classes, over 55s classes, sessions with apparatus, men only classes and children's programmes.

Reiki

This ancient Japanese healing technique is based on the principle that an unseen energy flows through our bodies. Reiki healers are able to channel this energy and transfer it through touch to relax and heal a patient. It's spiritual in nature, but it's not a religion, and people from all walks of life report feeling more focused, balanced and invigorated after treatment.

Glebe Healing Centre

1 Booth St
Annandale

9566 1222 | *www.glebehealing.com.au*

This natural therapies centre offers all kinds of healing therapies, including Reiki. Their treatment covers the organs, glands and lymph nodes, healing cells, rebalancing your energy and restoring vitality.

International House of Reiki

304 King St
Newtown

1800 000 992 | *www.reiki.net.au*

Treatments are held here every Wednesday and Thursday. Sessions are normally one-hour and the charge is $77 per treatment. A student clinic is also available on Wednesdays, for treatments at a reduced cost.

Usui Reiki Centre

2 Ernest Place
Crow's Nest
Outer North

0408 690 718 | *www.usuireikisydney.org*

Run on a donations basis, this centre offers Reiki healing at a venue of your choice. They also run regular teaching classes for those interested in becoming a Reiki Master, enabling you to practice on yourself and others.

Tai Chi

Tai Chi is a martial art with a difference. There are no flying kicks or one-inch punches; instead, it uses a series of graceful, flowing movements like a dance in slow motion. It aims to emphasise correct posture and balance, circulate invisible energy (or 'chi') around the body and create a balance between body, mind and emotions. Reported health benefits include better circulation, flexibility and a stronger immune system.

Sydney School of Tai Chi

School of the
Performing Arts
King St
Newtown

9314 7375 | *www.sydneytaichi.net*

Get an introduction to the principles of Tai Chi with an eight-week beginners' course covering areas such as 'Loosening', 'Connection' and the 'Push Hands' techniques. Courses run regularly throughout the year, at a charge of $100 per person.

Various locations

The Tai Chi Society

9954 7266 | *www.taichisociety.com*

The Tai Chi Society runs eight-week beginners' classes in the eastern suburbs, inner west, northern beaches and north shore. You can choose from weekday, evening or weekend sessions, and after finishing a course you're free to do more intensive practice alone or in classes. The course costs $90 per person.

Yoga

Other options **Pilates** p.261

Yoga is popular in Sydney, with many variants to choose from. Styles include the aerobic movements of Ashtanga (focusing on strength and stamina), the very sweaty Bikram yoga (which takes place in 38 degree heat for flexibility and toxin release), and Iyengar (which uses props to help you achieve the correct positions). Most centres offer beginner courses, and mats and equipment are generally provided.

112 Darlinghurt Rd
Darlinghurst

Govindas Lotus Room

9380 5155 | *www.govindas.com.au*

This tranquil space offers some of the best yoga in Sydney. Featuring polished wooden floors, dim lighting and a cascading wall of water, the centre offers Hatha-style yoga, focusing on deep yogic breaths. The two teachers have years of experience. They run introductory courses and more advanced classes, as well as meditation, kirtan (chanting) evenings and special events. Booking is recommended.

144 Blues Pt Rd
McMahons Point
Outer North

North Sydney Yoga

9957 1855 | *www.northsydneyyoga.com*

Focusing on the discipline of Ashtanga Vinyasa yoga, this school runs regular six-week beginners' courses as well as casual classes for all levels. They also run prenatal yoga and Mysore classes; group classes in which you practice postures at your own pace, in rhythm with your breathing. The school has even been renovated using chemical-free paints to create the healthiest environment possible.

36 Lennox St
Newtown

Samadhi Yoga

9517 3280 | *www.samadhibliss.com*

This centre offers Kundalini yoga, meditation and Pranayama (yogic breathing techniques). They also run an eight-week beginners course, and mother and baby classes. They have regular yoga workshops, which are a great opportunity to experience the different styles and teachings of guest teachers from around the world.

63 William St
Darlinghurst

Sydney Yoga Space

9360 0577 | *www.sydneyyogaspace.com*

This central Sydney school teaches Iyengar yoga at three different levels for beginner, experienced and advanced students. They run regular introductory courses, as well as causal drop-in classes, workshops and retreats.

Various locations

Yoga Synergy

9389 7399 | *www.yogasynergy.com.au*

Yoga Synergy fuses Ashtanga Vinyasa, Iyengar, Tibetan yoga and medical science, in a moving meditation designed to improve cardiovascular fitness, strength and flexibility. Beginner courses and open classes get gradually tougher, with more challenging postures introduced over time. However, in every class students can choose an easy or hard version of each posture. Yoga Synergy has centres in Bondi, Newtown and Manly.

BIGGEST CHOICE OF BOOKS

MAGIC CHOICE OF BOOKS

EXCITING CHOICE
OF BOOKS

Phenomenal choice of books

UNBEATABLE CHOICE OF BOOKS

IN FULL COLOUR

SPECIAL CHOICE of books

THRILLING CHOICE OF BOOKS

Encyclopedic choice of Books

BALANCED CHOICE OF BOOKS

FANTASTIC
CHOICE OF BOOKS

BORDERS®

BIGGEST CHOICE OF BOOKS, STATIONERY AND MAGAZINES

Shopping

Shopping

Sydney has nonchalantly swept past Melbourne in recent years to take the crown as Australia's shopping capital. Shopping is the perfect pastime for a city often accused of being superficial and hedonistic, and many Sydneysiders consider it a serious leisure pursuit. There's an experience to suit every taste: wandering through the night markets in Chinatown, browsing Australian designer fashions, picking out a vintage clothing gem in Surry Hills, whiling away a rainy day in Gleebooks or picking up a bargain case of fine wine straight from the cellar door. If you love to shop, you'll love Sydney.

Pitt Street Mall in the city is the nucleus of shopping in Sydney – here you can find department stores like Myer and David Jones and a whole network of malls with enough shops to make your head spin. The nearby Queen Victoria Building offers a luxurious shopping experience beneath high ceilings and some ornately designed stained-glass windows.

The Rocks is a little touristy, but worth a look with its eclectic mix of markets, opal merchants, kitsch souvenir shops and international designers.

You won't save money by shopping in Sydney; most items like clothes, electrical goods and furniture cost the same as in the US and the UK, and international clothing and cosmetic brands may be more expensive. There are two major sales a year, in June and after Christmas, when you can fight the crowds for cut-price bargains, although many shops also run sales intermittently throughout the year. Shop attendants are quite relaxed and may not offer assistance unless asked.

While shopping in Sydney is not cheap, it is unique. Designer fashion, jewellery, art, vintage clothing, and beachwear all have a distinctive local flavour. Take a wander down Oxford Street to check out local designers like Sass and Bide, or Collette Dinnigan on nearby William Street, or head to one of the many Saturday markets to pick up a bargain from aspiring designers.

Sydney is also a haven for food lovers. The temperate climate means that most fresh produce, as well as specialty items like gourmet cheeses, are widely available. Thanks to a recent boom in the Australian wine industry, good quality wines are available at excellent prices, especially if you head north to the Hunter Valley and buy direct from the wineries.

Most shops are open seven days, usually until at least 17:00, and some have late-night shopping on Thursdays.

Galleries Victoria

Online Shopping

Online shopping is a popular pastime in Australia. If you want an item delivered to a Sydney address, use Australian sites to save time and money on shipping – it can be very slow and expensive to order from international sites like amazon.com. Ebay's Australian-based site www.ebay.com.au is hugely popular among Sydneysiders and has a massive range of items.

For new items, www.dstore.com.au sells everything from DVDs, cosmetics, furniture and flowers to computers. It accepts major international credit cards and ships to many countries overseas.

If you hate the supermarket you can order groceries online through www.coles.com.au, although you must spend a minimum of $30 plus a delivery fee. If you're looking for a gift or want to book a holiday, visit www.lastminute.com.au. It lists last minute specials and deals on a whole range of travel and lifestyle items. For more specific items, check the listing in What & Where to Buy on p.269.

International Returns
Generally, if you buy something in Australia, you will need to return it in Australia, rather than your home country. Similarly, Australian branches of multi-national chains are unlikely to take back something you bought at home.

Refunds & Exchanges

If you want to return an item, take it back within fourteen days in its original condition along with some proof of purchase. Under Australian law, retailers must give a refund if goods are faulty or become faulty soon after purchase, if the goods are unfit for their purpose or don't match the retailer's description or sample and if the retailer has offered special warranties or guarantees.

However, retailers are not obliged to give a refund if you change your mind, find the item cheaper elsewhere, were aware of a fault before buying the item or you damaged it yourself.

Consumer Rights

Consumer rights are taken seriously in Australia. The government-run website www.consumersonline.gov.au is an excellent resource that explains your rights when shopping, returning items, how to handle disputes, warnings about scams, and general advice about shopping, finance and buying cars, bikes, food and other products.

In the case of a dispute, try and settle with the retailer first. If that doesn't work, try the NSW Department of Fair Trading (www.fairtrading.nsw.gov.au, 9895 0111).

GST

All goods and services, except fresh vegetables and some medical items, attract the 10% goods and services tax, or GST. This is already included in the displayed price. It is illegal to add GST at the checkout.

If you are leaving the country (even if you are a citizen or resident) you can be refunded the GST paid on any item worth over $300 bought in the 30 days before your departure. To claim your refund, bring the item(s) along with your tax receipt to the airport in your hand luggage and go to the GST refund counter. For more information, visit www.customs.gov.au.

You can also avoid paying GST and other taxes by shopping at the airport duty-free shops like Downtown Duty Free. Most items are at least 10% cheaper than you would pay in a regular shop, and wine and perfumes can be up to 30% cheaper.

Shipping

Because of Sydney's relative isolation, shipping can sometimes be a slow and stressful, if not expensive, experience. Many online shops will ship items to overseas addresses (for example, www.dstore.com.au will ship large items to the UK, US and New Zealand), but few Australian shops will do so for a reasonable price. See the table of relocation companies on p.106 for more.

PackSend (www.packsend.com.au, 9290 1188) will package and ship most items anywhere in the world, including fragile items, large items, household goods or excess baggage. Companies like Wridgeways (www.wridgeways.com.au, 9645 7700) or King and Wilson (www.kingandwilson.com.au, 1300 368 893) can handle international removals and relocations. See p.106 for more.

It's worth getting quotes from a few different companies as prices and shipping times vary considerably. Generally, shipping large items to or from Australia takes several weeks unless you pay for express delivery.

267

How to Pay

Most shops accept credit cards, debit cards, Australian currency or EFTPOS, which is the most common form of payment. Many stores also accept EFTPOS transactions from international cards linked to Cirrus or Plus – check with your bank to see if your card is compatible.

No other currency but Australian dollars is accepted in Sydney. The most commonly accepted credit cards are Visa, Mastercard and Bankcard (including internationally-issued cards), American Express and Diner's Club are less commonly accepted, although major tourist destinations and department stores take them. Some shops impose a 1% surcharge on the use of credit cards.

Bargaining

Other options **Markets** p.306

Bargaining is rare in most Sydney shops. The exception is big-ticket items like white goods, TVs, stereos, cameras, computers and other electrical items. You can usually negotiate at least 10% off the price, except in large department stores.

Anything you buy second hand is almost always up for negotiation. If you are buying a second-hand car you can almost always knock between 10 and 20% off the price. Bargaining is not expected at the markets but if the item is slightly worn or you are buying more than one item, the seller may be willing to give you a discount.

Clothing Sizes

Women's Clothing							Women's Shoes					
Aust/NZ	8	10	12	14	16	18	Aust/NZ	5	6	7	8	9	10
Europe	36	38	40	42	44	46	Europe	35	36	37	38	39	40
Japan	5	7	9	11	13	15	France only	35	36	38	39	40	42
UK	8	10	12	14	16	18	Japan	22	23	24	25	26	27
USA	6	8	10	12	14	16	UK	3.5	4.5	5.5	6.5	7.5	8.5
							USA	5	6	7	8	9	10

Men's Clothing							Men's Shoes					
Aust/NZ	92	96	100	104	108	112	Aust/NZ	7	8	9	10	11	12
Europe	46	48	50	52	54	56	Europe	41	42	43	44.5	46	47
Japan	S	-	M	M	-	L	Japan	26	27	27.5	28	29	30
UK	35	36	37	38	39	40	UK	7	8	9	10	11	12
USA	35	36	37	38	39	40	USA	7.5	8.5	9.5	10.5	11.5	12.5

Measurements are approximate only; try before you buy

What & Where to Buy – Quick Reference

What & Where to Buy

Sydney is a great place to shop. You'll find everything from old second-hand stores and weekend markets with hidden treasures, to boutiques stocking the best of designer bling. From paintings to DIY, delis and department stores, this arty city is brimming with life and shops to cater to every taste.

Alcohol

Other options **Bars** p.352, **Drinks** p.313

A shop that sells alcohol in Sydney is known as a bottle shop or 'bottle-o'. Most offer a good selection of wines, beers (including local, imported and boutique), spirits and mixed drinks. Common outlets include Dan Murphy's, Vintage Cellars, Liquorland, and Porter's, which are franchises found all over Sydney with reasonable prices. These shops are usually open seven days, and typically close around 19:00. You can't buy alcohol in supermarkets, corner shops or petrol stations.

Australia is swimming in local wine and as a result, Sydney has plenty of quality wine at excellent prices. You can get a decent bottle for around $10, and some exceptional wines are available for under $20, although premium vintages can cost much more. In most shops you can save around 10% on the bottle price if you buy by the dozen. Many also hold free wine tastings at weekends and in the evenings. There will be a table set up with a few wines to taste and usually a sales person to discuss them with. Sometimes they can be a little pushy, so don't be afraid to say no. Tasting does not oblige you to buy; you can simply thank the attendant and walk away.

If you are interested in finding out more about Australian wines, *Quaff* by Peter Forrestal is a good guide to wines under $15, or the annual *Australian Wine Guide*, by Jeremy Oliver, reviews both popular and premium wines. You can also learn a lot on a wine tour, or by reading the wine columns in the *Sydney Morning Herald* and the *Daily Telegraph*.

Most shops also sell local, international and boutique beers. Cheaper beers include VB (Victoria Bitter) and Toohey's New, which cost around $10-$14 for a six pack. Good local beers include James Boags, Cascade, Little Creatures, James Squire and Hahn, which sell for around $14-$17 for a six-pack.

If you like to brew your own beer, shops like Brewcraft Retail Store and Brew-Maker (see table) sell home brew equipment and ingredients and give advice on how to best brew in Sydney's climate. Spirits such as vodka, whiskey and rum are almost all imported, so the range can be limited and more expensive than in Europe or America. Most 700ml bottles of spirits sell for $25 or more. Alcoholic drinks are labelled showing the percentage of alcohol they contain – around 5% for beer, 11% for wine and 25% for spirits.

Alcohol		
42 Harris Cellars & Deli	42 Harris St	9571 6466
Amato's Liquor Mart	267- 277 Norton St	9560 7628
Australian Wine Centre	1 Alfred St	9247 2755
Australian Wine Emporium	100 Cumberland St	9247 2229
Brewcraft Retail Store	116 Victoria Rd	9555 2294
Brew-Maker	3 Mount St	9665 3976
Chinatown Cellars	37 Ultimo Rd	9211 5544
CK Direct	Online only	1800 113 111
Dan Murphy's	Various locations	1300 723 388
Liquorland	Various locations	9624 6737
Porter's	Various locations	1800 688 226
Sydney Cellars	227 Broadway Rd	9660 9996
The Oak Barrel	152 Elizabeth St	9264 3022
Vintage Cellars	Various locations	1300 366 084
Woolworths Liquor	Various locations	9975 7933

269

Buying From The Cellar Door

The Hunter Valley is one of Australia's premier wine regions, famous for its varieties of chardonnay, semillon and shiraz. You can go on a wine tour (see p.200) or organise your own day trip to visit one of more than 40 wineries. Most wineries have a 'cellar door' where you can taste, tour the premises and buy wines direct. Major wineries like Tyrell's, Wyndham Estate and Lindeman's have cellar doors in the Hunter Valley, as do Brokenwood and Scarborough; along with boutique wineries like RidgeView, Krinklewood, Briar Ridge and Windsors Edge. You can usually save around 10-20% by buying direct from the cellar door, and it's great to be able to talk to the wine makers, see where the grapes are grown and how the wines are produced. Visit www.winecountry.com.au for more information.

When you enter any bottle shop you'll be met by a number of prominent signs explaining the various laws governing alcohol in Australia.

Firstly, you must be over 18 to buy alcohol, and this is strictly enforced. You risk a $5,000 fine if caught supplying alcohol to an under-18, and so does the proprietor. If asked for ID, you can show your passport or an Australian driver's licence. If you can't provide either, you may be refused service.

It is also illegal to supply alcohol to an intoxicated person in Australia, but this law is interpreted more loosely. Generally, someone unsteady on their feet or slurring their speech may be refused service at a bottle shop. Unsurprisingly, if you become aggressive or violent you will also be refused service.

Many pubs also sell take home alcohol – either via a small internal shop, a drive-through service attached to the side of the pub, or over the counter. Pubs need a special licence to sell 'takeaways', so not all establishments do. Pubs usually have a limited range of drinks and it can be more expensive, but the benefit is you can buy alcohol up until midnight – a good option if your local bottle shop is closed.

Cleanskins

A glut of Australian wines has led to a rise in the sale of 'cleanskins', sold cheaply through bottle shops and companies like CK Direct. A cleanskin is a bottle sold without the commercial label or winemaker's name. Wineries often offload excess bottles this way, but they can be a gamble. You may get something fantastic for under $10, or you may get something not much better than vinegar. It's important to only buy wines from cleanskin sellers who carefully select their wines, so it's best to avoid the large chain bottle shops. CK Direct sells a good range by phone and internet. The website has thorough descriptions of each wine, and staff can offer advice over the phone. An excellent range is available from $3-$20 per bottle with free delivery throughout Australia and a money back guarantee. See www.ckdirect.com.au.

137 Bondi Road
Bondi

Kemeny's

13 8881 | *www.kemenys.com.au*

Kemeny's is one of Sydney's best-known alcohol outlets. It offers a huge range and some of the best deals in town, with prices often more than 10% less than other shops. They stock a wide range of international and Australian wines. You can also order by phone or online and delivery to anywhere in Sydney costs $6.

599 Darling St
Rozelle

The Sackville

9555 7555

While drive-through bottle shops are common across Australia, lack of available real estate means they are rare around Sydney city. Like most drive-throughs the range isn't huge, but most popular brands are available.

99 Jones St
Ultimo

Ultimo Wine Centre

9211 2385 | *www.ultimowinecentre.com.au*

Billing itself as Australia's number one fine wine specialist, Ultimo Wine Centre is renowned for a comprehensive collection of premium wines. Both local and international brands are available and staff are well-versed in storage, varieties, vintages and food matching. It's not cheap – most wines are more than $20 per bottle, but you can be sure you're getting a first-class wine. There are free tastings in-store every Saturday from midday.

Art

Other options **Art Galleries** p.164, **Art & Craft Supplies** p.271, **Art Classes** p.220

From the Blue Mountains' Arthur Boyd to Brett Whitely's interpretations of Bondi Beach, Sydney has been widely celebrated on canvas.

There are a multitude of small galleries where you can buy works by renowned and upcoming artists. Eva Breuer (www.evabreuerartdealer.com.au) displays and sells works from many of Australia's most celebrated artists, as does the Tim Olsen Gallery (www.timolsengallery.com.au). The Aboriginal and Tribal Art Centre sells genuine Aboriginal paintings and art, while Boomalli is an Aborigine-owned collective of Sydney indigenous artists.

To commission portraits, Josonia Palaitis (JPStudios, 9550 4595, www.jpstudio.com.au) is one of Australia's most sought after portrait painters. See also Portrait Photographers on p.294

For more affordable art, many cafes and bars, like The Art House, regularly display exhibitions from low profile local artists, priced at $100 upwards. If original art is out of your price range, Matilda Prints has a large range of prints and photography that they will frame to order. Also try the Brett Whitely Gallery. Whitely was one of Australia's most important painters and while his works now sell for millions, the shop inside the gallery sells prints of his work for around $25.

Art		
Aboriginal & Tribal Art Centre	117 George St	9247 9625
Antique Print Room	QVB	9267 4355
Art Gallery of NSW	Art Gallery Rd	9225 1744
Arthouse Hotel	275 Pitt St	9284 1200
Boomalli	55-59 Flood St	9560 2541
Brett Whiteley Studio	2 Raper St	9225 1881
Byron McMahon Gallery	88 George St	9318 0404
Eva Breuer	83 Moncur St	9362 0297
Matilda Prints	151 Clarence St	9262 1262
The Metropolitan Museum of Art Store	QVB	9283 3799
Tim Olsen Gallery	76 Paddington St	9360 9854

Art & Craft Supplies

Other options **Art** p.271, **Art Classes** p.220, **Art Galleries** p.164

Art & Craft Supplies		
Bondi Road Art Supplies	179-181 Bondi Rd	9387 3746
City Scrapbooking	524 Parramatta Rd	9569 6392
Eckersley's	93 York St	9299 4151
Etelage	430 King St	9557 9089
Hobbyco	197 Pitt St	9221 0666
Oxford Art Supplies	221-223 Oxford St	9360 4066
Tapestry Craft	50 York St	9299 8588
The Bead Bar	80 George St	9247 5946
Tilly's	661 Darling St	9810 8309

If you prefer to make your own art, shops like Eckersley's sell a good range of oil paints, acrylics and watercolours as well as canvases, brushes and other materials. Tilly's in Balmain also has a good range of art and craft supplies, and helpful staff. If you're looking for beads, Etelage has a solid choice of handcrafted glass and wooden beads, and runs jewellery-making classes. City Scrapbooking supplies scrapbook materials and also offers classes.

Baby & Child Items

Items for babies and children are widely available in Sydney, and furniture including cots and chairs are built to comply with Australian safety standards.

Baby & Child Items

All For Kiddiz	163 Parramatta Road	9569 2255
Labella Baby	301 George St	9299 2791
My Baby Warehouse	305- 309 Parramatta Rd	9569 4244
One Fish Two Fish	251 Darling St	9818 2722
Osh Kosh B'Gosh	QVB	9267 6187
Pumpkin Patch	Birkenhead Pt	9181 4711
Shoes & Sox	Westfield Chatswood	9411 8840
Sydney Nappy Wash	Various locations	1300 303 600

Prices vary greatly; for example a jumpsuit could cost you anything from $2 to $200. Cheaper items are inevitably poorer quality, but that may not be an issue for rapidly growing babies and messy toddlers. More expensive items are generally better made and may be worth the investment if you intend to pass them down to younger children.

Cheap baby and kids' clothes are available from Target (www.target.com.au / 1300 130 000) and Kmart (www.kmart.com.au), who also sell a good range of furniture, accessories and toys.

Of course, in image-conscious Sydney there are also quality and designer kids' clothes available. If nothing but the best will do, fashion designer Collette Dinnigan has a children's range called Enfant, for babies to 4 year olds, available from David Jones (see p.304). Shops like One Fish Two Fish and Osh Kosh B'Gosh both sell hardwearing clothes made from good quality materials.

For nursery furniture, My Baby Warehouse (www.mybabywarehouse.com.au) and All For Kiddiz both sell a good range of baby furniture and accessories like cots, prams, chairs, car seats and toys.

Baby food and nappies are available from almost all supermarkets, but be aware that not all baby foods are created equal – some contain sugars and thickeners. Look for brands such as Motherly Cubes found in the freezer section, which are frozen pureed vegetables with no preservatives, thickeners or added sugar.

If you don't want to use disposable nappies, the Sydney Nappy Wash service (1300 303 600) supplies 100% cotton nappies along with a nursery bin, then picks up the dirty nappies and delivers fresh ones, for around $35 per week.

The Burkini

The latest craze to hit the stores is the burkini – a full-length two-piece lycra swimsuit with hijab head-covering suitable for Muslim women. It's not figure hugging enough to embarrass, but is tight enough to allow its wearer to swim freely.

Beachwear

Other options **Clothes** p.276, **Sporting Goods** p.295

Beachwear is an integral part of most local wardrobes. You'll find everything you need all year round in Sydney at department stores and surf shops located in beachside suburbs like Manly, Bondi and Coogee.

Walking around Campbell Parade in Bondi can sometimes feel like walking down a catwalk. Most locals interpret

Beachwear

Beach Culture	105 George St	9252 4551
Bikini Island Swimwear	38 Campbell Pde	9300 9446
Let's Go Surfing	128 Ramsgate Ave	9365 1800
Mambo Friendship Store	17 Oxford St	9331 8034
Rip Curl	Various locations	9264 6777
Roxy Store	175 Pitt St	9223 6999
Sue Rice	48 Ross St	9660 0488
Surf Dive 'N Ski	393 George St	9299 4920
Zimmerman	387 Oxford St	9357 4700

beach fashion with a mix of high-street, market or vintage clothing worn over swimwear. Sunglasses and a large bag to carry your towel and book are a must; accessories like hats and market jewellery are also popular. For footwear stick to sandals or thongs (flip-flops), which are also allowed in most local pubs and cafes. Most local women wear bikinis or one-pieces. Most local men wear boardshorts (boardies) or speedos (referred to as 'budgie smugglers').

If you're going to be swimming you'll need a durable pair of bathers that won't wash off in the first big wave, won't stretch, become transparent or rapidly fade and preferably look good for the fashion-conscious beachside suburbs. A quality pair of bathers should fit snugly (but not cut into the skin) and preferably be lined.

272

Cover Up
When buying beachwear don't forget to invest in a good hat, sunglasses, a light, long-sleeved top and a sarong that will protect your skin from the harsh Australian sun. There's nothing trendy about raw sunburnt skin.

Local brands like Rip Curl, Billabong and Mambo all make fashionable, good quality beachwear, priced from $50-$120 and women looking for innovative designs should also check out Seafolly and Tigerlily.

These brands are available in most beachwear shops like Rip Curl and Bikini Island Swimwear. Sue Rice (www.suerice.com.au) also specialises in custom made bathers in larger sizes for women, while Let's Go Surfing sells beachwear as well as wetsuits, surfboards, and snorkel gear.

Bicycles

Cycling in Sydney can be a challenge, with poor conditions and impatient drivers. But, a wide range of quality bikes are available. Centennial Park Cycles sells a good range of new and used

Bicycles		
Bicycle Inc	209 Castlereagh St	9283 5242
Bike Addiction	380 Pittwater Rd	9938 3511
Centennial Park Cycles	50 Clovelly Rd	9398 5027
Cheeky Monkey Cycle Company	3a Georgina St	9557 5424
Clarence Street Cyclery	104 Clarence St	9299 4962
PED Bicycles	19/200 Forbes St	9357 4990

bikes and rollerblades, while The Cheeky Monkey Cycle Company sells parts and accessories and does repairs; the staff are also passionate cyclists, so it's a great place to start networking.

Books

Other options **Second-Hand Items** p.294, **Libraries** p.236

Sydney has some wonderful iconic bookshops that are destinations in their own right; the thriving local literature scene centres on many of the city's locally-owned bookshops which are well-stocked and have knowledgeable staff.

Glebe is the city's best spot for book shopping, with Gleebooks, Sappho Books and Collins at Broadway Shopping Centre all within a short walk of each other and the second-hand book stalls at the Saturday Glebe markets. New books cost around $20-$40, but hardcover or specialty books may be more expensive.

Sydney also has an abundance of second-hand bookshops; prices are usually marked in pencil on the inside cover and tend to be around half of the price of a new book. Most major bookshops have an internal cafe with a small selection of light dishes, and many host book launches and literature and arts events throughout the year.

70 Norton St
Leichhardt

Berkelouw Books

9560 3200 | www.berkelouw.com.au

Berkelouw Books has been in Sydney since 1812, and have shops in Leichhardt and Paddington. Both stores have a range of new books, stationery and designer notebooks for sale, as well as a selection of second-hand books and CDs. The range of books varies but there is almost always a good collection of gardening, cooking and travel books, as well as standard fiction and non-fiction sections. Berkelouw boasts excellent coffee and a small range of lunch dishes and cakes are available. Keep your eye out for special events like Philosophy in the Café at the Leichhardt Berkelouw each week.

265 King St
Newtown

Better Read Than Dead

9557 8700

Better Read Than Dead stays open late and has a good selection of new books and all the general book categories are covered including fiction, non-fiction, biography, gardening, cooking, and travel. While there's no cafe, you'll find plenty of couches to sit on and browse potential purchases. The shop also sells a good range of novelty books, gift books and some stationery, and occasionally hosts book signings.

424 George St ◀
Darling Point

Dymock's

9235 0155 | *www.dymocks.com.au*

Dymock's is a bookshop chain with branches all over the city including Bondi Junction, Broadway, Burwood, Lane Cove, Neutral Bay, North Sydney and Parramatta. The shops are usually relatively small with only high-selling titles and popular categories like fiction, non-fiction, gardening, cooking, and travel on offer, with the exception of the city store which has a much better range of titles. Gift vouchers are available which can be redeemed at any Dymock's shop in Australia.

40 Hall St ◀
Bondi

Gertrude and Alice

9130 5155

With its wooden interior, sunken couches and wall-to-wall books, Gertrude and Alice second-hand bookshop feels cosy and unhurried; you can settle in for hours with a book, coffee and cake or Turkish bread. There is an excellent range including literature, travel, philosophy, gardening and culture but it does get crowded at weekends, especially during winter. You can also sell unwanted books here. Be aware though, the owners were considering closing down.

49 Glebe Point Rd ◀
Glebe

Gleebooks

9660 2333 | *www.gleebooks.com.au*

Gleebooks is one of Sydney's most renowned bookshops and a hub for writers, readers and literature events, and the two-storey shop has a huge range of books in almost every category. Upstairs you'll find more specific books like design, fashion, music, writing and the arts. You'll also find a good collection of specialist and international magazines and journals like *The New Yorker* and the *Australian Quarterly Essay*. Staff have an extensive knowledge of stock and can order books or magazines relatively quickly, depending on supply. You can also order online.

It's often worth keeping your eye on the windows for notices of literature events – many local and international authors do book readings and signings at Gleebooks which is open until 21:00 each day and all weekend.

191 Glebe Point Rd ◀
Glebe

Gleebooks Second-hand

9552 2526 | *www.gleebooks.com.au*

Glebe Second-hand has a good range of discounted and second-hand literature, pop fiction and children's books.

32 King St ◀
Newtown

Gould's Book Arcade

9519 8947 | *www.gouldsbooks.com.au*

Gould's Book Arcade is a local landmark in Newtown thanks to an extensive, if rambling, selection of new and second hand books, magazines, DVDs and videos, all managed by the unconventional local, Bob Gould.

If you're looking for a specific or out-of-print book (especially on history, art or politics) there's a good chance you'll find it at Gould's, but be prepared for a treasure hunt; while many sections of the shop are categorised, you'll find some corners are stacked with books to the ceiling, in no particular order. There's no cafe but staff are often happy to engage in long conversations, especially on slow days.

51 Glebe Point Rd ◀
Glebe

Sappho Books

9552 4498 | *www.sapphobooks.com.au*

Sappho Books is a huge two-storey second-hand bookshop right next door to Gleebooks. The range of titles available is excellent and includes travel, fiction, biography, non-fiction, sport, gardening, philosophy, media, war, design, arts, and rare and specialty books. Be prepared to pay at least $8 for any book you find, and much more for unique or hardcover books. There is a small cafe selling coffee and cakes, and a convivial atmosphere that encourages you to take a seat and muse over your choice.

Car Parts & Accessories

If you're keen to get someone else to fix up your car, better known repair franchises include www.midas.com.au, www.ultratune.com.au and www.lubemobile.com.au. Numbers are listed in the table on p.142 of the Residents chapter, under Vehicle Repair. This also has some info on the cost of getting your car serviced. If you're a keen revhead, and fancy a go yourself, there are plenty of shops waiting to accommodate you. www.sydney-city-directory.com.au or the yellow pages should list local spots. Allday (www.alldayperformance.com.au) is a good resource for those that want to fine tune their car's performance and appearance. Car Mate (www.carmate.com) on the Parramatta road sells body kits and Autobarn (www.autobarn.com.au) is a nationwide car parts superstore, with several branches around Sydney.

Car Parts & Accessories		
Allday Performance	Various locations	4333 3661
Autobarn	Various locations	9793 9455
Car Mate	Leichhardt	9723 1111
Everything GPS	202 Victoria Rd	9818 7040
Fast Fit Bullbars	601 Parramatta Rd	9569 4217

Cars

Other options **Buying a Vehicle** p.138

While driving in central Sydney can be a mighty pain, having a car becomes important once you get to the outer suburbs and beyond. For all the info you're likely to need to get on the road, turn to the Buying a Vehicle section in the Residents chapter (p.138). There are also tables of used and new car dealers to be found on p.138.

Clothes

Other options **Beachwear** p.272, **Hats** p.286, **Lingerie** p.289, **Shoes** p.295, **Sporting Goods** p.295, **Tailoring** p.296

Style varies from area to area; it is preppie on the north shore, vintage in the inner west, surf wear in the south and an eclectic mix of beachwear and designer in the eastern suburbs. If you're interested in current trends, the 'urban style' page in the Sunday *Sun Herald* gives a snapshot of some of the latest looks on Sydney's streets.

High Street
There are many high-street fashion shops selling quality, affordable clothes. For women, Sportsgirl, Portmans, and Witchery are good, while shops like General Pants Co and Just Jeans cater to men. All these shops have outlets in suburban malls, but if you're looking to do some serious high street shopping, head to Pitt Street Mall in the city.

Designer
Sydney fashion is relaxed yet glamorous. Local designers Wheels & Doll Baby, Zimmerman and Charlie Brown have all made an international impact. David Jones stocks Australian designers but brands like Armani, Louis Vuitton, Dolce & Gabbana are also available in Sydney, with shops concentrated around The Rocks and in Double Bay.

Vintage
Vintage clothes are a big element of Sydney style. Surry Hills is the city's vintage hub, with Grandma Takes A Trip (p.276), Mr Stinky and C's Flashback. Broadway Betty is also

275

Clothes

010 Maternity	Centrepoint	9293 1593	Hermes	Skygarden Centre	9223 4007
Absolute Fashion	MLC Centre	9233 5441	Hermes Paris	70 Castlereagh St	9223 5844
Adele Weiss	Chifley Plaza	9231 3511	House Of Cashmere	74 Castlereagh St	9231 5155
Akira	12a Queen St	9361 5221	Iceberg	64 Castlereagh St	9222 1822
Anthea Crawford	QVB	9264 5131	Ignazia	MLC Centre	9232 3787
Artwear By Lara S	77 George St	9247 3668	Industrie	239 King St	9519 7577
Barclay's Menswear	Centrepoint	9232 2260	Jeans West	Winston Hills Mall	9624 4892
Bardot	Central Plaza	9344 7072	Jigsaw	MLC Centre	9221 8407
Baubridge & Kay	Skygarden Centre	9223 6729	John Serafino	51 Pitt St	9251 3422
Bee Fashions	Centrepoint	9232 1543	Johnston & Bell	Skygarden Centre	9223 0084
Belinda	MLC Centre	9233 0781	Kookai	Sydney Central Plaza	9235 0293
Ben Sherman	Sydney Arcade	9222 1903	Lacoste Boutique	Harbourside	9280 0066
Betty Barckay	436 George St	9238 9960	Laura Ashley	Centrepoint	9232 2829
Big City Chic	Central Plaza	4721 7441	Louis Vuitton	155 George St	9251 8399
Bloch	Skygarden Centre	9231 4084	Lowes Menswear	Various locations	9267 2744
Broadway Betty	259 Broadway	9571 9422	Maloney Vince & Co	177 Elizabeth St	9264 8837
Blooms Design Co	QVB	9261 2462	Marcs	Mid City Centre	9221 5575
Calibre Clothing	139 Elizabeth St	9267 9321	Max Mara	Chifley Plaza	9223 2686
Capital L	333 South Dowling St	9361 0111	Mr Stinky	482 Cleveland St	9310 7005
Carla Zampatti	David Jones	9266 5338	Ojay	MLC Centre	9221 0403
Caviglia	64 Castlereagh St	9233 1997	Oxford	QVB	9264 2730
CEO	245 Pitt St	9267 1855	Peel	120 King St	9557 9400
Christopher Chronis	Central Plaza	9221 2691	Politix Menswear	Sydney Central Plaza	9231 1365
Country Road Clothing	142-144 Pitt St	9394 1818	Polo Ralph Lauren	QVB	9267 1630
Covers	David Jones	9266 5377	Portmans	135 King St	9223 8465
C's Flashback	180 King St	9565 4343	Posh Boutique	MLC Centre	9233 1261
Designer Labels Imports	MLC Centre	9238 6826	Prada Australia	15 Castlereagh St	9223 1688
Double Bay Clothing	83 Castlereagh St	9221 3237	R.M. Williams	389 George St	9262 2228
Dragstar	53a King St	9550 1243	Raza Vivre	Skygarden Centre	9283 3993
Easton Pearson	18 Elizabeth St	9331 4433	Reuben F Scarf	413 George St	9290 3966
Egg Maternity	28 Cross St	9363 2930	Review Clothing Stores	QVB	9264 4781
Emporio Armani	4 Martin Pl	8233 5858	Rivers	Skygarden Centre	9231 1066
Escada	46 Market St	9233 3311	Ron Bennett	245 Pitt St	9264 7485
Esprit Retail	9-13 Hay St	9211 6511	Sheike & Co	QVB	9283 8111
Farage	MLC Centre	9223 0241	Sisco	Skygarden Centre	9222 1122
Faster Pussycat	433a King St	9519 1744	Sportsgirl	Skygarden Centre	9223 8255
Filomena Natale	Skygarden Centre	9232 2048	Suite Boutique	Wynyard Station	9279 3503
Fletcher Jones	379 George St	9299 5961	Sussan	304 George St	9223 3326
French Connection	Opera Quays	9251 0602	Table Eight	Argyle Dept Store	9241 4554
Gant	145 King St	9221 4994	Tarocash	Centrepoint	9221 4639
Gianni Versace	128 Castlereagh St	9267 3232	Tuchuzy	90 Gould St	9365 5371
Giordano	Market City	9212 3948	Van Heusen	300 George St	9221 7333
Giorgio Bossi Italy	1 O'Connell St	9241 6875	Von Troska	Skygarden Centre	9235 0011
Great Australian Jumper Co	350 Kent St	9299 3388	Witchery	QVB	9267 2635
Gucci	MLC Centre	9232 7565	Xile Boutique	No.1 Martin Place	9233 8115
Henry Buck	23-25 O'Connell St	9232 4255	Yoshi Jones	134 King St	9550 1663

nearby (see table). But, some shops are seriously over-priced. True vintage clothes are usually pre-1980 and selected for their fabric, cut, shape or distinctive design. When you buy from a vintage shop it should be for two reasons; either it is totally unique, or you are buying an item for much less than it would cost new. If you're looking for good deals, you might be better off browsing through the donations at St Vincent de Paul's (p.276) or the Glebe and Rozelle markets (p.307).

Alternative
In Denial (74 Glebe Point Road, Glebe, 0410 511 635) sells a range of rave-inspired and eastern-style streetwear. Shopping there is a little like buying clothes in a club with the music blaring and low lights. Alternative jewellery is also available.

Petite and Plus Sizes
Options are fairly limited for those of an exceptional shape, but for plus-sized clothes, women can head to Towanda at 45 Market Street (9283 4848), men can try Big Guys at 46 Marion Street (9891 2266) or shop online at www.kingsize.com.au. Petite sizes are available in many fashion shops, especially those targeted towards the younger market, like Dotti at the Pitt Street Mall (9223 4028).

Maternity Wear
Expectant mums can head to Just Maternity (9266 0132) which has several outlets around Sydney or Egg Maternity in Double Bay. Big W in Winston Hills mall is a large discount store that stocks a maternity range and 010 Maternity in Westfield Centrepoint also has a good range and accepts giftcards.

Accessories
Accessories like sunglasses, jewellery, watches and scarves are available in most clothing shops but it's also worth checking out the markets in Glebe, Bondi and Paddington (see p.307) to find unique jewellery, bags and hats designed by locals.

348 Darling St
Balmain

Alfie's Little Brother Carter
9555 4100
The name might be a mouthful but Alfie's Little Brother Carter simplifies high-end fashion shopping, stocking many of the major designer brands for men and women. Here you'll find Sass & Bide, Alice McCall, Nobody Jeans, Paul Smith and The Magic Cape of Dynamite Boy so the shop is a great place to scope out up-and-coming designers as well as more established brands.

33 William St
Paddington

Collette Dinnigan
9360 6691
Arguably Australia's leading designer, Collette Dinnigan describes her collections as fun, sexy and beautifully crafted. Her clothes are renowned for their detail – fine beading, lace and handcrafted materials. She is famous for evening and bridal wear but also makes a wide range of skirts, jackets, tops, resort wear and eyewear. Just bring your credit card, as most designs start from $300.

263 Crown St
Surry Hills

Grandma Takes A Trip
9356 3322
Perhaps Sydney's best-known vintage clothing shop, Grandma Takes A Trip stocks a range of men's and women's vintage clothes and accessories including coats, suits, dresses, bags, sunglasses and jewellery and cufflinks. Don't expect to pick up serious bargains here; you won't find much for under $30, but every item is hand-picked for its

277

unique feel and design. The shop itself has a relaxed atmosphere and you're
encouraged to take your time and browse.

82 Gould St
Bondi

Ksubi/Tsubi
8303 1400

Ksubi has built a strong following among Sydneysiders with a range of relaxed-fit
jeans and street wear for both men and women, starting from $150 for a pair of jeans.
It was previously known as Tsubi but had to change names following a legal challenge
by US brand Tsubo.

80 Campbell Pde
Bondi

Mambo
9365 2255

Mambo is an Australian clothing brand with surf and street wear influences, perhaps
most recognised for its one-of-a-kind cartoons and bright prints. Mambo stores sell
everything from men's, women's and kids' t-shirts to jumpers, jackets, pants and
bathers. You'll see shops all over the city but if you want to save money check out the
outlet shop at Birkenhead Point in Drummoyne.

86 Gould St
Bondi

One Teaspoon
9365 1290

One Teaspoon is an institution for beachside fashionistas and you'll find a good range
of t-shirts, shirts, skirts and dresses in print fabrics perfect for the beach. The clothes are
very affordable considering the designer label and most retail for under $90. If you're
willing to spend over $300 you can book a personalised styling session after hours.

132 Oxford St
Central

Sass & Bide
9360 3900

If any designer outfit epitomises the Sydney women's look right now, it would have to
be Sass & Bide. Founded by locals Sarah-Jane 'Sass' Clarke and Heidi 'Bide' Middleton,
the shop has come a long way from its flagship stall at London's Portobello market.
With their figure-hugging jeans, quirky t-shirts with slogans like 'You owe me nothing',
floaty tops and lacy skirts, Sass & Bide is a favourite. Jeans start at around $180.

Various locations

St Vincent's de Paul
www.vinnies.org.au

St Vincent's de Paul, known as St Vinnie's or Vinnie's to Sydneysiders, is a charity-run
shop that sells second-hand clothes and wares donated by locals. The quality varies
greatly and there is always a large contingent of daggy clothes, but there are also many
gems that are true bargains; most items sell for well under $10. Vinnie's is also a great
place to look for fancy dress costumes like outrageous 80s ball gowns, odd-coloured
suits, old wedding dresses or
strange hats and glasses.

90 Gould St
Bondi

Tuchuzy
9365 5371

This well-established Bondi
fashion destination sells a
range of local and international
designs like Bettina Liano, Third
Millenium, Princess Highway
and Louis Epstein. Tuchuzy
stocks clothes for men, women

and kids, and while prices start very reasonably at $20 for some smaller items, most are priced at over $100.

147 Castlereagh St
Central

The Vintage Shop
9267 7135

The Vintage Shop in the city will please those looking for a genuine item of clothing from a bygone era. There are some real forgotten treasures here. Clothes are individually selected for their fabric, cut, and design and date from 1850 to 1980. The shop caters to both men and women with a good selection of dresses, shirts, pants, cardigans, hats, skirts and bags. A nice bonus is the advice offered by staff on how to care for your item.

Computers

Other options **Electronics & Home Appliances** p.280

The latest computer technology is usually available in Sydney as soon as it is released elsewhere – the exception is Apple products which can sometimes arrive months after their US release.

Computers are generally slightly more expensive than in the US. Very basic models start from around $500 while faster models with more memory cost over $1,500. For the very latest technology you'll pay over $2,000. Prices are almost always negotiable and you can usually save 10-20% if you bargain.

Computers		
Adelong Computers	127 York St	9260 3188
Apple Centre	Cnr Glebe Point Rd & Broadway	8586 1111
AUS Point Computers	149 Castlereagh St	9267 2535
Dick Smith	Westfield Bondi	9369 2576
Digital City	403 George St	9290 1510
Digital Video Technologies	5 Kiama St	9522 2244
Electronics Boutique	Centrepoint	9476 0988
Next Byte	66 Clarence St	9367 8585
Oriium Consulting	515 Kent St	1300 554 404
TEG Computers	33 Bligh St	9223 2360
Uniwell	20 Wallis Pde	9365 3092

Digital City has a good range of computers (including PCs and Macs), laptops, software and accessories, and will order special models or parts for you. Staff are not pushy and can give you sound advice on the pros and cons of different products. Next Byte (www.nextbyte.com.au) has shops all over the city selling PC computers and equipment, and is an authorised Apple reseller with a good range of Mac products, including iPods.

There are also several computer fairs selling discounted equipment held throughout the year at the University of NSW and Parramatta; visit www.computerfairs.com.au for upcoming dates.

Almost all new computers in Australia are sold with a one-year international warranty. If your computer is past warranty and needs repairs, try Nerds on Site (1800 696 373, www.nerdsonsite.com.au). This is a group of mobile computer repairers and technicians who will come to your home. Prices vary depending on the repairs required.

Costumes

Sydneysiders aren't shy about dressing up. This vibrant city brings out the festive spirit in everyone, from the smallest party among friends to major events like the Melbourne Cup. Don't be surprised to see whacky costumes strutting alongside the smart dresses and hats for this day at the races. For costume hire, head to Darlinghurst where you'll find Motley Costume Hire & Design and Mama Shirls or else see what The Costume Shop has to offer.

Costumes		
Costume Design Centre & Hire	288 Abercrombie St	9698 7440
Mama Shirls @ Team on Oxford	88 Oxford St	9357 2870
Motley Costume Hire & Design	39 Liverpool St	9269 6600
The Costume Shop	401 Cleveland St	9318 2511

279

Electronics & Home Appliances

Other options **Computers** p.279

There's an array of electronics and home appliance stores in Sydney, although prices are not likely to be cheaper than in the US or Europe. York Street and its surrounding area has many shops offering a whole range of deals, so do shop around. For hi-fi equipment and DVDs, try George's Electronics Retail & Duty Free, David Reid Electronics and JB Hi-Fi. For cameras, there are many shops on George Street – try CCC Camera House or Digital City.

When buying electronic items in Australia, it's worth checking if the warranty is international if you plan to take your goods back home with you. And, whether your new purchase will actually work in your home country. This might not stop you from buying but it may well influence how much you're willing to spend. Added extras such as guarantees and repair services vary from shop to shop. For home appliances, Bing Lee is a good bet and stocks everything from air conditioners to food mixers. You can also rent your white goods through Home Appliance Rentals. They offer a service of 'rent to buy', whereby you can pay for your goods in monthly installments while you use them. For second-hand items, see p.294.

Electronics & Home Appliances		
Audio Visual World	Various locations	9809 1777
Bing Lee Lifestyle	Skygarden Centre	9221 8028
CCC Camera House	416 George St	9232 4500
David Reid Electronics	127 York St	9267 1385
Digital City	309 George St	9299 7500
Gadgets	88 Pitt St	9223 0744
Georges Electronics Retail & Duty Free	56-58 York St	9299 2300
Home Appliance Rentals	Campbelltown	1300 137 336
JB Hi-Fi	Various locations	9267 8444
M Force Direct	87-89 Liverpool St	9267 3331
Powerland Electronics	Various locations	9734 9900
Quantum Energy	31 Market St	9261 5121
Tandy	127 York St	9267 1305

Eyewear

Other options **Sporting Goods** p.295

You need an Australian prescription to buy reading glasses in Sydney and they are readily available from optometrists. Many eyewear shops, like The Optical Superstore or Master Specs, have in-store optometrists. You may need to make an appointment and it will cost around $53, but if you are a resident this is refunded by Medicare. A basic set of frames starts from $50-$80, lenses start from $100 and for more complex glasses, or designer brands, expect to pay over $300.

Contact lenses are widely available in all forms and colours and you'll find sunglasses in many clothing shops. The Sunglasses Hut sells a wide range of sunglasses, including major designer brands. Most markets also have stalls selling sunglasses from around $10 a pair.

Eyewear		
Budget Eyewear Australia	428 George St	9815 2333
Eyecee	167 King St	9550 6711
Heming Scott & Donald	46 The Corso	9977 6700
Kingdom Optical	162-166 Goulburn St	9264 9133
Magicline Eyewear	410 Elizabeth St	9371 7444
Master Specs	310 George St	9387 5531
The Eyewear Collection	60 Margaret St	9251 1802
The Optical Superstore	436 George St	9238 0900
The Sunglasses Hut	Various locations	9223 8185

Flowers

Other options **Gardens** p.284

Flowers of all descriptions are widely available year-round in Sydney thanks to the favourable growing conditions in the region. Small bunches of flowers are usually available from supermarkets, corner shops and even petrol stations for around $10, but are not usually very fresh or vibrant.

Flowers

CBD Florist	580 George St	9267 8711
Circular Quay Florist	2 Alfred St	9247 5445
Eddy Avenue Florist	Central Station	9212 2897
Flowers All Hours	Various locations	1300 762 295
Flowers With Essence	320 Pitt St	9283 2727
Image De Fleur	265 Castlereagh St	9264 0640
Inbloom Florist	500 George St	9283 0022
Maurice the Florist	117 Macquarie St	9252 1451
Pearson's Florist	Various locations	9550 7777
Scent Fast Florists	21a Barcom Ave	1800 508 879
Urban Flower	1 Burwood Rd	1800 825 368

You can buy better quality arrangements from florists, including Australian native flowers. Expect to pay upwards of $25 for a small bouquet, $75 for a dozen roses, and up to $100 for a large bunch of striking blooms. Almost all florists are members of Interflora, who can deliver flowers almost anywhere in the world for an extra fee of between $10-$20. Urban Flower, also known as the Nite Florist, is worth remembering for its generous opening hours; from 07:00 to 23:00, every day of the year. Besides flowers they also sell and deliver hampers, chocolates and soft toys, and you can order over the phone. Pearson's is one of Sydney's best-known florists, with locations city-wide. Pearson's also runs flower-arranging courses and caters special events. One of Sydney's best-kept secrets is the Sydney Flower Market in Flemington, where farmers supply flowers to florists, but also the general public. See the market section on p.306 for more information.

Food
Other options **Health Food** p.286

Food lovers will delight in the superb range of fresh produce, whole foods and drinks available in Sydney. Whether you're looking for Asian greens or Italian antipasti, there's a multicultural array of food and drink to suit every taste.

Bakeries
Baker's Delight is an Australian franchise of bakeries found all across Sydney. Their success is down to reliable bread, cakes, tarts, rolls and pies, baked fresh every morning. Each Baker's Delight has the same range on offer: from white, brown, wholemeal, sourdough and Turkish bread to cheese and bacon rolls and 'pull apart' breads infused with cheese, spinach or other ingredients. You can buy breads whole or have them sliced to your liking, with most loaves selling for between $2.50 and $5.
Sonoma Bakehouse is famous for its sourdough bread, which is also a favourite of top Sydney restaurants. The range isn't huge but there's enough to cater for most tastes, including organic and gluten-free bread. There's also an internal cafe.

Coffee

The perfect cup of coffee is considered something of an art at Caffe Bianchi, which sells fresh roasted coffee blends (whole beans and ground), coffee machines, coffee paraphernalia and kitchenware. The coffee is reasonably priced from $5.50 for 250g – which is cheaper (and much better quality) than supermarket brands. It's open during regular business hours in the week and on Saturdays, but closed on Sundays. You can also order online www.caffebianchi.com (note the double 'f' in Caffe). They accept all major Australian credit cards.

Campos Cafe is tucked away behind the Marlborough Hotel and is easy to miss, but once you've tried the coffee it's hard to forget. You can order a freshly made coffee from one of the award-winning baristas while you select which beans you want to buy – sold whole, or ground to your liking. There is a huge range available, sourced from Africa, South America, and East Timor, (including Fair Trade coffee) selling for upwards of $8 per 250g.

Food		
About Life	605 Darling St	9555 2695
Barn Café & Grocery	731 Darling St	9810 1633
Bluestone Deli	60 Margaret St	9241 2577
Caffe Bianchi	Leichhardt Marketplace	9569 1671
Campus Cafe	193 Missenden Rd	9516 3361
Cavallaro's Sweet Indulgence	253 Macquarie St	9602 6055
Darrell Lea	398 George St	9231 3261
Denlen Gourmet Food	264 George St	9241 1519
Dong Nam A & Co	14 Campbell St	9212 6673
Earth Food Store	81a Gould St	9365 5098
Eilat At Hadassa	17 O'Brien St	9365 4904
Essential Ingredient	477 Pacific Highway	9439 9881
Foodtown Thai Kee Supermarket	393 Sussex St	9281 2202
Haigh's Chocolates	Strand Arcade	9221 6999
Ichiban-Kan Japanese Grocery	36 Nurses Walk	9247 2667
La Renaissance Café Patisserie	47 Argyle St	9241 4878
Le Breton Patisserie	519 Military Rd	9969 9654
Lindt Café	53 Martin Place	8257 1600
Macro Wholefoods	31-35 Oxford St	9389 7611
Quay Deli	5 Alfred St	9241 3571
Sonoma Bakehouse	215 Glebe Point Rd	9597 4133
Staffords Cheese Store	131 Balmain Rd	9564 2642
Sticky	Kendall Lane	9252 3337
T2	173 King St	9550 3044
The Tea Centre	The Glass House	9223 9909
TJ's Quality Meats	319 Darling St	9810 2911
Torres Cellars & Delicatessen	75 Liverpool St	9264 6862
Wintergarden Deli	1 O'Connell St	9241 4597

Tea

If you're a discerning tea drinker you'll adore The Tea Centre, which has over 185 teas and blends including black, green, oolong, herbal, fruit, special infusions and health teas. The Tea Centre sources tea from all over the world and supplies some of Australia's top restaurants and caterers. Prices start from $7.50 per 100g for English breakfast tea, $10.50 for 100g of most herbal teas and chai, or up to $20.50 for 100g of specialty teas like Ginger Kiss. There is not a teabag in sight here – tea is sold loose leaf to be brewed in teapots or strainers, which are also available. There are plenty of gift ideas, and if you can't make it to the city shop, staff will take orders over the phone for a $5-$10 postage charge.

T2 is a growing chain of speciality teashops found in many of Australia's trendy urban centres. T2 has an excellent range of loose-leaf teas available, including black, green, herbal and fruit, as well as teapots, teacups and tea strainers. At the front of the shop there are usually a range of special blends available for tasting. Teas cost upwards of $5 per 100g. Gift packs are also available.

Cheese

Australia is home to some of the world's best cheese makers but Sydney lived without a dedicated cheese shop until 2004, when Stafford's Cheese Store filled the gap. It doesn't disappoint. Stafford's sells hundreds of types of cheese, mostly sourced from Australia, although high quality international brands are also available. Prices fluctuate but don't expect to spend less than $10 for 250g. There's every type of cheese imaginable and staff are experts on the subject. Gift vouchers are also available.

Chocolate and Sweets

Tim Tam ◀

The Tim Tam is a much loved Aussie snack. It is a chocolate coated biscuit with a cream centre. The connoisseur consumer will bite a little off each end, and suck tea through the middle, using it as a straw. If mistimed, however, this can leave you with mucky fingers and a soggy biscuit.

Haigh's Chocolates sells a mouth-watering variety of handmade Australian chocolates. It's mostly small bite-size chocolates, but chocolate bars, gift boxes and other sweets are available. They are sold by weight and cost $9 for 100g, which will buy you five or six luxury chocolates.

Chocoholics will also find it hard to go past the world's first Lindt cafe, in Martin Place. There's a delicious array of Lindt chocolates, rich cakes and pastries. Cakes cost around $34 for an 8-person cake and up to $120 for a much larger one. There are also chocolate appreciation courses run in the evenings – ask the staff for details. Stop at the onsite cafe for one of Sydney's best hot chocolates. If you are ordering for a special event, make sure you call well in advance.

Sweet teeth will also be drawn to the colourful facade of Darrell Lea. It's still owned by an Australian family and maintains a homely, unhurried atmosphere. Here you can find a selection of fine chocolates, candies, and lollies to fulfill the strongest sugar craving.

Delicatessens

Delis here sell top-quality and premium foods; from antipasti such as olives, feta and sun-dried tomatoes; to premium pastas, meats, boutique oils, vinegars, coffee, juices, sauces and breads. You can also usually find specialty items you wouldn't get anywhere else, like duck's fat or saffron syrup.

The David Jones Food Hall in the city's Pitt Street Mall has an extensive delicatessen, see p.302 for more information.

About Life is all about gourmet and organic produce that you won't find in most chain stores. This is the deli with everything: from fresh fruit and vegetables, meats, seafood, Asian groceries, breads (including gluten-free), whole foods, cheeses, juices, oils, antipasti, vinegars and sauces.

The Barn Café & Grocery is another delicatessen gem found in the inner-west's Rozelle. It has a lovely country-grocer atmosphere. Fruit and vegetables are sourced directly from farms so are often much fresher than the supermarket produce. There is an impressive array of local and international deli items available, from antipasti to cheeses, meats, salads, spreads, cakes, tarts and pies. The friendly cafe attached offers cooking classes (children's classes are also available). The shop also does catering for events, gift hampers for special occasions, and has an online ordering system, visit www.thebarncafe.com.au.

The Essential Ingredient is a delicatessen and kitchenware megastore which stocks everything your kitchen will ever need – except fresh ingredients. The shop recently relocated from Camperdown to Crow's Nest to cope with an ever-increasing range. If you're looking for a specialty ingredient, chances are you'll find it here, as well as strainers, whisks and wooden spoons. The items are premium quality so expect to pay upwards of $8 for most food items.

Meat and Seafood

Meat is generally of high quality in Sydney. Coles and Woolworths (Hypermarkets, p.306) sell some organic cuts, but if you want the best, go to your local butcher. TJ's Quality Meats (see table, left) sells prime cuts of beef, lamb, chicken and pork sourced from Australia's top producers, including some organic ones. Glenmore Meats at 40 Wentworth Park Road in Glebe (9566 2400) also sells excellent quality meat.

283

Sydney Fish Market

For the best seafood, head to the fish markets in Pyrmont. This is where most fish shops source their produce. See Markets, p.306, for more information.

Kosher

Kosher cuts of meat are available from many butchers around Bondi (where Sydney's Jewish community is largely based), including Eilat At Hadassa.

Organic

You can buy organic food at many farmer's markets (see p.307), online via sites like www.organicfood.com.au, which delivers all over Sydney, and from some health stores (see p.286). Prices vary because of the higher cost of production, seasonal availability, growing conditions and the ups and downs of supply and demand. In general, you can expect to pay 50% above the price of regular produce if you are buying organic. Go to the Earth Food Store or Marco Wholefoods. Marco sells organic fruits, vegetables, meats and seafood, as well as non-organic produce and general delicatessen foods. Organic meat has also gained a following and organic beef, chicken and lamb are now available in most major supermarkets. See Meat and Seafood above and Hypermarkets p.306.

You can get a free directory of organic suppliers in Sydney. Just send an SAE (50 cents stamp) to: Catriona Macmillan, PO Box 3335, Tamarama, NSW 26.

Gardens

Other options **Hardware & DIY** p.285, **Flowers** p.280

The high number of renters and apartments mean that garden shops are very sparsely located near the city. But there are a few. The Annandale Garden Centre is good If you're simply buying a few pots and some shrubs. If you need more, you're better off heading to one of the large garden centres in the suburbs, which offer a much more extensive and affordable range of plants, shrubs and garden accessories. Flower Power has a good

Gardens		
Annandale Garden Centre	34-36 Booth St	9660 0874
Bunnings	179 Victoria Ave	9412 3533
Flower Power	Various locations	9747 5555
King Street Conservatory	416 King St	9557 7446
Linc's Bbq Heating & Furniture	128 George St	9477 3535
Rast Bros Nursery	31-37 Kissing Point Rd	9144 2134

selection of garden accessories, furniture and tools, as well as earth, mulch, fertiliser and pesticides. The Enfield shop is the closest one to the city, but there are also others in Bass Hill, Casula, Glenhaven, Moorebank, Mount Annan, Taren Point, Terrey Hills and Warriewood.

Gifts

Sydney is not shy about flogging cheesy gifts and trinkets to its hordes of tourists. The list of iconic Aussie gifts is long and a little bit tacky. You can go for fluffy kangaroos in the colours of the national rugby union team, wombat key rings, 'roo poo chocolate drops, possum-shaped macadamia nuts, proper ocker cork hats and almost anything else you can think of branded with the Aussie flag or bright gold and green. Much of this is to be found down by The Rocks and around Circular Quay, where the cruise liners dock and other tourists head in their droves. Aboriginal

Need Some Direction?

The *Explorer Mini Maps* pack a whole city into your pocket and once unfolded are excellent navigational tools. Not only are they handy in size, with detailed information on the sights and sounds of the city, but their price means they won't make a dent in your holiday fund. Wherever your travels take you, grab a mini map and you'll never have to ask for directions. Pocket the *Sydney Mini Map* to help find your way around your new home.

Gifts		
Australian Geographic	QVB	9257 0086
Best of Australiana	QVB	9261 2249
Luciana Art & Gifts	77 York St	9279 0792
Picolo Gifts	333 George St	9262 6219
Spring Row Gift Shop	115 George St	9247 1851
Wombat At The Rocks	27 Playfair St	9241 2632

items are also to be found down here, such as didgeridoos and boomerangs, just check for their authenticity. Some may have been hand crafted by a skilled Aboriginal artisan; others may have been factory made in Shanghai. A range of online gift services is also available in Australia; www.wishlist.com.au, www.toysandmore.com.au, www.interflora.com.au and wine through www.vintagecellars.com.au. For specific items, such as art (p.271) or toys (p.297), look under the individual section, as listed in the Quick Reference on p.268.

Handbags

There's a handbag for every occasion in Sydney, from designer pieces to handmade market items. Most fashion shops sell durable bags in the latest styles for $10 to $50. David Jones (p.304) sells some designer brands. You can buy original bags from the Bondi and Glebe markets (p.307) for

Handbags		
Chanel	70 Castlereagh St	9233 4800
Gucci	19 Martin Pl	9221 4218
Hunt Leather	MLC Centre	9233 8702
Hermes	77 Castlereagh St	9223 4007
Longchamp	MLC Centre	1800 083 355
Louis Vuitton	63 Castlereagh St	1300 883 880
Majestic Bags & Leather	100 Market St	9233 4675
MODO Handbags	273 George St	9241 3868
Park Avenue Handbags	168 Pitt St	9233 3108

around $30. If nothing but the best will do, head to Castlereagh Street. For vintage bags, try Grandma Takes a Trip (p.276).

Hardware & DIY

Other options **Outdoor Goods** p.292

There has been a DIY frenzy in Sydney in recent years, and the number of hardware shops has increased massively as a result.

If you're looking for tools, materials, fittings and paints you're best going to a hardware shop; Sunlite City Hardware has a good range of hardware, DIY and electronic items in the city.

Bunnings Warehouse (www.bunnings.com.au) is a chain of hardware warehouses located all around the city, which have just about every product available, as well as gift vouchers and registries for DIY nuts and they will beat any price found elsewhere by 10%. Other major franchises include Mitre10 (www.mitre10.com.au) and Home Hardware (www.homehardware.com.au), which also have stores across the city. Each of the websites listed has a store finder. If you'd rather shop somewhere independent, Booth and Taylor Hardware is an established local

Hardware & DIY		
Booth and Taylor Hardware	7 Booth St	9552 2910
Bunnings Warehouse	Various locations	9846 7100
Carrolls Hardware	163- 165 William St	9331 5555
Glenfords	1/4 Hollylea Rd	4625 2111
Hardware One	374 Pitt St	9264 8200
Home Hardware	Various locations	9839 0777
Mitre10	Various locations	9331 4689
Pauls City Hardware	163 Castlereagh St	9264 6200
Sunlite City Hardware	Various locations	9231 3331

shop with a good range of products. Almost all hardware shops also offer detailed advice, and many can recommend local professionals like carpenters or designers if your skills aren't up to the task at hand.

Hats

Ladies looking for a hat for the races (the rule to remember is straw for summer, felt for winter) are best served visiting the selection at Myer or David Jones, see p.304, or else Strand Hatters on George Street. See Table p.286 for a list of companies selling hats of all shapes and sizes.

If you're looking for an Akubra, Strand Hatters sells the genuine article alongside brands like Kangol and Harris Tweed. Here you can stock up on top hats, sombreros, tweed caps, French berets and 40s-style pork pie hats. The hats are made from quality fabrics like felt, fur and leather and start at around $30.

Hats		
Hat World Australia	683- 689 George St	9280 4930
Helen Kaminski	199 George St	9251 9850
Maya Neuman	94 Oxford St	9361 0905
Moray Millinery	191-195 Pitt St	9233 1591
Strand Hatters	412 George St	9231 6884

Health Food
Other options **Food** p.281

Health Food		
Discount Vitamin Centres DVC	143 King St	9233 8433
GNC Live Well	309 George St	9279 1770
Healthy, Wealthy, and Young	370 Pitt St	9268 0264
Pure Health	273 George St	9247 8889
Strand Health	The Rocks Centre	9252 2558
The Health Emporium	263-265 Bondi Road	9365 6008

Health foods, supplements and alternative medicines are widely available in Sydney. Vitamin and mineral supplements, soy products, gluten-free, and preservative-free products can be found in almost any supermarket but if you're looking for something more specific, The Health Emporium (www.healthemporium.com.au) sells a good range of organic fresh fruit and vegetables, whole foods and supplements. It also sells organic baby food, natural cleaning products and deli items. In the inner west, GNC Live Well sells a good range of health food items and some organic produce. For information on organic produce, see p.307, or Markets on p.306.

Home Furnishings & Accessories
Other options **Hardware & DIY** p.285

How you dress your home is just as important as how you dress yourself in some parts of Sydney, and there are loads of home furnishing and accessory shops as a result. Whether your style is minimalist, art deco or eclectic kitsch, there'll be a shop to fit your niche. You don't have to spend a lot of money to buy quality homeware in Sydney, although there are plenty of shops that cater to the designer home market.

If you're looking for basics, the Supa Centa mall in Moore Park is a good place to start, with IKEA, Harvey Norman, Fantastic Furniture and Domain stores all situated here (see p.288).

AES INTERNATIONAL

Individual Solutions...

...for individual clients

- Savings and Investments
- Offshore Banking
- Foreign Exchange
- Financial Planning
- Tax and Legal Advice
- Corporate Services

info@aesfinance.com   www.aesfinance.com

14 Rue Maunoir, 1207 Geneva, Switzerland, TEL:+41 22 534 9474

Home Furnishings & Accessories

Afghan Interiors	451 King St	9550 6666
Alan Landis Antiques	250 Pitt St	9267 7068
Arida	61 Macleay St	9357 4788
Beyond Furniture	375 Pacific Highway	9923 1123
Boodle & Dunthorne Royal Antiques	255 Pitt St	9267 7547
Carpeteria	17 Newland St	9389 4389
de de ce	263 Liverpool St	9360 2722
Fantastic Furniture	Various locations	9949 8702
FiftySixtySeventy	308 Trafalgar St	9566 1430
Gallery Orientique	Birkenhead Point	9181 4668
Harvey Norman	Various locations	8236 6600
Hills Floor Discount	146-152 Gloucester St	9894 1385
Homeware Gallery	7A Norton St	9560 5049
IKEA	1 Oulton Ave	8002 0400
International Floorcoverings	379 South Dowling St	9360 8655
James Lee Warner Furniture	32 Alice St	9519 6175
Karen Deakin Antiques	428 George St	9221 1404
Koskela Design	91 Campbell St	9280 0999
Laura Kincade	4 Bridge Rd	9692 0815
Mobler	28a Curlewis St	9365 0573
Newtown Furniture Haven	435 King St	9557 8455
Precision Flooring	1 Kings Cross Rd	8354 1500
Robert Heywood Modern Furniture	4 Bridge St	0411 501 777
Solid Grain Furniture	226 King St	9557 5682
Sunshine Screens	67-69 Lords Rd	9518 0111
Sydney Antique Centre	531 South Dowling St	9361 3244
Sydney Property Auction Centre	17 O'Connell St	9221 3405
The Classic Furniture Gallery	40 King St	9517 9990

Department stores like Myer (p.304) and David Jones (p.305) also have a good range of homeware and accessories, as does Target (p.272). Cheap furniture starts at around $100 for a new bookcase or basic wardrobe and $200 for a futon. You can get cheaper deals if you look for second-hand items, see p.294 for more information.

Newtown has an abundance of unique and affordable furniture shops. The Classic Furniture Gallery specialises in Javanese wood and recycled teak, including a range of bed frames, day beds, dining tables and carvings. There's also Afghan Interiors, which sells imported Asian-style furniture, right next door to the Newtown Furniture Haven, and down the road from Solid Grain Furniture, which specialises in wooden items.

The vintage boom has also extended to furniture, and shops like FiftySixtySeventy and Mobler sell designer vintage pieces to drool over. But vintage doesn't come cheap – even a simple lounge chair can be as much as $2,000 and many of these shops are only open at weekends.

If you're looking for classic furniture, Sydney Antique Centre is one of Australia's largest antique centres, and sells everything from dressers, bookcases, tables and chairs to antique clocks, bottles, books and dolls.

For new designer pieces, de de ce sells a good range of brands including Cappellini, Vola, Minotti and Knoll. Arida sells designer pieces with an artistic flair, including furniture from around the world, glassware and unique lamps. Koskela Design is an

Australian furniture designer with sleek, minimalist-looking pieces including beds, coffee tables, seats, cubes, rugs and lamps. For repairs and custom designs (including outdoor furniture), try the Homeware Gallery.

If you want to get some special flooring put down, try Carpeteria in Bondi, Hills Floor Discount in the city or else, go over to Darlinghurst where you'll find both International Floorcoverings and Precision Flooring. For children's furniture, see Childrens and Baby Items, p.271.

Jewellery, Watches & Gold
Other options **Markets** p.306

You can buy jewellery everywhere in Sydney – in clothing shops, markets, department stores and from independent sellers. Beads or cheap materials made into jewellery are popular among locals but Australia is the world's number one opal manufacturer, and Sydney is a great place to buy these unique multicoloured gems. A&H Australian Opal House and Australian Opal Market are good places to buy genuine stones, which come with a guarantee. You can get small, low-quality opals for as little as $30, but a good stone can cost thousands.

Silver and gold jewellery are not particularly cheap in Sydney, but the quality is generally good if you buy from a jeweller and for those with more to spend there's always Tiffany's. Most brands of watches are available including Tag Heuer and Rolex, but don't expect to get them cheaper than anywhere else. The Time Masters and The Hour Glass both sell a good range of watches.

Jewellery, Watches & Gold		
A & H Australian Opal House	QVB	9261 3193
Australian Opal Market	413 Sussex St	9212 5671
Camille Lucie	Westfield Bondi	9387 2244
Cartier	MLC Centre	9235 1322
Diamond World	Westfield Hornsby	9476 0524
Gregory Jewellers	MLC Centre	9232 8242
MLC Gifts	19 Martin Place	9231 3505
The Hour Glass	142 King Street	9221 2288
The Time Masters	70 Castlereagh St	9223 2788
Tiffany & Co.	28 Castlereagh St	9235 1777

Lingerie
Other options **Clothes** p.276

Lacy, racy, patterned, pretty and practical, there's a bra available for every occasion in Sydney. Australia is home to a number of celebrity lingerie designers, most famously Elle McPherson (Elle McPherson Intimates) and Kylie Minogue (Love Kylie). Elle McPherson Intimates includes an excellent collection of fashionable bras, briefs, g-strings, corsets and nightwear in well-fitting cuts while Love Kylie has more brazen designs. It's also a little less practical with more lace and frills, which look pretty but aren't always invisible under clothes.

Both Myer and David Jones (see p.304) have excellent selections of most major lingerie brands, including those mentioned above and Bendon, La Perla, Oroton, Calvin Klein and Loveable. If you're buying a gift, staff are very helpful at suggesting appealing designs and finding the right size.

Target (see p. 272) and Kmart (see p.272) also have a good range of cheaper brands like Antz Pantz. Bras N Things (www.brasnthings.com.au) is a chain store found in most malls, with a fair range of lingerie, nightwear and some fetish items. Gift vouchers are available.

Nightwear
Peter Alexander (www.peteralexander.com.au) is an Australian sleepwear designer that sells men's and women's pyjamas and nightwear almost exclusively by catalogue and the internet. The website can be a bit slow unless you have high-speed broadband, but the unique cuts and fabrics of the items, which are designed with the Australian climate in mind, are worth the wait. The items are good quality and well priced at around $40 for a pair of pyjama pants. Most credit cards are accepted and delivery to Sydney is prompt.

Lingerie		
Bras N Things	Various locations	1800 810 031
Can Can Lingerie	Sydney Central Plaza	9261 2460
Coucher Lingerie	Harbourside Centre	9221 1238
More Than a Handful	250 Pitt St	9267 4596
Peter Alexander	Various locations	1300 366 683

289

Fetish

For leatherwear, specialty lingerie and fetish clothing try www.adultshop.com.au, a Canberra-based company that sells a huge range of adult items. Most credit cards are accepted and packaging is discreet.

Perfect Fit

Most women find that the fit and cut of bras varies greatly between brands. If you're coming from overseas, get a proper fitting to find your Australian size. You'll find that most shops provide this service for free. Plus sizes might be frustrated by the range of fits available in department stores, but More Than a Handful offers specialised fittings for curvier women.

Luggage & Leather

Other options **Shipping** p.267

If you're buying a bag or suitcase, the Sydney Luggage Centre (www.sydneyluggagecentre.com.au) has just about every type of luggage imaginable, including backpacks, business bags, computer bags, handbags, duffle bags and suitcases. Brands range from cheap to designer, and repairs are also available. Cheaper suitcases are available from department stores like Target (p.272) and independent luggage shops dotted around the city.

Luggage & Leather		
Instyle	Westfield Parramatta	9476 2123
Bag Scene	Westfield Parramatta	9687 2822
Bag Station	Westfield Parramatta	9687 7588
Bags Bay	Westfield Liverpool	9822 5121
Bottega Venta	Chifley Plaza	9231 4148
Desa Leather	25 Willoughby Rd	9439 9220
Hunt Leather	MLC Centre	9233 8702
Sydney Luggage Centre	Various locations	9267 1139

Leather clothing is usually imported from overseas and is relatively expensive. You won't find leather jackets at the markets – you'll have to head to specialty shops like Desa Leather (www.desaleather.com.au) and Bottega Venta. Leather couches are available from most designer home furnishing shops, but can be impractical in sweaty Sydney summers.

Medicine

Other options **General Medical Care** p.116

There are pharmacies or chemists all over Sydney in shopping strips and malls, and most suburbs have at least one local chemist. Laws on prescription and over-the-counter medicines are strict, and it's unlikely you'll be able to get medicine anywhere other than where it is legally available.

Pharmacists in Australia are all university-qualified and can offer professional advice and assistance for most minor ailments so it's always worth asking them if you don't think a doctor is necessary. For most medicine you'll need a prescription, but many common pain relievers are available in supermarkets and over-the-counter. Paracetamol is sold as Panadol and Heron and is available in small quantities from supermarkets and service stations, as well as chemists. Pain relievers like codeine are available in small amounts over-the-counter at chemists, sold as Panadeine and Chemist's Own Pain Tablets. If you want higher strength codeine you'll need a prescription.

Cold and flu tablets containing pseudoephedrine are now only available by request at the chemist

Medicine		
All Night Chemist	20 Ware St	9724 1212
Priceline Pharmacy	World Square Shopping Centre	9268 0042
Rozelle Health & Beauty Pharmacy	Cnr Victoria Rd and Darling St	9810 7349
Twelve Hour Pharmacy	35 Norton St	9560 7008

and you have to provide photo ID to buy them but aspirin, cough medicines, and low-dose ibuprofen are widely available at supermarkets and chemists, where you can also find most allergy medicines.

Many chemists close at 18:00 and after that you can try the Twelve Hour Pharmacy, open from 09:00 to 21:30 every day, or Rozelle Health & Beauty Pharmacy, which is open late. If you're willing to drive you can try the All Night Chemist in west Sydney, but call before setting off if it's after midnight.

Mobile Telephones
Other options **Telephone** p.112

The major mobile phone service providers in Sydney are Telstra, Optus, 3, Virgin Mobile and Vodafone. All of these have shops where you can buy a phone, either by purchasing it outright, signing up to a monthly instalment plan for a year or more, or getting a phone with pre-paid credit. It's definitely worth shopping around and comparing call costs as well as the price of the phone as there are plenty of good deals to be found.

Mobile Telephones		
3	Various locations	13 3320
Allphones	Various locations	9268 0777
B Mobile	Various locations	9633 3513
Crazy John's	Various locations	13 2299
Mobile Select	Various locations	1300 134 131
Orange	Various locations	9283 9332
Telstra Shop	Various locations	12 5111
Vodafone	Various locations	1300 650 410

Most phones come with a one-year warranty, but if you have a phone under contract your service provider is obliged to repair it.

Mobile phone stores are found all over the city and in most malls. You can also order through websites run by most service providers.

Zone In

You'll need Region 4 DVDs for Australian DVD players. You can buy multi-region DVD players which play DVDs from any region and may be worth the extra money if you intend importing a DVD collection from overseas and buying new ones locally.

Music, DVDs & Videos

While some music and DVD shops have taken a bit of a beating thanks to internet downloads and iTunes, there are still shops catering for almost every taste. Sydney stores often have a good range of music, but don't have extras like live performances or in-store cafes.

Music, DVDs & Videos		
Dirt Cheap CDs	180 Campbell Pde	9365 5222
Fish Records	Various locations	9810 7345
Sanity	Pitt Street Mall	9221 2311
So Music	183 King St	9519 8622
Vintage Records	31a Parramatta Rd	9550 4667

New CDs and DVDs generally cost around $30, but an influx of cheap import stores mean many now retail for as little as $10.

Sanity (formerly HMV) in the city has one of the biggest ranges of music and DVDs. JB Hi-Fi (see Electronics and Home Appliances, p.282) has shops all over the city and has a massive range, including recent-releases for under $10. If you're looking for bargains, Dirt Cheap CDs sells all its CDs for the flat rate of $10. While it has many popular titles the range is somewhat limited.

For alternative music lovers, So Music has an excellent range of local music, blues, punk, rock and world music, as well as knowledgeable, music-loving staff. If you're into vinyl, head to Vintage Records. They sell a good range of new and second-hand records from $5 upwards.

Musical Instruments
Other options **Music Lessons** p.237, **Music, DVDs & Videos** p.291

The section of Parramatta Road that runs through Annandale is unlikely to inspire any album cover artworks, but this is the heart of the Sydney music scene. It's also where you'll find a good collection of instrument shops and congregating musos.

291

Music 101 sells new and used instruments and has a recording studio. Downtown Music sells mostly guitars and accessories as does Guitar World, and Jackson's Rare Guitars specialises in American guitars.

One you've bought what you need, if you feel the need for a little inspiration you could always grab a drink at the nearby Annandale Hotel, a hub for Sydney musicians. For more specialised instruments or classical music, try Allans Music in the city.

Musical Instruments		
Allans Music	228 Pitt St	9283 7711
Didj Beat Didjeridoos	14-15 Clock Tower	9251 4289
Downtown Music	141 Parramatta Rd	9569 2744
Guitar Crazy	183 Coogee Bay Rd	9665 8555
Guitar World	55 Parramatta Rd	9516 1650
Hutchings Pianos	5-7 Edgecliff Rd	9387 1376
Jacksons Rare Guitars	37- 39 Parramatta Rd	9565 5655
Music 101	101 Parramatta Rd	9519 2467
Sound Devices	265 Sussex St	9283 2077
The Music Place	500 Parramatta Rd	9550 0100

Outdoor Goods

Other options **Camping** p.223, **Hardware & DIY** p.285, **Sporting Goods** p.295

For the intrepid explorer, you can't get much better than Australia. The laidback lifestyle and great climate make getting out of the city ultra appealing and the natural beauty of it all makes it incredibly rewarding. Whether you're off bush camping or walking, trekking or fishing, you'll need to get kitted out properly before you go.

Your first stop should be Kent Street. Here you should be able to find everything you need, plus some extras you don't.

Mountain Equipment alone probably has everything you will need to get out there. From tents and hiking boots to baby carriers and hydration packs, if you've been to this place, there's really no excuse not to (www.mountainequipment.com) get outdoors.

Paddy Pallin is like an institution in Australia and as a result you'll find stores all over the country. There are two in the Sydney area, one in town and one in Parramatta. Here you'll also find outdoor gear and clothing. And even if you're only browsing, staff are happy just to chat about your next trip or share stories (www.paddypallin.com.au). If you're still not satisfied or are looking for something extra, Kathmandu is also in the area.

Further out, Kangaroo Tent City & BBQ in North Parramatta stocks all the gear, from furniture and patio heaters to the all-essential barbecue. For more information on sportswear, see Sporting Goods p.295.

Didgeridoos

If you want to learn to play the didgeridoo or 'didj', forget the straight painted pipes you find in souvenir shops. Authentic didgeridoos are produced in traditional communities and have an individual sound and an irregular shape. Aboriginal craftsmen carefully select part of a hardwood tree that has been hollowed out by termites, then cut and craft the instrument before finishing it with a rim of beeswax around the lip. Traditionally only played by men, mastering the didgeridoo (especially circular breathing) is tougher than it looks. Didj Beat Didjeridoo in The Rocks, (9251 4289, www.didjbeat.com) has a good range of authentic instruments and passionate staff who can give you playing tips.

Outdoor Goods		
Kangaroo Tent City & BBQ	596a Church St	9630 2888
Kathmandu	Town Hall	9261 8901
Mountain Equipment	491 Kent St	9267 3822
Paddy Pallin	507 Kent St	9264 2685

Party Accessories

Other options **Party Organisers** p.363

For a city so keen on celebrations, Sydney has relatively few specialist party shops, although party staples like balloons, party hats, and streamers are widely available at supermarkets. Chinatown also sells a colourful and dirt-cheap selection of lanterns, lights, firecrackers and colourful banners. See p.293 for more information.

Carnival &Toy Wholesaler sells a good range of party accessories, including items for kids' parties. Word of mouth is often the best way to find a party service to suit your needs, but you can also look online at www.sydney party.com.au. This huge directory covers everything from kids' parties and baby showers to security and corporate events.

Party Accessories		
Absolute Party Hire	38 Arden St	9664 1399
Balloon Saloon	327 Maroubra Rd	9344 9955
Born To Party	3 Spit Rd	9960 5666
Carnival & Toy Wholesaler	20 Bridge Rd	9660 7844
Partymoore	195b Burwood Rd	9745 2105
The Party Place	27 Babbage Rd	9417 0030

Perfumes & Cosmetics

Other options **Markets** p.306

Almost all major international brands of perfume and cosmetics are available in Sydney. The best place to start, especially if you are looking for specialty products, is Myer or David Jones (see p.304).

Most international brands are around 10-30% more expensive in Australia than you would find in Europe or the US. There are some good local brands worth a look – Napoleon Perdis (www.napoleoncosmetics.com.au), has a range of good bases, foundations, lipstick and eyeshadow. Model Co (www.modelco.com.au) is a fledgling Australian brand currently enjoying cult status around the world. The products are distinguishable by their hot pink packaging, and the self-tanner is particularly popular. Spas and beauty salons are

Perfumes & Cosmetics		
Lush	QVB	9283 5746
Mecca Cosmetica	56 Oxford St	9361 4488
Napoleon Perdis Cosmetics	Westfield Parramatta	9635 7761
The Perfume Connection	Sky Garden	9223 2227

found all over Sydney, including men-only spas. Some spas sell prestige brands of cosmetics, but usually only one particular brand, and at a premium price. See the Activities chapter, p.259 for more.

For budget shopping, Priceline has stores citywide (see www.priceline.com.au) with lower prices than most other retailers. Skincare, make-up and hair products are all available, including brands like L'Oreal, Garnier, Neutrogena, Dove and others.

At the other end of the scale, Mecca Cosmetica (www.meccacosmetica.com.au) has all the cult cosmetics and high-end international brands. They sell prestige make up, skin care, hair care, fragrances and men's cosmetics. For a more natural approach, Lush sells handmade products using largely natural ingredients and essential oils. The products are good quality and their luscious scents will leave you coming back for more. Lush specialises in moisturisers, soaps, massage oils and bath oils, priced from $2 to $30.

A Latte for Fido
Café Bones in Leichhardt (9402 9272, www.cafebones.com.au) is a wonderful dog-friendly cafe which serves coffee for owners and drinks for dogs. This is where animal lovers congregate for a chat after a long walk in the nearby park.

Pets

Other options **Pets** p.109

Sydney is a relatively pet-friendly city, although increasingly draconian pet laws in the inner city suburbs are making life harder for pet owners. Dogs, cats, fish, and birds are all widely available from pet shops; other animals like snakes and turtles are available from some specialty sellers but you may need a permit. Native Australian animals are protected and are generally not kept as pets. It's illegal to transport some native animals overseas without special permits, and strict penalties apply.

If you are considering getting a pet, you'll need to weigh up the breed and temperament of your animal carefully to fit in with your lifestyle and local council laws. Large or energetic animals won't enjoy living in a tiny apartment. Most councils ask that you have your dog or cat microchipped and registered.

293

Pets

Aqualand Aquarium	Westfield Parramatta	9893 7246
Aquatic Pet	Westfield Penrith	4721 5551
Burwood Pound	94 Coronation Pde	9747 3999
Central Pets & Aquarium	Cnr Evans & Rooty Hill Rd	9625 0982
Pet City	605-607 Botany Rd	9319 5006
Petbarn	124 Newbridge Rd	1300 655 896
Pets on Broadway	Broadway Shopping Centre	9280 1624
Sydney Dogs Home	77 Edward St	9587 9611

Thousands of animals are abandoned every year in Sydney, so if you get a pet, be prepared to commit to it.

Most pet shops maintain a reasonable standard of care and treat their animals humanely. Shops like Pets on Broadway have a good range of animals and fish. If you're not looking for a pure breed dog or cat you may be better off getting your pet from an animal shelter – this will not only save you money, but may save the life of a stray dog or cat. Try the Sydney Dogs Home (www.sydneydogshome.org) or the Burwood Pound. You can also ask your local veterinarian whether they have picked up any stray animals or know of any owners with puppies or kittens.

Portrait Photographers

Portrait Photographers

Bronwyn Challans	Glebe	9518 8448
Oneill Photographics	178 Military Rd	0413 514 825
Patrick Jones Photographic Studio	26 Rainford St	9331 2044
William Tell Photographers	493 Church St	9890 8188

Portrait photography is quite a big deal in Sydney. Snap-happy professionals tend to be rolled out for weddings, Christenings and all the other big family celebrations. Graduation is another event that commonly prompts people into getting a portrait done. Photographing newborns is becoming increasingly popular and Bronwyn Challans specialises in this (and capturing pregnant mums in full bloom) using only natural light. See her website, www.bchallansphotography.com.au, for more on her work.

Second-Hand Items

Other options **Books** p.273, **Cars** p.275

Hard Rubbish Day

Most Councils run a 'hard rubbish' day where residents can discard large household items, including furniture, on the roadside to be picked up and sent to a landfill. Second-hand furniture dealers often scour the streets on hard rubbish day (especially in up-market suburbs) to rescue quality items destined for the tip, and there's no reason why you can't either.

You can buy a lot of things cheaply second-hand in Sydney. However, used items have also been cannibalised by the popularity of 'vintage' pieces which means it's getting harder to find a bargain. Websites like eBay have some, as does the Trading Post (www.tradingpost.com.au), which sells larger items like furniture, sporting goods and outdoor equipment. Items bought through the Trading Post are almost always negotiable.

If you live in Bondi or Glebe you'll find you can pick up items of furniture, books and bric-a-brac for free on the roadside, all left behind by travellers. If you're not fussy it's worth keeping your eyes peeled: there are some real gems among the junk.

Second-hand furniture is available from shops like Peter Foley's Furniture or Brady's Used Furniture. If you're up for a treasure hunt you can also try Reverse Garbage, a non-profit collective selling all kinds of furniture and bric-a-brac that's been donated or discarded.

Second-Hand Items

Awesome Second Hand Furniture	265A George St	9601 6193
Blue Spinach Recycled Designer Clothing	348 Liverpool St	9331 3904
Brady's Used Furniture	500 Marrickville Rd	9560 1444
Peter Foley's Furniture	93-99 Bronte Rd	9389 9769
Reverse Garbage	142 Addison Rd	9569 3132
Rokit Gallery	80-84 George St	9247 1332
Route 66	255-257 Gouldburn St	9331 6686

Second-hand clothes are available from eBay, charity and second-hand shops. If you're after cheap clothes, forget trendy second-hand shops that tend to be pricier – instead head to shops like St Vincent de Paul (Vinnie's), The Salvation Army (the Salvos) or Wesley Mission. These shops also accept clothing donations, and all money raised goes towards charity projects.

Shoes

Other options **Beachwear** p.272, **Clothes** p.276, **Sporting Goods** p.295

From thongs to clogs to stilettos, there's a shoe for every foot and fetish in Sydney. Shoe shops are everywhere and most department stores also sell a good range. For sports shoes, try the Athlete's Foot. Shoe lovers after a mid-range bargain should start

Shoes		
Andrew McDonald	1/387 Oxford St	9358 6793
Aquila Shoes	Various locations	9232 3884
Athlete's Foot	Centrepoint	9221 2850
Bally	Westfield Bondi	9386 5580
Gary Castles Shoes	412-414 George St	9232 6544
Midas	QVB	9261 5815
Mollini	380a Oxford St	9331 1732
Platypus Shoes	47 The Corso	9977 1500
R.M. Williams	71 George St	9247 0204

looking in Pitt Street Mall, for a whole range of shoe shops as well as David Jones (p.304), which also sells brands like Jimmy Choo and Manolo Blahnik.
R.M. Williams (www.rmwilliams.com.au) is arguably Australia's most famous footwear designer and makes traditional leather boots and footwear for men and women. To newcomers, the shoes might not look gorgeous, but they are made with the best leather and are incredibly durable – one pair will last you years and years. In many country areas, a pair of R.M. Williams is a must-have fashion accessory.

Souvenirs

Other options **Gifts** p.285

Fluffy toy koalas, plastic boomerangs and brightly printed gum nut t-shirts are plentiful in Sydney. These types of kitsch souvenirs are called 'Australiana' by locals and are stocked in souvenir shops in areas like The Rocks, Bondi Beach and the airport. If you want something less tacky, items like framed photographs of Sydney Harbour and locally-made souvenirs are also available from The Rocks market, see p.308. Many souvenir shops contain Aboriginal artefacts that claim to be authentic, but this is disputable. Genuine Aboriginal arts and crafts are available from the Aboriginal & Tribal Art Centre.

Souvenirs		
Aboriginal & Tribal Art Centre	117 George St	9247 9625
Artwear By Lara S	77 George St	9247 3668
Ayers Rock Souvenirs	QVB	9283 7474
Gavala Aboriginal Art and Cultural Centre	Harbourside	9212 7232
Natural Selection Souvenirs	80-84 George St	9247 9174

Sporting Goods

Other options **Outdoor Goods** p.292

Australia prides itself on being a sporting nation, and Sydney's temperate climate and abundance of water, beaches and parks certainly makes it an ideal place to be outdoors.

Mini Marvels

Explorer *Mini Visitors' Guides* are the perfect holiday companion. They are small enough to fit in your pocket but beautiful enough to inspire you to explore. With detailed maps, visitors' information, restaurant, bar and shopping reviews, these mini marvels are simply a holiday must. Give the *Sydney Mini* to visiting friends and send them off to explore.

295

Sporting Goods

A1 Discount Fishing Tackle	407 Pitt St	9211 1926
All Referee, Umpire And Sports	40 Leighton Pl	9477 6666
Baker's Tennis Shop	155 Castlereagh St	9264 5288
Bicycles & Adventure Sports	722 George St	9281 6977
Canterbury International	Birkenhead Point	9719 9100
Golf Mart	32 York St	9299 3156
Inski	46 York St	9233 3200
Insport	Birkenhead Point	9719 9010
Kathmandu	Birkenhead Point	9181 5766
Larry Alder Ski & Outdoor	497 Kent Street	9264 2500
Mountain Designs	Birkenhead Point	9181 3922
Rebel Sports	Various locations	9211 5511
Speedo Outlet	Birkenhead Point	9181 2686
Sportspower	Winston Hills Mall	9624 1113
STM Snow & Surf	Cnr Bronte Rd and Birrell St	9387 4737
The Footy Shop	Harbourside Centre	9211 6861

Rebel Sport has a good range of sporting clothes and shoes as well as some equipment like footballs and tennis racquets.

If you're into sport, outdoor activities or camping, there's probably a specialty store somewhere in Sydney dedicated to your pursuit. For ski and snowboard equipment, visit Inski; for football equipment and memorabilia including Aussie Rules, rugby and soccer, head to The Footy Shop (www.footyshop.com.au). Tennis equipment is available from Baker's Tennis Shop. Golf Mart sells a good range of golfing equipment, accessories and fashion. For surfing and sailing equipment, try STM Snow & Surf. Fishermen can head to A1 Discount Fishing Tackle.

With the Royal National Park to the south, Blue Mountains in the West and Central Coast to the north, Sydney is at the heart of some excellent camping terrain. A group of camping and outdoor shops are concentrated in Kent and York Streets in the city just behind the QVB, most notably Larry Alder Ski & Outdoor. See Outdoor Goods, p.292.

Stationery

Stationery can be found at most newsagents, supermarkets and office supply shops. Generic stationery supplies are widely available but custom and more stylish supplies are harder to find. Officeworks stores (www.officeworks.com.au) are found all over the city and have a huge range of stationery, computers, office accessories and furniture at really cheap prices.

Just Office Stationery can custom-make office stationery and letterheads at reasonable prices. The Paperplace can provide more upmarket materials, as well as wedding stationery. Wills Quills can custom-make cards for all occasions.

Stationery

Express Office National	179a Military Rd	9909 1088
Just Office Stationery	32 York St	0416 083 995
Officewise	224 Headland Rd	9905 5931
Officeworks	Various locations	1300 721 591
Pennant Hills Printing & Stationery	3 Hillcrest Rd	9875 2466
Surry Office National	55 Denison St	1300 132 299
The Paperplace	11 Elizabeth St	9233 2979
Wills Quills	1/166 Victoria Ave	9411 2500

Tailoring
Other options **Clothes** p.271, **Textiles** p.297

Unless you are getting something very special made, tailoring clothes in Sydney is not a common practice because it's relatively expensive.

It's much cheaper to get your clothes tailored in nearby Asia if you have the opportunity to stop off there. Once they have your measurements, some Asian tailors will take phone orders and ship clothes to Sydney. Make sure you are buying from a trusted source however, or it might be money for nothing.

If you want to get something made in Sydney, get a quote first and ask if the price includes the cost of the material. Prices can vary greatly so it's worth shopping around. For fabric and dressmaking materials, try Spotlight at Birkenhead Point Shopping Centre, with shops also in Bondi Junction, Rockdale, Dee Why, Liverpool and Castle Hill selling a massive range of fabrics, homeware, wool, dress patterns and craft materials at very reasonable prices. Men can try Zink G.A. & Sons, while ladies looking to have a dress made can try Gloria Amparo. For alterations, try LookSmart in the Dymocks Building. Word of mouth is also a great way to find a tailor, so ask around for suggestions.

Tailoring		
Casa Adamo Finest Tailored Menswear	39 Norton St	9569 6419
F.F. Fashions	63 Great North Rd	9713 2088
Gina Thom Couture	30 Fisher Rd	9981 7041
Gloria Amparo Dressmaker	3/8 Boronia St	9906 7241
LookSmart	428 George St	9223 0111
Maloney Vince & Co	177 Elizabeth St	9264 8837
Spotlight	Various locations	9719 8353
Zink G.A. & Sons	56 Oxford St	9331 3675

Textiles

Other options **Tailoring** p.296, **Souvenirs** p.295

The areas around Market Street and Clarence Street are good for textiles, with shops such as Atelier Textiles. Saigon Fabrics is an upmarket shop that specialises in silks and laces. They cater for weddings and formal

Textiles		
Atelier Textiles	142 Clarence St	9299 5753
Hedrena Textiles	86-100 Market St	9223 2772
Saigon Fabrics	78 Erskine St	9299 0778
Tessuti	Pitt Street Mall	9262 1663

occasions. Set up by two sisters, they know their fabrics and will happily direct you to dressmakers and designers up to the job of creating your dream dress. Tessuti has several stores dotted around Sydney and does lovely fabrics, preferring natural fibres like silks, linens and wools. They import much of their stock from Europe. If you're willing to head out of town, Cabramatta has a good many stores that are less tough on the wallet. For more on tailoring, see p.297.

Toys, Games & Gifts

If you're looking for the latest must-have toy, most department stores and malls stock international brands like Disney, Barbie et al, if you're willing to brave the crowds. But Sydney is also home to a delightfully eclectic range of toyshops that stock more unconventional toys that are definitely worth a look. Two such shops are The Tin Soldier and Terrific Scientific. The Tin Solider has a whole range of traditional games like specialised chess sets, fantasy games, role playing games, figurines, as well as paints, dice and other accessories. And for the serious aficionado, the shop also has a good range of gaming and historical books. Terrific Scientific is a treasure trove of toys, games, and unusual gadgets for curious young minds. There's not a Disney toy in sight –

Toys, Games & Gifts		
Gallery In Toto	595 Darling St	9810 7500
Games Paradise	343-357 Pitt St	9267 2069
Hopscotch	701 Military Rd	9960 5733
Kidazzle	69 Lyons Rd	9719 9904
Lighten Up On Darling	440 Darling St	9555 9205
Monkey Puzzle Toy Store	13 Lackey St	9799 7101
Queen Victoria Card Shop	QVB	9261 2650
Tatti	33 Cross St	9362 4362
Terrific Scientific	51 Booth St	9692 9206
The Tin Soldier	46 York St	9279 2668

instead you'll find kaleidoscopes, ant farms, glow-in-the-dark rubber spiders, chemistry sets and a whole range of fascinating toys and gadgets. Frazzled parents will enjoy shopping in the relaxed, homely atmosphere that just can't be found in any department toy store, and if all gets too much you can always head next door for a coffee at the Gallery Café.

For card shops, try the Queen Victoria Card Shop at the QVB. Computer games are widely available. Shops like Games Paradise have the full range of the latest titles for computer, Nintendo, Xbox and PlayStation.

Wedding Items

Whether you're going traditional, simple or over-the-top, Sydney has shops that cater to all kinds of matrimonial plans.

Brides will do well to start their search for dresses in Leichhardt, which has a whole range of off-the-peg and designer bridal shops like Diane Lewis Bridal and Evermore

Wedding Items		
All The Rage Formal Wear	267 Parramatta Rd	9564 1442
Bee Ladies Wear	101 Castlereagh St	9232 1593
Brides of Piccadilly	210 Pitt St	9264 6562
Deseo Bridal & Evening Shoes	289 Parramatta Rd	9550 9246
Diane Lewis Bridal	150 Norton St	9550 9005
Evermore Bridal Boutique	265 Parramatta Rd	9572 6801
Farina Fashions Bridal Salon	428 George St	9222 2933
Millani Bridal Boutique	393 George St	9262 4090
Saigon Fabrics	78 Erskine St	9299 0778
Twinkle Diamonds	250 Pitt St	9261 5005
White Room Bridal	428 George St	9221 0962

Bridal Boutique. This area also has an abundance of formal shops like All The Rage Formal Wear, which can cater to bridesmaids. Deseo Bridal & Evening Shoes will also take care of footwear for the big day.

For designer gowns, try White Room Bridal, (www.whiteroombridal.com.au), which sells custom made designs as well as gowns from Pierre Cardin and Radiosa priced between $1,500-$4,000.

Department stores like Myer and David Jones run popular wedding gift registry services that can also be accessed over the internet. For stationery, try The Paperplace or Wills Quills; they can custom-make cards for all occasions. See Stationery on p.296. To help plan your wedding, a good start is www.easyweddings.com.au, which is a directory of wedding expos, dress shops and planning services.

Is getting lost your usual excuse?

Whether you're a map person or not, this pocket-sized marvel will help you get to know the city like the back of your hand… so you won't feel the back of someone else's.

Singapore Mini Map
Putting the city in your pocket

Places to Shop

The following section includes Sydney's main shopping malls, supermarkets, outdoor food and flower markets, as well as its quirkier suburban independent street boutiques. Welcome to the Sydney shopping Mecca.

Shopping Malls

Walking through any of Sydney's shopping malls may give you a strong sense of deja vu. Australia has more franchises than almost anywhere else in the world, which means that many malls house an identical collection of chain stores rather than independent shops.

Unless you have a particular affection for malls, there are few Sydney plazas that offer a really pleasant shopping experience. Most are clean and well maintained but lack atmosphere and unique flair, and can get crowded on holidays and at weekends.

The exceptions are parts of Pitt Street Mall, the Queen Victoria Building and the Italian Forum in Leichhardt, which offer a wider range of shops and a bit more individual charm.

Most malls have free parking, except in the city. Some of the larger urban malls like Bondi Junction and Broadway will give you two hours parking for free, and charge up to $10 per hour after that.

If you're shopping at Pitt Street Mall or anywhere in the city, leave your car at home – catch the bus or train and avoid the sluggish traffic, expensive parking and potential tickets.

In any mall throughout the city – small or large – you are almost guaranteed to find a supermarket, a bakery, a bank, a bottle shop, a few clothes shops, a homeware shop and at least one food outlet. Most of the larger malls have all of the above plus a food court, cinema, a department store like Kmart or Target, and more.

Shopping Malls		
Argyle Stores	The Rocks	9251 4800
Birkenhead Point	Drummoyne	9181 3922
Broadway Shopping Centre	Glebe	9213 3333
Centrepoint Shopping Centre	Pitt Street Mall	9229 7444
Chatswood Chase	Outer West	9411 6376
David Jones	Various locations	9266 5544
DFO	Outer West	9748 9800
Galeries Victoria	Central	9265 6812
Glasshouse	Pitt Street Mall	9223 8533
Greenwood Plaza	North Sydney	9923 0700
Harbourside	Darling Harbour	9281 3999
Imperial Arcade	Pitt Street Mall	9233 5662
Mid City Centre	Pitt Street Mall	9221 2422
MLC Centre	Central	9224 8333
Myer	Various locations	9238 9111
No.1 Martin Place	Central	9221 5073
Northbridge Plaza	North Sydney	9958 2648
Piccadilly	Central	9267 0722
Pitt Street Mall	Central	9286 0111
Queen Victoria Building	Central	9264 9209
Skygarden Centre	Pitt Street Mall	9231 1811
Stockland Shopping Centre	Various locations	9321 1500
Strand Arcade	Pitt Street Mall	9232 4199
Westfield Shopping Centre	Various locations	9231 9300
Winston Hills Mall	Outer West	9838 7822

300

Shopping Malls – Main

Roseby St

Birkenhead Point
9181 3922 | *www.birkenheadpoint.com.au*
It's almost a shame to build a shopping mall right on the edge of Sydney Harbour, but luckily Birkenhead Point, across the water from Balmain, makes the most of the view. It's a glittering location for an outlet mall, where major retailers offer discounted stock that is out-of-season or simply didn't sell. Australian designers Morrissey, Marcs, Alannah Hill and David Lawrence all have outlet stores here, as do fashion stores Cue, Witchery, French Connection, Jag, Mambo, Atelier and many more. Shops sell genuinely discounted items and you can pick up some real bargains. There's also a Spotlight store selling a huge range of textiles, art and craft materials; as well as shops that sell homeware, surfwear, lingerie and music. For locals there's a supermarket, grocer and chemist on the ground floor. When you get tired of shopping, try Clippers Cafe - it's a classic-style cafe that beats sitting in the noisy food court.

Opp Victoria Park
Central

Broadway Shopping Centre
9213 3333 | *www.broadway-centre.com.au*
Broadway Shopping Centre is a relatively new mall recognisable by its two soaring clock towers. The atmosphere among the three levels is light and bright, although the shops are mostly franchises you've probably seen elsewhere. Many inner-westies do their grocery shopping here thanks to two supermarkets, a grocer, a bakery, a bottle shop and two butchers which are usually open til 19:00. There's also a range of clothes shops, a large Collins bookstore (good for settling in at the internal cafe on really hot days), a food court, cinema, and a medical centre. Kmart is also here, open until late most nights.

345 Victoria
Ave
Chatswood

Chatswood Chase Shopping Centre
9419 6255 | *www.chatswoodchaseshopping.com.au*
If you live on the north side of the harbour, Chatswood Chase is the mall most convenient to you. It has over 130 shops including David Jones and Kmart. Like most malls the focus is on fashion, with a mix of designer and high street shops, as well as a food court, supermarket and some delis. You can drive here or catch the train, which stops nearby at the Chatswood interchange.

Pitt Street Mall

Pitt Street Mall

9286 0111 | *www.shopping-sydney.com.au*

Pitt Street Mall is an open walkway through one of Sydney's busiest shopping precincts in the CBD. The area includes department stores Myer and David Jones, plus other malls walled together including Mid-City Centre, Centrepoint Arcade (at the base of the enormous Centrepoint Tower), Skygarden, Glasshouse, and The Strand Arcade. Basically, Pitt Street Mall is the central catwalk through a labyrinth of mini malls which all interlink. It can be very easy to get lost. If you take the escalator underground from Myer and walk any distance you might find yourself coming up through the Queen Victoria Building on the other side of George Street. Thankfully there are plenty of maps to help you orientate yourself. There is a huge range of shops but the focus is on personal items like clothes, shoes, accessories, beauty products, books, CDs and DVDs. If you love to browse and compare prices, or simply like to have lots of choices, Pitt Street Mall is a great place to start a long day of shopping.

Queen Victoria Building

9264 9209 | *www.qvb.com.au*

With its lofty ceilings, ornate hand railings and patterned floors, the Queen Victoria Building (QVB) is an elegant shopping experience. The shops inside reflect the surroundings with sophisticated decor and higher prices. Brands like Calvin Klein and Polo Ralph Lauren mix with high street fashion and a good selection of arts and antiques shops. The QVB extends underground and you can walk through to Myer, Pitt Street Mall and Town Hall Station – but keep your wits about you because it's very easy to get lost. If you need any information, the concierge staff are very helpful (found on the ground floor and level two). They also run free daily tours, which take you through the design and history of the building. For a little side excursion, visit Queen Victoria's talking dog, found just behind the statue of Queen Victoria out front. Occasionally he pipes up with a little monologue that begins, 'Hello, my name is Islay…'.

Supa Centa

www.supacenta.com

Yes, the spelling is bad, but the Supa Centa, is a great one-stop location to buy furniture and homewares. There are a huge range of furniture shops including IKEA, Oz Design, Harvey Norman, Freedom Furniture, Fantastic Furniture and many more, including several bedding specialists and manchester (linen) shops. Bing Lee sells a wide range of white goods, furniture and electronics and will beat any price offered by other retailers. Be wary though, the staff can be a little pushy. The mall itself is fairly basic and while it has a few food outlets, there is no food court.

Westfield Bondi Junction

9947 8000 | *www.westfield.com*

This is like a luminous maze with over 3,000 shops interwoven over two large buildings. It's huge, dazzling and a little overwhelming. Take note of exactly where you've parked and exactly how you got there, because it's very easy to lose your car. Westfield Bondi is different to the other malls around Sydney because of its scale, but also because of more upmarket stores like Alannah Hill, Saba, Oroton and Morrissey. There are the usual high street fashion stores, as well as phone shops, furniture stores, electronics and games shops, food shops and supermarkets, a food court and cinema. Bondi Junction is the adjacent suburb to Bondi (it's a long and smoggy walk to the beach), and once you're outside Westfield, it's a pretty drab place to hang out. There's an open mall with a few discount shops where you might be able to snap up a bargain, but it certainly won't win any awards for design.

Small but indispensable…

Perfectly proportioned to fit in your pocket, these marvellous mini guidebooks make sure you don't just get the holiday you paid for, but rather the one that you dreamed of.

Explorer Mini Visitors' Guides
Maximising your holiday, minimising your hand luggage

Abu Dhabi • Amsterdam • Bahrain • Barcelona • Dubai • Dublin • Geneva • Hong Kong • Kuwait

EXPLORER

Shopping Malls – Other

Cnr Homebush Bay
& Underwood Rd
Outer West

DFO
9748 9800 | *www.dfo.com.au*
DFO, or the Direct Factory Outlet, houses a range of shops that sell excess stock and samples from fashion designers. The DFO outlet in Homebush is about 20 minutes drive west of the city. Stores include Lisa Ho, FCUK, Jag, Morrissey, Charlie Brown, Witchery, Tommy Hilfiger and many more. You can pick up plenty of bargains, but DFO is a somewhat drab mall with few other facilities. Still, it's a small price to pay for picking up a designer gown at 75% off the retail price.

Norton St
Leichhardt

The Italian Forum
9518 0077 | *www.italianforum.com.au*
Norton Street has long been billed as Sydney's little Italy, and the Italian Forum cemented this reputation. Designed to mimic an Italian plaza, with apartments overlooking a central restaurant precinct and network of shops, the Forum somehow managed to avoid being tacky and actually fulfils its brief. The feel is luxurious, relaxed, and very Italian. The central piazza is filled with restaurants, and live music and festivals are occasionally held here. There are designer clothing shops as well as an interesting shop called The Merchant of Venice, which stocks a dazzling selection of handmade masquerade masks, wall hangings and other beautiful oddities.

Cnr Marion &
Flood Sts
Leichhardt

Leichhardt Marketplace
9560 4488 | *www.marketplaceleichhardt.com.au*
Leichhardt Marketplace is less like a marketplace and more like a rabbit warren – it's not very big and the paths seem to branch off either downwards or upwards in every direction. While it's not a pretty place to shop, there are some worthwhile retailers here like coffee merchants Caffe Bianchi, Marketplace Continental Deli, and, if you're a resident, one of the few Medicare outlets near the city. It also has supermarkets, a food court, and a Target store.

86 -108
Castlereagh St
Central

Westfield Parramatta
9891 3929 | *www.westfield.com*
It once billed itself as the largest mall in the southern hemisphere, but apparently Westfield Parramatta no longer holds the title. It's still enormous though, with five levels of shops. These are mostly chain stores selling items at mid-level prices. Despite its size, the mall is easy to negotiate with an open-style layout that allows you to see the other levels so you've got a better idea of where you are. Parramatta is about 40 minutes west of the city and it's only really worthwhile shopping here if you live nearby or there's a specific shop you want to visit.

Department Stores

Unfortunately, most of Sydney's iconic department stores have been swallowed or closed down thanks to heavy competition from multinationals. There are a couple of Aussie survivors, but most of the department stores you will encounter in Sydney are international lower-priced chain stores like Target and Kmart. There are two major exceptions: Myer and David Jones.

Various locations

David Jones
9266 5544 | *www.davidjones.com.au*
Once considered the shopping domain of snobbish grandmothers, David Jones has repositioned itself in the last five years towards a much younger demographic.

David Jones is slightly more upmarket than Myer and sells a wider choice of designer brands. You can buy a huge range of items including cosmetics and perfumes, hats and accessories, women's, men's and kids' fashions, homeware and furniture. David Jones in the city also has one of Sydney's best delicatessens. The impressive and massive Food Hall stocks all kinds of premium and obscure foods and beverages, including some fresh produce and bakery items.

Various locations

Myer

9238 9111 | *www.myer.com.au*

Myer is Australia's most established department store, and has pride of place in the central shopping district of most big Australian cities, including Sydney. The first store was opened in Melbourne in 1900 by a poor Russian migrant named Sidney Myer and has been thriving ever since. The current store used to be called Gras Bros, but was bought out and renamed Myer a few years ago. The city Myer store has several floors, selling everything from cosmetics, shoes, fashion, accessories, homeware, furniture,

books, music, DVDs, toys and games. Myer is especially renowned for its extensive cosmetics and perfume selection, and is also a good place to shop if you are looking for an outfit for the races – they have a great range of hats. Most products are brand names, so you'll be paying more but getting good quality. The store also sells prestige brands like Manolo Blahnik shoes or Estee Lauder cosmetics. Myer has two annual sales, one starting the day after Christmas and the other in mid-winter, although smaller sales occur throughout the year.

Anzac Pde
Kensignton

Peter's of Kensington

9662 1433 | *www.petersofkensington.com.au*

Peter's of Kensington, about 5kms south of the city, is a Sydney institution. It sells everything you could possibly want for your home – towels, linen, kitchenware, knives, lamps, ornaments, glassware, cutlery and cookware. From hammocks to clothes hangers, Peter's will have them every colour, shape and style. Peter's is a beautifully designed store, and it's a pleasure to wander through the aisles of glittering and lustrous new products. There are regular sales with genuine discounts and you can often save up to 50% off the marked price. There's also an internal cafe with a good selection of food available.

305

Hypermarkets

Supermarkets are plentiful all over Sydney. The two main ones are Coles (www.coles.com.au) and Woolworths (Woolies, see www.woolworths.com.au), which sell most food items as well as fresh fruit and vegetables, fresh herbs, meat (including some organic), stationery, cleaning products, pet foods, some garden products and a small range of homeware and manchester (bedding). The fruit, vegetables and meat are good quality but are not as nice as you would find in a butcher, grocer or market. These supermarkets also have internal delicatessens, and are usually open seven days a week until late. Alcohol is not available in Australian supermarkets, but some stores have an adjacent bottle shop. The Coles stores located in the city, Newtown and Kings Cross are generally more expensive than suburban Coles stores.

Parking
Bigger suburban supermarkets tend to have large car parks attached, with spaces reserved near the door for the disabled and for parents with buggies. City centre stores do not, which can make doing a big shop a pain. Woolworths and Coles both offer home delivery through their website.

If you spend over $30 at Coles or Woolworths, your receipt will contain a barcode that gets you a 4 cents discount in petrol from specially marked service stations (see your local supermarket for details). Be warned though: a 4 cents discount in petrol will typically only save you around $2 on a tank, so it's not worth spending $30 just to get the discount.

Other supermarkets include IGA, which are independently owned supermarkets that have banded together under the IGA brand in the name of survival. These stores usually have a good range of products, although more limited than larger chain stores and sometimes more expensive.

Franklins and Bi-Lo are both no-frills supermarkets that sell lots of products, but in a limited selection of brands. Most do not sell fresh fruit and vegetables or meat. If you shop carefully you can save money compared to shopping at Coles or Woolworths, but the quality of some products may be lower.

ALDI is a recent German import to Australia, and is the cheapest of all supermarkets. The range is eclectic and the brands are mostly no-name imports. For example, you might find a stack of tinned tomatoes selling for 40 cents a can one week, and discount cat food the next. You might be frustrated trying to find specific items at ALDI, but it can be a good place to save money by buying in bulk. Remember to bring your own bags; otherwise you'll pay 15 cents per bag at the checkout.

Markets

Sydney has an excellent range of markets, mostly held at weekends. If you're looking for a unique gift, a cut-price designer outfit, locally made art or fruit and vegetables straight from the farm, head to your local market and you'll be sure to pick up a bargain.

Many markets have live music and food stalls, and are also a great place to just wander, talk to the stall owners and gently while away a weekend afternoon. The majority of markets are free.

Besides the markets listed here, there are also markets at The Rocks (North George Street), held on Saturdays and Sundays, which sell a range of locally made gift items like homeware, jewellery and accessories. The Rozelle markets (Rozelle Public School, Darling Street) held every Saturday is more of a 'trash and treasure' style market – while there are a few more professional stalls, many are simply locals selling bric-a-brac.

Bondi Primary School
Bondi

Bondi Markets

The Bondi markets epitomise Bondi in some ways: a bit crowded and full of young designers alongside old locals selling bric-a-brac. The markets sell clothes (new, local designer, vintage and second-hand), bags, sunglasses, jewellery, books, homeware and all kinds of eclectic items fashioned by carpenters, sculptors and photographers. International celebrities often zip through on whistle-stop tours of Australia, and plenty of local identities and wannabes also haunt the crowded pathways. Sundays, 10:00-16:00.

Glebe Primary School ◀ *The Glebe Markets*
Glebe

You can usually hear the Glebe Markets before you see them, thanks to the live local music that plays there every weekend. The Glebe Markets is one of Sydney's best for fun and atmosphere. If you don't want to buy anything it's nice to simply browse past the stalls selling jewellery, second-hand books, photo frames, handmade clothes and bags, sunglasses, vintage items and unusual gifts (wind chimes made from forks, anyone?). If you need a break there are also food stalls that sell freshly made Turkish, Indian and Mexican fare, and plenty of grassy spots to sit and watch the band. It does get busy, especially around midday. Parking is also a problem in the surrounding streets, and parking officers are vigilant – you're better off taking advantage of the three hours of free parking available at nearby Broadway Shopping Centre. Saturdays, 10:00-16:00.

Fox Studios ◀ *Farmers' Market*
Redfern

If you want your food fresh from the farm, follow many of Sydney's leading chefs and get down to the Fox Studios Farmers' market. Farmers come here from all over NSW, even as far away as Bega (six hours drive south of Sydney). If you're not tempted by the colourful array of fresh fruit and vegetables, you can always buy some free-range eggs, jams and jellies or homemade sausages. Prices are much cheaper than supermarkets, but vary because of seasonal changes. Wednesdays and Saturdays, 11:00-16:00.

Orange Grove ◀ *Organic Food Market*
Public School
Leichhardt

If you're into organic produce you can buy it fresh every Saturday from the Orange Grove markets. There's the usual range of fruit and veg, as well as meat, eggs, cheeses, tea, coffee, bread and a whole range of gourmet organic food. Orange Grove is tucked away at the far end of Leichhardt, near Darling Street in Rozelle. Saturdays, 08:00-13:00.

395 Oxford St ◀ *Paddington Markets*
Paddington

Fashion designers Collette Dinnigan and Nicole Zimmerman both started out selling their designs at the Paddington markets, and it's still a great place to check out budding Australian designers and pick up bargain designer clothing. Young designers often start out here to raise their profile and to see what customers like first hand. You can also get jewellery, hats, scarves, furniture, homeware and arts and crafts. Prices are probably a little more expensive than other markets. Saturdays, from 10:00-16:00.

Haymarket ◀ *Paddy's Market*
Central

Paddy's Market is an indoor market. Unlike other markets, many stallholders sell factory-produced goods imported from overseas rather than locally made items. There's a fresh fruit and vegetable market, as well as stalls that sell clothes, sunglasses, CDs, jewellery and souvenirs. The atmosphere is not as pleasant as other markets – it can feel dingy inside and is sometimes crowded, but you can save money by shopping here over the retail shops. Daily, 09:30-19:00.

Pyrmont Bridge Rd ◀ *Sydney Fish Markets*
Pyrmont

If you want to buy Sydney's freshest seafood, head to the Sydney Fish Markets. This is where Sydney's best chefs source their fish. You can buy prawns, snapper, rock oysters, Balmain bugs, and just about every other creature that swims in the sea. Get there early for the best and freshest deals, especially for prawns – by the end of the day the flavour can start to wane. Daily, 07:00-19:00.

307

Off Parramatta Rd ◀ *Sydney Flower Markets*
Outer West

The Sydney Flower Markets are where most florists source their flowers, but it's also open to the general public. You can get a beautiful array of fresh flowers direct from the growers, which is much cheaper than buying from a florist. If you arrive before 09:30 there's an entry fee of $8, after that it's free. Flemington is about 20 or 30 minutes' drive west of the city. Monday to Saturday, 05:00-11:00.

Open Air Markets			
Balmain Markets	Cnr Darling & Curtis Rd	Sat	08:30-16:00
Bondi Markets	Campbell Pde	Sun	10:00-16:00
Glebe Markets	Glebe Primary School	Sat	10:00-16:00
Paddy's Markets	Cnr Hay & Thomas St	Thu-Sun	10:00-18:00 on Thu 09:00-16:00 Fri, Sat, Sun
Sydney Fish Markets	Cnr Pyrmont Bridge Rd & Bank St	Mon-Sun	07:00-16:00
The Rocks Markets	North from Circular Quay railway station along George St	Sat, Sun	10:00-17:00

Streets/Areas to Shop

Sydney has been described as being a tribal city where every suburb walks to the beat of a different drum. It's certainly true that Sydney's best shopping strips cater to a wide range of tastes – from designer to bohemian and kitsch and touristy, there's a shopping experience for everyone.

Glebe Point Road, Glebe

Perhaps its proximity to Sydney University has meant Glebe Point Road is less about fashion and more about intellectual pursuits. There are bookshops galore, including Gleebooks, Sappho, Gleebooks Second-hand and the large Collins bookstore in nearby Broadway Shopping Centre, all open late most nights. It's also a good spot for music, with De Capo, which sells sheet music, Fish Records selling CDs, and X for second-hand CDs and records. It gets pretty busy on Saturdays thanks to the Glebe markets, but for the rest of the week there's quite a relaxed atmosphere.

Hall Street & Beyond, Bondi

While it's best known for the beach, Bondi's shopping credentials are rapidly on the rise. Bondi is a newcomer to the serious shopping trade – only recently have a number of shops opened that cater to the discerning and increasingly wealthy locals in this once working-class suburb. Shops like One Teaspoon and Tuchuzy will please those looking for designer fashion, and anyone looking for bathers will like Mambo, Rip Curl and Bikini Island. There's also the bookshop Gertrude and Alice, as well as several high street fashion shops and homeware shops.

King Street, Newtown

Walking down King Street in Newtown has a cosmopolitan, bohemian feel, although the shops are becoming increasingly trendy. It's a long road and you can buy anything from new and second-hand books, furniture, boutique fashion, shoes, homeware and much more. If you're looking for clothes, shops like Dangerfield, Quick Brown Fox and Elvis 4 Cleo sell a good range of boutique designs. You can also get books at Gould's, the Cornstalk Bookshop or Better Read Than Dead. If you're looking for something a little more unusual, Eastern Flair sells a whole range of imported Asian items like furniture, cushions, jewellery and home accessories. There are also a few locals selling poems and artworks by the side of the road. King Street has a relaxed, whatever-may-come kind of attitude, and it's also pleasant just to wander down the road with the sound of buskers playing in your wake.

Norton Street, Leichhardt

Norton Street was once a quiet suburban shopping strip until Norton Street Plaza and The Italian Forum opened up in 2000, and a host of other shops followed suit. There are designer fashion boutiques and shops selling Italian shoes. You can spend hours at Berkelouw bookshop browsing the new books downstairs or the second hand books and CDs upstairs. The Italian Forum also has a number of designer shops and eclectic merchants.

Oxford Street, Darlinghurst

Oxford Street was once the jewel in Sydney's shopping crown, but there's been a lot of hand-wringing about the state of the precinct recently – critics say business is on the wane. But the street running straight through Darlinghurst ('Darling-it-hurts' or just plain 'Darlo' to locals) still has plenty to offer. The focus is on upmarket fashion like Sass and Bide, as well as boutiques, vintage stores and art galleries among the trendy cafes and bars. Oxford Street is also the main street for the Gay and Lesbian Mardi Gras and while many have moved on, there is still a palpable gay and lesbian presence here.

The Rocks

In the shadow of the Harbour Bridge and next to Circular Quay, the shop facades in The Rocks are in the original terrace-style, dating back to the first white settlers. The same place where you can now buy a designer handbag may once have been the site of some convict conflict or a house wracked by the plague 200 years ago. While it caters well to tourists, you won't find many tacky souvenir shops (although there are a couple) – most shops here are at the designer end of the market. You can buy Aboriginal art, photographic prints of Sydney and clothing and accessories with prints from Australian artist Ken Done. If you're not after souvenirs there are designer shops like Louis Vuitton, bookshops, and the art shop at the nearby Museum of Contemporary Art in Circular Quay. It sells a curious range of arty products. There are markets at weekends.

More than 15 Million hits per month
Over 170 User Nationalities
123 Countries Covered

CONNECTING EXPATS WORLDWIDE

@llo' Expat

www.alloexpat.com
www.australia.alloexpat.com

Your Online Journey Begins With Us
Country Guide • Classifieds • Forums • Real Estate

Going Out

Going Out

Locals lead a hedonistic lifestyle. They love to eat, drink and socialise. In Sydney, there's something on every night of the week, whether it's the theatre, comedy or just having a laugh over a few schooners.

Sydney has two kinds of watering holes; down-to-earth pubs and swanky bars. The pubs are relaxed and convivial; the bars are showy and stylish.

Friday sees the suits knocking back Stellas in the CBD while Saturday night is when the clubbing and cocktail crowd comes out to play. On the weekend, a night out starts at around 20:00 and if you're up for a big one, you can stumble on until dawn.

The city's nightlife options range from the operatic to the utterly camp, and its restaurant scene is the best in Australia, if not the whole of Asia Pacific. We've tried to offer a taster of it all; giving you reviews of the bars, clubs and restaurants that we think should not be missed.

If you've just arrived and fancy a sharpener in an iconic setting, head to the Opera Bar, next to the Opera House. The crowd is unpretentious and the view is spectacular. If you don't mind the tourists (you are, after all, a resident now) grab a bottle of Aussie wine, watch the sun go down and congratulate yourself on your new life.

Eating Out

Sydneysiders take eating out very seriously. Accordingly, Sydney has an eclectic, buzzing cafe scene and there's always somewhere new opening. You're really spoilt for choice and the best part is; it's cheap (at least in comparison to Europe or the US). The most popular cafes are full at weekends and you'll often find you have to queue to get a table. People watching, latte in hand, is something of a local pastime.

Food wise, you can't beat Leichhardt or Haberfield for authentic Italian cuisine. For Thai or Lebanese, try Surry Hills and for Japanese, Neutral Bay is a good bet. For more detail, our restaurant reviews begin on p.315. For weekly updates, check out *The Sydney Morning Herald* (www.smh.com.au).

A meal at Sydney's most exclusive restaurant won't cost you more than $300 a head, and you can always eat for as little as $10 at your local Indian. Fast food spots and local cafes are popular with families but restaurants don't generally cater for children. Buffets are usually an exception, but are less popular since the rise of trendy, innovative restaurants.

Delivery

Sydney is a city where you can have any cuisine in the world delivered to your front door. There's no shortage of choice and you'll probably find your mailbox is permanently jammed with menus from local outlets. Indian, Thai, Chinese, Italian; take your pick. Also, if you order over a certain amount, delivery is often free. It's quick, easy and usually tasty too.

Local Tucker

'Mod Oz' is a fusion of Asian and European food. Australian chefs are very innovative, and mod Oz has become a recognised cuisine in its own right. Sydney benefits from its proximity to fresh Asian produce, along with high quality local meat, dairy and seafood. But of course, you can't go wrong with a meat pie from Harry's (see p.348) or a barbecue in your own back yard.

Cuisine List – Quick Reference					
African	315	French	324	Middle Eastern	338
Arabic / Lebanese	315	Greek	326	Pizzerias	339
Australian	316	Indian	328	Seafood	339
British	319	Italian	329	South American	341
Brunch	319	Japanese	331	Spanish/Portugese	342
Chinese	320	Korean	332	Steakhouses	343
Contemporary	321	Malaysian	333	Thai	343
Deli	323	Mediterranean	335	Vegetarian	345
Dinner Cruises	324	Mexican	337	Vietnamese	346

Top Picks – Quick Reference

Al Fresco		Cheap Eats		Hip Hangout		Cultural Experience	
Arabella	p.315	African Feeling	p.315	Bathers' Pavilion	p.347	Arabella	p.315
Baja Cantina	p.337	Bay Tinh	p.346	Billy Kwong	p.320	Arun Thai	p.343
Bel Parco	p.329	Brass Monkey	p.335	Brass Monkey	p.335	Bay Tinh	p.346
Doyles	p.340	Corinthian Rotisserie	p.326	Dragonfly	p.358	Café Gloria	p.342
Icebergs	p.335	Harry's Café de Wheels	p.348	glass brasserie	p.325	Casapueblo	p.341
La Cumbia	p.342	Ice Cube Grill	p.340	Hugo's Bar Pizza	p.339	Guillaume	p.325
Manly Phoenix	p.321	Koreana	p.333	Kirketon	p.322	Last Train to Bombay	p.328
Out of Africa	p.315	Laroche	p.316	Lotus Bar and Bistro	p.318	Longrain	p.322
Swell Restaurant	p.318	Malay Chinese	p.334	Ruby Rabbit	p.359	Mezzaluna	p.330
The Front	p.322	Thai Riffic	p.345	The Blu Horizon Bar	p.352	Steki Taverna	p.327
Zaaffran	p.329	Vera Cruz	p.337	The Victoria Room	p.354	Tagine	p.338

Drinks

Other options **Alcohol** p.269

Most restaurants have a licence – just make sure you bring your ID to show that you're over 18. The laws are strict and the fines hefty, so if you get caught drinking underage, expect to pay for it. Beer will cost you about $5, spirits $10 and soft drinks $4. Fruit cocktails are popular and it's common for people to ask for non-alcoholic mixes. The standard soft drinks are always available (coke, sprite, lemon squash and tonic) along with a variety of waters.

Wine is very popular, because of the cheap, good quality produce Australia churns out. Even earthy, spit-and-sawdust pubs will have a decent drop on offer. Bambini Wine Bar (www.bambinitrust.com.au) in the CBD was the Winner of 'Bar of the Year 2007 (Editor's Pick)' in *The Sydney Morning Herald* Good Food Awards. Gazebo Wine Garden (www.gazebowinegarden.com.au) in Elizabeth Bay has recently opened and is a huge hit with the locals. One of Australia's best food magazines, *Gourmet Traveller* recently rated these three wines as being amongst the best buys for 2007: 2005 McWilliam's Hanwood Estate chardonnay, south-eastern Australia; 2006 Pewsey Vale riesling, Eden Valley; 2003 Providence chardonnay, Tasmania.

BYO

Some restaurants will offer BYO or 'bring your own' alcohol. This may be because they don't have an alcohol licence, or to encourage people through the door. It is quite common, unless you go to an upmarket restaurant. Generally, BYO is more popular in mid-range spots like your local Thai or Indian. Corkage is always charged and ranges from a flat $4 to $6 per head to a dollar a bottle.

Hygiene

Most outlets are extremely hygienic, but you'll have a hard time finding out if a restaurant has been busted for letting bugs share your dinner. The City of Sydney council has ruled that it's not in the public interest to tell you. What we do know, is that in early 2006 the council reported a significant drop in health fines for restaurants. This, it claims, shows more food service operators are (literally) cleaning up their act. It's compulsory for every outlet to be checked, whether a large chain or a small independent.

Special Deals & Theme Nights

Australian's love any excuse to celebrate. Whether it's Christmas Eve or Saint Patrick's Day, there will be a party to go to. The city turns a dark shade of green for Paddy's day, and Australia Day and the December party season are celebrated with relish. If you're looking for a bite to eat, you'll often find that restaurants only offer set menus during these times, so that they can cater to the masses.

313

Going Out

Cheap Eats
Supermarket receipts often have vouchers offering cheap food, as does the website www.hotdockets.com. *The Sydney Morning Herald* runs its Good Food Month in October, and you can expect 10% off your bill at participating restaurants. The website www.your restaurants.com.au lets you download discounts onto your mobile phone.

Themed Nights
The quaint tradition of 'ladies nights' lingers on in Sydney. ScuBar (www.scubar.com.au, 9212 4244) leads the way with champagne at $2 a glass. The bar is always full of backpackers up for a giggle, and other theme nights include crab racing on a Monday and ping pong on Tuesdays. It's just off George Street, on Rawsons Place, near Central station. If you're after something a little fancier and a sweeping view across Sydney Harbour, head to Cruise Bar (9251 1188) in Circular Quay on a Wednesday night. Entry is free. On Thursday, there is a salsa themed night. At Gab Bar (www.hiltonsydney.com.au) in the Hilton Hotel, they are also keen on their speed dating, crab racing, ping-pong and weekly ladies nights. Keep an eye on the daily papers for more information on which places have theme nights.

Tax & Service Charges
If it's a public holiday, you can expect an additional 10% to be added to your bill. This is usually also the case on Sunday. Most restaurants and cafes expect an extra incentive to come to work while the rest of us are relaxing. The 10% Goods and Services Tax (GST) was introduced back in 2000 and is included in the price.

Tipping
Tipping is not as common as in the US or Europe. Bar staff, waiting staff and taxi drivers get paid quite well and do not generally expect a tip, although any extra is always appreciated. In restaurants and cafes, the plusher the place the more a tip will be expected. Up to 10% is fine, but don't feel obliged if service is poor. If you can, leave cash, as credit card tips do not always reach the staff. Regular cafes and coffee shops may also have a tip pot on the counter.

The Yellow Star
The natty yellow star seen to the right is our way of highlighting places that we think merit extra praise. It might be the atmosphere, the food, the cocktails, the music or the crowd, but any review that you see with the star attached is somewhere that we think is a bit special.

Independent Reviews
All of the outlets in this book have been independently reviewed by a team of food and nightlife experts who are based in Sydney. Their aim is to give clear, realistic and unbiased views of each venue without any back-handers, special treatment or underhandedness on the part of any restaurant owner, nightclub promoter, crafty PR guru or persuasive barista. If there's one thing the Explorer team thrives on, it's feedback. So if any of the reviews in this section have led you astray, or if your favourite local eatery doesn't grace these pages, then drop us a line on info@explorerpublishing.com and tell us all about it.

Restaurant Timings
Restaurant hours normally only change for public holidays, which are pretty sacred in Australia, and a lot of places close. Many restaurants do open on Christmas Day, but make sure you book well in advance - especially if you're headed somewhere a bit snazzy.

Vegetarian Food
Sydney has a range of buzzing veggie places to indulge in soy lattes and falafel burgers. Macro Cafe, see p.348, in Crows Nest serves fresh, organic fare and has become a local favourite with residents. In terms of restaurants, *The Sydney Morning Herald Good Food Guide* 2005 awarded Billy Kwong (p.320), the 'best vegetarian restaurant' prize because, 'Kylie Kwong makes vegetables exciting'. Another great place to go for a good veggie feast is Govindas (p.345), where a vegetarian buffet followed by a movie viewed on big, comfy couches will cost you less than $25. Glebe and Newtown are bursting with veggie options and you won't need to book; most restaurants have more than one vegetarian option but your best bet is Thai or Indian cuisine.

African

501 King St
Newtown

African Feeling

9516 3130 | www.africanfeeling.com.au

Chug back a homemade ginger beer as you settle into this small, cosy restaurant in the heart of alternative Newtown. With unfamiliar aromas wafting from the kitchen you may well forget you're in Australia. Roll your own fufu balls (yams mashed and shaped into balls, for dipping in sauces) while tapping your toes to the constant beats of the African drum. Dishes here cover traditional and modern African, with recipes from around the continent. Bring friends along to feast on the $30 banquet, or make it a dinner for two over an entree of corn bread and butter for just $6.50, followed by the West African spinach stew for $13.50. Non-meat eaters can get their fill with the vegetarian jungle, a combination of three veggie dishes.

43-45 East Esplanade
Manly

Out of Africa

9977 0055 | www.outofafrica.com.au

Morocco's tourist board claims the country's hospitality is second to none, and Out of Africa tries hard to prove them right. The north African cuisine here is excellent, served as you sit on brightly coloured cushions in the seaside suburb of Manly. Owner and chef Hassan M'Souli, is the author of the *Moroccan Modern* cookbook and has developed an extensive menu of Moroccan favourites, including a meatball tagine that is simmered in a flavour-filled tomato sauce, with onion, garlic, spices and poached eggs. He also holds cooking classes, which are much in-demand. Expect to pay around $24 for an ample main.

83 Spofforth St
Cremorne

Radio Cairo Café

9908 2649

Radio Cairo Café is a must visit for its traditional African dishes like sosaties; spicy apricot marinated lamb fillets, char grilled on a skewer and accompanied by chilli and sour cream. It also serves up Ethiopian and Ugandan delights. The naturally friendly and helpful staff add to the relaxed atmosphere. The decor is hip yet traditional and cool tunes hum away in the background. It's a restaurant worth travelling across town for and locals have learned to make their bookings a night in advance, often to follow a movie at the nearby Orpheum. Servings here are generous, and a $20 main should see you leaving fulfilled and perfectly chilled out.

Arabic/Lebanese

Other options **Middle Eastern** p.338

23 Glebe Point Rd
Glebe

Almustafa Lebanese Restaurant

9660 9006 | www.almustafa.com.au

Almustafa is a popular spot for birthdays and hen nights and can get quite raucous in the cushion room upstairs, as belly dancers shimmy to the cheers of partygoers. For $40 to $47 per head you can get all the mezze favourites such as dips, falafel, vine leaves and shish kebab, but if you just want good Lebanese fare without the hilarity, dine downstairs. Vegans are well catered for, with the kitchen also looking after coeliacs and those with food allergies. All dishes at Almustafa are also completely gluten free.

489-491 King St
Newtown

Arabella

9550 1119 | www.arabella.com.au

Arabella lovingly brings a taste of Beirut to Sydney. Decked out in chic, modern style, but with a more traditional cushion room, the restaurant comes alive to the

315

beat of belly dancers on Friday and Saturday nights. While the chef will suggest you feast on a mixed grill with sides of hummus, tabbouleh and fresh Lebanese bread, the lamb shawarma is just as good, marinated in a blend of spices and homemade red vinegar. Banquets here start at $35 per person, which includes enough food to keep you well and truly satisfied.

Arax

670 Willoughby Rd
Willoughby
Outer North

9958 1518

The wood fired pizzas here, served up with lashings of hummus or baba ghanoush, have been served to loyal customers for three decades. But if you're not so keen on mixing Italian with Lebanese, there are plenty of other offerings on the menu. Besides the traditional mezze and spiced lamb, the grilled fish (marinated in olive oil, spices and a hint of lemon) is divine. Come Saturday night, the pleasant decor is further brightened up by exuberant belly dancers.

Emma's on Liberty

59a Liberty St
Enmore
Outer West

9550 3458

This restaurant is crowded for one reason: it's good. You could easily eat alone at Emma's in artsy Enmore, but the food here is so authentic and spot on, you'll want to share it. And with mains starting at just $12, it's very affordable. While service can be slow thanks to the throng of people who pass through the doors, it's worth waiting to order the $32 banquet, served with endless Lebanese bread. If you do order from the menu, best start with a helping of dips featuring baba ghanoush and hummus drizzled with olive oil. It's so good, you'll be tempted to lick the plate.

Laroche

61-67 Haldon St
Lakemba
Outer West

9759 9257

Laroche is a magnet for Lakemba locals, who head there for the fresh Lebanese fare. It's best to book if you want to take up one of the modest restaurant's 50 seats, as most are taken up from breakfast through to lunch. For just $12, you could easily fill two tummies, with a mixed plate of baba ganoush, hummus, kefte, falafel, pickled turnip, tomato, mint, olives, shish kebab and shish taouk, served with Arabic bread and a soft drink to wash it all down. If you're unfamiliar with the menu, staff here will happily explain each dish. Don't leave without trying the Lebanese coffee.

Summerland

457 Chappel Rd
Bankstown
Outer West

9708 5107

The food never seems to end at Summerland, and nor do the good times. Families have been coming back to this entertainment restaurant for years, with photographic proof proudly pasted on the walls. While some come for the belly dancers and singers, regulars will tell you it's the authentic cuisine that brings them back. If you dare, order big with the $30 or $40 banquet. This is a challenge for even the hungriest of patrons, with its freshly baked breads, dips, salads, tender barbecued meats, falafel, cheeses, kefte kebab and sausage, all washed down with Arabic coffee. The lunchtime banquet menu is even more affordable, starting at just $18.

Australian

Aperitif

7 Kellett St
Kings Cross

9357 4729

There's something delightfully different about Aperitif, from its high ceilings right down to its Riedel stemless glasses. This sleek bar and restaurant, neatly tucked away in the midnight madness that is Kings Cross, is for those who want to combine outstanding sommelier-chosen wines with great food, all created by French chef, David Bitton. Once perched on the velvety-soft, red, bench-style seating, or in the more intimate rear bar, choose from 40 imported wines, 28 of which are offered by the glass (or even by the half glass). You can match these to dishes such as Claire de Lune Sydney rock oysters, a substantial paella of Spanish rice with chicken and seafood or the grilled mussels, tomato, saffron and pimientos. Be sure to ask the obliging staff to serve up some chilled asparagus soup with goat's cheese curd – it's delicious. Or, try the French or Mediterranean tapas. The kitchen stays open well past midnight.

252 George St
Central

Est

9240 3010 | *www.merivale.com*

Shoulder your way past the showy, suit-wearing crowd (as much part of the Establishment Hotel as its high ceilings and grand decor), and make your way to Est for an elegant evening under the talented care of chef, Peter Doyle. Known widely as the founding father of modern Australian cuisine, Doyle and his staff are top class. It is everything you'd expect from a restaurant that received three prestigious chefs hats from *The Sydney Morning Herald Good Food Guide* 2007. This is a very glamorous dining experience. You could start with a beautifully presented nage of Moreton Bay bug (that's lobster soup), snow peas, black fungi, lemongrass and kaffir lime for $33. Then follow with a pan-roasted John Dory fillet and grilled white scallop with a sherry, carrot juice and dessert wine sauce for $47. If you still have room, choose the caramelised French toast with caramel poached pear and ice cream for $22.

69 Bynya Rd
Whale Beach
Outer North

Jonah's

9974 5599 | *www.jonahs.com.au*

Follow in the footsteps of the rich and famous with a night at Jonah's, overlooking spectacular Whale Beach. A long-time haven for visiting stars (think Laurence Olivier and Vivian Leigh), this fine dining establishment and boutique is charming without pretension. Slide into the soft blue bench seats and catch the sunset over the ocean, as you're waited on by highly trained staff that manage to make you feel as if your conversation is never interrupted. Under the direction of George Francisco, the menu is very well priced for such high quality. The roasted ocean trout and blue eye trevalla crepinette (a kind of fish wrap) with potatoes, wilted spinach and foie gras sauce is great for $38. Those with a sweet tooth shouldn't leave without a helping of the Belgian triple chocolate layered cake with mocha rum sauce for $17.

2/411 Bourke St
Surry Hills

Le Pelican

9380 2622 | *www.lepelicanrestaurant.com*

The French bistro design here is so authentic you expect to see cuddling couples feeding each other spoonfuls of brioche. Chef Jean-Francois Sabet, who was once seen on the television show *My Restaurant Rules*, has mixed French and mod Oz to create dishes dictated by whatever fresh produce is picked up at the markets each morning. Le Pelican only opened in 2006, but it doesn't seem to have taken long for word to get out. Tables fill quickly, so it's essential to book if you want to experience the innovative menu, which comes complete with charming service.

James Craig Rd
Superyacht Marina
Rozelle

Liquidity

9810 3433

If you can stop ogling the luxury yachts for long enough, you'll find that this sleek marquee restaurant is just as fancy. Family friendly without forsaking class, Liquidity has solid lunch and dinner menus complemented with a well-chosen wine selection. A meal of pan seared scallops with buffalo mozzarella, ratatouille, prosciutto and aged balsamic dressing, followed by a mixed seafood grill can be completed with one of the fabulous desserts, which will leave you with a contented smile on your face. You can then make your way home by water taxi, which one of the friendly staff will order for you.

22 Challis Ave
Potts Point

Lotus Bar and Bistro
9326 9000 | www.merivale.com
In Greek mythology, the lotus was thought to induce a reluctance to depart. This is the case here, down a side street in trendy Potts Point. It seems that most who saunter in through the thin timber-panelled entry into the dainty eating area were born cool, or at least know how to play the part. But they also know the work of a good chef when they taste it. Lauren Murdoch inspires with succulent servings of salmon entree, ample enough to make you wonder if it's actually the main, followed by barramundi, which tenderly falls apart with the slightest touch. Lotus is slick and airy, adorned with modern tables and chairs in blank white, leaving the eye to appreciate the metallic Florence Broadhurst design that covers the walls. While service leaves a lot to be desired, the affordable mains, from around $29, will ensure you'll return.

71-73 Stanley St
Leichhardt

Pello
9360 4640 | www.pello.com.au
You might expect to pay more for the fine food at Pello, cleverly concocted by chef Thomas Johns. The bistro-style restaurant, complete with a small terrace that offers a view of Sydney's Little Italy below, is a groovy place where you could easily sit for hours as you marvel over the modern European-influenced meals. An entree of almond crusted coral trout with celery puree, fennel, tomatoes and baby leeks for $22 is a good place to start, followed by a main of braised globe artichokes, gratinated white onion, potato, mushrooms and Gruyere for $32. Desserts are called indulgences at Pello, and it's no wonder with the likes of the delectable pear tarte with sweet wine and ice cream for $15.

465 Bronte Rd
Bronte

Swell Restaurant
9386 5001 | www.swellrestaurant.com.au
From the tactility of the waiting staff, to the sound of the crushing waves at nearby Bronte beach, Swell is a sensory experience. From early morning breakfasts of pesto scrambled eggs with smoked salmon and sourdough toast to romantic evenings over pan-fried goats cheese gnocchi with pumpkin, squash and sage butter, you'll have decided to return before the meal has even ended. Chef Daud Kendall rightly shows off his version of mod Oz, which is influenced by flavours of the Mediterranean, Asia, France and Spain. Swell also hosts taster and wine dinners designed, they say, for 'adventurous lovers of great food and wine'. Their Italian week and Bastille Day food festivities are well worth a visit.

828 Pittwater Rd
Dee Why
Outer North

Top BBQ
9982 8088
It doesn't matter how busy it gets here, the hungry folk just keep coming. While they may not line up for the ambience (it's all multi-coloured lights and bare furnishings), the fresh food is definitely worth the trip. From the salt and pepper calamari to the

piled-high plate of barbecue pork, you'll find plenty of reasons to schedule a return visit to this popular restaurant in seaside Dee Why. Ask the obliging staff to suggest their favourites, which you can enjoy with an in-house or BYO wine.

British

99 Glebe Point Rd
Glebe

A'Mews
9660 4999 | www.amews.com.au
This inner-city gem, which offers a mix of modern French and English dishes, knows how to turn it on without emptying the pockets of its loyal diners. With its three levels, A'Mews is roomy enough to dine with friends, yet quiet enough to share a romantic dinner for two. If you can't decide from the enticing menu (with dishes such as pumpkin, red onion and blue goats cheese risotto with roasted chestnuts) you can go for the $60, six-course taster. You'll soon understand why so many critics have sung the praises of this timber-decked delight. It's worth leaving space for dessert too. Choices include mascarpone and honey parfait with poached stone fruit and chocolate sabayon (French for zabaglione) with brandied cherries.

141 Belmore Rd
Randwick

Restaurant Balzac
9399 9660 | www.restaurantbalzac.com.au
The name may suggest otherwise, but this is French with a British touch. Dessert-lovers will be tempted to start with the baked triple cream cheesecake and work backwards to an entree of Pacific oysters, but every dish served here is as delightful as the next. Wine connoisseurs are also well looked after, with a list that takes you from New Zealand to France. The naked sandstone walls are prettied up with tasteful furniture and linen-decked tables, adding class to the clean, crisp decor and warm ambience. Choose from two taster menus at $80 per head, or $125 with matching wines. Functions are also popular, with a five-course menu available for $70 per head.

Brunch

If you live in Sydney for any length of time, you will 'do brunch'. The meal between breakfast and lunch is a popular social occasion at weekends, when the brunching set (from sociable singles to families) perch on sidewalks for gourmet goodies and strong coffee. Some of the more popular spots include Bills in Darlinghurst, Surry Hills or Woollahra, Yellow in Potts Point or Ripples in Kirribilli. Most places require you to pre-book in order to guarantee a seat and prices are often higher in the smarter suburbs. Many cafes and restaurants also apply a surcharge on Sundays, so expect to see up to 10% added to your bill.

Celebrity Chefs

Sydney has a number of restaurants owned by well-known chefs. The most notable is probably Tetsuya's (p.332), owned and run by Tetsuya Wakuda. The ten-course taster menu is $160 per person, plus drinks. Kylie Kwong has been billed as Australia's answer to Jamie Oliver. Her Asian restaurant, Billy Kwong (p.320), is always packed. A few doors up you'll find Bills (p.321), owned by celebrity chef Bill Granger. Scrambled eggs at Bills are a Sydney ritual. glass brasserie (p.325) at the new Hilton is led by celeb restaurateur Luke Mangan.

Brunch		
Alliance Francaise	Central	9267 1755
Bambini Trust Café	Central	9283 7098
Bathers' Pavilion	North Sydney	9969 5050
Bill's	Mosman	9328 7997
Café Giulia	Glebe	9698 4424
Café Sopra	Redfern	9699 3174
Jellyfish	Manly	9977 4555
La Renaissance Café Patisserie	Central	9241 4878
Lindt Café	Central	8257 1600
Macro Wholefoods Café	Bondi	9004 1240
Maltese Café	Darlinghurst	9361 6942
Pancakes on The Rocks	The Rocks	9247 6371
Ripples Café	Kirribilli	9929 7722
Sean's Panorama	Bondi	9365 4924
Simmone Logue	Double Bay	9327 5700
The Vinyl Lounge	Potts Point	9326 9224
Yellow Bistro & Food Store	Potts Point	9357 3400

Chinese

Billy Kwong
355 Crown St
Surry Hills

9332 3300

If you're not too concerned with a lack of elbowroom or perching on stools, it's worth the wait to score a table at this truly tiny eatery. Owner, chef and media personality Kylie Kwong has successfully married organic and biodynamic Chinese cuisine with Sydney swank. Over a glass of BYO wine, order the banquet to really get a taste for what the fuss is all about, or opt for the famous duck, a Kwong speciality. It's no wonder *The Sydney Morning Herald Good Food Guide* 2007 named this modern Chinese eatery a favourite.

China Doll
6 Cowper Wharf Rd
Woolloomooloo

9380 6744 | www.chinadoll.com.au

There's something about this place on Sydney's historic finger wharf that makes you want to roll your lunch into dinner. The calming Iain Halliday-designed decor, the city skyline view and the well-proportioned modern Asian dishes served up by attentive staff combine to make the China Doll experience beautiful. Considering its well-to-do location, prices here don't hurt as much as you might expect. You can order an entree of steamed vegetable wontons with Chinese black vinegar for $16, tuck into steamed Tasmanian salmon fillet with black bean, lemon and chilli for $33 and finish off with a dessert of sago pudding (a kind of tapioca) with fresh passionfruit for $12. Complete the China Doll experience with an Asian-inspired cocktail, such as the 'china white'. It's an interesting mix of juniper, jasmine tea and fresh lychees, finished with elderflower and martini bianco, and costs $16.

Friendship Oriental
477-479 King
Georges Rd
Outer West

9586 3288

You can be certain your dinner will be served fresh at this longstanding, bustling restaurant. The catches of the day can be viewed and selected from the sizeable fish tanks, before heading to your plain but neat table. Then watch the staff work their magic in the open kitchen. All the expected Chinese dishes are available, as well as many more authentic offerings. Service keeps up with the steady influx of customers and as its name suggests, Friendship Oriental is very amiable.

Golden Century
393-399 Sussex St
Darlinghurst

9212 3901 | www.goldencentury.com.au

As large as its reputation, this local favourite keeps its doors open until 04:00, welcoming a steady stream of patrons eager to have their spin of a lazy Susan (the turning table top). Ingredients are fresh – a tank-lined wall has a show of live seafood, from plump prawns to pipis (a local shellfish). The extensive menu also caters well to meat lovers and while it may take a few attempts for your order to be heard above the chatter and noodle slurping, it'll be well worth the effort. Golden Century also has outlets in Fox Studios and Star City.

186-188 Victoria St
Potts Point

Jimmy Liks

8354 1400 | *www.jimmyliks.com*

It's dimly lit, with little room to swing a chopstick, and Jimmy Liks' fans wouldn't have it any other way. Sling back a few Asian-inspired cocktails at the lengthy bar, before moving to the restaurant for the sumptuous Jimmy's Selection. With its ample servings of tender chicken, pork, beef and crab, this $50-per-head feast is most impressive. Be warned though: the food is so good at this hip joint, you could find your full belly begging for an early night, rather than the party you'd planned at nearby Kings Cross.

Westfield Bondi Junction
Bondi

Kam Fook

9386 9889 | *www.kamfook.com.au*

It's worth enduring the clattering noise here for the excellent food. The yum cha (a type of Chinese breakfast tapas) has locals lining up as early as 11:00 to score a table at either the roomy Bondi Junction branch or the 600-seat, Chatswood restaurant. Tear yourself away from the seafood on show in the wall-lined fish tanks, and take your pick from the yum cha trolleys that cruise the room. If a la carte is more your thing, a portion of san choy bow (pork mince with mushrooms and water chestnuts) could easily serve two. The entertainment comes from traditionally-clad Chinese musicians. While it's not the cheapest Chinese tucker in town, you can still get your fill for around $20, with entrees starting at $6 and mains at $15.

Manly Wharf East Esplanade
Manly

Manly Phoenix

9977 2988 | *www.phoenixrestaurants.com.au*

One of the newest restaurants in the Phoenix chain (others are at Castle Hill, Rhodes and the CBD), the modern Chinese served here is as good as the view. The famous wharf lends itself perfectly to a relaxed catch up with friends over plentiful and fresh $24 per head yum cha or, for those who choose to linger longer, the $88 taster menu.The Singapore chilli snow crab is good or, if you don't mind a bit of a kick, the beef fillet cubes with wasabi sauce are excellent. Leave your car at home and sample some of the well-chosen in-house wines - you can get there and back by taking the easily accessible ferries, buses or jet cat.

Contemporary

433 Liverpool St
Darlinghurst

Bills

9360 9631 | *www.bills.com.au*

To find out what all the fuss is about, you could buy one of Bill Granger's wildly popular cookbooks and try to master his recipes yourself. Or, just add your footprints to the well-worn path that leads to Bills in Darlinghurst. Mention this iconic cafe to any knowing Sydneysider, and the word you're most likely to hear is 'breakfast'. Whether it's to catch-up with friends or have a business meeting, Bills is a regular hangout for residents and tourists alike. The perfect scrambled eggs ($11.80) and sweet corn fritter with roast tomato, spinach and bacon ($16.80), will take you through to dinnertime. With two other Bills outlets in Surry Hills and Woollahra, its never been easier to get in on the action.

321

Catalina

1 Sunderland Ave
Rose Bay

9371 0555 | www.catalinarosebay.com.au

To call yourself a true Sydneysider, make a booking at sun-drenched Catalina Rose Bay, which has become a much loved dining institution over its 12 years in business. There's no need to snazz up the sleek, minimalist interior to get the crowds here; no one would notice anyway. It's the seafood packed menu (there's plenty for meat lovers too) and romantic water view of pretty Rose Bay that keeps residents coming back. Dine from Wednesday to Sunday and you can test your chopstick skills with master sushi chef Yoshinori Fuchigami's sushi and sashimi menu.

This award-winning spot, which is also popular for corporate functions and weddings, just seems to get better and better.

The Front Restaurant and Bar

11 Hickson Rd
Walsh Bay
Darling Harbour

8298 9999 | www.mirvachotels.com

If you're keen for fine dining, but aren't so fussed about getting all dressed up, try The Front Restaurant and Bar at The Sebel Pier One – Sydney's first over-water hotel. Tucked away from the hurried crowds at The Rocks nearby, this romantic, alfresco setting looks over Walsh Bay. For $60 you can savour perfectly seared scallops with smoked salmon and tempura avocado, slow roasted lamb shank with kumara mash followed by chocolate cherry bombe dessert. There's also an impressive selection of Australian wines.

Kirketon Dining Room & Bar

207 Darlinghurst Rd
Darlinghurst

9557 0770 | www.kirketon-diningroom.com

Inspired by the iconic brasseries of Paris and the rich atmosphere of New York's most famed French grills, Kirketon Dining Room and Bar is a breath of fresh air on the contemporary dining scene. With its dark leather booths, antique French mirrors, aged brass finishes and low lighting, you quickly get a sense that what you're about to experience is something special – and it is. Chef Jocelyn Rivière turns out delights like beetroot and horseradish cured salmon for entree and pan-roasted ocean trout with fennel puree, broad beans, green olives and oven-dried tomatoes for main. The Kirketon is also a great place to share champagne cocktails with friends; try the delicious bar snacks like crisp fried salt cod croquettes with aioli. Mains here start at $28. It's truly a must visit.

Longrain

85 Commonwealth St
Surry Hills

9280 2888 | www.longrain.com.au

One step inside the 100-year old converted warehouse that is Longrain, and you'll understand why many a Sydneysider has put this restaurant and cocktail bar on their favourites list. Chic without trying to be cool, luxurious without being lavish, you can expect consistency in the Asian-influenced cuisine and swift service. Since opening in 2001, it has regularly been awarded the prestigious two chefs hats by *The Sydney Morning Herald Good Food Guide*. Many of its industrial features still exist, but are softened with an excellent collection of Australian art and photography. Menu prices are what you'd expect of such a restaurant, but still not overly pricey. Enjoy a banquet with friends, at a reasonable $44 or $55 per head, which includes dishes such as crab and mango salad and duck red curry with ginger and lychees.

Strangers with Candy

96 Kepos St
Redfern

9698 6000 | *www.strangerswithcandy.com.au*

There's nothing like a splash of colour to lift your mood. But it's not just the bright red walls that put a smile on your face at this quirky Redfern restaurant. Add to the mix some sprightly service and lovingly prepared food and you've got yourself a recipe for a relaxed breakfast, lunch or dinner. Once an old corner terrace, Strangers with Candy is now a popular meeting place for workers and weekenders who want a guaranteed good time over a BYO bottle of wine. Don't pass up an ample serving of crispy pan-fried fish cakes, topped with tomato salsa, salad and prosciutto.

Sugaroom

1 Harris St
Pyrmont

9571 5055 | *www.sugaroom.com.au*

With a name that echoes the sugar refinery that once occupied this building, you'll still find plenty of sweetness at the Sugaroom. Greg Anderson, who has worked as golfer Greg Norman's private chef, delights Pyrmont's eager foodies. You can either dine indoors or out, overlooking the city harbour and its twinkling lights. You can order beautifully presented dishes like pan-fried Atlantic salmon fillet with crab risotto and fennel salad or just chill with a sugadream cocktail over a bar snack of kingfish carpaccio. Lovely for romantic dinners for two, Sugaroom is also a top spot for functions, such as weddings and cocktail parties. Main meals here start at $26.

Will and Toby's

8-13 South Steyne
Manly

9977 5944 | *www.willandtobys.com.au*

There's nothing fish and chips about this seaside restaurant, with its impeccable service, tantalising menu and wines to match. Brothers Will and Toby, who opened their first bistro and bar in Darlinghurst five years ago, have excelled themselves in Manly with an open, airy venue that makes the most of the beach view. Its whitewashed walls and comfy bench seats in seaside hues of blue and white are relaxing, so take your time as you choose from the modern menu. Whether you want the full dining experience, or just to wander off the sand for a bite to eat, it's hard to pass up the reasonably priced cuttlefish risotto with fennel and dill ($19), or the warm caramelised onion and goats cheese tart ($16). However, the real showstoppers here are the desserts, such as the frozen pistachio nougatine with candied zest and fresh fruit.

Deli

Leading a hectic lifestyle in Sydney doesn't mean you can't sit down to a gourmet meal at home, even if you didn't make it yourself. Delis are an ever-popular option for those who want quality food fast. Thanks to the city's multicultural population, you can get just about any cuisine you like, sold in upmarket food halls, specialty shops and produce markets. It's worth the trip to suburbs such as Haberfield, Leichhardt, Marrickville, Bankstown and Petersham, where you can fill your shopping bag with

Italian sausages, handmade breads, cheeses, pastries, pasta, olives and oils. Popular outlets include Deli on Market (30-32 Market Street, 9262 6906) in the city, Gusto Delicatessen (16 Hall Street, 9130 4565) in Bondi and Luigi Brothers (372 New South Head Road, 9363 0050) in Double Bay. See Delicatessens on p.282.

Dinner Cruises
Other options **Boat Tours** p.194

Pyrmont Bay Wharf ◄
Pyrmont

Rhythmboat Cruises
9879 3942 | *www.rhythmboat.com.au*
While you could just book a Rhythmboat cruise for the spectacular harbour view, you'll also be guaranteed a good meal and lots of entertainment. The comedy cruise costs $69 and for that you can fill up on a three-course meal while enjoying the routines of some of the country's most talented funny men. If your dancing shoes need a workout, opt for the Friday and Sunday night salsa cruises, where you can sit back and watch the colourful show or hit the dance floor yourself. Rhythmboat Cruises also hold special Christmas party functions.

37 Bank St ◄
Pyrmont

Vagabond Cruises
9660 0388 | *www.vagabond.com.au*
While you can whoop it up extravagantly on one of the three Vagabond vessels, you can also keep it casual with a barbecue meal. Seating from 30 to 300, these cruises are popular with Sydneysiders who want to show visiting guests why their harbour is so great, and those who are just after a good night out. The jazz and Latino cruises are particularly popular. Make the most of the Sydney summer and dine alfresco on the deck or book a boat for a special occasion. Vagabond is popular for wedding receptions, hen nights, Christmas parties and school formals.

French

100 Market St ◄
Central

360 Bar and Dining
9235 2188 | *www.360dining.com.au*
Book well in advance for a table at the southern hemisphere's highest restaurant; it's worth the wait. With a revolving floor that ensures a bird's-eye view of the city from every table, 360 is a unique experience. Executive chef George Diamond uses hard to source ingredients and claims guests experience something 'exclusive and intrinsically special'. He's right. You'll be back for the sensational Atlantic salmon fillet with cauliflower puree, caramelised fennel, deep-fried oyster and bearnaise sauce ($45), accompanied with a side of roast lyonnaise potatoes and thyme. Choose from carefully selected wines, which are sure to add to the relaxation brought on by the dim lighting and dark, hand-carved mahogany surrounds. It's all cleverly put together by award-winning designer Michael McCann.

324

27 O'Connell St
Circular Quay

Bilson's Restaurant

8214 0496 | www.bilsons.com.au

You're allowed to have high expectations when it comes to Bilson's, which sits in the foyer of the Radisson Plaza. Widely known as the 'godfather of Sydney dining', chef Tony Bilson obviously doesn't let the pressure get to him and consistently dishes up sensational French fare that's way above the culinary fads. The restaurant's romantic surroundings make it a great choice for first dates, with its calm lighting and attentive yet unobtrusive service. The whole experience may make you feel like a million dollars, but you don't have to part with last week's wages to come here. Yes, it is easy to tot up the bill, but you can also order mains, such as the jewfish chowder, local lobster and Hawkesbury calamari for around $30.

488 George St
Central

glass brasserie

9265 6068 | www.glassbrasserie.com.au

This place is as famous around Sydney as its chef Luke Magnan. You get an inkling that you're about to experience something special as you're welcomed into the striking earth-coloured dining room. Even if your table isn't beside the 13-metre floor to ceiling window overlooking the QVB, the experience is still impressive. But, it's the food that really steals the show. With an emphasis on local and seasonal produce with a French twist, Magnan, who can be seen cruising the floor greeting his enthusiastic diners, is on to a winner. Entrees start at $17.50 for half a dozen oysters, while a main of fig tart, red onion jam, blue cheese and truffled sour juice dressing will set you back about $23.50. Don't forget to ask the sommelier to select one of the 10,000 Australian, international and boutique wines to go with your meal.

Opera House
Central

Guillaume at Bennelong

9241 1999 | www.guillaumeatbennelong.com.au

Housed in the southern shell of the Sydney Opera House, Guillaume at Bennelong's fame is about more than its location. Tear your attention away from the view long enough to study the menu and you'll discover plenty of mouth-watering reasons why this restaurant wins so many awards (it recently picked up the prestigious three hats in the 2007 *Sydney Morning Herald Good Food Guide)*. Food here is mod Oz with a classical French influence. Opt for a romantic dinner for two in the intimate booths or at a private dining table. Otherwise, gather with friends over canapes at the bar before settling into the curved cocoa-coloured bench seats. Don't leave without a serving of the nougat ice cream with hazelnut, almond and strawberry coulis.

107 Pitt St
Central

Industrie – South of France

9221 8001 | www.industriebar.com.au

You'll find it hard not to gravitate toward the slick, cushion-scattered bench seats here. With its sexy, contemporary interior of exposed brick walls, ambient lighting and industrial-inspired furnishings, Industrie is a cool spot for breakfast, lunch, dinner or just a drink. The all-day menu, which is available until midnight, features French and Mediterranean flavours in dishes such as the galette a la citrouille en galette; a beetroot scented rice with haloumi, pumpkin, pine nuts and rocket pesto. Cheese lovers might like the assiette de fromages with poppy seed cracker bread to finish.

17 Alexander St
Crows Nest
Outer North

La Goulue

9439 1640

Impeccable service and consistently great French food are the hallmarks of La Goulue's. Surprisingly, you don't have to spend a mint to experience it, as mains start at just $26. Chef Wayne Smith may not be French, but he certainly has a flair for producing their rich

325

fare. Take your favourite bottle, or choose from the restaurant's own selection, as you sit in inviting, simply decorated, bistro-style surrounds. One great dish is zucchini flowers stuffed with lobster cream sauce.

758 Darling St
Rozelle

La Grande Bouffe
9818 4333 | www.lagrandebouffe.com.au
Rest your tired feet with a French feast at La Grande Bouffe, a touch of country France in Rozelle. The perfectly presented food bursts with traditional French flavours, from the breakfast menu of fresh crepes with raspberry coulis and fromage frais to the taster menu with escargots, tomato consomme and creme brulee. You can sit outside and watch the world go by, as you peruse the extensive local, national and international wine list. Or, as night falls, dine with friends in the dimly lit, polished-timber interior. Mains start at $29.

355 Crown St
Surry Hills

Marque Restaurant
9332 2225 | www.marquesrestaurant.com.au
It's an intimate space at Marque, with egg lamps exuding a gentle light over the chocolate-coloured room. The French cuisine served here pushes the boundaries of the traditional, with dishes such as the subtle almond jelly, served with firm crabmeat, almond gazpacho, prune oil and sweetcorn custard. Follow up with potato and smoky mackerel mille-feuille, served with olive truffles and hazelnut sauce. Besides the innovative cuisine, Marque is also home to an award-winning wine list, which the sommelier is happy to match with each of your courses.

Greek

283 Marrickville Rd
Marrickville

Corinthian Rotisserie
9698 6895
You can't get much more authentic than this. The Giannakelos family has run this Marrickville favourite for what seems like forever, offering up lashings of Greek home-style food. In fact, with its blue and white interior, which oozes the charm of an authentic Greek tavern, you could easily believe you're there. Service here is warm and friendly; everything you would expect from an old-style, family-run business. The local Greek community visit in droves for the traditional moussaka and plentiful homemade dips for $8. This licensed eatery is open until around 03:00 on weekends and 01:00 on weekdays.

251-253 Elizabeth St
Central

Hellenic Club
9264 5792 | www.hellenicclub.citysearch.com.au
Escape the city rush and enjoy the Hyde Park view over a lengthy lunch or relaxing dinner. This place has been delivering solid Greek favourites for 50 years, winning new fans with its quality and simplicity in a club-like environment. While dining in Sydney central can often take some financial planning, you can tuck into a three-course meal here for $27.50 and entrees start at just $6. If you want good Greek super quick, line up at the bistro before settling into a game of pool with friends. Function planners have also made good use of the third floor social room over the years, which is let out free of charge.

149 Enmore Rd
Newtown

Kafenes
9557 7580
In a strip teeming with eateries all competing for the public's dinner dollars stands Kafenes, a Greek diamond in the rough. While it's tempting to fill up on the flavoursome

eggplant dip, scooped onto generous servings of pitta bread, it's worth waiting for what's to come. Traditional to the core, this busy restaurant serves up all the favourites like moussaka, souvlaki and loukanika complemented by authentic Greek salads. A short stroll from the popular Enmore Theatre, if you don't have time to compete with the crowds, be sure to plan your visit for when there aren't any shows on. Even at peak periods, the service at Kafenes is fast and friendly.

Mezes at Omega

161 King St
Central

9223 0242 | *www.omegarestaurant.com.au*

Unless you plan to take a group of eight or more to dinner, you can't make a booking at Mezes at Omega, which serves up a modern take on classic Greek food. The decor matches the contemporary cuisine and chef Peter Conistis' menu is very affordable, with dishes from around $6 to $24. While widely known for his modern interpretations, there are still plenty of Greek classics on the menu, such as moussaka and herb roasted yellow fin tuna with zucchini fritters and tzatziki. Finish up with a sweet treat of home-made Turkish delight over tea or coffee with petit fours.

Perama

88 Audley St
Petersham

9569 7534 | *www.perama.com.au*

Can't afford a trip to Greece? Do the second best thing and head to Perama in Petersham. Delightfully decked in blue and white, this busy Greek restaurant is said to be one of Sydney's best. After a finger-licking feast of mezze, stuffed vine leaves and lamb, you may well agree. You can try finishing with the baklava ice cream just to make sure. Those with a real hunger won't go past the $45 banquet, which includes barbecued haloumi cheese, fried calamari, chicken oregano and Greek coffee to finish. Or, if you prefer, take a Keo St John Commandaria port from Cypress as a digestive. While meat steals the show, there are plenty of options for vegetarians, which the service savvy staff are happy to point out.

Steki Taverna

2 O'Connell St
Newtown

9516 2191

It's loud and fabulously festive inside Steki Taverna, with its live entertainment and excitable customers. You won't leave hungry whether you opt for the ample seafood platter for a main, or choose to tuck into a tender, slow-cooked lamb. If, after a dance or two on the nearby stage, you've worked up a second hunger, you can opt for the traditional bougatsa (a filo wrapped semolina custard with icing sugar and cinnamon) or indulge in some sugary sweet Turkish delight. This is not a spot for a quiet meal, but is good food served in a jolly atmosphere.

Zeus Restaurant

2/33 Terminus St
Castle Hill
Outer West

8850 6100 | *www.zeusrestaurant.citysearch.com.au*

Locals love Zeus for its big welcome and piled-high plates of good Greek fare. A restaurant for the whole family, the little ones are well catered for with smaller servings of Greek classics such as moussaka and souvlaki. Vegetarians are equally well served, with a dish that has layers of char grilled eggplant, zucchini, semi-dried tomatoes, baby spinach and perfectly grilled haloumi cheese. Fans of seafood can go for the baby calamari tossed in lemon and olive oil, served with garlic and dill or the mussels simmered in a mild chilli with fresh tomato and basil sauce. The latter comes with a side of crusty bread to soak up the dregs. If you can't decide, you can't go wrong with the seven-course banquet for $40 per head.

Indian

Aki's
1/6 Cowper Wharf Rd
Woolloomooloo

9332 4600 | *www.akisindian.com.au*

Expect more than just a traditional Indian feast at Aki's. Chef Kumar Mahadevan has received rave reviews for his menu at this multi-levelled, modern restaurant, which boasts flavour-filled offerings such as jumbo prawns and tropical snake beans, gently simmered in a sauce of coconut milk, turmeric, fennel, curry leaves and ginger. Prices here are a pleasant surprise, considering its sought-after waterfront location. Starters range from $11.80 to $21.80, while $18.80 will buy you a main of whole baby eggplant and fried banana chillies, crushed coriander seeds, crushed black pepper, cumin and tomatoes. Arrive early to enjoy pre-dinner drinks in the cocktail lounge area upstairs.

All India Restaurant
The Bijou
2a Rowntree St
Balmain

9555 8844 | *www.all-india.com.au*

You can count on being spoiled for choice here. The open kitchen serves up generous helpings of well-ordered favourites such as butter chicken with sides of fluffy garlic naan, as well as tempting set menus of pappadams, seekh, cochin beef, vegetable korma, rice and naan bread at $19.90 per person. All India also caters for private functions, from weddings to corporate, with the private dining room seating up to 110 people. If the welcoming staff can't tempt you with some wine from the extensive list, or if you prefer to end your meal with something sweet, opt for the chai, an Indian tea of cardamom and mild spices warmed with milk.

Bukhara
Cnr Cross & Bay St
Double Bay

9363 5510

Go beyond butter chicken at Bukhara. With its Indian and Mauritian-inspired menu, this popular restaurant is known for stepping outside the traditional, with tantalising offerings such as calamari with mustard seeds and onions, or the beautiful texture and flavours of the crab Creole – baby deep fried zucchini flowers bursting with gingered crab meat. The atmosphere here is conducive to an enjoyable dinner with the whole family or an intimate outing for two. You can peer through glass windows into the busy kitchen to see the chef work his magic. Neatly dressed staff add to the pleasant Bukhara experience with swift, friendly service.

Last Train to Bombay
469 Pacific Highway
Crows Nest
Outer North

9460 6664

Even the Bollywood movies playing on the wall-mounted television won't drag your attention away from the fine fare at the Last Train to Bombay. Owner Harry Virk has brought together four chefs, each specialising in different Indian cuisines: northern,

Aki's   *All India Restaurant*

southern, Tandoori and Chaat (traditional street food), resulting in a menu that will take you on a journey you won't want to end. While it's hardly the place for a romantic dinner, service is fast and you're guaranteed to leave with a full belly and not too much of a dent in your wallet. And it's certainly a test of willpower to forgo one of the 40 desserts on display.

Oh! Calcutta!

251 Victoria St
Darlinghurst

9360 3650 | *www.ohcalcutta.com.au*
Loyal diners have been returning to Oh! Calcutta! for almost 20 years, thanks to its delectable cuisine and welcoming atmosphere. It's a short stroll from Kings Cross Station, and the immaculately dressed staff serve up a saag paneer like you've never tasted and a duck curry that will melt in your mouth. But if you really want to get a proper taste of what this place is all about, first timers should try the taster menu. It features three entrees, three mains, rice, accompaniments and bread for $47.90 per person, or the seafood option for $55 per person. If you've still got room, finish off with a mixed plate of Indian sweets for $12.90. Fully licensed with an ample list of local and imported beverages, you can also BYO.

Surjit's

215 Parramatta Rd
Annandale
Outer West

9564 6600
You don't have to be a cricket fan to eat at Surjits, but you'll definitely enjoy it that bit more if you at least have an appreciation for the game. Owner Surjit has created a shrine to his favourite sport, displayed side-by-side with his other passion: Indian food. Inside this eatery, with its stark white decor and basic timber seating, you can study the cricket memorabilia and biographies just as you would the extensive menu. Think generous helpings of tandoori chicken and palak paneer (and perhaps a story or two from Surjit on how he fed the Indian team when they were in town). While service can be a little slow, the authenticity of the north Indian food makes it worth coming back for more.

Zaaffran

345 Harbourside
Shopping Ctr
Darling Harbour

9211 8900 | *www.zaaffran.com.au*
If you adore good Indian food, but want to try a restaurant that has something extra, look no further than Zaaffran. Set in tourist-friendly Darling Harbour, with glorious Cockle Bay views, the restaurant is easy to reach by foot or ferry should you choose to linger over a few glasses of wine. Perfect for an intimate dinner or a bigger get together, Zaaffran is a vegetarian's paradise, with a big percentage of its menu dedicated to vegan fare. Meat lovers however, will rave about the free-range chicken tandoori, grilled with besan, mace, nutmeg, cardamom and yoghurt. The whole menu steps carefully and very successfully outside its traditional Indian heritage. Despite its popularity and positive reviews it's very affordable, with mains starting at $15.50.

Italian

Other options **Pizzerias** p.339, **Mediterranean** p.335

Bel Parco Ristorante & Bar

Bicentennial Park
Outer West

9763 7530 | *www.belparco.com.au*
With modern Italian fare, including a great selection of traditional wood-fired pizzas, the restaurant has enthusiastic diners coming from miles away. Set in Australian native parklands, it's easy to believe you're far from the city's traffic troubles, leaving you to enjoy the food in peace. Wednesday nights at Bel Parco are all about the pizza, served

with the chef's special calzone and a local draught beer, all for $20. Come Thursday it's risotto that steals the show with the cauliflower and prawn variety or the daily special served with a glass of house wine for $25.

Ecco Ristorante

2 St Georges Cres
Drummoyne

9719 9394 | *www.ecco.com.au*
Set in Drummoyne Sailing Club, Ecco's water views, hearty traditional dishes and chilled atmosphere, all combine for a very relaxing experience. The food is just how mamma would make it and there are plenty of options on offer – from the starter of wild mushrooms, confit garlic and watercress, to a main of pesce al forno (a whole roasted fish with lemon and parsley). For those who can't decide, the three set menus are always a popular choice, ranging from $65 to $85 per head. Don't give up your seat before trying the risotto dessert, with white chocolate, pistachio and strawberry syrup.

Elio

159 Norton St
Leichhardt

9560 9129 | *www.elio.com.au*
Lunch or dinner at Elio's is like being part of a large Italian family, with loads of traditional Italian fare served up by smiling staff. The restaurant courtyard with its creeping vines is a touch of Tuscany in Sydney's Little Italy. Inside, it's a modern tale, with sleek surrounds where families and friends come for Italian staples such as linguini con vongole (linguini with Tasmanian baby clams, chilli, garlic and white wine). There's also an extensive wine list, or if you'd prefer, start your Elio experience with a well-shaken dry martini from the bar.

Grappa

267-277 Norton St
Leichhardt

9560 6090 | *www.grappa.com.au*
There are so many authentic Italian restaurants to choose from that knowing where to pull up a pew can be tricky. But some, such as Grappa, have a reputation that keep pizza and pasta lovers coming back for more. The decor may be anything but traditional, but the nosh here is every bit Italiano, such as the white anchovies with fennel crostini starter and the veal involtini with caponata for main, or a dessert of a trio of homemade sorbets or ice cream. To wash it all down, there's everything from highball coolers to martini and vermouths, and of course, a wide selection of grappa.

Mezzaluna

123 Victoria St
Potts Point

9357 1988 | *www.mezzaluna.com.au*
There's much more to Mezzaluna than the great views. Those who haven't been fortunate enough to venture past the deceivingly small frontage are missing out on a wonderful tribute to northern Italian food, prepared by the Polese family. You could start with crisp fried zucchini flowers stuffed with ricotta, gorgonzola and parmesan, served with a tomato, olive and pine nut salsa ($23.50), followed by west Australian scampi baked and served with Spanish onion, saffron and lemon dressing, ($46). Desserts are a mouthful in more ways than one. The strati di marscapone con mango, gelatina di lamponi e meringa is layers of mango marscapone and raspberry jelly topped with meringue and passion fruit syrup. Book well in advance if you want to watch the sunset fall over the city.

Pilu at Freshwater

Moore Rd, Harbord
Outer North

9938 3331 | *www.piluatfreshwater.com.au*
Feel the day's stresses melt away as you're ushered to a table overlooking Freshwater beach. The view here is beautiful. Inside the heritage-listed beach house is chef Giovanni Pilu, who has been dishing up unforgettable Sardinian fare since 2004. Try

delights such as the tender calamari filled with baby squid, pine nuts, fregola pasta, olives and mixed herbs. This is also a popular choice for weddings, with its immaculately landscaped gardens and wedding packages tailored to suit.

Japanese

161 Middle Head Rd
Mosman

Goemon Sushi Café

9968 4983 | *www.goemon.com.au*

Think twice about turning up without a booking at Goemon. There's little room to move in this tiny eatery, but its loyal diners don't seem to mind, since it serves up possibly the freshest sushi and sashimi in Sydney. Favourite dishes here include the tempura gyoza dumplings, salmon and spicy leek wrap or the grilled eel with mirin and honey soy sauce. With polite, fun staff, it's hard not to fall for this Japanese gem. Entrees here start at $3.50 for miso soup, while mains start at $15.

336 Victoria Ave
Chatswood
Outer North

Makoto

9411 1838

It's worth the short wait to join the ride on this sushi train. With conveyor belts that continue as far as the eye can see, the selection of sushi and sashimi they carry will please even the most discerning. Immaculately clean, there's rarely an empty seat inside this sleekly decorated restaurant and you're always welcomed with a warm Japanese greeting. If the passing plates aren't enough to tempt, you can also order a la carte from the kitchen. Beware, it's hard to let the green tea brulee pass you by. If you go Monday to Wednesday every dish aboard the train costs under $2.70.

Overseas Passenger
Terminal
Circular Quay

Ocean Room

8273 1277

Everything about this restaurant is inspired by the ocean, from the clever modern design, with a live aquarium wall, to the beautifully presented menu. Combined with the knockout harbour view, it's easy to see why the Ocean Room has become so popular. While chef Raita Noda presents the expected Japanese staples such as sushi and sashimi, he also surprises with rich Mediterranean flavours. Try tuna, poached in olive oil with crystallised orange crust and fennel with kaffir salad, or the $90 per head tasting menu if you really can't decide. Functions are also a speciality here, with a private dining room upstairs with glass from floor to ceiling.

136 Wairoa Ave
Bondi

Raw Bar

9365 7200

If you need a break from the beach, take a seat at this modern Japanese eatery. Food here is fresh and fast and comes complete with that Bondi vibe. Loyal diners, who flock here for generous servings, will tell you not to pass up the bento box with teriyaki chicken, sushi, sashimi, tempura and miso for around $24, but the prawn tempura rolls really do the trick. There are no reservations here; it's first come, first served.

331

Tetsuya's

529 Kent St
Central

9267 2900 | *www.tetsuyas.com*

Tetsuya's reputation precedes itself. You often need to book months in advance to secure a place at this much talked about Franco/Japanese experience. Awarded the prestigious three chefs hats from *The Sydney Morning Herald Good Food Guide* 2007, the restaurant continues to hold its own with unforgettable dishes. Examples include tartare of tuna on sushi rice with avocado or the lobster ravioli with crab and shellfish essence. The two elegantly plush dining rooms fittingly overlook a Japanese garden, while private dining rooms can also be reserved.

Toko

362 Oxford St
Paddington

9380 7001 | *www.toko.com.au*

More than just a sushi conveyor, Toko is an excellent way to break up a day of shopping on trendy Oxford Street. Reminiscent of a cool bar with its metallic finishes and modern lighting, it's also home to a variety (43 in fact) of sushi tempters like the nori rolls of cuttlefish or prawn. There is also an extensive hot menu serving up dishes like soba duck soup. For a sweet treat, sample a serving of tempura banana with green tea and vanilla bean ice cream.

Wagamama

Various locations

9356 2166 | *www.wagamama.com.au*

Wagamama works because you're assured flavoursome, classic Japanese fare every time. With four outlets dotted around the city centre, as well as one in Parramatta and at the international airport, it's easy to feed the whole family and have enough change leftover for the train tickets. Modelled on traditional ramen (meaning quick cooking noodle) bars, which have been around in Japan for hundreds of years, main meals here cost around $15. Service is quick and pleasant and children are more than welcome. If you can't keep away, join the frequent noodler programme to earn dollar-saving points with every visit.

Yoshii

115 Harrington St
The Rocks

9247 2566 | *www.yoshii.com.au*

There's passion in the food at this beautifully decked out restaurant, from the contemporary lunch and dinner menus to the sushi bar. Tokyo-born chef Yoshii Ryuichi marries the traditional with the modern by serving up dishes like Japanese yam braised in rice water and bonito stock (that's the dried fish flakes), served with shavings of foie gras and duck mince. It's pretty rich, but delicious. The popular sushi bar menu starts at $100 for seasonal kobachi (appetisers), seasonal nigiri sushi, miso soup and desserts. These are all works of art on a plate and enough to feed a few people.

Korean

Haroo

155 Miller St
North Sydney

9922 1993

Korean at heart with a hint of Japanese, Haroo is small in size, but mighty big on taste. While business people frequent the restaurant during the day, those after an intimate dining experience fill the cosy rooms at night. Most tables have traditional barbecues for those who want an authentic Korean experience, and the extensive menu has some of the best tempura this side of the bridge. Lunchtime crowds push the friendly staff to the limit, but the service at Haroo is usually efficient and meals are delivered to your table piping hot.

501 Victoria Ave
Chatswood
Outer North

Koreana
9413 4408

Forget your backyard barbecue for a moment and grill Korean style. This place serves up tender marinated meats and veggies that simmer away right before your eyes. While you can dine a la carte, first timers should try the barbecue to discover what Korean food is all about. For as little as $34, two people can feast on beef, pork and chicken with sides of kimchee (fermented cabbage) and miso. It's enough to fill the most famished of customers. Tucked away in the business district of busy Chatswood, Koreana boasts welcoming, efficient staff and a family-friendly atmosphere that will have you coming back whenever you get the urge for traditional Korean food.

36 Glebe Point Rd
Glebe

Mu Kung Hwa
9660 0744

First glance may suggest there's nothing fancy about this popular Korean eatery, but the food proves otherwise. Here, the barbecue reigns supreme, with hotplates on each of the simple tables so you can fry to your heart's content. The servings are generous and the meats are marinated in rich sauces. Banquets are also a popular choice here, served up almost as soon as the cork has been popped on your bottle of BYO. The filling seafood and shallot pancake is also a popular choice.

325 Church St
Parramatta
Outer West

Parra Gardens
9633 2663

If you fancy a good sing-song after a Korean meal, head to Parra Gardens. Popular for its traditional Korean menu, it's also frequented by karaoke lovers who can sing up a storm in the adjoining function room. The Japanese influence goes beyond the entertainment, with some of the dishes coming straight from Japan. But it's the ample portions of the Korean barbecue that's the real winner here, with dinner cooked in front of you. Try the mixed seafood hotpot with tofu and Asian vegetables. It's served swimming in a broth that you'll be slurping until the last spoonful. If you're not sure about what to choose, the set menus, from $6 to $13, are always a good option.

Malaysian

121 Avoca St
Randwick

Asian Style
9399 3825

The home-cooked delights dished up at this eastern suburbs gem are unlikely to leave you disappointed. The family-run restaurant takes your dining experience beyond the fresh ingredients and fine food, with friendly service that will have you wondering why it can't be like this every time you eat out. The peaceful, intimate surroundings, decked out with padded walls, will allow you to concentrate on the beautifully prepared meals. Options include the water spinach kangkong (it's a kind of stew) and traditional desserts. The chef also offers a range of specials, separate from the usual menu choices.

201 Sussex St
Darling Harbour

Chinta Ria, Temple of Love
9264 3211 | *www.chintaria.com*

It's busy at Chinta Ria. It doesn't matter what day of the week it is, you'll witness (along with the gigantic Buddha in the entrance), hoards of hungry diners looking for a decent Malaysian meal without an exorbitant price tag. Considering its prime location, with stunning views of Cockle Bay, you'd expect to pay more than $16 for the curry laksa, swirling with fine strands of vermicelli and soft hokkien noodles, tossed together with fried bean curd puff, slices of fishcake, chicken and sugar snap peas. Entrees here start at just $7. While the basic seating and happy chatter from nearby diners might not keep you there for hours on end, the authentic dishes will ensure you come again.

Green Gourmet

115-117 King St
Newtown

9519 5330 | *www.greengourmet.com.au*

Don't expect to find meat of any kind at this vegan Asian eatery. But with tofu this good, the most dedicated carnivores should be kept (relatively) happy. The family-run restaurant takes pride in 'nourishing the body and mind' with freshly prepared vegan food at reasonable prices. If it's all a bit new to you, you could start with the steamed barbecue 'not pork' bun, $2.80, before moving on to the soft tofu and soy nugget, presented in a clay pot and dressed with fresh mushrooms and soy sauce for $12.80. Gluten intolerants flock here for the $5.20 dessert menu, with such sweet delights as steamed lotus seed coconut dumpling, or the green tea moon cake with tofu ice cream, all enjoyed in simple surroundings.

Kuali

115 Longueville Rd
Lane Cove
Outer North

9418 6878 | *www.kuali.com.au*

If your two passions are shopping and eating, you're on to a winner at family friendly Kuali. Even if you're not into retail therapy, it's still worth making your way through a sea of shoppers to experience the formidable Malaysian fare. Once settled at your simple table, you can start with a helping of the grilled otak otak, a delectable spicy mackerel mousse, for $6, followed by the chef's special of kajang satay with duck, and a side of roti bread to soak up the last dregs. If it's your first visit and you're not sure what to order from the extensive menu, you can't go wrong with the mud crab in Kuali chilli sauce.

Malay Chinese Takeaway

64 Castlereagh St
Central

9232 7838

As city folk and students elbow their way to some of the best Malay Chinese food in Sydney, it's obvious this is no place for an intimate dinner. But at these prices, you won't really care. The faded paintwork becomes unimportant once your $10 laksa is served up, which happens almost as soon as you've placed your order and taken a number. It's cash all the way at this family-run restaurant, with no cards of any type accepted. Loyal diners, who rarely leave without ordering the traditional mee siam (vermicelli in a spicy sweet and sour gravy), also love the fact that it's BYO and there's no corkage fee.

Temasek

71 George St
Parramatta
Outer West

9633 9926

You don't go to Temasek, tucked away inside a busy suburban mall, for five-star service. When the traditional food is this good, however, you can understand why families come here again and again. Word spread quickly, prompting the restaurant to open a second dining area to cope with the demand. You're ushered past vintage travel posters to your chrome chairs, where you're encouraged to order almost as quickly as you're handed the menu. If you can't decide, order a serving of almond butter king prawns for $29, or the fried calamari, marinated in garlic, tamarind and chilli. Widely thought of as one of the best Malaysian eateries in Sydney, Temasek is worth the trip. The food is good enough to make the slightly surly and occasionally brusque service seem like a charming novelty.

Mediterranean

Other options **French** p.324, **Greek** p.326, **Spanish** p.342, **Italian** p.329

185 Elizabeth St
Central

Bambini Trust Café

9283 7098 | www.bambinitrust.com.au

Everything is large at Bambini Trust Café, from the grand pillared entrance to the servings of pumpkin ravioli and ricotta with browned butter and sage. While dinner here isn't easily forgotten, those in the know also head to this immaculate city cafe to sample the breakfast menu. You could try the house bircher muesli with fresh fruits or the perfectly poached eggs with smoked salmon or ham, topped with spinach and creamy hollandaise. Come winter, a serving of the vanilla rhubarb porridge, washed down with a Cremcaffe roast can help you face rush hour, which you may have forgotten is waiting just outside.

115a Cronulla St
Cronulla
Outer South

Brass Monkey

9544 3844 | www.brassmonkey.com.au

Good food and music fuse at this intimate venue, tucked away in the beachside suburb of Cronulla. As the lights dim, you can dine on Mediterranean mainstays such as tapas and mezze, while toe tapping to local and international jazz, funk, blues, roots and pop acts. Mains are well priced, with the $35 mixed platter of lamb and chicken skewers, falafel with tahini dip, dolmades (vine leaves), spinach triangles with hummus and bread perfect for two. The $14 pizzas are also popular here, with such toppings as avocado, spanish onion, spinach, basil, roma tomato, salami and mozzarella on a thin margarita base. Shows start at just $10.

7 Hickson Rd
Central

harbourkitchen&bar

9256 1661 | www.harbourkitchen.com.au

With its views over the Opera House, you'll need to book well in advance to secure a table at this delightful restaurant in the Park Hyatt hotel. Whether you choose to lunch the day away, or soak up the sunset over dinner, it's hard to imagine ever being disappointed in this restaurant, with its floor to ceiling glass windows and impeccable service. The Tony Chi decor brings the kitchen to its guests, with the open-style giving diners a look into how their meals are prepared. Chef Danny Drinkwater has created a modern menu, with Mediterranean-inspired flavours; a must-try is his signature dish of cumin-crusted veal fillet, soft porcini polenta and spiced tomato. Finish off with the exquisite moscato and mascarpone sour cherry trifle. Entrees start at $16, with mains from $33.

1 Notts Ave
Bondi

Icebergs Dining Room and Bar

9365 9099 | www.idrb.com

Sydneysiders go to Icebergs as much for the celebrity spotting as they do for the Mediterranean fare and million-dollar views. Overlooking iconic Bondi Beach, this fashionable piece of real estate has greeted the likes of Elle MacPherson and other international celebs. If you dine in the evening, catch the sun setting over the ocean as you tuck into a serving of stingray, silverbeet, asparagus and shitake and wood ear mushrooms prepared by chef Robert Marchetti. While the valet parking adds to the distinctive experience, the wine list will have you considering your transport options.

East Esplanade
Manly Wharf
Manly

Manly Wharf Hotel

9977 1266 | *www.manlywharfhotel.com.au*

To some, the Manly Wharf Hotel is as famous as the green and yellow ferries that dock near its door. Designed to bring the outdoors in, with glass doors that open wide to ensure the sea breeze sweeps through to the bar, this is the place to experience Manly dining at its relaxed, family-friendly best. Grab one of the large timber outdoor tables

and place your order for a pepperoni pig pizza, $15, topped with chilli roast pork belly, pepperoni, tomato ragu and provolone cheese. Or stick with the sea theme and choose the tender salt and pepper squid, $14, or traditional beer battered fish and chips, $19, with a splash of lemon tartare sauce. Then all you have to do is take a number and enjoy the sea and sunshine until the efficient staff bring your order to the table. Kids are also well catered for, with a special 'little ones' menu with goodies such as mini cheese and tomato pizza.

25 Bligh St
Central

Miltons

9232 0007 | *www.miltons.com.au*

With its long white leather bench seats, crisp linen tablecloths and ambient lighting, Miltons would be the ideal backdrop for a sexy music video – if you could keep the hungry diners out that is. A favourite with tourists and locals alike, this restaurant spreads its charm over two levels. Upstairs is for private dining and pre-dinner cocktails while downstairs is the main eating space. Here, classic meets contemporary with warm timber finishes, marble and limestone, creating an ambience to match the Mediterranean cuisine. Try starting with an antipasto plate of marinated seafood, vegetables and cured meat from $17 and don't miss out on the saffron risotto with king prawns, calamari, black mussels and clams for $30. Then there's the must-try vanilla bean creme brulee with raspberry coulis for $12.50.

38-42 Frazer St
Leichhardt

Viscardi's

9555 6088 | *www.lemontage.com.au*

It's easy to lose track of the time at Viscardi's, as you dine overlooking the calm waters of Iron Cove. Smiling waiters serve plentiful helpings of fresh Mediterranean fare in the Tuscan-inspired courtyard or indoors, among the its chocolate leather seats and crisp, white-tiled floors. As the only restaurant on the water's edge in Leichhardt, it seems only fitting the seafood here is special. Sample a side of grilled yellow fin tuna, cold potatoes, olives, french beans with basil-lime vinaigrette for $18 that goes perfectly with a main of grilled river scampi dressed in olive oil and lemon for $44. If you can, skip the sweets and savour the assorted Italian cheeses that come with a selection of breads including pugliese, crostini and woodfire ciabatta for $20.

Mexican

140 Avoca St
Randwick

Azteca's
9398 1020

If you've always longed for a real taste of Mexico but can't afford the airfare, book a table at Azteca's. Unashamedly decked out with ponchos and sombreros, the world seems a more colourful place thanks to this family-run restaurant. While owner José Cruz serenades his guests, partner Anne Leeson cooks up a storm in the kitchen, with traditional favourites such as chicken fajitas with lashings of avocado, sour cream, refried beans, onions and rice. A starter will cost you from $5.20, and mains from $13.30, making it an affordable and fun night out.

43-45 Glebe Point Rd
Glebe

Baja Cantina
9571 1199

Quench your thirst for authentic margaritas at one of Sydney's newest Mexican offerings. The inviting rear courtyard at Baja Cantina is a great place to chill out on a summer's day with a meal of traditional Mexican staples such as enchiladas, nachos and burritos. Servings are well priced and ample enough to fulfil, but thankfully leave enough room for an icy cold jug of traditional sangria or, if you'd prefer, an Aussie beer for just $3.50. Word has spread quickly and there's usually a roaring crowd come weekends, so it's wise to book ahead.

180 Anzac Pde
Kensington

Juanita's
9663 5013

It's good times all the way here, where it's easy to get in the party mood over generous helpings of Mexican food. The atmosphere at Juanita's is as bright as the orange building it operates in. While Sydney may not have perfected the truest of Mexican fare, those who keep coming back to this Kensington favourite will tell you it's not far off it. Saturday nights are busy, so be sure to book ahead. Once settled, you can get a liberal helping of guacamole, frijoles and chilli conquefo for $14.90. On Sundays and Mondays, there's an 'all-you-can-eat' tacos and fajitas frenzy for just $19.90.

403 King St
Newtown

Newton's Cucina
9519 8211

Ask any true lover of Mexican food where to find a decent, authentic meal and you're likely to hear about this modern Tex-Mex joint. While Newton's may not sound like its roots began anywhere close to Mexico, don't let the name fool you. From the fajitas to the nachos, the food here is as authentic as you'll get in Sydney, a city where good Mexican restaurants are hard to find. Servings are generous enough to share, with mains hovering around $29. And although the dishes may be Mexican, you won't find sombrero-clad walls.

314 Military Rd
Cremorne

Vera Cruz
9904 5818

This is one Mexican eatery where they've swapped kitsch for cool, with modern, white decor dressed up with hot pink neon lights and slick bench seating. This is not a typical cantina with fake roadsigns and cowboy frippery and their refusal to slip into stock Mexican restaurant tackiness also stretches to the food. This is subtle Mexican, with fresh ingredients and zingy nuances of flavour. It's very different to the starchy tortillas and heavy doses of chilli that you get elsewhere. Sizeable portions are served up quickly by attentive staff. Mains here are all $25.50.

Middle Eastern
Other options **Arabic/Lebanese** p.315

579 Crown St
Surry Hills

Café Mint
9319 0848 | *www.cafemint.com.au*

It really doesn't matter about the lack of space at Café Mint – it's the menu that grabs your attention. Settle in with a glass of BYO on the bench seating, before perusing a menu that boasts an eclectic mix of Middle Eastern fare. Start with the mezze plate of gourmet dips, gherkins, roasted herby tomatoes and eggplant, followed by the potato and roast garlic ravioli with spicy lamb mince, pine nuts and mint yoghurt. You might want to add a side of rocket, pear, walnut and goats curd for good measure. Café Mint opens early, with those in the know clambering to get a taste of the breakfast couscous with honey yoghurt, spiced fruit, pistachios and warm milk for $10.90.

40 Hall St
Bondi

Gertrude & Alice
9130 5155

JK Rowling could have written Harry Potter in a place like this. With its cosy surroundings and second-hand books, it's easy to lose an afternoon to eating and reading, completely oblivious to the Bondi buzz just outside. Regulars will tell you not to pass up a helping of the flourless chocolate cake, washed down with a freshly brewed coffee, while the Mediterranean and Middle Eastern mainstays such as the open sandwich with olives, tomato and haloumi cheese are also popular.

The Promenade
Darling Harbour

Sumac
9281 2700 | *www.sumacrestaurant.com.au*

Tastes of the Mediterranean, Middle East and north Africa collide in a flavour explosion at Sumac. Swipe just-baked Turkish bread through mounds of plentiful dips on a mezze plate that also boasts chargrilled quail and superb vine leaves. If by chance the bread and dips aren't enough for you, try the fried almond crumbed haloumi in quince sauce. If you're after a quiet meal, it's best to come here for lunch. At night, the bar brings in patrons eager to start their evening with one of Sumac's exotic cocktails, such as the marrakechita with triple sec, tequila and preserved lemon.

679 Darling St
Rozelle

Tagine
9810 6108 | *www.tagine.com.au*

Tagine takes its name from a north African stew of spiced meat and vegetables, slow cooked in a shallow, earthenware dish. For around $25 you can discover what all the fuss is about, whether you go for the meatballs with raisins in spicy tomato salsa, lamb shoulder with new potatoes and roasted garlic or calamari, or the seafood medley with its spicy capsicum and tomato puree. To complete your meal, try the oh-so-sweet feteer meshaltet, an Egyptian delicacy of pastry smothered in butter and dished up with honey, double cream and molasses. With the friendly service and great atmosphere, Tagine can be hard to leave.

231 Victoria St
Darlinghurst

The Victoria Room
www.thevictoriaroom.com

A few too many glasses of champagne here and you could well forget which era you're living in. Elegantly dressed with antique leather-buttoned couches, velvet booths and splashes of brocade, whether you choose to dine or drink here, you'll vow to be back. With its old-world charm comes impeccable service and a well-priced menu. You'll find dishes such as spicy Moroccan meatballs for $14 and veal melinasi for $19. This place is also known for its high tea, where Sunday brunchers come to catch up over champers and finger-sized sandwiches. Ever innovative, The Victoria Room recently opened its supper room for late-night dining – perfect for a civilised snack after the theatre or movies and open until 01:30.

Pizzerias
Other options **Italian** p.329

Various locations

GPK
9953 6064 | www.gotogpk.com.au
Thankfully there are six GPK (Gourmet Pizza Kitchen) outlets in Sydney; this kiddie-friendly place deserves to be shared. The perfectly balanced menu gives plenty of choice for all, including vegetarians, without being overwhelming. If you choose to eat on the run, pull up a pew in the bar-like waiting area and mull over the many magazines while sipping on a complimentary beverage. Expect the same service with each visit; friendly and as quick-as-can-be.

33 Bayswater Rd
Kings Cross

Hugos Bar Pizza
9357 4411
Rub shoulders with the hip crowd at this classy hangout and enjoy what may well be the best pizza you've ever had. Dubbed home to 'the world's best' at the 2005 New York Pizza Challenge, Hugo's is about more than just good Italian pie. Catch up with pals in the cosy sunken lounge area, complete with fireplace, or liven it up with a rhubarb and star anise cocktail at the onyx bar. Decked with slick leather benches, Hugo's Bar Pizza is also popular for functions, including weddings, and can cater for up to 140.

500 Crown St
Surry Hills

Pizza e Birra
9332 2510
There are plenty of good times to be had at Pizza e Birra. A happy crowd swill golden ale and share their life happenings over wood-fired pizzas, topped with the usual Italian favourites, as well as a variety of other tempting dishes from fish to steak. But before you hurry straight to the mains, a pre-dinner snack of chargrilled calamari or eggplant meatballs is worthwhile, as you relax into the comfortable wooden, bistro-style seats. While you may have to wait to pull up a pew because of the no booking policy, once you're in, chances are you won't want to leave.

Pizzerias		
Dolce Ristorante	Various locations	9232 1306
Fedele's Pizza Restaurant	Outer North	9889 7770
Il Cuore	Outer West	9746 8746
Papa Luigi's Italian Restaurant & Pizzeria	Various locations	8338 8500
Rozelle Pizzeria	Rozelle	9818 7166
Toppings Restaurant & Cafe	Outer North	9499 3181

Seafood

Blackwattle Bay
Pyrmont

Blackwattle Bay
9004 1100 | www.sydneyfishmarket.com.au
You can't get much fresher than this. Pull up a seat at one of the many dockside cafes and watch the fishermen bring in their daily catch. It's hard to resist ordering after being tempted with fresh oysters that are shucked before your eyes. The lively market atmosphere, with its wholesale and retail fish markets, on the shores of Blackwattle Bay, is a top spot for families and seafood lovers who enjoy a spot of people watching. For those who want to learn how to prepare their own, there's also the popular seafood cooking school.

Customs House
31 Alfred St
Central

Café Sydney

9251 8683 | *www.cafesydney.com.au*

You'll be hard pressed to find a Sydneysider who hasn't at least heard of this popular spot, and its spectacular harbour views. The dishes take their inspiration from Japan, Italy, India, Morocco and Thailand and the theme is ultimately seafood, to be enjoyed indoors or out on the sheltered terrace. The menu is extensive and includes a tempting seafood platter for $135. It gets busy with office workers during the day but is also popular for special occasions, and you can either hire out a private dining room for 14 or the whole venue.

11 Marine Pde
Watsons Bay

Doyles

9337 2007 | *www.doyles.com.au*

There's the Sydney Harbour Bridge and the Opera House. Then there's Doyles. Opened as Australia's first seafood restaurant in 1885, this Watsons Bay restaurant has a panoramic view of the harbour and its landmarks. This, though, is easy to ignore once the tucker is delivered by a cheery waiter. This is excellent, unpretentious, freshly prepared seafood; from the jumbo prawns to the fish chowder and freshly shucked oysters. The healthy portions will challenge the most gluttonous appetite and there's a good range of Aussie wines and ice cold beers to help wash it all down. Despite the celebrity status (and visitors) Doyles retains the air of a cosy seaside chippy. There are also outlets at Circular Quay and the Fish Market.

19-21 Pirrama Rd
Jones Bay Wharf
Pyrmont

Flying Fish

9518 6677 | *www.flyingfish.com.au*

Whether you're dining or simply want to have a drink with friends, you'll feel all the more glamorous just for the experience here. Head chef Peter Kuruvita delights with his much celebrated fare, which starts with seafood tapas and ends seemingly hours later with a dessert plate followed by coffee and petit fours. Group functions are a specialty, held in the Wine Room with its two-story loft style space or in the Arcadia Room, which can host up to 20 guests on two tables. Flying Fish also caters well to vegetarians and for those who prefer their fish Japanese-style, the raw bar is a must. Mains start at $37.

2/21 Broughton St
Kirribilli

Garfish

9922 4322 | *www.garfish.com.au*

From snapper pie to the spanner crab with basil gnocchi, you're guaranteed freshness without fuss at Garfish. Specialising in lesser-known fish species has ensured a roaring and returning trade, with the restaurant expanding to meet demand. There are also outlets in Crows Nest and Manly, but back in Kirribilli, it's rare to find an empty seat, either inside the small yet chic dining room or at the outside tables, shaded by large umbrellas. Breakfast is also popular at Garfish, with diners ordering up waffles with banana, ricotta and passionfruit, washed down with well-made coffee.

Imax
31 Wheat Rd
Darling Harbour

Ice Cube Seafood Grill Bar

8267 3666 | *www.icecubeseafood.com.au*

Even at full capacity, the service at Ice Cube is as slick as the interior. While many choose to sit indoors and ogle the wall-sized wine collection, for others, the chance to sit next to busy Darling Harbour is too good to refuse. Just when you think the Ice Cube experience couldn't get better – out comes the food. The taster plate starter at just $20 per head is full of fresh, perfectly pan-cooked seafood. The mains continue to please, with hearty, tasty servings that will leave you full, yet somehow wanting more. Don't leave without a serving of tiramisu. If you love to people watch, arrive early and have a drink at the adjacent Ice Cube Bar.

Ice Cube Seafood Grill

Flying Fish

Café Sydney

Doyles

93-95 North Steyne
Manly

Jellyfish
9977 4555

Manly locals love Jellyfish for its casual class. Here, eating a breakfast of smoked salmon and eggs is an experience rather than just a meal and one coffee will never be enough. Come dinner, the ocean views go perfectly with the menu of fresh seafood, from the snapper to the seared kingfish. The experience is made all the more enjoyable thanks to the friendly, upbeat staff who would never hurry you from your seat, despite the eager patrons looming in line.

South American

474 Cleveland St
Surry Hills

Casapueblo
9319 6377 | *www.casapueblorestaurant.com*

This busy restaurant, with its whitewashed walls and well considered decor, is a slice of South America in Sydney. The owners have made the most of the space in this small terrace house to accommodate the ever-increasing crowd who come for Zulma Otero's authentic cuisine. Start with the tapas, which can include anything from potatoes with peanuts, cheese and chilli to crumbed mussels stuffed with spice. Move on to a main of pastel de choclo – a beef, chicken and corn casserole. The chaja, a traditional meringue and cream dessert, is worth leaving room for. If your visit to Casapueblo puts you in the party mood, you'll be pleased to know they also offer a catering service.

14 Gardeners Rd
Kingsford
Randwick

La Cumbia

9662 8231 | *www.lacumbia.com.au*

You won't leave hungry after a visit to La Cumbia, which cheerily serves hearty dishes inspired by the cuisines of Mexico, Columbia, Peru and Spain. Meatlovers will rejoice at the endless choices here, including the bandeja paisa, a Columbian meal of beans, rice, beef mince, pork, egg, fried banana, avocado and Spanish chorizo. In addition to great tapas, there's also a party menu. Whatever you go for, you should be looking at around $25 per head. There's also a selection of Columbian beers available, from $4.50.

Spanish/Portuguese

Other options **Mediterranean** p.335

54 West Esplanade
Manly

Alhambra Café and Tapas Bar

9976 2975

Pull up a pew and dine alfresco at Alhambra, as Manly's famous ferries pull up just outside. While the big boats put on a show, there's also a jovial atmosphere inside this popular restaurant, with flamboyant flamenco dancers and Spanish guitarists entertaining a happy crowd from Thursday to Saturday. The food, prepared using the best of Moroccan and Spanish know-how, is also worth celebrating. You can sample the Charmoula sardines marinated in a blend of herbs and Moroccan spices then pan fried and served with Spanish onion and fresh tomato salsa for just $14. Or you can go for dishes like chargrilled swordfish with olive and caper salsa, topped with capsicum jam and lemon sauce and potato scallops for $26.

82 Audley St
Petersham

Café Gloria

9568 3966

Judging by its popularity with the Portuguese community, Café Gloria is doing something right. Take comfort in the chunky pine furniture and sample authentic Portuguese food, dished up in healthy-sized servings. You'll definitely manage to find space for the red bean stew (feijoada) of bacon, pork, beef and salami served with piles of rice and you may even push the limits and order from the array of tempting desserts – all for a moderate fee.

423 Pitt St
Central

Encasa

9211 4257 | *www.encasarestaurant.com*

Encasa's roaring trade has much to do with its tasty tapas at affordable prices in a city where finding good Spanish food is difficult. You may be sharing elbowroom with hungry students, backpackers and knowing locals, all keen to discover what all the excitement is about. For $6.50 you'll get a good serving of olives stuffed with preserved lemon before heading for the mains, which start at $19. If you want to ensure a seat, be sure to book ahead, particularly on the weekend. On most busy nights, with no booking you can expect to wait for up to half an hour.

Cnr Liverpool and
George Sts
Central

Grand Taverna

9267 3608

You're guaranteed sizeable servings of hearty Spanish sustenance with a visit to Grand Taverna, tucked away in Sydney's Spanish quarter. Those who know about it flock to this pub restaurant for cheap eats over a cold brew, whether it's a local beer or a jug of sangria ($16). The tasty tapas of marinated baby octopus, barbecue and spicy prawns and garlic mushrooms is a popular choice as a shared starter, as is the $28 banquet as a main. Servings here are generous – for $40 you'll be assured of a mixed seafood platter that well and truly fills the gap.

Steakhouses

Other options **South American** p.341

Various locations

Hog's Breath

9130 8045 | *www.hogsbreath.com.au*

A franchise eatery it may be, but there's good reason why this Australian steakhouse went from one to 68 restaurants within 17 years. The steak is good enough to convert a vegetarian; the cuts are slow cooked over 18 hours and then seared on a high temperature chargrill before being served. The saloon-style restaurant, with its novel hog's tail fries, is Australian in heritage, yet feels more American in style, with old-school Hollywood celebrity memorabilia and United States number plates tacked to the timber walls. After dinner, you can finish off with a drink in the separate bar area.

9 Cowper Wharf Rd
Woolloomooloo

Kingsleys

1300 546 475 | *www.steak.com.au*

Vegetarians need not venture into Kingsleys, unless they're happy to dine on seafood. With steaks seared to perfection, locals depend on this restaurant, with its city skyline and Woolloomooloo Bay views, when they're craving a sizable serving of meat. Seafood lovers shouldn't go past the soft shell, mud or snow crabs. These are served cold with mayonnaise, teamed with Maryland lemon butter or wok fried with a hot, sticky tomato, black bean and chilli sauce. You can wash it all down with a selection of local and imported beers.

80 Henry St
Penrith
Outer West

Madisons Chargrill

4721 2222 | *www.madisonschargrill.com.au*

The service is as good as the succulent steak at this award-winning restaurant, where it's a genuine challenge to clean your plate. With the generous portions, you'll be thankful that there's plenty of room to spread out here, with wide, linen-clothed tables and dining chairs you'd expect to find in a well-to-do home. Enjoy Angus grain steaks cooked to perfection, an extensive selection of house wine and if you still have some space left, try the delectable strawberries smothered in chocolate.

1 Martin Place
Central

Prime Restaurant

9229 7777 | *www.gposydney.com*

Make sure you take a big appetite (and perhaps a bigger than usual budget) to Prime, in the cool depths of the city's GPO building. The sandstone interior, with large leather bucket seats and crisp tablecloths sets the stage for a truly chic and unique experience. Recognised for its excellence, the steak here is served just how it should be and there's a sommelier on hand to help you match a wine to your meal. Non-carnivores can choose from the ample seafood offerings, including Sydney rock oysters with an eschalot dipping sauce at $35 per dozen. If you're in an extravagant mood, you can't beat the 450g Wagyu Chateaubriand, served with gratin potatoes and sauce bordelaise for two at $170.

Thai

28 Macleay St
Potts Point

Arun Thai

9326 9135 | *www.arunthai.com.au*

Loyal fans have been coming to this relaxed haven to escape the busy streets of Potts Point for two decades. Arrive early to enjoy Thai tapas and drinks at the bar area, before being seated by the attentive staff at linen-clothed tables. For those who're after a hit of true Thai spice, the pla nung manow, from the chef's signature menu

selection, is a must-try, with its steamed wild barramundi fillet swimming in lemongrass, garlic, chilli and lime juice. Vegetarians are well catered for too, with fresh dishes such as pad snow pea and pad poy sein – stir fried mixed vegetables with vermicelli, mushrooms, snow peas and bean curd.

Arun Thai

Bank's Thai

91 Enmore Rd
Enmore

9550 6840

Expect only authentic Thai food and decor at this busy restaurant, which has expanded to keep up with demand. A great venue for birthday celebrations and get togethers, meals won't break the bank and are served up by consistently friendly staff, no matter how rushed they become. You can enjoy the popular salt and pepper squid as you settle into the courtyard, roof garden or main restaurant area with a bottle of BYO wine, before moving on to a simmering curry of prawns, banana chillies and coconut. Vegetarians will love the fried rice.

Nu's

178 Blues Point Rd
North Sydney

9954 1780

Sydneysiders are spoiled for choice when it comes to Thai restaurants, but recently opened Nu's is a much-welcomed addition. It has quickly become known for its traditional dishes, creatively infused with flavours that sing of the Mediterranean, France and Asia. The $9 Thai tapas is a great way to start your culinary excursion here, as you ponder a menu that features dishes of deep fried snapper, chargrilled scallops and wok-fried pork hock, prepared by talented Thai chef Nu Suandokmai. Before opening this romantic two-storey restaurant, he kept Adelaide's appetite for clever Thai satisfied with his first restaurant. Service here is fast and friendly without fault. A must visit.

Oceanic Thai

309 Clovelly Rd
Clovelly

9665 8942 | *www.oceanicthai.com.au*

If you really need an excuse to visit the relaxed seaside neighbourhood of Clovelly, Oceanic Thai should be it. Once your eyes have adjusted to the moody lighting, cast them towards the brief menu, with starters for just $4.50 and mains for $26. You could try the smoked silver perch with its caramelised salty crunch to start before moving on to a fish and radish and sour orange curry. Then allow the savvy staff to serve you a plate of Thai desserts for two; it's a sound investment of $18.

Spice I am

90 Wentworth Ave
Surry Hills

9280 0928 | *www.spiceiam.com*

A first glance might suggest this small and crowded eatery in Surry Hills is more of a cheap cafeteria than a quality restaurant, but don't be too hasty to judge. It has been awarded a Thai Select mark by the Thai government for its authenticity and quality. Executive chef Sujet Saenkham's passion is obvious with every bite. From the melt-in-your-mouth hor mok (Phuket-style steamed fish mousse) to the koong mah-karm (deep fried king prawns in tamarind sauce) it's hard to make a wrong choice. As the name suggests, food here is hot, so be sure to tell the very efficient staff if you'd prefer yours mild.

346 New South Head Rd
Double Bay

Thai Riffic

9362 9546

There are a few Thai Riffic's dotted around Sydney, from the north shore to the Shire. It doesn't really matter which one you visit, you're always guaranteed fresh, wholesome Thai. Filling and affordable, there's little need to order a starter, with main dishes costing around $20. With its heavy, timber bench seating, scattered with Balinese-style cushions, Thai Riffic is a popular lunchtime meeting place. At night, the quick, obliging staff keep the hordes of regular diners content.

Vegetarian

College St
Cook and Phillip Park
Central

Bodhi in the Park

9360 2523

You can relax here all afternoon in the courtyard as you tuck into vegetarian yum cha or other Asian delights. Bodhi in the Park is a tranquil escape from the city buzz and the alfresco dining makes it perfect for a weekend catch up with friends. Yum cha ranges from $4.50 to $7.50. While service can be patchy and aloof at times, the menu makes up for it.

112 Darlinghurst Rd
Darlinghurst

Govinda's Restaurant and Cinema

9380 5162

You're guaranteed to be well fed and well entertained at Govinda's, where locals flock to feast on plentiful vegetarian food before catching a movie in the boutique cinema. For just $16.90, you can sample the ever-changing Indian menu, which always features favourites such as dal soup, vegetable curry and cauliflower pakoras. For just an extra $7.90 you'll be ushered upstairs, where you can lounge on upholstered cushions on the floor. Beyond the meals and movies, Govinda's is a treasure trove of all things holistic, with meditation classes, yoga and various workshops on offer.

182 King St
Newtown

Green Palace

9550 5234

With its generous portions, you'll be hard pushed not to leave food on your plate at Green Palace. Thai chef Kijja Silanuluck started out cooking his flavoursome food at some of the city's temples. Today he ensures a continuous flow of loyal customers with his crispy faux duck salad and enticing curries, washed down with Thai iced tea. Cuisine here is cooked with care and served by friendly staff who are only too happy to talk you through the menu. You can't help but leaving Green Palace feeling more centred and zen, and very full.

612 Darling St
Rozelle

Iku Wholefood Kitchen

9810 5155 | www.iku.com.au

They use more than 200 organic and biodynamic ingredients in the food prepared at Iku, making it one of Sydney's favourite vegetarian outlets. With stores all over the city, it has never been easier to sit down to a lasagne of mushroom, tofu, garlic and chives and a casserole of adzuki bean, pumpkin and ginger. This healthy crew take their philosophy beyond gluten-free, chemical-free, fresh ingredients. The cleaning products used in the central Marrickville kitchen are environmentally sound, while any water used is filtered (they're even happy to invite customers into the kitchen to see for themselves). With such care taken in the selection and preparation, you would expect to pay more than $8.50 for a curry of spicy tamarind tofu-tempeh, or $7 for a sesame and vanilla fudge tart.

Vietnamese

Bay Tinh
316-318 Victoria Rd
Marrickville
Outer West

9560 8673

Many have wondered if chef Van Tinh Tran realises that his loyal customers would pay much more for his authentic Vietnamese tucker. If you stop long enough to peer through the yellowing lace curtains, you'll quickly realise there's much more than meets the eye here. As the newspaper reviews taped to the front window will tell you, Tran once cooked for dignitaries in his home country and later brought his culinary skills Down Under. You can't go wrong with a serving of beef cubes, deep fried fish or vegetable spring rolls, served up by traditionally dressed staff who turn your order around quickly.

Phamish
354 Liverpool St
Darlinghurst

9357 2688

People don't mind waiting for a seat at vibrant Phamish, with its spritely red walls and friendly order-at-the-counter service. Get in early if you want to be guaranteed a table, where you (and up to six friends) can dine on the much-ordered salt and pepper squid, duck pancakes and swimmer crab dumplings, all over a bottle of BYO wine. While it's not a restaurant where you can linger for hours well after the meal has ended, Phamish is great when you're after a filling feed before a night out.

Phuong
87 Willoughby Rd
Crows Nest
Outer North

9439 2621

They must be doing something right here; this is one of Sydney's longest serving Vietnamese restaurants. While the cheap prices have ensured customers keep coming back, it's more the quality of the fresh, flavoursome dishes that makes this one a favourite. To start, you could try the freshly prepared rice paper rolls, a tasty combination of pork, prawns, chicken, lettuce, bean sprouts, vermicelli and mint. If you're dining with friends, you won't go wrong with the $25 banquet, served inside or out at this consistently busy restaurant. While the decor may not have changed in 30 years, those who love it wouldn't want it any other way.

Red Lantern
545 Crown St
Surry Hills

9698 4355

There's a modern take on traditional at Red Lantern, where diners frequent the dark timbered interior for vegetarian rice flour crepes and salt and pepper calamari. Staff are well versed in the menu and you may want to skip lunch so you can fit it all in. It's constantly busy here and competition for tables is stiff, but once you're in, you'll see what all the fuss is about. When you've placed and paid for your order, make your way back to the table of comfy red stools and wait for your mild goat curry or seared roast duck with Asian greens and tamarind plum sauce to arrive.

Tran's
523 Military Rd
Spit Junction
Mosman

9969 9275 | *www.transrestaurant.com.au*

Good times and great food are a given at Tran's; just ask the regulars who fill the tables each night. Ancient cooking styles of southern Vietnam, with hints of a French and Chinese influence, are served up in the softly-lit surrounds under the direction of Lanna Tran, who takes pride in her fresh food. She even grows her own herbs, using them to create the delicate flavours of the ever-changing menu. Favourites include the crisp rice pancakes, lemongrass pork belly with rice noodles, mint, lime juice and fish sauce and the che chuoi (banana stewed in coconut cream with tapioca). The restaurant also holds special banquet nights to celebrate events like the Vietnamese New Year.

Cafes & Coffee Shops
Other options **Afternoon Tea** p.349

Arty Latte
Bathers' Pavilion (p.347) has opened a small art gallery upstairs, while downstairs there is a renowned cafe and restaurant. This is always busy and right on the beach. The Art Gallery of NSW (p.366) has a great cafe, which overlooks Woolloomooloo wharf. Similarly, the Museum of Contemporary Art (p.167) has a cute coffee shop. It's worth a cappuccino.

As one of the world's most eclectic food capitals, Sydney is bursting at the seams with cafes. Through the week these become a second home to office workers, but come the weekend the vibe is decidedly more relaxed. Chairs and tables spill out onto the pavements, regardless of location, and you'd be hard pressed to find a corner without a cafe. Families are welcome and catered for in most cafes here, which generally open at the crack of dawn, particularly on weekends. The ever-popular Bathers' Pavilion in Balmoral opens at 07:00 and closes late to keep up with the demand for cafe-style dining. The food served is strongly influenced by the city's multicultural population, and many places also cater to those with diet restrictions such as gluten and lactose intolerances. And for coffee or gourmet food-on-the-go, chains such as Starbucks are dotted all over the city and its suburbs.

4 The Esplanade
Balmoral Beach

Bathers' Pavilion
9969 5050 | www.batherspavilion.com.au
It's not just the stunning location that attracts people here, owner and chef Serge Danserau's menus are amongst the best in town, and this, combined with the friendly and efficient staff ensures the crowds keep pouring in. Bathers' Pavilion is considered as much a city landmark as the Harbour Bridge. Once a changing shed for swimmers, it's now a welcoming and stylish haven of private dining rooms with an a la carte restaurant, bar and cafe. Of a weekend, the latter bustles with hungry brunchers who are more than willing to perch at the bar, coffee in hand, in wait of the next table. Try the eggs Benedict, which are possibly the best in Sydney. This is one restaurant you'll be back to again.

316 Victoria Ave
Chatswood
Outer North

Café Andronicus
9413 1494
The food here is good but the coffee is even better. Andronicus is a cafe that consistently seems to be near full capacity, both day and night. While the cement floors were made for easy cleaning, they do little to dull the noise from the traffic outside, or the buzz of fellow diners. Still, you can drown out the din with your own chatter, in between a look at your favourite newspapers, which hang alongside glossy magazines on the wall. Service here is kept at a steady, cheerful pace and you're never made to feel you've overstayed your welcome, no matter how many hours pass by. If you're on for a lazy day, be sure to order a chai latte between coffees for a really sweet treat.

1/2 Danks St
Waterloo

Danks Street Depot
9698 2201 | www.danksstreetdepot.com.au
There's always something new to try here, thanks to Jared Ingersoll's menu, which changes daily. Hungry patrons fill the long room with its clean, modern lines, waiting to sample new and exciting dishes. Favourites include the slow-cooked broccoli served on scrambled eggs and toast with feta and parsley for breakfast, and the pan roasted salmon fillet with soy beans wakami, baby spinach and horseradish vinaigrette for lunch. They also do a mean cocktail here and have an extensive list of imported beers. Lunchtime mains start at $12.50.

347

Cowper Wharf Rd
Woolloomooloo

Harry's Café de Wheels
9357 3074

If it's traditional Aussie takeaway tucker you're after, follow in celebrity footsteps and make a stop at Harry's. This 60-year-old Aussie icon has fed many an A-lister, tourist and local after a night out on the town with its authentic meat pies with mash and peas, as well as hot dogs and pasties. On the walls you'll see its colourful history, full of photographs of the celebrities who've been there. Don't expect five-star cuisine from this must-visit eatery – it's plastic knives and forks all the way. Shutters stay open 24 hours.

61 Annandale St
Annandale

Hopscotch
9560 2698

People come here as much for the scrabble and kid's games as the food. This is where the little ones are welcome and your teapot gets refilled free of charge. Locals come for relaxed weekend brunches, where they can sit inside or out, as they catch up on the latest with the Sunday papers. This charming eatery is so popular that a short wait for a table is guaranteed, but that's no worry to the regulars who know only too well what's in store. The friendly, chatty staff serve up great coffee over eggs cooked to perfection, served with salmon that's smoked in-house. If the kids get restless, there's plenty here to keep them occupied, leaving you to enjoy the last crumbs of the delicious homemade cake.

31-37 Oxford St
Bondi

Macro Wholefoods Café
9004 1240 | *www.macrowholefoods.com.au*

There's something about Macro that makes you feel healthier just for walking through the Crows Nest or Bondi Junction doors. The cafe, and adjoining organic market, are abuzz with weekend workout-ers, famished friends and families in search of an organic meal that's more than just a carrot on a plate. Fussy foodies love it for its varied menu, which incorporates all tastes and tolerances, from gluten-free to soy. Don't leave without experiencing the buckwheat pancakes with berries and bananas or the scrambled tofu, washed down with a cup of dandelion tea.

MCA Café

140 George St
The Rocks

9241 4253 | *www.culinaryedge.com.au*

It's alfresco dining at its absolute finest at the MCA Café, with its sunny Circular Quay views and modern Asian menu. People watch, with the Opera House as a backdrop, as you dig into freshly shucked oysters and sip on well chosen wines by the glass. This is consistently popular with lunchtime crowds, so it's a good idea to prebook. While the sometimes-frosty service may deter you a bit, the roasted barramundi with cauliflower puree, chestnuts, oyster mushrooms and seared scallops will ensure a return visit. If it's just a coffee you're after, try it over a dessert of peach, raspberry and marscapone trifle. Entrees at MCA Café start at $18 and mains at $25.

Plonk! Beach Café

Ferguson's Marina
Spit Bridge
Mosman

9960 1007 | *www.plonkbeachcafe.com.au*

If it's a sunny Sydney day, this is a great place to do lunch with family or friends. The polished timber-decked floors add to the seaside ambience of this popular licensed cafe-cum-restaurant, where service is attentive and the simple, straightforward menu is ample enough to satisfy. Be sure to take along a bucket and spade so the kids can frolic on the nearby stretch of sand while you savour the last spoonfuls of flourless orange and almond tart from the tempting dessert menu. Entrees start at $9.50, mains from $20 and sweets from $10.

Well Connected

35 Glebe Point Rd
Glebe

9566 2655

Brunchers, lunchers and evening diners spill out onto the streets where they sit on retro-styled chairs, poring over the latest news in the local rag. Flip-flops are welcome at this relaxed cafe, which serves up filling brekkie greats such as eggs Benedict with ham (or salmon if you prefer). The lunchtime crowd meld into the burgundy swivel bucket chairs as they feast on various sarnies - either vegetarian or bursting with fillings of bacon, lettuce, tomato and avocado. Also great for just a catch up with friends over well-brewed coffee and cake, this brightly painted eatery could cure the most dire of hangovers.

Yellow Bistro & Food Store

57 Macleay Street
Potts Point

9357 3400

The walls are certainly yellow here, but it's more than just the paintwork that makes this place shine. A slice of homemade pie will cost you around $13 (try owner Lorraine Godsmark's much talked about date tart), but every last mouthful is worth it. Washed down with a perfectly brewed coffee, or a good glass of wine, it's easy to lose a couple of hours here on a lazy Saturday afternoon. If you're looking for food-to-go, Yellow is a must-visit for its home baked delights. Vegetarians are also well catered for here.

Afternoon Tea

Other options **Cafes & Coffee Shops** p.347

To escape the city, many locals drive to the Blue Mountains for high tea. The most popular place is the Mercure Grand Hydro Majestic Hotel (www.hydromajestic.com.au). Built in 1904, it overlooks the magnificent Megalong Valley. If you'd prefer to stay in

---

Hidden Charges

In most places, you shouldn't get any nasty surprises with the bill. Remember that on public holidays you'll always pay a 10% surcharge and some places even add 10% on Sundays. A Goods and Services Tax (GST) of 10% is always included in the final price. If bottled water is on the table, you'll be charged. Tap water is safe to drink, so if the waiter does bring bottled water that you didn't order, feel free to send it back. Bread is always complimentary unless you order garlic or herb varieties, when the price should be on the menu.

Sydney, The Tearoom (www.thetearoom.com.au) at the Queen Victoria Building does silver service morning and afternoon tea, which is served daily from 11:00. Also check out The Harbour Kitchen (www.harbourkitchen.com.au), which combines afternoon tea with monthly fashion shows.

Internet Cafes
Other options **Internet** p.113

It seems wherever there's electricity, there's a computer with internet access in Sydney. Besides the countless hostels and hotels that offer the service, there are also plenty of stand-alone outlets that can be found. Expect to pay around $3 per hour during the day and, in most cases, a cheaper rate at night. Getting online is easiest in suburbs such as Bondi, Kings Cross and Chinatown thanks to their big backpacker populations. Those who would prefer to avoid the masses can experience a more personalised service at outlets such as the more pricey Well Connected Internet Café – one of the city's first, with comfy lounges and good coffee. Other favourites include the Global Gossip chain, which is also good for international phone calls (www.globalgossip.com.au) and City Hunter (www.cityhunter.com.au). See p.113 for more on internet access.

Internet Cafes		
B Game Internet Cafe	Outer West	9831 6577
Beachnet Internet Cafe	Outer North	9984 8806
Cafology	Outer West	9554 7055
City Hunter	Various locations	9261 0768
Connect On King	Newtown	9517 4726
Cyber Hut	Outer South	9344 6777
Dc Productions	Outer West	9896 0033
Eastwest Network	Central	9797 9729
Global Gossip	Various locations	
Netplanet Cybercafe	Bondi	9386 4936
Well Connected	Glebe	9566 2655

Fruit Juices
Other options **Cafes & Coffee Shops** p.347

Sydney likes to think of itself as a healthy city, which has encouraged franchise and independent juice bars to pop up everywhere – from shopping malls to beachside strips. While the bigger juice companies have been reprimanded for promising their fruity blends will lead you to a slimmer butt and a stress free life, it hasn't damaged the $150 million industry, with a thirsty Sydney public continuing to guzzle away. Favourites include Australia's biggest, Boost Juice (www.boostjuicebars.com), as well as a selection of smaller bars including Sejuiced (www.sejuiced.com.au) in Bronte and La Passion Du Fruit (9690 1894) in Surry Hills. Stressed-out suits line up morning and night for their shot of wheatgrass, while workout mums can't get enough of their skinny smoothies with a burst of TD5 – a Boost Juice yoghurt which is said to be lower in calories.

The world has much to offer.
It's just knowing where to find it.

If you're an American Express® Cardmember, simply visit
americanexpress.com/selects or visit your local homepage, and click on
'offers'. You'll find great offers wherever you are today, all in one place.

selects

AMERICAN
EXPRESS

THE WORLD OFFERS. WE SELECT. YOU ENJOY.

Drinking & Driving

Unless you injure someone, it's unlikely that you will go to jail for a first offence. But, you'll have your licence suspended for a minimum of three months and a fine of up to $5,000. Zero tolerance applies to all learner drivers and those on provisional one or two licences. More details can be found on p.136. For taxis, check the table on p.44 and for other public transport options go to p.40.

Bars

Other options **Pubs** p.355, **Nightclubs** p.358

While the true Aussie male can still find a traditional corner pub that serves up his favourite brew on tap, the Sydney bar and pub scene also caters to those after something a little swankier. Whether it's the best cocktails in town (try the Water Bar at the Blue Hotel in Woolloomooloo, 9331 9000) or somewhere to munch on traditional tapas over imported champagne (try Hugos in Kings Cross, see p.339), you can find it in Sydney. Competition is fierce for the drinker's dollar. Big bucks have been spent on award-winning architecture with moody lighting, drawing in crowds from the inner city and beachside suburbs alike. You won't have to look far to find a pub or bar that offers half-price drinks at happy hour or with a widescreen television to catch the latest game. The only challenge is finding a seat in your chosen spot. Weekday workers tend to hit their favourite local from around 16:00 on Fridays. You'll find many an expat frequenting the Coogee or Bondi bar scene at hip outlets such as Ravesi's (9365 4422), but there are plenty of other choices for those looking for a taste of home. The Elephant and Wheelbarrow in Paddington (9360 9668) is a favourite for its classic British offerings, from the dinner and drinks down to the decor.

Door Policy

Sydney bouncers share from the excess of self importance suffered by door staff across the world. As anywhere, if you're a bit mouthy or drunk, you're less likely to cross the velvet rope.

It's fine to wear jeans and a t-shirt to the down-to-earth bars, but at the more pretentious ones, you won't get in if you're not dressed the part. You need to be over 18 and ID checks are frequent so make sure you bring your license or passport along. Men will find it harder than women to get past the bouncers, so it's easier if you're in a mixed group. You generally don't have to be a member to get in anywhere, unless it's full, in which case members get priority. To join most places, just grab a form from staff or log onto the bar's website.

Dress Code

The look is more casual Down Under than in Europe but as always, dress code changes from one place to the next. Women can wear almost anything they like but men should stick to collared shirts if they're going anywhere classier than the local pub and swap trainers for shoes. In summer, when the heat is soaring, stick to short sleeved tops. Air-conditioning is generally at a good temperature so you don't need to worry about bringing a jacket. In winter a warm coat is essential, as Sydney does get cold.

Shangri-La Hotel
176 Cumberland St
The Rocks

The Blu Horizon Bar

9250 6000 | *www.shangri-la.com*

The cocktails waiting at the top of the Shangri-La Hotel are well worth the 36-storey ride. While hotel guests make up much of the clientele here, it's also a popular spot for Sydneysiders looking for a well-made drink in a sexy bar. You can order one of 300 cocktails, mixed to perfection by the world champion flair bartender and a team of mixologists. While it's not the cheapest place in town, it's worth paying that bit extra for the spectacular views.

24 Darlinghurst Rd
Kings Cross

The Bourbon

9358 1144 | *www.thebourbon.com.au*

It's all about polished pub grub and people watching at this once rundown Kings Cross favourite. While Russell Crowe has been known to hang out here, it's not just the celeb set that come for the big mounds of beef nachos with guacamole and sour cream ($14). Locals love the $10 lunches, served every day, which guarantee a feed of 250-gram prime rib, fries or mash, a choice of sauces and a green salad on the side. The modern seating, in fresh hues of lime and chocolate with splashes of red, is quickly filled when $3 happy hour arrives, from Monday to Thursday between 18:00 and 21:00. Check the website for the up-to-date entertainment calendar.

18 Opera Quays
Circular Quay

Bubble Champagne Cocktail Lounge

9251 0311

Sydney's first and only dedicated champagne lounge, Bubble is home to 30 of the best varieties, making it a must-visit for its sumptuous cocktails. The A-listers, suits and eastern suburb socialites flock here for its signature cocktail, Bubblicious – a mix of Plymouth gin, raspberries, lemon juice and a touch of sugar, topped with champagne. With its Circular Quay view, Bubble is a top spot for a relaxed and fun night out with friends.

Quay Grand
63 Macquarie St
Circular Quay

ECQ Bar

9256 4000

It's swanky but not too pompous at the ECQ Bar. Choose from the extensive wine and cocktail list as you order from the delicious $26 tapas menu, which features chargrilled Turkish bread, guacamole, tapenade, marinated olives and all of the usual trimmings. For those who get the midnight munchies over a glass of chilled ale, you can also order the more filling wedges and sour cream. Private functions are also popular here, with ECQ catering for up to 100 guests with canapes, from $28 per person.

86 Walker St
North Sydney

The Firehouse

8904 9696 | *www.firehousehotel.com.au*

As its name suggests, The Firehouse once housed the big red trucks, but much to the locals' delight, it's now a funky bar. While North Sydney can seem like a ghost town once the workers have clocked off, the full rooms of The Firehouse would suggest they've all come here to enjoy dinner or the $14 cocktails. You can sit upstairs in the lounge, garden or airy balcony after you've ordered from the bar, or head down to the cocktail lounge, with its comfortable sofas and leather stools.

15 Kellett St
Kings Cross

Iguana Bar and Restaurant

9357 2609

In colourful Kings Cross, with its bright lights and ladies of the night, sits the Iguana Bar. It's the perfect spot for those looking for a filling Aussie meal, a late night snack or just a drink at the dimly lit bar. Considered a city celebrity haven since way back, you can check out the photo evidence plastered to the walls. Local fare, from kangaroo to barramundi, is on the menu, which easily impresses the tourists and satisfies the locals. The prices will leave you with more than enough change to keep the party going.

16-18 Cross St
Double Bay

JAM Wine & Tapas Bar

9327 3533

Moroccan-inspired JAM Wine and Tapas Bar in well-to-do Double Bay is not your typical boozer. The supper club-cum-restaurant-cum lounge is a chilled out meeting place for suits looking for classy after-work sips, or for friends wanting to catch up over a $17 cocktail. Settle in with a furry chinchilla on your lap (the cocktail that is) while

353

you choose from the tempting tapas on offer, including generous servings of mussels, prawns, and baby clams in a white wine, tomato and garlic sauce. Or, if the bubbles from the French champagne are bouncing around on an empty stomach, ensure your longevity with a crisp pizza of roast pumpkin, Persian feta, pine nuts and rocket pesto.

3 Lime St
King Street Wharf
Darling Harbour

The Loft Bar

9299 4770 | *www.theloftsydney.com*

The Loft Bar is as well dressed as its beautiful clientele. Laze back into large leather sofas with your drink in hand, surrounded by dazzling, light-filled, timber panelled walls and Sydney water views. The Loft's cocktail selections are endless and take their inspiration from flavours of the Middle East, Mediterranean, Far East and the Americas, overseen by leading mixologist Garth Foster. The eastern breakfast martini is a must, with its quince jam, shaken with Absolut citron, cointreau, orange bitters and garnished with an orange twist.

255 Darling St
Balmain

The Monkey Bar

9810 1749 | *www.monkeybar.com.au*

Catch the ferry to Balmain and enjoy a beer with the locals at The Monkey Bar. This popular watering hole is home to lively entertainment and good food, from its function rooms, bistro and courtyard. Whether it's your first visit or your 50th, the friendly staff will make you feel right at home. Sophisticated, yet relaxed, The Monkey Bar, which also has an outlet in Chatswood, serves up modern Australian cuisine combined with a decent selection of Australian and New Zealand wines. While it's great for a catch up with friends, it's also popular for a romantic dinner.

231 Victoria St
Darlinghurst

The Victoria Room

www.thevictoriaroom.com

It's pretty classy at The Victoria Room, a popular meeting place for after-work drinks or proper weekend catch-ups. The antique furniture and vintage style sets the scene for a very polite champagne supper. The velvety sofas and deep armchairs give a sense of old fashioned decadence that is very deliberate and very good fun. The high teas are particularly popular, as patrons lose an afternoon to quaffing fine champagne, tea and scones.

Cocktail Lounges

The bars in Sydney do fantastic cocktails. Lotus Bar (p.318) in trendy Potts Point is still the place to go for cocktails and the atmosphere is surprisingly unpretentious and low-key. The most popular drink here is the celestial martini (Plymouth gin, elderflower cordial, apple juice, limejuice, and kaffir lime leaf). Lotus recently won the *Bartender* magazine Cocktail Bar of the Year award for 2006. Other cocktail spots worth checking out include Bubble (p.353), Blu Horizon (p.352) and Icebergs (p.335) at Bondi for views of Sydney's most iconic beach.

Sports Bars

Cheers Bar (www.cheersbar.com.au) on George Street is well known and if a big game is on this place will be heaving. Even if you're not a rugby fan, you'll still have a good night out at the Wallaby Bar (www.wallabybar.com.au). The Dolphin (www.dolphinhotel.com.au) in Surry Hills has recently been renovated and always pulls in a friendly crowd. The focus is, naturally, on Australian sports. Cricket and rugby take precedence over everything else, although the English premiership does get quite good coverage. Fans of other sports may struggle to follow their team back home. A list of pubs showing SKY Channel Australia (which shows more international sport) is on p.355.

354

Pubs

Other options **Bars** p.352

The pub is an Aussie institution, and wherever you find yourself in Sydney, it's unlikely you won't have to search too far for a drink. The law used to be that only hotels could serve alcohol in Australia, so all of Sydney's oldest and most traditional drinking dens have some sort of digs upstairs, though these are rarely still hired out. Most neighborhoods will have a local hotel where you can meet the natives, though some are more salubrious than others. Hotel's in the inner-city suburbs have become fairly trendy and are as likely to serve Thai fishcakes and European lagers as pies and VB. The welcome is likely to be friendly wherever you find yourself. Even at the city's shabbiest pubs, the atmosphere will be nothing more than raucous and is unlikely to be intimidating.

Beer

While there isn't a particular beer that can be pigeonholed as iconic to Sydney, there are a host of great Australian lagers that locals love. James Boags (Tasmania), Cascade Premium (Tas), Coopers (South Australia) and Redback (Western Australia) are good premium beers. Standard Aussie beers like Victoria Bitter (Victoria), Tooheys New (NSW), XXXX (Queensland) and Swan (WA) are iconic in their home states but aren't rated that highly elsewhere. Two NSW boutique beers worth trying are St Arnou and Little Creatures. There are two sizes of beer, midis and schooners and prices start at about $2.

267 Oxford St
Darlinghurst

Beauchamp Hotel

9331 2575

Many an Oxford Street shopper has stopped off for a quick thirst quencher at the Beauchamp. With its second-floor courtyard surrounded in creeping vines and mirrors, this sexy hotel has a bit more about it than most pubs. Head downstairs and you'll discover a basement decked in heavy, comfortable lounges filled with a funky, twenty and thirty-something clientele. Once you're done lounging, there's a popular pool area. The staff here are charming, friendly and handle the demanding weekend crowds with aplomb.

456 Darling St
Balmain

The Cat & Fiddle

9810 7931 | *www.thecatandfiddle.net*

The Cat & Fiddle is best known for its live music, and many of the city's better live bands have made their mark here first, with most going on to feature on the pub's album releases *Live at the Cat*, volumes one and two. The music is typically indie, blues and rock, but beyond all that, people come here to share stories over a drink at one of the two large bars, where, despite its popularity, finding a seat never seems a problem. The food at The Cat & Fiddle is good pub grub at affordable prices, ensuring you'll be back for more.

470 Crown St ◀
Surry Hills

The Clock Hotel

9331 5333

The Clock Hotel is always abuzz with a loyal crowd who come here to mingle over drinks or for a quality meal. The food ranges from good pub grub to more sophisticated, Mediterranean-style tapas. This multi-level boozer features the Street Bar, where you can really relax and watch the world go by, the Pool Bar where you can mix it with the cool crowd, and the Balcony Bar where you can sip on cocktails and be a tad more bling. There are 18 wines available by the glass here, while beer lovers can choose from bottled and premium beers on tap.

381 Clovelly Rd ◀
Clovelly

The Clovelly

9665 1214 | *www.clovellyhotel.citysearch.com.au*

It's always busy at this much-loved watering hole, where a beer's a beer and dressing up isn't necessary. There are four large bars to do your drinking at and normally enough life at any one of them to keep you entertained. There's also decent food at the hotel's restaurant. You can take the whole family to the Level One bar, with its pool tables and cushioned lounges, but the Garden Lounge is more popular, with views out over the Pacific Ocean or nearby gardens. The main bar has widescreen televisions showing sport, and if that doesn't take your fancy, you can stroll through to the bar next door and gawp at the wall-sized tropical fish tank.

1 Willoughby Rd ◀
Crows Nest
Outer North

The Crows Nest Hotel

943 6487 | *www.crowsnesthotel.com.au*

Whether you want to dance the night away to live cover bands, settle with friends in the lounge, perch at the bar or try your luck on the pokies, you can do it all at the Crowie. Situated at the five-way intersection in popular Crows Nest on Sydney's north shore, the pub is well known for its entertainment and as a hot spot for after work drinks. Inside it has comfortable booth lounges and ambient lighting given off by large pendants that hang from the ceiling. Those who want to kick on can keep their seat, or slide over to the Junction Bar, where you can people watch through the floor to ceiling windows as you sip a well-muddled cocktail.

360 Victoria St ◀
Darlinghurst

Green Park Hotel

9380 5311 | *www.green-park-hotel.com*

This corner pub in trendy Darlinghurst is as relaxed and traditional as Sydney hotels come. It's a no-nonsense boozer with a blue-tiled, dark timbered interior and an energetic (and often noisy) feel. It's mix of local characters, trendy eastern suburbanites and gay boys and girls, giving it a vibrant atmosphere. This is a place to settle in with pals and play a friendly game of pool (they also hold competitions here), or take advantage of the take-away food service from nearby Burgerman so you don't lose your seat. It's open until 02:00, Monday to Saturday and the new outdoor area is a great spot for a beer on a sunny day. Sunday afternoons at the Green Park are a big tradition among the city's gay community.

118 Military Rd ◀
Neutral Bay

The Oaks

9953 5515 | *www.oakshotel.com.au*

You could spend days at The Oaks, without needing to head home. With so many rooms, there should always be something to entertain you. Have your fill of beautifully prepared meats in the steakhouse, devour every last scrap of the fresh, flavour-filled gourmet pizzas or play pool with pals in the Cue and Cushion bar. If this doesn't take your fancy, take a step back in time to the 1930s inspired Nineteenthirtysix bar, where you're encouraged to sit over a casual drink and get lost in conversation. The huge, family-friendly courtyard is one of the most popular areas of The Oaks, its main feature a large oak tree, twinkling with fairy lights.

The Paddington Inn

338 Oxford St
Paddington

9380 5913

This landmark pub is one of the city's, or at least Paddington's, favourites. The grand, high ceilings sit above a smiling crowd that has long enjoyed its well-stocked bar and enticing bistro. A popular spot for a break from shopping during the day, The Paddington Inn comes alive as the sun sets, filling with a fashionable crowd. Refurbished almost 10 years ago, the pub's dark timber interior and gold leaf bar top are offset with gentle lighting. Once past the more casual front end of the pub, keep walking to the sunken open kitchen area and bar for food. The Inn has a good selection of tap and bottled beers, as well as a wine list that changes with the menu. The cocktail menu is also popular.

The Slip Inn

111 Sussex St
Central

9240 3000 | *www.merivale.com*

Those who know (and you'd be hard pressed to find a Sydneysider who doesn't) will tell you The Slip Inn has a fairytale to tell. It was here during the 2000 Olympics that Aussie girl Mary Donaldson met Frederick; the Crown Prince of Denmark and her future husband. While most will not find a stray European royal bumbling about the place, there is still a fun time to be had. Stylish and brimming with city slick, The Slip Inn boasts bars, a lounge, club area and, if you work up an appetite, good food. Loyal fans also quickly fill the Tuscan-inspired courtyard for after-work drinks or to get their weekend party started.

The Tilbury

**Cnr Nicholson and
Forbes Sts**
Woolloomooloo

9368 1955 | *www.thetilburyhotel.com.au*

Don't expect a traditional pub here. The Tilbury is as sexy as its cocktails, from the Frenchito (fresh mint and limes, muddled and shaken with vodka, Chambord and pineapple juice) to the Senorita, (bursting with fresh berries in a pool of tequila and Chambord and cranberry juice). The open-style bar, with its whitewashed walls and inviting furniture, plays funk and soul on Thursdays, laid back grooves on Fridays and disco on Saturdays. Come Sunday, the casual but well-dressed crowd make their way to the pool deck, where sounds of jazz fill the air.

Kirketon Dining Room & Bar (p.322)

357

Nightclubs
Other options **Bars** p.352

Some of the hottest nightclubs in Australia pump their tunes in Sydney. From the country's biggest, Home, see p.358, in Darling Harbour, to trendy clubs like Ruby Rabbit in Darlinghurst, there are plenty of good times to be had. Dress codes tend to be smart casual (no sneakers, tidy shoes and collared shirts), and generally depend on the mood of the bouncers patrolling the door. While Kings Cross will always be the favourite destination of tourists and loyal locals for some guaranteed good nightclub action, the city's sprawling suburbs also boast their fair share of happening hotspots, from stand-alone venues to the local RSL. The country's best-known DJ's spin alongside their international counterparts at such haunts as The Chinese Laundry, p.358, Home and Suzie Q's, p.359. Paying a cover charge is standard in Sydney; you can expect to pay anything from $5 to $30 just to get a look in.

81 Sussex St
Central

Bristol Arms Retro Nightclub
9262 5491

It's not just the five floors and seven bars that bring the happy young things to Retro Nightclub. As its name suggests, the tunes here are reflective of eras past – from the 60s through to the 90s. Here, Michael Jackson is still cool and Madonna young. The huge dance floors quickly fill to the beats of the in-house DJs, making Retro one of city's most popular nightspots. In this place it doesn't matter if you don't do cool and the bus stop isn't anything to do with public transport.

111 Sussex St
Central

Chinese Laundry
9240 3000 | *www.merivale.com*

As the party gets started at the well-frequented Slip Inn upstairs, clubbers-in-the-know are warming up in the cool depths of Asian-inspired Chinese Laundry down below. The underground nightclub is a magnet for local and international DJs, as well as live musicians, who belt out their tunes to an appreciative, party-hard crowd. Fun-loving staff pour their liquor with passion and add to the overall friendly vibe of the place.

1 Earl Pl
Potts Point

Dragonfly
9356 2666

The well-heeled set, from high fashion model types to celebs, have been known to add sex appeal to this already classy establishment (think Nicole Kidman, Jamie Foxx, the Black Eyed Peas and Usher among other A-listers). Celebrity hype aside, there's a lot more to Dragonfly than expensive furniture, myriad mirror balls and jagged, stone walls. The curious and the loyal come here for a thumping dance floor and private booths, to get away from the nearby loud and gaudy Kings Cross and for a sophisticated, slinky vibe.

Cockle Bay
Darling Harbour

Home
9266 0600 | *www.homesydney.com*

Home is Sydney's superclub, and its modern decor and futuristic architecture overlook the waters of Darling Harbour and the city skyline. As weekends roll around, a sea of drinkers and dancers fill the multilevel main room, but for a chilled cocktail and a break from the beats, they hit the 'padded cell', silver room. Internationally renowned DJ's fill the roster from Thursday to Saturday nights. Functions are also a speciality at this nightclub, with private events catering for up to 2,100 people. The views from the roof terrace make for a refreshing break from the largeness downstairs. Home also stages regular gay events, including the world-famous 'Queer

Nation' parties, which have a different theme every night. These are big nights for serious partygoers, and they're usually held on long weekends so you've plenty of time to recover. They attract a wide range of clubbers and famous DJs and the venue has a distinct Ibiza feel.

39 Darlinghurst Rd
Kings Cross

Moulin Rouge

8345 1711 | www.moulinrougesydney.com.au

Everyone is happy at Moulin Rouge, a cool and homely underground nightclub in the depths of Kings Cross. As with most worthy nightspots in Sydney, you can expect to join the lengthy queue before you're granted entry. But once you're in, the sexy vibe and inviting, eclectic surrounds reminiscent of its Parisian namesake will make you forget all about the short wait (and quite possibly, the time). If you stay to stumps over cocktails and canapes, you'll be hitting the pavement just as the sun does at 06:00. Head here for Rouge Rock-R every Friday and DJ sounds of Moulin Nights every Saturday.

231 Oxford St
Darlinghurst

Ruby Rabbit

9326 0044 | www.rubyrabbit.com.au

Three storeys of sophisticated nightclub action await at Ruby Rabbit, where the cool crowd don't necessarily know it and the thirty-somethings love to show off their moves. The Florence Broadhurst-covered walls may be narrow, but there's still plenty of room to strut your stuff and to elbow your way to the slender bar for a drink of local and imported beers, cocktails and wine. Celebrity spotting isn't unusual at the Rabbit, where the music's loud and guaranteed to get you in the party mood. This pretty party place has also played host to music awards, fashion parties, product launches and after parties.

169 Oxford St
Darlinghurst

Suzie Q's

9331 7729 | www.suzieqs.com.au

Disco balls make a comeback at Suzie Q's, where modern decor meets antique charm. The laidback attitude that oozes from this slick city bar keeps the young professional crowd filling the couches. From there they can move onto the dance floor that throngs to the beat of local and international DJs, varied enough to keep any musical tastes satisfied. The extensive drinks menu also aims to please, with some of the city's most talented bar staff on hand to mix it just how you like it. Suzie Q's is open from Thursday to Sunday.

Moulin Rouge   *Ruby Rabbit*

3 Bridge Lane
Central

Tank

8295 9966 | www.tankclub.com.au

Nominated in the top eight nightclubs in the world by the House Music Awards, Tank is swimming with cool tunes and a cool crowd to match. The three bars, two dance floors and VIP area (with private booths) are the second home to keen clubbers and the international DJ's who entertain them. To keep up with the young, sophisticated crowd, you'll need to dress the part – you can wear jeans and sneakers with one condition: they must be deemed funky by the door staff. Show up early here if you don't want to spend too long in the line. For the latest gig guides, see the Tank website.

62-64 Kellett St
Kings Cross

Tonic Lounge

8354 1544 | www.toniclounge.com.au

The only bad thing about Tonic is closing time. The club fills a charming two-storey terrace house with a dressed up interior of shabby chic and Victorian grandeur. This effortless plushness should not put you off. Tonic is much less pretentious than it could be, and you won't be frowned on if you're not as well styled as the cool interior. The friendly staff are fond of sharing the good times with

you, often making their own DJ requests and getting groovy when the mood takes. In between dances, you can sit back with a well mixed pepper and strawberry martini in one of the velvet booths.

Cnr Abercrombie and Broadway
Central

Purple Sneakers

9211 3486 | www.purplesneakers.com.au

Think jam-packed dance floors, sweaty bodies and a house party vibe and you'll have an idea of what Purple Sneakers is all about. It's a cheap night out with a cover charge of just $10 (and is free before 20:00; doors open at 19:30) and goes on until the very wee hours. With everything from hip hop to rock, electro, indie and disco this place caters to a broad selection of Sydney's music loving crowd. The mix of moods and tunes here is eclectic and changeable. If you don't like the type of music on the night, don't worry; just come back a few hours later and it's likely to have switched dramatically. The mood though, should be the same jolly vibe.

2 Roslyn St
Potts Point

Ladylux

9361 5000 | www.ladylux.com.au

The first thing that hits you about Ladylux is the gloriously garish mock flock wallpaper. The pink, Florence Broadhurst designed floral swirls make the place look lavish and trendy, while the dinky little alcoves are grand spots to cosy up and chat and drink. The dancefloor also sees a lot of action. Nights vary through the week, with a tendency towards funky house, and international DJs are flown in regularly. They occasionally offer free drinks to get people in the door. The one constant though is a giggly and glamorous crowd. You can email or view the website for extra info.

Gay & Lesbian

It's difficult to imagine a city with a more high profile gay scene than Sydney. Since the first, troubled gay rights marches of the 1970s, today's gay Sydney has become a vibrant, open and colourful community, with a scene focused around Oxford Street and the suburbs of Darlinghurst, Surry Hills and Newtown.

Gay culture has merged with the mainstream here. The main 'gay areas' have become the city's trendiest spots and gay and straight bars sit side by side. Across the city, the famed Gay and Lesbian Mardi Gras is a highlight of Sydney's summer calendar.

Oxford Street is much more about mixed venues than exclusively gay hangouts. In Newtown, the scene is more grungy and diverse. It's also home to the Imperial, the bar made famous by the film *Priscilla, Queen of the Desert*, which still holds weekend drag show tributes.

The age of consent is the same for both heterosexual and homosexual (16), and while there are occasional reports of gay-bashings and homophobia, particularly in some of the city's western suburbs, Sydney's residents are generally open and accepting. See also the Green Park Hotel on p.356 and Home on p.358. These are straight, but attract a gay crowd.

Fag Tag is worth a mention, though it isn't a bar or club. It's actually a group that takes over – or 'fag-tags' – non-gay venues around Sydney, organising parties and events for everyone on their mailing list. Their parties are well known and much loved and they always attract a wide following of what they proudly call 'gays, lesbians, friends, sisters, siblings, cousins, ex-fags, hags, can't-decides and closets'. Previous venues have included the famous Opera Bar of the Opera House, as well as all manner of other places around the city. Visit their website and join their mailing list for forthcoming event details. See www.fagtag.com.au.

Taylor Square
Darlinghurst

Arq

9380 8700 | www.arqsydney.com.au

Arq is one of the main spots. It's a split-level venue with a mezzanine-encircled dance floor and bar, and a smaller, more intimate bar downstairs with pool tables and lounge seating. It has a slick, sophisticated feel, attracting a like-minded crowd of pretty-boy gym bunnies, and it's also one of the more popular venues for straight clubbers who like a mixed, party atmosphere. It's open from Thursday to Sunday nights and entry is between $5 and $20.

324 King St
Newtown

Bank Hotel

9557 1692

This bar cum club cum restaurant has had a multi-million dollar refurbishment. The (slightly pricey) Thai restaurant downstairs is popular and serves great food while the multi-level beer garden is great for a few chilled out drinks. The mid-priced cocktails are heavenly and should get you in the mood to shake a few moves in The Velvet Room upstairs (think blue satin drapes and chocolate walls). More of a girl's night out on Wednesdays, the rest of the week this place draws a mixed crowd. Open Sunday to Tuesday from 10:00-00:00, Wednesday and Thursday from 10:00 till 02:00 and from 10:00 to 04:00 on Fridays and Saturdays.

77 William St
Kings Cross

Club 77

www.club77sydney.com

This small, smokey club has been on the go for over ten years now and is something of a Sydney institution. Open til late from Thursday to Sunday, it fills up quickly and gets pretty hot so don't overdo the layers. Tunes swing towards the alternative. Celebs have been known to pop in from time to time, and Lily Allen has performed here.

361

117-123 Oxford Street
Darlinghurst

The Columbian Hotel
9360 2151

Primarily a bar for gay men, the Columbian also attracts a significant lesbian crowd. The large windows on the ground floor are grand for gawping out and watching the world go by, or looking in and watching the lively crowd. The bar upstairs is a little more sedate, with cosy loungers and alcoves. This is a well-liked, fairly unpretentious spot.

34 Erskineville Rd
Erskineville

The Imperial
9519 9899

Made famous by the movie *Priscilla, Queen of the Desert* (where the opening scenes were shot), this bar has three distinct areas: a front pub bar, which is a little rough around the edges, a dark but fun basement club bar, and the main back bar, which is home to the regularly-staged drag shows. These are definitely worth checking out, being almost as amusing and outrageous as the performances in the movie that put this bar firmly in the public eye. Be prepared for a grungy but refreshingly unpretentious gay and lesbian crowd.

Taylor Square
Darlinghurst

Manacle
9331 2950 | *www.manacle.com.au*

As the name suggests, this dark, underground venue is a leather bar, attracting a mature and mixed bag of mostly male visitors. There's no dress code so you don't need to be kitted out to get in. The walls of its two bars are adorned with all kinds of leather and fetish memorabilia, and the place gets pretty busy from Friday through to Sunday. It's open Wednesday to Sunday from 20:00 and also runs regular daytime club events and after-parties.

85 Oxford St
Darlinghurst

The Midnight Shift
9360 4319 | *www.themidnightshift.com*

One of Sydney's best-established clubs, the Midnight Shift, or 'The Shift' as it's generally known, is a split-level venue with a bar downstairs and club upstairs. While the bar is less popular, the club can get very busy, especially on Saturday nights when the dark and dingy surroundings are filled with a bare-chested, mostly male crowd. The dance floor gets pretty crowded and sweaty, though not usually until well after midnight. Entry to the bar is free, but it'll cost you around $20 to get into the club at weekends.

41 Oxford St
Darlinghurst

Slide
8915 1899 | *www.slide.com.au*

One of the newer additions to Sydney's strip of gay bars and clubs is Slide, housed in the Art Deco surroundings of what used to be a bank (the sliding glass doors are now the only recognisable element). Today it's a sophisticated bar, club and restaurant, attracting a young, trendy, mixed crowd who make full use of the bar's split level surroundings and small, though often packed, dance floor stage. It's open until 03:00 Wednesday to Friday, and closes at 04:00 on weekends. Cover charges vary.

175 Oxford St
Darlinghurst

Stonewall
9360 1963

This always packed bar is especially popular with younger guys and it's also home to all kinds of drag shows, which are staged most nights of the week. It has three levels – a ground floor bar with show stage, a middle level bar with more laid-back dance music and a top level with music catering to a more hardcore crowd. You'll often need to queue to get in, and on Friday to Sunday nights, the line of eager young things can seem to go on forever.

Parties at Home

Just as eating out is commonplace in Sydney, so is entertaining at home – from backyard barbecues to fancy dress parties. Costume shops can be found in many a suburb (see p.292) or can be brought straight to your door from companies like www.mobilefancydress.com.au. Red Balloon Days (www.redballoondays.com.au) offers a 'cocktail party at home' package. For $1,092 you and 10 friends can sit back while an internationally trained chef and barmen serve you canapes and cocktails over five hours and then clean up once the party's over. For children's birthday parties, see www.party-oz.com.au, which covers entertainers and costumes, food and decorations.

Explorer Online

Now that you own an Explorer book you may want to check out the rest of our product range. From maps and visitor guides to restaurant guides and photography books, Explorer has a collection of carefully crafted products just waiting for you. Check out our website for more: **www.explorer publishing.com**

Party Organisers

Of course, for the biggest dos, it's best to get in the pros. If you need your garden turned into a medieval courtyard, would like to have a private party at the Opera House or just want a raucous hen or stag party, there is likely to be a firm here to look after you. Most of the firms listed are general party planners that will do corporate and private bespoke events as well as weddings. Distinctive, Nightingales and Majstro are specialist wedding planners and don't tend to do the other bits. For more on wedding related formalities, see p.66 of the Residence chapter. Go to p.298 of the Shopping chapter for details of where to get your frock and p.280 for florists.

Party Organisers

Angels Dreaming	www.angelsdreaming.com.au	9550 5550
Distinctive Weddings	www.distinctiveweddings.com.au	9703 0341
Elite Events	www.eliteevents.com.au	9487 3859
Events with Panache	www.eventswithpanache.com.au	9659 8238
Majstro	www.majstro.com.au	1300 364 917
Nightingales Wedding Designers	www.wedding.au.com	9212 7118
Susan Stanford Special Events	www.susanstanfordevents.com.au	9328 3358
Time 2 Celebrate	www.time2celebrate.com.au	9264 4384

Caterers

From classy canapes to fast and friendly party food, there are plenty of companies around that are ready and willing to give you a quote. Award-winning caterer Zest, headed by chef Lucy Haynes, is a very popular choice for those who want innovative food served at weddings or parties at home. Zest, which has its permanent home at the Royal Motor Yacht Club, has lunch and dinner menu options as well as cocktail party, roving dinner, cocktail buffet and conference package options. Gastronomy, with its Asian and European influences, has also picked up a few awards and is a popular caterer to anything from grand corporate events to smaller, less public gatherings (including weddings). High-end caterers also supply well-trained, well-dressed serving staff. Meanwhile, for a backyard feast, companies such as Spit Roast King provide hearty dishes that will keep guests well and truly satisfied.

Caterers

Avocado Group	9882 3244
Earth Catering	9557 1422
Finger Foods	1300 368 453
Flavours Catering and Events	1300 368 605
Gastronomy	9663 4840
Spit Roast King	9150 7581
The Roos Brothers	9436 1133
Toast Food	9241 7300
Trippas White Catering	9252 7555
Zest	9327 3441

Prostitution

Prostitution was legalised in NSW with the Disorderly Houses Amendment Act 1995. Licensed brothels are now allowed to operate in certain zones. Customers can ask to see the licence of any premises used for prostitution. Street solicitation remains illegal. SWOP (Sex Workers' Outreach Project, see www.swop.org.au) promotes AIDS and STD awareness and gives information to sex workers. WorkCover (www.workcover. nsw.gov.au) checks the health and safety conditions in brothels. The legal age for a sex worker is 18. To visit a male prostitute, clients must be over 18. To visit a female prostitute, they must be over 16.

Cabaret & Strip Shows

It's easy to find a touch of Parisian nightlife in Sydney, with quality cabaret shows staged on sea and land. Sydney Showboats (www.sydneyshowboats. com.au) is popular for its extravagant performances, with many of its stars having danced their way straight from the Moulin Rouge. Meanwhile, showy suburbs such as Newtown offer their very own version (think *Priscilla, Queen of the Desert*) in corner pubs and restaurants. The Imperial (p.362) was the inspiration for Precilla, and continues to show drag acts. In Kings Cross there's a slew of adult clubs that line the famous strip (www.kingscrossonline.com.au). These range from the saucy to the seedy and many are knocking shops with clientele after extras, so may not be the best spot for a giggling mixed group on a night out. Table dancing club, Dancers Cabaret, on Bayswater Road has long been a magnet for those seeking a bit of raunch (www.dancers.com.au).

Casinos

From the grand Star City to pubs and RSL (Returned Services League) clubs lined with poker machines (pokies), it's easy and legal to place a bet in Sydney once over 18 years of age. While 2.1% of the Australian adult population has a gambling addiction, the rest spend an average of $1,000 each year trying to become instant millionaires. The largest and most popular is Star City Casino (www.starcity.com.au) in Darling Harbour, where you can eat, sleep, drink, party and, of course, lay your wager. It's open 24 hours, so you can flutter on until dawn. While legal gambling is confined to casinos and pubs, the wartime game of two-up brings gambling to the street every ANZAC Day on April 25. It's hard not to get into the two-up spirit either, as the beer flows from early afternoon until the wee hours.

Cinemas

Films take six to 12 months to reach Australia after they've been released in America. Hoyts and Greater Union cinemas are the main multiplexes, popular for Hollywood blockbuster films. The quirky, art-house cinemas such as Dendy are good for foreign films, as are Palace Cinemas. Govinda's (p.364) in Darlinghurst has big, comfy pillows to lie back on while you watch and a great veggie buffet. Movie tickets generally cost around $16. And if you go on 'cheapie Tuesdays' as the locals call it, you won't pay more than $10.

Film festivals are popular, the most notable being the Sydney Film Festival. The French Film Festival also always sells out, especially on opening and closing nights. The Italian Film Festival has screenings in a number of cinemas around the city. Budding producers can have a go at entering their reels at Tropfest, the largest short film competition in the world, which runs every February. For festival details, see p.177.

During the summer, outdoor cinemas are really popular. The Moonlight Cinema at

Cinemas			
Dendy	Various locations	9247 3800	www.dendy.com.au
French Film Festival	Various locations	9267 1755	www.frenchfilmfestival.org
Govinda's	Darlinghurst	9380 5155	www.govindas.com.au
Greater Union	Various locations	9218 2421	www.greaterunion.com.au
Hoyts	Various locations	1900 946 987	www.hoyts.ninemsn.com.au
Italian Film Festival	Various locations	1300 306 776	www.italianfilmfestival.com.au
Moonlight Cinema	Paddington	1300 551 908	www.moonlight.com.au
Palace Cinemas	Various locations	9360 8599	www.palacecinemas.com.au
St George	The Domain	1900 933 899	www.stgeorge.com.au
Sydney Film Festival	Various locations	9318 0999	www.sydneyfilmfestival.org
Tropfest	The Domain	9368 0434	www.tropfest.com

Entertainment

Aussie Flicks

For a relatively small nation, Australia punches above its weight in the world of cinema. It has produced box office successes like *Priscilla, Queen of the Desert, Mad Max, Strictly Ballroom, Happy Feet* and *Crocodile Dundee*. It has also had some big cult hits with T*he Castle, Sirens Chopper* and *Romper Stomper*. But, the country's biggest stars like Nicole Kidman, Russell Crowe and Cate Blanchett have to go to the US to make it big and the industry is suffering from something of an investment slump. To arrest this, the Australian Government, which gives about $140m to the industry each year, is looking at changing tax incentives to encourage private investment. *Variety* magazine says private investment in Australian films last year amounted to just $8 million; 7% of the total. But, iconic films are still being made and those listed above should not be missed.

Picture Perfect

They say a picture can speak a thousand words, so if you can't sum up the sights and sounds of a city in a sentence then grab a copy of one of Explorer's stunning *Mini Photography Books*. Showcasing a unique view of world cities, these books will make sure you take home more than just memories from your next trip.

Centennial Park screens classics like *Breakfast at Tiffany's* as well as new blockbusters. For a movie with a view, the open-air cinema at Mrs Macquaries Chair at the Royal Botanic Gardens overlook Sydney Harbour. Cinema times are listed in all the major daily newspapers and all films are rated. Few films are banned here.

It's no longer scenes of the outback that dominate Australian cinema. Although it has taken a long time and many brave moves to get to where it is today - the first time Aboriginal actors were put in lead roles was not until 1955 with the Charles Chauvel (controversial) film, Jeddah. Today, Australian cinema continues to explore Australian racial and political issues, the Aussie identity and the country's many cultures. In 2005 it held a slowly growing 2.8% share of the worldwide box office (according to MPDAA), following a sharp decline in 2004. The fate of Australian cinema on the world stage is uncertain, given the Hollywood monopoly, but with the new generation of budding directors and actors just starting out, it's more a case of watch this space.

Comedy

Aussies tend to reckon they're a witty bunch, and a number of clubs and pubs host comedy nights in Sydney. In Glebe, The Harold Park (9660 3688) is always a laugh, as is Mic in Hand (www.micinhand.com), which has developed a bit of an underground following. Held in the A Friend in Hand pub (www.friendinhand.com.au), this is a place where anyone can get up on stage. Otherwise, the Fringe Bar (9360 5443) on Oxford Street on a Monday night is hilarious, and they serve great food too. The Australian Youth Hotel (9692 0414) runs a weekly comedy night, which is always very Australian, and the perfect place to sit back and enjoy a few beers. The cream of Sydney's comedy crop though is the Laugh Garage (www.thelaughgarage.com) in Parramatta.

The Big Laugh Comedy Festival (www.biglaughriverside.com.au) runs from March 22 to April 1, overlapping with CRACKER (www.crackercomedy.com.au). Mic in Hand (www.micinhand.com) has developed an underground following with the Glebe locals.

Concerts

Other options **Theatre** p.366

All the big names come to Sydney: Kylie, Coldplay, The Rolling Stones and the Red Hot Chili Peppers have all performed here. Most major events are held at The Sydney Entertainment Centre (see table on next page). To keep an eye on upcoming concerts, good websites include www.sonybmg.com.au, www.inthemix.com.au, www.moshtix.com.au and www.sydneyolympicpark.com.au.

The best place to see Australian bands is at grungy festivals like The Big Day Out (www.bigdayout.com) or Homebake (www.homebake.com.au). See p.177 for more on these. Favourite groups include Silverchair, Eskimo Joe, The Hilltop Hoods, Scribe, Gotye, Björn Again, The Butterfly Effect and Bob Evans, among others.

Mini Marvels

Explorer *Mini Visitors' Guides* are the perfect holiday companion. They are small enough to fit in your pocket but beautiful enough to inspire you to explore. With area information, detailed maps, visitors' information, restaurant and bar reviews, the lowdown on shopping and all the sights and sounds of the city, these mini marvels are simply a holiday must.

In summer, Sydney is a haven for live music and outdoor concerts. The Basement always has a good line up and past acts have included James Brown. Field Day (www.fuzzy.com.au) is a festival held every New Year's Day, while Good Vibrations (www.goodvibrationsfestival.com.au) takes place in Centennial Park in February.

For live bands, The Sandwich Club (www.sandwichclub.fm/blog) is a group of guys that write a blog on all the latest and greatest bands. They hold a night at Candies Apartment in Kings Cross on the last Thursday of every month and invite up-and-coming bands to play. With entry for as little as $5, it's a cool, cheap night out. Art After Hours, every Wednesday night from 18:30 at the Art Gallery of NSW is a great, culture packed evening featuring a mix of films, lectures, art exhibitions and live music. The Enmore Theatre always has a good line up of local and international bands and DJs as does the Metro Theatre. For classical music and opera, The Opera House always has a good line up.

Concerts			
Art Gallery of NSW	The Domain	9225 1744	www.artafterhours.com.au
Metro Theatre	Central	9550 3666	www.metrotheatre.com.au
Sydney Entertainment Centre	Darling Harbour	9320 4200	www.sydentcent.com.au
The Basement	Circular Quay	9251 2797	www.thebasement.com.au
The Enmore Theatre	Newtown	9550 3666	www.enmoretheatre.com.au
The Opera House	Central	9250 7111	www.sydneyoperahouse.com

Fashion Shows

Come May, the fashion-savvy, celebrities and media descend on Sydney for Australian Fashion Week (www.mafw.com.au), where the nation's designers parade their latest collections. But if stilettos and sequins aren't on your radar, there are plenty of other non-fashion shows to keep you busy. From wedding fairs to home and boat shows, the Sydney Convention and Exhibition Centre (www.scec.com.au) at Darling Harbour hosts the majority.

Theatre

From the grand Sydney Theatre Company to the Belvoir Street Theatre, there's plenty of stage action in Sydney. The city caters to all tastes – from small productions to million-dollar shows with A-list stars. Expect to pay anywhere from $15 to $80 for tickets, depending on the scale of the production. Theatre schools often put on end of term shows, where students put their skills to the test in front of a live audience on stages such as The Pilgrim, which is home to the Sydney Art Theatre in the city. The National Institute of Dramatic Art (NIDA) is one of the top schools. Small theatre production companies include Tamarama Rock Surfers, Company B and Griffin Theatre Company. The Darlinghurst Theatre is also popular for its acting classes and live productions. The Opera House is a little maligned for its acoustics, but while you live here, you really should make sure you see a show there.

Theatre			
Belvoir Street Theatre	Surry Hills	9698 3344	www.belvoir.com.au
Domain Theatre	The Domain	9225 1700	www.artgallery.nsw.gov.au
Sydney Art Theatre	Central	9261 8981	www.sat.org.au
Sydney Opera House	Central	9250 7777	www.sydneyoperahouse.com
Sydney Theatre Company	Various locations	9250 1777	www.sydneytheatre.com.au
The Darlinghurst Theatre	Darlinghurst	8356 9987	www.darlinghursttheatre.com

When you're lost what will you find in your pocket?

Item 71. The half-eaten chewing gum

When you reach into your pocket make sure you have one of these minature marvels to hand… far more use than a half-eaten stick of chewing gum when you're lost.

London Mini Map
Putting the city in your pocket

Abu Dhabi · Amsterdam · Bahrain · Barcelona · Dubai · Dublin · Geneva · Hong Kong · Kuwait

EXPLORER

DIGITALGLOBE™

C L E A R L Y   T H E   B E S T

61 cm QuickBird Imagery is the highest resolution satellite imagery available. We offer products and resorces to both existing GIS users and the entire next generation of mapping and multimedia applications.

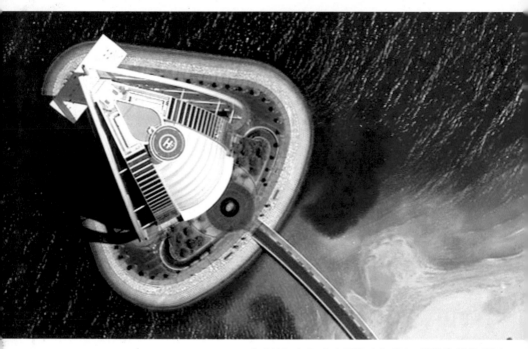

Burj Al Arab, Scale 1:2500, dated May 2003 © DigitalGlobe

MAPSgeosystems

DigitalGlobe's Master Reseller serving the Middle East and East, Central and West Africa

MAPS (UAE), Corniche Plaza 1, P.O. Box 5232, Sharjah, UAE.
Tel : +971 6 5725411, Fax : +971 6 5724057
www.maps-geosystems.com

For further details, please contact quickbird@maps-geosystems.com

Maps

User's Guide

This section has three detailed maps (numbers 2,3 and 4) of the Sydney CBD and its immediate surroundings to the east and south. They are intended to help you get your bearings when you first arrive, and give you an idea of where we're talking about in the main chapters of the book. The overview on page 375 shows where these areas cover. They are blown up nice and big, at a 1cm=80m scale. We've included the main hotels from the General Information chapter (see p.31 onwards) along with schools, hospitals, shopping centres, heritage sites and parks. See the legend below for an idea of which is which. We've also put on the CityRail stations (look out for the familiar logo) Light Rail (the green dots) and Monorail (the red dots).

You might also have noticed that some of the area write ups in the Residents and Exploring chapters have map references. They refer to maps 2,3 and 4. And, for the bigger picture, the map on page 372 gives you a view of the state of New South Wales. There's even a map of the whole of Australia sitting opposite this very page. Page 382 has a ferry map, and our inside back cover has a CityRail map.

More Maps

Beyond these maps and our own very nifty **Sydney Mini Map** *(see right for details) there are a number of street directories to be found in Sydney's bookshops and newsagents. The* Gregory's *Sydney* Compact Street Directory *has been in print for more than 20 years and is well known by locals. See www.gregorys-online.com for more. UBD (www.ubd.com.au) have been printing their full size book for even longer.*

Need More?

We understand that this residents' guide is a pretty big book. It needs to be, to carry all the info we have about living in Sydney. But, unless you've got the pockets of a clown, it's unlikely to be carried around with you on day trips.

With this in mind, we've created the **Sydney Mini Map** as a more manageable alternative.

This packs the whole city into your pocket and once unfolded is an excellent navigational tool. It's part of a series of Mini Maps that includes cities as diverse as London, Dubai, New York and Barcelona. Wherever your travels take you, you'll never have to ask for directions again. Visit our website, www.explorerpublishing.com for details of how to pick up these little gems, or nip into any good bookshop.

Online Maps

There are a few websites that have searchable maps of Sydney: www.street-directory.com.au is worth a look, but the navigation can be a bit tricky. The site www.whereis.com.au is a bit more user-friendly and Schmap maps (see www.schmap.com and download Sydney) are also pretty good. Hardcore map fans tend to like Google Earth (download from http://earth.google.com) for its satellite images, powerful search facility and incredibly detailed views, but the street directory isn't very detailed.

Map Legend

■	Hotel/Resort
□	Education
□	Park/Garden
■	Hospital
■	Shopping
■	Heritage/Museum
■	Pedestrian Area
■	Built up Area/Building

SYDNEY	Area name
40	Road No
▬	Highway
▬	Major Road
═	Secondary Road
═	Other Road
●—	Light Rail Station
- - ● - -	Monorail Station
—⊛—	CityRail Station
▬▬	State Border

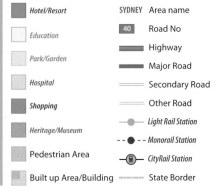

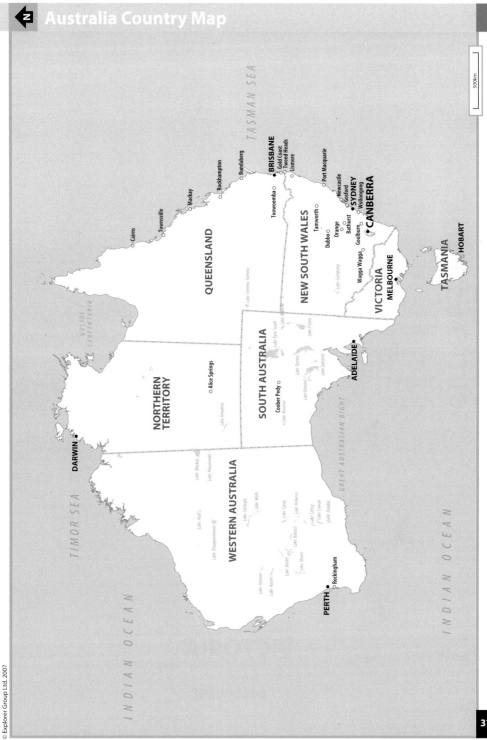

500km

TASMAN SEA

Cairns
Townsville
Mackay
Rockhampton
Bundaberg
BRISBANE
Gold Coast
Tweed Heads
Lismore
Toowoomba
Port Macquarie
Newcastle
Gosford
SYDNEY
Wollongong
Tamworth
Orange
Bathurst
CANBERRA
Dubbo
Goulburn
Wagga Wagga
Lake Gumphang

QUEENSLAND

NEW SOUTH WALES

Lake Yamma Yamma

MELBOURNE

VICTORIA

TASMANIA

HOBART

GULF OF CARPENTARIA

NORTHERN TERRITORY

Alice Springs

Lake Amadeus

SOUTH AUSTRALIA

Coober Pedy
Lake Eyre South
Lake Eyre North
Lake Blanche
Lake Torrens
Lake Gairdner
Lake Everard
Lake Frome

ADELAIDE

GREAT AUSTRALIAN BIGHT

DARWIN

TIMOR SEA

WESTERN AUSTRALIA

Lake Mackay
Lake Macdonald
Lake Amadeus
Lake Hopkins

Lake Corrigin
Lake Wells
Lake Carey
Lake Rebecca
Lake Ballard
Lake Lefroy
Lake Cowan
Lake Dundas
Lake Barlee
Lake Moore
Lake Disappointment
Lake Argyle
Lake Annean
Lake Austin

Rockingham

PERTH

INDIAN OCEAN

INDIAN OCEAN

© Explorer Group Ltd. 2007

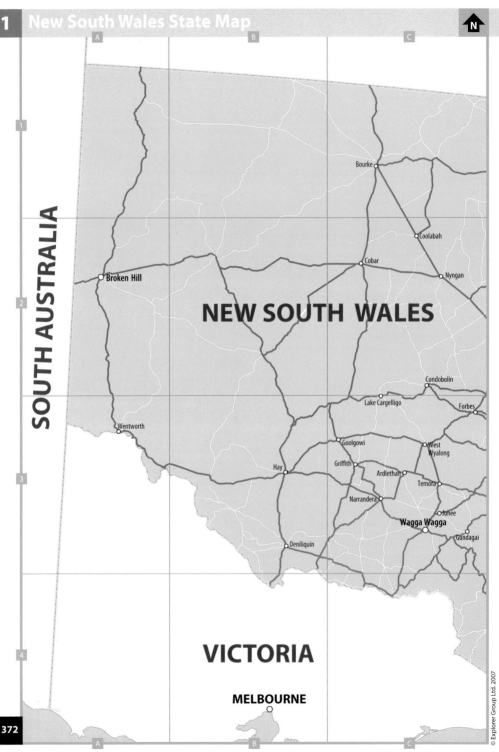

© Explorer Group Ltd. 2007

Sydney Explorer 1st Edition

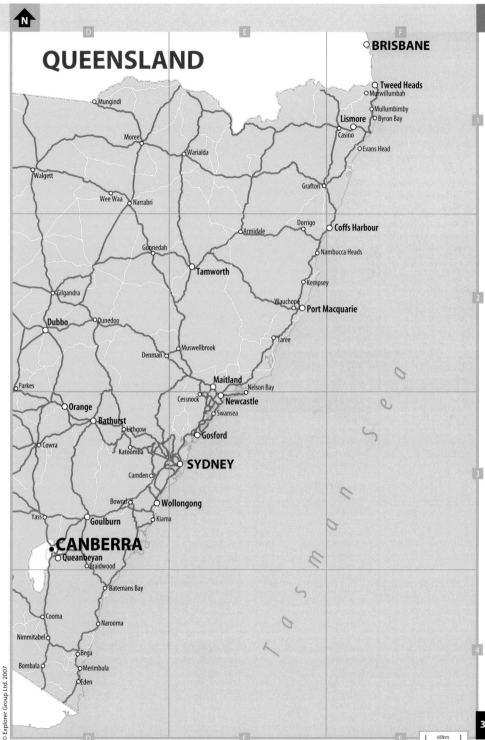

QUEENSLAND

BRISBANE

Mungindi

Moree

Warialda

Tweed Heads
Murwillumbah
Mullumbimby
Lismore
Byron Bay
Casino
Evans Head

Walgett

Wee Waa
Narrabri

Grafton

Dorrigo
Coffs Harbour

Armidale

Nambucca Heads

Gilgandra

Gunnedah

Tamworth

Kempsey

Wauchope
Port Macquarie

Dubbo

Dunedoo

Parkes

Denman

Muswellbrook

Taree

Maitland
Nelson Bay

Orange

Cessnock
Newcastle
Swansea

Bathurst

Cowra

Lithgow

Gosford

Katoomba

SYDNEY

Camden

Bowral
Wollongong

Yass

Goulburn
Kiama

CANBERRA
Queanbeyan
Braidwood

Batemans Bay

Cooma

Narooma

Nimmitabel

Bega

Bombala

Merimbula
Eden

© Explorer Group Ltd. 2007

Tasman Sea

60km

Area & Street Index

The table below contains a list of the main areas and streets in Sydney. The coordinates for each area refer to where the name appears on our map, rather than a geographical centre. Surry Hills, for example, continues for some way beyond the limits of Map 4.

Where streets extend beyond one grid reference, we've done the same. So George Street is given as Map 3, grid reference E3, but actually extends from the Rocks all the way to Central station.

Pull-Out Map

Tucked away in the back of this guidebook is a massive pull-out map of the city that you now call home. It gives a bigger picture of Sydney, stretching from Coogee in the south east to Ryde in the north west and from Earlswood in the south west up to the golden sands of Manly.

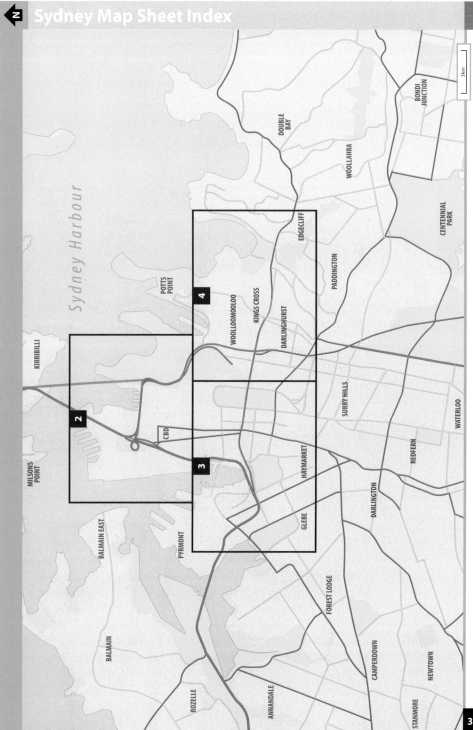

3km

Sydney Harbour

BONDI
JUNCTION

DOUBLE
BAY

WOOLLAHRA

CENTENNIAL
PARK

EDGECLIFF

PADDINGTON

4

POTTS
POINT

KINGS CROSS

WOOLLOOMOOLOO

DARLINGHURST

KIRRIBILLI

SURRY HILLS

WATERLOO

2

CBD

REDFERN

MILSONS
POINT

3

HAYMARKET

DARLINGTON

GLEBE

BALMAIN EAST

PYRMONT

FOREST LODGE

BALMAIN

CAMPERDOWN

NEWTOWN

ROZELLE

ANNANDALE

STANMORE

© Explorer Group Ltd. 2007

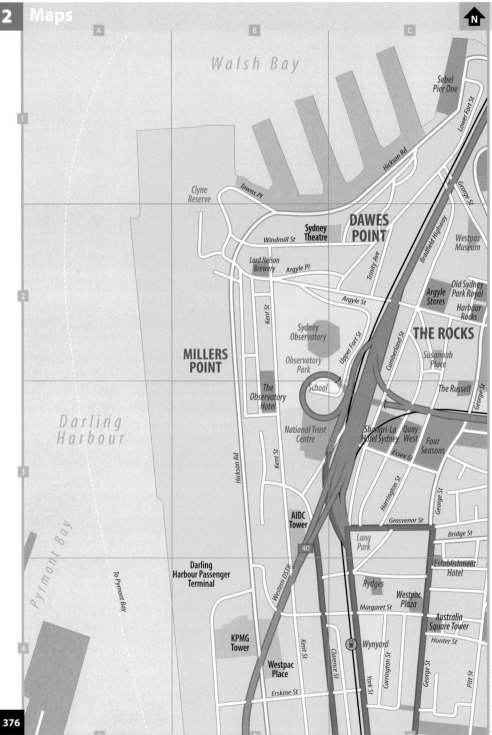

N

Walsh Bay

Sebel
Pier One

Clyne
Reserve

Towns Pl

Hickson Rd

George St

Lower Fort St

DAWES
POINT

Windmill St

Sydney
Theatre

Trinity Ave

Bradfield Highway

Westpac
Museum

Lord Nelson
Brewery

Argyle Pl

Argyle St

Old Sydney
Park Royal

Argyle
Stores

Harbour
Rocks

MILLERS
POINT

Kent St

Sydney
Observatory

Upper Fort St

Cumberland St

THE ROCKS

Observatory
Park

Susannah
Place

The
Observatory
Hotel

School

The Russell

George St

Darling
Harbour

National Trust
Centre

Shangri-La
Hotel Sydney

Quay
West

Four
Seasons

Essex St

Hickson Rd

Kent St

Harrington St

George St

AIDC
Tower

Grosvenor St

Bridge St

Lang
Park

Establishment
Hotel

Pyrmont Bay

To Pyrmont Bay

Darling
Harbour Passenger
Terminal

Western DSTR

40

Rydges

Margaret St

Westpac
Plaza

Australia
Square Tower

Hunter St

KPMG
Tower

Kent St

Clarence St

Wynyard

York St

Carrington St

George St

Pitt St

Westpac
Place

Erskine St

© Explorer Group Ltd. 2007

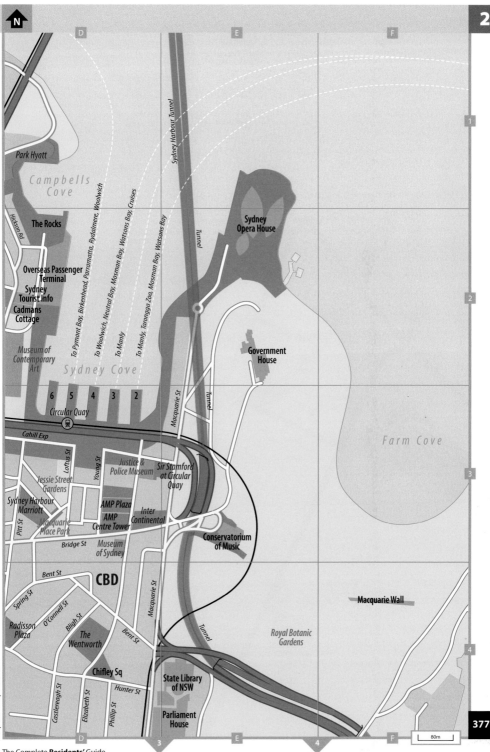

Park Hyatt

Campbells
Cove

The Rocks

Hickson Rd

Overseas Passenger
Terminal

Sydney
Tourist Info

Cadmans
Cottage

Museum of
Contemporary
Art

Sydney Cove

6 5 4 3 2

Circular Quay

Cahill Exp

To Pymont Bay, Birkenhead, Parramatta, Rydalmere, Woolwich

To Woolwich, Neutral Bay, Mosman Bay, Watsons Bay, Cruises

To Manly

To Manly, Taronga Zoo, Mosman Bay, Watsons Bay

Sydney Harbour Tunnel

Tunnel

Sydney
Opera House

Government
House

Farm Cove

Macquarie St

Tunnel

Jessie Street
Gardens

Sydney Harbour
Marriott

Macquarie
Place Park

Pitt St

Loftus St

Young St

Justice &
Police Museum

Sir Stamford
at Circular
Quay

AMP Plaza

AMP
Centre Tower

Inter
Continental

Conservatorium
of Music

Bridge St

Museum
of Sydney

Bent St

CBD

Spring St

O'Connell St

Bligh St

Macquarie St

Bent St

The
Wentworth

Radisson
Plaza

Macquarie Wall

Royal Botanic
Gardens

Tunnel

Chifley Sq

Castlereagh St

Elizabeth St

Phillip St

Hunter St

State Library
of NSW

Parliament
House

© Explorer Group Ltd. 2007

80m

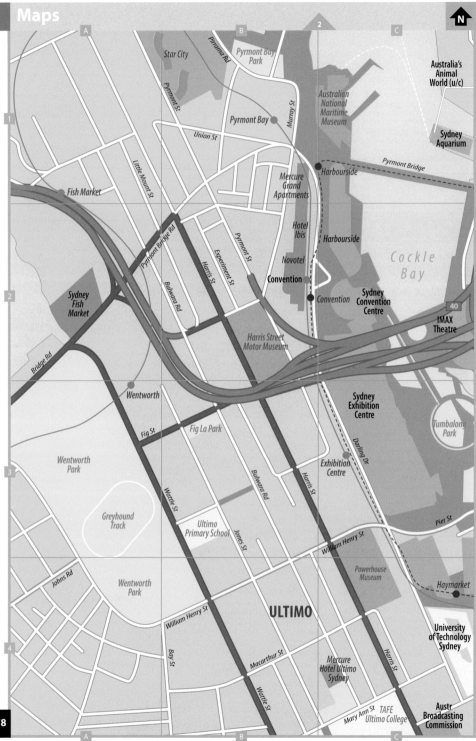

© Explorer Group Ltd. 2007

Sydney Explorer 1st Edition

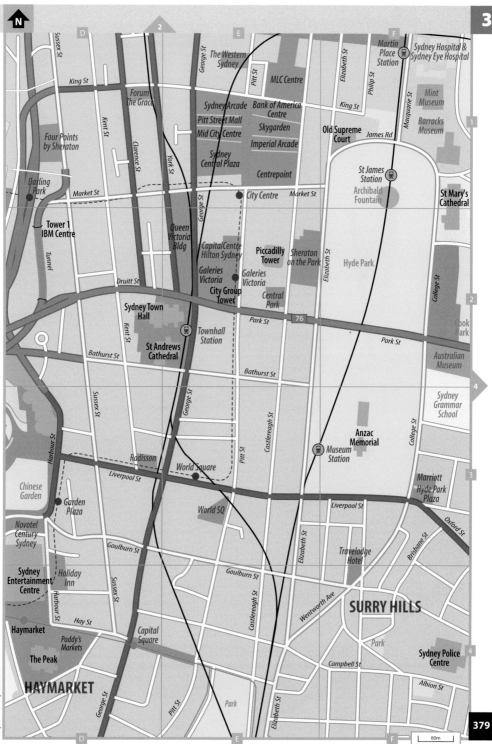

© Explorer Group Ltd. 2007

The Complete **Residents'** Guide

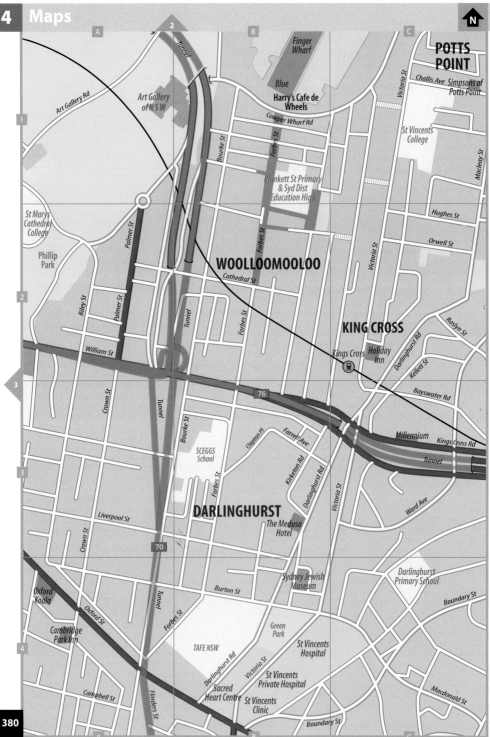

N

POTTS
POINT

Finger
Wharf

Blue

Harry's Cafe de
Wheels

Challis Ave Simpsons of
Potts Point

Art Gallery Rd

Art Gallery
of N S W

Cowper Wharf Rd

Victoria St

St Vincents
College

Mackey St

Bourke St

Forbes St

Plunkett St Primary
& Syd Dist
Education High

Hughes St

St Marys
Cathedral
College

Orwell St

Forbes St

Palmer St

WOOLLOOMOOLOO

Victoria St

Phillip
Park

Cathedral St

KING CROSS

Roslyn St

Riley St

Palmer St

Forbes St

Tunnel

Kings Cross

Holiday
Inn

Darlinghurst Rd

Kellett St

William St

76

Bayswater Rd

Crown St

Tunnel

Millennium Kings Cross Rd

Bourke St

Clapton Pl

Farrell Ave

Tunnel

Kirketon Rd

SCEGGS
School

Forbes St

Darlinghurst Rd

Victoria St

Ward Ave

DARLINGHURST

The Medusa
Hotel

Liverpool St

Darlinghurst
Primary School

Crown St

70

Sydney Jewish
Museum

Boundary St

Burton St

Oxford
Koala

Tunnel

Green
Park

St Vincents
Hospital

Fortes St

TAFE NSW

Victoria St

Macdonald St

Oxford St

Cambridge
Park Inn

Darlinghurst Rd

St Vincents
Private Hospital

Sacred
Heart Centre

St Vincents
Clinic

Campbell St

Flinders St

Boundary St

© Explorer Group Ltd. 2007

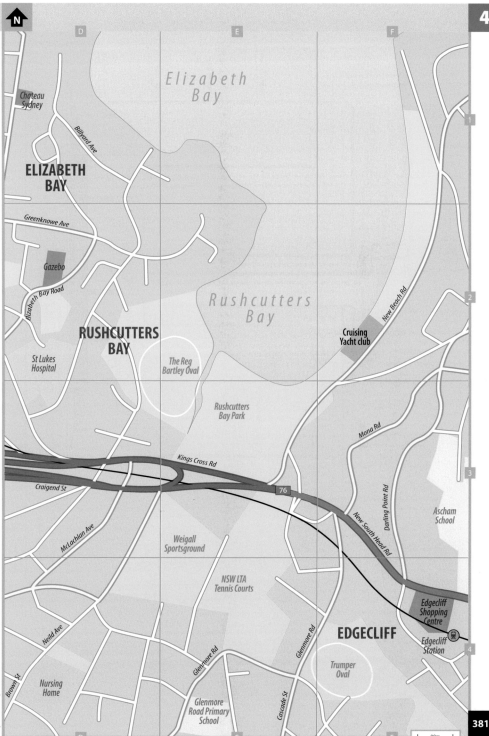

N

Elizabeth
Bay

Chateau
Sydney

Billyard Ave

**ELIZABETH
BAY**

Greenknowe Ave

Elizabeth Bay Road

Gazebo

**RUSHCUTTERS
BAY**

St Lukes
Hospital

Rushcutters
Bay

The Reg
Bartley Oval

New Beach Rd

Cruising
Yacht club

Rushcutters
Bay Park

Mona Rd

Kings Cross Rd

Craigend St

76

McLachlan Ave

Weigall
Sportsground

New South Head Rd

Darling Point Rd

Ascham
School

NSW LTA
Tennis Courts

Neild Ave

Brown St

Nursing
Home

Glenmore Rd

Glenmore Rd

Cascade St

Glenmore Rd

EDGECLIFF

Trumper
Oval

Edgecliff
Shopping
Centre

Edgecliff
Station

Glenmore
Road Primary
School

1

2

3

4

80m

© Explorer Group Ltd. 2007

Sydney Ferry Map

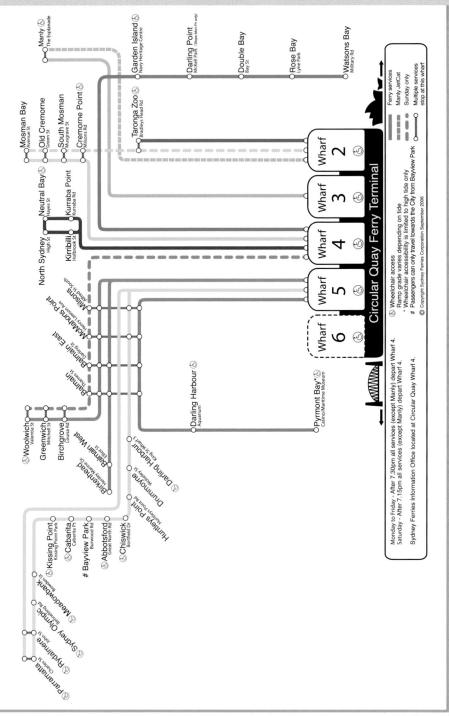

Index

Index

387

Index

Index

The *Sydney Explorer* Team

Lead Editor Matt Farquharson
Deputy Editors Katie Drynan & Helen Spearman
Editorial Assistant Mimi Stankova
Lead Designer Hashim Moideen
Cartographer Noushad Madathil
Photographers Pete Maloney, Matt Farquharson, Paul Campbell & Simon Jackson
Proofreaders Joanna Holden-MacDonald & Monica Degiovanni

Publisher
Alistair MacKenzie

Editorial
Managing Editor Claire England
Lead Editors David Quinn, Jane Roberts, Matt Farquharson, Sean Kearns, Tim Binks
Deputy Editors Helen Spearman, Katie Drynan, Tom Jordan
Editorial Assistants Ingrid Cupido, Mimi Stankova

Design
Creative Director Pete Maloney
Art Director Ieyad Charaf
Senior Designers Alex Jeffries, Motaz Al Bunai
Layout Manager Jayde Fernandes
Designers Hashim Moideen, Rafi Pullat, Shefeeq Marakkatepurath, Sunita Lakhiani
Cartography Manager Zainudheen Madathil
Cartographer Noushad Madathil
Design Admin Manager Shyrell Tamayo
Production Coordinator Maricar Ong

Photography
Photography Manager Pamela Grist
Photographer Victor Romero
Image Editor Henry Hilos

Sales and Marketing
Area Sales Managers Laura Zuffa, Stephen Jones
Marketing Manager Kate Fox
Retail Sales Manager Ivan Rodrigues
Retail Sales Coordinator Kiran Melwani
Distribution Executives Abdul Gafoor, Ahmed Mainodin, Firos Khan, Mannie Lugtu
Warehouse Assistant Mohammed Kunjaymo
Drivers Mohammed Sameer, Shabsir Madathil

Finance and Administration
Administration Manager Andrea Fust
Accounts Assistant Cherry Enriquez
Administrator Enrico Maullon
Driver Rafi Jamal

IT
IT Administrator Ajay Krishnan R.
Software Engineers Roshni Ahuja, Tissy Varghese

Explorer Publishing & Distribution
Office 51B, Zomorrodah Building, Za'abeel Road
PO Box 34275, Dubai, United Arab Emirates
Phone: +971 (0)4 335 3520, **Fax:** +971 (0)4 335 3529
info@explorerpublishing.com
www.explorerpublishing.com

Contact Us

Reader Response
If you have any comments and suggestions, fill out our online reader response form and you could win prizes. Log on to **www.explorerpublishing.com**

General Enquiries
We'd love to hear your thoughts and answer any questions you have about this book or any other Explorer product. Contact us at **info@explorerpublishing.com**

Careers
If you fancy yourself as an Explorer, send your CV (stating the position you're interested in) to **jobs@explorerpublishing.com**

Designlab and Contract Publishing
For enquiries about Explorer's Contract Publishing arm and design services contact **designlab@explorerpublishing.com**

PR and Marketing
For PR and marketing enquries contact **marketing@explorerpublishing.com** **pr@explorerpublishing.com**

Corporate Sales
For bulk sales and customisation options, for this book or any Explorer product, contact **sales@explorerpublishing.com**

Advertising and Sponsorship
For advertising and sponsorship, contact **media@explorerpublishing.com**

Quick Reference

Embassies, Consulates & Immigration

Argentina	9262 2933
Austria	9251 3363
Belgium	9327 8377
Brazil	9267 4414
Canada	9364 3000
China	8595 8000
Czech Republic	9371 8878
Denmark	9247 2224
Department of Immigration and Citizenship	13 1881
Egypt	9281 4844
France	9261 5779
Germany	9328 7733
Greece	9221 2388
Hungary	9328 7859
India	9223 9500
Indonesia	9344 9933
Israel	6273 1309
Italy	9392 7900
Japan	9231 3455
Korea, Republic of	9210 0200
Netherlands	9387 6644
New Zealand	8256 2000
Norway	9200 2159
Pakistan	9299 3066
Papua New Guinea	6273 3322
Philippines	9262 7377
Poland	9363 9816
Portugal	9262 2199
Russia	9326 1866
South Africa	6273 2424
Spain	9261 2433
Sweden	9262 6433
Switzerland	8383 4000
Thailand	9241 2542
Turkey	9328 1155
United Kingdom	9247 7521
USA	9373 9200

Helplines

Alcohol and Drug Information Service	9361 8000
Domestic Violence and Sexual Assault	1800 200 526
Kids Helpline	1800 551 800
Mental Health Central Sydney	1800 636 825
Mental Health Northern Sydney	1300 302 980
Mental Health South Eastern Sydney	1300 300 180
Mental Health Western Sydney	9840 3047
Rape Crisis Centre	9819 7357
Sexual Abuse Help Line	13 1200
Youthline	9633 3666

Sydney Airport

Duty Free	1800 733 000
Flight info (text flight number to)	1990 0747
Quarantine	1800 020 504
Visitor Centre (and lost property)	9667 6050

Emergencies

Emergency dentists	9369 7050
Pharmacy finder	9467 7100
Poisons Information Centre	13 1126
Police Assistance Line	131 444
Police, fire, ambulance	000
State Emergency Service	13 2500

Main Government Hospitals

Canterbury Hospital	9787 0000
Children's Hospital at Westmead	9845 0000
Manly Hospital	9976 9611
Prince of Wales Hospital	9382 2222
Royal Hospital for Women	9382 6111
Royal Prince Alfred Hospital	9515 6111
St Vincent's Hospital	8382 1111
Sydney Children's Hospital	9382 1111

Public Transport

CityRail	13 1500
CountryLink	13 2232
Monorail and Light Rail	9285 5600
Roads and Traffic Authority	13 2213
Sydney Buses	13 1500
Sydney Coach Terminal	9212 3433
Sydney Ferries	13 1500

Taxi Companies

Legion Cabs	13 1451
Premier Cabs	13 1017
RSL Cabs	9581 1111
Silver Service Taxis	13 3100
St George Cabs	13 2166
Taxis Combined Services	13 3300
Wheelchair Accessible Taxis	1800 043 187

Operator Services

Directory enquiries	1223
International enquiries	1225
Operator services	1234
Reverse charges	12550
Talking clock	1194

Interstate & International Calls

International calls	0011
NSW and ACT area code	02
NT, SA and WA area code	08
QLD area code	07
VIC and TAS area code	03

Credit Cards (Lost & Stolen)

American Express	1300 132 639
MasterCard	1800 120 113
Visa International	1800 450 346

Sydney Explorer 1st Edition